READERS, TEACHERS, LEARNERS

D1402893

READERS, TEACHERS, LEARNERS
Expanding Literacy Across the Content Areas

Fourth Edition

William G. Brozo
The University of Tennessee

Michele L. Simpson
University of Georgia

Upper Saddle River, New Jersey
Columbus, Ohio

Library of Congress Cataloging in Publication Data

Brozo, William G.
    Readers, teachers, learners: expanding literacy across the content areas / William G.
Brozo, Michele L. Simpson.— 4th ed.
        p. cm.
    Includes bibliographical references and index.
    ISBN 0-13-097855-8 (pbk.)
        1. Reading (Secondary)— United States. 2. Language arts (Secondary)— United States.
I. Simpson, Michele L. II. Title.

LB1632 .B7 2003
428.4'071'273—dc21

                                                                                2002021940

Vice President and Publisher: Jeffery W. Johnston
Editor: Linda Ashe Montgomery
Editorial Assistant: Evelyn Olson
Production Editor: Linda Hillis Bayma
Text Design and Production Coordination: Tiffany Kuehn, Carlisle Publishers Services
Design Coordinator: Diane C. Lorenzo
Photo Coordinator: Kathleen Kirtland
Cover Designer: Ali Mohrman
Cover image: Superstock
Production Manager: Laura Messerly
Director of Marketing: Ann Castel Davis
Marketing Manager: Krista Groshong
Marketing Coordinator: Tyra Cooper

This book was set in Garamond Book by Carlisle Communications, Ltd. It was printed and bound by
R.R. Donnelley & Sons Company. The cover was printed by The Lehigh Press, Inc.

Photo Credits: Scott Cunningham/Merrill, pp. 32, 98, 208; Anthony Magnacca/Merrill, pp. 304, 360, 402; Anne
Vega/Merrill, pp. 2, 254; Tom Watson/Merrill, pp. 54, 158; Todd Yarrington/Merrill, p. 440.

Pearson Education Ltd.
Pearson Education Australia Pty. Limited
Pearson Education Singapore Pte. Ltd.
Pearson Education North Asia Ltd.
Pearson Education Canada, Ltd.
Pearson Educación de Mexico, S.A. de C.V.
Pearson Education—Japan
Pearson Education Malaysia Pte. Ltd.
Pearson Education, *Upper Saddle River, New Jersey*

**Copyright © 2003, 1999, 1995, 1991 by Pearson Education, Inc., Upper Saddle River, New Jersey
07458.** All rights reserved. Printed in the United States of America. This publication is protected by Copyright
and permission should be obtained from the publisher prior to any prohibited reproduction, storage in a
retrieval system, or transmission in any form or by any means, electronic, mechanical, photocopying,
recording, or likewise. For information regarding permission(s), write to: Rights and Permissions Department.

10 9 8 7 6 5 4 3 2 1
ISBN 0-13-097855-8

For Carol, Hannah, and Genevieve

—William G. Brozo

For Tom

—Michele L. Simpson

PREFACE

In every case, it is the reader who reads the sense, it is the reader who grants or recognizes in an object, place or event a certain possible readability; it is the reader who must attribute meaning to a system of signs, and then decipher it. We all read ourselves and the world around us in order to glimpse what and where we are. We read to understand, or to begin to understand. We cannot do but read. Reading, almost as much as breathing, is our essential function.

—Alberto Manguel (1996)

Those of us who "cannot do but read" are part of a culture of letters dating from the first Sumerian tablets of the fifth millennium B.C. to Greek scrolls; from the codices of St. Augustine to CD-ROMs. Every word read is part of a history of language and sense filled with tales of anarchy, censorship, triumph, and passion. To read and write, then, is to become part of that history and, moreover, to learn from the voices of the past.

Just as the printing press and mass production of books, plays, and pamphlets revolutionized conceptions of literacy in the Renaissance, today new communications technologies are changing the ways we think about what it means to be literate. At the same time, researchers are calling attention to social, cultural, and multicultural dimensions of literacy, leading many to assert that literacy should no longer be defined as mere reading and writing but something much more complex, fluid, and multifaceted. In this new edition of *Readers, Teachers, Learners* we draw significant inspiration from current theorizing about multiple literacies. This is done while continuing to show deference to and honor the lifeworlds of middle and secondary school teachers who struggle daily to make their instruction more responsive to the needs of young adults.

Acknowledging that each literate act has historical, sociological, political, and cultural connections, we remain true in this edition to the primary thrust of the three that have come before it, which has been to emphasize the importance of traditional print literacy as a foundation for discourse flexibility and critical thinking. We were reminded recently of how far our sophisticated literate sensibilities can take us after reading descriptions by successful women of their earliest memories of critical book experiences (Copper-Mullin & Coye, 1998). Books about Madeline, the Cat in the Hat, Gigi the Merry-Go-Round Horse, and the Bobbsey Twins marked entry points into literacy for Supreme Court Justice Ruth Bader Ginsburg, Civil Rights activist Ruby Bridges, NASA astronaut Dr. Ellen Baker, and Pulitzer Prize winner Ellen Taaffe Zwilich. From the first stirrings of excitement brought about by these print encounters as children, they have traveled vast distances from their points of entry on a transformative journey of self-discovery and professional accomplishment. It is this same journey we hope all young adults are offered the opportunity to take. It is a journey that cannot be short-circuited, as each of us knows who began so modestly down our own literate paths. And now after years of traditional print explorations we have come to appreciate the true benefits of our literate journeys—expanded consciousness, discourse flexibility, intellectual curiosity, and the ability to read and understand the stories, histories, and philosophies of the ages.

To confer the bounties of expansive literacy ability and sustain and engage today's middle and secondary students in reading and writing is no mean feat. Adolescents have grown up in a world in which information is electronically and visually mediated—so much so that the very need for print literacy is becoming increasingly challenged. We agree with Stephen Hearst (1998) who notes:

> Pictures work supremely well as symbols and expressions of our deepest feelings, but language is the indispensable tool in the exercise of reason, in the precise expression of thought. The need to state the obvious is itself a symptom of how images have taken over ground precisely held by language. And in a mature democracy, where every vote carries equal weight, the achievement of critical literacy, the ability to judge and weigh the truth or falsity of things, is not merely desirable, it is of the essence. (p. 101)

We expand in this book on the position taken in previous editions that alternative information sources and traditional literacy can be complementary. Students should be guided to read critically so they can view critically.

Revising *Readers, Teachers, Learners* continues to be a labor of love for us since reading is our passion. The exhilaration of residing in the world between a book's covers is all the incentive we need to return to this pastime each and every day. We know all too well, however, that countless American adults and youths habitually avoid reading. Gustáve Flaubert said, "Read in order to live," but too many among us are choosing to live without reading. To be a nonreader in today's perplexing, information-laden world brings serious consequences. Beyond the more intangible benefits of regular reading, nonreaders lose reading skills, are less capable of understanding complex text, may be less likely to access higher education or find well-paying jobs, and may fail to impart positive values of literacy to their children. Being an active reader, on the other hand, can expand life and career options and enlarge one's sense of self.

This book, as with each of its predecessors, is about widening life and career options for students in the middle and upper grades through literacy. We make one overarching assertion in this book: Teachers of all subjects can create engaging learning environments where readers and learners use literacy for personal pleasure, as a tool for academic achievement, and to expand critical consciousness. To demonstrate the viability of this assertion we continue in this fourth edition to communicate to teachers through teachers. With fresh and exciting reading, writing, and literacy research as a backdrop, we have tried in a collaborative spirit to empower teachers with the confidence to make their own best decisions about the learning that goes on in their classrooms. As in our previous three editions, we have made a serious effort to avoid prescribing, offering "canned" answers, or making injunctions that demand certain behaviors from content-area teachers. To do so would be to ignore the realities and exigencies teachers must face in the everyday world of middle and secondary school.

We hope another vital message of the book has been made more vivid in this edition: that teachers inform us as much as we inform them. In a very real sense, the growth and improvement of adolescents' language processes will depend on the strength of the transactions between teachers in higher education and teachers in public schools.

In this edition we present even more actual teaching scenarios than in the first, second, and third editions, including additional examples from content areas such as math, science, art, music, and kinesiology. In each of the scenarios we demonstrate the valuable lessons to be learned from content-area teachers struggling and succeeding as they implement stimulating reading, writing, and learning strategies. Theory and research frame these vignettes and examples, which provide glimpses of teachers making literacy and content acquisition work.

IMPORTANT UPDATES AND NEW FEATURES

Anyone familiar with our previous editions will immediately notice some major revisions in this book in both format and content.

Format

- **Expanded Marginal Gloss**—The notes in the margins that signal important content and ideas are fuller and have been improved upon by the addition of references to our book's website. At this site, readers will find a variety of supporting information, such as useful Internet sites (see description that follows).

- **Revised Anticipation Guides**—The statements in these interactive guides have been revised to reflect changes in chapter content. Asking readers of our book to fill in the guides before each chapter and then return to the guides after reading and studying each chapter offers direct experience with a strategy we strongly advocate teachers use with their own students.

Content

- **A New Companion Website**—Accompanying this new edition is a user-friendly website that provides readers a variety of helpful resources. Within each chapter, marginal gloss directs readers to the website where readers may access chapter objectives, discussion questions, links to other helpful Internet sites, and other relevant links.

- **New "Meeting the Needs of Diverse Learners in the Content-Area Classroom" Segments**—New to this edition and appearing throughout most chapters are special boxed features entitled "Meeting the Needs of Diverse Learners in the Content-Area Classroom." This boxed material describes content-area teachers working with students who have extra learning needs. Our goal with this approach is to help reinforce the idea that struggling adolescent readers/learners are deserving of responsive instruction in every classroom. As a consequence of placing students with reading and learning differences directly within the context of regular classroom instruction, a separate chapter for these students was no longer necessary.

- **More Actual Teaching Vignettes**—By incorporating material from what was a separate chapter for struggling readers and learners throughout the book, we have been able to reduce the total number of chapters while expanding and enriching the 11 that comprise this new edition. A benefit to readers has been an increase in the number and type of actual teaching situations, scenarios, and vignettes, making it easier to envision application of the strategies we present.

- **Updated Chapter on Technology**—As developments in school-based applications of information and communications technologies increase at an ever quickening pace, it is imperative that the most current strategies that link reading and learning in middle and secondary school with computers be shared. This chapter is filled with outstanding new ways teachers in the content areas are employing computer technology to increase student motivation, expand opportunities for language development, and make learning more accessible and memorable.

- **New and Updated References to Professional and Young Adult Literature**—Readers of this fourth edition will be especially pleased with all of the updated references to the most current thinking and supporting literature for the ideas and strategies we present. Although this book is clearly a practical teaching guide, we want all of our readers to be mindful of the scholarship that undergirds the strategies we advocate. In addition, many new exciting young adult books are cited with suggestions and examples of how these resources can be incorporated into the content classroom.

ASSUMPTIONS UNDERLYING THE READING AND WRITING STRATEGIES

As with the previous editions, a major theme of this book is that teachers who employ language-based strategies are more likely to engender active learning and expand literacy for students in the middle and upper grades. Throughout the book we describe strategies that exploit students' beliefs and backgrounds and provide students with new, imaginative experiences that will help them find reasons to learn. The strategies we discuss demonstrate how teachers can help students to become independent and active learners. Above all, the strategies in this book are intended to make learning fun and accessible for all.

Our selection of strategies for this fourth edition was guided by our belief that students can become engaged and purposeful learners when provided opportunities for sustained reading and writing and when they are made to feel welcome as active participants in content classrooms. Students are likely to become active members of a classroom community when teachers create learning experiences that are positive and authentic, when they make learning meaning centered, when they work with students to shape the nature of learning, and when they give students personally meaningful reasons to learn.

The following assumptions form the foundation on which our ideas for teaching and learning rest.

1. **Teaching is more than dispensing information, because learning is more than receiving and remembering information.** Learning is the construction of meaning, an active process on the part of the learner. Teaching is creating classroom contexts that support the knowledge construction process.

2. **A major goal of education should be the development of critical thinkers and active, independent learners.** Students should be provided opportunities to play active roles in the meaning-making process. Students should be engaged in learning experiences that help them critically evaluate their worlds and participate in active problem solving of real-world concerns.

3. **To be literate is to use literacy as a tool for learning.** In supportive learning environments students can learn to use literacy as a vehicle for meaningful and functional learning.

4. **Content and process should be taught simultaneously.** Students should be led to see that *what* is learned is inextricably tied to *how* it is learned.

5. **Content-area teachers need to develop students' will to learn.** Literacy and learning skills are of little help if students are unmotivated to learn. Motivation results when teachers create interesting learning environments and help students develop their own personally relevant reasons for learning.

ORGANIZATION OF THE BOOK

This text is designed to help you teach your content more effectively and to develop independent learners who can think about your content in creative and critical ways. This text is also designed to help you envision the possibilities for exciting teaching and learning in your classroom. To this end, we have filled this fourth edition of our book with even more practical examples, teaching scenarios, and classroom dialogs. Retaining the informal tone we established in previous editions, we share our own teaching experiences as well as those of many middle and secondary school classroom teachers. We provide many alternatives, not with the intent that you should adopt every one, but with the expectation that you will select the strategies that best suit your subject area, your students, and your teaching style.

As in previous editions, Chapter 1 provides a thorough description of major trends in literacy, themes in this new edition, and the important foundations of language-based teaching and learning. Chapters 2 and 3 are critical in that they explain the processes involved in developing active learners. We recommend that you read these first three chapters before reading the others, because the remaining chapters build on the foundations we establish in Chapters 1, 2, and 3.

Readers of our previous editions will notice the overall sequence of chapters has remained the same. However, by incorporating material on special needs students throughout the book, we were able to eliminate Chapter 11 which exclusively discussed the topic. Thus, the former Chapter 12, "Becoming an Effective Content Literacy Professional," is now the new Chapter 11. Sequencing chapters for a book on content-area reading is never easy. Most users of our book recognize, however, that after the first three foundational chapters, there is a great deal of flexibility and interchangeability with respect to the order in which Chapters 4 through 11 are considered. For instance, content in Chapter 6 devoted to vocabulary theory, research, and strategies, while containing ideas and examples related to content in other chapters, can stand alone and be placed appropriately within a preferred instructional sequence. The same may be said for Chapter 7 on writing, Chapter 8 on young adult literature, Chapter 9 dealing with study reading, and Chapter 10 focused on the use of technology in content learning. We have kept "Classroom Assessment of Literacy Growth and Content Learning" as Chapter 4 in this edition, though some might prefer to deal with assessment issues near the end of a course of study with the book.

Regardless of the content that you teach or plan to teach, each chapter can provide you with insights into effective classroom interactions and practical examples of teaching strategies. Even when these examples of strategies and classroom applications do not come from your particular subject area, they can be invaluable as guides for helping you modify instructional practices within your own classroom context. Therefore, we recommend that you read each one and instead of thinking about how a particular strategy can be implemented exactly as explained and presented here, consider how it might be adapted to your content, students, classroom, and teaching style.

Woven throughout the 11 chapters of this new edition are many common threads. For instance, although we devote an entire chapter to writing in the content areas (Chapter 7), writing strategies are offered in nearly every chapter. The same holds true for using young adult literature and trade books to engender interest and spice up content learning (Chapter 8). In the case of strategies for struggling adolescent readers and learners, instead of retaining a separate chapter on this topic, we provide teaching examples throughout the book within special sections entitled "Meeting the Needs of Diverse Learners in the Content-Area Classroom."

Chapters 3 through 11 continue to include case studies. Encountered first after the chapter introduction, you will be asked to consider a particular problem or issue from an actual teaching scenario related to the content of the chapter. At the conclusion of the chapter, the case study is revisited, and you are invited to offer teaching or problem-solving suggestions. This process makes your reading and study more interactive, and we hope you will become better able to envision the potential applications of the strategies in genuine classroom environments. We urge you to take full advantage of the case studies as you read and reflect on chapter information.

ACKNOWLEDGMENTS

This preface would be incomplete without recognizing the supporting role of the Merrill/Prentice Hall editorial and production staff. A very special thanks to Linda Montgomery, our editor. Without her generosity of time and advice and faith in the power of our message about content-area literacy, this fourth edition would never have become a reality. Thanks as well go to our production editor Linda Bayma, our copy editor Karen Bankston, and Dan Parker for his patience and wizardry in designing our Companion Website. We are, of course, indebted to our diligent reviewers—Thomas W. Bean, University of Nevada, Las Vegas; Carole L. Bond, University of Memphis; Marian Jean Dreher, University of Maryland; Kovider Mokhtari, Oklahoma State University; and David G. Petkosh, Cabrini College—whose helpful insights made this fourth edition an even better text than its predecessors. A word of gratitude to Debra Coffey, whose tireless library and Web searches helped update our references. Finally, we thank all the students, teachers, and colleagues whose experiences inspired us and continue to influence our work. In particular, we want to thank Jan, Rafalar, Guy, and all the superb teachers at Winter Park High School in Florida for what we learned from you.

In physics they call it the "butterfly effect"—small influences creating dramatic effects—derived from the idea that the mere flap of an insect's wing in your backyard might ignite a chain of meteorological events leading to a hurricane on the other side of the globe. This book is dedicated to small influences that bring about big changes in the way students and teachers in middle and secondary schools interact and the quality of student learning.

REFERENCES

Copper-Mullin, A., & Coye, J. M. (1998). *Once upon a heroine: 400 books for girls to love.* Chicago: Contemporary Books.

Hearst, S. (1998). Television and its influence on reading. In B. Cox (Ed.), *Literacy is not enough: Essays on the importance of reading.* New York: Manchester University Press.

Manguel, A. (1996). *A history of reading.* New York: Viking.

ABOUT THE AUTHORS

William G. Brozo is a professor of language and literacy at the University of Tennessee. He earned his bachelor's degree from the University of North Carolina and his master's and doctorate from the University of South Carolina. He has taught reading and language arts in junior and senior high school in the Carolinas. He is the author of numerous articles on literacy development for young adults as well as *To Be a Boy, To Be a Reader* (International Reading Association), a book of strategies for helping teen and preteen males become active readers. Dr. Brozo serves on the editorial review boards of the *Reading Research Quarterly* and *Reading Research and Instruction* and the editorial advisory board of the *Journal of Adolescent & Adult Literacy.* He is also a member of the Commission on Adolescent Literacy. Dr. Brozo regularly speaks at professional meetings around the country and consults with teachers and administrators to discuss ways of enriching the literacy culture of middle and secondary schools and making teaching more responsive to student needs.

Bill lives in Knoxville, Tennessee, with his wife and daughter and their standard poodle, Teddy. He is an aficionado of opera and Renaissance music and drama. He runs daily to stay fit.

Michele L. Simpson is a professor of reading at the University of Georgia where she teaches learning strategy courses to undergraduates and instructional methods courses to doctoral students across a wide spectrum of academic disciplines such as chemistry, biology, history, and mathematics. After receiving her bachelor's and master's degrees from the University of Northern Iowa, she taught speech, reading, and language arts to students in junior and senior highs in Illinois, Iowa, and Michigan. In Iowa she was recognized as the Reading Teacher of the Year, the first secondary teacher to win such an award. Michele has co-authored two textbooks on learning strategies and vocabulary development and has contributed numerous chapters to edited books such as the *Handbook of Reading Research* (Vol. 3). In addition to making presentations at national and international conferences, she has published more than 50 articles in journals such as the *Journal of Adolescent & Adult Literacy* and the *Journal of Literacy Research.* She keeps current with the demands of public schools by collaborating with her husband, a middle school language arts teacher, and by consulting with school systems such as Winter Park High School in Orange County, Florida.

Michele lives in Athens, Georgia, with her husband and Siamese cat named Red Chief (if you know O'Henry, the author, you understand the cat's name). When she is not teaching or writing, she enjoys running, biking, and maintaining her Hatha Yoga regime.

DISCOVER THE COMPANION WEBSITE ACCOMPANYING THIS BOOK

THE PRENTICE HALL COMPANION WEBSITE: A VIRTUAL LEARNING ENVIRONMENT

Technology is a constantly growing and changing aspect of our field that is creating a need for content and resources. To address this emerging need, Prentice Hall has developed an online learning environment for students and professors alike—Companion Websites—to support our textbooks.

In creating a Companion Website, our goal is to build on and enhance what the textbook already offers. For this reason, the content for each user-friendly website is organized by chapter and provides the professor and student with a variety of meaningful resources.

FOR THE PROFESSOR—

Every Companion Website integrates **Syllabus Mansqer**™, an online syllabus creation and management utility.

- **Syllabus Manager**™ provides you, the instructor, with an easy, step-by-step process to create and revise syllabi, with direct links into the Companion Website and other online content without having to learn HTML.

- Students may log on to your syllabus during any study session. All they need to know is the web address for the Companion Website and the password you've assigned to your syllabus.

- After you have created a syllabus using **Syllabus Manager**™, students may enter the syllabus for their course section from any point in the Companion Website.

- Clicking on a date, the student is shown the list of activities for the assignment. The activities for each assignment are linked directly to actual content, saving time for students.

- Adding assignments consists of clicking on the desired due date, then filling in the details of the assignment—name of the assignment, instructions, and whether it is a one-time or repeating assignment.

- In addition, links to other activities can be created easily. If the activity is online, a URL can be entered in the space provided, and it will be linked automatically in the final syllabus.

- Your completed syllabus is hosted on our servers, allowing convenient updates from any computer on the Internet. Changes you make to your syllabus are immediately available to your students at their next logon.

Common Companion Website features for students include:

FOR THE STUDENT—

- **Chapter Objectives**—outline key concepts from the text
- **Interactive Self-quizzes**—complete with automatic grading that provides immediate feedback for students

    After students submit their answers for the interactive self-quizzes, the Companion Website **Results Reporter** computes a percentage grade, provides a graphic representation of how many questions were answered correctly and incorrectly, and gives a question-by-question analysis of the quiz. Students are given the option to send their quiz to up to four email addresses (professor, teaching assistant, study partner, etc.).

- **Web Resources**—links to www sites that relate to chapter content
- **Learning Network**—the Pearson Learning Network offers a wealth of additional resources to aid in their understanding and application of content

- **Message Board**—serves as a virtual bulletin board to post—or respond to—questions or comments to/from a national audience
- **Chat**—real-time chat with anyone who is using the text anywhere in the country—ideal for discussion and study groups, class projects, etc.

To take advantage of the many available resources, please visit the *Readers, Teachers, Learners: Expanding Literacy Across the Content Areas,* Fourth Edition, Companion Website at

www.prenhall.com/brozo

BRIEF CONTENTS

CONTENTS

Chapter 3   Comprehension Strategies: The Tools of Content-Area Teachers   53

Chapter 4   Classroom Assessment of Literacy Growth and Content Learning   97

Chapter 5 **Initiating Students to New Learning** **157**

Chapter 7   Writing as a Tool for Active Learning   **253**

Chapter 10   Expanding Literacy and Content Learning Through Computer Technology   401

Chapter 11   Becoming an Effective Content Literacy Professional   439

CHAPTER ONE

Readers, Teachers, Learners: An Introduction

ANTICIPATION GUIDE

Directions: Read each statement carefully and decide whether you agree or disagree with it, placing a check mark in the appropriate *Before Reading* column. When finished reading and studying the chapter, return to the guide and decide whether your anticipations need to be changed by placing a check mark in the appropriate *After Reading* column.

	BEFORE READING		AFTER READING	
	Agree	*Disagree*	*Agree*	*Disagree*
1. Students are better able to read at higher levels than in the past.	_____	_____	_____	_____
2. Literacy means being able to read words correctly.	_____	_____	_____	_____
3. All teachers should reinforce literacy skills for students.	_____	_____	_____	_____
4. *Aliteracy* means being unable to read.	_____	_____	_____	_____
5. Literacy can be used to achieve social and economic improvement.	_____	_____	_____	_____
6. Learning is most effective when students learn on their own.	_____	_____	_____	_____
7. Traditional print literacy is unaffected by communication technologies.	_____	_____	_____	_____

...[P]lausible argument, substantiated over three hundred years of insight and research, is that knowing is an activity, not a condition or state, that knowledge implies the making of connections, not an inert body of information, that both teachers and students are learners, that discourse manifests and realizes the power to learn, and that teaching entails creating incentives and contexts for learning, not a reporting of data. Specifically, learning is the process of an individual's mind making meaning from the material of its experience.

—Knoblach and Brannon (1983)

This book is about readers, teachers, and learners in middle and secondary school; it is about contexts for learning; and it is about how students can be supported in their use of language processes for gaining greater understanding of course content and gaining greater control over their literate futures.

Our purpose in this chapter is fourfold: (1) to share our philosophy of literacy; (2) to build a case for why literacy processes should be integral to middle and secondary content classroom instruction; (3) to describe what we believe to be the important foundations of language-based teaching; and (4) to lay out the assumptions about literacy and learning underpinning the strategies and ideas contained in this text.

Go to *http://www. prenhall.com/ brozo*, select Chapter 1, then click on Chapter Objectives to provide a focus for your reading.

WHAT IS LITERACY AND ITS ROLE IN MIDDLE AND SECONDARY SCHOOL?

To be literate in middle and secondary school means many things. It means using literacy to bring pleasure and expand one's sense of self. It means using literacy to become a more fully realized and participatory citizen in a democratic society such as ours. It means being able to use reading, writing, speaking, and listening to acquire and apply knowledge in content-area classrooms. And increasingly it is coming to mean using multiple literacies, including technological literacy, to access information and create products of new learning.

With regard to using literacy for pleasure and personal growth, it seems to us that middle and secondary school teachers must take as much care in reaching adolescents as they do in teaching them the curriculum. As if to confirm a long-held supposition about the relationship between reading widely for pleasure and reading achievement, recent national reading test results clearly demonstrate that middle- and upper-grade students who read for pleasure achieved higher scores on the test (Donahue, Voelkl, Campbell, & Mazzeo, 1999). A big part of reaching students is to trust the voices of our students, to be learners ourselves, and to take risks. Glasgow (1996) and others (Hill & Van Horn, 1995; Jimenez & Gamez, 1996; Stewart, Paradis, Ross, & Lewis, 1996) have found that one of the best ways to reach young adults at all ability levels is through books. Sharing books that help students work through a personal or interpersonal crisis, that excite their imaginations, or that support their "need to know" communicates the clear message that the teacher cares about students and values reading and learning outside the traditional boundaries of the school or class curriculum. To be a companion in literacy, however, requires that we ourselves read and know books. Linda Rief, a junior high school teacher, talks about how she rediscovered reading in a summer course and how she was shocked into awareness of her own reading habits:

To be a companion in students' literacy requires that we as teachers read and know books.

> She asked each of us to bring five favorite books we were currently reading, or had recently read, to the first class. I couldn't find five recently read

books. I realized I wasn't reading. I thought I didn't have time. That scared me. Reading was part of my curriculum. How could I have neglected it so badly? (1992, p. 3)

Becoming knowledgeable about books, and regularly reading and writing ourselves, puts us in the perfect position to introduce young adults to the pleasures and functional uses of literacy.

Helping students become critical, participatory citizens may be one of the most important, yet most neglected, aspects of literacy teaching and learning in middle and secondary schools (Goodman, 1992; Muspratt, Luke, & Freebody, 1997; Willinsky, 1990). This may be due to the way schools are structured. Gregory and Smith (1987) sum up the plight of American schools:

> In our view the typical American . . . school is much more effective as an instrument for controlling and confining . . . than as a means for teaching. . . . Very little of the . . . school experience is congruent with the findings of learning research or of common sense. Rather, it is about the fragmentation of knowledge, the emphasis on coverage at the expense of establishment of personal meaning, the tyranny of a time schedule that precludes lengthy discourse or introspection, and a concept of mass education that emasculates attempts to individualize learning. (p. 5)

The harshness of these criticisms makes us uncomfortable; yet, many students and parents appear to agree with them (Bintz, 1993). This book is an attempt to counter the diatribes of biased researchers and a critical public by presenting numerous examples of effective teaching and useful learning in middle and secondary schools.

One tool adolescent boys and girls must have to become more self-actualized adults is skillful and critical reading ability. As the U.S. House of Representatives Committee on Education and the Workforce (Forgione, 1999) found, reading ability is a powerful variable in the lives of youth that can contribute either to a virtuous cycle of successful living or a grinding cycle of constant difficulty and failure. Reinforcing this finding, Hofstetter, Sticht, and Hofstetter (1999) discovered that regardless of cultural background, people in society who achieve and exercise power over their lives spend more time reading than those who have less power or feel powerless. Reading, the authors assert, leads to knowledge, which is associated with power regardless of most barriers that citizens otherwise face. In other words, active literacy makes it possible for individuals to more readily acquire knowledge, which is the great equalizer in terms of access to the power levers in personal and community life.

Reading ability is a powerful variable in the lives of youth.

We believe our prescient forebears, such as Thomas Jefferson and Benjamin Franklin, foresaw the critical role schools could play in preparing students to be intelligent, functioning members in the democratic process. In fact, more than 200 years ago, they suggested that the biggest threat to national security was an uninformed populace. Literacy teaching and learning in junior and senior high schools could provide the necessary experiences for adolescents to take on the political, social, and economic challenges in the near and long term. Making literacy and learning meaningful on a sociopolitical level could help students look more critically at their own lives, as well as the lives of their neighbors and society, and imbue them with the courage to become involved in the improvement of our political, social, and economic condition (Gee, 2000; King & Brozo, 1992; Lankshear, 1993).

With regard to learning content material, unfortunately, students are rarely taught reading, writing, and reasoning processes that enable them to use these literacy skills as tools for learning in their daily schoolwork (Bean, 2000; Bintz, 1993). A traditional perspective of reading development assumes that students become fluent readers by third or fourth grade, just about the time they begin encountering textbooks in science, social studies, and health. But the processing demands of simple stories, which comprise nearly all of the material for reading instruction in the early grades, contrast sharply with the processing demands of expository texts from which middle and secondary students are expected to read and learn. Consequently, when students experience difficulty with expository reading in their content classes, it is often assumed that they have not learned to read properly, and they may be recycled through a program of basic reading skills. This practice leaves little hope of ever developing interested or sophisticated readers. When we consider the complexity of textbook reading, even greater time should be devoted to providing instruction in processing expository text at the middle and secondary levels than is provided for story reading at the elementary level (Vacca & Alvermann, 1998).

Processing demands of simple stories contrast sharply with those of expository text.

Finally, helping middle and secondary students exploit what would appear to be their natural interests in new technologies becomes one more tool for teachers to foster literacy and content learning (Alvermann, 2000). Mindful of the need to ensure young adults are print literate in the traditional sense, Luke and Elkins (1998) remind us that:

> . . . new technologies do not simply replace or erase older systems of communication. Rather they have a transformative, hybrid effect. . . . The advent of TV and the Internet are not a fait accompli, nor are they, as many teachers working in print traditions are convinced, simply negative forces to be oppressed at all costs. Rather they are still evolving, shapeable technologies that can be used for both constructive and quite destructive social and cultural consequences. (p. 5)

Middle- and upper-grade educators are turning more and more to electronic media, exploring their possibilities for engaging disaffected learners and integrating alternative information sources with traditional texts to improve students' understanding and appreciation of content-area topics.

Thus, reading is meaningful for adolescents when they can apply literacy processes for pleasure and personal growth, for better understanding of and influencing their world, for expanding comprehension of content textbooks and other school-related reading materials, and for using information and communication technologies in the process of learning. The development of these critical reading, writing, reasoning, and technology skills cannot be left to reading teachers or

Teachers in all subject areas are responsible for students' literacy growth.

English teachers alone. Teachers in all academic areas should be responsible for reinforcing literacy skills as they apply to the understanding of their particular content as well as helping adolescents appreciate the personal pleasures of literacy (Moore, Bean, Birdyshaw, & Rycik, 1999). As far back as 1926, Olive Gray offered this observation concerning the importance of content-area reading:

> In his school work a pupil needs facility in the rapid, exact reading of subject matter more than he needs any other type of reading ability that he may be led to acquire. The facility that is needed does not usually result from general training in reading. Even training in reading the subject matter of one field does not provide sufficient ability to read other types of material. (p. 607)

Although we are certainly not the first to make these admonitions, the idea that all teachers should assume responsibility for supporting students' various needs to be literate and ways of using literacy remains quite difficult for some to grasp (Wade & Moje, 2000). Yet, the stakes are too high for any of us not to take advantage of the powerful role we can play in the literate lives of adolescents. The fact is that none of us—teachers and students alike—at any point in time have "arrived" as readers, writers, and thinkers. Instead, our literacy skills are in a continual process of growth and refinement. Furthermore, it is in all teachers' best interests to nurture literacy growth for their students because the record shows irrefutably that better readers are better achievers in all subject areas (Campbell, Hombo, & Mazzeo, 2000).

DEFINITION OF LITERACY: A MODEST PROPOSAL

Given the multifarious nature of literacy, perhaps it is futile to attempt to include all of its dimensions in a single terse definition. We believe, therefore, that it is more helpful to define literacy by sharing scenes, contexts, and instances of literacy teaching and learning. In other words, we try in this book to make the concept concrete by demonstrating how teachers and students in middle and secondary schools continually stretch the boundaries of literacy possibilities. As you might infer, we believe there is no single best static definition of literacy. Nonetheless, we outline in general terms the variables inherent in literacy acts in schools. Following is our modest definition of literacy, which will form the basis for all of the discussion and methods in this book. This definition combines current theory and research with our own and others' teaching experiences.

Literacy (including traditional conceptions of reading, writing, speaking, and listening, as well as technologically based literacies) is a meaning-making and meaning-using process. Meaning is constructed through the interaction between the learner (in all of his or her complexity), the text (in all of its complexity and in all of its various forms of presentation), and instructional variables within the context of the learning situation. **Meaning** is used in direct relation to the level of interest in the learner and the level of functionality of the learning. The degree of interaction and use varies as a function of factors such as the learner's culture, prior knowledge, skills and strategies, motivation and interests, the type of text, the classroom environment, the instructional strategies, the meaningfulness of learning activities, and a host of other contextual factors.

Notice in this definition that our overall goal as learners is to make sense of our world through the use of literacy. Like all good thinkers, your ability to make meaningful interpretations of this book and use what you learn from it is directly related to:

1. how much you already know about the topic of literacy (prior knowledge)

2. how much experience you have with printed language (prior knowledge about the organization and structure of texts)

3. how interested and motivated you are in reading this text

4. what strategies you employ for studying and retaining the ideas and information (computer technology skills, such as navigating the Internet, chat room and message board experiences)

5. what your purpose is for reading it in the first place

6. how the instructor uses the book (if you are reading it for a college course), structures the literacy context, and provides classroom experiences for learning the concepts and strategies in the book

7. how well we as authors have communicated to you as the reader

As classroom teachers, the more instruction we provide that braids literacy processes with the curriculum (Guthrie, Cox, Anderson, Harris, Mazonni, & Rach, 1998) that is connected to the interests and experiences of the learner (Marshall, 2000), that allows for the exploration and generation of engaging texts (Many, Fyfe, Lewis, & Mitchell, 1996), and that makes learning meaningful and functional (Eccles, Wigfield, & Schiefele, 1998), the more we improve how students make and use meaning.

Teachers can help students improve how they make and use meaning.

The remainder of this chapter is devoted, first, to describing some growing trends on the middle and secondary school landscape to clarify why content-area literacy is so important. Next, we describe important foundations of language-based teaching that undergird the cases, scenes, and strategies offered in this text.

THE LITERACY AND LEARNING LANDSCAPE

The literacy and learning landscape in American middle and secondary schools resembles a geological landscape in that some of its terrain has remained quite stable while other areas are in the throes of change. For example, achievement levels in reading, math, and science show a pattern of relative stagnation over the past 20 to 30 years, whereas rapid, ever expanding developments in communication and information technologies have created upheaval among traditionally minded teachers and scholars. All of us have been forced to ask fundamental questions about the importance of print literacy and the very roles of classroom teachers themselves within this continually changing environment. The fact that this continuous change brings with it a need to regularly redefine the nature of literacy and learning has profound implications for middle and secondary school teachers and learners (Leu, 2000). Given these developments, even as we attempt to sketch the terrain of secondary reading and learning as we see it today, by the time you read this, "today" is many days in the past. Nonetheless, trends can be discerned and are worthwhile to consider as we try to anticipate the future challenges of our work as teachers of young adults.

Four growing trends in this landscape deserve our serious consideration. First, national assessment data on reading and writing continue to point to the fact that many middle and secondary school students cannot read or write beyond basic levels. This means more and more adolescent learners are struggling to survive. A second and insidious trend is that growing numbers of able readers are choosing not to read. This phenomenon is called *aliteracy.* Third, technology and electronic media are more influential than ever in the lives of young people and are shaping their perspectives on reading and learning. Finally, middle and secondary schools are becoming increasingly accountable for the achievement of their students as determined by high-stakes testing. Taken together, these trends pose many awesome challenges for middle and secondary school educators concerned about the literacy and knowledge growth of their students. Each is developed in more detail in the following discussion.

Low Levels of Literacy

Middle and high school students are expected to possess proficient vocabulary and comprehension skills necessary for understanding complex subject-area materials. However, despite the national emphasis on improving reading ability of children in the primary grades, many young adults who exited their elementary years with adequate reading skill find the reading demands placed on them at higher grade levels too taxing (McCray, Vaughn, & Neal, 2001). Furthermore, a majority of students who experienced reading difficulties in elementary school continue to struggle well into adolescence (Greene, 1999). Confirmation for these assertions comes from the National Assessment of Educational Progress (NAEP). A congressionally mandated project of the National Center for Education Statistics of the U.S. Department of Education, NAEP has been conducting nationwide surveys of the reading competency of 9-, 13-, and 17-year-olds since 1969 and of writing competence in the same grades since 1984. With its most recent reading assessment in 1999 (Campbell et al., 2000), we now have 30 years of data acquired over 10 administrations of NAEP reading. The following major trends have emerged:

Go to Web Resources for Chapter 1 at *http://www. prenhall.com/brozo* and look for National Assessment of Educational Progress.

■ The average reading proficiency for 13- and 17-year-olds has increased only slightly since 1971.

■ Virtually all students displayed rudimentary reading skills and strategies characterized by the ability to perform relatively uncomplicated, discrete reading tasks successfully. However, very few students in any assessment reached the highest levels of reading proficiency, reflecting their difficulty in comprehending passages that are more lengthy and complex or that deal with specialized subject matter.

■ For African American and Hispanic students at ages 13 and 17, gains in average reading proficiency have been extremely modest since 1984, while gains from 1971 to 1984 were dramatic. African American and Hispanic students in these age groups scored on average 30 points below those of similar aged white students, reversing a trend toward narrowing the gap that was only 20 points in 1988.

Many adolescents continue to have difficulty reading and writing at proficient and advanced levels.

Data from the most recent NAEP writing assessment for 8th and 12th graders (Greenwald, Persky, Campbell, & Mazzeo, 1999) paint a picture similar to the one in reading. Among the major findings are the following:

■ Despite successes junior and senior high schools may believe are occurring in writing instruction, the majority of students at both grade levels continue to have serious difficulty generating effective informative, persuasive, or narrative writing.

■ A majority of all students, but particularly those who were African American and Hispanic, did not reach proficient or advanced achievement levels. Most students in all categories demonstrated writing competency at the basic level.

These findings clearly demonstrate that middle and secondary students are not making the kinds of reading gains all of us would like to see. These data also point to the fact that students in larger numbers than should be acceptable are finding themselves in science, social studies, math, and language classes barely able to read, write, and process information at an appropriate level to be successful (Alvermann, 2000; Greenleaf, Schoenbach, Cziko, & Mueller, 2001).

Also, it would appear that not enough attention to writing as a regular and important form of communicating and meaning making is being given in junior and senior high schools. Attention to fostering higher levels of literacy and problem-solving abilities among young adults seems imperative because our world is becoming increasingly complex and increasingly challenges the intellectual and creative energies of all our citizens (Forgione, 1999).

There is some good news on this front, however. American eighth-grade students performed above the international average in math and science as compared with 37 other participating nations, both in 1995 and in 1999 (National Center for Education Statistics, 2000). Also, our fourth and ninth graders compare quite favorably to students in other countries in reading achievement. The International

Association for the Evaluation of Educational Achievement (IEA), in its International Reading Literacy Study (Binkley & Williams, 1997), found that American fourth graders ranked among those of the top three countries, behind Finland and Sweden, outperforming those of such industrialized nations as Germany and France. American ninth graders fared less well but were among the top 10 countries in the study. Results such as these from international studies of reading achievement among elementary and secondary school children help erode the myth that students in the United States are inferior to those from other countries.

A word of caution should be added to this discussion, however. IEA emphasizes that the tests used to measure reading comprehension focused almost exclusively on lower levels of thinking. In other words, to demonstrate success on the IEA test, students had to answer "questions directly related to the passage" (Binkley & Williams, 1997, p. 14). On the other hand, successful performance on NAEP's tests of reading required students to interpret and examine passage meaning, summarize, develop their own ideas about text information, and evaluate limitations of documents. In some ways, therefore, the IEA study corroborates the NAEP results. In both cases, students performed fairly well on measures of reading comprehension requiring lower levels of thinking; advanced literacy skills were found wanting on the NAEP test, though they were not measured on the IEA test.

We believe advanced literacy skills will develop when teachers place a special emphasis on helping students make thoughtful, critical elaborations of ideas and understandings that come from the materials they read and from their prior knowledge and experiences. To accomplish this, classroom teachers must shift away from learning that requires only simple memorization and superficial reading (Alvermann, 2000; Greenleaf et al., 2001).

Nearly every year, the national science and math teachers' associations call for a move away from teaching science and math as a collection of minute facts and details, which students tend to memorize for quizzes and tests and then forget, toward improving the way students think and reason about science and math and making this content more functional and meaningful. These points were reinforced when data from the Third International Mathematics and Science Study (Forgione, 1999) showed that the relative international standing of U.S. students declined as they progress through school. To explain why, the researchers placed the blame on the mathematics and science curricula in American middle and high schools. The basic problem, they say, is the "lack of coherence, depth, and continuity—for covering too many topics at the expense of in-depth understanding" (p. 12). Instead, they argue for an approach that teaches fewer topics well and initiates students to these topics in earlier grades. We strongly endorse this recommendation because, like these educators, we believe that as students' thinking abilities improve, their interest in and motivation to learn science and math will increase and their ability to learn and retain important science and math facts will improve.

One recommendation for developing in-depth understanding of content is to teach fewer topics well.

Science and math educators are not alone in their desire to transform the learning of that content from a rote exercise to a functional, problem-solving process. Similar curricular recommendations have been made by national social studies organizations under the banner of "globalism," whereby students are led to see how broad social, political, and economic issues relate to their everyday experiences.

In all the subjects students study, countless opportunities exist for developing higher level literacy and thinking skills. Classrooms that create experiences for students to tap their own prior knowledge, to connect their experiences with the topic, to develop their own interpretations of what they read, to question, rethink, self-assess, and elaborate on text information and ideas are likely to expand literacy and content learning (Bean, 2000).

The NAEP results also make clear the need to support students in their literacy efforts at home. Students at all three grade levels demonstrated higher reading proficiency if they (1) had a wider array of literacy materials in their homes, (2) read for fun on their own time, (3) had more frequent home discussions about their studies, (4) watched less television, and (5) read five or more pages each day of homework (Campbell et al., 2000).

Aliteracy

Barbara Hoover (1989), a syndicated columnist, tells a seriocomic story of falling in love with an attractive, enjoyable, and affectionate man. Not long into the relationship, however, she discovered that he owned just four books—a couple of business manuals, a dictionary, and a success guide. Her better judgment clouded temporarily by the newness of the romance, she minimized this observation and started bringing her own books to read during idle moments in their time together. After a couple of difficult years, they finally broke up. It was then, she says, that she realized an important truth: "There are two kinds of people: those who read and those who don't. And sometimes they run out of things to say to each other" (p. 3B).

Although more and more money is spent on ensuring children learn how to read, a growing number of people, like Hoover's ex-boyfriend, are in fact reading less and, in some cases, choosing not to read at all. This decision of literate individuals not to use their literacy has come to be known as **aliteracy.**

Studies in the 1980s (Thimmesch, 1985) revealed that the average college student had not read a book in four years after graduating; that fewer than 25% of Americans could be characterized as moderate to heavy readers (defined as reading 10 to 30 books or more per year); and that, for the most part, even teachers were not reading.

Students, parents, and teachers who know how to read but are out of the habit may be considered aliterate.

Today, there is even wider evidence for the phenomenon of aliteracy (Weeks, 2001). In a new Kinsey-style report on American reading habits (Carvajal, 1999), these ominous discoveries were made:

- In 1992 at the start of the study, almost 51% of those surveyed reported reading on average 1 hour per day. By 1999, the rate had dropped to 45%.

- Overall, fewer people are reading with any regularity, with those over 50 reading about twice as much per day as those in their 20s and younger.

These survey results are all the more troubling when we consider that Americans have a cultural heritage rooted in literacy. European settlers brought with them either the habit of reading or the desire for state-based/public schooling. Schools would be the sites where their children could learn to read and enjoy the benefits a lettered education would bring them (Soltow & Stevens, 1981). Passions for literacy were often so strong newcomers to the early colonies took great risks to include books among their personal stowage on the arduous sea voyage from the Old World. Louis Wright (1957) writes:

> Since freight was high and even the most elementary essentials of life had to be transported, the wonder is that the emigrants found room for such luxuries as books. But the fact is that they did. We can imagine the bewildered worry of many a pioneer, pondering the relative importance of an extra pair of books or a stout folio as he chose his indispensables for the Great Venture. The choice of books brought by the first settlers, or imported as soon as they had established themselves in the wilderness, provides a significant clue (of literacy) as an intellectual and social value. (p. 126)

Books and reading were tantamount to survival for many early American immigrants.

Books and reading were tantamount to survival for many early American immigrants. That kind of devotion to print literacy is difficult to come by today. It is the rare conversation among young people and adults alike that centers on the newest book read. Book talk has been replaced by conversation about last evening's TV shows or the latest movie or computer game, leading Sven Birkerts (1994) to ask: "In our zeal to embrace the wonders of the electronic age, are we sacrificing our literary culture" (p. 4)? Teachers, parents, and all concerned adults should ask themselves this sobering question when they reflect on how best to entice adolescents into the reading club and ensure they remain lifelong members.

Aliteracy is a phenomenon that appears to cut across socioeconomic status; the young and the old, the rich and the poor, the successful and the unsuccessful all have their share of able readers who prefer not to read (Carvajal, 1999). For example, interior decorators and homebuilders in wealthy suburbs report that large homes are being built and remodeled without libraries, studies, or bookshelves. The owners simply aren't reading. Instead, these homes are being furnished with lavish entertainment centers (Hoover, 1989). Even past U.S. presidents, such as Ronald Reagan and George Bush, might be characterized as aliterates because they knew how to read but simply chose not to. When interviewed at the end of his administration, Reagan was hard pressed to remember the last time he had read a book, let alone what the title was. And Bush boasted that when he read he liked to look through fishing magazines (even as his wife, Barbara, headed a national drive for literacy). We are not trying to single out these two presidents for criticism but rather to draw attention to how pervasive aliteracy has become in our country.

While speaking of political figures, studies have shown people who rely exclusively on video to size up political candidates make far more subjective judgments than people who rely largely on written accounts about those candidates and the issues (Minow & Lamay, 1996). This increasing proclivity toward evaluating candidates based on their television presence has far-reaching implications. For instance, we're coming to discover that, more often than not, political candidates who outspend their opponents in campaigns win elections. The great bulk of campaign spending, especially at the state and national levels, is for television advertising. Although our more cynical instincts tell us that this may have always been the case, increased television viewing may actually be playing into the hands of politicians with the deepest campaign chests. All of us would agree that a democracy is on a less than firm foundation if its citizenry elects not the representatives who have the best ideas, but those who have the most money. Politicians appear to be well aware of these contemporary truisms of campaign financing, as evidenced by the alarming number of scandals related to their obsession with raising money.

The impact of aliteracy even reaches our political system.

It is difficult for adults, whether parents, teachers, successful businesspeople, or politicians, to impart the love of reading or even a positive attitude toward reading to American youth unless they themselves value literacy enough to make it an integral part of their lives.

With respect to secondary school students, recent national surveys (Libsch & Breslow, 1996) of high school seniors' reading habits reveal an overall decline since 1975 in the reading of books and other nonassigned material. A disturbing increase was noted by the investigators for both females and males in the number of seniors reading fewer magazines and newspapers on a daily basis and no books at all, as compared with teens from past surveys. Others (Beers, 1996; Schumm & Saumell, 1994) corroborate these survey findings with evidence of their own for widespread aliteracy among young adults. All agree that we know aliteracy is a serious problem, but questions about how it starts, how it can be prevented from spreading, and how it might be prevented in the first place have yet to be clearly resolved.

We argue, therefore, that teachers are foot soldiers in the fight against aliteracy. Those of us who work directly with middle- and upper-grade students are in the best position to foster positive perceptions and attitudes toward literacy while giving students regular and frequent opportunities to practice and grow as literate learners.

The Technological Classroom

Nicholas Negroponte (1995), in his book *Being Digital*, says "Computing is not about computers any more. It is about living" (p. 6). The implications of this pronouncement for teachers and learners in middle and secondary schools are considerable. Today, it is commonplace for students to have computers in their homes and know more about them and have more facility with their wide-ranging capabilities than many adults (Hollingsworth & Eastman, 1997). No longer is there a question about whether technology will play a role in the literacy and content learning of students but rather to what extent it will. Given the ubiquitous nature of electronically networked information resources in the day-to-day lives of teen and preteen youth, many educators believe schools should be sites for exploiting these new technologies to better prepare students for a rapidly changing future (Leu, 2000).

Techno-visionaries (Herreid, 2000) see a world of the next 30 years where virtual classrooms link students across the world and electronic personalities become the teachers. Schools as we know them will disappear in the 21st century, they say, as newer more technologically nimble institutions emerge that push the visual and conceptual barriers away to address the real needs of students (Harris & Sullivan, 2000). Advocates of this new vision (McDonough, 2000) exhort schools to begin designing all classrooms in ways that make technology user friendly. Teachers are also admonished to develop expanded computer knowledge and skills well beyond simple word processing, e-mail, and spreadsheet applications (Rickelman & Caplan, 2000).

> *Technology is not a quick fix for literacy and learning problems but, when used effectively, can be part of the solution.*

To be sure, not all educators and scholars share the dream that technology may hold for today's youth. Some, like Jane Healy (1999), worry that children and young adults are becoming subjects of an enormously sanguine experiment, involving getting and keeping kids on computers. She wonders if technology will indeed improve the quality of learning for adolescents and prepare them for the future, or whether the unmitigated positive regard for computers is a desperate effort to find a "quick fix" for a multitude of problems facing teachers and learners we have been unable to address.

Regardless of one's opinion on the matter of transforming middle schools and high schools into high-tech learning environments, information and communication technologies are here to stay. How teachers integrate computers and other electronic media into the content classroom while expanding literacy and a consciousness of active learning for all students is the ultimate challenge they will face in this new century.

High-Stakes Testing and Teacher Accountability

Like death and taxes, some are loath to say, testing has become a fact of life. Few like to have to administer tests, fewer like to take them; yet, the trend across the nation, at least in the near term, is for more rather than less testing to occur in middle and secondary schools. Recent presidents have built testing priorities into their education agendas. Some prefer a national test of basic skills accountability, whereas others want each state to develop its own measures. During the 1990s, educators in virtually every state committed an enormous amount of time and energy to develop descriptions of standards at every level and for every content area (McGill-Franzen, 2000), while at the same time putting into place major statewide testing programs to determine the degree to which students met the standards (Haertel, 1999).

Many teachers and parents have maligned what they perceive as the rampant and inappropriate use of standardized tests as a tool for school reform (Barksdale-Ladd & Thomas, 2000). In many states, teachers' and administrators' very jobs have been placed in jeopardy because of their students' test scores

(Sheldon & Biddle, 1998). The result has been to design curricula around the expectations of the tests. Test-driven instruction for students in the content areas does have its brighter side, according to some (Hargis, 1990), especially when such tests cover critical material and are designed well (Smith, Stevenson, & Li, 1998).

Our concern is that mandated, high-stakes, standardized testing will reduce the curriculum to the inculcation of a collection of "knowledge widgets," at the unfortunate expense of critical learning. Supporters of critical learning (Gee, 2000; Luke, 1998) talk about the need to infuse school curricula with a literacy perspective whereby reading and writing become processes for educating students to be critical participatory citizens. In this view (King & Brozo, 1992), school learning should provide the context for students to become critical and self-determined thinkers. Unfortunately, as increasing testing, economic, and political pressures dictate the teaching and learning possibilities for teachers and students, teachers often find themselves in the role of information disseminator, forced to find ever more efficient means to "cover the material."

Standardized testing and the development of critical literacy seem to be at odds.

Symptomatic of a curriculum that has become devoid of a critical component is the preoccupation among policy makers that adolescents get a job or do better than Japan (Gee, Hull, & Lankshear, 1996). This single-minded thinking about the purpose of schooling reflects the prevailing condition of much of our content-area curriculum. Middle and secondary schools that make it a priority to educate students to make choices and think critically can help students develop the confidence and conviction that they can make a difference in the world (Hull, 2000). This sense of power can result from instruction concerned with making connections between and among teachers and students, within and among classrooms, and inside and outside of schools. Critical literacy fosters an understanding of the ways we are all interconnected and interdependent and teaches that in caring for others we are in fact caring for ourselves (Goodman, 1992).

When conceptualizing a curriculum of critical literacy that attends to the real-world needs, concerns, and aspirations of youth, we can't help but think of the monumental problems facing us as a nation that beg for creative and humane solutions. Those same problems could be the focus of our curriculum in middle and secondary schools: for example, conditions of urban and rural poverty, overpopulation and world hunger, environmental degradation, unresponsive government, and the energy crisis. We believe that schools can become sites for entertaining, working toward, and remedying the social, political, economic, and environmental ills of our communities, nation, and world. How this vision might be realized within a standards- and test-driven school order will be the challenge for us all.

In the end, regardless of their supporters and detractors, testing and assessment are not going away anytime soon. Perhaps a sensible balance for middle and secondary school teachers is to retain a critical stance on assessment while preparing students for their inevitability (Christensen, 1999). We have seen excellent teachers of young adults develop sensible and effective strategies for dealing with high-stakes tests. First and foremost, they ensure the important content of the subject area is learned in interesting, meaningful, and critical ways, but they also reserve a portion of the curriculum to helping students develop techniques for dealing with tests (McColskey & McMunn, 2000).

In the concluding section of this chapter, we outline five essential foundations of language-based teaching. Based on our own teaching experience, our work with other teachers, and our knowledge of the research and applied literature in literacy, we believe adherence to these foundations holds great promise for meeting the challenges posed by falling levels of literacy, aliteracy, the technological revolution, and high-stakes testing.

FOUNDATIONS OF LANGUAGE-BASED TEACHING

Language-based teaching involves much more than the narrow notion of reading and writing techniques. It is a philosophy of teaching that sees the teacher's role, regardless of content area, as one of exploiting language in all its dimensions to facilitate students' own knowledge construction and use.

Following are the five foundations we consider essential for effective language-based teaching:

1. Language-based teachers understand that learning is a social process.
2. Language-based teachers know that the best learning occurs when it is whole, functional, and meaningful.
3. Language-based teachers know that students improve their reading and writing when given abundant opportunities to use reading and writing as vehicles for learning.
4. Language-based teachers understand the importance motivation plays in learning.
5. Language-based teachers are continually moving toward better literacy and content teaching.

Foundation 1: Language-Based Teachers Understand That Learning Is a Social Process

It has long been recognized that we know what we know only when we reflect our knowledge in others (Blumer, 1969). Harste (1988) offers these insights into the significance of the social nature of learning:

> I am convinced that we know nothing by ourselves. It is only in juxtaposition with others that we know, and know what we know differs from others' knowledge. (p. 13)

Literacy is a social process (Green, 1990; Myers, 1992; Turner, 1995). Social processes fashion social languages (Gee, 2000) that are "used to enact, recognize, and negotiate different socially situated identities and to carry out different socially situated activities" (p. 413). From this point of view, literacy is understandable only when it is viewed in relation to others. For instance, when Monica, a 10th grader, confides in her English journal that her boyfriend has been unfaithful, she might write: "I'm feeling really angry today because Jack, my boyfriend, or should I say my ex-boyfriend, is seeing someone else." After school, on the walk home with her best friend, Tara, Monica tells her: "I found out today that Jack's hangin' with Christi. That scumbag is dead!" For her English teacher, Monica uses socially accepted discourse conventions; while talking with her friend away from school space, she uses another culturally distinctive language form that defines herself and her friend as socially intimate partners.

Social learning promotes intextual tying.

To be literate, then, is to be part of a social context. Even when you curl up with a book in the "private" act of reading, you are not alone—you are interacting with an author who holds other ideas, points of view, and styles of expression. A useful construct here is **intertextuality**, or ways in which an individual's construction of meaning depends on other meanings (Hartman, 1995; Lenski, 1998). It has been demonstrated (Bloome & Egan-Robertson, 1993; Saunders, 1997; Unrau & Ruddell, 1995) that when teachers provide for intertextual tying, when they exploit the social world of the classroom and socially derived texts from their students, greater language learning takes place. By providing students opportunities to observe another author at work and to talk with that author, they will make connections between their own and others' spoken and written texts in order to develop and expand on their own ideas.

The instructional implications of the social nature of learning are many and varied. On a general level, students can build shared meanings of literacy, language, and concepts when they are encouraged to make use of demonstrations provided by their peers and teachers and are given opportunities to interact informally with other authors and learners in the classroom community. On a practical level, the classroom itself should be arranged to encourage social interaction among student meaning makers. Instead of arranging desks in rows, forcing students to talk to the back of others' heads and making easy eye contact only with the teacher, we recommend a more flexible seating arrangement that encourages student-student dialoguing and problem solving. One such approach is cooperative learning, which has been found to improve not only the academic achievement of students but also their level of interpersonal attraction.

Cooperative Learning

Johnson and Johnson (1989) describe three basic learning experiences that students are likely to have in schools: individualistic, competitive, and cooperative. Of the three, cooperative learning has been shown to be superior for facilitating a teacher's constructive use of student interaction, alleviating the monotony of the traditional teacher-directed classroom, improving academic achievement and content learning, building student self-esteem, and improving pro-social behavior (Slavin & Cooper, 1999).

 Go to Web Resources for Chapter 1 at *http://www.prenhall.com/brozo* and look for cooperative learning.

Cooperative learning groups consist generally of three or more students grouped heterogeneously and linked by a common goal. The emphasis in the groups is on the completion of an academic assignment and the promotion of social skills. Cooperative learning has become immensely popular since the early 1980s because of its positive effect on achievement, self-esteem, interpersonal dynamics, and motivation. Figure 1.1 presents the essential elements for successful cooperative learning.

Cooperative learning promotes constructive meaning making through student interaction.

The use of cooperative groups as a dynamic method for teaching content-area comprehension and learning has been consistently supported by a history of voluminous research (Slavin, 1996). Cooperative learning has been shown to help students assume greater responsibility for their learning and approach learning tasks with more confidence (Slavin & Cooper, 1999). In heterogeneous classroom situations, where social interaction plays an important role in the facilitation of learning (Jordan & LeMatais, 1997), cooperative learning provides students who view themselves as unsuccessful learners, when grouped with others of low ability (Ediger, 1995; Thorpe & Wood, 2000), the opportunity to

FIGURE 1.1 Essential Elements of Cooperative Learning

1. *Positive interdependence:* "We sink or swim together!"
   Methods to promote this attitude include
   - mutual goal
   - group accountability
   - shared/limited materials
   - group rewards
   - complementary and interconnected roles
   - division of labor
2. *Individual accountability:* "No hitchhiking!"
   Methods to promote this attitude include
   - individual tests
   - random selection of a group member
   - random selection of one paper
3. *Face-to-face interaction*
   - eye to eye, knee to knee
   - oral exchange
   - conducive physical arrangement
4. *Appropriate use of collaborative skills*
   - skills should be taught
   - skills should be practiced
   - students should be motivated to use skills
   - skills should be assessed by teacher or group members

make significant contributions to group decisions. Further, cooperative learning gives students the opportunity to share what they have learned, to listen to the ideas and opinions of fellow students, to be taught by their peers, and to assume the role of teacher (Johnson & Johnson, 1996; Schniedewind & Davidson, 2000). As a result of cooperative learning, greater literacy and content learning have been observed in a variety of classroom contexts (Bowen, 2000; Chang & Mao, 1999; Hendrix, 1999).

Given the support in the professional literature for cooperative learning, one would think this approach has the potential for solving nearly all classrooms ills. Clearly, cooperative learning is not a panacea (Blumenfeld, Marx, Soloway, & Krajcik, 1997). Some (Randall, 1999) wonder whether we have popularized the approach to the point that has blinded us to its drawbacks. Others (Cohen & Lotan, 1995; Leonard & McElroy, 2000) recommend teachers ensure the following in order to increase the likelihood of successful cooperative group learning and interaction:

- Make certain that all students have a role to play.
- Clearly define roles and make them all high status and equally important.
- Make certain students consider everyone's thinking.
- Carefully monitor each group to determine all students are actively involved.

When teachers in middle and secondary schools use cooperative learning appropriately, they communicate to students that their input is equally valued and that their contributions broaden the understanding of the content for all learners in the classroom community. We demonstrate applications of this powerful teaching and learning strategy throughout this book.

Foundation 2: Language-Based Teachers Know That the Best Learning Occurs When It Is Whole, Functional, and Meaningful

The term **whole** in this principle has many different aspects. In one sense, it refers to complete and genuine text sources that students read and write. Commercially prepared learning materials, such as textbooks, are bound by countless restrictions that result inevitably in "pointlessly arid prose" (Tyson-Bernstein, 1988). Genuine text, on the other hand, is created by authors who simply have an urge to communicate their perspectives and information on a topic. Consider, for instance, the difference between the treatment of the Vietnam War in a 10th-grade history textbook compared with Elizabeth Becker's (1992) *America's Vietnam War: A Narrative History*. The textbook, because of space limitations, offers only a few pages on the topic. The textbook publisher makes sure that issues about the war that might be considered too controversial are not included; concerns about readability force the authors of the textbook to exclude certain imaginative terms and phrases. By comparison, Becker's book provides an in-depth, critical view of the issues surrounding the Vietnam War, from the history of American involvement to the fall of Saigon. Unbounded by publisher restrictions, such as those placed on textbook authors, Becker presents the topic in a lively and engaging way that is sure to draw adolescent readers into a more thoughtful study of Vietnam. Although textbooks often form the core of learning in most secondary classrooms, we suggest that textbooks alone aren't enough because they fail the test of wholeness.

With respect to writing, we advocate that teachers allow students to compose complete texts through the writing process (discussed in detail in Chapter 7). Instead of being confined to certain topics and forms of writing, as often as possible students should be free to select the discourse mode best suited to their needs of expression. For example, in writing about the Vietnam War, students required to write a two-page report on the battle of Dien Bien Phu or the Gulf of Tonkin incident would likely be less engaged in and enthusiastic about learning than if they were asked to put themselves in the place of a participant or a victim of the war (e.g., a Viet Cong villager, a witness to the My Lai massacre, an American living in Canada to avoid the draft, a parent of a soldier who is missing in action) and write, for instance, a letter, diary entry, or story. Better yet, students could be asked to respond in writing, using a variety of discourse options that help them rework the content. When given options, students may choose to write poetry, song lyrics, or dialog for a drama to be enacted impromptu by a small group. In this way, students become much more invested in the learning process as they develop a sense of ownership of their ideas and their learning.

Students own their learning when allowed to choose their discourse mode.

Another aspect of whole learning is the notion of **integrated learning.** Students should be involved in activities and projects that require integrating reading, writing, speaking, and listening. Writers workshops (see Chapter 7), for example, can be used to bring all the language systems to bear on learning content material. Integration also refers to tying together learning from many areas of the secondary school curriculum. This aspect of holistic teaching can be the most challenging for secondary teachers, largely because of the highly departmentalized nature of most junior and senior high schools. Consider this example of integration: Students learning about the Vietnam War could be learning about the U.S. government's evolving foreign policy as it relates to Southeast Asia in one classroom, the culture and customs of Southeast Asia in another, and the economic ramifications of the war in another. Students meanwhile could read works of fiction by Southeast Asian authors or about this region and its people. Making the curriculum whole allows students to see the interconnectedness of content in order to develop a broader understanding of topics. We present strategies for teachers working together to bring cohesion to the curriculum in Chapter 11.

Webster's dictionary defines **functional** as "connected with." We like this definition because it implies that when teachers make learning functional, students connect with it. They find linkages between classroom content, on the one hand, and needs and purposes in their personal lives, on the other. We

Functional learning is tied to students' lives.

agree with Edelsky, Altwerger, and Flores (1991), who argue that "learners' purposes and intentions are what drives learning" (p. 25). If the sole purpose of learning is external to the learner (e.g., pleasing the teacher, getting a good grade), then it doesn't really matter what is learned. In content-area classrooms where the purposes of learning are always and unilaterally determined by the teacher, we have seen a condition of "learned helplessness" (Diener & Dweck, 1978) set in. Students can become so conditioned to respond only to teachers' directives that they rarely, if ever, initiate learning, attack problems independently, or seek out information on their own. By contrast, students in classrooms that support their own explorations of functional learning are engaged, enthusiastic, and independent.

An excellent example of functional learning comes from a senior high school French class where the teacher provided the necessary support for students to explore their career options in a French language profession or aspects of French culture about which students desired more information. One student, Deanna, interviewed translators from international businesses (e.g., Michelin) and gained insights into the educational and experiential prerequisites for such a career. Terrell read about and spoke directly to French poets and writers whose topics dealt with race relations in France. Kimme's interest in becoming a buyer for a major department store led her to study the French fashion world. And Charles looked into French wines and cuisine with the intent of using this knowledge to conduct eating tours in France. These students kept a log of their information-gathering process, including following leads, phone conversations, and written correspondence, as well as personal reflections on their research. They also shared their findings with the class. Their demonstrations clearly reflected the power of making learning functional.

Meaningfulness refers to ways of making learning personally meaningful for the learner. If we assume that the only way to make students learn is to force them to learn, then we may be left with no choice but to use force every time we try to teach. Think about an alternative self-fulfilling prophecy. What if we demonstrated trust in students' own natural curiosity, their own need to know more, their ability to make meaning? Imagine the transformation that might take place in classrooms where students are supported in their efforts to find meaningful connections to their own lives and their realities outside school with topics and content being considered in school. In working with Chicago youth, we discovered that students who were considered problems became engaged in learning when they were supported in their efforts to bring their real-world issues and concerns into the classroom. Using a reader-response writing strategy (described in detail in Chapter 7), students in an eighth-grade social studies class read magazine and newspaper articles about problems common to most inner-city communities and then wrote responses connecting their own experiences with those in the readings. Raymond, a former "graffiti artist," responded to an article in the *Chicago Tribune* about gangs and graffiti by relating it to his experiences. Raymond claimed that although most graffiti artists were not gang members, the mayor was linking all of them to gangs to mobilize more resources to eradicate graffiti. The teacher of this class found that by supporting her students' efforts to bring their lives into the content of their writing, students like Raymond became more engaged learners and more animated participants in class discussion.

Foundation 3: Language-Based Teachers Know That Students Improve Their Reading and Writing When Given Abundant Opportunities to Use Reading and Writing as Vehicles for Learning

Earlier, we described the result of aliteracy: Children and youth adopt the attitude that using literacy is not critical to functioning in the adult world. As one avoids literacy experiences more and more, one's reading, writing, and critical thinking skills wither. Frank Smith's (1985) pithy axiom that "We learn to read by reading" (p. 88) captures the essence of this principle. All of us must take responsibility for expanding literacy for our students. This is not the purview of any single teacher or of parents alone. And to do so, we must all be prepared to involve students in literacy experiences that contribute to their language development and their ability to think more expansively about themselves and their worlds.

Middle and secondary school learning environments that embody this principle of language-based teaching possess characteristics of immersion, demonstration, interaction, and transaction. **Immersion** refers to involving students in environments that are language-rich, filled with real-world artifacts of the adult literate community and opportunities for critical analysis of school, text, and personal truths. **Demonstration** reminds us that teachers should know the literacy processes from the inside out to credibly model teaching as learning and teaching as inquiry. **Interaction** refers to giving students opportunities to learn from one another, value one another, and critique one another's truths. The teacher's truths should be subject to the same level of scrutiny as anyone else's. **Transaction** suggests that for students to learn principles of cooperation, participation, and critical citizenship, they should be directly involved in shaping the curriculum so that it is more closely aligned with their personal and career needs and goals.

In content-area classrooms, this principle means that teachers create supportive learning environments for students to use the language processes of reading, writing, speaking, and listening to better understand the curriculum. Such an environment would likely include process writing (see Chapter 7) wherein students work together to write drafts, receive feedback, and rewrite until their work is ready to be graded and/or published. A content-area teacher who encourages students' literacy growth while expanding their knowledge of content also makes available to students and makes integral to the curriculum a variety of resources, such as multimedia, electronic databases, trade and reference books, textbooks, and, as mentioned, a variety of literacy material from the adult world. Not only can these alternative reading materials generate more enthusiasm for reading and learning, but they are also excellent resources for broadening students' understanding of topics as they read and consider the topics from various perspectives.

In middle and secondary classrooms where this principle is practiced, teachers in all content areas provide sustained, uninterrupted periods for students and themselves to read and write. In this way, a literate culture is developed wherein teachers model healthy, adaptive literacy behavior while nurturing the literacy habits of their students.

All content-area teachers can create opportunities for sustained, uninterrupted reading and writing.

Virtually every chapter of this book offers ideas and strategies for getting students more actively and frequently involved in using the language systems as vehicles for learning and for personal growth and pleasure.

Foundation 4: Language-Based Teachers Understand the Importance of Engaged Learning

Engaged learning or motivation is a topic researchers of learning can never ignore. Behaviorists may try to argue that children can be taught to learn school-based information and content much the same way they can be taught to dribble a basketball or swim the breast stroke—that is, by breaking down learning into minute parts and steps, working discretely with each one until all have been mastered before putting the parts together into a meaningful whole. Missing, of course, in the behavioral approach to instruction is whether or not the learner has the will to master discrete parts of learning. Without a student's acquiescence, all of our attempts at drill and practice of small, fragmented parts of learning will meet with disappointment. A principal offered these enlightened words to us recently on this topic: "We can force students to attend school, but we can't force them to learn."

Not surprisingly, motivation has remained one of the most popular areas of interest to researchers and practitioners in literacy and content learning (Guthrie & Wigfield, 2000). Over the past couple of decades, research has offered us many important new insights into how to motivate students to read by using interesting books (Allington & Guice, 1997; Elley, 1992; Guthrie, Alao, & Rinehart, 1997) and how this motivation can translate into significant improvement in reading achievement (Baker & Wigfield, 2000; Taylor, Frye, & Maruyama, 1990).

Content teachers can help students develop the will to learn.

Turner (1995) has provided extensive research-based descriptions of school contexts that are motivating for students. These motivating contexts consist of the "six Cs" (Turner & Paris, 1995):

Choice.   When students can choose the tasks and texts they are interested in, they spend more energy trying to learn and understand the material.

Challenge.   Moderately challenging tasks, as opposed to simple, feel-good tasks, are often the most engaging and cognitively useful to students.

Control.   Students need to have some control of their learning in order to develop independence and versatility as learners.

Collaboration.   Social interaction and cooperation are fundamental to motivation because they increase effort and persistence.

Constructing meaning.   Active meaning construction promotes motivation by placing responsibility on students to make sense of their learning. When students are denied this responsibility, they often become passive and nonparticipatory.

Consequences.   Students should be helped to see the connection between effort and outcome. When tasks are controllable, students are more likely to take responsibility for them and more willing to learn from mistakes.

As you proceed through this book, pay attention to how the teachers in the many scenarios we describe incorporate the six Cs into their instructional approach.

Foundation 5: Language-Based Teachers Are Continually Moving Toward Better Literacy and Content Teaching

A theme running throughout this book is that language-based teaching is a process. This book is meant to encourage and support content-area teachers as they move from teaching practices that focus exclusively on content to those that develop and apply students' language processes and, in this way, help students come to value literacy as an integral part of their lives. Advocates of a content/ process model of middle and secondary school teaching for improving students' ability to learn content material, as well as for expanding students' sense of themselves as learners and as critical, independent decision makers, have been around for some time (see Herber, 1978). Nonetheless, changes in the ways teachers teach junior and senior high students have been slow and painstaking. Administrators, professors, "experts," teachers, and students all share some of the responsibility for this uneven progress. Some (Moje, Brozo, & Haas, 1994; O'Brien, Stewart, and Moje, 1995) explain how the realities of middle and secondary school teaching, including curricular demands and institutional and peer pressures, can seem to leave teachers little choice but to employ efficient but unengaging and unauthentic instructional methods (e.g., lecturing, objective testing). We understand the realities of change and, therefore, emphasize the value of making transitions.

After working with a junior high school teacher, Robin, for a year as she implemented cooperative learning for the first time after 12 years of teaching, we found that two overarching generalizations hold true with regard to making transitions in teaching: transitions take time, and they involve helping students make transitions.

Transitions Take Time

Effective content-area teachers are always seeking new ways of infusing their instruction with language-based strategies.

Robin wanted to change but found that when her students didn't respond in ways she had expected, she became filled with self-doubt and wondered about returning to an information dissemination model of teaching. It was only after 3 or 4 months of the school year, as her students began to take on their cooperative roles with enthusiasm and independence, that she saw the tangible benefits of this new approach to teaching and learning. Robin realized that through exploration, experimentation, and reflection she eventually appreciated the powerful transformation taking place in her classroom. As Robin allowed time for change, students began to change; these positive changes in the students then made it easier for Robin to accept and support further transitions to more language-based, cooperative teaching.

Transitions Involve Helping Students Make Transitions

We often forget, in our enthusiastic support of teacher change, that as challenging as it may be for teachers themselves to make the transition to new models of teaching, it may be even more challenging for students in a changing classroom environment. In Robin's classroom, we discovered that students were not prepared initially for the demands of cooperative learning and, therefore, could not make an abrupt transition from their role as receivers of information to active participants in shared learning. As discussed, the interrelationship between the students' reluctance to change and Robin's perseverance to work through change was critical. What helped was Robin's willingness to provide more modeling, more opportunities for students to take risks and experiment with their new roles. Perhaps most critical, however, was the self-assessment that was built into the process of cooperative learning. Through this process, students were able to take a new look at themselves as learners and turn to Robin for support. In this process, too, Robin watched herself change from "purveyor of truth" to someone who created the process and environment that allowed students to see each other as learning resources.

SUMMARY

This opening chapter has set the stage for the ideas, examples, and strategies presented in this book. We have discussed the challenges all of us must face in attempting to encourage middle and secondary students to become active, full participants in the learning process. Findings from national reports on literacy skills and on the literacy habits of adolescents and adults present an ever shifting landscape that will require middle and secondary school teachers to be flexible, creative, and student-centered. Low levels of literacy are apparently becoming acceptable in our schools, and an attitude of indifference toward reading appears to be growing among adults; meanwhile, our youth are becoming increasingly passive learners. At the same time, as testing and accountability pressures mount, the potential power of literacy as a tool for promoting social, political, and economic transformation may continue to be sacrificed in middle and secondary schools. Finally, literacy itself is being redefined by information and communication technologies.

Go to *http://www.prenhall.com/brozo,* select Chapter 1, then click on Chapter Review Questions to check your understanding of the material.

To thrive in this new landscape, we suggest that teachers, with the help of their students, create learning environments in content classrooms that are language based, where students use literacy and technology to acquire new knowledge, to grow personally, to find pleasure, and to transform themselves and their world.

REFERENCES

Allington, R., & Guice, S. (1997). Literature curriculum: Issues of definition and control. In J. Flood, S. B. Heath, & D. Lapp (Eds.), *Research on teaching literacy through communicative and visual arts*. New York: Macmillan.

Alvermann, D. (2000). *Grappling with the big issues in middle grades literacy education*. Keynote address at the Conference of the National Educational Research Policy and Priorities Board, Washington, DC.

Baker, L., & Wigfield, A. (2000). Dimensions of children's motivation for reading and their relations to reading activity and reading achievement. *Reading Research Quarterly, 34,* 452–477.

Barksdale-Ladd, M., & Thomas, K. (2000). What's at stake in high-stakes testing: Teachers and parents speak out. *Journal of Teacher Education, 51,* 384–399.

Bean, T. (2000). Reading in the content areas: Social constructivist dimensions. In M. Kamil, P. Mosenthal, P. D. Pearson, & R. Barr (Eds.), *Handbook of reading research* (Vol. 3). Mahwah, NJ: Lawrence Erlbaum Associates.

Becker, E. (1992). *America's Vietnam war: A narrative history.* New York: Clarion Books.

Beers, K. (1996). No time, no interest, no way: The three voices of aliteracy. *School Library Journal, 42,* 30–41.

Binkley, M., & Williams, T. (1997). *Reading literacy in the United States.* Washington, DC: U.S. Department of Education.

Bintz, W. (1993). Resistant readers in secondary education: Some insights and implications. *Journal of Reading, 36,* 604–615.

Birkerts, S. (1994). *The Gutenberg elegies.* New York: Fawcett Columbine.

Bloome, D., & Egan-Robertson, A. (1993). The social construction of intertextuality in classroom reading and writing lessons. *Reading Research Quarterly, 28,* 304–333.

Blumenfeld, P., Marx, R., Soloway, E., & Krajcik, J. (1997). Learning with peers: From small group cooperation to collaborative communities. *Educational Researcher, 25,* 37–40.

Blumer, H. (1969). *Symbolic interactionism: Perspectives and method.* Englewood Cliffs, NJ: Prentice Hall.

Bowen, C. (2000). A quantitative literature review of cooperative learning effects on high school and college chemistry achievement. *Journal of Chemical Education, 77,* 116–119.

Campbell, J., Hombo, C., & Mazzeo, J. (2000). *NAEP 1999 trends in academic progress.* Washington, DC: National Center for Education Statistics.

Carvajal, D. (1999, July 12). In search of readers, publishers consider age. *New York Times,* C1.

Chang, C. Y., & Mao, S. L. (1999). The effects on students' cognitive achievement when using the cooperative learning method in earth science classrooms. *School Science and Mathematics, 99,* 374–379.

Christensen, L. (1999). High stakes harm. *Rethinking Schools, 13,* 14–18.

Cohen, E., & Lotan, R. (1995). Producing equal-status interaction in the heterogeneous classroom. *American Educational Research Journal, 32,* 99–120.

Diener, C., & Dweck, C. (1978). An analysis of learned helplessness: Continuous changes in performance, strategy, and achievement cognitions following failure. *Journal of Personality and Social Psychology, 34,* 451–462.

Donahue, P., Voelkl, K., Campbell, J., & Mazzeo, J. (1999). *NAEP 1998 reading report card for the nation.* Washington, DC: National Center for Education Statistics.

Eccles, J., Wigfield, A., & Schiefele, U. (1998). Motivation to succeed. In W. Damon (series Ed.) & N. Eisenberg (Ed.), *Handbook of child psychology: (Vol.3) Social, emotional, and personality development* (5th ed.). New York: Wiley.

Edelsky, C., Altwerger, B., & Flores, B. (1991). *Whole language:What's the difference?* Portsmouth, NH: Heinemann.

Ediger, M. (1995). Cooperative learning and heterogeneous grouping. *Reading Improvement, 32,* 135-143.

Elley, W. (1992). *How in the world do students read?* Hamburg, Germany: International Association for the Evaluation of Educational Achievement.

Forgione, P. (1999). *Achievement in the United States:Are students performing better?* Washington, DC: National Center for Education Statistics.

Gee, J. P. (2000). Teenagers in new times: A new literacy studies perspective. *Journal of Adolescent & Adult Literacy, 43,* 412-420.

Gee, J. P., Hull, G., & Lankshear, C. (1996). *The new work order:Behind the language of the new capitalism.* Boulder, CO: Westview.

Glasgow, J. N. (1996). Motivating the tech prep reader through learning styles and adolescent literature. *Journal of Adolescent & Adult Literacy, 39,* 358-367.

Goodman, J. (1992). Towards a discourse of imagery: Critical curriculum theorizing. *The Educational Forum, 56,* 269-289.

Gray, O. (1926). Teaching pupils to read arithmetic and other subject matter. *The Elementary School Journal, 26,* 607-618.

Green, J. (1990). Reading as a social process. In J. Howell, A. McNamara, & M. Clough (Eds.), *Social context of literacy.* Canberra, Australia: ACT Department of Education, Canberra.

Greene, J. (1999). Another chance: Help for older students with limited literacy. *Perspective, 25,* 5-10.

Greenleaf, C., Schoenbach, R., Cziko, C., & Mueller, F. (2001). Apprenticing adolescent readers to academic literacy. *Harvard Educational Review, 71,* 79-129.

Greenwald, E., Persky, H., Campbell, J., & Mazzeo, J. (1999). *NAEP 1998 writing: Report card for the nation and the states.* Washington, DC: National Center for Education Statistics.

Gregory, T., & Smith, G. (1987). *High schools as communities:The small school reconsidered.* Bloomington, IN: Phi Delta Kappa.

Guthrie, J., Alao, S., & Rinehart, J. (1997). Engagement in reading for young adolescents. *Journal of Adolescent & Adult Literacy, 40,* 438-446.

Guthrie, J., Cox, K., Anderson, E., Harris, K., Mazonni, S., & Rach, L. (1998). Principles of integrated instruction for engagement in reading. *Educational Psychology Review, 10,* 177-199.

Guthrie, J., & Wigfield, A. (2000). Engagement and motivation in reading. In M. Kamil, P. Mosenthal, P. D. Pearson, & R. Barr (Eds.), *Handbook of reading research* (Vol. III). Mahwah, NJ: Lawrence Erlbaum Associates.

Haertel, E. (1999). Performance assessment and education reform. *Phi Delta Kappan, 80,* 662-666.

Hargis, C. (1990). *Grades and grading practices.* Springfield, IL: Charles C. Thomas.

Harris, P., & Sullivan, M. (2000). Plugging in high-tech takes a new vision for education. *The Education Digest, 66,* 33-36.

Harste, J. (1988). Tomorrow's readers today: Becoming a profession of collaborative learners. In J. Readence & R. S. Baldwin (Eds.), *Dialogues in literacy research.* Chicago: National Reading Conference.

Hartman, D. (1995). Eight readers reading: The intertextual links of proficient readers reading multiple passages. *Reading Research Quarterly, 30,* 520-561.

Healy, J. (1999). *How computers affect our children's minds—for better or worse.* New York: Touchstone.

Hendrix, J. (1999). Connecting cooperative learning and social studies. *The Clearing House, 73,* 57-60.

Herber, H. (1978). *Teaching reading in the content areas.* Englewood Cliffs, NJ: Prentice Hall.

Herreid, C. F. (2000). The last teacher. *Journal of College Science Teaching, 29,* 423-427.

Hill, M., & Van Horn, L. (1995). Book club goes to jail: Can book clubs replace gangs? *Journal of Adolescent & Adult Literacy, 39,* 180-189.

Hofstetter, C., Sticht, T., & Hofstetter, C. (1999). Knowledge, literacy and power. *Communication Research, 26,* 58-80.

Hollingsworth, H., & Eastman, S. (1997). Homes more high tech than schools? *Educational Technology, 37,* 46-51.

Hoover, B. (1989, April 16). Is anybody reading? *The Detroit News,* Section E, p. 1.

Hull, G. (2000). The changing world of work. *Journal of Adolescent & Adult Literacy, 42,* 26-29.

Jacobson, J. (1990). Group vs. individual completion of a cloze passage. *Journal of Reading, 33,* 244-251.

Jimenez, R., & Gamez, A. (1996). Literature-based cognitive strategy instruction for middle school Latina/o students. *Journal of Adolescent & Adult Literacy, 40,* 84-91.

Johnson, D., & Johnson, R. (1989). *Cooperation and competition:Theory and research.* Edina, MN: Interaction Book Company.

Johnson, D., & Johnson, R. (1996). Cooperative learning and traditional American values: An appreciation. *NASSP Bulletin, 80,* 63-66.

Jordan, D., & LeMatais, J. (1997). Social skilling through cooperative learning. *Educational Researcher, 39,* 3-12.

King, J., & Brozo, W. G. (1992). Critical literacy and the pedagogies of empowerment. In A. Frager & J. Miller (Eds.), *Using inquiry in reading education.* Oxford, OH: College Reading Association.

Knoblach, C. H., & Brannon, L. (1983). Writing as learning through the curriculum. *College English, 45,* 465-474.

Lankshear, C. (1993). Curriculum as literacy: Reading and writing in *New Times.* In B. Green (Ed.), *The insistence of the letter: Literacy studies and curriculum theorizing.* Pittsburgh: University of Pittsburgh.

Lenski, S. D. (1998). Intertextual intentions: Making connections across texts. *The Clearing House, 72,* 74-80.

Leonard, J., & McElroy, K. (2000). What one middle school teacher learned about cooperative learning. *Journal of Research in Childhood Education, 14,* 239-245.

Leu, D. (2000). Literacy and technology: Deictic consequences for literacy education in an information age. In M. Kamil, P. Mosenthal, P. D. Pearson, & R. Barr (Eds.), *Handbook of reading research* (Vol. III). Mahwah, NJ: Lawrence Erlbaum Associates.

Libsch, M., & Breslow, M. (1996). Trends in non-assigned reading by high school seniors. *NASSP Bulletin, 80,* 111-116.

Luke, A. (1998). Getting over method: Literacy teaching as work in new times. *Language Arts, 75,* 305-313.

Luke, A., & Elkins, J. (1998). Reinventing literacy in "New Times." *Journal of Adolescent & Adult Literacy, 42,* 4-7.

Many, J., Fyfe, R., Lewis, G., & Mitchell, E. (1996). Traversing the topical landscape: Exploring students' self-directed reading-writing-research processes. *Reading Research Quarterly, 31,* 12-35.

Marshall, J. (2000). Research on response to literature. In M. Kamil, P. Mosenthal, P. D. Pearson, & R. Barr (Eds.), *Handbook of reading research* (Vol. III). Mahwah, NJ: Lawrence Erlbaum Associates.

McColskey, W., & McMunn, N. (2000). Strategies for dealing with high-stakes state tests. *Phi Delta Kappan, 82,* 115-120.

McCray, A., Vaughn, S., & Neal, L. (2001). Not all students learn to read by third grade: Middle school students speak out about their reading disabilities. *The Journal of Special Education, 35,* 17-30.

McDonough, J. (2000). Engaged learning. *American School & University, 72,* 60-64.

McGill-Franzen, A. (2000). Policy and instruction: What is the relationship? In M. Kamil, P. Mosenthal, P. D. Pearson, & R. Barr (Eds.), *Handbook of reading research* (Vol. III). Mahwah, NJ: Lawrence Erlbaum Associates.

Minow, N., & Lamay, C. (1996). *Abandoned in the wasteland: Children, television, and the first amendment.* New York: Hill & Wong.

Moje, E., Brozo, W. G., & Haas, J. (1994). Portfolios in high school classrooms: Challenges to change. *Reading Research and Instruction, 33,* 275-292.

Moore, D., Bean, T., Birdyshaw, D., & Rycik, J. (1999). Adolescent literacy: A position statement. *Journal of Adolescent & Adult Literacy, 43,* 97-112.

Muspratt, S., Luke, A., & Freebody, P. (1997). *Constructing critical literacies: Teaching and learning textual practice.* Cresskill, NJ: Hampton Press.

Myers, J. (1992). The social contexts of school and personal literacy. *Reading Research Quarterly, 27,* 297-333.

National Center for Education Statistics. (2000). *Pursuing excellence: Comparisons of international eighth-grade mathematics & science achievement from a U.S. perspective, 1995 & 1999.* Washington, DC: Department of Education.

Negroponte, N. (1995). *Being digital.* New York: Vintage Books.

O'Brien, D., Stewart, R., & Moje, E. (1995). Why content literacy is difficult to infuse into the secondary school: Complexities of curriculum, pedagogy, and school culture. *Reading Research Quarterly, 30,* 442-463.

Randall, V. (1999). Cooperative learning: Abused and overused? *The Education Digest, 65,* 29-32.

Rickelman, R., & Caplan, R. (2000). Technological literacy in the intermediate and middle grades. In K. Wood & T. Dickenson (Eds.), *Promoting literacy in grades 4-9.* Boston: Allyn & Bacon.

Rief, L. (1992). *Seeking diversity: Language arts with adolescents.* Portsmouth, NH: Heinemann.

Saunders, L. (1997). Lingering with Dicey: Robin's song. *Journal of Adolescent & Adult Literacy, 40,* 548-557.

Schniedewind, N., & Davidson, E. (2000). Differentiating cooperative learning. *Educational Leadership, 58,* 24-27.

Schumm, J., & Saumell, K. (1994). Aliteracy: We know it is a problem, but where does it start? *Journal of Reading, 37,* 701-707.

Sheldon, K., & Biddle, B. (1998). Standards, accountability, and school reform: Perils and pitfalls. *Teachers College Record, 100,* 164-180.

Slavin, R. (1996). Research on cooperative learning and achievement: What we know, what we need to know. *Contemporary Educational Psychology, 21,* 43–69.

Slavin, R., & Cooper, R. (1999). Improving intergroup relations: Lessons learned from cooperative learning programs. *The Journal of Social Issues, 55,* 647–663.

Smith, F. (1985). *Reading without nonsense.* New York: Teachers College Press.

Smith, M., Stevenson, D., & Li, C. (1998). Voluntary national tests would improve education. *Educational Leadership, 55,* 42–44.

Soltow, L., & Stevens, E. (1981). *The rise of literacy and the common school in the United States: A socioeconomic analysis to 1870.* Chicago: University of Chicago Press.

Stewart, R., Paradis, E., Ross, B., & Lewis, M. (1996). Student voices: What works in literature-based developmental reading. *Journal of Adolescent & Adult Literacy, 39,* 468–477.

Taylor, B., Frye, B., & Maruyama, G. (1990). Time spent reading and reading growth. *American Educational Research Journal, 27,* 351–362.

Thimmesch, N. (1985). *Aliteracy.* Washington, DC: National Enterprise Institute.

Thorpe, L., & Wood, K. (2000). Cross-age tutoring for young adolescents. *The Clearing House, 73,* 239–242.

Turner, J. (1995). The influence of classroom contexts on young children's motivation for literacy. *Reading Research Quarterly, 30,* 410–441.

Turner, J., & Paris, S. (1995). How literacy tasks influence children's motivation for literacy. *The Reading Teacher, 48,* 662–673.

Tyson-Bernstein, H. (1988). *A conspiracy of good intentions.* Washington, DC: Council for Basic Education.

Unrau, N., & Ruddell, R. (1995). Interpreting texts in classroom contexts. *Journal of Adolescent & Adult Literacy, 39,* 16–27.

Vacca, R., & Alvermann, D. (October, 1998). The crisis in adolescent literacy: Is it real or imagined? *National Association of Secondary School Principals Bulletin,* 4–9.

Wade, S., & Moje, E. (2000). The role of text in classroom learning. In M. Kamil, P. Mosenthal, P. D. Pearson, & R. Barr (Eds.), *Handbook of reading research* (Vol. III). Mahwah, NJ: Lawrence Erlbaum Associates.

Weeks, L. (2001, May 14). Read all about it, or maybe not—Millions of Americans who can read choose not to. Can we do without the written word? *The Washington Post,* C1

Willinsky, J. (1990). *The new literacy.* New York: Routledge.

Wright, L. (1957). *The cultural life of the American colonies: 1607–1763.* New York: Harper & Row.

CHAPTER TWO

Active Learners Across the Content Areas

ANTICIPATION GUIDE

Directions: Read each statement carefully and decide whether you agree or disagree with it, placing a check mark in the appropriate *Before Reading* column. When finished reading and studying the chapter, return to the guide and decide whether your anticipations need to be changed by placing a check mark in the appropriate *After Reading* column.

	BEFORE READING		AFTER READING	
	Agree	*Disagree*	*Agree*	*Disagree*
1. Students' beliefs about learning and knowledge influence how they read and study.	____	____	____	____
2. What you know about a topic has little influence on how much you will remember once you begin reading.	____	____	____	____
3. Narrative writing and expository writing place equal demands on readers.	____	____	____	____
4. Most middle school and secondary school textbooks have been written so that they are very easy to understand.	____	____	____	____

Active learning works not only because it helps motivation and feedback but also because active learners are more likely to be attentive and to be thinking about the topic, relating new knowledge to previous learning, and elaborating the implications of what they have learned.

—McKeachie (1994)

ltrough McKeachie offered this opinion about active learning almost a decade ago, it still resonates with many individuals concerned about whether or not high school students are graduating with the necessary higher level comprehension and critical thinking skills. This chapter describes a model of active learning that can apply to all content-area classrooms where readers and teachers focus on understanding, critical thinking, and learning. Because we know that many middle school and high school teachers use discussions, demonstrations, projects, and activities to help them teach their course objectives and may never use the traditional textbook, we wish to stress the universality of this model of active learning. Rather than focusing on just higher level comprehension or critical thinking strategies oriented only to textbooks, we propose a model that will assist students in their meaning-making processes for any content-area class and any text, written or oral. Hence, when we discuss texts in this chapter and the other chapters, we refer to all the written and oral texts from which students must learn. The five theoretical principles that guide students' active learning from these texts are as follows:

Go to *http:// www.prenhall. com/brozo*, select Chapter 2, then click on Chapter Objectives to provide a focus for your reading.

Principle 1:   Active learners use their prior knowledge as they interact with text.

Principle 2:   Active learners summarize and organize as they interact with text.

Principle 3:   Active learners think critically about text and create their own elaborations.

Principle 4:   Active learners are metacognitively aware.

Principle 5:   Active learners possess and employ a wide range of reading and learning strategies.

In this chapter we provide the background and rationale for these five principles of active learning. We also discuss the characteristics of materials that can assist students in their reading and learning. Then in Chapter 3 we return to these principles and provide examples of strategies and approaches that teachers in secondary schools can use with their students to assist them in learning content-area concepts. We would be remiss if we did not also point out that almost every chapter in this textbook presents practical ideas and strategies for promoting active learning across the content areas.

FIVE PRINCIPLES THAT PROMOTE ACTIVE LEARNING

Principle 1: Active Learners Use Their Prior Knowledge as They Interact With Text

Active learners know that what they take from a text depends on how much they bring to it. In other words, what learners already know, their prior knowledge, and what they want to know will affect the ease or difficulty of their meaning making or understanding and their subsequent learning. This premise is consistent with a **schema-theoretic** perspective of comprehension (McNamara, Miller, & Bransford, 1991). **Schemata** (plural of **schema**) are abstract frameworks that organize knowledge in memory by putting information into the correct "slot," each slot containing related parts (Wilson & Anderson, 1986). For instance, the schema for going to an airport probably includes taxis, ticket counters, crowds, the smell of jet fuel, claiming baggage, and so on. These clusters of related knowledge in memory—of experience, ideas, and feelings— guide our interpretations, inferences, expectations, and attention as passages are comprehended. It is theorized that learners comprehend a text when they bring to mind a schema that gives a good account of the objects and events described in the message. Schemata guide comprehension; without them, we could make little sense of a text. Without some unifying idea to help tie together the information, without connections to our own prior knowledge and experience, without a foundational understanding of the concept, we might as well be looking at words in a foreign language.

What students know about a topic influences their understanding.

To demonstrate the important role schemata play in students' comprehension and meaning making, read the following passage and see if you can activate an appropriate schema to help you understand it.

> The southpaw touched the rubber, kicked, and dealed. The big number 38 sent one up the chute. Smith raced from the hot corner and camped under it. He tripped, however, on the artificial turf, and it fell behind him and just in front of Murphy from left—38 had a two-bagger on a Texas leaguer. Cries of "kill the bum" echoed throughout the place as number 16 strode up. He was a sub for the DH and stood in, brandishing a 40-ounce stick menacingly. He crushed one through the hole at short. Perez stabbed at it, but it rolled all the way to the warning track. Number 38 touched home, and it was over.

Did you understand this passage? What does it mean if you can't understand it? Chances are that you had no difficulty with saying the words, so much of the difficulty you may have had making sense of this short passage can be attributed to an underdeveloped schema: a lack of prior knowledge about baseball, especially baseball terminology.

Middle school and high school students often experience difficulty comprehending technical concepts because of their limited prior knowledge. Conversely, students with extensive prior knowledge of a given topic will likely understand and learn more, whether that information comes from a textbook or a class discussion. Of course, prior knowledge occurs in degrees and is not necessarily an all-or-none condition. In a classic study of prior knowledge, Bransford and Johnson (1972) presented the following statement to students from differing sociocultural backgrounds:

> Jane decided not to wear her matching silver necklace, earrings, and belt because she was going to the airport. (p. 719)

Students from backgrounds that had provided them with many direct and related prior experiences with airports and airplane travel had no problems explaining Jane's reasoning: The heavy jewelry could trigger the metal detector; therefore, she left it at home. Students from backgrounds that precluded opportunities for visiting airports and flying, however, came up with explanations such as "She was afraid of getting ripped off." The point of this research, as well as of other related studies, is that the amount of information students possess on any topic may vary widely, leading to alternative interpretations.

What is more, many students do not automatically draw on their prior experiences when learning in school settings. For many students, learning is a compartmentalized procedure in which the different subjects they study and their own background knowledge may never interact or come together. For example, what students have learned in a seventh-grade physical education class about the role of adrenalin in a competitive event may never be used when they study human glands in a science class. Hence, teachers must cue and encourage students to use their prior knowledge from one setting in another.

Although most researchers agree that prior knowledge facilitates comprehension, some have shown that students may possess "incorrect" prior knowledge or "naïve" conceptions that can interfere with learning important information (Guzzetti & Hynd, 1998). For example, many of us have entrenched beliefs about the laws of motion that are not scientifically defensible. Researchers have also found that many students are likely to hold on to their misconceptions even when they watch demonstrations that prove otherwise (Guzzetti & Hynd, 1998). These findings reinforce the critical importance of exploring students' prior knowledge for and conceptions of topics before they read a text or listen to a lecture. In this way, you can discover any misconceptions and create instructional conditions that enable students to reject their existing misconceptions and to learn content-area concepts.

Chapter 5 offers teacher-proven techniques to help students tap prior knowledge and change misconceptions.

To summarize, active learners use their schema or prior knowledge flexibly to construct meaningful interpretations of texts. The instructional implication of the importance of prior knowledge for middle school and secondary school teachers can be simply stated: To maximize learning, teachers need to assist students in developing relevant background knowledge and in relating their own experiences to what they learn. In the next chapter and in Chapter 5, we examine some teaching approaches for helping students activate and use relevant prior knowledge.

Principle 2: Active Learners Summarize and Organize as They Interact With Text

As you were reading about the first principle of active learning, you were unconsciously doing what active readers do on a routine basis when they grapple with challenging or novel ideas. That is, you were reading carefully in order to summarize the key ideas or overall meaning of those paragraphs. All of us summarize many times during the course of a day. Summarizing is condensing information and ideas using our own words; without it, communication would be tediously protracted. Another important reading process involves students in making associations and organizing information for their future use. We focus on these two important processes—summarizing and organizing—for the second principle of active learning.

Across the content areas, the ability to summarize text is perhaps one of the most essential reading skills because it provides the foundation for a wide array of other thinking processes (e.g., organizing, synthesizing). Unfortunately, many middle and high school students are not adept in summarizing what they have read (Nist & Simpson, 2000). Rather than summarize a concept using their own words, many students resort to memorizing irrelevant details, missing the "big picture" of what they have read or heard during a class discussion.

Fortunately, summarizing has been investigated over a period of time, and researchers have discovered that skilled readers use certain rules in constructing main ideas for paragraphs and passages (e.g., Brown & Day, 1983). These rules include:

- deleting irrelevant or unimportant information
- generalizing categories for lists of items or actions
- selecting key idea statements when the author provides one
- constructing key ideas statements if none are provided

These rules have important implications for content-area teachers who are frustrated with students' passive reading approaches. Brown and Day (1983), for example, found that when struggling readers were trained to use the same processes used by skilled readers, their ability to summarize and comprehend text improved significantly. Furthermore, they discovered that these processes could easily be demonstrated and modeled for students. In Chapter 3 we will visit the classroom of a content-area teacher who did just that to help her students. You will also find alternative ideas for teaching and reinforcing the processes involved in summarization throughout this textbook (e.g., Chapter 7, Writing as a Tool for Active Learning; Chapter 9, Study Strategies).

Struggling readers can benefit from training in summarizing.

As you have been reading, you have been using the structure or organization of this chapter to help you identify and summarize important ideas. That is, you may have focused on ideas marked by typographical features such as bold-face headings, or you may have noted information that we cued using words such as *furthermore* or *in summary*. We know from the research that skilled readers use text organization to aid their understanding, especially when they find the material they are reading unfamiliar or somewhat challenging (Goldman & Rackstraw, 2000). More specifically, skilled readers use all of these signals to organize what they read:

- summary statements
- previews or introductory statements

- typographic clues such as underlining, italics, and boldface print or headings
- pointer words and phrases, such as "the most important reason why"
- enumeration devices (e.g., *first, furthermore, finally*)
- connectives (e.g., *because, the reasons why, however, the consequences*)

You might find it surprising to know that a majority of adolescents do not understand and capitalize on these signals that authors use to explain and organize their ideas (Chambliss, 1995). Among the many explanations for this situation is that secondary students have had far more experiences with the **narrative** or story format of writing than they have had with the **expository** or explanatory format of writing. In fact, we teach children to read with stories because they are already familiar with the structure of stories.

Stories or narrative text have predictable structures or patterns, called **story grammars** (Mandler, 1987). For instance, stories have settings; they have characters; the main character is usually en route to a goal; to reach his or her goal, the main character must confront obstacles, essentially conflict; and the conflict is resolved in some way. Apparently, as readers or listeners receive constant exposure to well-structured stories, they internalize these grammars in the form of a story schema, which assists them in understanding and writing stories.

Because most of us prefer the narrative structure, interest in stories rarely wanes throughout our lives. However, most textbooks and classroom presentations do not typically use a narrative structure. Rather, most learning situations in school are organized around an expository or explanatory structure that is more formal and demanding than our oral language. Try to recall the last time you relished the opportunity to crack open one of your textbooks before going to bed. Most of us rarely do, and the same is true of students.

Adolescents find expository text more challenging and "boring" than narrative text.

We have observed students plowing through their assigned government and science reading, eager to finish so that they can put down the book. Students in middle and secondary school must learn to deal with the formal expository styles of writing and speaking if they are to be successful readers and learners. By helping them develop an understanding of how writers organize expository text, we can improve their comprehension (Goldman & Rakestraw, 2000).

For quite some time, researchers have been identifying the general structures of expository text and demonstrating the importance of students using this information in order to enhance their understanding (e.g., Armbruster, Anderson, & Ostertag, 1987). Although several organizational structures exist for expository text, Meyer's (1979) system, which examines five groups of logical relationships, is representative and highly inclusive:

- *Antecedence/consequence or covariance showing a causal relationship between ideas.* For example, a paragraph taken from a biology textbook explaining the direct and indirect cell damage caused by radiation would be organized using the antecedent/consequent pattern.

Texts have predictable structures or organization.

- *Response relationships, including problem-solution, question-answer, and remark-reply.* For example, in an ecology textbook, one chapter is devoted to the problems caused by water and air pollution, and the next chapter focuses on possible solutions to the problems caused by the pollution.

■ *Comparison relationships dealing with likenesses and differences between ideas.* For example, in a chapter about igneous rocks, students learn how intrusive and extrusive rocks are similar in some ways but different in others.

■ *Collection relationships showing that ideas are related to each other by a common factor or factors.* In a geometry class it is important for students to understand that triangles, quadrilaterals, pentagons, hexagons, octagons, and decagons are all examples of polygons and, hence, have the same common features. Such reasoning is an example of the collection relationship or pattern of thinking.

■ *Description relationships presenting attributes or explanations of a topic.* This type of relationship exists in all content areas. For example, when a physical education teacher explains a sport such as tennis to her students, she probably not only presents the goals and rules of the game but also describes the characteristics of an expert tennis player. She provides descriptions and attributions because she knows they will help her students understand the nuances of tennis.

We should point out, however, that authors rarely write an article or textbook chapter using one organizational pattern. The same would be true for a visual or auditory presentation of content material. Even so, when teachers provide direct instruction on how to use text structure as an organizing device for meaning making, students will benefit (Goldman & Rakestraw, 2000). To sum, then, active learners are those individuals who can summarize and organize important ideas, whether it be from a demonstration, a film, or a challenging textbook assignment.

Students may not realize that lectures and films have an organizational structure, too.

Principle 3: Active Learners Think Critically About Text and Create Their Own Elaborations

Mr. Kuzak, a ninth-grade science teacher, told his students to write a summary of a section in their textbook that discussed water and land pollution. He likes to give this assignment early in the year to determine which of his students have difficulty in thinking about scientific concepts. Susan's and Derrick's summaries in Figure 2.1 typify what Phil receives from his first-year students. Which student is the active learner? What did that student do to make his or her summary better?

As you probably determined, Susan's summary is more effective than Derrick's for several reasons. What reasons did you list? If you listed any of the following, you identified some of Susan's thinking processes.

Most classes have more "Derricks" than "Susans."

■ Susan focused on the overall structure of the section—the four types of pollution and the solutions to water pollution. Derrick focused on details and facts, with no sense of organization.

■ Susan used personal examples (e.g., the Alaskan oil spill) that were not included in the text. Derrick's summary used only textbook information,

Susan's Summary

According to this section of our textbook, there are four sources of water pollution: agriculture, industry, domestic, and other sources such as oil spills. Perhaps the most dangerous source of pollution comes from industry, though oil spills, such as the one in Alaska, have certainly had a large impact on our wildlife and on our economy. Pesticides, fertilizers, and animal waste, the three types of agricultural pollution, are usually not direct but indirect. A notorious example of a pesticide is DDT. There are three kinds of industrial pollution: chemical, thermal, and radiation. The problems associated with radiation seem to be the most severe in that skin cancer and leukemia are possible results of exposure. Organic waste and detergent builders are the main sources of domestic pollution. Both seem to have an adverse effect on our lakes and rivers so that the balance of nature is upset. This section of the chapter ended by discussing some solutions to the problem of water pollution—all of which are costly but very important.

Derrick's Summary

This section of the chapter discussed different kinds of water pollution. Pesticides such as DDT are dangerous to use because they are not biodegradable. Some nitrates are toxic to animals and humans. Nitrates can be reduced to nitrites, which interfere with the transport of oxygen by hemoglobin in the blood. Mercury vapor is highly toxic and can be absorbed through the lungs. There are two types of radiation cell damage, direct and indirect. Detergents and organic wastes can also harm our water sources. Oil spills hurt our aquatic life.

FIGURE 2.1   Susan's and Derrick's Summaries on Water Pollution

even though water pollution is a highly controversial and often debated topic in the news today.

■ Susan formed some conclusions and drew some inferences from the text. For instance, she inferred that radiation is the most dangerous form of water pollution.

In sum, Susan's summary provided more evidence of critical thinking and elaborations than did Derrick's summary. When students think critically about what they read or hear, they identify the author's purpose, assumptions, and perspectives. Then they assess those elements using universal criteria and standards such as clarity, accuracy, precision, relevance, depth, and logic (Ennis, 1996).

Taking a slightly different perspective, Wineburg (1991) proposes that critical readers engage in three basic processes: sourcing, contextualizing, and corroborating. Sourcing requires students to analyze the credentials of the writer and to consider how the bias of the source might affect what is being said (e.g., What expertise does this individual have on this topic?). Contextualizing involves students in placing a piece of text into a time period and determining how the time and place may have had an impact on what the author said (e.g., Did Malcolm X's statement about civil rights change once he studied the Muslim religion?).

Wineburg, a historian, provides an alternative view of critical thinking.

Corroborating involves students in comparing and contrasting viewpoints stated in one text with other texts they have read or encountered (e.g., Do all authors agree that the United States was attacked during the Tonkin Gulf Incident?). Hynd (1999), who has studied both high school and college students as they read history texts, suggests that Wineburg's schema represents the "heart of thinking critically about what one encounters in everyday life" (p. 432).

When students think elaboratively about text, they add information that is not explicitly stated (Pressley, 2000). Students can think elaboratively in various ways about the texts they read or listen to in class. They can:

- *compose* titles, headings, and subheadings when they are missing
- *develop* questions
- *relate* text to personal experiences
- *seek* interrelationships across text
- *create* examples, analogies, or metaphors
- *make* predictions or form inferences
- *apply* principles to new situations

Students who think critically about text and create their own elaborations will increase their understanding of content-area concepts (Simpson, Olejnik, Tam, & Supattathum, 1994). We know, however, that more middle school and secondary students are like Derrick than like Susan. This widespread tendency of students to be passive, noncritical consumers of information has caused many groups, such as the International Reading Association, to recommend that content-area teachers work together to "effectively support adolescents' development of advanced reading strategies" (Moore, Bean, Birdyshaw, & Rycik, 1999).

Throughout this book you will find practical strategies to help your students think critically about content-area concepts.

Fortunately, content-area teachers can use a variety of strategies to help students move toward a more sophisticated level of thinking in order to become active learners. Most of these teacher-directed strategies begin by providing students with examples, demonstrations, and activities that require them to go beyond memorization. Then, gradually, students are challenged to accept responsibility and ownership in initiating their own critical and elaborative thinking. In Chapter 3 we discuss how classroom teachers can teach students to think critically and elaboratively about concepts and ideas. However, we want to remind you that throughout this textbook you will find numerous activities and techniques that challenge students to engage in higher levels of thinking.

Principle 4: Active Learners Are Metacognitively Aware

Thus far, we have discussed three characteristics of active learners. Briefly, active learners use their prior knowledge to make sense of what they are learning, they summarize and organize ideas, and they elaborate and critically think about what they are learning. The fourth principle describes active learners as those who are metacognitively aware.

Think about a typical reading experience: You're moving through a passage on automatic pilot, absorbing information and ideas, seemingly without effort.

Suddenly, your eyes fix on the word *propinquity.* Within a mere 2 or 3 seconds, you realize you don't know what the word means, quickly reread the sentence in which it was found, and decide that, at least for the time being, its definition is not critical to your present level of comprehension. Back on automatic pilot, you realize after two more paragraphs that the meaning of *propinquity* has become more significant. You return to the word, frame its meaning in context, guess, and finally consult a dictionary.

This scenario essentially describes the process of **monitoring**, one aspect of metacognition. According to Baker and Brown (1984), **metacognition** is the "knowledge and control we have over thinking and learning activities" (p. 2). Students who can self-monitor their reading or listening can detect errors or contradictions in a text, identify topics or ideas they do not understand, and use a variety of task-appropriate reading and learning strategies to "fix up" or alleviate their difficulties in understanding (Simpson & Nist, 2001).

Self-monitoring plays a vital role in determining whether or not students have successful reading experiences. In fact, research indicates that novice and expert readers and successful and less successful students differ substantially in their monitoring abilities (Afflerbach, 2000; Nist & Simpson, 2000). There also appear to be developmental differences in students' ability to self-monitor. Researchers have found that older students seem better able to regulate and control their understanding processes than younger students (Pressley, 2000).

Students can be taught how to monitor their understanding.

These findings do not mean, however, that you can expect your students to be able to monitor their reading, listening, and understanding. As Alexander and Jetton (2000) have suggested, many students focus on "doing the reading rather than mastering the content" (p. 299). We have found from our research that entering college first-year students are also passive learners who are "doing" rather than thinking about, monitoring, and evaluating their understanding (Simpson & Nist, 2001). Fortunately, high school and middle school students can profit greatly from some form of self-monitoring training. For example, when Rosenshine, Meister, and Chapman (1994) reviewed the studies that focused on teaching students to monitor their learning through self-questioning, predicting, summarizing, and clarifying, they found consistently strong effects.

In addition to self-monitoring, metacognition involves **task knowledge** and **self-knowledge**. *Task knowledge* can be classified according to the products that teachers require of students and the thinking processes involved in completing the products (Doyle, 1983). Typical products include tests, papers, classroom discussions, projects, experiments, and demonstrations. Each product requires certain types of thinking processes, making some products more challenging than others. For example, some multiple-choice tests require students to memorize certain facts and details. The following question illustrates a factual test question in a science course:

What are the two basic types of igneous rocks?

a.   clastic sedimentary and breccia

b.   intrusive and extrusive

    c.   metamorphic and organic

    d.   foliated and nonfoliated

Other tasks require higher levels of thinking because they involve drawing conclusions, taking a stand on an issue, or applying a concept to a new situation. The following question, taken from a 10th-grade psychology course, illustrates an application-level question concerning Freud's concept of a defense mechanism:

> Theo has a girlfriend whom he accuses of being unfaithful. Interestingly, Theo is the one who has been unfaithful because he has been seeing three other girls. Which defense mechanism is Theo using when he accuses his girlfriend of being unfaithful?

    a.   rationalization

    b.   denial

    c.   projection

    d.   repression

The correct answer to the question, (c), required students to understand the concept of defense mechanism, the various kinds of defense mechanisms, and examples of each. Questions such as these require students to think and elaborate on what they read in their texts or hear in class discussions so that they can identify new situations or examples of concepts.

When students understand the tasks you assign, the learning becomes easier for them.

Thus, task knowledge involves an understanding of the product to be created and the thinking processes involved in creating it. When active learners possess task knowledge, they realize that understanding directions to a physics laboratory experiment, for example, requires a different kind of reading and thinking than does understanding a poem, such as "Richard Cory," so that they can write a paper for their English teacher. Students who understand the academic tasks specified by their teachers and select the appropriate strategies and approaches to accomplish those tasks are generally the ones who are academically successful (Pressley, 1995; Simpson, Hynd, Nist, & Burrell, 1997).

Students with **self-knowledge** understand themselves as readers and learners. Specifically, they are aware of their motivations, beliefs, and strengths as they read, listen, and think about ideas. Motivation is perhaps the most important aspect of self-knowledge because it contributes to students' views of themselves as individuals who control what and how much they learn. When students hold strong, positive views of themselves as learners, they have what Zimmerman (2000) and others have described as strong **self-efficacy**. Students with strong self-efficacy are more likely to choose learning strategies and approaches that require them to think critically and elaboratively (Pintrich & Garcia, 1994; Zimmerman, 2000). In contrast, students with low self-efficacy are those who tend to give up quickly, doubt their ability when they confront a difficult or novel situation, and resort to memorization, even when it is not appropriate.

Another important aspect of self-knowledge consists of the beliefs that students have about what constitutes knowledge and learning. According to Schommer, Calvert, Gariglietti, & Bajaj (1997) who have conducted extensive research with secondary school students, these beliefs, or personal **epistemologies**, include several knowledge dimensions. For example, some students may perceive knowledge to be absolute, something handed down by authority that can be acquired quickly, with little effort. In contrast, other students view knowledge acquisition as a tentative, gradual process derived from reason and thought after considerable effort on their part.

Students' beliefs about learning influence how they read and study.

How students define knowledge has an impact on how they proceed with their reading and learning in a content area (Hofer & Pintrich, 1997; Simpson & Nist, 2001). For example, if students believe that reading in biology requires them to focus only on definitions, more than likely they will memorize definitions to words such as glucose rather than employ elaborative strategies that involve them in searching for relationships between key concepts (e.g., glucose, glycogen, insulin). Hence, as teachers, it is important for us to know what students believe about knowledge, learning, and reading and to nudge those beliefs from simple to more complex.

Metacognition is probably the mind-set that makes learning possible. Students who are metacognitively aware are the ones who understand all the nuances of academic tasks, who can monitor their learning in order to identify when they do not understand, and who can identify strategies to help them learn more effectively. Most important, students who are metacognitively aware are the ones who see themselves as individuals who control what and how much they learn. In Chapters 3 and 9 and elsewhere in this textbook, we discuss strategies that content-area teachers can use to encourage their students to become more metacognitively aware.

Principle 5: Active Learners Possess and Employ a Wide Range of Reading and Learning Strategies

Strategies are the behaviors or actions that students use during learning to influence their understanding, thinking, and retrieval of new information or concepts (Weinstein & Mayer, 1986). To be effective, students need strategies to make sense out of their texts, monitor their understanding, and clarify what they do not understand. In addition, to cope with the difficult tasks that demand higher levels of thinking, middle school and secondary school students need strategies to help them elaborate, organize, and synthesize information from multiple sources. Such a list of requirements implies that no one technique or strategy will work for students in all situations (Nist & Simpson, 2000). Rather than a generic approach, active learners have a repertoire of strategies and know when to select the most appropriate one(s) for the subject area and for the task described by the teacher.

No one best strategy or technique guarantees the development of active learners.

To select the most appropriate strategy, active learners must have three different kinds of strategic knowledge (Paris, Wasik, & Turner, 1991). The first is **declarative** knowledge. For example, a student with declarative knowledge of previewing knows that previewing is done before reading and that it involves such steps as reading the introduction and summary. The second kind of strategic knowledge is **procedural**. Active learners with declarative and procedural knowledge of the preview strategy can preview and describe the steps for previewing in detail. In addition to these two types of strategic knowledge, active learners possess **conditional** knowledge, perhaps the most critical form of strategic knowledge (Zimmerman, 2000). When active learners have conditional knowledge, they know when and why to use various strategies. Thus, with the previewing strategy, they know that it may be appropriate to preview only certain texts. Active learners know that the time involved in previewing a chapter before they read is time well spent because it allows them to check the author's organization, establish what they may already know about the topic, set purposes for reading, and divide the reading into meaningful chunks. Students must develop all three kinds of strategic knowledge if they are to control and transfer the strategies we teach in the classroom to their own reading and learning tasks outside the classroom (Simpson & Nist, 2001; Zimmerman, 2000).

If you want students to try a new technique, show them how and why.

In sum, students must have a wide repertoire of strategies to match the different types of academic tasks and texts they will encounter across the content areas. In addition, students must know where, how, and why they should use these strategies. Throughout this textbook, we discuss a variety of strategies and explain ways in which they can be taught. In the next section we discuss in more detail one factor that has a significant impact on students' choice of strategies and whether they have difficulties understanding what they read—the textbook.

THE ROLE OF THE TEXTBOOK IN ACTIVE LEARNING

Most content-area teachers, especially those new to a school system, inherit the textbook they will be using with their students. They begin the school year hoping that this textbook will include the most pertinent and recent information and that their students will find the ideas easy to follow, yet engaging. Unfortunately, this perfect textbook scenario rarely occurs. In fact, there probably is no such thing as a perfect textbook, but we know from the research that some textbooks are more effective or "**considerate**" of the reader than others (Anderson & Armbruster, 1986). Hence, it is important to understand the qualities of a considerate textbook because you will be asked several times during your career to make a recommendation for an upcoming textbook adoption.

Fry's readability formula is one of many formulas for determining a textbook's "reading level."

Before we examine some of those qualities of effective textbooks, we want to discuss one criterion that is often used in selecting textbooks—**readability.** The readability of printed material has been interpreted to mean that challenging texts are ones that have long sentences and difficult, long words. Conversely, easy materials are those with shorter sentences and shorter words. Readability formulas such as Fry's (1968) use these easily quantifiable indices to yield either a grade level or a score similar to a reading level. Many textbook writers, editors, and publishers have attempted to lower the reading level of their textbooks by asking the authors to use short, simple sentences and fewer multisyllable words. The goal, of course, is to sell more books because school districts want "readable" materials.

An example will demonstrate what happens when authors are asked to rewrite something using readability indices. The two paragraphs that follow provide explanations of why leaf openings close. Which one best explains the concept and thus is more considerate? Which one is "easier" according to a formula such as Fry's?

Version One

In the evening, the light fades. Photosynthesis slows down. The amount of carbon dioxide in the air space builds up again. This buildup of carbon dioxide makes the guard cells relax. The openings are closed.

Version Two

The fading light of evening causes photosynthesis to slow down. A plant's ability to "breathe," however, does not depend on light and thus continues to produce carbon dioxide. The carbon dioxide in the air spaces builds up again, which makes the guard cells relax. The relaxing of the guard cells closes the leaf openings. Consequently, the leaf openings close in the evenings as photosynthesis slows down. (Anderson & Armbruster, 1984, p. 206)

Which version best explained the concept of why leaf openings close? More than likely, you answered that Version Two was more considerate because the author explained in detail how changes in light affect plants. You could probably almost visualize what happens as night falls from the author's description. Which version was "easier" according to a readability formula? Version One was "easier" because it contained only 5 sentences, 35 words, and 52 syllables. A quick check on Version Two would reveal that it contained only 4 sentences, more words per sentence, and far more multisyllable words than Version One. In the first version, the author's use of short, simple sentences often obscured the relationships among the ideas in the text. In the second version, the author echoed words that ended the previous sentence by placing them at or near the beginning of the following sentence (e.g., *leaf openings*) and inserted words that tied together the text and made the relationships more obvious (e.g., *consequently*). Those features in Version Two are features of an effective, considerate textbook (Alexander & Jetton, 2000; Anderson & Armbruster, 1986).

Unfortunately, many middle school and secondary school textbooks are similar to Version One and have a high degree of inconsiderateness. They contain misleading titles and subtitles, lack explicit main ideas, omit crucial information, contain contradictory information, and are ambiguous (Pressley, Yokoi, van Meter, Van Etten, & Freebern, 1997). Thus, when selecting a textbook, teachers should focus on whether it is considerate rather than on superficial features that may give the impression of considerateness but actually make the text less readable.

Although no textbook is perfect, some are more considerate and have better learnability characteristics than others. Those characteristics include (Alexander & Jetton, 2000):

Consider these characteristics when you select a textbook.

- The authors effectively communicate their purpose or aim.

- The authors consider the audience of their textbook and provide sufficient background information, a judicious use of well-defined technical words, and referents for any figurative or literary allusions (e.g., *myths*).

- The authors have a focus and share that focus with the readers via an overall organization or macrostructure (e.g., headings, subheadings, main ideas that are linked to each other).

- The authors have a focus and share that with the readers via a microstructure that provides development via examples, anecdotes, supporting details, explanations, and quotations from primary sources.

- The authors use a style of writing that is clear and explicit.

Theresa, an eighth-grade health education teacher, was provided the opportunity to select a new textbook for the upcoming school year. Her department chairperson gave her a checklist (see Figure 2.2) to use in judging the textbooks that were sent to her and her colleagues from the various publishers. As you can tell from a quick perusal of the checklist, it incorporated many of the learnability characteristics discussed above. Theresa found the checklist extremely helpful in reviewing the many textbooks because she had specific characteristics to evaluate that went beyond the mere coverage of content in the field of health. After a careful and thoughtful evaluation of the possible new adoptions, Theresa and her colleagues selected the text they believed would best maximize the learning potential of their students. Admittedly, they had hoped to find the perfect health education textbook but soon realized that such a book did not exist. Rather, they decide to provide supplementary sources for their students on topics they wished to stress that were not contained in the textbook and to use specific comprehension building strategies to facilitate their students' understanding of the concepts.

This textbook offers ideas to overcome inconsiderate texts.

You might be teaching in a situation where you are presently using a textbook that is not considerate. Perhaps you are teaching in a situation where the school district cannot afford new textbooks for quite some time. What we want to stress is the fact that effective teaching can help your students read, understand, and learn, even if the textbook is less than desirable. In Chapter 3 we discuss many of these teaching strategies that can help your students overcome the barriers of inconsiderate text and become more actively involved in the meaning-making process.

Directions: Check the column that best describes the textbook's use of these characteristics that promote active and successful learning.

	Excellent	Good	Poor
1. Difficult new vocabulary words are highlighted, italicized, underlined, or defined in the margins.	___	___	___
2. Concepts are presented clearly in relatively direct and understandable sentences.	___	___	___
3. The chapter's main idea(s) or purposes for reading are explicitly stated at the beginning.	___	___	___
4. The authors present a list of objectives, questions, or organizational structure to guide the students while reading/studying.	___	___	___
5. The authors use explicit and appropriate words to signal the text's structure and organization (e.g., *on the other hand*).	___	___	___
6. The authors use practical real-life situations, examples, or analogies that students can relate to and in which they have an interest.	___	___	___
7. The authors use boldface headings and subheadings that are logical to the concepts being discussed and useful to students with little or no prior knowledge.	___	___	___
8. The authors internally summarize key concepts and present useful summaries at the end of the chapter.	___	___	___
9. The authors help students use appropriate prior knowledge by reviewing or reminding readers of previously learned concepts (e.g., *in the last chapter we discussed . . .*).	___	___	___
10. The text includes quotations from primary sources and authorities to support and add interest.	___	___	___
11. When there are questions at the end of the chapter, different kinds (e.g., true–false) of questions are supplied that require higher levels of thinking (e.g., on my own) and responses using students' own words.	___	___	___
12. The table of contents shows a logical development of the subject matter.	___	___	___
13. Captions under graphs, tables, diagrams, and pictures are clearly written.	___	___	___
14. Math and science problem examples match the concepts and steps previously discussed.	___	___	___
15. The authors inform the students when information contained in graphs, tables, or diagrams is not also contained in the text.	___	___	___
16. When the text refers to a graph or table, that aid is on the same page as the textual reference.	___	___	___
17. The authors suggest other resources and activities for students motivated to explore the area or for students who have difficulties with specific objectives or specific tasks.	___	___	___

FIGURE 2.2   Criteria for Measuring a Textbook's Learnability

OTHER INFLUENCES ON ACTIVE LEARNING

In Chapter 1 we gave considerable attention to the idea that learning does not take place in a vacuum; rather, students become active learners within supportive learning environments that teachers create. It is important to keep in mind, therefore, that students will not develop all the characteristics of active learners described previously unless teachers actively promote independent learning within a classroom context that is inviting, engaging, and nurturing of students' risk taking.

You can create an environment that fosters active learning in a variety of ways. Most important, you need to model or demonstrate the strategic behavior you want your students to emulate. For example, if you want them to use a specific strategy in solving math story problems, you must demonstrate and explain that process so that it becomes external and accessible. The mental steps you intuitively employ must be made explicit to your students; otherwise, the chances of their understanding and applying the strategy to their own story problems will be greatly reduced.

You can also encourage active learning by providing students with challenging and diverse tasks that require them to think critically and elaboratively. Students will not try out new strategies if they believe their usual routines will work. Their resistance to change makes sense if you think about it. Would you change your tennis serve if you were constantly winning all your matches? Moreover, you should stress that learning is often hard, even for the most capable learners. If students view learning as difficult but not impossible, they will be more likely to use active learning strategies. Of course, the key to these two instructional principles is finding the balance between assigning your students impossible tasks and inviting them to engage in challenging tasks that they can accomplish with your support. Throughout this textbook, you will read about teachers who have found that delicate balance necessary for encouraging their students to become active learners.

SUMMARY

Go to *http://www.prenhall.com/brozo*, select Chapter 2, then click on Chapter Review Questions to check your understanding of the material.

In this chapter we have proposed a holistic perspective of active learning. We have suggested that active learners are strategically involved in the reading process. More specifically, we outlined five important principles that characterize active learners. These five principles are not discrete and mutually exclusive, as in the skills model of reading comprehension, but rather are interactive and interdependent. The first principle concerns learners' use of prior knowledge to interact with text. The second principle focuses on active learners who summarize and organize what they read. The third principle explains how active learners think critically about text and create their own elaborations in order to enhance their understanding and recall. The fourth principle explains how active learners who are metacognitively aware monitor their understanding, understand their academic tasks, and view themselves as learners who have control of what and how much they learn. The fifth principle states that active learners possess and use a wide variety of strategies that encourage them to make sense of what they read, monitor their understanding, and clarify what they do not understand.

In Chapter 3 we address these five principles within a methodological framework. We explain and demonstrate how you can use and devise specific strategies for your classroom. Some of these strategies will be teacher directed and some will be student initiated. As you read the remaining chapters of this book, you will be frequently reminded of how a particular strategy is intended to force students out of familiar passive roles and impel them to become active participants in the learning process.

REFERENCES

Afflerbach, P. (2000). Verbal reports and protocol analysis. In M. Kamil, P. Mosenthal, P. Pearson, & R. Barr (Eds.), *Handbook of reading research:* (Vol. 3, pp. 163–180). Mahwah, NJ: Lawrence Erlbaum Associates.

Alexander, P., & Jetton, T. (2000). Learning from text: A multidimensional and developmental perspective. In M. Kamil, P. Mosenthal, P. Pearson, & R. Barr (Eds.), *Handbook of reading research:* (Vol. 3, pp. 285–310). Mahwah, NJ: Lawrence Erlbaum Associates.

Anderson, T. H., & Armbruster, B. B. (1984). Content area textbooks. In R. Anderson, J. Osborn, & R. Tierney (Eds.), *Learning to read in American schools: Basal readers and content texts.* Hillsdale, NJ: Erlbaum.

Anderson, T. H., & Armbruster, B. B. (1986). Readable textbooks, or, selecting a textbook is not like buying a pair of shoes. In J. Orasanu (Ed.), *Reading comprehension: From research to practice.* Hillsdale, NJ: Erlbaum.

Armbruster, B., Anderson, T., & Ostertag, J. (1987). Does text structure/summarization instruction facilitate learning from expository text? *Reading Research Quarterly, 22,* 331–346.

Baker, L., & Brown, A. (1984). Metacognitive skills and reading. In P. D. Pearson (Ed.), *Handbook of reading research.* New York: Longman.

Bransford, J., & Johnson, M. (1972). Contextual prerequisites for understanding: Some interesting investigations of comprehension and recall. *Journal of Verbal Learning and Verbal Behavior, 11,* 717–726.

Brown, A., & Day, J. (1983). Macrorules for summarizing text: The development of expertise. *Journal of Verbal Learning and Verbal Behavior, 22,* 1–14.

Chambliss, M. (1995). Text cues and strategies successful readers use to construct the gist of lengthy written arguments. *Reading Research Quarterly, 30,* 778–807.

Doyle, W. (1983). Academic work. *Review of Educational Research, 53,* 159–199.

Ennis, R. (1996). *Critical thinking.* Upper Saddle River, NJ: Prentice Hall.

Fry, E. B. (1968). A readability formula that saves time. *Journal of Reading, 11,* 513–516, 575–578.

Goldman, S. R., & Rakestraw, J. (2000). Structural aspects of constructing meaning from text. In M. Kamil, P. Mosenthal, P. Pearson, & R. Barr (Eds.), *Handbook of reading research:* (Vol. 3, pp. 311–335). Mahwah, NJ: Lawrence Erlbaum Associates.

Guzzetti, B., & Hynd, C. (1998). *Theoretical perspectives on conceptual change.* Mahwah, NJ: Lawrence Erlbaum Associates.

Hofer, B., & Pintrich, P. (1997). The development of epistemological theories: Beliefs about knowledge and knowing and their relation to learning. *Review of Educational Research, 67,* 88–140.

Hynd, C. (1999). Teaching students to think critically using multiple texts in history. *Journal of Adolescent & Adult Literacy, 42,* 428–437.

Mandler, J. (1987). On the psychological reality of story structure. *Discourse Processes, 10,* 1–29.

McKeachie, W. J. (1994). *Teaching tips* (9th ed.). Lexington, MA: D. C. Heath.

McNamara, T., Miller, D., & Bransford, J. (1991). Mental models and reading comprehension. In R. Barr, M. Kamil, P. Mosenthal, & P. D. Pearson (Eds.), *Handbook of reading research* (Vol. 2). New York: Longman.

Meyer, B. J. (1979). Organizational patterns in prose and their use in reading. In M. L. Kamil & A. J. Moe (Eds.), *Reading research: Studies and applications.* 28th Yearbook of the National Reading Conference. Rochester, NY: National Reading Conference.

Moore, D., Bean, T., Birdyshaw, D., & Rycik, J. (1999). Adolescent literacy: A position statement. *Journal of Adolescent & Adult Literacy, 43,* 97–111.

Nist, S., & Simpson, M. (2000). College studying. In M. Kamil, P. Mosenthal, P. Pearson, & R. Barr (Eds.), *Handbook of reading research:* (Vol. 3, pp. 645–666). Mahwah, NJ: Lawrence Erlbaum Associates.

Paris, S., Wasik, B., & Turner, J. (1991). The development of strategic readers. In R. Barr, M. Kamil, P. Mosenthal, & P. D. Pearson (Eds.), *Handbook of reading research* (Vol. 2). New York: Longman.

Pintrich, P. R., & Garcia, A. (1994). Self-regulated learning in college students: Knowledge, strategies, and motivation. In P. R. Pintrich, D. R. Brown, & C. E. Weinstein (Eds.), *Student motivation, cognition, and learning.* Hillsdale, NJ: Erlbaum.

Pressley, M. (1995). More about the development of self-regulation: Complex, long-term, and thoroughly social. *Educational Psychologist, 30,* 207–212.

Pressley, M. (2000). What should comprehension instruction be the instruction of? In M. Kamil, P. Mosenthal, P. Pearson, & R. Barr (Eds.), *Handbook of reading research:* (Vol. 3, pp. 545–561). Mahwah, NJ: Lawrence Erlbaum Associates.

Pressley, M., Yokoi, L., van Meter, P., Van Etten, S., & Freebern, G. (1997). Some of the reasons why preparing for exams is so hard: What can be done to make it easier? *Educational Psychology Review, 9,* 1–38.

Rosenshine, B., Meister, C., & Chapman, S. (1994). Reciprocal teaching: A review of the research. *Review of Educational Research, 64,* 479–530.

Schommer, M., Calvert, C., Gariglietti, G., & Bajaj, A. (1997). The development of epistemological beliefs among secondary students: A longitudinal study. *Journal of Educational Psychology, 89,* 37–40.

Simpson, M. L., Hynd, C. R., Nist, S. L., & Burrell, K. I. (1997). College academic assistance programs and practices. *Educational Psychology Review, 9,* 39–87.

Simpson, M. L., & Nist, S. L. (2001). Encouraging active reading at the college level. In M. Pressley & C. Block (Eds.), *Reading comprehension instruction.* New York: Guilford Publications.

Simpson, M. L., Olejnik, S., Tam, A., & Supattathum, S. (1994). Elaborative verbal rehearsals and college students' cognitive performance. *Journal of Educational Psychology, 86,* 267–278.

Weinstein, C. E., & Mayer, R. E. (1986). The teaching of learning strategies. In M. C. Wittrock (Ed.), *Handbook of research on teaching.* New York: Macmillan.

Wilson, P. T., & Anderson, R. C. (1986). What they don't know will hurt them: The role of prior knowledge in comprehension. In J. Orasanu (Ed.), *Reading comprehension: From research to practice.* Hillsdale, NJ: Erlbaum.

Wineburg, S. S. (1991). Historical problem solving: The study of cognitive processes used in the evaluation of documentary and pictorial evidence. *Journal of Educational Psychology, 8,* 73–87.

Zimmerman, B. J. (2000). Attaining self-regulation: A social cognitive perspective. In M. Boekaerts, P. Pintrich, & M. Zeidner (Eds.), *Handbook of self-regulation* (pp. 13–39). San Diego, CA: Academic Press.

CHAPTER THREE

Comprehension Strategies: The Tools of Content-Area Teachers

ANTICIPATION GUIDE

Directions: Read each statement carefully and decide whether you agree or disagree with it, placing a check mark in the appropriate *Before Reading* column. When you have finished reading and studying the chapter, return to the guide and decide whether your anticipations need to be changed by placing a check mark in the appropriate *After Reading* column.

	BEFORE READING		AFTER READING	
	Agree	*Disagree*	*Agree*	*Disagree*
1. If students will not read their assignments, then teachers should lecture on those concepts.	_____	_____	_____	_____
2. The best way to teach students how to monitor their learning is by having them answer questions at the end of a chapter.	_____	_____	_____	_____
3. Most students believe that answers to all questions will be found in the text.	_____	_____	_____	_____
4. The brighter students are the ones who profit most from instruction on how to think critically.	_____	_____	_____	_____

To fail to teach students strategies they do not use and from which they could benefit is to fail the students, to neglect to show them ways of reaching reading and studying in optimal ways. To teach crops and arithmetic facts and science principles and battles without teaching students how they can learn more about any of this or about other content is to risk that children will not become effective independent learners.

—Garner (1988)

As discussed in Chapter 1, we believe that the major goal of education should be the development of critical thinkers and active learners who can use the literacy processes to pursue knowledge and solve problems. To become active learners, students need strategies that involve them in the process of constructing meaning in reading and writing and using new understandings in a functional way. In this chapter we present teacher-directed comprehension strategies for facilitating the growth of active learners across all the content areas. Comprehension should not—and cannot—be taught in isolation from the material from which students are trying to learn. This is especially true in middle school and in high school.

The five principles outlined in Chapter 2 provide the organizing framework for this chapter. The first principle of active learning is discussed briefly here because Chapter 5 deals in depth with the importance of building students' readiness to learn. The fifth principle of active learning will be discussed in detail in Chapter 9, Study Strategies. None of these five principles, however, are mutually exclusive. That is, a strategy discussed under the first principle—helping students use prior knowledge in the meaning-making process—could easily help your students with the second, third, fourth, or fifth principles describing active learning. In fact, each chapter in this book will in some way present another approach to helping your students become active readers and writers and, thus, effective independent learners.

Before we examine these approaches, however, we will address an issue that troubles many of the teachers with whom we interact—students who do not read their assignments. In the first section, Building a Context That Supports and Requires Active Reading, we share some ideas, collected from our own teaching experiences and from a variety of secondary-level teachers, that encourage and nudge students into reading and interacting with text. But, first, consider this case study.

 Go to *http://www.prenhall.com/brozo*, select Chapter 3, then click on Chapter Objectives to provide a focus for your reading.

CASE STUDY

Charles teaches 10th-grade general biology in a large consolidated high school in the Midwest. After 3 years of teaching, he has noticed that many of his students (1) generally have a difficult time understanding the textbook, (2) do not complete homework reading assignments, and (3) seem to be trying to memorize information while failing to learn to observe and think about scientific phenomena. Charles is highly interested in discovering ways to help his students become more enthusiastic about science learning and better able to deal with and benefit from textbook reading.

Midway through the first semester of the new school year, Charles has begun a 2-week unit on genetics. Within the unit he wants to emphasize students' understanding of genetic engineering and the implications of this technology for their personal lives. In the preceding 2 months, his students studied the scientific method, the cell, and classification of living things, including the life cycle and basic requirements of life.

Case studies in this textbook provide an opportunity to apply concepts and techniques to new situations.

To the Reader:

As you read and work through this chapter on comprehension strategies, think about and be prepared to generate some strategies that could help Charles accomplish his goals. Consider how the strategies described in this chapter and those generated from your own experience and imagination could be adapted to the teaching and learning of science material.

BUILDING A CONTEXT THAT SUPPORTS AND REQUIRES ACTIVE READING

Students cannot improve their reading comprehension if they choose not to read.

The findings from classroom observational studies, the comments gleaned from interviews with students and teachers, and the results from surveys such as the NAEP all point to the fact that students are not reading their texts in or out of class (Wade & Moje, 2000). The NAEP, for example, determined in its research that adolescents reported reading for all their courses a total of five or fewer pages per day (Campbell, Voelkl, & Donahue, 1997). The graduating seniors and college first-year students we work with frequently tell us that the NAEP estimate of five pages a day is a bit high and that they were able to earn high grades in their courses with far less reading. Are these seniors that knowledgeable? Do they already know the basic concepts in our chemistry, English literature, and economics courses so well that their engagement in reading is unnecessary? The answer to those two rhetorical questions is "no." Students choose not to read when they realize that their teachers will provide them the necessary course information in the form of lectures, discussions, review sheets, or outlines that they can download from websites.

Breaking that cycle of dependency and passivity is troublesome for many teachers who want their students to become active, independent learners. It is also troublesome for administrators and parents who realize that students will never become fluent, critical readers if they do not open their texts and begin the process of reading and thinking about ideas. Although there is no panacea for this dilemma, we know from our experiences and from those of other content-area teachers that several practical techniques can build a context for active reading and learning. These techniques are embedded in three basic guidelines.

Explain Expectations and Roles

Students need to understand their role and your role in the learning process. That is, it is important for teachers to explain their role as one who creates activities to support and extend their students' understanding and mastery of major concepts. Students should also be told that they are expected to read text material outside of class and to bring their questions and concerns to class. If they choose not to read their assignments, students should be reminded that "safety nets" are not available. In other words, students should not expect you, as the teacher, to tell them the needed information via a lecture or review sheet.

These notions will be tested and challenged by the students, so it is important for you to be tenacious and steadfast. Equally important, however, is the second guideline that emphasizes the necessity of front-loading all assignments.

Front-Load All Assignments

In Chapter 5 we share a variety of strategies and techniques for preparing students for their learning tasks. These techniques share in common the importance of building interest and motivation, setting meaningful purposes for learning, activating and building students' prior knowledge, and preteaching any difficult vocabulary. These are all important aspects of front-loading. In addition, you might consider sharing the following important information when you give a reading assignment to your students:

Experienced teachers know that giving a detailed, explicit reading assignment is extremely important.

1. How should they read? Should they skim the assignment? Or should they read slowly, pausing to study all charts and graphs?

2. What should they focus on when they read? Definitions? Examples? Theories? Themes? Functions? Trends? Descriptions? Causes and effects? Comparisons and contrasts? Significant events?

3. How should they approach a difficult section? Should they use a diagram that explains the concept? Should they refer to their notes from the lab experiment? Or should they read the chapter summary before they begin reading?

4. How could they break up their reading into smaller chunks?

5. How long should it take them to read the assignment?

6. What will be expected of them once they have read the material? Should they come prepared to write? To discuss? To ask questions?

Implicit in all these suggestions is the belief that giving an assignment is more than announcing what pages need to be read. If you want students to read, you must prepare them. Once you have front-loaded the situation, you are then ready to require students to demonstrate and monitor their understanding, the third and final guideline.

Expect Students to Demonstrate and Monitor Their Understanding

If students know they will be held responsible for their reading assignments and you take the time to front-load these assignments, they will read them. We know that this sounds terribly simplistic, but it works, especially when teachers use a bit of ingenuity to ensure that their expectations are met. Although there are a variety of clever activities, we have found these two to be particularly effective: the **pop quiz with a card** and the **one-minute bucket activity.**

The pop quiz with a card is a quiz given at the beginning of the hour over the assigned reading. The students are told during the assignment-making process that they should jot down the key ideas from their reading on an index card and that they can use this one index card in case there might be a pop quiz the next day in class. Some teachers have even provided students models and examples of possible index cards to make sure they are not writing everything like a medieval monk. The quizzes are typically brief (three to five short-answer questions) and focus on key ideas, but most important, they are randomly administered. That is, the students never really know when a quiz might be given, and that randomness helps to guarantee that students will read. Teachers have told us that only the grade-conscious students initially did their index cards and read the assignments. But gradually, over time, the presence of index cards grew exponentially, so that the majority of students were reading and creating their index cards. Another serendipitous result to the "pop quiz with an index card" activity is that students are actually coming to class, armed with questions about information they did not understand. In other words, they were monitoring their understanding, an important characteristic of active learners.

You can hold students accountable for their reading assignments in a variety of ways.

The second activity, the one-minute bucket activity, originated with a biology teacher but can be used by any content-area teacher who expects students to read their assignments. A bucket is placed on a chair inside the classroom door; slips of paper are next to the bucket. Students are told that they must write their name on a slip and place it in the bucket. They know that there will be a drawing at the beginning of class and the persons selected will be responsible for summarizing a concept from the assigned reading or for working a problem on the board. This task can be part of the students' participation grade for the day. Once class begins, the teacher asks the students to close their books and draws a name from the bucket. That student is then responsible for explaining the concept to the entire class; many teachers like students to stand by their seat or to go to the board so they might use the board as their visual prop. Other teachers have told us that they permit students a "life-line" or the assistance of one student of their choosing. Generally, it is useful to have three or four quick drawings from the bucket. The students' explanations certainly will help you understand how well they understood what they read and whether or not they did read. The bucket activity also provides some very "teachable" moments and an excellent way to "prime the pump" with weary adolescents.

Obviously, you can use a variety of ways to require students to demonstrate and monitor their understanding, and we invite you to discover them as you read the rest of this book (e.g., index/exit slips). Please remember that we are not suggesting that teachers not teach. Rather, we are suggesting that students read their assignments and come to class armed with questions and concerns so that teachers can clarify and extend their students' understanding of concepts.

ACTIVE LEARNERS USE THEIR PRIOR KNOWLEDGE AS THEY INTERACT WITH TEXT

In Chapter 5 you will find many more prior knowledge-building strategies.

The principle that active learners use prior knowledge as they interact with text (as discussed in Chapter 2) is concerned with the extent to which students *apply* appropriate schemata during the reading process. You can use a variety of strategies to help students engage and use relevant prior knowledge as they read. In this section, we discuss one very effective approach, the Content Area DR-TA.

Content Area Directed Reading-Thinking Activity (DR-TA)

The **Content Area Directed Reading-Thinking Activity,** or **DR-TA** (Haggard, 1985) was developed to activate students' prior knowledge about a topic and to involve them actively in what they are learning. Although the steps or procedures of the DR-TA are flexible and can be modified for almost any situation or content area, students are usually involved in (1) activating their prior knowledge, (2) predicting what will be discussed in the text, (3) reading, and (4) confirming and revising their predictions with the information they learned from the text.

Phil, a sixth-grade science teacher, uses a modification of the DR-TA with his students because he believes that it arouses their curiosity and motivates them to read more intently. When he taught a unit on humans and the environment, he started by asking his students to meet with their study partner to brainstorm and list all the information they predicted would be covered in the unit. After a few minutes of brainstorming, Phil led a large-group discussion in which the study partners shared their lists as he wrote them on the board. As you can see in Figure 3.1, their ideas were very concrete, focusing on personal experiences. Chanda and her study partner listed ideas that pertained to littering because their youth group had just finished a project in which they volunteered to remove litter from the county road near their church.

Phil followed up the prediction step of DR-TA by suggesting that the students organize these predictions around possible problems that we have with

---

Ideas Brainstormed

smelly garbage
litter
rats in garbage cans
garbage pits
a trip to a landfill
a dirty lake by my grandmother
unclean air in Chicago—my sister lives there
clay soil in Georgia
farmers using irrigation to grow cotton
the high cost of food
tainted food, like hamburgers and apples
not enough rain
oil on the beach in Brunswick
dead whales
people dying from bad food or water
newspapers, cartons, cigarettes on roadsides
picking up trash on Saturday morning

FIGURE 3.1 Students' Brainstorming as a Part of a Content Area Directed Reading-Thinking Activity (DR-TA) Lesson

our environment and possible solutions to these problems. He asked them to reread the list and identify the problems first. As the students volunteered their responses, he made another list on the board under the heading "Problems." When he asked the students to identify possible solutions, several of them pointed out that their predictions did not include any solutions except for the one about Chanda's church group. "Can you think of any solutions to our environmental problems besides picking up trash?" Phil asked. The students then volunteered the idea of recycling, and Phil added that to the "Solutions" list.

At this point, Phil told the students to read the first five pages of the chapter, which focused on the use and misuse of natural resources and the consequences of pollution. He directed them to "read carefully in order to determine the accuracy of our predictions and to identify information that we can add to our problems and solutions lists." Because Phil likes to have his students start their assignments during class, he gave them the last 10 minutes to begin their reading.

The next day, Phil asked the students to copy the list of predictions on the board. He then asked them to identify situations in which the predictions matched the information in the text that they had been assigned to read. As the students eagerly volunteered, he placed a check mark by the relevant information on the master list. Then Phil told them to meet with their study partner to identify the problems or solutions discussed in the text but not included in their original predictions. After allowing 5 minutes for the partners to work, Phil led a large-group discussion of the problems related to pollution and the environment. Figure 3.2 illustrates the information the students added to the master list.

Phil uses the Content Area DR-TA because he likes the fact that his students are engaged in brainstorming, discussing, writing, and reading to verify their predictions. In addition, he believes that the steps involved in DR-TA help his students become more aware of the active role they must assume when reading content-area material.

The Content Area DR-TA not only provides considerable diagnostic information about students and their prior knowledge but also, because it is an excellent stimulus for student discussion and writing, promotes more critical reading and thinking. In the next section, we discuss strategies that help students summarize and organize as they interact with text, the second principle.

ACTIVE LEARNERS SUMMARIZE AND ORGANIZE AS THEY INTERACT WITH TEXT

Many teachers will tell you that the students who frustrate them the most are those passive students who rarely do the reading or assignments but listen well enough in class to "just get by." For these passive nonparticipants, learning is memorization of facts, and teachers are the dispensers of information. Although there is no panacea for passivity, a beginning point for all content-area teachers is to help their students become active learners who summarize and organize as they read. In this section, we will discuss the following four comprehension

Problems in Our Environment	Solutions to the Problems
Before We Read	*Before We Read*
dead whales	picking up trash
people dying from bad food or water	
newspaper, cartons, cigarettes on	
roadsides	
oil on beaches	
dirty water in lakes and oceans	
unclean air	
smelly garbage	
After We Read	*After We Read*
mercury from industrial waste	landfills with liners
acid mine waste	outlawing chemicals
pesticides with DDT	sewage treatment
detergents with phosphates	contour farming
fertilizers with phosphates	reclamation projects
animal wastes	public awareness
thermal pollution	
radiation	

FIGURE 3.2   Students' Ideas Before and After Reading Organized into a Problem–Solution Format

enhancing strategies: verbal demonstrations, process guides, expository passage organizers, and charting. These strategies are intended to help students summarize and focus on key ideas and use a text's structure and organization to sense connections and understand relationships between content-area concepts.

Verbal Demonstrations of the Active Reading Process

Although a majority of adolescents can read the words in their texts, they struggle with the understanding process because they are passive readers who are cruising through on automatic pilot. Passive readers do not think as they read and thus have difficulties understanding difficult and unfamiliar content-area material. We have found in our experiences, as have other teachers and researchers, that verbal demonstrations or think-alouds help older learners understand how they should read actively and how they should modify their reading approaches for the different content areas. When teachers provide their students verbal demonstrations, they externalize what is internal by reading, thinking, and reporting out loud the processes and strategies they are using to understand a particular piece of text. These verbal demonstrations can focus on how to summarize and organize ideas as well as a variety of other higher level reading and thinking skills.

Regularly demonstrate how to read and think in your content area.

The students in Loris's seventh-grade language arts class were having difficulty in making the transition from narrative text (i.e., stories) to the expository material contained in their textbooks. They were reading passively, focusing on minute, irrelevant details. Loris decided that she would help her students focus on key ideas and learn the steps involved in summarization by providing them a verbal demonstration. For the demonstration she selected a passage she knew was difficult and challenging. She distributed the short passage and, without having previously rehearsed it, began reading and thinking aloud as she attempted to summarize the key ideas. Loris believes that demonstrating the summarizing process with brand-new text gives students a glimpse of how she struggles to make meaning and to reveal the genesis of her summary thinking. She has discovered that by giving only polished summaries, she misses the opportunity to teach her students the strategies she used to construct them—that is, the process of working from confusion to understanding.

After her verbal demonstration, a student in the class offered Loris his history textbook and asked her to summarize a subsection from his reading assignment for the upcoming week. Selecting a short section entitled "The Yellow Press," Loris made copies and distributed them the next day. Without rehearsing, she then made sense of the text and the decisions behind what to include in her summary. Compare the textbook segment with Loris's think-aloud while modeling the summarizing process.

The Yellow Press

While supporters of the rebel cause were active in the United States, newspaper tycoons William Randolph Hearst and Joseph Pulitzer were carrying on a circulation war. Each was determined that his paper would outsell the other. So both began to play up Spanish "atrocities." Legitimate accounts of suffering in the concentration camps were mixed with fake stories of wells being poisoned and little children being thrown to the sharks. American correspondents, who were not allowed to enter areas where fighting was going on, would sit around the bars of Havana and make up reports about battles that never took place. One, artist Frederic Remington, who had been illustrating reporters' dispatches, cabled Hearst saying that war between the United States and Spain seemed very unlikely. Back came Hearst's reply, "You furnish the pictures and I'll furnish the war."*

Loris's Verbal Demonstration

Loris: Remember that I'm looking at this section without having read what comes before, so I'm reading it in isolation. You would have read the entire chapter. But I can clearly see by looking at the other subheadings on these couple of pages that the topic is about Cuba and its struggle for independence from Spain around the turn of the century.

---

*Jordan, W. D., Greenblat, M., & Bowes, J. S. (1985). *The Americans, the history of a people and a nation*. Evanston, IL: McDougal, Littell. Copyright 1985. Used by permission of the Publisher.

Okay, right from the start, the term *yellow press* means something like bad journalism or false reporting. This is something I just already know, so I'm thinking that the section will describe false reports about the Cuban-Spanish war. I don't remember much about that time in history except for Teddy Roosevelt and his Rough Riders, so I'll have to read on to find out which side the press is writing bad news about. *(Loris reads the first three lines aloud.)* I know of Hearst and Pulitzer and the fact that they made their fortunes in the newspaper business. Remember Patti Hearst? She's part of that family . . . and you've heard of the Pulitzer Prize for journalism and fiction writing, haven't you?

I've learned here that they were reporting falsely about the Spanish to make them look bad and capitalize on all the Cuban supporters in the United States who might buy their papers. I figured this out because it said they wanted "to outsell the other" so they played up Spanish "atrocities." *Atrocities* are terrible acts of inhumanity, like the Nazis' concentration camps, and the word is in quotes, which tells me that it's being used in a sarcastic or exaggerated way. *(Loris reads the next sentence.)*

These are examples of the exaggerated stories about how the Spaniards were supposedly torturing helpless Cubans, throwing babies to sharks, and poisoning water. Because these are specific examples, I probably won't include them in my summary. *(Loris reads the last three sentences.)*

Okay, so the reporters made up the false stories, and the last example points up how far Hearst was willing to go. He would actually lie about a war between the United States and Spain just to sell more papers.

I noticed Remington was an illustrator. He's famous for his paintings of Western scenes, cowboys and Indians.

Now I'm going back to create a summary for this. First, I'm thinking about what the overall point is . . . something like how newspapers reported lies during the Cuban war of independence just to sell more papers. With this idea in mind, I'm going to *delete* some specific details here, like the fake stories of atrocities and the fact that the reporters sat in bars and thought up their stories, and even the last example about Hearst and a make-believe war. *(As she reported aloud on her thinking, she went to the board and crossed out the lines she wished to delete.)* Instead I want to group or *categorize* these things with an expression like, well, I could use this one: "The press printed false stories about Spanish atrocities."

So I might say in my summary *(Loris writes using a grease pencil and an overhead transparency while saying the words aloud)*: "During the Cuban war of independence, major U.S. newspapers were competing with one another to sell the most papers. To do this, some papers printed false stories about Spanish atrocities."

Now, if it's important to remember that Hearst's and Pulitzer's papers were the primary ones engaged in false reporting, then I suppose they should be mentioned in the summary.

Student: You said that when we summarize, we should also look for topic sentences if the author gives them to us, so couldn't you just take the first three lines of that section, since they say just about what you've said?

Loris: They do sound similar, don't they? If those three sentences said it all for you, then I guess there would be no reason why you couldn't use them. But one thing I'm trying to encourage you all to do is to put the information into your own words as much as possible because, by paraphrasing, you can usually save on words and condense even more. I suppose if I were summarizing this entire chapter, then mention of the Cuban war of independence in my first sentence would not be necessary either, and I could cut it out.

As this session demonstrates, allowing students to eavesdrop on her thinking and decision making provided students with a model for interacting with Loris in constructing summaries for other pieces of text. Working and struggling together, they added and deleted information, created topic sentences, and tied together remaining ideas into condensed paragraphs.

For more ideas on how to teach and reinforce summarization, see Chapters 7 and 9.

Like other teachers who have taught students how to summarize, Loris uses a variety of activities to teach and reinforce the steps of summarization. Once students feel somewhat comfortable summarizing, Loris asks them to share their own summaries with their classmates to help each other. Loris has also given students models of summaries to evaluate. We have used this activity and have found it productive to provide two or three versions of a summary, ask students to rank them from best to worst, and give a rationale for their decisions. This activity can be done in pairs or in small groups.

We have seen that verbally demonstrating the processes involved in summarizing key ideas is a very effective strategy for Loris's students. You will find numerous other examples in this book of teachers verbally demonstrating and modeling across a wide variety of content areas and in a number of classroom settings.

Process Guides

Process guides are similar to verbal demonstrations in that they provide students models and suggestions on how they should summarize and organize key content-area concepts. These guides, however, are written suggestions that "walk" students through the processes involved in reading like an expert in biology or an expert in history. The process guide is a particularly effective and efficient way to begin a semester because it provides students the necessary assistance and scaffolding as they adjust their reading approaches to a particular content area.

You can provide a variety of suggestions in a process guide. Some of these suggestions might guide students in how to read their assignment (e.g., skim, slow down, notice the graph) and some suggestions might point out an important idea or relationship that students must understand. The following are examples taken from a variety of content areas:

1. Page 93, paragraphs 3–6: Pay special attention to this section. Make sure you identify three reasons for Hunter's actions.

2. Page 145: Notice the three subtopics under the boldface heading titled "Involvement in Vietnam." These three subtopics represent three reasons for our involvement. What are those three reasons?

3. Page 22: Study the graph. Be prepared to explain the processes represented in the graph. HINT: Read the graph from top to bottom.

4. Read the summary on page 223 BEFORE you begin to read. Why? The section's key ideas are highlighted for you.

5. Page 99: Skim the first three paragraphs. Then slow down and read very carefully about the two hormonal control systems. Make sure you can explain the two systems using your own words.

6. Page 11, paragraph 4: This paragraph explains why settlers chose this spot for their homes. There are three reasons why—the authors cue these reasons with words like "first" and "furthermore." Make sure you know the three reasons.

The process guide can be modified to any content area.

As you can see, the process guide can accomplish a variety of goals. One marine biology teacher we know, Christina, described the process guide as being a "personal tutor for each of my students." Christina was concerned that a majority of her students were trying to memorize all the details when they were reading. Some of her students seemed to give up on their reading or chose not to read, hoping she would summarize the information for them. Christina wisely decided not to lecture on the information contained in the book. Rather, she decided she would help her students learn the concepts in her course while modeling the processes involved in reading biology material. Her solution was the process guide.

To prepare the process guides, Christina began by asking herself what she wanted her students to know when they finished reading a chapter. Once she identified those major concepts and ideas, she then read the chapter carefully so she could identify potential problems her students might have as they read. As she read, she realized that many of them would skip the important charts and graphs, some of which illustrated important information not contained in the written presentation. She also realized that they needed to focus on key ideas and summarize those ideas, using their own words. Armed with that diagnostic information, Christina wrote her suggestions, cued to certain pages and paragraphs for the chapter on the sea floor. As illustrated in Figure 3.3, her guide offered specific reading suggestions and asked the students to jot down brief responses to her probes.

Christina introduced the guide to her students with an explanation as to its purpose. After demonstrating how to answer the first two questions, she gave her students 10 minutes at the end of the period to begin their reading and thinking. As the students read the text and their process guide, she circulated the room, guiding and prompting. Before the bell rang, she assigned her

READING AND PROCESS GUIDE FOR CHAPTER TWO

Directions: The purpose of this guide is to help you with the processes of reading like a "scientist." Read the suggestions and answer the questions AS YOU READ pages 33 and 34. Remember that reading science material is very different from reading a newspaper or short story—you will need to read more deliberately and to focus on definitions, examples, characteristics, and processes.

1. Begin your reading by examining Figure 2.17. Read the caption. You should now know the 3 parts to a continental margin.

2. Now focus on the first major boldface heading titled "Continental Margins." Read the first paragraph and be prepared to write a description of a continental margin and the 3 parts to a continental margin.

   Description of a continental margin:

   3 Parts:

3. The first subheading on page 33 is titled "The Continental Shelf." Read the two paragraphs in this section. Be prepared to list below the characteristics of a continental shelf.

   Characteristics of the continental shelf:

   • The shallowest part of the continental margin
   • Biologically very rich
   •
   •
   •

4. Did your characteristics of the continental shelf include the following key terms: *submarine canyons* and *shelf breaks?* If you have not examined Figure 2.18, DO THIS NOW! Remember that figures and graphs are very important in science and often present information NOT in the text. What do you learn from Figure 2.18? (HINT: You will obtain an example of a concept.)

5. The second subheading on page 33 is titled "The Continental Slope." Read this paragraph and then write a description of the continental slope, the second part of the continental margin.

   Description of the continental slope:

6. The third subheading on page 33 is titled the "The Continental Rise." Read this paragraph and then write a description of HOW a continental rise is formed.

   Steps in forming a continental rise:

7. Read the italicized summary on page 33. Does this information make sense to you? It should.

8. On page 34 you will find another boldface heading— "Active and Passive Margins." Before reading these 3 paragraphs, examine Figure 2.19. Read the caption. Again, an example is provided. What country is given as an example of active and passive margins? _____

FIGURE 3.3   Reading and Process Guide for Marine Biology

9. Read the first 2 paragraphs under the boldface heading— "Active and Passive Margins." These paragraphs explain how continental margins and habitats are influenced by plate tectonic processes. Obviously, you will need to be able to explain an active and passive margin and how they are formed. Make sure you stop to read Figure 2.20 when the authors ask you to do so.

  How active margins are formed:

  Characteristics of active margins:
  • Steep, rocky shorelines
  •
  •

  Examples of active margins:

10. Now, read the last paragraph for this section. What do you predict this paragraph will describe? _____ _____ What should you know when you finish this paragraph? (HINT: Look above at what you had to know for active margins.)

  Write the key idea for this paragraph:

FIGURE 3.3   Reading and Process Guide for Marine Biology—*Continued*

students to finish their reading and hinted at the possibility of pop quiz over the material. As she informed us, her announcement that students could use their completed process guide if there were a quiz motivated most of her students to do the reading.

Of course, Christina is not planning on writing process guides for all her chapters because she is hoping that her students will soon "figure out" how to read her biology materials. To her critics in her department who suggest she is telling her students too much, she responds that she is merely guiding her students in how to read and think and encouraging many of them to open their books. Another way in which Christina and other content-area teachers can encourage students to read actively is through the use of the expository text organizer.

Expository Passage Organizers

Expository passage organizers (EPOs) are another useful way to help students become active learners who summarize and organize as they read. EPOs were designed to help students understand the structure of expository text (Miller & George, 1992). Providing organizers for reading and writing expository text has been shown to improve students' comprehension and recall (Goldman & Rakestraw, 2000; Mayer, 1996) as well as their writing and their attitude toward writing.

AIDS: How a Virus Becomes an Epidemic

Directions: Complete the following EPO by looking back at the passage.
Passage Pattern: Problem–Solution

Introduction—Problem—Paragraph 1

Detail: HIV can be passed to another person during sexual intercourse if body flu-
ids are exchanged.

Detail: Blood-to-blood contact _____

Detail: Mothers with AIDS _____

Main Idea: HIV enters the body in only three ways.

Body—Solution—Paragraph 2

Main Idea: _____

Detail: AZT has been shown to interfere with the production of HIV.

Detail: Natural immune substances _____

Body—Solution—Paragraph 3

Main Idea: Scientists continue to search for better ways to treat the infections that
attack people with AIDS.

Detail: Chemotherapy, radiation _____

Detail: Antibiotics _____

Detail: Early detection of HIV can improve the chances of successful treatment.

Conclusion—Result—Paragraph 4

Main Idea: With no scientific cure in sight, changing behavior in the face of this
growing danger may be the best preventive act.

Detail: _____

FIGURE 3.4   EPO for a Problem–Solution Text

EPOs help students understand relationships between ideas.

Teachers in a variety of content areas can design EPOs that match their particular texts or lessons. For example, in the EPO in Figure 3.4 a seventh-grade health teacher provided his students with an EPO for a problem–solution text on AIDS. Here is how the EPO was generated and how the teacher used it with his students:

First, he identified the various structural elements of the text—in this case, a chapter from a book entitled *AIDS: How It Works in the Body* (Greenberg, 1992), by (1) listing the overall passage pattern (problem–solution); (2) labeling the critical components of the text structure (e.g., introduction, problem, body); and (3) providing the partially completed main idea and detail statements within each of the critical components. As students work through the chapter, they fill in the remaining information on the EPO, such as additional details and/or main idea statements.

The teacher uses EPOs such as the one on AIDS not only to promote students' understanding and recall of text material but also to further develop their expository writing skills. The organization of the EPO helps students conceptualize the overall structure of the author's ideas about AIDS from the specification of the problems to a discussion of particular solutions. The teacher extends the utility of EPOs by writing an essay himself using an expository text pattern consistent with the cause–effect patterns in the text and then fashioning an EPO for it. Both the essay and the EPO are shared with students and critiqued. Using EPOs to interact with text helps students recognize that their expository writing should have an overall organizational pattern as well. In recognizing how authors produce well-written exposition, students learn to model their compositions on these excellent examples. For instance, in the problem–solution essay on AIDs, students see how the author's citing of the problem is a main idea and her elaborations on the problem are supporting details. They notice how the author uses examples to support points and become better at providing appropriate supporting examples when composing their own expository texts.

Charting

A critical aspect of instruction designed to promote active learning is for teachers to phase out of their instructional role and for students to phase in and take on more responsibility for their own learning. One method that supports this transfer is charting, a strategy that eventually can be used by students once teachers have provided sufficient examples and guided practice.

Charting helps students summarize key ideas and visually sense the interrelationships between these ideas. The chart in Figure 3.5 is one that Tad, a biology teacher, used to help his sophomores understand a film they had watched about recent research and experiments involving the pituitary gland. Tad first distributed the partially completed chart and described how the act of creating a chart can help improve understanding and recall. He then told his students to complete the chart after viewing the film. The next day in class, he asked his students to work in small groups to check and discuss the information in their charts. After allowing students to work in small groups, he brought the class together for a discussion of the function and location of the pituitary gland. During the rest of the unit entitled "Hormones, Nerves, and Muscles," he created a variety of charting formats so that his students could see their versatility. Tad's long-term plan was to require his students to work in pairs to create their own charts for the next unit of study.

Tad relied on the structure of his supplementary materials and the textbook to organize the charts for his units of study. Although this organizational structure suited his instructional objectives and his students, you may have to make some adjustments, depending on the extent to which the information in your units of study is explicitly organized. Charting then becomes one way of imposing order on information that may not be organized in a suitable way for your students.

The Pituitary Gland				
Hormone	Function	Location	Scientific Name	Chemical Composition
TSH	influences the thyroid by negative feedback	anterior lobe; I of 4 tropic hormones	thyroid-stimulating hormone	glycoprotein
FSH	stimulates ovarian follicle	anterior lobe; I of 4 tropic hormones	follicle-stimulating hormone	glycoprotein
ACTH				
LH				
Growth				

FIGURE 3.5   Sample Chart for Biology Chapter

Students can create charts to help them learn in math, biology, and many other classes.

Ann, a math instructor, uses charting to improve her students' skills in solving word problems. The following motion problem is typical:

> The speed of a stream is 4 miles per hour. A boat travels 6 miles per hour upstream in the same time it takes to travel 12 miles downstream. What is the speed of the boat in still water?

To help her students achieve the reading precision necessary for motion problems, Ann asks them to organize the data in a chart with the headings t, r, and d, representing time, rate, and distance. She explains her lesson this way:

> My students already know that $R \times T = D$. I also have them represent rate downstream as $b + c$, where b is the rate of the boat, c is the rate of the current or stream, and $b - c$ is the rate upstream. I point out how the boat and current work together downstream, hence $b + c$, and against each other upstream, hence $b - c$. Therefore, before looking at the specifics of the problems, the student can make a chart as follows:

	t	r	d
upstream		$b - c$	
downstream		$b + c$	

My students then can read further and fill in the appropriate information, so the chart looks like this:

	t	r	d
upstream		$b - c$	
downstream		$b + c$	

Here is the process they follow. Four is substituted for the stream speed. Six and 12 are substituted for distance up- and downstream, and the time is represented as distance divided by rate. To set up an equation, students must look for a relationship, and hopefully they read "same time," so they set the representations for time equal to each other. In other words, the equation is:

$$\frac{6}{b - 4} = \frac{12}{b + 4}$$

My students seem to catch on to these motion problems much quicker with the charting technique.

Ann knows that she needs to maximize the interactions between her students and their math textbook by employing a variety of strategies that help them focus on key ideas and organize those ideas in a meaningful manner. Organizing formats like Ann's and Tadd's can be found elsewhere in this textbook, so we urge you to note them in subsequent chapters (i.e, Chapters 7 and 9).

Content teachers can also help facilitate students' independent learning by encouraging them to think critically and elaboratively about concepts—the third principle of active learning. In the next section we discuss this important principle.

ACTIVE LEARNERS THINK CRITICALLY ABOUT TEXT AND CREATE THEIR OWN ELABORATIONS

As noted in Chapter 1, it is imperative that adolescents become critical readers if they are to thrive and survive in society. Critical readers think about, interpret, and analyze what they read, all processes that require students to go beyond the memorization of details found in a text. In the next section we will share four techniques that encourage students to think critically about text and to create their own elaborations. However, we also wish to remind you the techniques and strategies in other chapters of this textbook will assist content-area teachers with this third principle of active learning. For example, Chapter 7, the chapter on writing, includes numerous ideas for promoting critical thinking across the content areas.

Throughout this book you will find numerous ideas for encouraging your students to think critically about content-area concepts.

Identifying Sources of Information in Answering Questions

One important way you can encourage your students' elaborative and critical thinking about content-area concepts is through a questioning strategy that sensitizes them to the fact that understanding is more than the memorization of facts and details. Using a questioning framework known as **question–answer relations (QAR)** (Raphael & Pearson, 1985), students learn how to locate and use many sources of information when answering questions along the continuum of text processing.

- *Right There:* The answer can be found in the text. The question cues the reader by echoing words from the text. The information source is mostly text based.

- *Think and Search:* The answer is not directly stated but requires the reader to combine ideas in the text with prior knowledge to form inferences.

- *On My Own:* The source of information for answering this type of question is the reader's prior knowledge. Processing is almost entirely reader based.

QAR refutes the common misconception held by students that the text tells all. Reliance on the text as the sole source of information limits students' interactions with text and consequently their depth of understanding. If students are asked questions at the think-and-search and on-my-own levels of processing, they will remember textual information and ideas at those levels; if they are asked questions at the right-there level, they will likely remember only information at the verbatim-recall level.

Students can be taught how to read materials beyond the surface level.

To provide you with firsthand experience with identifying sources of information for questions, following is a QAR activity for you to complete. The experience will give you a much better grasp of the processing requirements placed on students in a typical QAR exercise. Read the following passage; then group the questions and answers according to the source of information for answering them (right there, think and search, on my own).

The Story of Buck Billings

"Buck" Billings left Teddy's Rough Riders the very day peace was signed with the Spanish. There were wild stories about gold in the Klondike, and he couldn't wait to claim his stake. In the port of Havana he planned to pick up a boat to Tampa, then head north by train. After 3 days' trek through mosquito-infested swamps, he found that all the boats were packed with soldiers and civilians leaving for the States. He hopped aboard a ship bound for Venezuela. From there he found passage on a banana boat heading for South Carolina. The boat was turned back by a hurricane and forced to dock in Santiago Harbor. On a small sailing vessel he was finally able to reach the southern coast of Florida. He walked for 2 days to a train depot. After several weeks, he made it through the southern plains and eventually arrived in Denver, the town of his birth. Since it was already November, he moved back into his Aunt Dolly's boarding house, where he planned to stay for the next 4 months. During that winter, however, his yellow fever returned, and he succumbed to it on the first day of the new year.

1. Why was the boat forced to turn back? (Because of a hurricane)
2. Where is Aunt Dolly's boarding house? (Denver)

3. Where is the Klondike? (In Alaska)

4. Where was Buck's ship forced to dock after the hurricane? (In Santiago Harbor)

5. If Buck intended to head back to the States, why did he take a boat to Venezuela? (Because all the boats heading for the States were packed, and he thought he could get back to the States from Venezuela)

6. Where did Buck get yellow fever? (Cuba)

7. What was the boat carrying that was heading for South Carolina? (Bananas)

8. Did Buck make it to the coast of South Carolina? (No, the boat was forced back by a storm.)

9. Where was Buck the day peace was signed with the Spanish? (Cuba)

10. Who is Teddy? (Teddy Roosevelt)

Think about how you categorized these questions and answers as you read our categorization and rationales. We placed questions 1 and 4 in the right-there category because these questions cue the reader to the answers with words taken directly from the relevant sentence in the text.

Questions 2, 5, 7, and 8 we identified as think-and-search questions. Question 2 requires the reader to combine ideas from two sentences—the one stating that Buck arrived in Denver and the next one stating that Buck moved back with his aunt. The inference is that Buck is from Denver and has lived with his aunt before. To answer question 5 also requires some inferential reasoning. Buck was unable to go directly north to the States because all the ships were filled. By heading south first, he hoped to get there from Venezuela by avoiding Cuba altogether. Unfortunately, he found himself back in Cuba anyway. Question 7 asks the reader to make a low-level inference that connects the words in the question "What was the boat carrying?" to the sentence in the text that refers to the boat heading for South Carolina as a "banana boat." To answer question 8, the reader must combine information from two sentences—one stating that Buck was on a boat bound for South Carolina and the next one stating that the boat was forced to dock in Santiago Harbor. To answer "no" to this question requires more inferencing than may initially meet the eye. Notice that the reader must realize that Santiago Harbor is not in South Carolina, and because no other mention of South Carolina is made in the passage, it can be assumed that Buck never arrived there.

We grouped questions 3, 6, 9, and 10 in the on-my-own category. Certainly, to answer question 3, the reader must already know the geographical location of the Klondike. The text provides no clue. If the reader also realizes that peace with the Spanish over Cuba was signed at around the turn of the century, this knowledge could reinforce the time frame for the Alaskan gold rush. To know that Buck probably contracted yellow fever in Cuba (question 6) means that the reader has prior knowledge that yellow fever is a tropical disease and that many soldiers suffered and died from it as a result of their experiences in the war with

Spain over Cuba. To answer question 9, the reader must integrate several bits of textual information with a great deal of prior knowledge. The reader must possess knowledge about the Rough Riders and Teddy Roosevelt and know that they fought the Spanish in Cuba. Question 10 requires prior knowledge related to question 9; certainly, the reader must know that it was Teddy Roosevelt who commanded the Rough Riders.

Teaching Question–Answer Relations Using Cooperative Learning

The ultimate goal of QAR is not simply to train students to identify information sources for answering questions. Instead, QAR training should be seen as a method of sensitizing students to the idea that there are various ways of thinking about a text. Through QAR they can use their existing knowledge to interact more elaboratively and meaningfully with the texts they read.

Following is a description of an actual eighth-grade science classroom in which students were involved in cooperative learning experiences for reinforcing their understanding of QAR. Beth, the teacher, exploits the powerful learning potential of cooperative groups throughout the school year with nearly every topic she and her students explore. Students in this class develop a deeper understanding of science content through interactions with their peers by speaking, listening, reading, and writing. All students are provided greater opportunities to articulate and reinterpret text concepts and vocabulary, raise questions, discuss answers, and become more active class members.

Use a variety of grouping methods and teach students the rules for group interactions.

The topic the class was considering was "What Makes Ice Ages?" Beth first asked students to form into their **study reading groups,** three to a group. Her students were used to many different grouping arrangements that allow them to move in and out of groups, interacting with different students, depending on the purpose of the group. For instance, two other common grouping patterns in Beth's classroom were **interest groups** and **research groups**. Beth briefly rehearsed the "Rules for Group Membership," which students had in their notes and which were also written in bold letters on the side wall bulletin board.

- Each member must be strongly committed to doing the work and carrying out his or her specific role within the group.
- Each member should understand and follow the directions for completing assigned work.
- Each member should respect other members' input.
- A member who disagrees with another member should defend his or her own point of view, giving specific reasons based on the text or on personal experience.
- No member should dominate or withdraw; every member should add something to the discussion.
- Each member should be positive and encourage other members.

Beth then introduced the idea of QAR using an overhead transparency to focus the discussion. She discussed with the students how becoming more sensitive to the sources of information for answering questions can improve their ability to get more out of their textbook reading. She explained each of the levels of QAR and provided a handout with the labels and explanations. Beth asked students to open their science textbooks to the beginning of the section on ice ages. Using an overhead transparency, she presented a series of questions accompanied by answers covering the first page of this section. In their groups, students discussed among themselves why a question belonged in a particular category. Afterward, students shared their responses and rationales with the whole class. Beth allowed students to debate their answers, providing support, feedback, and demonstrations of her own thinking in identifying information sources for the questions.

The next phase of QAR instruction involves assigning responsibilities to each of the three group members. Beth asked each student in the groups to generate questions with answers for one of the three levels of QAR. The questions were written on the next page of the text. The groups then went over their questions, helping each other focus on the appropriate question for the assigned level. Beth then asked groups to exchange questions, emphasizing that the questions not be labeled. The groups worked with their new questions, determining sources of information and rationales. During this time, Beth sat in on each group's discussion, answering questions, providing necessary input, and reinforcing group efforts. Questions were given back to their owners with comments. Students then reworked their questions based on input from the other groups.

To get a better idea of the kinds of group discussions students had as they worked cooperatively on identifying QARs, refer to the following excerpt. This discussion took place between three students trying to determine whether a question required think-and-search or on-my-own processing.

Student 1: The question is, "If the greenhouse effect is true, what kind of climate will Chicago have in 50 years?"

Student 2: What's the answer?

Student 1: It says "6 to 12 degrees warmer. Like Florida."

Student 3: How are we supposed to know that?

Student 1: We can figure it out. We have to look in the book first to make sure it doesn't tell us about Chicago.

Student 3: I don't remember anything about Chicago.

Student 2: It doesn't, I'm looking right now. I can't find anything about it.

Student 1: It does say that if carbon dioxide keeps getting worse, the world temperature is going to go up. You see where I am, on page 128.

Student 3: It's for sure not a right-there or in-the-book question.

Student 1: Does it say by how many degrees? I'm looking down here. Yeah, here it is. It says that "if carbon dioxide levels continue to increase at the present rate, in 40 to 50 years the greenhouse effect will cause temperatures worldwide to increase by about 6 to 12 degrees centigrade."

Student 2: So, big deal, that doesn't sound like very much. How could that make us as warm as Florida?

(Students attend to the text.)

Student 3: Look, I found this part up here that says that a 100 million years ago the earth was a lot warmer even at the poles. So maybe if the poles were warm, we would be really warm too. What do you think?

Student 1: I like it. This is a hard one.

Student 2: So we're saying it's what, an on-my-own type or a think-and-search?

(They ponder.)

Student 3: I think it's sorta like both. You can find some of the information in the book, but you have to figure it out by yourself when it comes to the part about Chicago.

Student 1: Don't we have to say one or the other?

Student 3: I don't think so. She said they could be one or the other or anywhere in between.

(Student 1, designated as the recorder, writes down the group's rationale. They move on to the next question.)

QAR training promotes sensitivity to various information sources for answering comprehension questions; thus, students learn to process text in a more elaborative fashion. To move toward greater independence in reading comprehension, students should be generating their own questions that reflect the important information and ideas in the text. In Chapter 9, self-questioning is discussed as a strategy for improving students' understanding and metacognitive awareness.

Using Study Guides

To facilitate students' elaborative processing and to promote more critical thinking, teachers can provide students with **study guides** (Herber, 1978). Study guides are designed to stimulate students' thinking during or after their reading, listening, or involvement in any content-area instruction. Guides also help students focus on important information and ideas, making their reading or listening more efficient.

To find out why these study guides are better than the traditional guide, do the sample in Figure 3.6.

If you are not familiar with study guides, we invite you to complete the sample in Figure 3.6. First, look at the guide and directions. Then read the passage that accompanies it. After reading, complete the guide.

Now that you have finished the guide, a few comments are in order. Did you notice that, like QAR questions, the statements seemed to require a greater

Directions: Read the following passage; then read the statements about it. In the space to the left of each statement, put an *A* if you agree with the statement and a *D* if you disagree. Base your decisions on the information and ideas in the passage, as well as on what you already know about the topic.

Jesse Jackson's Broadening Political Base

In 1984, during his first presidential campaign, Jesse Jackson identified a constituency of the American public he believed had been, up to that time, underrepresented. Minorities of all colors and ethnic backgrounds, as well as women, the poor, and other groups, rallied around Jackson and were to become his *rainbow coalition.* Jackson claimed that politicians had forgotten about these groups of Americans. He charged that many were victims of poverty, homelessness, joblessness, poor working conditions, low salaries, sexual harassment, and subtle and overt racism. Many had chosen not to vote out of hopelessness. They looked at the slate of presidential candidates, claimed Jackson, and despaired, realizing that none had their concerns at heart.

In spite of grass-roots support and impassioned oratory, Jackson lost his bid for the presidency in 1984. Many said the country was not ready for a black president. However, political analysts speculated that Jackson's lack of success was attributable more to his narrow appeal than to his color. Indeed, in the 1988 presidential election, Jackson broadened his political base of support and mounted a far more serious challenge for the Democratic Party nomination. While holding on to the rainbow coalition, he reached out to farmers, factory workers, and the Democratic mainstream. He brought many delegates to the Democratic National Convention in Atlanta, where he brokered his political power and exerted leverage on Michael Dukakis to help shape the Democratic planks and platform.

Level I

_____ Jackson broadened his political base of support in 1984.
_____ Jackson first ran for president in 1984.
_____ The Democratic National Convention was held in Atlanta in 1982.
_____ The rainbow coalition was made up of the white middle class.

Level II

_____ Jackson might have been more successful in 1984, but the country was not ready for a black president.
_____ Jackson charged that the presidential candidates engaged in racism.
_____ Jackson supported equal pay for women.
_____ Affordable housing would not have been on Jackson's platform in 1984.

Level III

_____ Presidential candidates who appeal to farmers and factory workers are likely to be fairly successful.
_____ Jackson should continue to broaden his political base of support if he expects to be successful in 1996.
_____ Americans will not vote for a black president in the foreseeable future.
_____ Jackson lost his bid for the presidency in 1988.

FIGURE 3.6   Sample Study Guide Activity

degree of mental activity as you moved from level I to level III? The reason is that the statements were written to tap various levels of comprehension. We think about a text as existing on a sliding scale or continuum. On one end of the continuum is the kind of text processing that requires recall of directly stated material. We might call this **text-based processing** or **memory-level comprehension** because the information is based almost entirely on the text. To respond to level I of the study guide, you employed mostly text-based processing because the answers were basically right there. As we move along the continuum, processing becomes less and less text based and increasingly reader based. By **reader based**, we mean that comprehension requires readers to connect their prior knowledge about a topic with the information in text. Level II of the guide required you to combine your prior knowledge with textual information to form inferences. At level III, comprehension of these statements that seem to go far beyond the directly stated information in the text required you to rely heavily on prior knowledge and to process text in an elaborative fashion by applying and predicting. Thus, the goals of a study guide are to help learners assimilate information into their existing schemata and to think critically about ideas.

Something else you may have noticed about your study guide experience is that the statements in the guide form an excellent basis for class discussion. In fact, we urge you to take advantage of the discussion-generation potential of study guides; otherwise, students might eventually come to view them as just more busy work. The important advantage of study guides for teachers is that students must read the assigned textbook and think about the assignment rather than skim or scan the pages for answers to text-based questions. In short, students who are required to complete study guides cannot come to class unprepared; the guides force them to become active learners.

A few other important features of study guides are especially pertinent. To make guides more motivating and attractive to students and, consequently, to increase the likelihood that they will complete them and use them, the response formats should require students to do very little writing other than make a simple mark or check or write a few words. The idea is that guides should not resemble the typical discussion questions students are used to seeing and are forced to respond to with extensive written answers. The extent of the response on the guides should not, however, be construed as indicating the extent of thinking demanded of students. A colleague puts it well, describing study guides as "short on responding but long on thinking." As you undoubtedly noticed when working through the level III statements in Figure 3.6, your single-letter responses were made after considerable mental activity. In the directions to the guide, you are asked to base your responses on evidence from the text and your prior knowledge. Emphasis on this point will discourage students from responding arbitrarily, especially when they will be held accountable for their work in small-group or whole-class discussions.

Finally, like most strategies, study guides can become drudgery if misused or overused. Use discretion in employing them. Not every text lesson or topic will demand or lend itself to guides. A science teacher's point about study guides is instructive: "I use them with topics that typically give my students the most difficulty. They agree that it helps them organize the information and ideas and prepares them for my tests. But I don't use them all the time because other approaches work well too." Study guides are only one way to promote elaborate text processing.

Designing and Teaching With Guides

There are no set procedures for creating study guides. The types of guides are as varied as the teachers who construct them. In this section, we present various examples of teacher-constructed study guides from many different content areas. However, although guides can take a number of different forms, you must make some important and necessary decisions before designing them:

1. Read the text material thoroughly and decide what information and concepts need to be emphasized. You will be reminded of this step at several points throughout this book because it is the same process you should go through when, for instance, deciding key vocabulary to teach, appropriate readiness activities, and relevant trade books to accompany the text.

2. Determine how much assistance your students will need to process the information at an elaborative and meaningful level. If students already possess a basic understanding of the content, your guides can focus exclusively on higher levels of critical thinking. If, on the other hand, your students lack a basic understanding of the content, then guides should focus more on key ideas.

3. Ask yourself, "What format will stimulate my students to think about the content in an elaborative fashion, as well as motivate and appeal to them?" In our experience, the more imaginative the guide, the greater the chance that students will be enthusiastic about the guide and use it appropriately.

It is critical to prepare students to use study guides. If you simply distribute guides and tell students to complete them, you are setting yourself up for disappointment. Students need grooming and coaching to take full advantage of study guides. We recommend that you begin by "walking through" one of the guides, explaining its features, intent, and benefits. Allow students to meet in small groups and complete the guide in class under your supervision and with your assistance. Engage the class in discussion based on their responses to the guide, and use this feedback to provide additional explanation and to make any necessary modifications to the guide. Above all, keep in mind your purpose for using study guides. They should not be used as tests because promoting a right-or-wrong attitude among students undermines your intent—to encourage elaboration and critical thinking. It is important, however, that students be responsible for rationalizing and defending their responses to the guide. Make this an integral part of the study guide activity. Finally, at every opportunity, reinforce the connection between the mental activity required to complete the guides and your expectations of how and what students should be learning.

Examples of Guides From Various Content Areas

Study guides have been used successfully by teachers and students in nearly every content area with a wide variety of topics. As you look over the following guides, observe the format of each and reflect on how students are encouraged to think critically about the concepts. In addition, consider how you can adapt

Make sure you examine the examples from other content areas.

Directions: Below you will find a copy of today's want ads from the *Maycomb Daily Times,* a fictitious newspaper straight from the pages of *To Kill a Mockingbird.* Below each ad, write the name of the character from the novel that you feel would best fit the ad's description. All ads apply to at least one character, and some ads may have more than one responder. Be prepared to justify your answers.

Wanted: Individual who is interested in donating baked goods to be sold at the next PTA meeting to raise money for a school function.

_____

The Caucasians of America need information on the ghetto life of African Americans in contemporary America. Only those with personal experience need apply.

_____

Needed: Local newspaper is in need of an owner. Must have experience in printing, distribution, and sales.

_____

Gun Club looking for good shooter to give seminar.

_____

Help! The Kane County Rehabilitation Center is looking for a spokesperson for its drug unit.

_____

Child abuse is a crime. Report all cases to authorities.

_____

Wanted: A disciplinarian. A child whom everyone considers a BRAT needs some old-fashioned disciplining.

_____

Teacher needed. Patience a plus but not necessary. Will train.

_____

The rape crisis hotline is a free public service for the community. If you know of anyone who needs our help, encourage them to call us.

_____

Pen pals are wonderful. If you know of anyone who is interested in being a summer friend, a winter writer, send us his/her name.

_____

Seamstress Opening. Easy mending duties. Pick your own hours. Work at home if it's more convenient.

_____

Stop being a neighborhood gossip. Join Tale Enders today. Nobody likes to hear what everyone else has been up to.

_____

FIGURE 3.7   Study Guide for Literature: *To Kill a Mockingbird*

these formats to fit the textbooks, films, demonstrations, or discussions you use in your classroom.

Literature.   The study guide in Figure 3.7 was developed by an English teacher for her sophomores as they completed their analysis of characters in *To Kill a Mockingbird.*

Directions to Students: Check which vehicle is affected most by the following adverse surface conditions. Be prepared to defend your decisions in class discussion.

	Automobile	**Motorcycle**
1. Loose gravel	_____	_____
2. Gravel surface	_____	_____
3. Sand on pavement	_____	_____
4. Snow	_____	_____
5. Mud	_____	_____
6. Washboard	_____	_____
7. Potholes	_____	_____
8. Wet pavement	_____	_____

Directions to Students: Answer the following question:
How can a motorcycle operator compensate for the shortcomings of the machine under adverse surface conditions?

FIGURE 3.8 Study Guide for Automobile and Motorcycle Safety

Driver's Education.   For a unit in a driver's education class, students were provided with the guide shown in Figure 3.8 to help them compare and contrast the characteristics of motorcycles and automobiles. The information was presented in a film rather than a textbook. After the film, the students were asked to answer the questions that followed each section. These questions then served as a stimulus for classroom discussion.

Foreign Language.   In the final example of content-area study guides shown in Figure 3.9, you can see that guides can even be applied to foreign languages to promote more critical thinking. The Spanish teacher who constructed this guide found it to be very useful in helping her students expand their understanding of the central character. The guide is presented in English but was, of course, given to her students in Spanish.

A Final Word About Study Guides

As this section has demonstrated, study guides can be a very effective and versatile means of promoting higher level thinking about the concepts in your content area. In addition to their usefulness in promoting learning from text, they can be used for lectures, films, and demonstrations. But they are just one means. And, as we have pointed out, they are teacher initiated. Here and in other sections of this book, we emphasize the importance of developing independent readers and learners. Therefore, we present a variety of strategies for teaching students how to generate their own guides and study aids, such as maps, summaries, and other study products that reflect elaborative processing of text and promote long-term retention (see Chapter 9).

Study guides can be used for classes that use alternative means of presenting information to students.

Directions: In your reading about Sor Juana, you discovered that she could be considered one of the first advocates of the feminist movement. In addition, she was a very caring person, and her strong convictions often led her to step into situations on behalf of other people. *Evaluate* the following statements according to whether Sor Juana would agree or disagree with them. Just for fun, also consider your own reactions. Use the numbers 0–5 (5 = *total agreement;* 0 = *total disagreement*). You will be asked to justify your reactions in the class discussion.

Sor Juana   **Me**

_____   _____   1. The greatest contribution of women to society is that of producing babies.

_____   _____   2. Although men and women are physically different, there is very little difference in their intellectual capacities.

_____   _____   3. If a job that a man holds is essentially the same as the job held by a woman employed by the same company, the man should receive a higher salary because he is most likely the main breadwinner for his family.

_____   _____   4. There is no excuse for racial or religious discrimination. If you suspect that either of these situations is occurring in your community, you should talk to your neighbors about it.

_____   _____   5. If you are passing in front of a store and see a robbery taking place, you should discreetly enter the store, assess the situation, and, if possible, somehow try to overpower the thief.

_____   _____   6. Because of past discrimination, society should now make certain allowances for women. For example, companies should be strongly urged to hire a woman when given the choice between a man and a woman with equal qualifications.

_____   _____   7. Although both men and women are eligible for the armed services, only men should be assigned combat roles.

_____   _____   8. If a company is marketing something that you believe may be harmful, you should discuss your feelings with the manager of the store that is selling the product. If he continues to sell the product, you should picket his store.

FIGURE 3.9   Study Guide for a Foreign Language: Spanish Article "Sor Juana Ines de la Cruz: Monja y Feminista"

Using Discussion Webs to Encourage Critical and Elaborative Thinking

As teachers, we all remember one situation in which we anticipated a lively discussion among our students because we had assigned them an intriguing selection to read. In addition, we entered the classroom armed with a list of thought-provoking questions to help stimulate the discussion. Unfortunately, the discussion fell flat because we did the talking and the students did the listening. Some teachers have given up on discussion because of these memories or of other memories of situations where certain students monopolized the discussion while others daydreamed. Discussion, however, can be a positive and productive experience for students and teachers with appropriate preparation.

One strategy that prepares students for discussion is the *Discussion Web* (Alvermann, 1991). Discussion Webs encourage students to think critically because they are examining alternative points of view and offering evidence to

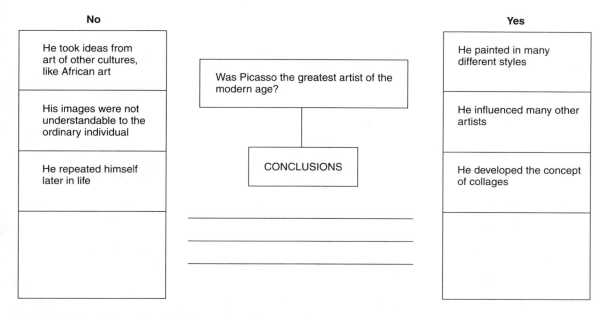

No

He took ideas from art of other cultures, like African art
His images were not understandable to the ordinary individual
He repeated himself later in life

Was Picasso the greatest artist of the modern age?

CONCLUSIONS

_____

_____

_____

Yes

He painted in many different styles
He influenced many other artists
He developed the concept of collages

FIGURE 3.10   Discussion Web for an Art Class

support those views. As illustrated in Figure 3.10, the Discussion Web is literally a visual or graphic representation of the thinking processes the students will go through during their discussion. In the center of the Discussion Web is the central issue or question that the students are to discuss in class. The question should be stated so that there is more than one point of view. The example in Figure 3.10 was created by Raymond, an art teacher who wanted his students to consider the central question "Was Picasso the greatest artist of the modern age?" On either side of the Discussion Web are spaces for students to list the reasons why they believe that either "yes" or "no" is the answer to the central question.

When Raymond used the Discussion Web with his art students, he followed these steps recommended by Alvermann (1991):

1. Prepare students for reading or listening by activating their prior knowledge, setting purposes and questions, and asking students to make predictions.

2. Have students read the selection, listen to the lecture, or watch the demonstration or video.

3. Introduce the central question and the Discussion Web. Ask students to work in pairs in discussing both points of view. The partners should take turns jotting down their reasons in the two support columns. Instruct the partners to allow equal time for both sides of the issue.

4. After the partners have jotted down a few of their reasons, combine the partners into groups of four. The four students will compare their

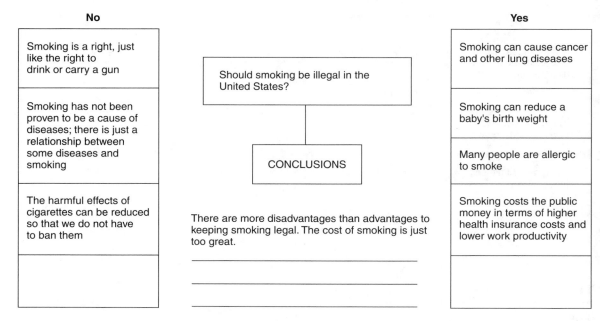

FIGURE 3.11   Discussion Web for a Health Course

Discussion Webs, with the ultimate goal of reaching a consensus. Remind the students to keep an open mind and to listen to the members of their group. If they cannot agree on a point of view, they can offer a minority report as well as a majority report.

5. When the groups have reached a consensus or the students' participation seems to be waning, give them a 3-minute warning. Within those 3 minutes, they are to decide who will report their views to the large group and what the individual will say.

6. Ask each spokesperson to report what his or her group decided and why.

7. After the whole-class discussion has ended, assign students to write their own responses to the central question in the blanks provided under the Conclusions section of the Discussion Web (see Figure 3.10).

Discussion Webs can be used before or after reading or writing assignments.

Discussion Webs can be used in a variety of ways. Raymond created the Discussion Web in Figure 3.10 as a way of encouraging students to discuss ideas after they had viewed a video on influential artists in the modern art movement. He tells us that he particularly likes the Discussion Web because all the students participate actively in class, even the introverted ones who are afraid to speak up. Raymond believes that most of the students feel more comfortable speaking and sharing their views because they have had time to rehearse what they wanted to say as they worked with their partner and the group of four.

Discussion Webs can also be used as a follow-up to a reading assignment. Figure 3.11 illustrates how a pair of eighth-grade students completed a Discussion Web after reading an assignment on smoking for a health and wellness course. Finally, many teachers report using the Discussion Web to help students brainstorm and prepare for their writing assignments. This use of the Discussion Web has been validated in research studies. For example, Rubin and Dodd in their classic study (1987) found that that oral language activities that required students to debate and switch sides during the debates improved the fluency and organization of their writing. In sum, Discussion Webs seem to have many advantages for content-area teachers who want less passivity and more critical thinking in their classroom.

Challenging and Thinking Critically About Texts

Students do not typically question or challenge what they read, especially their textbooks. Researchers, for example, have found that many high school and college students believe that the ideas in their history textbooks are absolutely true, immutable, and nondebatable (Hynd, 1999; Simpson & Nist, 1997). In order to feel comfortable challenging texts, students need to interact with a variety of sources on a topic, not just one source. When students encounter multiple texts on an issue or concept, they are more likely to discern differences across the authors, to note omissions, and to detect the voices of the various authors (Hynd, 1999). However, we should stress that providing students multiple sources on a topic, such as the Vietnam Conflict, will not guarantee that students will immediately begin to think critically about what they are reading. Content area teachers will need to model and guide their students through important critical thinking processes (e.g., sourcing, contextualizing, and corroborating) while they are reading (Beck, McKeown, Hamilton, & Kucan, 1997).

Researchers have found that students accept information in their textbooks without question.

Mary Beth, a high school instructor who teaches anatomy and kinesiology to juniors, decided to do just that. She began by locating several articles on the Internet concerning dieting and nutrition. One particular article intrigued her because it was written by an individual with a medical degree who was touting a particular diet program and book that could be purchased on the Internet for a considerable sum of money. Moreover, the author offered several statements in the article that contradicted what her students had learned from their textbooks and discussions during class. The second article Mary Beth selected for her students focused on less glamorous but more research-based methods of dieting such as exercising and using common sense with food choices. The author, however, was not a doctor or researcher.

With a third article she located on the Internet, Mary Beth began the mini-unit by introducing four critical thinking guidelines she wanted to stress: the authority and intent of the author and the accuracy and objectivity of his or her ideas. After modeling and discussing these four guidelines in conjunction with the third article, Mary Beth then informed the students that they, too, would have the opportunity to challenge an Internet author. She placed the students in pairs, giving them their own article to read. Their assignment was to read the article and to come to class prepared to teach their partner about the other article.

The next day Mary Beth provided the partners 10 minutes to meet and teach each other about their article. After 10 minutes she placed the students in groups of four and distributed the handout titled "Challenging the Author" (see Figure 3.12). The groups of four were given 20 minutes to discuss the nine questions. Mary Beth circulated around the room listening to the discussions and guiding their participation, when necessary. She then rang a bell and gave the groups the task of reaching an agreement of how they would "rate the author" (see Part Two). The students were also instructed to fill out Part One and to select a spokesperson who would report back to the class.

Needless to say, the students were all actively engaged in the discussion of the articles and in the rating of the authors. And, as Mary Beth hypothesized, two of the groups rated the article by the medical doctor as superior solely on the basis of his "authority." At the end of the hour Mary Beth helped the students debrief the experience and discussed how they might use these four guidelines in their own reading, whether it be on the Internet or in magazines and newspapers.

You need not teach anatomy to use these techniques and guidelines on critical thinking with your own students. Any content-area teacher can design a similar lesson using the Internet or any source that provides students an alternative viewpoint or an alternative development of an idea. In the next section we examine the fourth principle of active learning—the importance of building metacognitively aware students.

Go to Web Resources for Chapter 3 at http://www.prenhall.com/ brozo and look for ideas on how to evaluate websites.

ACTIVE LEARNERS ARE METACOGNITIVELY AWARE

We close this chapter by examining strategies that will help students monitor their understanding and correct situations in which they are having comprehension difficulties, important processes involved in becoming metacognitively aware. In order to address this fourth principle of active learning, we examine three strategies: reciprocal teaching, fix-up strategies, and DRAW.

Reciprocal Teaching and Self-Monitoring

To understand a text, you need to split your mental focus. On the one hand, you need to focus on the material itself. At the same time, however, you need to constantly monitor your processing to make sure you are comprehending and learning (Pressley, 2000). Unsophisticated readers and learners generally do not monitor their understanding and are unsure about what to do once they have determined that they are lost or confused (Simpson & Nist, 2001). Fortunately, teachers can help students become more metacognitively aware. One such strategy is reciprocal teaching, an instructional approach that has been found to be extremely successful with at-risk middle school and high school students (Brown & Palincsar, 1982). In classrooms where *reciprocal teaching* takes place, the teacher and student take turns generating questions and summaries and leading a discussion about sections of a text. Initially, the

Reciprocal teaching is a powerful and encompassing technique that will benefit all students.

PART ONE DIRECTIONS: Think about the following questions as you read the article you were assigned. These questions force you to think critically about an author's authority, intent, accuracy, and objectivity. If you think of additional questions that would be useful to you and your group members, write them in the blank lines.

Authority

1. Who is the author or producer of this information?
2. What are the author's qualifications? Are these credentials credible? Are these qualifications sufficient to discuss the content presented in the article?

Intent

3. What is the author trying to say here? What is the message?
4. Did the author explain and support the ideas in a clear fashion? Explain.

Accuracy

5. When was this article written? What do you know about this time period?
6. Can this information be verified by another source? Explain.
7. Is this information consistent with what you already know about the topic? Why or why not?

Objectivity

8. Is there any sort of bias evident in this article? Explain.
9. Is the author's motivation for writing clear to you? What do you think that motivation was?
10. OTHER QUESTIONS:

PART TWO DIRECTIONS: After answering the questions listed above and listening to your peers during the discussion, RATE the author of this article/essay. Complete the grid below so it represents what your group decides. You must reach a consensus and be prepared to defend your rating. Select a spokesperson for your group.

RATE THE AUTHOR

	1	2	3	4	5
	Low		Average		High
Authority					
Intent					
Accuracy					
Objectivity					

TOTAL SCORE: _____

FIGURE 3.12   Questioning and Challenging the Author

teacher models questioning, summarizing, clarifying, and predicting activities while encouraging students to participate at whatever level they can manage. Gradually, students become more capable of contributing to such discussions and assume more responsibility for their own learning.

Rob teaches a study skills course as one component of exploratory classes for sixth graders. In the class, Rob spends many sessions discussing and modeling what active learners do when they read and think about content-area concepts. Here we provide an excerpt of Rob and his students interacting during reciprocal teaching.

Rob began by modeling his active learning processes with a short segment from a science textbook chapter about lightning. He allowed his students to eavesdrop on his thought processes as he attempted to make sense of the chapter.

Students sat at desks arranged in a horseshoe shape, with their copies of the chapter, as Rob commented after reading the first short paragraph:

> What I understand here is that up until very recently we haven't known much about lightning, but now things are changing. I'll probably read something about the technology we're using to figure out how lightning occurs.

During reading he shared comments such as this:

> Right now I'm staring blankly at the page trying to gather my thoughts. I'm not reading anything new. I think I'm just cycling these things around to see if anything seems reasonable.
>
> I'm looking again for key words like *positive* and *negative particles* and *cumulonimbus cloud*. They're going to tip me off as to the big point.

When Rob finished the first major section of the chapter, he attempted to summarize:

> Okay, the first thing is, I went over it and skimmed through the section again, so I can remember where I saw the important things.
>
> It's [the passage] talking about how technology is helping us to better understand lightning so that we can figure out how to protect ourselves from it.

He paused periodically and posed questions to himself ("What's the main idea here?" or "Does that make sense?"). Often after finishing a paragraph, he stated the gist. He made predictions about where the text was going next, and his soliloquy included connecting what he was reading with his store of prior knowledge and personal experiences.

In the next excerpt, Rob and his students were reading and discussing paragraphs from their social studies textbooks. They took turns asking questions about the topic and summarizing. The first paragraph they discussed was about Commander Peary and his quest for the North Pole.

On finishing reading of the short text segment, students immediately responded:

> *Student 1:* I have a question about this. What year did Peary write his diary?
>
> *Rob:* Not a bad beginning, but I would consider that a question about details. Try to avoid the kind of question you can answer by looking word for

word in the paragraph. See if next time you can ask a main idea question, and begin your question with a question word like *how, why, when*. Go ahead, try that.

Student 2: What if I ask, Why is Peary's diary important?

Rob: A very good question. Notice how your question seems to be getting at the most important idea in the paragraph.

Student 3: And you can't answer it by just looking at the words.

Rob: Right. Very good work! Now, can anyone give me a summary statement for the paragraph?

Student 4: Well, the only way we really know if Peary got to the North Pole is from his diary.

Rob: And why is that?

Student 4: Because there was no one else around who knew for sure where they were.

Student 5: You can't bring back any proof you were there.

Rob: Okay, that explains why some think Peary may not have made it to the Pole first. Isn't that an important part of the summary? (Several students agree.)

Rob: Let me try to make a summary for you. The most important thing we have learned is that we have to take Peary at his word when he said that he reached the North Pole because we don't have any other evidence to support that he did. Does that make sense? Have I left out anything important? Those are important questions to always ask yourself.

Rob's reciprocal teaching approach seems to be successful because it forces the students to respond, which allows him to evaluate their understanding and provide appropriate feedback. Also, by responding orally, the students are given the opportunity to self-diagnose their understanding and improve their ability to self-question, summarize, clarify, and predict, all processes leading to active learning. Rob does not merely talk to his students about how to read and then tell them to open their texts and read that way. Instead, he demonstrates how he reads and constructs meaning and, through interactions with students, gives them greater responsibility for learning from text.

Middle school and high school students need to learn strategies for monitoring their understanding in all their courses. In addition, they must learn strategies for fixing up the situations in which they are lost or do not understand a concept. In the next section, we outline some fix-up strategies.

Fix-Up Strategies

Metacognitively aware learners know when their understanding breaks down and what techniques to use to reduce their confusion (Simpson & Nist, 2000). **Fix-up strategies** are the observable or "in the head" techniques that active learners use when they are trying to increase their understanding of a particular content-area concept. To illustrate the importance of fix-up strategies, read the following passage and then list all the techniques you used or would use to understand what you had read:

> Recent developments in the self-worth theory of achievement motivation attest to the potential heuristic value of maintaining Atkinson's original quadripolar model. In essence, self-worth theory argues that the need for self-acceptance is the highest human priority and that, in reality, the dynamics of school achievement largely reflect attempts to aggrandize and protect self-perceptions of ability. (Covington & Roberts, 1994, p. 161)

What techniques did you include in your list? Some of the more common fix-up strategies include:

1. rereading the confusing sentence or paragraph
2. reading more slowly
3. reading ahead to see if the information becomes clearer
4. looking back at previous paragraphs, headings, or introductions to see if the author explained the concept in another way
5. referring to visual aids provided by the author, such as maps, charts, pictures, or graphs
6. making a picture in your mind of the concept being discussed
7. drawing or sketching the concept being discussed
8. looking for text examples that clarify difficult abstractions
9. checking alternative sources such as other textbooks or references

Active learners need a variety of ways to fix up their comprehension breakdowns.

Most middle school and high school students have limited fix-up strategies, and the ones they do use are usually passive, emphasizing rereading and rote memorization of information. Teachers, however, can assist students by modeling and demonstrating effective fix-up strategies appropriate to their content area. If students can see that it is normal to experience comprehension difficulties and that even experts must solve these problems, they are more likely to incorporate the strategies into their behaviors and routines. In addition, teachers can assist students by reiterating in class the diverse ways in which they can improve their comprehension and learning. For example, we know a sixth-grade science teacher who lists fix-up strategies on poster board for all his students to see, and a 10th-grade algebra teacher who gives her students a bookmark listing the fix-up strategies she wants them to use when they are attempting to solve word problems.

The DRAW Activity

DRAW (Agnew, 2000) is an acronym that stands for what students will be doing during class in response to a reading assignment or any other learning activity (e.g., a lab, discussion): Draw, Reflect/Review, Attend, and Write. That is, students will draw from a hat or box a question to answer and then review and reflect in order to answer their selected question. After giving the students a set period of time, the teacher then asks the students to attend and participate in the class discussion of the questions. Once the class has discussed all the questions and all the students have shared their answers, the final step, write, involves students in writing answers to some of the questions in the form of a quiz. The questions for the quiz come from the questions originally in the hat/box; the teacher randomly selects two or three of the questions for the students to answer and the students answer the questions without looking at their notes. Agnew, the developer of DRAW, explains that the four-step approach has encouraged her students to read and think more critically and to monitor their understanding of important concepts.

The teachers we have worked with have found DRAW to be a highly motivating activity, especially for struggling readers. Darren used this technique in his ninth-grade global studies class. Most of the students were struggling readers or students who had recently learned English as their second language. Darren followed these steps to build his DRAW lesson:

1. Assign students to read an essay, article, or chapter excerpt and make sure to front-load the assignment. In Darren's case the students had just finished a brief newspaper article on religion.

2. In preparation for the class discussion over the assigned material, write a series of numbered questions, making sure they exist along the continuum of text processing (i.e., right-there, on-my-own). On the day of the discussion distribute the Question Sheets to each student.

3. Cut one Question Sheet into strips containing individual questions. These question strips are mixed and placed in a small box or hat.

4. During class the following day ask each student to draw one question slip from the hat/box. Darren modified this step and placed the students in pairs to work together on their question.

5. Give students a specified amount of time to review and reflect on their question. At this point it is important to remind students that they are responsible for answering the question and sharing that answer with the class. They may use their class notes during this phase, but this is optional. Darren let his students use their notes and the article because a lot of his questions were written on higher levels of thinking. Darren and other teachers suggest that students be given a specific time frame (e.g., 10 minutes) and a 1-minute warning so they can gather their thoughts for the discussion.

6. During this step, remind students to attend to the discussion in order to prepare for the subsequent quiz over the assigned material. Distribute the Question Sheets to the class and suggest that they take notes during the discussion. Begin the discussion by asking the student or pair that drew the first question to read it aloud, explain the answer, and share how they arrived at the answer. Facilitate and guide

TEACHING DIVERSE Learners

The DRAW activity is also an excellent way to review for an exam.

the discussion by asking the class to discuss whether they agree or disagree and to explain why.

7. When all the questions have been discussed, ask the students to put away their Question Sheets. Darren permitted his student to use their Question Sheets, but modified the activity so that students who did not use their Question Sheets during the quiz received 2 extra-credit points on the quiz.

8. Take up the question slips distributed to the students and place them back in the hat/box.

9. Ask the students to take out a piece of paper and to write the answers to the questions drawn from the hat/box. Read a few of the questions aloud, but not all of them. Darren drew five questions so all the students had a chance to demonstrate their understanding of the newspaper article.

10. The students hand in the quiz for a grade, participation points, or extra credit. After collecting and grading the quiz, discuss any concepts/ideas that are still problematic for the students. Darren used the DRAW quiz as one of their pop quizzes that he gives at least once a week.

In addition to encouraging students to monitor their understanding and to think critically about concepts, DRAW has been found to have other advantages. Some teachers have told us that they use the DRAW activity, along with the pop quiz with an index card, as a technique for making sure their students read their assignments. Other teachers have reported that DRAW works well in situations where students do not have textbooks per se, but instead have been learning about concepts from discussions, demonstrations, videos, or computer simulations. For example, music, health, and physical education instructors have found DRAW to be an excellent review activity.

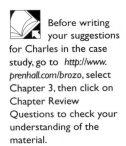 Before writing your suggestions for Charles in the case study, go to *http://www.prenhall.com/brozo*, select Chapter 3, then click on Chapter Review Questions to check your understanding of the material.

To sum, you can use a variety of strategies to encourage your students to monitor their understanding and to fix up or solve situations in which they are lost or confused. If you are interested in identifying additional strategies for helping your students become more metacogitively aware and in control of their learning, Chapter 9, Study Strategies, is an excellent resource.

CASE STUDY REVISITED

Charles, the biology teacher introduced at the beginning of this chapter, was searching for ways to engage his students in more meaningful interactions with his course content. Now that you have read this chapter, propose strategies that may help Charles move his students toward more elaborative and meaningful processing of text material related to the topic of genetic engineering.

Charles decided to use a variety of readiness strategies to introduce his students to the new content and gain their interest. He began by exposing them to alternative source material for exploration of the topic. He captured his students' interest by reading aloud daily from a science fiction novel, Hayford Peirce's *Phylum Monsters,* about a genetic engineer called a "life-stylist." The novel helped motivate the class to dig deeper into the content.

Charles also presented examples of exciting experiments done by genetic researchers. For example, he read to students about researchers at the University of California, San Diego, who in 1986 took the gene that makes fireflies glow and inserted it into the DNA of tobacco. The researchers were then able to raise tobacco plants that glowed in the dark.

Charles asked his students to read articles on genetic engineering in news magazines and to summarize the key ideas on index cards. He reminded the students to include in their summaries the advantages and disadvantages for this technology. Using the Discussion Web strategy, students met in pairs and groups of four to discuss and prepare what they would say to the whole class on the central question of whether genetic engineering was morally responsible.

When he assigned a section on genetics from the textbook for all the students to read, Charles took class time to carefully front-load the assignment. Then, on the next day, he gave the students a pop quiz with an index card to make sure they were reading and thinking about the key ideas. Finally, Charles helped his students write to the Food and Drug Administration explaining their views on the subject of genetically engineered food.

As a result of these efforts to prepare students for and introduce them to their new learning, Charles saw his students become active learners. They read and participated with enthusiasm and were motivated to work together in small groups and as a class to explore further the topic of genetic engineering.

————◄○►————

SUMMARY

Focusing on the principles of active learning, this chapter has described a range of practical strategies that all content-area teachers can use to enhance their students' comprehension of text. The first principle of active learning is concerned with students' use of their prior knowledge as they interact with text. The second principle focuses on how active learners summarize and organize as they read. The third principle concerns how active learners think critically about text and create their own elaborations. The fourth principle deals with how active learners are metacognitively aware. The fifth principle, discussed in more detail in Chapter 9, emphasizes the importance of students having a variety of reading and learning strategies to meet the varying demands of the courses they are studying.

Ideally, Chapters 2 and 3 will help form the foundation of your lessons and units of instruction. Many of the same strategies discussed in this chapter appear at other points throughout the book; many new strategies for helping students learn more effectively will also be presented. Nevertheless, all of the strategies are based on the principles of developing active, independent readers and learners. Consequently, in later chapters, we demonstrate that comprehension is at the heart of reading and learning across the content areas. In Chapter 4, assessment and teaching comprehension are presented as integral instructional activities. In Chapter 5, we discuss how schema activation and development will help teachers prepare their students for learning. In Chapter 6, we show how effective vocabulary instruction develops contextual and conceptual understanding of important textual information and ideas. In Chapter 7, writing is seen as a tool for expanding the comprehension and learning of text material and course content. In Chapter 8, literature is discussed as an alternative and a companion to the textbook for building prior knowledge, generating interest, and expanding comprehension. Chapter 9 demonstrates how students can make comprehension more permanent with student-initiated learning strategies.

REFERENCES

Agnew, M. (2000). DRAW: A motivational reading comprehension strategy for disaffected readers. *Journal of Adolescent & Adult Literacy, 43,* 574–576.

Alvermann, D. E. (1991). The Discussion Web: A graphic aid for learning across the curriculum. *The Reading Teacher, 45,* 92–99.

Beck, I., McKeown, M., Hamilton, R., & Kucan, L. (1997). *Questioning the author: An approach for enhancing student engagement with text.* Newark, NJ: International Reading Association.

Brown, A., & Palincsar, A. (1982). Inducing strategic learning from texts by means of informed, self-control training. *Topics in Learning and Learning Disabilities, 2,* 1–17.

Campbell, J., Voelkl, K., & Donahue, P. (1997). *Report in brief: NAEP 1996 trends in academic progress.* Washington, DC: National Center for Education Statistics.

Covington, M. V., & Roberts, B. W. (1994). Self-worth and college achievement: Motivational and personality correlates. In P. R. Pintrich, D. R. Brown, & C. E. Weinstein (Eds.), *Student motivation, cognition, and learning.* Hillsdale, NJ: Erlbaum.

Garner, R. (1988). *Metacognition and reading comprehension.* Norwood, NJ: Ablex.

Goldman, S., & Rakestraw, J. (2000). Structural aspects of constructing meaning from text. In M. Kamil, P. Mosenthal, P. Pearson, & R. Barr (Eds.), *Handbook of reading research* (Vol. 3, pp. 311–335). Mahwah, NJ: Lawrence Erlbaum Associates.

Greenberg, L. (1992). *AIDS: How it works in the body.* New York: Franklin Watts.

Haggard, M. (1985). An interactive strategies approach to content reading. *Journal of Reading, 29,* 204–210.

Herber, H. (1978). *Teaching reading in the content areas.* Englewood Cliffs, NJ: Prentice Hall.

Hynd, C. (1999). Teaching students to think critically using multiple texts in history. *Journal of Adolescent & Adult Literacy, 42,* 428–437.

Mayer, R. E. (1996). Learning strategies for making sense out of expository text: The SOI model for guiding these cognitive processes in knowledge construction. *Educational Psychology Review, 8,* 357–371.

Miller, K., & George, J. (1992). Expository passage organizers: Models for reading and writing. *Journal of Reading, 35,* 372–377.

Pressley, M. (2000). What should comprehension instruction be the instruction of? In M. Kamil, P. Mosenthal, P. Pearson, & R. Barr (Eds.), *Handbook of reading research* (Vol. 3, pp. 545–561). Mahwah, NJ: Lawrence Erlbaum Associates.

Raphael, T. E., & Pearson, P. D. (1985). Increasing students' awareness of sources of information for answering questions. *American Educational Research Journal, 22,* 217–235.

Rubin, D. L., & Dodd, W. M. (1987). *Talking into writing: Exercises for basic writers.* ERIC Clearinghouse on Reading and Communication Skills: National Council of Teachers of English.

Simpson, M. L., & Nist, S. L. (1997). Perspectives on learning history: A case study. *Journal of Literacy Research, 29,* 363–395.

Simpson, M., & Nist, S. (2000). An update on strategic learning: It's more than textbook reading strategies. *Journal of Adolescent & Adult Literacy, 43,* 528–541.

Simpson, M., & Nist, S. (2001). Encouraging active reading at the college level. In M. Pressley & C. Collins-Block (Eds.), *Reading comprehension instruction.* New York: Guilford Publications.

Wade, S., & Moje, E. (2000). The role of text in classroom learning. In M. Kamil, P. Mosenthal, P. Pearson, & R. Barr (Eds.), *Handbook of reading research* (Vol.3, pp. 609–627). Mahwah, NJ: Lawrence Erlbaum Associates.

CHAPTER FOUR

Classroom Assessment of Literacy Growth and Content Learning

ANTICIPATION GUIDE

Directions: Read each statement carefully and decide whether you agree or disagree with it, placing a check mark in the appropriate *Before Reading* column. When you have finished reading and studying the chapter, return to the guide and decide whether your anticipations need to be changed by placing a check mark in the appropriate *After Reading* column.

	BEFORE READING		AFTER READING	
	Agree	*Disagree*	*Agree*	*Disagree*
1. Standardized tests have more disadvantages than advantages.	____	____	____	____
2. Assessment is an activity that occurs primarily at the beginning of the school year.	____	____	____	____
3. Reading specialists should be the ones to assess students' literacy strengths and needs.	____	____	____	____
4. Assessment should focus only on students' reading and writing weaknesses.	____	____	____	____
5. Students should be involved in assessment activities.	____	____	____	____
6. Assessment can inform teaching and learning.	____	____	____	____

There are two primary functions of assessment: optimal learning for all, and a just society. Achieving the former (centrally dependent on teachers as assessors) would accomplish most of the latter. To make serious progress toward this goal, we need a contextualized theory of assessment that is grounded as firmly in moral and social theory as it is in theories of language, literacy, learning, and caring.

—Johnston (1993)

More than 20 years of theory development and research has characterized literacy as an interactive, context-bound, purposeful process of meaning construction (Bissex, 1980; Clay, 1975; Gee, 2000). During the same time, we have progressed in our understanding of what literacy behaviors should be assessed, how that assessment should be represented, and which participants or stakeholders should be involved (Johnston, 1993). At the middle and high school levels, these changes have translated into an emphasis on teachers defining what it means to be literate and knowledgeable in their classrooms and designing a variety of performance-based activities and authentic opportunities to assess their students as they interact with content-area concepts (Clark & Clark, 2000). More important, the recent advances in assessment theory and research point out what teachers have always known: "In successful schools, assessment goes on continually and in a way that helps, not hinders, the search for better educational policies and teaching practices" (Apple, 1999, p. 28).

In this chapter, issues and strategies of assessment are presented relative to one basic assumption: The goal of literacy assessment is to provide teachers with knowledge about how best to improve and support learning for students and self-knowledge for learners that will allow them to become more reflective, active, and purposeful learners. We demonstrate how your assessments can reveal to you and your students important information about students' thinking, language processes, and their content knowledge. Because assessment guides and informs instruction and can be integrated into the daily flow of instructional events in the classroom, this chapter provides a foundation for assessment strategies that appear in later chapters. It also builds on the comprehension strategies discussed in Chapters 2 and 3 by demonstrating how assessments can be used to reveal useful information about students' literacy and learning processes.

We are also mindful, however, of two assessment issues that teachers must address on a daily basis. The first issue concerns the proliferation of standardized tests and basic skills competency exams, which more and more states and school districts are mandating (Olson, 1998; Rothstein, 2000). As we pointed out in the first chapter, this trend in standardized testing is in direct response to growing popular and political pressures on schools to meet higher standards and be accountable for those standards (Lewis, 2000). One gauge of our expanding testing culture is the fact that the Department of Education spends more on the National Assessment of Educational Progress (NAEP, described in Chapter 1) than on any other initiative (Hoff, 2000). To help prepare you to deal with this issue, we describe sensible ways middle and secondary school teachers can accommodate the realities of and benefit from standardized testing. Along with this discussion, we provide a brief primer on standardized reading tests. The second issue concerns the factors involved in grading and ways in which grades can be better used for the improvement of instruction. We'll examine ways in which the grading process can be used to communicate more effectively about genuine academic growth to both students and their parents.

Go to *http://www.prenhall.com/brozo*, select Chapter 4, then click on Chapter Objectives to provide a focus for your reading.

Assessment should improve instruction and student self-knowledge.

CASE STUDY

Terri is a seventh-grade general science teacher interested in discovering more about her students' ability to comprehend textbook information. After attending in-service workshops on content-area assessment procedures, she began to recognize the need for alternative assessments to the chapter check tests in her science textbook. After 5 years of teaching, she discovered that she was relying more and more on these tests for grading purposes and less and less on other "views" of her students as learners and knowledge seekers. Moreover, the results of these tests were not providing Terri with information about why students performed the way they did. She had no way of discovering whether success or failure was tied in any way to students' study processes or to their ability to understand the science text.

The in-service presenter emphasized the need to tie content material to the processes for learning it effectively. Suggestions were made concerning ways teachers could teach and assess at the same time using the class textbook. Terri decided to use this information to develop teaching strategies for improving students' thinking about text structure.

To the Reader:
Think about Terri's concern as you read this chapter, and be prepared by the end of this chapter to suggest possible assessment/teaching solutions for her.

GUIDELINES FOR LITERACY ASSESSMENT

The following five guidelines are based on a synthesis of current research and theory about assessment of literacy and learning. These guidelines should determine how you will assess the students in your content area and use that information to plan instructional units.

Assessment Is a Process of Becoming Informed About Authentic Learning

Authentic learning refers to learning that is functional and meaningful. As we stated in Chapter 1, the extent to which students use learning beyond the boundaries of the classroom is directly related to its perceived functionality. For authentic learning to occur, assessments should be rooted in activities that have genuine purposes (Avery, Carmichael-Tanaka, Kunze, & Kouneski, 2000; Geocaris & Ross, 1999). In this way, acquiring information about student learning does not become an end in itself but is an evolving process of gathering feedback for the teacher and student so that instruction can become more engaging, more tied to real-world issues and concerns, and more personally meaningful.

What do we want to know about students that requires us to assess them? We want to know under what conditions they learn best, what instructional strategies we can employ to facilitate their learning, and how to encourage independent, active reading. We also want students to discover more about themselves as learners so that they can expand their abilities as literate knowledge seekers.

Middle school and high school teachers want to know whether or not their students are likely to profit from textbook reading, daily instruction, process writing, research projects, and so on. The assessment tools we use for these purposes should therefore be designed to provide insights into students' reading, writing, and thinking strategies with the actual texts they must use daily and in the actual, authentic contexts of their use. In this way, the information gained from assessment can be immediately translated into action, such as promoting elaborative processing (Chapter 3), activating and building relevant prior knowledge (Chapter 5), teaching key concepts and vocabulary (Chapter 6), facilitating thinking and reflection through writing (Chapter 7), developing text study skills (Chapter 9), or improving other important reading, writing, and learning processes.

Authentic assessment can be immediately translated into teacher and learner action.

Assessment of Literacy and Content Learning Should Use Multiple Data Sources Across Multiple Contexts

A basketball coach who wants to find out how well new recruits can play the game does not give a paper-and-pencil test. The players are required to perform various tasks on the court, and their ability is assessed while being directly observed. By making multiple assessments of **situated performances** (Valencia, McGinley, & Pearson, 1990), a coach can learn the most about a player's true ability and potential. So it is with the assessment of literacy and learning in content-area classrooms (Lawrence & Pallrand, 2000; Nickell, 1999; Serri, 1999).

A sixth-grade health education teacher may feel that she has all the information needed about a student's reading ability when given the test results of the Comprehensive Test of Basic Skills (CTBS). But what do percentiles and grade equivalents have to do with reading and learning from a health education textbook? Perhaps very little, and for obvious reasons. First, the comprehension passages on a test like the CTBS may not cover health issues such as nutrition or exercise. Second, the kind of reading demanded by reading comprehension tests is significantly different from the way a student would read and study a health education textbook. For example, on the test, a student reads one or two paragraphs under strict time limitations. In contrast, the reading assignment in the health education class may require the student to spend an entire week reading and discussing a 20- to 30-page chapter, allowing enough time to learn the material. Finally, the CTBS measures reading performance with multiple-choice questions. The health education teacher may require students to write out answers to short and long essay-type questions.

Rather than relying on one source of information about students, teachers need information from multiple sources in order to plan appropriate instruction. For example, a science teacher could test her students' ability to process and understand the textbook information and could observe the students'

Multiple assessment approaches can account for all dimensions of student learning.

problem-solving abilities and use of experimentation through field notes and logs (Haines, 2001). The advantage of determining students' progress and understanding with the actual materials used in the science class is that the teacher would then have a much clearer idea about how to modify her instruction to improve students' learning.

This example reinforces an important point we made in Chapter 1: Literacy ability is context bound. No single test (whether the CTBS or any other paper-and-pencil test) can adequately reflect the teaching-learning process. As a former student of ours said, the old "clump theory" of literacy no longer makes sense. Traditional views of literacy held that all of us possess a given, measurable quantity, or clump, of literacy ability and that reading tests could accurately weigh our clumps. As our conceptions of what it means to be literate have changed to include the social, dynamic, generative, and idiosyncratic nature of literacy, the most commonly used formal measures of reading and writing have remained largely decontextualized (Fuchs, 1999). To assess in ways consistent with our best thinking about literacy and content learning, our assessment repertoire must be expanded to include multiple demonstrations of ability in situated contexts of authentic teaching and learning.

Assessment Is a Continuous Process

A high school teacher of students with learning disabilities recently complained that she is often excluded from the decision-making process concerning student needs and placement. She said decisions are made about students based on clinical testing in language competencies, intelligence, and behavior, with virtually no input from the teacher who is working closely with and observing the students every day. One of her students, she said, is entirely capable of regular education course work, according to her observations, because he is an excellent reader and possesses some good study skills. When she talked with the clinician, she was shown the student's reading test scores on the Woodcock Reading Mastery Tests (WRMT), which placed him nearly 3 years below his grade placement of 10th grade. It is unlikely, she was told, that he had improved as much as she claimed in the 1 month since he was tested. The question comes down to this: Whose assessment—the clinician's WRMT or the teacher's observations—is more reflective of the student's true ability?

Considering our point about the important influence of context on learning performance, isn't it possible that the context itself—that is, the conditions under which literacy activities and tasks are assessed—has influenced the 10th-grade student's reading test performance? The answer is an unequivocal "yes." Several years ago, we discovered that students will often demonstrate much better recall and supply richer information when retelling a story or text to a friend or fellow student than to a teacher, researcher, or test giver (Carey, Harste, and Smith, 1981). We also have known for some time that when a student is excessively anxious about a task because the perceived consequences of failure are threatening, there is generally a concomitant decrease in performance (Stiggins, 1999). The LD teacher's student could have been very threatened by the clinical setting while taking the WRMT, resulting in an artificially low estimate of his reading ability. On the other hand, the student may have perceived the LD teacher in a nonthreatening way and the classroom as a supportive environment. In this context, the student may have demonstrated his true ability. To reiterate, we believe that any test is only a small sample of behavior, and when a single test or observation occurs in isolation (i.e., by a clinician with one test at one point in time), there is insufficient grounds for drawing meaningful diagnostic conclusions.

In addition to the influence of context on reading performance, there are other reasons why reading assessment should be a continuous process. Any test result or observed score is partly a reflection of the test taker's true ability, or true score, and a host of other factors we did not plan to measure, referred to as the **error score**. Contextual factors, as in the preceding case with the student with learning disabilities, are among many contributions to the error score. The reader's health, attitude, tendency to guess, prior knowledge, the test's ability to communicate, and the quality of the test questions, to name a few, are all factors that influence to some degree a test taker's score. Unfortunately, we can never be absolutely certain how much of the observed score is composed of an error score. This critical issue should be considered before we base major decisions on one test or observation—especially if that test or observation is isolated from the conditions under which actual reading tasks are performed—because the observed score may not measure a student's true ability.

All of what we have just said can be applied to classroom teachers who rely exclusively on end-of-chapter, -unit, or -year tests to make decisions about grading and student progress. Learning is a continuous and dynamic process that takes place over time and changes with each new instructional situation (Stiggins, 1999). Based on international studies of testing and achievement, William (2000) asserts that "if schools used assessment during teaching, to find out what students have learned, and what they need to do next, on a daily basis" instead of focusing on easily measurable outcomes on standardized tests, student achievement would rise. Therefore, to obtain more useful and meaningful information on your students' literacy and learning abilities, we recommend that you base instructional decisions on long-term observations and assessments. Later in this chapter, we provide guidelines and details for assessment formats that use day-to-day information gained from observing students and gathering reflections of their progress over time. Only with such important assessment data can we expect to build a supportive classroom learning environment.

Since learning is a dynamic process, the best assessments occur in multiple contexts and over time.

Assessment Should Include Students' Interests and Belief Systems

Carmen begins every new school year with an activity designed to help her eighth graders get to know one another. Using a strategy called "My Bag," Carmen and her students bring in bags filled with objects and items that represent who they are. Students form groups of three or four and share these items. Carmen asks students not to do a show-and-tell but to use an item to elicit questions. For example, Juanita took an onyx ring out of her bag and passed it around for her group members to inspect. Soon students were asking her questions: "Where'd you get it?" "Was it your mom's?" "What kind of stone is that?" Juanita revealed that the ring belonged to her *tia,* her aunt, with whom she had a very close and friendly relationship; she said the ring was given to her just before her aunt died. In another case, Carlos showed his group a model car and a screwdriver. Before long, he was responding to questions that allowed him to go into great detail about his interest in fixing cars with his older brother and his plan to be an auto mechanic.

While students go through the My Bag activity, Carmen circulates throughout the room, taking note of students' interests, desires, needs, and concerns, such as Juanita's relationship with her aunt and Carlos's interest in auto repair. Armed with this knowledge, Carmen tailors certain writing, reading, and group projects to her students' needs and desires. She alludes to particular characteristics of students revealed through the My Bag exercise during class activities, which helps demonstrate her interest in and concern for her students and builds a caring atmosphere in the classroom. In the end, Carmen, too, shares her bag, allowing students to get to know their teacher as a real person who has goals, desires, and interests, just as they do. Carmen has found that in being part of the My Bag activity herself, she can establish an initial foundation on which trust and cooperative problem solving can be built.

Through the use of the My Bag strategy, Carmen gathers invaluable assessment information about her students' interests and beliefs in a highly personal, unique, and enjoyable way. While gathering information about how students process text, we should be equally concerned with discovering their habits, interests, and attitudes to reinforce and reward students' use of reading and writing for self-development and learning and for joy and escape. The benefits that result from putting students in touch with books that match their interests cannot be denied.

An acquaintance described how he had been diagnosed as a remedial reader every year from second to seventh grade. Teachers were beginning to lose hope of ever teaching Tom how to read beyond a rudimentary level. His difficulty affected his achievement in all subjects. Then a particularly enlightened math teacher discovered that Tom's favorite activity was performing magic tricks. The teacher brought Tom some books on magic from the library. He read them. He began reading more and more books on magic. Soon his ability to read and understand other books improved. Eventually Tom graduated from high school with a good grade average and finally earned a baccalaureate degree from the University of Illinois, a prominent and respected institution. The lesson here is obvious: By discovering students' interests and introducing them to books that match their interests, we stand a chance of developing enthusiastic and competent readers.

Obtaining information about students' real-world needs and interests—in other words, what they do and what concerns them when they are outside of school—can be as useful in planning ways to teach and reach your students as

Teachers can use students as curricular informants to make instruction more responsive to their needs.

information about their reading/writing processes and content knowledge. Interest is one of the most potent motivators for young adults, and teachers can take full advantage of this fact in a number of ways (Brophy, 1998; Stipek, 1996). One obvious strategy is to introduce students to reading materials related to their interests. These materials may be tied to the topic of study in your classroom or may simply be relevant to students on a personal level. In Chapter 8 we explain how teachers can take full advantage of young adult literature to help meet students' needs.

In addition to assessing students' interests, teachers need to identify their beliefs systems about learning and how they view themselves as learners (Schommer, Calvert, Gariglietti, & Bajaj, 1997). Students with naive conceptions about learning and how knowledge is acquired tend to believe that learning is something that is simple and happens quickly, with very little effort (Nist & Simpson, 2000). As a result, they are less likely to use strategies that engage them in elaborative levels of thinking, choosing instead to use rote-level strategies emphasizing the memorization of facts. For example, because many students believe that knowledge about science is simply the memorization of isolated facts, they tend to focus on those facts without thinking about the interrelationships between them and the concepts they represent. This type of learning is obviously something that students can do in a rather superficial fashion rather than invest any mental effort.

These implicit beliefs about learning have a subtle impact on how students comprehend what they read, problem solve, and persist when assigned difficult tasks by their teachers. In addition, Schommer (1994) has found an association between students' grades and their naive conceptions of learning. In her study of 1,000 high school students, a regression analysis that controlled for general intelligence indicated that the more students believed in quick learning, the more likely they were to have a low overall grade point average. Later in this chapter, we will present some assessment activities that will help you identify students' interests and beliefs about reading and learning and discuss how you can use that information to inform your teaching.

Effective Assessment Involves Students in Self-Reflection and Self-Evaluation

Traditionally, assessment has been interpreted as a professional activity that teachers "do to students" rather than an ongoing activity that involves both students and teachers in the improvement of instruction. Currently, literacy educators recommend that students be involved in assessing their own strengths and needs since that self-reflection and evaluation are important to students' development as independent learners (Alexander & Jetton, 2000; Zimmerman, Bandura, & Martinez-Pons, 1992). For example, several studies have shown that at-risk students can improve their academic achievement and intrinsic motivation if they are taught how to set goals and evaluate their progress toward those goals (D'Agostino, 1996).

There are a variety of ways you can involve students in self-evaluation and self-reflection, one of which is journal writing. These journal entries can be assigned at the beginning of the school year or can be required of students as part of an instructional unit, especially after they have received feedback on how they performed on an exam. For example, Ann, a seventh-grade math teacher, asks all her students to complete a mathematics autobiography as their first entry in their journal (additional information about Learner Autobiographies can be found later in this chapter). She uses the following directions, which can be modified to fit almost any content area:

Learner Autobiographies can help students self-evaluate their expanding content knowledge.

> Write your math autobiography. Think and write about the experiences you have had that relate to mathematics. These questions may be used as guides.
>
> 1. How did you feel about math in elementary school?
> 2. What are your experiences with effective and ineffective math teachers?
> 3. Is there one particular experience that stands out?
> 4. What were or are the attitudes of your family members toward math?
> 5. Was there a time when you liked math? Hated it? Why did you feel the way you did?
> 6. Did you have any special strategies for getting through (or around) math classes? Have these strategies worked for you? Why or why not?
> 7. Is there one particular experience you feel is responsible for your present feelings about math?

Ann tells us that she quickly learns a great deal of useful information about her students' attitudes, anxieties, and mathematical strategies from this initial journal entry. She then uses classroom observations of her students, as well as their homework and test performance, to validate these self-reports. One of her students, Zena, is the author of the following entry. You will note that this journal entry provided Ann with some useful insights about Zena as she evaluated herself.

> When I was in elementary school I had a little trouble with adding and subtracting. I now have difficulties with my multiplication tables. Story problems really bother me so my mother tries to help me with these. I still am nervous about math, especially if the test is timed. In stores I always make sure they give me the correct change, but I have trouble figuring out the prices on clothes when they have sales.
>
> If I have good teachers I do great, but when I have poor teachers I do bad. I had a teacher who didn't like me and tried her hardest to make me fail her class. My parents told me to just do the best I can and not to worry about how the teacher feels about me. My father and brothers are all good in math, so I am the only math dummy in our house.
>
> I like math when I understand it, but if I don't understand it, I don't like it. I usually am afraid to ask questions when I am lost—so please be patient with me.

These five guidelines should assist you in determining the assessment procedures appropriate for your content area and your students. Before we describe additional assessment procedures that you can incorporate into your classroom routine, we need to address two controversial issues—standardized tests and grading.

OUR STANDARDIZED TESTING CULTURE

The hardest part about my job is trying to get these students ready for the test in one short semester. And all the while I'm doing it, I'm wondering if they'll be able to take away anything useful at all from my class.

Ronnie, a high school science teacher, revealed to us his frustration about standardized achievement testing at the beginning of the school year. A seasoned teacher with impeccable credentials, vaunted reputation, and practical experience in a nuclear physics laboratory, Ronnie had come to realize how easy it was to find himself teaching to a test, in spite of his own better judgment. To respond to his concerns with blandishments such as, "Well, that's reality; you're not alone, everyone else is trying to deal with it," sounds hollow and patronizing, especially to such a highly skilled and knowledgeable professional. In spite of the compellingness of the arguments outspoken critics (Kohn, 2001; Ohanian, 1999) of standards and testing have made, any of us would justifiably be accused of being in denial if we failed to acknowledge the pervasiveness and significance of standardized testing in middle and secondary schools today. Like Ronnie, our personal biases about the ultimate value of standardized tests aside, we all must learn to make the most of this political and institutional reality. As a result of our own search for more meaningful uses of such tests, here is one potential benefit and one documented benefit resulting from sensible school- and teacher-level strategies based on standardized testing.

Benefit 1: Widespread Measures of Accountability Will Bring About Needed Reforms

In a recent survey of parents' views about testing (Lewis, 2000), 59% believed that schools place too much emphasis on standardized test scores, even while they generally endorsed spending time on test preparation provided important skills and knowledge were being measured. As standardized testing occurs ever more frequently and with high-stakes consequences in schools, there is growing consensus that the proper role of assessment in bringing about proposed educational reforms must be determined.

In response to warnings about the misuse of tests, the American Educational Research Association (AERA) has released new Standards for Educational and Psychological Testing. These comprehensive standards say the following conditions for testing must include:

- protection against high-stakes decisions based on a single test
- adequate resources and opportunities for learning

- full disclosure of likely negative consequences of high-stakes testing programs
- opportunities for meaningful remediation for students who fail high-stakes tests
- appropriate attention to students with language differences and disabilities
- sufficient reliability and validity for each intended use
- alignment between the test and the curriculum
- validity of passing scores and achievement levels
- ongoing evaluation of the intended and unintended effects of high-stakes testing

 Go to Web Resources for Chapter 4 at *http://www.prenhall.com/brozo* and look for standardized testing and standards-based education.

Former undersecretary of the U.S. Department of Education, Marshall Smith (Lewis, 2000), acknowledged at a recent conference of the Center for Research on Evaluation, Standards, and Student Testing that opportunities for young people should not depend on "one determining episode in [their] life" like a high-stakes test. The strongest feature of the American educational system, he continued, is its willingness to give young people second or more chances to succeed.

Benefit 2: Standardized Test Scores Can Be a Tool for Teaching and Learning

One might successfully argue that if standardized tests are not likely to disappear anytime soon, then a serious effort should be mounted to help teachers see the connection between test scores and daily classroom practices. We would like to describe two scenarios: one concerning a high school's use of low-stakes standardized testing to sensitize teachers to discrepancies between their students' reading abilities and their textbooks' readabilities, and the other demonstrating how high-stakes test results were incorporated into a composite view of students in the middle grades in order to design customized literacy interventions.

Foothills High School, within view of the Smoky Mountains, set ambitious reading goals for the 2000–2001 academic year. Among them was that all students would be reading at grade level. When the school received Goals 2000 funding for its proposed reading project, school personnel called on us for assistance. The first thing we were forced to say to the teachers and administrative team was that elevating all students to grade-level achievement was unrealistic. Any of us familiar with Matthew effects (Stanovich, 1986) in reading and learning knows that as students move up in grade level the spread of achievement widens. Consequently, it is not uncommon to find students in high school reading as much as five or six grade levels below their grade placement, especially in regular history, science, and math classes. Moving those students up to a grade placement standard in one or two years is simply not feasible within most secondary school settings. Nevertheless, we needed to find out the reading achievement levels of the Foothills High students, and the most efficient means for doing so was to conduct schoolwide standardized testing.

We administered either the Nelson-Denny or the Gates-McGinitie Reading test depending upon previous year's high-stakes competency test results. These tests were intended as low-stakes indicators of the students' overall reading ability levels, because the results would be used only internally by school personnel and would not be used for determining whether students had met state or district reading and language standards. Test results were revealing to teachers, particularly when the ability levels of students in their classes were compared with the readability levels of their textbooks. For example, Hugh became quite alarmed when he observed that 7 out of 22 students in his 9th-grade Algebra I class were reading at the 7th-grade level or below. In fact, two of his students scored at the 4th-grade level on the Gates-McGinitie. Meanwhile, the readability of his class textbook was between the 9th- and 10th-grade level. This meant that whenever Hugh gives textbook reading assignments several of his students are likely to have difficulty or be unable to read the assignment at all, unless provided plenty of instructional support.

As with Hugh, many Foothills High teachers were surprised to discover how many of their students were reading below their grade placement—in too many cases, far below their expected grade level. This revelation was made possible only as a result of low-stakes standardized testing. This is not to say the teachers were completely unaware of their students' general abilities in their classrooms. In fact, when they compared student test performance with the grades they were achieving in their classrooms, there was a clear pattern of consistency. What teachers couldn't say for certain without reading test data is who specifically was in need of further reading diagnosis and special instructional support. This was most true in the case of science and math teachers who might have fewer occasions to observe their students reading. Also, the test results were provided the teachers early in the new school year, before enough time had elapsed for them to know with certainty who might be struggling with textbook reading assignments.

We were able to turn these standardized test results into useful information in two critical ways: (1) the teachers became much more sensitive to the importance of finding ways to accommodate the reading needs of low-performing students in their classrooms; and (2) we were able to identify students for further literacy assessment. As a result of testing and discovering who was in need of special literacy assistance, Foothills High created small-group classes to improve the neediest students' reading skills. As significantly, Foothills High teachers began using alternative and modified texts for their low-performing students as one way to ensure these students were in fact engaged in genuine reading and were expanding their knowledge base about important class topics. For instance, the science faculty put together a collection of easier reading texts from a website. The history teachers created a similar alternative set of readings on virtually every class topic that were within the reading ability ranges of their struggling readers from websites.

Once again, it is unlikely that any of these developments would have occurred had it not been made clear through standardized reading testing that

Go to Web Resources for Chapter 4 at *http://www. prenhall.com/brozo* and look for easier reading content materials.

perhaps as many as 20 to 25% of Foothills High students were reading two or more years below grade placement.

TEACHING DIVERSE Learners

MEETING THE NEEDS OF DIVERSE LEARNERS IN THE CONTENT-AREA CLASSROOM

In a very different setting, inner-city Chicago, researchers (Chen, Salahuddin, Horsch, & Wagner, 2000) have been assisting the teachers and staff of Garfield School in the process of turning standardized test scores into a tool for improving teaching and learning and setting educational goals. Garfield serves nearly 700 students, kindergarten through eighth grade. Most are African American and most are eligible for the free or reduced lunch program. In 1996 Garfield was placed on academic probation by the Chicago Board of Education for its low reading scores on the Iowa Test of Basic Skills (ITBS). At that time, only 14% of Garfield's students were reading at or above national grade-level norms.

The researchers found interesting patterns of scores that differentiated student performance by grade level and particular reading skill. For example, students in the upper grades, 5 through 8, had higher achievement than those in the lower grades. Also, when specific skills were analyzed, upper-level students were closer to the national norms than lower-level students in factual, inferential, and evaluative meaning. It was critical to conduct a detailed analysis of students' reading scores in order to find explanations for Garfield's test results and offer appropriate and feasible recommendations for change.

The researchers took the next step of conducting thorough evaluations of local schools demographically similar to Garfield but with higher test scores on the ITBS. Their goal was to discover possible contributing factors to the students' better performance in those schools. They learned that all of the other schools had the following characteristics in common:

■ All had a comprehensive, well-defined schoolwide reading program.
■ All had a designated reading coordinator in their buildings.
■ All observed daily reading periods from 60 to 90 minutes.

Standardized test analysis led to a set of recommendations for Garfield that included incorporating the features contributing to success in other schools into their own school. After doing so, the following year's ITBS scores increased nearly five percentage points. The researchers explained this result by emphasizing the importance of using test data to improve school reading programs, especially when test score analysis (a) is used as the entry point for the assessment-intervention process, (b) helps teachers recognize their responsibility for improving instruction provided to whole groups and individuals, and (c) leads to faculty support services that directly enhance the quality of curricula and teaching.

Some schools have shown that standardized test results can be used to set schoolwide goals and improve instruction.

Taken together, the use of low-stakes standardized test results at Foothills High and the critical local use of high-stakes test results at Garfield School demonstrate the possible benefits these data might provide teachers and students, even while recognizing their limitations. In the next section of this chapter we explore more closely technical and logistical considerations of standardized testing that can help you better understand the results derived from such tests and improve the way you communicate the results to others.

Standardized Reading Achievement Tests: What You Should Know

Question

Audrey strained to see the people who were coming through the crowd. Somewhere down there her parents were waiting to welcome her after her voyage.

   a. Audrey is standing in a crowd, waiting to meet a plane.
   b. Audrey is in a crowd, walking toward her parents.
   c. Audrey is on a ship, looking out at a crowd waiting for the ship.
   d. Audrey is looking at a ship on which her parents are arriving.
      (*Reading Yardsticks,* Form B, 1981, p. 11)

Does the preceding question format look familiar? It should. All of us have taken some form of a reading test that contained short passages and multiple-choice comprehension questions that were similar to this example. We ascribe almost magical qualities to standardized reading tests. They are objective measurements, simple to administer and score, with comprehensive tables and charts for deriving a variety of scores. And with more than 100 reading tests on the market, they are accessible and widely discussed in the media. In this section we will discuss the characteristics of standardized tests, outline their uses and potential limitations, and offer some suggestions on how you can communicate with parents and the public about the standardized tests your school administers to students.

Although reading tests have been around since the beginning of the last century, only since the 1930s has the question format become the most popular method of assessing comprehension and the basis for current standardized tests of reading achievement (Readence & Moore, 1983). Educators over the past 50 years have regarded the question-answering format as the most convenient, objective, and cost-effective means of comprehension assessment. Why is so much attention given to reading assessment? Most educators and a majority of the public agree that raising students' literacy level is an extremely important goal of public schooling (Lewis, 2001). Since the accountability movement of the 1970s, and given the current glut of national reports, a prominent area of attention for educational improvement initiatives has been literacy (National Reading Panel, 2000). To measure the effectiveness of these initiatives, educators have come to rely on students' standardized test scores.

What is a standardized reading achievement test? The term **standardized** means that the test was administered and scored under standard and uniform testing procedures. It is typically constructed by test specialists working with curriculum experts and teachers. Before the test is made available to schools and teachers, it is given to a large number of students, who represent the group for whom the test was intended. This representative group of students is called the *norm group.* The norm group's scores on the test are transformed statistically into *standard scores,* which are usually made available in tabular form in the test's users manual. These standard scores allow teachers and schools to compare their students with a national group of students or with other similar students in their state. The most common standard scores used by schools to interpret student performance on reading achievement tests are grade equivalents and percentiles. A **grade-equivalent** interpretation of a student's reading achievement test score is indicated in terms of years and months—for instance, 10.6, or 10th grade, 6th month. When interpreting reading test performance in terms of a **percentile**, we describe a student's score as a point at or below which a given percentage of other scores falls. For example, a student who scored at the 80th percentile scored as well as or better than 80% of the students in the norm group.

The norm group of the standardized tests you use should be similar to the students in your classes.

The Uses and Potential Limitations of Standardized Tests

Many of the criticisms of standardized tests focus on how the test scores will be used. Teachers and parents, for example, worry that students will be placed in classes on the basis of one standardized test. What needs to be remembered, however, is that standardized tests, like any other assessment instrument, are only one data source or sample of students' behaviors, skills, and strategies. As the assessment guidelines have suggested, any instructional decision about a student is best made using a variety of sources of information.

If standardized tests should be considered as only one source of information about students, why are these tests given? What are their uses? Why do school districts, school boards, and the public clamor for some form of standardized tests? Standardized tests do have their uses. At the district level, they can be used by principals and superintendents to evaluate a special program or intervention to determine its effectiveness. In addition, the data from a standardized test can often inform administrators and teachers about large-scale trends at the district level. These trends can reflect the skills that are being taught effectively and those that need more emphasis. For example, in Maria's school district, the middle school teachers and administrators examined the results of the Iowa Basic Skills Exam for the sixth graders' strengths and weaknesses. As a result of their analysis, they identified vocabulary as a goal for the next school year because the sixth graders scored much too low on this subtest.

Standardized test results can be a starting point for further diagnosis and assessment.

Standardized test results can also be used by the classroom teacher. Some teachers use these scores as a large-scale screening device to determine possible groupings or skills that need emphasis for the class and for individual students. For example, when Maria examined the test results for Joseph, an incoming sixth grader, she saw these scores:

| Vocabulary | 5.1 | grade equivalent |
| Comprehension | 2.8 | grade equivalent |

Joseph's scores suggest that he needs work on reading comprehension but that his vocabulary background is not a contributing factor to his low score on comprehension. Maria hypothesized that Joseph may need help with active reading for main ideas to improve his comprehension. Of course, Maria used that information as a preliminary hunch. She verified that hunch with her own assessment activities to learn more about the strengths and skill needs of Joseph and the other students in her sixth-grade language arts classes.

Maria used her own assessment activities because she is aware of the limitations of standardized tests:

1. They are only an estimate of a student's reading ability.

2. Each test measures reading in a different way, which means that a student might have five different scores on five different tests.

3. They do not provide information about how students read and learn in their content-area classes.

4. They may contain linguistic or cultural bias that can influence the test scores for students from different cultures or students whose primary language or dialect is not English.

These limitations, of course, can apply to any teacher-designed assessment instrument or activity. Hence, sensitivity to the uses and limitations of standardized tests should help you in planning your own assessment activities.

Communicating With Parents and Students About Standardized Reading Test Results

School districts have an obligation to inform students and parents of reading achievement test results. It is their right to know. Whereas some testing experts have argued that the distribution of assessment results should be limited to those who are prepared to use them, classroom teachers in science, math, history, and language arts may be given printouts of their homeroom students' reading test scores. Furthermore, it is not uncommon for the classroom teacher to be asked by students and parents to explain test scores. These facts point to the need for all teachers to become informed about what these scores mean and how they can be used. Following are several suggestions for reporting and explaining standardized reading test results to students and/or parents. These suggestions come from our own experience as middle school and high school teachers as well as the experience of others.

1.   Put parents at ease. Welcome them and make sure that they are comfortable. If possible, meet where there is good lighting and privacy.

2.   Before presenting information to parents, find out what information they have already received from other teachers, counselors, or administrators. Failure to

do so may put you in the uncomfortable position of contradicting a colleague, having to change your position, or reporting redundant information.

3. Before presenting information, determine exactly what kind of information the parent wants.

Teachers should help parents understand standardized test results are only one view of a student's abilities.

4. If assessment information is inadequate or contradictory, be willing to admit the weaknesses of evaluation based on these data.

5. Urge parents not to fixate on standard scores but instead pay close attention to a variety of data sources, such as the student's previous work and the teacher's evaluations.

6. If necessary, explain the limitations of grade equivalents. They are too easily misinterpreted to be given to parents indiscriminately. These norms are often **extrapolated**; that is, they are often estimates based on trends in scores established by the norm group. In other words, if a 10th grader obtains a grade equivalent of 5.5 (5th grade, 5th month) on a reading achievement test appropriate for 10th graders, it is unlikely that students at the 5.5 grade level were actually in the norming group for the 10th-grade test. Therefore, this grade equivalent is merely an estimate based on the hypothetical performance of students at the 5.5 grade level if they had taken the 10th-grade test. As you can tell from this explanation, grade equivalents are very difficult to explain and interpret properly. Another limitation of grade equivalents is that the amount of error may be anywhere from half a year to a full year and a half. So a score of 10.0 could be as low as 8.5 or as high as 11.5—we simply do not know for sure.

7. When explaining percentile scores, make it clear that they are not to be confused with percentages of questions answered correctly. It might be best to say, "In comparison with 10th graders throughout the United States, John is in the upper 10 to 15%, as measured by the Iowa Silent Reading Test when this test was taken last October."

There is no need for classroom teachers to become test and measurement experts simply because occasionally they may be asked to administer and interpret the scores of standardized reading tests. By combining some basic knowledge about these tests with common sense, you can improve your chances of communicating effectively with students and parents.

TEACHERS' GRADES: A FORM OF ASSESSMENT AND EVALUATION

Grades are another important assessment issue that teachers must address. Some have suggested that most of the time teachers spend on assessment during the school year is for giving grades (Hargis, 1999). Hargis (1990) provides a compelling critique of typical grading practices, revealing countless myths and flaws. Although many of us might not prefer the traditional grading process, grading probably will always be with us. Mindful of this, we offer some thoughts and guidelines based on what we as teachers have done and what we have observed other teachers do when they grade. Most important, the uneasiness and ambiguities connected with grading can be lessened if we place grading in the proper context. That is, grading should only be a minor part of student assessment (McKeachie, 1994). The major part of assessment and evaluation is the qualitative information we communicate to students and parents on a regular basis. We will, however, examine both aspects of assessment—the quantitative grade we compute and the qualitative information we share.

Grading should only be a minor part of student assessment.

Our observations and conversations with teachers have helped us develop some basic guidelines that make the quantitative aspects of assessment and evaluation easier.

1. *Make explicit how you will determine a course grade.* Teachers need to make explicit what factors are considered in determining students' course grades. That is, will the course grade be based solely on a student's performance or achievement on tests? Will a student's effort count? How much will homework count? What role will a student's participation in class discussion or a cooperative project play in computing a grade? We cannot answer these questions for you, but you should consider them all carefully and then make sure that students and parents understand at the beginning of the school year the factors that you include when you assign a grade.

These seven guidelines will help you grade more effectively by using grades for quantitative assessment.

2. *Make explicit how you will evaluate an assignment.* Although grading is subjective, it can become more objective if you tell students in advance what you expect from them in their work or assignments. The more information you give them on how you will evaluate a lab report on an experiment or a summary of an article, the more comfortable students will be about the grade they receive. Specifically, students need to know in advance the value of the assignment and what a quality product or performance looks like. If, for example, the assignment is to write a summary of a newspaper article, the students could be told the following:

> The summary you will write is worth 20 points. Your summary should be at least six sentences in length and should include the author's thesis and an explanation of how the thesis was developed. A summary with these characteristics will receive the full 20 points.

Some teachers like to use a checklist that specifies the evaluation criteria. The checklist in Figure 4.1 is an example used by a vocal music teacher who asked her students to find a current article in a magazine or newspaper that critiqued some type of musical performance. Notice that she informed the students on how the total points for the assignment would be awarded. She tells us her students also use the checklist as a way of checking and monitoring their own work before they hand it in to her.

3. *Award credit when students try out new strategies or approaches.* Students will not be risk takers if they realize there is an inherent penalty for trying out new strategies or approaches. Hence, it is important to acknowledge these risks and to award proper credit. If, for example, a student tries to develop a map

Directions: Use this checklist to evaluate your assignment before you hand it in to me. The criteria listed below should help you locate strengths and weaknesses in your work. I will also be using the checklist to evaluate your assignment.

_____ 1. The references were listed on the index card correctly and completely. (WORTH 6 POINTS)
_____ 2. The two articles were appropriate to the assignment. (WORTH 4 POINTS)
_____ 3. There was a complete and accurate summary of the key ideas of the two articles you read. (WORTH 10 POINTS)

TOTAL POINTS:

COMMENTS:

FIGURE 4.1   Checklist for Library Project

for a chapter rather than outline it, as he usually does, provide the student with substantive feedback on his first attempts at mapping. If the map is not adequate because it overlooks some key points or interrelationships, still award as much credit as possible or allow the student to revise and modify the strategy before a grade is assigned.

4. *Include grading opportunities for both the process and the product.* Although college professors assign grades only for tests, quizzes, and the papers students write, middle school and high school teachers have the opportunity to include in their grading procedures more than just a final product. Sometimes more important than a product is the process of learning because it acknowledges students' attempts to construct meaning in a particular content area. Those attempts to construct meaning might include strategies to improve recall and understanding, journal entries about difficult concepts, classroom discussions about controversial ideas, or essay revisions. Portfolio assessment (described in detail later in this chapter) is another way in which the process is valued as much as the product.

Teachers also gave us several guidelines on how to communicate qualitative information to students about their performance in a particular content area. The following three guidelines seem particularly pertinent:

5. *Provide students with a variety of qualitative feedback.* The qualitative information connected with assessment and evaluation can occur in many forms. Most common are the comments teachers write on papers, the responses they offer to students' statements or queries, or the checklists they develop to describe the qualities of an activity or strategy that students have completed. The key, however, is to provide students with a variety of feedback in a format that makes sense to them.

Instead of grades, qualitative feedback should comprise most of the information students receive on their learning efforts.

6. *Provide students with timely feedback on their work.* We are sure you remember receiving a paper in one of your college writing classes that the professor took 3 weeks to grade. The grade at that point meant little because you had almost forgotten what you had written. Obviously, effective feedback must occur as soon as possible after students have completed a task if they are to improve their performance and learn. Admittedly, this is difficult because middle school and high school teachers might receive work from more than 100 students a day. Grading students' summaries or providing them with information on their progress becomes very time intensive. However, substantive and timely feedback can be provided in a variety of ways.

Checklists are one way to give students quick feedback on how they performed on a particular assignment. Rather than write the same comment 50 times, the checklist allows the teacher to indicate quickly the strengths and weaknesses of an assignment. In addition to the checklist in Figure 4.1, you will find other examples of checklists teachers have devised throughout this textbook.

A second way to make sure that students receive qualitative information about their work in a timely fashion is to create a symbol system and then limit your comments for a particular assignment to that set of symbols. For example, if you have been teaching students how to write a summary that includes the steps and the findings of a lab experiment, the following symbols might be useful in providing students with information about their efforts:

GES: Good explanation of the steps of the experiment

MNS: More information needed on the steps

GEF: Good explanation on the findings

MNF: More information needed on the findings

Some teachers complain that students do not read the qualitative information they are given, but instead focus only on the grades awarded. One middle school language arts teacher told us that she circumvents that difficulty by not writing the letter grade on the assignment until the student writes a response to her comments. Once she reads the student's comments, she places a grade on the paper. Regardless of how it is handled, quick, substantive feedback is important to the learning process.

7. *Involve students in the evaluation process.* Interestingly, all of the qualitative information discussed thus far has emphasized the teacher's responsibility, not the student's responsibility or participation. Assessment, however, should include students in self-reflection and evaluation activities. As we mentioned in the guidelines earlier in this chapter, students should play an active role in setting goals and evaluating whether they have reached those goals. When students are involved in evaluating their work in a content area, they are more likely to link their performance with effort rather than ascribe it to luck or chance or the whims of a teacher.

Taylor, an eighth-grade art teacher, realizes the importance of actively involving students in evaluating their own work. Therefore, she asks her students to evaluate their projects before they hand them in to her for feedback and a grade. She begins the process by asking her students to examine a few projects of her former students. Then she asks them to brainstorm some qualities that make certain projects more memorable than others. Once the class has listed all the possibilities, Taylor returns on the next day with a checklist containing the qualities the students have brainstormed and a few she has added herself. She tells her students to use this checklist to evaluate their own project and then to write a brief paragraph explaining what new techniques they have tried out. Although Taylor does not use a checklist for every project, she and her students find the experience useful.

As we stated earlier, grading is only a minor part of assessment and evaluation. The major part is the qualitative information we share. In the next section, we examine a variety of ways to gather information about students in authentic situations.

AUTHENTIC ASSESSMENT OF LITERACY AND CONTENT LEARNING

Earlier in this chapter, we referred to authentic learning. We now use this term, **authentic assessment**, to refer to a functional purposeful process created by teachers and students for discovering genuine learning needs and documenting genuine learning growth. Over the past several years, we have been collecting what we consider to be some of the best examples of authentic assessment. These examples not only reflect creative methods of discovering how students read and think, but are also consistent with current perspectives on how best to

Authentic assessment can occur only when students are engaged in authentic learning.

teach and assess literacy and learning processes. Because these assessments are devised and/or adapted by teachers, often in collaboration with students, they invariably yield richer and more meaningful information about student learning than could be gained from traditional testing practices (Geocaris & Ross, 1999). Furthermore, using authentic assessment helps you rely on your own assessment skills and individual judgment and exercise your own professional prerogative in making important instructional decisions (Clark & Clark, 2000).

One of the key principles of reading assessment discussed earlier is to embed assessment in the contexts of actual literacy and learning activities so that the results of assessment will have direct and immediate instructional implications. To this end, middle school and high school teachers need to devise their own approaches to assessment to determine the extent to which their students can read and learn from the various materials used in the classroom and use this new learning in functional and purposeful ways. The approaches teachers have employed to accomplish this goal have taken a number of forms, but all have these four critical characteristics in common:

1. They assess literacy and learning processes with the materials used in the classroom and in the actual contexts of their use.

2. They are so closely related to instruction that assessment and instruction become virtually indistinguishable.

3. They reflect the essential role of the teacher's judgment in student evaluation.

4. They develop students' abilities to think metacognitively and self-reflect.

In the following sections, we will examine successful authentic assessment procedures that middle school and high school content-area teachers are using with their students. Each one possesses characteristics of effective assessment listed previously.

MEETING THE NEEDS OF DIVERSE LEARNERS IN THE CONTENT-AREA CLASSROOM

Paul, a high school history teacher and highly informed professional, read about the experiences of two Minneapolis teachers in one of his professional journals (Avery, et al., 2000) who were facing similar curricular and cultural issues as he. Like the teachers in the article, Paul taught American history to regular-education 10th graders. During the course of the year-long class, he included a unit on immigration of the 1900s, as did the teachers about whom he read. Because his school is culturally diverse, he took advantage of the unique ethnic and experiential backgrounds of his students by having them trace their families' journey to the United States and share these stories with their classmates. Some who had only recently moved to this country themselves described exotic customs, animals, and natural terrain of their homelands or told vivid and poignant tales of life in countries ravaged by disasters, war, and poverty. Others recounted exciting, though often harrowing, events surrounding their passage to the states.

Paul took note of how his students who were new residents tended to become especially engaged and animated during study of the topic of immigration. It was also clear to him that more than any other time during the year students seemed to develop a strong sense of community. He realized, however, as the teachers in the article realized, that the unit could be even more critical with the inclusion of a greater degree of authenticity, both in terms of instruction and assessment.

As we have noted earlier, authentic learning occurs when students are engaged in focused inquiry and become seekers of their own knowledge. This is more likely to happen when the problem, issue, or topic can be tied to their lifeworlds. To achieve greater authenticity, Paul devised an immigration assessment activity inspired by the work of the teachers in Minneapolis, with the following characteristics:

- Students were required to organize, synthesize, interpret, explain, and evaluate complex information related to immigration in the United States.

- Students were required to consider alternative solutions, strategies, perspectives, and points of view as they explored the issue of immigration in the United States.
- Students were required to address the issue of immigration based on how they experienced it.
- Students were required to demonstrate their understanding of the critical issues of immigration through extended writing.

Diverse learners, like all students, deserve authentic learning and assessment experiences.

Paul's authentic assessment task first required students to carefully record important immigration data for all their classmates. This information was placed on a chart (see Figure 4.2). Next, students further organized and analyzed the data to determine if any trends could be discerned. Students then compared the patterns of immigration in the class with patterns described in their history textbook used to study the topic of immigration. The students' final product was a paper that described their findings and the significance of their results. Paul provided the class with a scoring rubric (explained in this chapter) describing the four areas to be evaluated: data-driven assertions, analysis of historical versus class immigration patterns, significance of the findings, and format/style.

With these activities, Paul had found a way to bridge the remote and lifeless facts of 20th-century immigration presented in the textbook with the current experiences of recent immigrants in his class. The relevance of the activities to the lifeworlds of Paul's students engendered a heightened level of engagement with the content resulting in his class asking, discussing, and seeking answers to critical questions such as: Who are today's immigrants? Why do some groups seem to assimilate into American culture more readily than others? Why are some targets of racism and discrimination? Which structures and institutions help or hinder an immigrant's transition to American society? Answers were found by reading excerpts from Sherry Garland's *Shadow of the Dragon* (1993) about a teenage boy from Vietnam living in Houston who, in spite of all his efforts to "fit in," gets pulled back into the turbulence of his native culture when a cousin arrives from a Vietnamese prison camp. Other answers were found by listening to guest speakers such as the Russian Community Center volunteer who described efforts to help many living in the perilous, war-torn Balkans and Chechniya seek asylum in the United States. Still more answers were gathered by exploring through the Internet the precise language of current U.S. immigration policy.

While Paul saw abundant evidence of his students connecting political history with personal history, the authentic assessment activities also helped Paul modify his typical approach to teaching from one of information disseminator to that of facilitator of his students' own inquiry. Observing the direct benefits to students' knowledge growth and pro-social behavior convinced Paul of the value of authentic teaching and evaluation.

Student	Place of Origin	Destination	Year	Related Events	Reasons	Struggles Upon Arrival	Traditions Embraced or Rejected
Omar	Hebron, Palestine	Houston, TX	1997	War, land scarcity, discrimination	To live with my uncle, escape war	Poor English skills and poor grades in school	Christmas Ramadan Fast food
Felipe	Matamoros, Mexico	Houston, TX	1992	Corrupt government, poverty	To find a good job for my father	Gangs and drugs	American football Tamales

FIGURE 4.2   Personal Immigration Histories

Authentic Assessment in Math

Darlene's seventh-graders were the beneficiaries of their teacher's affiliation with the Middle School Math through Applications Project (MMAP), funded by the National Science Foundation. The goals of MMAP are to offer middle school teachers a projects-based math curriculum that invites students to explore how professionals, such as architects and biologists, use math. Assessment of newly learned math concepts and skills is embedded within the context of the projects and focuses on four critical questions designed to encourage reflective thinking and accountability:

- What have we learned?
- How do we know we have achieved quality work?
- Whom do we hold accountable for our learning?
- How does evaluation help us learn more?

One of the MMAP units Darlene modified for her science class was the Antarctica Project. In this unit, students were assigned the task of designing a research station for scientists on the boundless icesheet of the southern polar cap. In groups of two to three, students drew floor plans, made considerations for optimizing insulation and heating efficiency as part of construction and supply expenses, and explored safety and quality of life issues. Along the way, the seventh graders were asked to apply critical math concepts, such as function, area, scale, and variable.

At the close of each day's activities, Darlene invited the class to brainstorm the math terms heard or used as they worked on their projects. In this way, students were able to reflect on what they had learned. As she wrote the terms on the board she urged students to provide examples from their research station design work. For instance, after writing Mateen's word "function," Darlene asked him how it applied to his classwork that day.

"Okay, it's like you need more insulation if you don't want to spend as much on heating the station."

"In other words function refers to relationship?"

"Yeah, you know, one thing goes up and one goes down."

The quality of student work is considered relative to agreed-upon standards. For example, when one of Darlene's students, Maya, presented her group's plan for a staircase in the research station, a classmate, Joy, determined it was too steep to allow occupants to take normal steps. Since several students had designed stairs in a similar way, Darlene led the class in a discussion of ways math could be used to establish space parameters for a person to walk up and down. This process of critical self-evaluation permitted Darlene's students to assess their own design features, create a set of shared definitions of quality design based on important mathematical concepts, and modify their designs to improve the overall project.

Darlene built into the project a brief presentation from each group at about the midway point. Her goal was to encourage accountability through peer critique. During Denny and Tremain's presentation, students found a significant de-

Go to Web Resources for Chapter 4 at *http://www. prenhall.com/brozo* and look for authentic teaching and assessment in math.

sign flaw. "According to your scale, that table is 20 feet long! They don't have that kind of room in there, do they?" Upon closer examination, Denny and Tremain saw their error and made notes for redesigning the station. In another presentation, the class politely challenged a group's inclusion of only one entry door for the research station. "I know it'll save on heat, but what if the scientists have to escape because of a fire or something?"

Holding each other accountable leads to increased personal accountability. Giving students the license to critique their own and other's work encourages reflective learning and helps students internalize a process of self-evaluation. Furthermore, students come to see assessment as a tool for improving achievement.

Finally, to demonstrate how evaluation can be used as a tool for learning, Darlene distributes examples of anonymous student work from previous years. The class is invited to critique completed Antarctica research station designs by applying the key math concepts discussed and used in their own research station projects. Darlene provides a rating sheet that asks student evaluators to find answers to important math questions, then rate the station design on criteria of quality. For example, in Figure 4.3, to rate the level of quality of space efficiency on a Likert-type scale, notice how students must first answer the math questions: What is the total area of the research station? What is the area of each separate work and living space? What are the ratios between total area and separate work and living space areas? Answers to these questions must be placed on the evaluation sheet to accompany a rating score. A final question asks students to justify their evaluations by answering the question: Why did you rate this criterion the way you did?

Darlene has found the process of placing students in the role of evaluator greatly improves their skills as self-assessors. When students view their own work critically at all stages of development, ultimately they are likely to produce superior work. This is certainly the case with Darlene's students who, she says, achieve levels of thinking about math and problem solving that would not be possible without authentic learning and assessment.

Authentic Assessment in Science

An assessment strategy used by Jerome in 12th-grade astronomy measures his students' abilities to make connections across concepts and processes. Expertise in science, as in any content domain, requires "connected understanding" (Schau, Mattern, Zeilik, Teague, & Weber, 2001)—that is, the development of rich, accurate, and accessible sets of organized knowledge. As we have pointed out, assessment tasks that prompt simple recall of disparate facts may be easy for most students to tackle but give teachers a one-dimensional view of content mastery. Mastery of subject matter should also be gauged by assessing how competent students are in synthesizing new information, noticing direct links among related units of information, and inferring connections.

An assessment format that serves Jerome's purpose of measuring his students' connected knowledge of astronomy is a fill-in concept map. This strategy

Directions: Evaluate the Antactica Research Station design by first answering questions 1–3. Next, rate the design from 1 (to a limited extent) to 5 (to a great extent). In the space below each ranking, explain why you ranked the design criteria the way you did.

1. What is the total area of the research station? _____

2. What is the area of each separate work and living space? _____

_____

3. What are the ratios between total area and separate work and living space areas? _____

_____

4. The total area of the research station is appropriate for its purpose.

    1...2...3...4...5

    Explain rating: _____

5. The living space is appropriate for the research station.

    1...2...3...4...5

    Explain rating: _____

6. The work space is appropriate for the research station.

    1...2...3...4...5

    Explain rating: _____

7. Ratios of work and living space to overall space of the research station are appropriate for its purpose.

    1...2...3...4...5

    Explain rating: _____

8. The research station design is drawn to scale.

    1...2...3...4...5

    Explain rating: _____

9. Cost and function variables have been appropriately accounted for in the research station's design.

    1...2...3...4...5

    Explain rating: _____

FIGURE 4.3   Rating Scale for Quality of Space Efficiency for an Antarctica Research Station

entails creating a partially completed graphic that depicts networks of related concepts and requesting students complete the graphic by supplying the appropriate missing terms in their correct places in the graphic. In Figure 4.4 Jerome's students are asked to use the word list at the top to complete the map. You will observe in this example 10 blank bubbles with only seven key terms,

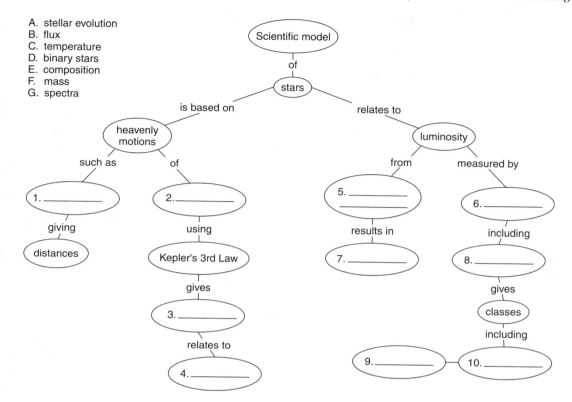

A. stellar evolution
B. flux
C. temperature
D. binary stars
E. composition
F. mass
G. spectra

FIGURE 4.4 Science Bubble Map

which means some terms will be used more than once. Jerome scores the concept map based on the percentage of correct responses to the total number of blank bubbles.

Since Jerome's approach to teaching astronomy and all his science subjects is to facilitate knowledge connections, his use of concept maps for assessing his students' abilities to demonstrate critical links in their new knowledge lends further authenticity to his efforts. An added benefit is that his students like completing the maps, especially those with lower levels of communication skills.

Using concept maps as a teaching and assessment tool helps students make critical knowledge connections.

Creating a Portfolio Assessment Culture: Process and Product

As part of a year-long portfolio teaching/assessment research project in collaboration with a high school French and English teacher, we had local professionals speak to students about the importance of portfolios in their work and lives. Frank, a local architect, began his talk to a group of industrial arts, art, and foreign language students by saying, "We are all walking portfolios." Students smiled.

"I mean, look around. Each of you projects a certain image by the way you dress, wear your hair, walk, and talk, and this image is open to evaluation and judgment by peers, parents, teachers, and potential employers," Frank continued. "That's why you leave the jeans and sneakers at home when you go to a job interview."

Frank's points were extremely helpful because they solidified for students the idea that portfolios are more than a product, a thing, a container of stuff. They are a concept and a process. In our debriefing session after Frank's presentation, students made comments such as "I'm beginning to get the picture that portfolios are anything we want them to be to help someone see what we're capable of." "Like Frank said, I can evaluate my own work and then put together a portfolio that projects the image I want."

We'll return to our experiences and the results of our portfolio research project (Moje, Brozo, & Haas, 1994) a bit later in this section. First, we will briefly explore the definition and history of portfolios and discuss some of the hows and whys of their use.

A portfolio culture involves teachers supporting and students documenting authentic learning over time.

Portfolios for instruction and assessment remain popular with teachers in nearly every field. We're sure most of you are by now quite familiar with the term and have, perhaps, even used portfolios in your own teaching. One of the best working definitions of a portfolio we have seen was developed at the Northwest Regional Educational Laboratory (Arter, 1990):

> A portfolio is a purposeful collection of student work that exhibits to the students (and/or others) the student's efforts, progress or achievement in (a) given area(s). This collection must include: (1) student participation in selection of portfolio content; (2) the criteria for selection; (3) the criteria for judging merit; and (4) evidence of student self-reflection. (p. 2)

Portfolios are a relatively recent and unique innovation in the areas of literacy and content learning (Kish, Sheehan, Cole, Struyk, & Kinder, 1997; Lockledge, 1997). Although in fields such as commercial art, modeling, photography, and journalism, portfolios have been used for some time to showcase artistic and professional achievement (Tierney, Carter, & Desai, 1991), portfolio assessment in writing emerged only in the early 1980s with the work of Judy and Judy (1981) and Elbow and Belanoff (1986) in a first-year writing course. The growth in portfolio assessment in educational circles during the decade of the 1990s was remarkable. However, in recent years, the idealism of using portfolios to document literacy growth and content learning (Camp & Levine, 1991; DeFina, 1992; Murphy & Smith, 1991) has diminished somewhat as the reality of their implementation has become clearer to measurement specialists (Koretz, 1998) and practitioners (Parsons, 1998; Simon & Forgette-Giroux, 2000) alike.

Like many educational innovations, when just a few short years ago it was nearly impossible to pick up a literacy journal or an applied journal in the natural sciences, social sciences, and math without finding an article on portfolios, today the situation is quite different. This is not to say that portfolio assessment is a flawed approach to teaching and documenting student achievement. On the contrary, portfolios offer teachers an excellent vehicle for meeting the calls by education experts for performance-based measures of reading and learning (Bol, Nunnery, Stephenson, & Mogge, 2000). Nonetheless, researchers and practitioners are now taking a more prudent and, perhaps, a more realistic view of the benefits and difficulties of portfolio assessment and teaching.

Why has the allure of portfolio assessment persisted in spite of the challenges it poses? Put simply, portfolios offer an assessment framework that reflects our current understanding of the process of literacy and content learning. We know, for instance, that:

1. Learning takes place over time—portfolios are collections of learning demonstrations at many points during the learning cycle.

2. Learning occurs in multiple contexts—portfolios sample work from a variety of teaching-learning situations.

3. Effective learning occurs when learners are engaged in meaningful, purposeful learning activities—portfolio teaching/assessment provide teachers an ideal way to promote authentic learning.

4. Effective learning requires personal reflection—portfolios have self-reflection built into the process.

Proponents (Murphy, 1997; Phelps, LaPorte, & Mahood, 1997; Reese, 1999), including ourselves, suggest that the following five questions be answered when planning to establish a curriculum that includes portfolio teaching/assessment.

What Will the Portfolio Look Like?

All portfolios should have a physical structure as well as a conceptual structure. Physically, a portfolio may be structured chronologically, by subject area, or by style of work. Some (Herman & Morrell, 1999) are even experimenting with electronic portfolios using the Internet and a special website. The *conceptual structure* refers to your goals for student learning. After identifying goals, you should decide the best ways to document students' work relative to the goals.

Portfolios should have a physical and conceptual structure.

What Goes in the Portfolio?

To determine what goes in the portfolio, several related questions must be answered first: Who will evaluate the portfolios (parents, administrators, teachers)? What will these individuals want to know about student learning? Will portfolio samples document student growth that test scores cannot capture? Or will they further support the results of test scores? What is the best evidence that can be included in the portfolio to document student progress toward goals? Will students include their best work only, or will the portfolio contain a progressive record of student growth, or both? Will the portfolio include drafts, sketches, and ideas in unfinished as well as finished form?

Because portfolio assessment is authentic in that it represents genuine, meaningful learning activities in the classroom, work samples should come from the variety of daily and weekly assignments and projects in which students are engaged. If you are documenting the literacy progress of a seventh grader, for example, then his portfolio would likely contain samples from a writing folder; excerpts from journals and literature logs; early and final drafts of written reports and themes; and copies of assignments from various content areas that required reading and writing.

A 10th-grade biology student's portfolio might include lab reports documenting her ability to conduct an experiment and analyze and interpret the results, actual project hardware, photographs and logs from field work, and questions and hypotheses for further scientific inquiry.

A math student in the eighth grade might include in his portfolio documentation of his improving ability to understand increasingly complex story problems or algebraic equations, samples of computations, descriptions of certain mathematical properties, explanations of why certain mathematical processes work, and evidence of using math to solve everyday problems.

Becky, a high school physics teacher, requires her students to demonstrate mastery of each objective she hands out at the beginning of a new unit. Typical objectives might ask students to determine the average speed of an object in motion or explain changes in velocity and acceleration of a ball when it is thrown up and returns to the thrower. Students need to provide evidence in their portfolios of ways in which the critical physics concept under investigation reveals itself in the real world. Becky allows evidence such as:

- a written description and analysis of an experiment or demonstration conducted either in class or at home
- a written description and analysis of an article or a picture from a newspaper or magazine that shows the concept in action
- a photograph, graph, or drawing accompanied by an explanation of why it qualifies as evidence of the physics concept
- a digital video or CD-ROM of the concept in action accompanied by audio or written narration explaining it.

In addition to work samples, portfolios should contain reflective records. Vital to the process of learning through portfolio teaching/assessment, **reflective records** are documentation of students' personal reflections and self-evaluations. Students should study their portfolios at various points throughout the year, focusing on a single work, a set of revisions, evidence of growth in a particular area, or the portfolio materials as a whole. In reflecting on these samples, students should ask themselves questions such as the following:

Students reflect on and evaluate their own products of learning.

Why did I select this piece of work?

Is this a sample of my best work?

What special strengths are reflected in this work?

What was particularly important to me during the process of completing this work?

What have I learned about (math, science, history, writing, etc.) from working on this piece or project?

If I could continue working on this piece or project, what would I do?

What particular skill or area of interest would I like to try out in future works?

Self-evaluative questions concerned solely with writing might include the following:

How has my writing changed since I wrote this?

If I revised this, what would I change?

What have I learned since I wrote this report that I would include in a follow-up report?

How did drafting and revising help me develop this essay?

How have I used this process to create other essays and reports?

Answers to these questions in the form of comments and reflections then become part of the student's portfolio. Students should also date their work and comment briefly on why it was included in the portfolio.

You should also include brief notes about why certain samples of students' work were chosen. At the same time, you should keep personal and anecdotal records of students' work and progress based on classroom observations, inspection of portfolio samples, and conferences on the portfolio with students, parents, and other teachers. These records can complement students' reflective records. Given most middle school and high school teachers' severe time constraints, record keeping of this kind can often pose the biggest challenge in portfolio assessment.

Jenny, an 11th-grade English teacher, handles record keeping by writing brief comments on adhesive name-tag-sized labels from rolls she can hold in her hand. She then affixes her comments to the work sample in the portfolio. Comments on each label include identification of the sample, why the activity was completed, why the sample was included, and brief notes about what the sample shows about a student's progress toward achieving instructional and personal goals. Jenny has found her system to be more manageable than others she has tried, especially because she can also hold the roll of labels during classroom activities and make observational and anecdotal records on them quickly and unobtrusively. Later, these notes, too, can be placed in students' portfolios.

Many teachers have found the use of checklists and questionnaires essential for analyzing portfolios and keeping records on them. A math teacher uses the following set of questions to assess students' math work samples:

- What mathematics did the student learn?
- How does this relate to what the student has learned before?
- Of the math the student has done lately, what areas of strength and confidence are exhibited in this work?
- What aspects of this work reflect a lack of or incomplete understanding?

Name	Project	Self-Evaluation	Reference Skills	Improvement

FIGURE 4.5   Portfolio Criteria Checklist

A seventh-grade history teacher uses an overall checklist such as the one shown in Figure 4.5 to keep track of his students' progress relative to portfolio criteria established in collaboration with his class.

How and When Will Samples Be Selected?

It's important to establish a clear and efficient system for selecting materials to go into and come out of the portfolio throughout the school year. Most teachers make these decisions at the end of a unit, grading period, semester, or school year. These are all good times to keep and add work samples that provide the clearest and most compelling evidence of student growth and achievement and, where appropriate, to eliminate other samples. Many teachers have found time lines helpful in making the entire class aware of when portfolio checks, revisions, and new entries will occur. In this way, students are brought into the decision-making process about what to include in their portfolios and further develop the ability to monitor their own progress. As stated, the more students are brought into the teaching-learning process, the more responsibility they take for their own learning.

Time lines help teachers and students keep track of progress in portfolio development.

The physics teacher, Becky, schedules at least one day per week for her students to use class time to work on their portfolios. The time is spent talking with individual students about their portfolio evidence, monitoring peer sharing and brainstorming, and assisting students in setting up and photographing experiments that generate data for their objectives. To ensure efficient use of in-class portfolio time, Becky requests that students submit in writing at least a day in advance what they intend to photograph and any special arrangements or supplies that will be needed.

How Will Portfolios Be Evaluated?

It is essential that evaluative criteria be established relative to the learning goals you and your students set up beforehand. We recommend that the greater part of a student's portfolio be evaluated on the basis of growth, in terms of both academic achievement and self-knowledge, instead of on the basis of comparison with other students' work.

The evaluation process typical in most middle school and secondary classrooms or schools where portfolio assessment occurs looks like this:

1. The teacher discusses and negotiates goals of portfolios with students.
2. Teacher and students develop guidelines and procedures for showcasing portfolios.
3. A showcase portfolio is developed by students with assistance and feedback from peers.
4. Students develop self-evaluation comments and present their portfolio.
5. Students evaluate their portfolio according to criteria they help develop with the teacher (e.g., evidence of improvement, evidence of effort, quality of self-evaluation, range of projects, presentation, future goals).
6. The student submits his or her portfolio to the teacher, who reviews it along with the student's self-evaluations and peer criteria scores. A grade is awarded.
7. The portfolio is returned to the student.

Figure 4.6 shows a **portfolio grade sheet** (Krest, 1990) that can be used to record individual grades for each writing sample and portfolio grades for students' progress.

Becky, the physics teacher, gives her students a time line with due dates for submitting possible items to be included in their portfolios and for the final portfolio. She also gives her class two scoring rubrics: one for evaluating the overall portfolio, which counts toward 70% of students' final grades, and another for evaluating peers, worth 30% of the final grade.

After about two weeks into a new unit, Becky conducts a portfolio preview to check students' progress. She writes comments on the portfolios in progress and returns them to students promptly so they can make necessary changes. Her students appreciate this feedback, while others who might be having difficulty find this deadline motivates them to get to work.

On the day final portfolios are due, Becky assigns students to groups of three to share their work. Students take turns presenting for about 5 minutes and then evaluate their peer's portfolio presentations. Presenters explain how their portfolio documents support the unit's objectives while the peer reviewers, the other students in the group, listen, peruse, and evaluate. Becky moves about the

Due Dates: _____
_____
_____

Name: _____

	Date	Portfolio Grade	Sample	Comments
HP:*				
MP:				
LP:				
HP:				
MP:				
LP:				
HP:				
MP:				
LP:				
HP:				
MP:				
LP:				

*HP = high priority; MP = middle priority; LP = low priority

FIGURE 4.6   Portfolio Grade Sheet

room constantly to listen in on the presentations, occasionally asking a clarifying question or challenging an assertion, and to monitor group activity. When finished with their presentations, students hand in their portfolios, and Becky grades them according to an evaluation checklist that includes the critical documentation criteria. Evaluating portfolio previews and using a checklist limits Becky's grading time to 10 minutes or so per portfolio. This approach to evaluation has resulted in very few students questioning their grades.

How Can Portfolios Be Passed On?

Portfolios create opportunities for teachers to have in-depth conversations about individual students' skills and needs.

As many teachers have noted, one of the special advantages of portfolio assessment is that the records of student progress can be passed on to succeeding teachers. In this way, the portfolio process promotes continuity in a student's education and collaboration among teachers at various grade levels. We suggest that as the school year draws to a close, you get together with other teachers at the next grade level to discuss their expectations and to find out what kind of information from portfolios would be most helpful to them in determining student accomplishment. In this process, you can make decisions about what to include or exclude before passing on portfolios. This is also a good time to have a conference with students about their portfolios in terms of the kind of work they believe would best reflect their growth and achievement for next year's teacher.

A Study of Portfolio Assessment: What We Learned

In this section, we discuss the findings of our own research about the benefits of portfolio teaching and assessment. We are vitally concerned about the extent to which the strategies and ideas we offer are implemented in real classroom settings by real teachers. Given this concern, much of our own research over the course of our careers has been devoted to discovering how teachers implement instructional innovations.

We conducted a 6-month-long research project during which we worked with and observed an experienced high school French teacher, Jayne, as she implemented portfolio instruction and assessment (Moje, et al., 1994). Our goal was to gain insights into the potential effectiveness of the strategy and the teacher change process itself. Furthermore, we hoped to develop a better understanding of the realities of using portfolios in a secondary school classroom where an individual teacher was attempting to put ideas from the literature into practice.

Our findings suggest that students—their input and voices—are often omitted from reports on the effectiveness of portfolios. Another factor not often accounted for in the rhetoric of educational change is the response and cooperation of students themselves. Yet, we discovered that without student cooperation and involvement, portfolio teaching and assessment is as vulnerable to failure as any other highly touted instructional innovation that has come before it. Perhaps the most important insight we gained from our experience in Jayne's classroom was that *students, like teachers, need scaffolding for change.* In other words, we can't always expect students to take advantage of new strategies simply because we think they should. The change process must include them as well; therefore, we need to prepare students for change, support them as they move through the change process, and provide them with ample opportunities for reflection on and critique of the change process.

With these general findings in mind, and based on our numerous conversations and interviews with several students from Jayne's classroom, we (Moje et al., 1994) offer the following guidelines for implementing portfolios with middle school and secondary school students:

1. Start with simple activities.

2. Negotiate firm deadlines.

These five guidelines will help content-area teachers succeed with their first attempts to use portfolios.

3. Encourage students to set concrete goals.

4. Provide initial resources.

5. Integrate other classroom activities with the portfolios.

Start With Simple Activities

We suggest that you begin to use portfolios by asking students to complete simple, short writing activities. The activities can take any form. For example, in an advanced algebra class, students could make journal entries that allow them to reflect on their reasons for taking the advanced class, or they could prepare goal statements or biographies that link the class to their needs and interests. Starting with simple activities with foreseeable deadlines will allow students to work up slowly to more comprehensive projects.

Negotiate Firm Deadlines

When students are not used to the cognitive ambiguity and uncertainty of the portfolio process, it is important to help them set deadlines to keep them focused on their work. Despite the fact that the portfolio is designed to be an ongoing activity as opposed to a finite project, students who are accustomed to due dates may require your guidance in setting deadlines to get work completed and to meet project goals.

Encourage Students to Set Concrete Goals

Rather than expecting all students to be able to generate their own projects and samples for the portfolios, we suggest that you conduct conferences with students to create a plan of action. Such a plan would provide students with short-range goals that could be accomplished according to agreed-on deadlines, giving students a clearer view of their progress toward long-range goals. Plans of action can also provide students with a means of self-assessment because students would be able to evaluate both their progress toward meeting steps in the plan and the wisdom of the steps they chose.

Provide Initial Resources

Providing initial resources is critical in classrooms where portfolios will comprise project materials and samples. Students who are not used to conducting extended research that might require finding contacts, following up leads, making phone calls, and the like will need an initial source of specific information to get them started. These sources can help students sustain their research efforts while helping them learn valuable reference skills in the process.

Integrate Other Classroom Activities With the Portfolios

Many teachers feel the necessity of covering certain concepts that are integral to their content area by means of direct instruction to ensure that the concepts are learned. Jayne, for example, felt it was necessary to continue using the French text and to provide direct instruction in grammar and vocabulary. She understood that students might be unprepared for complete immersion in the portfolio project and consequently moved back and forth between the two types of teaching. The stark contrast, however, between the teacher-led instruction and the student-led portfolios created tension and ambiguity among students.

Although Jayne wanted the portfolio writings to be applications of the book lessons, students didn't readily make the connections on their own. On reflection, Jayne decided that she could have tied together activities in a variety of ways. For example, she could have demonstrated the grammar rules the students read about in the textbook by pointing out the uses of grammatical structures in their portfolio writing samples. Integration helps students see the utility and value of portfolios as an integral part of the learning process in content classrooms.

Perhaps the most outstanding benefit of portfolio assessment is that it invites students and teachers to be allies in the assessment process. When a portfolio culture is established, there is a good chance that students will become more concerned, thoughtful, and energetic learners. At the same time, teachers will find renewed enthusiasm for providing support and guidance of others' learning while growing as learners themselves.

OTHER INFORMAL ASSESSMENT OPPORTUNITIES

In addition to using portfolios in the classroom, content-area teachers have other ways of assessing their students' strengths and needs. Some of these assessment opportunities involve students in reading and thinking about content-area concepts, some involve students in writing, and some involve students in completing self-report instruments.

Assessment by Observation

Suggesting to teachers that they assess through observation is like asking them to breathe or walk; it comes so naturally to most of them that its importance and power as an assessment strategy is often overlooked. Unfortunately, assessments based on teachers' intuition about, interaction with, and systematic observations of students has been devalued (Johnston, 1990).

Observational assessment is an excellent source of the critical information the classroom teacher needs to make important instructional decisions. Assessing through observation requires that teachers become more sensitive to the entire instructional situation: the reader, the text, the tasks required of the reader, the processes needed to complete the tasks, and the environment in which the tasks occur. Assessments conducted as students interact with text and complete daily assignments, engage in class discussions, or work cooperatively to solve problems can provide a rich source of information about students' relative strengths

Systematically observing students provides teachers with critical information for making responsive instructional decisions.

and needs, as well as how instruction can be modified to facilitate learning (Valencia & Wixson, 2000). For instance, teachers can make minute-by-minute decisions and lesson adjustments during classroom learning as they discover which students lack appropriate prior knowledge, fail to understand key vocabulary, or need further concept development (Johnston, 1992).

Observing students over time in a variety of classroom situations can provide teachers with an objective, unbiased view of students. Earlier, we discussed the limitations of making instructional decisions based on a single assessment at one point in time—specifically, that single assessments are not reliable measures of a student's true reading and learning ability. In contrast, observational assessments are ongoing and occur within the context of normal classroom activities while students are engaged in learning content-area concepts.

To determine the extent of students' understanding or lack of understanding and set the scene for observation, many teachers ask students to either write or talk about a concept at the beginning of class. For example, Phil, a seventh-grade science teacher, determines how much his students learned from their reading assignment by asking them to meet in pairs and list all the words they can recall about a topic, such as the six different kinds of forces. With this activity, one student talks as the other student writes down the words that his or her partner says. After 2 minutes, the roles are switched and the process begins again. To increase the interest in the activity, Phil sets a kitchen timer, which clicks away as he walks about the room listening to what the students are saying and watching what they are writing.

Phil tells us that this **word fluency activity** helps him to determine quickly which students have read the assignment and which ones understand the concepts. With this diagnostic information, Phil can plan more effective lessons and activities for his students. In addition to the word fluency activity, many other comprehension and vocabulary strategies can be used to create rich observation opportunities. These strategies are discussed in Chapters 3 and 6.

In addition to capitalizing on teachable moments, teachers can structure their observations with the use of a checklist. For example, Phil created an observation checklist (Figure 4.7) to collect information on which students may be having difficulty reading his textbook and laboratory activity booklet. With this checklist, he can determine accurately and reliably which individuals need special assistance.

Observation checklists can help determine which students need special assistance.

Another teacher put together her observation checklist (Figure 4.8) based on what she believed to be characteristics of good readers. With the knowledge she gains about her students' strategies for processing their textbook and other reading material, she determines the relative need for reading and study skills instruction for the group and for individuals.

Because these observations occur as a natural part of the content-area lesson, students can demonstrate their true ability. Teachers can obtain highly relevant and useful data by measuring what they choose to measure in the classroom context where students perform actual reading, writing, and learning tasks. The checklists shown in Figures 4.7 and 4.8 are examples of more systematic attempts to assess through observation. They can and should be modified to fit your particular assessment needs.

Student:

1. Avoids eye contact with me, especially when I'm asking questions of the class over the reading assignment.

2. May create the impression that he or she knows the answer to my question by looking intently and flagging his or her hand.

3. During oral reading of the textbook, tries to be the first one to read to get it over with.

4. During oral reading, tries to be the last one to read or tries to avoid being called on to read.

5. Frequently forgets to bring to class books and other materials that may be used for oral reading or needed to do in-class work.

6. Twists and turns restlessly in seat, often talking with neighbor.

7. Attempts to disrupt class.

8. Uses manipulative techniques within and outside of class to try to create a positive perception of his or her ability in spite of poor performance.

9. Uses neighbor for information about assignments and answers to questions.

FIGURE 4.7   Behavioral Clues to Students Needing Special Assistance

Student:

1. Uses prior knowledge to help construct meaning from text.
2. Draws inferences at the word, sentence, paragraph, and text levels.
3. Provides many plausible responses to questions about text.
4. Varies reading strategies to fit the text and the reading situation.
5. Synthesizes information within and across text.
6. Asks good questions about text.
7. Exhibits positive attitudes toward reading.
8. Integrates many skills to produce an understanding of text.
9. Uses knowledge flexibly.

Source: Adapted from P. D. Pearson & S. Valencia, "Assessment, Accountability, and Professional Prerogative," in J. Readence & R. S. Baldwin (Eds.), *Research in Literacy: Merging Perspectives.* © Copyright 1986, National Reading Conference.

FIGURE 4.8   Characteristics of Good Readers

The Content-Area Inventory

The **Content-Area Inventory** is extremely valuable because it asks students to demonstrate their thinking and learning processes as they read content-area textbooks or any written/oral material teachers may use in their courses (Rakes & Smith, 1992). The results of this type of assessment are far more informative

Discovering students' study, reading, and thinking skills early in the year can lead to effective teaching.

than commercially prepared tests, we believe, because the assessment is based on material students will be using throughout the year. Hence, when teachers use the Content-Area Inventory, they quickly discover which students will have difficulty reading and thinking about the assigned materials used in their course. Moreover, the information gained from a Content-Area Inventory can help teachers identify skills that students will need to be taught to succeed in a particular content area.

Although the Content-Area Inventory can be developed in a variety of ways, traditionally it has had two main sections. The first section usually measures students' skills in using book parts, using reference skills, and reading illustrative materials such as diagrams, tables, and charts. As students answer these questions, they are free to use all the parts of the textbook necessary. For the second section, the students read silently a lengthy excerpt from the textbook and then answer a series of questions with the textbook closed. These questions in the second section measure students' skills in understanding technical and general vocabulary words and comprehending what they have read. Music, art, and physical education teachers may wish to have students complete a listening task in this section rather than a reading task since listening skills are more crucial in these content areas.

To develop your own Content-Area Inventory, use the following steps:

1. Identify the essential reading, writing, listening, and thinking skills essential to your course.

2. Select a typical excerpt from the textbook or material the class will probably be reading in your course. The selection need not include the entire unit or story, but it should be complete within itself and not dependent on other sections of the chapter. In most cases, two or three pages will provide a sufficient sample of students' behaviors and skills.

3. Read the selection and design at least 25 questions for the first and second sections. These questions should reflect the skills you intend to assess and should be open-ended so that students have to use their recall and writing skills to answer them.

4. To make sure you have created a reliable instrument with no ambiguities, ask a colleague to read the excerpt and answer your questions. Then debrief the experience with the colleague and revise accordingly.

5. Prepare a student answer sheet and a key, noting specific page references for discussion purposes after the testing is completed.

The Content-Area Inventory in Figure 4.9 was developed by a driver's education department in a large metropolitan high school. The teachers had determined that it was important for students to be able to use their textbook effectively, to interpret illustrative materials, to understand technical vocabulary, and to identify and paraphrase the key ideas of what they had read. The driver's education teachers administered this assessment during the first week of class at the beginning of the school year. With the results, they were able to determine

Using Book Parts

1. On what page does the unit (section) entitled "When You Are the Driver" begin?
2. On what pages can you find information on smoking and driving?
3. In what part of the book can you find the meaning of *kinetic energy?*

Understanding Graphs and Charts

1. According to the chart on page 61, what is the second most important cause of rural fatal accidents?
2. What does the chart on page 334 imply about the relationship between speed and fuel consumption?
3. Using the chart on page 302 and your own weight, determine what alcohol concentration in your blood would make you legally drunk.

Vocabulary in Context

1. What does the word *converse* mean in the following sentence?
   Do not take your eyes off the road to *converse* with a passenger.
2. What does the word *distracting* mean in the following sentence?
   He should avoid *distracting* the driver.
3. What does the word *enables* mean in the following sentence?
   It *enables* you to carry out your decisions promptly and in just the way you planned.

Summarizing and Sensing Key Ideas

1. Write a one-paragraph summary of the section entitled "A Defensive Driver's Decision Steps" on page 101. Be sure to include the key ideas and any other pertinent information. Use your own words as you write the summary.
2. Using your own words, state the key idea of the following paragraph:

   Not only does a defensive driver have to see all hazards and decide on his defense, he also has to act in time. A defensive driver's thinking shows in his actions as he drives. He anticipates hazards and covers the brake in case a stop is needed. He has both hands on the wheel so that he will be ready to act.

3. Write one or two sentences stating the key idea(s) of Chapter 18, "Controlling Your Emotions and Attitudes."

Creating Study Aids

1. Imagine that you will have a multiple-choice and short-answer test on Chapter 18. Organize the material in that chapter by taking notes on it or by creating some form of study aid.

FIGURE 4.9   Content-Area Inventory for a Driver's Education Textbook

to what extent students could use their text as a resource and comprehend and process the textual information at a meaningful level. This knowledge led to specific instructional approaches such as cooperative grouping, direct process instruction in comprehension and concept knowledge, and training in designing and using study aids based on text and lecture information.

The teachers in this department have pointed out that it is important to explain the purposes of the Content-Area Inventory to the students. That is, the students should do their best work because the information from the inventory will help in planning appropriate instruction. In addition, students should be told that they will be reading silently and then answering short-answer questions without the assistance of the textbook.

One middle school team of teachers told us that they observe students as they read in order to note any who are demonstrating behaviors indicating frustration. For example, they make anecdotal notes of their students who appear to use excessive lip movements and who seem restless and generally inattentive. These behaviors may identify students who are experiencing difficulty comprehending what they are reading.

Teachers can gain additional information about students by observing them as they complete the Content-Area Inventory.

You can choose to grade the Content-Area Inventory in class the next day, using that time to discuss the questions and answers with the students, or you can choose to grade the inventory outside of class. Once the Content-Area Inventory has been graded, total the number of items each student answered correctly in both sections. Enter that total in your gradebook and use the following criteria for interpretation:

80% of the items correct—the student will probably be able to use and comprehend the textbook or materials

79–65%—the student will need some assistance in the form of teacher-directed strategies

Below 65%—the student will require significant assistance because the textbook or material is too difficult

Some teachers like to use a yellow highlighter to note in their gradebook which students are finding the content material too difficult.

The Content-Area Inventory will also help you see patterns in the skills for which students will need additional teaching and reinforcement. Rosa, a sixth-grade math teacher, developed a Classroom Summary Form to help her see these patterns. As illustrated in Figure 4.10, Rosa listed one class of her students on the vertical axis. On the horizontal axis she listed the reading skills she wants her students to master in her math course. Then she placed a check mark in the appropriate column for the students who missed more than half of the questions on a specific skill. For example, any student who missed three Content-Area Inventory questions about Understanding Math Symbols received a check on the Classroom Summary Form. Rosa believes that this additional analysis helps her identify the reading and problem-solving skills that most of her students will need to be taught to succeed in mathematics. An added advantage of the Content-Area Inventory is that it can be created for any course, regardless of whether you present the objectives and information to your students in written form or in the form of discussions, lectures, labs, and demonstrations.

Assessment Activities Using Students' Writing

Writing is a powerful communication tool because it mirrors what we understand and think about certain ideas. Writing is also permanent, allowing us to reflect upon the meanings that we attempted to construct on paper or on a computer

Classroom Summary Form: Content-Area Inventory

Names	Using Parts of the Book					Following Directions				Understanding Math Symbols				Understanding Vocabulary				Noting Main Ideas				Drawing Conclusions				
	1	2	3	4	5	6	7	8	9	10	11	12	13	14	15	16	17	18	19	20	21	22	23	24	25	26
Jason	✓					✓	✓	✓		✓	✓	✓		✓		✓	✓	✓	✓	✓	✓	✓	✓	✓	✓	✓
Tamika						✓	✓			✓	✓			✓		✓						✓	✓	✓	✓	✓
Jorge													✓		✓	✓								✓		
Michelle													✓		✓	✓						✓	✓	✓	✓	✓
Tyrone	✓	✓	✓	✓	✓	✓	✓	✓	✓	✓	✓	✓	✓	✓	✓	✓	✓	✓	✓	✓		✓	✓	✓	✓	✓
Gareth			✓			✓	✓	✓	✓	✓	✓	✓		✓	✓	✓	✓	✓	✓	✓		✓	✓	✓	✓	
Avery						✓	✓	✓	✓	✓	✓			✓										✓		
Judd		✓				✓	✓	✓	✓	✓	✓			✓	✓	✓	✓	✓	✓	✓		✓	✓	✓	✓	✓
Chanda	✓	✓				✓	✓	✓	✓	✓	✓			✓	✓	✓	✓	✓	✓	✓		✓	✓	✓	✓	✓
Jennifer																										

Place a check mark under the number of the question that was missed and alongside the name of the student who missed it.

FIGURE 4.10 Classroom Summary Form: Content-Area Inventory

screen. Hence, it is logical to use writing activities as one way to assess students' comprehension of a text (Afflerbach, 2000; Brozo & Brozo, 1994). In the next section, we will consider how you can use summary writing and autobiographical entries as assessment tools. Other assessment and teaching ideas that capitalize on the power of writing are found in Chapter 7.

Summary Writing

Written summaries can reveal metacognitive and other important thinking processes.

When students write a summary of what they have read or listened to, they must think metacognitively, make inferences, select important ideas, and form gists (Brozo & Curtis, 1987; Pressley, 2000). The following letter from P. T. Barnum to General Ulysses S. Grant (*Sequential Tests of Educational Progress,* 1957) was given to ninth-grade American history students at the beginning of a unit on entrepreneurs of the late 19th century. The teacher asked his students to read the letter and then, without looking back, summarize the key ideas and any other relevant information.

> Honored Sir:
>
> The whole world honors and respects you. All are anxious that you should live happy and free from care. While they admire your manliness in declining the large sum recently tendered you by friends, they still desire to see you achieve financial independence in an honorable manner. Of the unique and valuable trophies with which you have been honored we all have read, and all have a laudable desire to see these evidences of love and respect bestowed upon you by monarchs, princes, and people throughout the globe.
>
> While you would confer a great and enduring favor on your fellow men and women by permitting them to see these trophies, you could also remove existing embarrassments in a most satisfactory and honorable manner. I will give you one hundred thousand dollars cash, besides a proportion of the profits, if I may be permitted to exhibit these relics to a grateful and appreciative public, and I will give satisfactory bonds of half a million dollars for their safe-keeping and return.
>
> These precious trophies of which all your friends are so proud, would be placed before the eyes of your millions of admirers in a manner and style at once pleasing to yourself and satisfactory to the best elements of the entire community. Remembering that the momentoes [*sic*] of Washington, Napoleon, Frederick the Great, and many other distinguished men have given immense pleasure to millions who have been permitted to see them, I trust you will in the honorable manner proposed, gratify the public and thus inculcate the lesson of honesty, perseverance, and true patriotism so admirably illustrated in your career.
>
> I have the honor to be truly your friend and admirer,
>
> *P.T. Barnum*

The three types of summaries produced by the students are representative of the responses obtained by the history teacher. Here is one example:

Honored sir: The whole world respects you with honor. All are anxious that you should live happily with care. While the whole world worries about the manliness in declining the money tendered you by friends, they respect you to manage with honorable manner.

This response revealed to the teacher a couple of possibilities. First, because the student apparently tried to simply rewrite the letter, the student may have misunderstood the directions. Second, this response could also reflect a reader who, being incapable of understanding the surface logic of the letter (let alone the implied ideas), may have resorted to a strategy intended to disguise this possible serious lack of comprehension by simply writing down the words of the letter. In any case, the history teacher had what he believed to be a student who needed definite follow-up, and he immediately got together with the student for further assessment and discussion.

Another student submitted this summary:

The passage was a letter sent to Ulysses S. Grant from P. T. Barnum. The letter outlined how Barnum wanted to bring his attractions before millions of admirers with the permission of Ulysses Grant. Barnum was willing to pay $100,000 and a portion of the profits if he was so permitted to be allowed to show his trophies to the American public. Barnum promised $500,000 in satisfactory bonds to Ulysses Grant for safekeeping and return to demonstrate how serious Barnum was in bringing his trophies to the people.

Barnum started his letter to Ulysses Grant [by saying] that the people as well as himself respected his position of President and wished him the best of health. Barnum also finished his letter in the same fashion, comparing Grant with other great men such as Frederick the Great, Washington, and Napoleon.

What appeared obvious to the history teacher in this response was that the student had a good grasp of the basic information in the letter. The student recalled the significant details and followed the surface logic of Barnum's proposal to Grant. What is not reflected in this response, however, is any indication that the student appreciated the subtlety and irony in Barnum's letter. Also, this reader apparently had little prior knowledge of the topic because no additional ideas or information, beyond those included in the text, were provided.

A third student turned in this summary:

The letter from P. T. Barnum to Grant was first a letter honoring and showing Grant how much his public loved him. In other words, a real snow job. Because in the latter part of the letter, Barnum gives Grant a proposal of, first, paying Grant one-hundred thousand dollars to let Barnum exhibit his oddities, or as Barnum puts it, his trophies. Second, Barnum pledged to pay a half a million dollars in bonds for Grant's protection of his trophies. The whole letter came out to be a bribe on Barnum's part. But in real life it worked in favor of Barnum. The reason that one can tell this letter was a real snow job is because Grant wasn't everything Barnum said he was.

The teacher felt this was an impressive response. It reflected not only a basic understanding of the facts of Barnum's proposal, but also an understanding of Barnum's power of persuasion by heaping what history perhaps has proven unfounded, lofty praise on Grant. This student's ability to pick up on the underlying themes and rhetorical devices in the letter indicates a good deal of relevant prior knowledge about the topic and the skill to bring that prior knowledge to bear in constructing a multilevel understanding of the text.

Students who show signs of lacking relevant prior knowledge or the literacy skills to interpret the assessment passage meaningfully may be given special assistance. You can provide these students with additional or alternative reading opportunities from books that are content related, including some that are easier and more enjoyable to read than the textbook, to help build prior knowledge. Cooperative learning experiences are helpful for improving students' interpretive powers. Beyond the revelation of your students' reading performance with the texts used in your classrooms, written summaries have another advantage: An entire class can be assessed at one time. This advantage in efficiency, however, can be a disadvantage for students who are poor writers. An alternative to written summaries is to assess students' comprehension of text by having them summarize orally what they remember and learned from the text.

Content-area teachers may employ several tactics to quickly evaluate student summaries.

To read and evaluate their students' summaries quickly and efficiently, some teachers have developed scoring rubrics or checklists. Although these scoring devices for writing will be discussed in more detail in Chapter 7, it would be useful to discuss two different approaches. One approach is based on the assumption that within any paragraph, some ideas are more important, more central to the overall meaning than others. Thus, it is possible to rank these ideas on a scale of importance (Winograd, 1984); for instance, an idea of great importance might have a ranking of 3, while an idea of little importance might have a ranking of 1. Suppose you and I are going to read a passage about pollution. The author of the passage makes a few major points about the global consequences of pollution and presents several examples of pollution. After reading, in my summary I mention three specific examples of pollution, whereas your summary includes two of the author's major points and one specific example. Although we both recalled three ideas, your retelling would receive a higher rating because you recalled two major ideas.

A second approach to scoring summaries is more holistic. A holistic scoring rubric was developed by a 10th-grade English teacher (Figure 4.11). His scoring guide for the summaries included many aspects of reading, such as comprehension, metacognitive awareness, strategy use, level of text involvement, and facility with language.

Learner Autobiographies

The Learner Autobiography is an effective method for discovering more about students' interests and belief systems (Gilles et al., 1988). The idea is that students need opportunities to examine their personal histories as readers, writers,

Directions: Indicate with a check mark the extent to which the student's summary includes evidence of the following:

	No Evidence	Some Evidence	Significant Evidence
1. Includes verbatim information.			
2. Includes inferred information.			
3. Includes most important ideas.			
4. Connects prior knowledge with text information.			
5. Makes summary statements and generalizations.			
6. Indicates affective involvement with text.			
7. Demonstrates appropriate use of language.			
8. Demonstrates sense of audience or purpose.			
9. Indicates control of the mechanics of speaking.			
10. Indicates creative impressions or reactions to text.			

FIGURE 4.11   Scoring of Students' Summaries

and learners both in and out of school. By exploring their past, students might better understand their current approaches and beliefs about learning. To help students reflect on their past experiences as language users and learners, we recommend the following approach:

1. In small groups, ask students to brainstorm their past as readers, writers, and learners. They should try to remember about a time, person, school year, class, event, assignment, textbook or other book, teacher, friend, relative, or the like.

2. After brainstorming, students should write about that event, time, or person that had a positive or negative impact on their thinking and feeling about literacy and learning.

3. Be sure students focus on two questions: What happened that influenced the way you read, write, and learn now? How do you feel about that influence now?

Students and teachers can use Learner Autobiographies to reflect on past experiences with learning subject matter.

4. Students should be allowed to write as much as necessary to describe and reflect fully on their past influences and experiences related to how they currently think about themselves as readers, writers, and learners.

5. After thinking and writing, students could be allowed to exchange their drafts with members of their brainstorm group for comment, questions, and feedback.

6. Volunteers could be asked to share their autobiographies.

7. We recommend that you also take part in this activity by writing and sharing your autobiography with the class.

If you feel uncomfortable using these procedures with the Learner Autobiography, you can ask students to write parts of the Autobiography throughout the school year. For example, we know one physics teacher, Hector, who asks his students to write on an index card what they think it means to read, study, and learn in a physics course. He does this activity at the beginning of the class period the first week of classes. After collecting and reading the index cards, Hector discusses with his students his perceptions of what it means to read and learn in physics.

During the school year he follows up this initial assignment by asking students to write on other topics such as these:

This week I really liked _____ because _____; what really confused me this week was _____; and I would like to know more about _____ because _____.

These brief assignments on index cards have two advantages. First, students react positively to them because the required amount of writing seems less intimidating. For Hector, the index cards allow him to assess quickly what his students are thinking, learning, and feeling as they study physics.

The information gained from autobiographies and other writing tasks from your students can help you make instructional decisions, deconstruct maladaptive attitudes and beliefs about literacy, target certain activities and projects to particular students, and improve and support healthy attitudes about literacy and learning.

Self-Report Inventories and Questionnaires

Inventories and questionnaires are the simplest and most direct way of acquiring information about students' skills, interests, attitudes, and belief systems. Although self-report instruments have been criticized because students tend to use the cues embedded in the questions to determine how they should answer in order to be judged competent (Garner, 1987), you can reduce these potential limitations by using a variety of techniques. For example, ask *what* your students do but not *why*, and ask the question in two different ways to validate the consistency of their responses.

Some inventories and questionnaires, such as the Interest Inventory I (Figure 4.12) and the Survey of Study Strategies (Figure 4.13), require students

---

Directions: Put a check mark on the line to the left of each activity you like to do in your spare time.

Interests Outside of School

_____ Television	_____ Volunteer work	_____ Dancing	_____ Cooking
_____ Outdoor games	_____ Reading	_____ Socializing	_____ Music
_____ Watching sports	_____ Hobbies	_____ Movies	_____ Motorcycles
_____ Hiking and camping	_____ Playing sports	_____ Computer and Internet	_____ Cars
_____ Video games	_____ Fishing or hunting	_____ Traveling	_____ Other(s):

FIGURE 4.12   Interest Inventory I

merely to read and place a check mark in the appropriate place. Other inventories, like the Interest Inventory II (Figure 4.14), ask students to write more elaborate answers to questions regarding their interests. The Writing Strategies Questionnaire in Figure 4.15 has been used by middle school and high school teachers to discover important past experiences their students have had with writing and how they think and feel about writing.

Although your students' attitudes about themselves as learners in your classroom may be difficult to uncover with one simple inventory or questionnaire, they are a starting point for acquiring more in-depth information about your students. The key is that opportunities are provided on a regular basis for students to explore and share their underlying beliefs and attitudes toward literacy and learning. Remember, the examples of inventories and questionnaires we have presented are merely suggestions of the kinds of issues and questions you may find relevant to your teaching situation. We urge you to use these suggestions to develop your own inventories that suit your particular need to know more about your students.

Self-reports of students' attitudes toward learning should be obtained often, using simple, teacher-made instruments.

CASE STUDY REVISITED

Terri, the seventh-grade science teacher introduced in the case study in the beginning of the chapter, wanted to find a classroom-based assessment strategy of her students' ability to understand their science text. Now that you have read about and explored a variety of assessment approaches in this chapter, reflect again on Terri's concerns and generate a few suggestions for meeting her assessment needs. Afterward, read about what she actually did to assess her students.

In our discussion of schema theory in Chapter 2, we pointed out that for students to succeed in school, they need to have a well-developed sense of how authors structure ideas in narrative, especially in expository texts. These schemata for text structure help readers predict, assimilate, and retrieve text information—three critical reading processes. As we discovered, middle school and high school students may have a very good sense of how stories are structured but a relatively poor sense of the structures of complex expository texts they are likely to find in their social science and science books.

Before writing your suggestions for Terri, go to *http://www.prenhall.com/brozo*, select Chapter 4, then click on Chapter Review Questions to check your understanding of the material.

Your Name: _____

Date: _____

SURVEY OF STUDY STRATEGIES

	Strongly Agree	Agree	Neutral	Disagree	Strongly Disagree
Time Management					
1. I put off my homework until the last minute.					
2. I plan regular times to study.					
3. I study less than an hour a day outside class.					
4. I cram for tests the night before the exam.					
5. I study with the radio, stereo, or TV on.					
6. I have a specified and quiet place for study.					
Remembering and Understanding					
1. I examine each of my textbooks for its overall organization.					
2. I look over a chapter before reading it in detail.					
3. I have to read a chapter several times before I understand it.					
4. I'm halfway through a chapter before I understand what it is about.					
5. I do not know which information in a chapter is important and which is not.					
6. My mind wanders to other things while I am reading an assignment.					
7. I have trouble remembering what I read.					
8. I try to set purposes and questions to be answered in my reading assignments.					
9. I find reading difficult because of the big words.					

FIGURE 4.13   Survey of Study Strategies

	Strongly Agree	Agree	Neutral	Disagree	Strongly Disagree
Note Taking and Listening					
1. I take notes on my assigned readings.					
2. My notes on my textbooks are unorganized and messy.					
3. My notes don't make any sense to me.					
4. I don't know what to write down in my notes.					
5. I can't find information in my notes when I need it.					
6. I don't get much out of lectures.					
7. I find myself doodling or writing letters during lectures.					
8. I can't pick out important ideas from a lecture.					
9. I review my lecture notes as soon as possible after class.					
Test Taking and Test Preparation					
1. I study the wrong things for a test.					
2. I do not perform well on tests.					
3. I have mental blocks when I take a test.					
4. I know how to prepare for an essay exam.					
5. I have an effective strategy for approaching my upcoming exams.					
6. I know techniques for memorization.					
Reading Rate Strategies					
1. I hurry through all my assignments as quickly as I can.					
2. My reading speed is fast enough for my assignments.					
3. It takes me a long time to read any assignment.					
4. I can scan for specific information with little difficulty.					
5. I read most material at the same rate.					
6. I read as quickly as most people in my class.					

FIGURE 4.13   Survey of Study Strategies–Continued

Directions: Finish each sentence so that it tells something about you. You may write as much as you wish to finish each sentence.

1. After school I like to _____
2. On weekends I like to _____
3. _____ is my favorite TV show because _____
4. The kind of music I like is _____
5. When I graduate from high school, I want to _____
6. If I could go anywhere in the world, I'd go to _____ because _____
7. If I could take only one book with me on a trip to Mars, that book would be _____ because _____
8. I have seen the movie _____ and wish I could find a book similar to it because _____
9. I have reread the book _____ because _____
10. When I read the newspaper or a magazine, I like to read _____ because _____

FIGURE 4.14   Interest Inventory II

1. If you knew someone was having trouble writing, what would you do to help?
2. What would a teacher do to help that student?
3. If you were told you have to write an essay due in 1 week, what would you do to make sure it is done on time and is well written?
4. Think about someone you know who is a good writer. What makes that person a good writer?
5. What is the best advice you've ever been given about writing?
6. How did you learn to write? When? Who helped you?
7. What would help you improve your writing?
8. Do you think you're a good writer? Why or why not?
9. Why do people write? What are your reasons for writing?
10. Does the writing you do in school interest you? Why or why not?

FIGURE 4.15   Writing Strategies Questionnaire

Mindful of the problems students have in thinking like writers, Terri decided to combine some of the suggestions she obtained from an in-service workshop with her own ideas. From the workshop she learned how to construct a Content-Area Inventory using the materials from her course. The excerpt she selected was about rocks, a typical reading assignment that required students to identify types and characteristics, similarities and differences. Because Terri wanted to assess how well students could read to determine these writing patterns, her Content-Area Inventory contained many items like the following:

1. According to the paragraphs you have just read, what are two types of igneous rocks?

2. According to the paragraphs you have just read, what are some characteristics of these types of rocks? Name one characteristic of each rock.

3. According to the paragraphs you have just read, how are these types of rock different?

4. What words or phrases did the author use to cue you that the rocks were different in some ways? One such phrase was very different. What was the other?

In addition to the information she gained about her students from the Content-Area Inventory, Terri carefully observes her students in a variety of settings. For example, she pays special attention to the following signals that her students understand text organization and structure:

- As students are summarizing or discussing an assignment, she determines whether they are using the author's organizational structures as their ideas or comments unfold.

- When students are writing responses to text reading, she looks for indications that they are using text structure knowledge as a framework for developing their writing.

Terri has also found useful a classroom activity that her students really enjoy. She gives her students articles that have been cut up at paragraph boundaries and scrambled and tells them that they will be reading a text that is mixed up. Working in pairs, students are asked to put the article back together in the original fashion. While doing so, they are asked to think out loud and explain their decisions during the text reconstruction process to their partners. Terri moves about the room and listens to each pair of students to monitor their progress and provide assistance through modeling or questioning. She looks for evidence that her students grasp the problem–solution pattern employed by the author. Her evidence comes from students' comments and statements such as these:

Number 5 has to go near the end because it sounds like a summary of the problems with deforestation in developing countries.

By combining text reconstruction activities with the Content-Area Inventory and classroom observations, Terri has learned a lot about her students and why they perform the way they do. This information has helped her realize the importance of using a variety of strategies to help her students understand important concepts in science. Furthermore, she has found what researchers before her have found (Goldman & Rakestraw, 2000; Mayer, 1996)—that familiarity with expository text structure enhances comprehension and that knowledge of text structure can be directly taught.

———◦———

SUMMARY

Assessment of literacy and content learning is a process of becoming informed about teaching and learning to improve instruction for the teacher and to increase self-knowledge for students. In this chapter we emphasized the importance of authentic assessments that integrate process and content and help make the boundary between assessment and teaching nearly indistinguishable. Because content-area teachers need a variety of practical assessment activities and instruments, we described how teachers have created assignment-based assessment strategies, employed portfolio approaches, and used other methods, such as classroom observations during teachable moments, students' writing, checklists, and the Content-Area Inventory.

In this chapter we also made clear the importance of middle and secondary school teachers finding ways to take advantage of and make more meaningful standardized testing. When results from standardized reading and achievement tests heighten teachers' sensitivity to the needs of struggling readers and learners, then curricular and instructional changes might be made to improve learning progress for these students. This was the case in two settings, Foothills High and Garfield School.

Finally, we stressed that when process assessment of literacy is integrated within the content classroom, the result is that assessment and teaching become nearly indistinguishable. Therefore, throughout this book we discuss strategies in relation to how they can be used to assess and teach particular literacy/learning processes. For example, in the next chapter, our discussion of effective strategies for preparing students for content-area assignments includes how assessment of prior knowledge and building prior knowledge can be complementary. In Chapter 6, we describe vocabulary strategies that have built-in assessments for the teacher and self-assessment for the student. This holds true for Chapter 7, in which we demonstrate how students' writing can be used in assessment and development of comprehension. Many of the strategies for teaching with trade literature, developed in Chapter 8, can be used to reveal what students are learning. In Chapter 9, strategies for developing text study processes are interwoven with teacher assessment and self-assessments of these strategies. Finally, in the last chapter, we discuss the role of assessment as a tool of reflection in improving teaching effectiveness.

REFERENCES

Afflerbach, P. (2000). Verbal reports and protocol analysis. In M. Kamil, P. Mosenthal, P. D. Pearson, & R. Barr (Eds.), *Handbook of reading research* (Vol. 3). Mahwah, NJ: Erlbaum.

Alexander, P., & Jetton, T. (2000). Learning from text: A multidimensional and developmental perspective. In M. Kamil, P. Mosenthal, P. D. Pearson, & R. Barr (Eds.), *Handbook of reading research* (Vol. 3). Mahwah, NJ: Lawrence Erlbaum Associates.

Apple, M. (1999). Teacher assessment ignores social justice. *The Education Digest, 65,* 24–28.

Arter, J. (1990). *Using portfolios in instruction and assessment.* Portland, OR: Northwest Regional Educational Laboratory.

Avery, P., Carmichael-Tanaka, D., Kunze, J., & Kouneski, N. (2000). Writing about immigration: Authentic assessment for U.S. history students. *Social Education, 64,* 372–375.

Bissex, G. (1980). *Gyns at work: A child learns to write and read.* Cambridge, MA: Harvard University Press.

Bol, L., Nunnery, J., Stephenson, P., & Mogge, K. (2000). Changes in teachers' assessment practices in the new American schools restructuring models. *Teaching and Change, 7,* 127–146.

Brophy, J. (1998). *Motivating students to learn.* Boston: McGraw-Hill.

Brozo, W. G., & Brozo, C. L. (1994). Literacy assessment in standardized and zero-failure contexts. *Reading and Writing Quarterly, 10,* 189–200.

Brozo, W. G., & Curtis, C. L. (1987). Coping strategies of four successful learning disabled college students: A case study approach. In J. Readence & R. S. Baldwin (Eds.), *Research in literacy: Merging perspectives. Thirty-sixth yearbook of the National Reading Conference.* Rochester, NY: National Reading Conference.

Camp, R., & Levine, D. (1991). Portfolios evolving: Background and variations in sixth-through twelfth-grade classrooms. In P. Belanoof & M. Dixon (Eds.), *Portfolios: Process and product.* Portsmouth, NH: Boynton/Cook.

Carey, R. F., Harste, J. C., & Smith, S. L. (1981). Contextual constraints and discourse processes: A replication study. *Reading Research Quarterly, 16,* 201–212.

Chen, J. Q., Salahuddin, R., Horsch, P., & Wagner, S. (2000). Turning standardized test scores into a tool for improving teaching and learning: An assessment-based approach. *Urban Education, 35,* 356–384.

Clark, D., & Clark, S. (2000). Appropriate assessment strategies for young adolescents in an era of standards-based reform. *The Clearing House, 73,* 201–204.

Clay, M. (1975). *What did I write?* Auckland, New Zealand: Heinemann.

D'Agostino, J. V. (1996). Authentic instruction and academic achievement in compensatory education classrooms. *Studies in Educational Evaluation, 22,* 139–155.

DeFina, A. (1992). *Portfolio assessment: Getting started.* New York: Scholastic.

Elbow, P., & Belanoff, P. (1986). Portfolios as a substitute for proficiency examinations. *College Composition and Communication, 37,* 336–339.

Fuchs, L. (1999). Connecting assessment to instruction. *Schools in the Middle, 9,* 4–8.

Garland, S. (1993). *Shadow of the dragon.* New York: Harcourt.

Garner, R. (1987). *Metacognition and reading comprehension.* Norwood, NJ: Ablex.

Gee, J. P. (2000). Discourse and sociocultural studies in reading. In M. Kamil, P. Mosenthal, P. D. Pearson, & R. Barr (Eds.), *Handbook of reading research* (Vol. 3). Mahwah, NJ: Lawrence Erlbaum Associates.

Geocaris, C., & Ross, M. (1999). A test worth taking. *Educational Leadership, 57,* 29–33.

Gilles, C., Bixby, M., Crowley, P., Crenshaw, S., Henrich, M., Reynolds, F., & Pyle, D. (1988). *Whole language strategies for secondary students.* New York: Richard C. Owen.

Goldman, S., & Rakestraw, J. (2000). Structural aspects of constructing meaning from text. In M. Kamil, P. Mosenthal, P. D. Pearson, & R. Barr (Eds.), *Handbook of reading research* (Vol. 3). Mahwah, NJ: Lawrence Erlbaum Associates.

Haines, S. (2001). Signs of success: Improving student achievement on performance-based assessments. *The Science Teacher, 68,* 26–29.

Hargis, C. (1990). *Grades and grading practices: Obstacles to improving education and to helping at-risk students.* Springfield, IL: Charles C. Thomas.

Hargis, C. (1999). *Teaching and testing in reading: A practical guide for teachers and parents.* Springfield, IL: Charles C. Thomas.

Herman, L., & Morrell, M. (1999). Educational progressions: Electronic portfolios in a virtual classroom. *T.H.E. Journal, 26,* 86–89.

Hoff, D. (2000, February 16). Test-weary schools balk at NAEP. *Education Week, 19,* 1,11.

Johnston, P. (1990). Steps toward a more naturalistic approach to the assessment of the reading process. In S. Legg & J. Algina (Eds.), *Cognitive assessment of language and mathematics outcomes.* Norwood, NJ: Ablex.

Johnston, P. (1992). *Constructive evaluation of literate activity.* New York: Longman.

Johnston, P. (1993). Assessment as a social practice. In D. J. Leu & C. K. Kinzer (Eds.), *Examining central issues in literacy research, theory, and practice. Forty-second yearbook of the National Reading Conference.* Chicago: National Reading Conference.

Judy, S., & Judy, S. (1981). *An introduction to the teaching of writing.* New York: Wiley.

Kish, C., Sheehan, J., Cole, K., Struyk, R., & Kinder, D. (1997). Portfolios in the classroom: A vehicle for developing reflective thinking. *The High School Journal, 80,* 254–260.

Kohn, A. (2001, January 10). TIMSS rivalry: Competitiveness and quality are often antithetical. *Education Week,* 57.

Koretz, D. (1998). Large-scale portfolio assessments in the US: Evidence pertaining to the quality of measurement. *Assessment in Education, 5,* 309–334.

Krest, M. (1990). Adapting the portfolio to meet student needs. *English Journal, 79,* 29–34.

Lawrence, M., & Pallrand, G. (2000). A case study of the effectiveness of teacher experiencee in the use of explanation-based assessment in high school physics. *School Science and Mathematics, 100,* 36–47.

Lewis, A. (2000). Standing firm on standards. *Phi Delta Kappan, 82,* 263–264.

Lewis, A. (2001). Raising achievement. *The Education Digest, 66,* 71–72.

Lockledge, A. (1997). Portfolio assessment in middle-school and high-school social studies classrooms. *The Social Studies, 88,* 65–69.

Mayer, R. E. (1996). Learning strategies for making sense out of expository text: The SOI model for guiding these cognitive processes in model construction. *Educational Psychology Review, 8,* 357–371.

McKeachie, W. J. (1994). *Teaching tips* (9th ed.). Lexington, MA: D. C. Heath.

Moje, W., Brozo, W. G., & Haas, J. (1994). Portfolios in a high school classroom: Challenges to change. *Reading Research and Instruction, 33,* 275–292.

Murphy, S. (1997). Who should taste the soup and when? Designing portfolio assessment programs to enhance learning. *The Clearing House, 71,* 81–84.

Murphy, S., & Smith, M. (1991). *Writing portfolios: A bridge from teaching to assessment.* Markham, Ontario: Pippin.

National Reading Panel. (2000). *Teaching children to read.* Bethesda, MD: The National Institute of Child Health and Human Development.

Nickell, P. (1999). The issue of subjectivity in authentic social studies assessment. *Social Education, 63,* 353–355.

Nist, S., & Simpson, M. (2000). College studying. In M. Kamil, P. Mosenthal, P. D. Pearson, & R. Barr (Eds.), *Handbook of reading research,* (Vol. 3). Mahwah, NJ: Lawrence Erlbaum Associates.

Ohanian, S. (1999). *One size fits few: The folly of educational standards.* Portsmouth, NH: Heinemann.

Olson, L. (1998, February 11). The push for accountability gathers steam. *Education Week,* 17.

Parsons, J. (1998). Portfolio assessment: Let us proceed with caution. *Adult Learning, 9,* 28–30.

Phelps, A., LaPorte, M., & Mahood, A. (1997). Portfolio assessment In high school chemistry: One teacher's guidelines. *Journal of Chemical Education, 74,* 528–531.

Pressley, M. (2000). What should comprehension instruction be the instruction of? In M. Kamil, P. Mosenthal, P. D. Pearson, & R. Barr (Eds.), *Handbook of reading research,* (Vol. 3). Mahwah, NJ: Lawrence Erlbaum Associates.

Rakes, T. A., & Smith, L. J. (1992). Assessing reading skills in the content areas. In E. K. Dishner, T. W. Bean, J. E. Readence, & D. W. Moore (Eds.), *Reading in the content areas: Improving classroom instruction.* Dubuque, IA: Kendall/Hunt.

Readence, J. E., & Moore, D. W. (1983). Why questions? A historical perspective on standardized reading comprehension tests. *Journal of Reading, 26,* 306–313.

Reading yardsticks. (1981). Level 14—Grade 8. Chicago: Riverside.

Reese, B. (1999). Phenomenal portfolios: A first year teacher uses portfolios to encourage concept mastery. *The Science Teacher, 66,* 25–28.

Rothstein, R. (2000, May 24). Tests alone fail to assure accountability of schools. *New York Times,* p. B12.

Schau, C., Mattern, N., Zeilik, M., Teague, K., & Weber, R. (2001). Select-and-fill-in concept map scores as a measure of students' connected understanding of science. *Educational and Psychological Measurement, 61,* 136–158.

Schommer, M. (1994). An emerging conceptualization of epistemological beliefs and their role in learning. In R. Garner & P. A. Alexander (Eds.), *Beliefs about text and instruction with text.* Hillsdale, NJ: Erlbaum.

Schommer, M., Calvert, C., Gariglietti, G., & Bajaj, A. (1997). The development of epistemological beliefs among secondary students: A longitudinal study. *Journal of Educational Psychology, 89,* 37–40.

Sequential tests of educational progress. (1957). Princeton, NJ: Educational Testing Service.

Serri, P. (1999). Practical assessment: Realistic assessment strategies help educators attain curricular objectives. *The Science Teacher, 66,* 34–37.

Simon, M., & Forgette-Giroux, R. (2000). Impact of a content selection framework on portfolio assessment at the classroom level. *Assessment in Education, 7,* 83–101.

Stanovich, K. (1986). Matthew effects in reading: Some consequences of individual differences in the development of reading fluency. *Reading Research Quarterly, 21,* 360–406.

Stiggins, R. (1999). Assessment, student confidence, and school success. *Phi Delta Kappan, 81,* 191–198.

Stipek, D. (1996). Motivation and Instruction. In D. C. Berliner & R. C. Calfee (Eds.), *Handbook of educational psychology.* New York: Macmillan.

Tierney, R., Carter, M., & Desai, L. (1991). *Portfolio assessment in the reading-writing classroom.* Norwood, MA: Christopher Gordon.

Valencia, S. W., McGinley, W., & Pearson, P. D. (1990). Assessing reading and writing. In G. Duffy (Ed.), *Reading in the middle school.* Newark, DE: International Reading Association.

Valencia, S., & Wixson, K. (2000). Policy-oriented research on literacy standards and assessment. In M. Kamil, P. Mosenthal, P. D. Pearson, & R. Barr (2000). *Handbook of reading research* (Vol. 3). Mahwah, NJ: Lawrence Erlbaum Associates.

William, D. (2000). Education: The meanings and consequences of educational assessments. *The Critical Quarterly, 42,* 105–127.

Winograd, P. (1984). Strategic difficulties in summarizing texts. *Reading Research Quarterly, 19,* 404–425.

Zimmerman, B. J., Bandura, A., & Martinez-Pons, M. (1992). Self-motivation for academic attainment: The role of self-efficacy beliefs and personal goal setting. *American Educational Research Journal, 29,* 663–676.

CHAPTER FIVE

Initiating Students to New Learning

ANTICIPATION GUIDE

Directions: Read each statement carefully and decide whether you agree or disagree with it, placing a check mark in the appropriate *Before Reading* column. When you have finished reading and studying the chapter, return to the guide and decide whether your anticipations need to be changed by placing a check mark in the appropriate *After Reading* column.

	BEFORE READING		AFTER READING	
	Agree	*Disagree*	*Agree*	*Disagree*
1. One of the most neglected phases of a content lesson is readiness.	____	____	____	____
2. Most students are automatically motivated to learn new content.	____	____	____	____
3. Students can be helped in setting purposes for reading by being told what to read.	____	____	____	____
4. Writing can be used to prepare for learning.	____	____	____	____
5. Teachers do not have time for readiness activities.	____	____	____	____

*It is clear that very little improvement may be expected from formal drill . . .
unless at the same time provision is made for the enrichment of experience,
the development of language abilities, and the improvement of thinking.*

—Ernest Horn (1937)

When Ernest Horn made these comments more than 60 years ago, workbooks and skills kits were beginning to flood the reading materials market. These materials were designed to drill students on reading skills and were based on the assumption that drill alone would develop competent readers. Horn's insights into the complex interactions between learners' experiences, language abilities, and cognitive strategies, on the one hand, and the extent to which the context supports meaningful learning, on the other, continue to be verified through scholarly research (c.f. Bean, 2000; Hartman, 1995; Wilkinson & Silliman, 2000). Today teachers and researchers agree that to create the best conditions for learning, students need to be prepared to learn.

In Chapters 2 and 3, we discussed several important principles of active learning and demonstrated how many useful strategies can be employed by middle and secondary school teachers to promote literacy growth and increase content learning. In this chapter, we explain the important role the preparation phase plays in learning in the content classroom. We argue that when students are adequately prepared for and actively engaged in literacy and content learning activities, their enthusiasm for learning increases and their comprehension of the material improves.

Our primary focus in this chapter is on strategies, ideas, and guidelines for preparing students to learn in middle and secondary school classrooms through reading and writing. Since learning at this level must occur as a result of exposure to a variety of information sources, we describe classroom readiness strategies that can apply equally effectively to (a) a chapter from a textbook or novel, (b) a guest speaker, (c) a video, (d) an experiment, (e) a field trip, (f) a discussion or debate, (g) a computer-based learning activity; or (h) a lecture. We hope that the principles of effective readiness instruction and the numerous classroom examples described in this chapter will stimulate your own innovative approaches to setting the stage for and engaging students in new learning.

Go to *http://www.prenhall.com/brozo*, select Chapter 5, then click on Chapter Objectives to provide a focus for your reading.

CASE STUDY

Theresa is an eighth-grade social studies teacher. She has noticed that her students appear to have become increasingly uninterested and passive over the past 10 years. Although she has typically taught units from the textbook, her efforts to enlist students in learning social studies content have been moving further and further from the text—with encouraging results. For instance, early in the school year she employed some new strategies to help students develop a broader sense of community responsibility. To her delight, the class took off with the strategy, exhibiting a level of enthusiasm Theresa hadn't seen for some time.

Theresa is in the process of planning a unit on early Native Americans. Last year was the first year she deviated from the textbook approach to teaching about native peoples by having a member of a local Huron tribe talk to the class about history and customs. He also shared costumes and artifacts. This year she would like to do more to help students develop a better understanding of what we know about the early

Take full advantage of these interactive case studies. They can help you solve problems and provide a focus for reading the chapter.

Native American cultures and how we learn about these cultures. She wants to devise active, hands-on approaches to engage her class in the study of this important topic.

To the Reader:
As you read and work through this chapter, think about possible strategies and teaching approaches Theresa might use to engage her students in learning about early American cultures. Be prepared to offer your suggestions when we revisit this case study at the conclusion of the chapter.

GUIDELINES FOR EFFECTIVE READINESS INSTRUCTION

Engender Interest and Motivation

A self-evident and empirically grounded truth about learning is that students will expend the energy necessary to learn if they are interested in the material (Eccles, Wigfield, Schiefele, 1998; Mosenthal, 1999; Renninger, Hidi, & Krapp, 1992). This is certainly not a recent revelation. More than 80 years ago, John Dewey promoted the idea that when students are interested in a topic or activity they will learn "in a whole-hearted way" (1913, p. 65). Unfortunately, although we all pay lip service to this principle, we often fail to put it into practice. Perhaps it is the lack of attention to basic principles of motivation for learning that is contributing to a nationwide, and perhaps even a worldwide, decline in students' interest in reading as they move into and through middle and secondary school (Bintz, 1993; McKenna, Kear, & Ellsworth, 1995).

Over the past few years, there has been a resurgence of interest among researchers and practitioners in the influence of motivation on literacy and learning (Guthrie & Wigfield, 2000; Hidi & Harackiewicz, 2000). The realization that students must have both the *skill* and the *will* to learn has led to a variety of instructional practices designed to support the affective as well as the cognitive aspects of literacy development and school achievement (Cameron & Pierce, 1994; Frager, 1993). Teachers who motivate for learning do not automatically assume that all students eagerly desire to learn. Instead, they prepare students for learning by helping them become active participants in the learning process, demonstrating how the content can relate to students' lives and concerns, and providing opportunities for students to enjoy learning (Moje, 2000; Ruddell, 1995).

Because textbook prose is lifeless, students need strategies to make required reading more engaging.

Another important consideration in sparking motivation and interest in learning for middle and secondary school teachers is the role of the textbook (Alexander & Jetton, 2000). If you spend any time working with textbooks, you will soon notice that invariably the prose is abstract, formal, and lifeless (Tyson-Bernstein, 1988). To expect students to relish textbook reading is, we believe, unrealistic. Therefore, every effort needs to be made to get students interested in the textbook topic (Hidi & Baird, 1988; Schiefele, 1996; Wade,

Schraw, Buxton, & Hayes, 1993). This can be accomplished with language experiences, films, games, role-playing, guest speakers, field trips, multimedia, writing, reading-related texts, and fictional works, to name just a few ways. Interest-promoting strategies such as disrupting learners' expectations, challenging them to resolve a paradox, and introducing novel and conflicting information or situations have also been shown to be effective (Mathison, 1989). The unexpected benefit of your efforts to develop imaginative, unique, interest-engendering activities is that you will become more interested in the content as well. And as you know, the more enthusiastic you are about learning, the greater your chance of awakening interest in your students.

Activate and Build Relevant Prior Knowledge

As we saw in Chapter 2, relevant prior knowledge makes up, by and large, one's schema, or networks of related information. Pearson and Johnson (1978) describe the process of activating and building relevant prior knowledge as one of "building bridges between the new and the known." This simple yet elegant concept is neglected far too often in instructional plans.

To demonstrate the importance of relevant prior knowledge for successful reading and learning, we have an assignment for you. Read the following passage and be prepared to discuss the main points, the supporting details, and the relationships between the themes in the passage and other related passages you have read.

> It is highly unsettling for some to come into close contact with them. Far worse to gain control over them and to deliberately inflict pain on them. The revulsion caused by this punishment is so strong that many will not take part in it at all. Thus there exists a group of people who seem to revel in the contact and the punishment as well as the rewards associated with both. Then there is another group of people who shun the whole enterprise: contact, punishment, and rewards alike.
>
> Members of the first group share modes of talk, dress, and deportment. Members of the second group, however, are as varied as all humanity.
>
> Then there is a group of others, not previously mentioned, for the sake of whose attention all this activity is undertaken. They too harm the victims, though they do it without intention of cruelty. They simply follow their own necessities. And though they may inflict the cruelest punishment of all, sometimes—but not always—they themselves suffer as a result. (Gillet & Temple, 1986, p. 4)

Do you have any idea what this passage is about? Every time we ask our students to read it, they first try desperately to impose a sensible interpretation on the words, offer possibilities that leave them uncomfortable, and finally give up, resorting to protests that sound all too familiar to any classroom teacher: "This is too hard." Most complain that this reading exercise is unfair because the passage has too many unclear referents, which makes it impossible to understand with any certainty. The typical guesses we get vary widely: parents and children, concentration camps, corporal punishment, and teachers and students.

Teaching without warm-up activities puts students at a disadvantage when trying to learn new information.

With this exercise, we have been able to simulate for you how many students must feel when given reading assignments without direction, warm-up, or any of the relevant background knowledge necessary for interpreting the statements in the passage. We know that secondary students often finish textbook readings and come away as bewildered as you probably were about the preceding passage.

By the way, the title of the passage is "Fishing Worms." Does that help? Go back and reread it now, and notice as you read how all the ideas seem to fit together, how meaning jumps automatically into consciousness. The title acts as an organizer, a unifying theme, and brings to mind a schema for fishing and worms, which, as discussed in Chapter 2, provides a slot in memory for filing the information presented in this text. Now imagine a ninth grader trying to grapple with the ideas and facts in the following text segment. Without any preparation for this text, the student might find it as unintelligible as the previous passage, sans title, was for you.

A systematic examination of all known rock types shows that two principal kinds predominate. The first are *igneous rocks,* formed by the cooling and crystallization of liquids from deep in the crust or upper part of the mantle, called *magmas.* The second are *sedimentary rocks,* formed by compaction and cementation of sediment derived from the continuous erosion of the continents by water, atmosphere, ice, and wind. Most of the sediments are deposited in the sea along the margins of continents. As the marginal piles of sediment grow larger and are buried deeper, increasing pressure and rising temperature produce physical and chemical changes in them. The resulting *metamorphic rocks,* however, generally show whether they were originally sedimentary or igneous rocks. When a sedimentary pile becomes thick enough, material near the bottom may melt to form *magma.* The newly formed magma, being less dense than the rock from which it was derived, will tend to rise up, intruding its parents, and as it cools and crystallizes it will form a new igneous rock.*

What can a teacher do to build a schema and thereby prepare students for reading and learning about rocks in a unit on geology? The possibilities are many and are limited only by the teacher's imagination. The teacher could provide direct experience with rock types by bringing actual examples to class to hold and study. An expert on local geology might give a class demonstration. A field trip to observe natural rock formations could be planned. Students could be asked to find and bring to class examples of rock types. The teacher might prepare a graphic representation of the key vocabulary in the passage depicting the relationships among the ideas. Other high-interest, topically related materials such as VanRose's (2000) *Volcano and Earthquake,* Claybourne's (2000) *Read About*

---

*Adapted from Stokes/Judson/Picard, *Introduction to Geology: Physical and Historical,* 2e, © 1978, pp. 73–75. Adapted by permission of Prentice Hall, Inc., Upper Saddle River, New Jersey.

Volcanoes, or Bredeson's (2001) *Mount Saint Helens Volcano,* a brief but superbly written account of that sensational eruption and its aftermath, could be read before tackling the text. These are only a few suggestions.

For some topics, students will already possess a great deal of background knowledge but simply need to be reminded of what they know. For instance, a class of sophomore history students fails to comprehend the full significance of Julius Caesar's move to publish the activities of the Roman senate. The teacher writes on the board "Jay picks his ears," "Myra sniffs glue." Jay and Myra, students in the class who have secretly agreed to participate in the put-on, begin protesting vehemently as the others roar. "The point," the teacher says, "is, how many of you would like to have your foolish acts made public?" Caesar felt that the senators were behaving without decorum, she goes on to explain, and believed that having their behavior posted for all to read would pressure them into changing their ways. She then apologizes to Myra and Jay for libeling them. The teacher, in this example, using information gained from what we might call on-the-spot assessment, modified her instruction to include a concrete example to make her point clearer. The teacher was able to prepare her students for new learning by linking new information from a historical study of 2,000 years ago—a disparate culture and time—with the experiences and attitudes of adolescents today.

Exploit readiness by analogy as a way of tapping into everyday experiences, feelings, and behaviors of today's adolescents.

With other topics, students will have great gaps in knowledge that will need to be bridged before they can be expected to profit from their reading and learning (Carr & Thompson, 1996; Gaultney, 1995; McKeown, Beck, Sinatra, & Loxterman, 1992). We often take too much for granted when we assign readings or begin lectures or lab activities. We assume students have all the prerequisite knowledge for easy assimilation of the new ideas and facts they will encounter. For instance, in spite of the popularity of a topic such as baseball, many students do not possess a sophisticated baseball schema. Two early and now "classic" studies on the role of prior knowledge in comprehension demonstrated that students who were similar in reading ability performed differently on a comprehension exercise concerning a passage about baseball, depending on their level of prior knowledge about that subject (Spilich, Vesonder, Chiesi, & Voss, 1979). Similarly, Hayes and Tierney (1980) found that high school students who had difficulty reading and recalling newspaper reports of cricket matches improved their performance dramatically when they received instruction on the nature of the game of cricket before reading the newspaper reports. Findings such as these have been replicated in numerous studies over the past decade (Pressley, 2000; Symons & Pressley, 1993; Tobias, 1994).

Help Set Meaningful Purposes for Learning

Thirty years ago, Illich advocated a curriculum that engendered "self-motivated learning instead of employing teachers to bribe or compel the student to find the time and the will to learn" (1970, p. 104). Three decades later Illich's recommendation is as viable as ever (Deci, Koestner, Ryan, & Cameron, 2001; Guthrie & Wigfield, 1997). Students become independent knowledge seekers when they perceive what they are learning to be personally meaningful and relevant to their lives and futures. On one level, then, we are suggesting that meaningful purposes for learning can be established only when the learning itself is meaningful.

On a practical level, setting meaningful purposes for learning is essential to remaining focused on an activity. For example, consider this often-repeated scenario. You are assigned a textbook chapter to read as homework. As you read, you realize that your eyes just seem to be moving over words; you're not sure what to concentrate on or what to gloss over. You decide to try to remember facts, but you're not sure why. You realize that you have not been given any direction on *how* to read. In other words, you have not been provided a *purpose* for reading, and figuring out what you are expected to recall as a result of your reading becomes a matter of guesswork. Unfortunately, by studying the facts of the chapter, you guessed incorrectly. Your examination on the chapter is an essay test with conceptual questions. There is a bright spot in this story, however. At least you attempted to set your own purpose for reading, even though you were not provided with one. Many students have not learned to establish a reason for reading before they begin a reading assignment. We have a responsibility for setting clear expectations for students when making reading assignments and for showing students how to read to meet those expectations. Furthermore, we all need to provide instruction in helping students learn how to set their own purposes for reading.

Help students recognize the link between what you're asking them to learn and their own personal need to know.

This guideline applies equally to lectures, labs, and other learning experiences in addition to reading. Students should be made aware of what they are about to learn and, more important, why the content is being discussed and studied. To tell students that "You must learn this because I say so" is not a meaningful purpose for learning. Instead, try to make students aware of real-world purposes for learning. That is, by linking the learning of course content to students' own needs, issues, concerns, and interests inside and outside of school, we can show them the function and meaningfulness of learning (Edwards, 2001). In the next major section of this chapter we offer several examples of middle and secondary school teachers using creative means to make learning purposeful for their students—by demonstrating for the athletes in a math class how math can be used to compile sports statistics, for example.

Preteach Critical Concepts and Vocabulary

With some content, particularly content for which students have limited schemata, deciding how much to preteach can seem overwhelming. Obviously, all new concepts and all unfamiliar terms cannot be taught. Some researchers (Anderson & Nagy, 1992; Nagy, 1997; Nagy, Anderson, & Herman, 1987) have speculated that if teachers concentrated on teaching students unfamiliar words, that is all they would have time to do every day! We recommend here, as we recommend throughout this book, that when deciding what to preteach—or, for that matter, when deciding on any content to teach—emphasize the *most important* ideas and information to be learned. Not all information is vital; not all of it needs to be taught directly, nor should it be. Normally, students are under the impression that every idea and each bit of information in a chapter is of equal importance. The ways in which you prepare students to learn can help dispel this misconception.

CHANNELING KNOWLEDGE AND INTEREST WITH READINESS STRATEGIES

Direct Experiences

While the learning styles debate goes on, one self-evident truth about teaching and learning is that nothing beats direct experience for anchoring new information in memory. As students move through the grades, content becomes increasingly abstract and disconnected from their day-to-day lives. Simple narratives become replaced by complex expository prose; neighborhood and community topics fade away as world-level issues are introduced; and manipulatives disappear as students are asked to master complex scientific and mathematical processes using mental operations. Yet, middle and secondary school students continue to need *grounded* approaches to learning that help them make tangible connections to increasingly abstract ideas and processes. Concrete, firsthand learning activities become **experiential referents** for future learning.

Experiential referents as shared readiness experiences bind a community of learners and allow teachers to regularly remind students, as a topic is further explored, that "we have all done this together, we have all witnessed this phenomenon, we have all made this common discovery." Frequent references to shared experiences increase students' chances of making connections between what they learned as a result of the experience and the new information they're encountering.

Direct experiences, to which students' subsequent learning might be anchored, can include any type of field trip. Middle and secondary school teachers in the Detroit area, for instance, often take advantage of the living history museum of Greenfield Village. On more than 100 acres, Henry Ford preserved such American relics as Edison's New Jersey laboratory with the original light bulb and phonographic inventions, the Wright brothers' original bicycle shop, and Henry Ford's garage where his first automobile was built and where the garage wall had to be broken open to allow clearance for the car. Additionally, there are active wheelwrights, coopers, glass blowers, and blacksmiths, along with an original inn serving food in the style of the 1850s. This is a grand site for providing students with a firsthand look at the history of the 19th century. Outside of Seattle, teachers can take students to authentic Indian villages to see dwellings, totems, customs, dress, and more. Along the Texas Gulf, students and teachers journey frequently to the seashore to witness whooping cranes and roseate spoonbills in their winter habitat, endangered species of all kinds in the Aransas Wildlife Refuge, the state aquarium, and the University of Texas marine

As field trips become harder to arrange, consider virtual field trips via the Internet.

biology research center on Padre Island. But even as field trips become less and less common in schools due to costs, logistics, and liability, creative ways can be devised to bring hands-on learning into the classroom.

Judy, a sixth-grade science teacher, borrowed her school's old home economics room with its four ovens for a class experiment. She arranged several food items, mixing bowls, and pizza tins on a table at the front of the room. She told her students that they were home alone and were hungry for pizza; however, without money to buy a pizza and no pizzas in the freezer, they would have to create one with the ingredients on the table. Judy divided the class into groups of three, gave each group a sheet for recording the steps involved in their pizza-making adventure, and told them to get started. Under her watchful eye, the groups discussed and gathered, mixed, poured, stirred, baked, and laughed their way through this discovery process. After the fun, Judy asked each group to show off its "pizza," identify its ingredients, and describe the steps taken to create it. Brave volunteers stepped forward to taste test the pizzas. After the class cleaned up and resettled, Judy gave the groups a handout with a detailed description of the five steps of the scientific method. On a poster board with the same five steps listed, she and the students wrote out how the steps they took to create their pizzas corresponded with the steps in the scientific method.

Judy's hands-on class experience satisfied several goals of readiness instruction. First, it immediately generated a great deal of enthusiasm on the part of the class. Second, students were allowed to become purposeful learners as they searched for the best possible ingredients and steps to create pizzas from scratch. Finally, the pizza-making activity provided students with an experiential referent for their ongoing study of the scientific method. In fact, throughout the next several days and weeks, Judy constantly referred back to the pizza-making adventure to remind students of a related aspect of the scientific method they were studying.

MEETING THE NEEDS OF DIVERSE LEARNERS IN THE CONTENT-AREA CLASSROOM

In our personal experience with eighth-grade Mexican American students from the barrio, we have discovered the crucial role direct experiences can have on their motivation for and quality of learning (Brozo, Valerio, & Salazar, 1996). Throughout a unit on Hispanic American culture, we had students explore their cultural roots within their families and with the help of community members.

Before the unit began, we took the students on a walking field trip just two blocks away from their school to visit Gracie's garden. Gracie possessed extensive Mexican folk knowledge of the healing powers of plants and herbs. As the eighth graders and we walked through her garden, she explained in a mix of English and Spanish how for generations the native peoples of South Texas, which was once part of Mexico, kept themselves healthy and cured ailments ranging from indigestion to urinary tract infections with "green medicines." Students also went to the local university to participate in Cinco de Mayo ("The Fifth of May," a Mexican American holiday) festivities. There the eighth graders enjoyed a talk and demonstration from a local Mexican American scholar on the curative benefits of herbs and plants. These experiences helped provide the students with a common reference and relevant background information for the stories and books we read about Mexican American folk medicines and culture.

Another way we were able to integrate direct experiences into the unit while taking advantage of community and cultural resources was through Integrated Parent Involvement Packets (IPIPs) (Prouty & Irby, 1995). The IPIPs we used were packaged in a three-ring binder. Introducing the IPIP was a letter to the parents thanking them for taking the time to participate in the unit. On the flip side of the letter was a sign-out chart with a place for the parents' and students' signatures when they completed the IPIP. Next, there was an explanation of what was required to complete the IPIP successfully. This was followed by a story by a Hispanic author along with a short biography of the author. The stories reflected authentic Hispanic cultural experiences and were meant to be read aloud by the parents and the students to one another (Hayden, 1995).

The final component of the IPIP was a hands-on activity for student and parents to share. The activities were typically suggested by the IPIP readings. For example, in one of the stories we included in the IPIPs, Sandra Cisneros's (1990) "Three Wise Guys: Un Cuento de Navidad," a Mexican American family celebrates Christmas with the smell of cinnamon in the holiday air. We then asked parents and students to make cinnamon sticks from the ingredients we provided in a zippered plastic pouch in the IPIP binder. After reading Rudolpho Anaya's (1990) "Salomon's Story," which contains information about brewing traditional teas from local herbs, parents and students were given directions and ingredients for making their own native tea, manzanilla.

Overall, our efforts to involve students directly in learning experiences based in community–school collaboration during the Hispanic culture unit resulted in the eighth graders exhibiting greater enthusiasm for learning, improved literacy behavior, and heightened awareness of their positive cultural identity.

Experts recommend that the more diverse the students, the more content should be related to their culture and experiences.

Role-Playing and Simulations

Brian introduced the study of carbon bonding to his chemistry class through one of the most unique and clever activities we have ever witnessed. With the desks moved to the walls of the classroom leaving a large open area in the middle, Brian asked his students to stand up and then distributed paper bag vests to each of them that were labeled with a large, colorful *H, C,* or *O* (for *hydrogen, carbon,* and *oxygen*). After students donned the vests, he gave a fellow teacher a printed square dance call. He then pulled out a fiddle from its case, and with

When planning readiness activities, for the most part, the more novel and creative, the better.

everyone set, he started to play the "Carbon Bonding Hoedown" as the square dance caller called the moves. Meanwhile, students moved around the room searching for partners; by the conclusion of the square dance, all carbon atoms had bonded appropriately, as represented by the students and their vests. Everyone had fun with this activity, and it formed a meaningful introduction to the exploration of the topic. It also provided the class with a memorable experience to which Brian could refer as they progressed through the study of carbon atoms and carbon bonding.

In another example of role-playing in a chemistry classroom, Ron was preparing his students for a series of lessons on covalent bonding. To help them better understand this concept, he exploited the class's knowledge of marriage, reasoning that just as the bonding of two people in matrimony has certain conditions, so too does the bonding of atoms.

Ron split his class into two groups, telling one they represent the Doe family and the other, the Smith family. The Does were asked to select a groom for a marriage ceremony, and the Smiths were asked to select a bride. Ron gave each family an index card with background information to establish a context for forging a successful marriage contract between the two families. As it happens, the two families have had a long-standing dispute, the resolution of which depends upon the terms of the marriage agreement being acceptable to both groups. The Does own land whereas the Smiths own seeds. The groups appointed negotiators to meet and work out the contract. Once both families agreed to the terms, the happy couple was joined in matrimony amid a festive class atmosphere. Ron even brought out a cake for the occasion.

While the class settled down to enjoy the confection, Ron put the activity in chemical terms. Using the graphic display in Figure 5.1, he explained that all

FIGURE 5.1 Marriage Bonding as an Analogy for Covalent Bonding

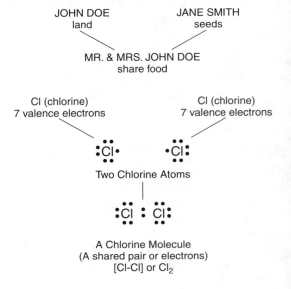

atoms strive to become noble gases by having eight valence electrons. Two atoms will come together and share a bond to reach this goal. He went on to ask the students to imagine the Doe and Smith families are atoms and the seeds and lands are electrons. As long as the couple stays married and share that bond, they will share the seeds and land between the families. Both families will have food and will prosper together. At the atomic level, when atoms share electrons and form a noble gas, the result is covalent bonding.

MEETING THE NEEDS OF DIVERSE LEARNERS IN THE CONTENT-AREA CLASSROOM

Inclusion is the law, which means you will be responsible for teaching students with learning disabilities in your classroom.

Martin's role as a special education teacher has changed over the past few years. At one time all students were pulled out of their regular classes and provided separate modified instruction in math, science, history, and English in a self-contained environment. Today, Martin's caseload of special education students is attending all regular classes where he provides instructional and classroom management assistance to teachers and direct help for his students. His overall goal is to sensitize the regular education teacher to the need to modify ways information is disseminated and to help create an engaging learning environment that will hold the attention of his special learners.

In a 10th-grade history class, for example, Martin worked with the teacher on a readiness activity that had been successful in his self-contained setting. One of his principal objectives for a unit about how the American colonies gained their freedom is to develop a thorough understanding of the concept of *taxation without representation*. Martin knew that in the past his students were reasonably excited about the topic, but he found in his assessments that they failed to grasp the significance of the essential concepts leading to a full understanding of the antecedents and consequences of the American Revolution. Martin also knew that the more he transformed lifeless textual information into something tangible and personal, the greater the students' involvement and the more they seemed to learn.

As a motivator and as a way of personalizing the concept, Martin and the history teacher had the class participate in a simulation activity. They called it a *government experiment* as they handed out written directions and guided the class through them. The students were divided into two groups: one was called the "Oros" and the other the "Bindus." Martin appointed himself the king of the Oros, while the history teacher joined the side of the Bindus. Each group was given a set of directions for electing representatives to make laws or rules. The Bindus were told they could only make rules that applied to themselves, whereas the Oros could impose rules on the Bindus if they chose. Each group also was given a lump sum of 1,000 play dollars for its treasury.

Martin, as king of the Oros, immediately began imposing laws on the Bindus that roughly paralleled the Stamp Act and the Tea Act. The "Paper and Pencil Rule" taxed every Bindu 5 dollars for every pencil, pen, and piece of paper used; the "Pop Rule" taxed the Bindus 10 dollars for having a soda or any other drink in class (the history teacher permitted his students to have soft drinks in the classroom). Interestingly, the turn of events in the history classroom resembled what had happened between the British and the American colonies. Complaining fell on deaf ears, so at first the Bindus gave in to the Oros' rules. Soon, however, the Bindus began to protest— first by not bringing paper or pencils to class and then by simply ignoring the rule and disdainfully using as many sheets of paper and pencils as they wished. The same thing happened with their soda drinking. Soon the Bindus were challenging the Oros' authority by drinking without paying taxes. By week's end, the Oros were debating among themselves as to whether they should drop the taxes or impose penalties and stiffer taxes, while the Bindus were prepared to resist at all costs.

At this point, Martin asked the class to analyze its situation. The history teacher and the Bindus argued that it was extremely unfair for a separate group of people to tell them what to do. They said they wanted and were able to take care of themselves. One student put it succinctly to the Oros: "What gives you the right to tax us?" The Oros had never really considered this question. They behaved as though there was only one way to behave. Martin and the history teacher took advantage of the students' self-discovery about what can happen when one group imposes rules on another group against its will by having the students draw parallels to the conditions that led to war between the British and the colonies. They asked students to divide a sheet of paper in half. On one side, they were to list the rules imposed by the Oros and the Bindus' reactions to those rules. Then, as they read and studied the chapter, they were to list on the other side of the sheet the events that took place in colonial America just before the Revolutionary War.

In yet another excellent simulation experience, Jennifer prepared her sixth graders for the study of westward expansion by setting up a wagonmaster election. After asking four students to join her, she formed groups of three with the rest of the class. The groups were given a scenario describing that they were pioneers in the 1850s about to go on an adventure to the West. Before they took their trip, however, they needed to select the best possible wagonmaster for the job. Groups were given rating sheets with critical criteria for a good wagonmaster, such as being experienced in dealing with Indians, knowledgeable about the best water sources and smoothest trails, and so on. Meanwhile, the four students Jennifer had chosen were to be the individuals vying for the job of wagonmaster. Each was given a name, a brief biography, and a few minutes to prepare for his pitch to the pioneers. When ready, each character, like "Calico Cody," told the groups in impassioned tones why he was the best suited for the job, given the many successful wagon trains he had led back and forth across Indian territories. After all wagonmaster candidates presented themselves, the pioneers checked their ratings and voted on their top choice. This activity and the discussion that followed served as a highly motivating and instructive way to prepare students for the topic.

Debates and Discussions

As we have said throughout this book, there are obvious differences between classrooms where students are expected to be passive receivers of information and ideas and classrooms where students are active participants in the learning process. Being a good lecturer in the middle and upper grades is not enough; students learn and remember best when they participate in the dialog about class topics (Barton, 1995; Parker, 2001). Samuel Johnson put it best more than 200 years ago when he said; "The seeds of knowledge may be planted in solitude, but must be cultivated in public" (Boswell, 1979, p. 121).

Providing young adults plenty of opportunities to engage in public discourse is often a goal of middle and secondary school teachers, but it presents dilemmas that act to limit the extent to which discussion techniques are employed in content-area classrooms (Larson, 1999). For example, In spite of our numerous demonstrations of ways to conduct class discussions, teachers often respond that it's never as easy for them as we make it appear. They are often hesitant to plan discussions because some of their students act immaturely. Yet, they believe that immature discussants need to engage in discussions if they are ever to become skillful at it. And they are right. The reluctance is based on the fear that students will get out of control. One teacher told us flatly, "A Friday afternoon discussion, forget it!"

Nonetheless, teachers can take measures to increase the likelihood of successful classroom discussions. For instance, Patty, a seventh-grade language arts teacher, spends a considerable amount of time at the beginning of each school year teaching her students about respect and about listening. She stresses that it is important to her that each student in her class has a voice, but of equal importance is that students allow others to have a voice as well. Building community at the front end of a new year pays rich dividends during the remainder of the year in the form of students who are more considerate of one another, who are more willing and comfortable risk takers, and who appreciate the importance of the social construction of knowledge (Larson, 1999).

Teachers who desire to exploit the learning potential of class discussion often tend to undermine it by doing most of the talking and asking most of the questions (Alvermann, O'Brien, & Dillon, 1990; Barton, 1995). These practices inhibit rather than foster the enrichment of understanding through the exchange of viewpoints. The goal is to encourage and orchestrate discussions that result in more student–student interaction patterns rather than student–teacher patterns (Guzzetti & Williams, 1996; Wyatt & Willis, 2000). The following alternatives to questioning and teacher-dominated discussions provide strategies for increasing student involvement in class talk and discussion:

Students will improve their abilities to debate and discuss when given frequent opportunities to do so.

- Make a declarative or factual statement.
- Make a reflective statement.
- Describe the student's state of mind.
- Invite the student to elaborate on a statement.
- Encourage the student to ask a question.
- Encourage students to ask questions of one another.
- Maintain a deliberate silence.
- Encourage other students to answer questions posed to you.
- Help students link new information to their prior knowledge.
- Model good listening strategies.
- Allow for small-group brainstorming first before whole-group interaction.

Because family conversation and discussion are rare today, class discussions are all the more crucial for building mental and verbal abilities.

The following example demonstrates how a teacher can employ effective student-centered discussion strategies in preparation for reading and learning.

An economics class preparing to read and learn about the effects of a recession on the economy watched as the teacher wrote the word *recession* in large letters on the board. Without saying anything, he waited for students to react, question, and elaborate. In no time, students began to make associations with the word. These initial associations with the concept provided students with the opportunity to find associations with their prior knowledge. As students answered, the teacher wrote their responses on the board while purposely avoiding reacting to every response. Responses such as "inflation" and "higher gas prices" were typical, but everyone was surprised to hear the word "grounded" shouted out by a student in the corner. Instead of asking a question himself, the teacher asked if anyone had a question for this student. Students were eager to find out what "grounded" had to do with recession and pressed the student for an explanation. She explained that she had once inflated her parents' already whopping phone bill during a financially tight period that she said was caused by a recession. Her parents punished her by taking away her phone privileges and restricting her after-school activity for a couple of weeks. By using discussion as a readiness-to-learn activity, the teacher helped students develop an awareness of their network of associations and allowed them to listen to one another, weigh, reject, revise, and integrate ideas in their own minds. The grounded student's contribution turned out to be profitable because the textbook chapter they were assigned to read devoted a major section to the everyday, personal effects of a recession.

After the discussion, the teacher restated students' initial associations with the concept. This allowed students to reflect on their own thinking and offer any new ideas about the concept *recession*. They could verbalize associations that had been elaborated or changed through the discussion and probe their memories to expand on their prior knowledge. Interestingly, several other personal connections with the topic were discovered. One student talked about having to limit his "cruising" because he couldn't afford to waste gas. Another mentioned that his brother had to put off buying a house because interest rates were too high. When the class ended, the students had a better idea of how much they knew about the topic, and the teacher, who encouraged student-centered discussion, had a good picture of his students' existing knowledge. With this information, the preparatory phase of instruction can be adjusted.

Middle and secondary school teachers can use many other simple discussion techniques to energize the content-area classroom and heighten enthusiasm for learning (Green, 2000). Here are some of the best that we have witnessed.

■ *Turn-to-Your-Neighbor-and-Discuss.*   This is simple to implement. Before beginning an exploration of new content, ask students to consider a problem or question or make a prediction, then turn to the classmate sitting next to them and discuss a response. Limit the time for a response so students will start thinking quickly and stay on task. Thirty seconds to a minute may be best, though with weightier questions and problems, more time may be needed. As students are discussing, move around the room to monitor their conversations and encourage equal participation. After the brief discussions, you can ask students to share their ideas without necessarily revealing the exact nature of the content to be presented. We have seen this strategy used successfully to overcome the problem of only the effusive students answering a whole-class discussion question. When all students are given even a brief opportunity to think and say something about a topic with one other, they seem to be better prepared to offer their comments afterward to the whole class.

The turn-to-your-neighbor-and-discuss strategy can help all students become more involved in classroom discussions.

■ *Think-Pair-Square-Share.*   This discussion strategy is very similar to the one just described. After being given an issue, problem, or question, ask students to think alone for a short period of time, then pair up with someone to share their thoughts. Then have pairs of students share with other pairs, forming, in effect, small groups of four students. Again, your role as teacher is to monitor the brief discussions and elicit responses afterward. Be sure to encourage student pairs not to automatically adopt the ideas and solutions of their partners. These short-term discussion strategies actually work best when a diversity of perspectives are expressed.

■ *Round Robin.*   After placing students in or forming groups of three to five, pose a problem or question and have each one go around the circle quickly sharing ideas or solutions. You can give students one opportunity to "pass" on a response, but eventually every student must respond. This technique is used most effectively when, after initial clockwise sharing, students are asked to write down on a single piece of paper each of their responses. This allows all opinions and ideas of the groups to be brought to the teacher's and the rest of their classmates' attention. It also provides a record of the group's thinking, which might be used in grading.

■ *Inside-Outside Circles.*   We have immensely enjoyed participating in this discussion strategy, so much so that we use it often in our own university classes. It offers a novel format and can bring about face-to-face dialoging between students who might never have the opportunity otherwise.

Students stand and face each other in two concentric circles. The inside circle faces out and the outside circle faces in. After posing a readiness problem or question, ask students to discuss ideas and answers with the person standing most directly in front of them. The interesting aspect of this technique is that at any time you can ask the inner or outer circle to rotate until you say "stop." Then the discussion can begin anew. After a few rotations, we randomly ask individual students to share their own ideas or those of the person(s) with whom they have been discussing. The advantage of this strategy is the variety of inputs possible through simply rotating the circles of students. Be sure to make enough space in the room for this discussion activity, and move about the circle to listen in on students' brainstorming.

A variation on the Inside-Outside Circles technique is one called **Line-Ups**. When classroom space is too limited for two concentric circles, you can get essentially the same benefits of this approach by forming two lines of students close enough together so that they can face each other and discuss. Instead of rotating circles as in the previous technique, have one of the lines move down. When this happens, students on the ends will not have someone directly in front of them, so they can walk around to the end of the other line to begin a conversation with a new student.

■ *Value Lines.* This approach to readiness discussion is especially useful when preparing to present students with content that evokes strong responses and controversy or when you want students to take a stand on an issue. You can begin by creating an imaginary line or symbolic line in the classroom. We have seen teachers isolate a row of desks in the middle of the room to create a line. A long strip of colored paper or even a piece of yarn can work. Next, you read a statement or make an assertion and ask students to move to one side of the line reserved for those who agree with it and the other side for those who disagree. Then have the students turn to another person on their side of the line and discuss why they agree or disagree with the statement. After a short while, have students converse with someone across the line to share why they believe the way they do. At any time, you can ask pairs of opposing conversants to give their opinions and ideas. As you monitor discussion, encourage respectful disagreements and polite arguing.

■ *Fishbowl Discussions.* With this technique, a small group of students is asked to discuss an issue or problem while another group of students looks on. The idea of the fishbowl is that the outside group must listen but not contribute to the deliberations of the students "in the fishbowl." At some point during the discussion, those looking in should be given an opportunity to discuss among themselves their reactions to the conversation they observed. Then you can ask both groups to share with the entire class the nature of their discussions. This approach to discussion allows the outside group to assess and critique the ideas of the fishbowl discussants.

■ *Mock Trials.* A much more elaborate debate strategy as compared with those described previously is conducting a mock trail in the classroom (Beck, 1999).

Pennie's seventh-grade class was poised to read the breathtaking courtroom chapters in Harper Lee's (1960) English-curriculum stalwart, *To Kill a Mockingbird*. Instead of a teacher-led oral review to bring students to the point of this new episode in the novel, she organized the class for a simulated court scene of their own. Here was the premise for the defense:

You are lawyers representing 18-year-old Michael Soo in a court case. Michael, a Korean American, along with his father and brother are being charged with theft of a motorcycle owned by 19-year-old John Adams.

Here are the facts presented to you by Michael Soo:

On the morning of Thursday, October 12, 2000, Michael met Mr. Adams in Mr. Adams's driveway to look at a Suzuki motorcycle John was selling. Michael test-rode the bike and then negotiated a purchase price with John of $2,000. Because his father was going to help pay for the motorcycle, Michael hoped he would return the following day, Friday, to buy the motorcycle.

Michael went home, and when his father returned from work at 6:00 p.m., he talked with him about buying the motorcycle. Michael's father said before he would help pay for the bike, he would need to see it first.

Michael, his father, and his younger brother drove to John Adams's house around 8:30 p.m. to look at the bike. There were no lights on in the house. Michael rang the doorbell, but no one answered. Michael's father aimed the truck so the headlights would shine on the motorcycle that was parked in the driveway. The three of them then inspected the bike.

Michael's father told Michael he wouldn't pay $2,000 for the motorcycle because he didn't think it was worth that much money. John Adams had not returned by the time Michael, his father, and brother drove home. It was 9:15 p.m. Michael decided he would keep looking for a better deal on a Suzuki motorcycle.

Two days later, Saturday, police officers came to Michael's house asking questions. They explained that John Adams's motorcycle had been stolen and that Michael, his father, and brother had been seen late Thursday evening at the scene of the crime. The Soos denied any involvement, explaining their purpose for being at John Adams's home Thursday evening.

Granting a police request to look around, the officers found in the Soo's garage hundreds of motorcycle parts and two or three partially built motorcycles. Many of the parts had the Suzuki name and logo on them. The Soos explained that motorcycles were their hobby and that they had owned several Suzuki motorcycles in the past. Unfortunately, they could not find receipts of purchase for any of the motorcycles or parts.

Michael, his father, and brother were then issued a warrant for their arrest for stealing John Adams's motorcycle.

It is your job as a legal team to prove the Soos are being falsely accused because they are Korean American.

Pennie formed several groups and made certain each student had a role. For instance, there were teams of lawyers representing the Soos and John Adams,

Go to Web Resources for Chapter 5 at *http://www. prenhall.com/brozo* and look for mock trials.

witnesses, and a jury. Other individuals played the part of a judge, a bailiff, and Michael and John. Her students performed their roles with flare and feeling, swept up in the moment by an imaginary setting and list of accusations that seemed all too real. When the jury found in favor of the plaintiff, John, the stage was set perfectly for reading about what was to happen to Atticus, Bob and Mayella Ewell, and Tom Robinson. With this readiness strategy, Pennie had created a context that brought the issue of racial prejudice into the present day, set the role-play in a place similar to the one in the novel, and made the role-play characters ones the students might recognize from their own communities and neighborhoods. Pennie's students couldn't wait to find out if Tom Robinson's fate would be similar to Michael's in their role-play.

Cheng, a ninth-grade teacher, used writing, cooperative learning, and a class debate in the form of a mock trial to arouse students' interest in the topic of equal rights and opportunities in their American citizenship class. Cheng introduced students to the topic by dividing them into two groups. First, he had the students read about laws and regulations developed in the United States to promote equal opportunity. Then he distributed a written scenario of discrimination to Group 1 and an alternative version of the same scenario to Group 2.

Group 1: You are the lawyers representing the Jackson family in a court case. Mr. and Mrs. Jackson wanted to buy a large house in an upper-middle-class suburb of a major city. They found a house for sale by the owner that was just the right size for themselves and their two children. The Jacksons called in advance to set up an appointment to see the house. The owner, Mr. Simon, was discourteous when the Jacksons arrived and let them into his house only after telling them he was convinced it would soon be sold to another party.

The Jacksons were very impressed with Mr. Simon's house. They were told by their bank that if they chose to buy the house, they would be approved for a loan. When the Jacksons contacted Mr. Simon the next day to make an offer, he told them he was not going to sell it to them. When asked why, he said flatly that he "preferred not to."

Mr. and Mrs. Jackson were very upset. They felt that they were being denied the house because they were African American.

As the lawyers for the Jacksons, your job is to convince the judge that Mr. Simon was discriminating against the Jacksons on the basis of their race. In your group:

1. List as many reasons as you can why the Jackson family should be allowed to buy Mr. Simon's house. Make sure your arguments make sense and seem fair.

2. Choose a spokesperson who will present your case to the judge.

Group 2: You are the lawyers representing Mr. Simon in a court case. Mr. Simon is a hard-working, law-abiding citizen who has owned his large suburban home for 17 years.

Go to Web Resources for Chapter 5 at *http://www. prenhall.com/brozo* and look for *To Kill a Mockingbird.*

Mock trials increase students' motivation to learn and can move them to higher levels of critical literacy.

A couple of months ago, he came home from work late in the evening. As he attempted to unlock his front door, he was accosted by two men, who forced him inside at gunpoint. For the next hour, one of the thieves held a gun to his head while the other raced through the house taking valuables and money. Before leaving, the men took Mr. Simon's wallet, watch, and jewelry, then knocked him unconscious. The two robbers were African American.

Word of the incident swept through the all-white suburb, where fear was mixed with disgust.

Mr. Simon decided to sell his house and move to a more rural part of the state to get away from the crime influence of a nearby large city. An African American family, the Jacksons, looked through his house and wanted to buy it, but Mr. Simon chose not to sell to them.

Mr. Simon is now being sued by the Jacksons because they feel they were unfairly discriminated against because of their race.

As the lawyers for Mr. Simon, your job is to convince the judge that he, as owner of the property, has the right to decide who may or may not purchase his home. In your group:

1. List as many reasons as you can why Mr. Simon has the right to make the decision he made. Make sure your arguments make sense and seem fair.

2. Choose a spokesperson who will present your case to the judge.

Cheng gave both groups enough time to generate arguments and formulate a defense for their respective clients. He then identified himself as the judge and asked the spokesperson for the Jacksons and Mr. Simon to present their cases. Afterward, Cheng invited further comment from the rest of the class. He thanked the groups for their fine work and said the next step would involve doing more research on how similar cases were resolved in the past. At this point, Cheng directed the students to a section in their textbook that discussed several similar discrimination cases and asked them to read it carefully for homework.

By having his students work together to think about, write, and present their ideas and beliefs, Cheng used conflicting perspectives to generate arguments and discussion about the topic of equal rights. After this activity, students brought a heightened level of enthusiasm and interest to their textbook reading assignment because they were eager to discover how discrimination cases similar to theirs had been resolved in the past.

Pennie's and Cheng's class readiness activities demonstrate clearly how student talk can lead to meaning making and intertextual tying—critical prerequisites for future learning. With simple and effective class discussions as students begin to explore a new topic, teachers can assess how much students already know about the topic and vary the degree or emphasis of preteaching relative to what they discover. In addition, teachers who use discussion create a learning environment that fosters a free exchange of different viewpoints, which helps students actively shape their own knowledge and enrich and refine their understandings of a topic (Alvermann et al., 1996; Barnitz, 1994; Unrau & Ruddell, 1995).

Guest Speakers and Performers

We watched the eyes of a group of seventh graders grow to saucer proportions as a local ornithologist walked into the classroom with a great horned owl on one arm and an osprey on the other—both nearly 2 feet tall! The guest speaker explained the life habits of these birds of prey and gave demonstrations. Students asked questions and were nearly able to touch the birds as they gathered around the speaker. It was a memorable day for Diane's science class, especially when the osprey unexpectedly let out a loud whistling call. Thus began Diane's unit on birds of prey.

Guest speakers and performers bring firsthand learning to the classroom.

A group of Alamo battle reenactors tumbled into Hector's eighth-grade history classroom, including a Mexican soldier, a Tennessee volunteer, and a Texas frontiersman. Outfitted in authentic attire, carrying authentic weaponry, and remaining in character for the entire class period, these three performers talked about their lives and the events at the Alamo as though the battle had happened yesterday. Thus, students began the study of the Alamo with the help of these memorable guests.

In both of these cases, Diane, the science teacher, and Hector, the history teacher, were clever enough to recognize the power of bringing into class members of the community with expert knowledge. Students began their study of the topics with increased anticipation, excitement, and a store of useful new knowledge to help them better negotiate the texts and ideas to follow.

We believe that guest speakers and performers are perhaps the most underused resources teachers can gather. Even in the remotest communities there is a wealth of knowledge to be tapped—individuals who lived through critical times in history, local authors and artists, and members of the political, industrial, and scientific worlds. Often local municipalities have information services about local experts. Colleges and universities have public information offices with names and addresses of professors and notes on their areas of expertise. We recently contacted a city office for information about local Native American groups and were put in touch with a couple of organizations that supplied guest speakers to a ninth-grade teacher's classroom.

We agree with those (Hoss, 1991; Poling, 2000) who advise that to get the most out of guest speakers and performers, students and guests should be prepared. Students should be given time to generate questions, while guests should know in advance your expectations for their visit, how much time they will have, and any special requests. These preparation procedures can avoid potential problems such as embarrassing comments, rambling, or information unrelated to the topic.

Lindy Poling (2000), a high school social studies teacher, has found that guest speakers in her classroom motivate students to think more critically and provide them a personal and humorous perspective on the curriculum. Being prepared, however, is critical, and she recommends:

- contacting local organizations that provide effective guest speakers (e.g., local universities, public information offices of local municipalities, veterans and civic organizations)

- screening the guest beforehand to make certain their background truly matches the objectives of the classroom content

- preparing the guest by informing them about what students have been studying in relation to the topic of their expertise and what particular aspects of their expertise you would like emphasized in the presentation.

- establishing a careful question and answer plan that requires students to generate questions in advance and submit them to you for screening and possible forwarding to the guest speaker

Toni, a high school chemistry teacher, invited to her class a woman friend who was an organic chemist in the research and development department of a large local company. She had her students spend a couple of class periods preparing for the guest speaker by first brainstorming their areas of interest about which the guest would likely have information; these included original discoveries and patents, new and future uses of polymers, employment opportunities for women in chemistry, and the day-to-day operation of an R&D department. Toni then asked her students to form small groups based on their interests and generate a set of 10 questions each that they would like answered by the guest chemist. Toni looked over the questions and helped each group refine its list to five good questions. Meanwhile, Toni contacted her friend and told her what the students were most interested in learning. This information made it possible for the chemist to prepare effectively for the classroom visit.

When the day arrived, the school newspaper and science club wanted to cover the presentation, so a video camera was set up to record the event. The chemist gave a brief overview and then asked for questions. Each group was given the opportunity to ask all five of its questions in a set to avoid forcing the guest speaker to jump from topic to topic in a disjointed way. She brought in examples of products developed by her center, and diagrams, notes, and computer graphics on future developments. She talked from experience about her interest and schooling in chemistry and the process of gaining employment in the company. She described how patents are obtained and showed the class some of the patented products for which she was responsible. Finally, using a CD-ROM presentation, she took the class through a computer-simulated field trip of her R&D center.

Reading Young Adult Literature to Build Prior Knowledge and Generate Interest

Teachers often ask how they can get their students interested in topics that are treated so lifelessly in the textbook they lose their students to boredom. Take a topic in science, for example, such as laws of motion or environmental pollution. In such a case, many teachers would be inclined to simply assign the textbook reading, show slides or a video, and then lecture, although they know that students' interest will be minimal. As an alternative, we suggest that they

Go to Web Resources for Chapter 5 at *http://www. prenhall.com/brozo* and look for fiction and nonfiction books in the content classroom.

consider reading aloud or asking students to read one of the many outstanding books that deal with science topics, such as Homer Hickman's (1998) *Rocket Boys: A Memoir* and Abner Shimony's (1997) *Tibaldo and the Hole in the Calendar*. In addition to galvanizing the students with their narrative, these stories indirectly provide readers with a living context for science that makes the facts and details more palatable.

Students can also be introduced to topics with nonfiction books. Many teens, especially boys, prefer nonfiction to fiction (Brozo, 2002; Herz & Gallo, 1996). Unfortunately, their experiences with nonfiction in school are usually limited to textbooks (Clary, 1991; Matulka, 1997), which may contribute to their lack of interest in the first place. Many junior and senior high students are never exposed to nonfiction books that have been written specifically for them. The numbers of nonfiction titles for adolescents grows annually, making it easier for classroom teachers to identify appropriate books to incorporate into their content lessons.

In addition to the Hickman memoir mentioned previously, Richard Maurer's (1995) *Rocket! How a Toy Launched the Space Age* would be an outstanding nonfiction companion in preparation for the study of laws of physics in the science classroom. Lawrence, Rochelle, and Jack Sutin's (1996) *Jack and Rochelle: A Holocaust Story of Love and Resistance* could be offered as a prelude to the study of the Nazis and the Jews during World War II. An autobiography, this gripping account of a young couple who survived the Holocaust is filled with facts and details that help students better understand this tragic period in world history. Relevant prior knowledge of boreal ecosystems could be acquired by reading *Born Naked* (Mowat, 1995), Farley Mowat's own affectionate story of growing up in rural Canada and experiencing the wilds with his famous environmentalist father, Angus. For students about to begin a creative writing unit, *The Abracadabra Kid: A Writer's Life* (Fleischman, 1996) is a splendid prelude. This autobiography of a popular young adult writer tells in a brisk and appealing style how he began as a boy magician and ended up an award-winning writer of books for young adults. Fleischman's experiences and his numerous practical tips combine to make this an inspiring book for aspiring adolescent writers. With nonfiction books such as these, students develop schemata while reading an interesting and palatable alternative to the textbook. (See Chapter 8 for a comprehensive discussion of strategies for using trade books in the content classroom.)

Purpose-Setting Strategies

Many highly effective classroom strategies have been designed to help middle and secondary students set purposes for their reading and develop an anticipatory set for their reading and learning. In this section, we demonstrate how five particularly useful strategies—prediction, KWL, anticipation guides, lesson impressions, and SQPL—can be used to help students set meaningful purposes for and encourage higher level thinking about class topics. Furthermore, these strategies induce students to attend to topics more closely, interact with them in more meaningful ways, and combine their world knowledge with new information, resulting in broader understandings.

Prediction

One excellent way of helping students set their own purposes for reading is with prediction activities (Dermody & Speaker, 1999). Anderson (1984) has proposed that this technique is consistent with a schema-theoretic perspective of optimal reading because it helps students integrate meaningfully what they already know with what is presented on the printed page. Using a **prediction** technique, students either simply generate some form of prediction in advance of reading or read titles, headings, subheadings, or a short segment of text and, based on this limited information, predict what they expect to read in the passage. In this way, they become aware of their prior knowledge and begin to organize what they already know about the subject at hand. By making predictions, they anticipate what they will find in the text, leading them to read for the purpose of finding out if their predictions are corroborated. Countless methods can be used to help students anticipate the content of their reading.

A wonderful example of the effectiveness of using prediction for purpose setting was provided by a senior high journalism teacher. He was instructing students in editorial writing by sharing examples of editorials and analyzing them. He handed out a sheet of paper with the title "A No-Lose Proposition," by Stanley J. Lieberman, and the first paragraph, which read:

> America is the most litigious society in the world. We are suing each other at an alarming and increasing rate, and we have more lawyers per capita than any other nation. Since 1950 the number of lawyers in America has increased 250 percent. We have well over half a million lawyers—one for every 450 people. In New York state the ratio is one lawyer per 18. By contrast, the ratio in West Germany is one lawyer per 2,000.

After reading this material, the students worked in small groups and discussed the possible directions the editorial might take, given the title and the first paragraph. Each group was to make two predictions. The teacher moved around the room, listening in on each group, assisting when asked. Next, each group's predictions were presented to the whole class while the teacher wrote them on the board. A lengthy and immensely beneficial discussion then ensued, which included a class-derived definition of *litigious* and an impassioned defense of lawyers by a student whose father and mother were attorneys. An impressive amount of background and related knowledge poured out, as did the exchange and exploration of biases, opinions, and beliefs. The teacher played a facilitative role during the discussion. He prodded when necessary, refocused the conversation when it seemed to stray too far from the task of determining what the author was likely to say in the passage, and clarified points and details. When the debate over which predictions were likely to be verified by the text wound down, the students were eager to finish reading the editorial. Three agreed-on predictions remained on the board, and the students were reminded to read and discover to what extent, if any, the text supported them. After reading, the class discussed the accuracy of their predictions. No one had foreseen that the author would make a pitch for mediation as a way to unblock a clogged court system, although one prediction anticipated some kind of workable solution to this problem based on the editorial's title.

Reflect for a moment on how the preceding scene differs from the way a typical reading assignment is given—with little or no preparation or direction. By the time these students were ready to read the editorial, they had activated and elaborated their schemata for *lawyer* and related legal issues. They had developed an interest in the topic through small-group and whole-class discussions that challenged beliefs and biases and piqued curiosity. And they had developed their own purposes for reading. As a result, attention to the text and comprehension could not help but improve.

Schema theorists say reading comprehension involves constant hypothesis testing. Predictions are like hypotheses that can be confirmed, refined, extended, or rejected using evidence from the text. In this process, original predictions give way to new predictions as new information from the text is encountered, thus setting further purposes for reading.

Many variations on the prediction theme can help students develop an anticipatory set for the text information. In a 12th-grade sociology class preparing to read about the benefits and limitations of day-care centers, the teacher posed this problem:

> If you were a parent who needed to work to keep the family going, yet you desperately wanted to spend more time with your children, what would you do?

Channel students' natural desire to have the "full story" with innovative and thought-provoking prediction prompts.

In cooperative learning groups, the students talked among themselves, proposing solutions to the problem. After the entire class discussed possible solutions, their strengths, and their limitations, the teacher invited them to read the essay and find out how a working parent handled this dilemma. The students now had a purpose for reading.

In a seventh-grade health class, students working in cooperative groups were asked to generate as many words as they could within 3 minutes related to the concept *necessities to sustain life*. At the end of the 3 minutes, students were asked to arrange their words into subcategories and to be prepared to explain the logic behind them. One group clustered their words around *necessities for the body* (oxygen, food, water), *necessities for the heart* (relationships, religion), and *necessities for the mind* (books, music, art). Another group categorized their words with *work* and *fun*. After this exploration of what they already knew about the topic, students were asked to use their words and categories to predict what the reading assignment would be about. Once again, we see how this prediction strategy helped students develop purposes for reading.

Remember, prediction strategies can work equally well before lectures and experiential, hands-on activities such as labs and field trips.

From these examples, you can see that the list of ways of helping students set purposes for reading is limited only by the teacher's imagination. Other variations on the prediction strategy include KWL anticipation guides, lesson impressions, and SQPL.

KWL

KWL focuses on the student as a strategic learner and is based on three principal components: (1) recalling what is *known,* (2) determining what students *want* to learn, and (3) identifying what is *learned* (Carr & Ogle, 1987; Ogle, 1986). We strongly endorse this strategy because it can be carried out before, during, and after reading. Before reading, the student activates background knowledge and sets a purpose for reading; during reading, the student thinks critically about information and monitors learning; and after reading, the student integrates and consolidates the information read. Here we focus on the before-reading benefits of the strategy.

To give you a better idea of the kind of thinking involved in the KWL strategy, let us assume you were asked by the professor using this book to employ the strategy for Chapter 5, the chapter you are reading now. First, you would be directed to read the title, "Initiating Students to New Learning," and in small cooperative groups or as a whole class, you would brainstorm and discuss ideas and information you already hold in prior knowledge about the topic. Through discussion, a good deal of known information will be generated, and unresolved points and unanswered questions also will likely emerge. These will be saved and referred to later as issues about which you desire further information. After brainstorming and discussing, you would have a collection of ideas and facts about the chapter topic listed on a chart in the *K* (what is *known*) column.

In the next phase before reading, you would be asked to generate questions you would like answered by the text. Questions come from the brainstorming and discussion, as well as anticipated information you think will be encountered in the text. These questions comprise the entries in the second column on the chart, *W* (what you *want* to learn). By developing questions in this way, you will tend to define for yourself your purpose for reading. The result is that your reading and self-monitoring during reading will be more focused. As you read, you will pause periodically to monitor your comprehension by checking the questions from the *W* column that can be answered by what you have read. As new information is encountered, additional questions can be added to the list. Thus, purposes are refined and extended throughout reading.

Figure 5.2 depicts what you might have generated for the first two columns of the KWL chart. As you read, you would note in the *L* column new information and information that helps answer the questions you posed in the *W* column. After reading, you would be asked to discuss what you have learned from your reading. You would review the questions asked before and during reading to determine if and how they were answered. For example, in Figure 5.2, the first three questions in the *W* column can be answered fairly thoroughly with the information in this chapter. For the last question, which would remain unresolved

K (Known)	W (Want to Know)	L (Learned)
Reading readiness is important for beginning readers.	What can the classroom teacher do to prepare students for reading assignments?	
Schema theory says prior knowledge for a topic makes it easier to read about that topic.	Why is readiness important for secondary school reading?	
One strategy is to read the introduction and conclusion before reading the chapter.	What are all the things that should be done during readiness?	
	Is Directed-Reading-Thinking-Activity a good readiness strategy?	

FIGURE 5.2   KWL Chart for Chapter 5

because this chapter does not specifically discuss the Directed-Reading-Thinking-Activity strategy, you would be encouraged to conduct some personal research to gather further information about this aspect of the topic. Perhaps the professor would direct you to additional secondary reading methods textbooks or to journal articles that deal with the topic of using Directed-Reading-Thinking-Activity as a prereading strategy.

KWL is a tried and true readiness strategy for countless teachers around the country.

The KWL strategy can be applied in a variety of content areas with a range of text material. Figure 5.3, for example, is a KWL chart created by an eighth grader reading about the formation of mountains. In this example, note that the student appeared to have little prior knowledge on the topic. As a result of a liberal exchange of ideas in small groups and with the whole class, she asked some excellent questions (in the *W* column) that were answered by the reading. In cases in which students' questions cannot be answered by the text, many teachers will ask students to pursue answers to these questions through research and present their findings to the class.

Students will develop the ability to use the KWL strategy on their own through instruction that gradually shifts responsibility for initiating the strategy from you to your students (Kiefer, 2001). After you introduce the strategy with a textbook example and model KWL thinking by describing how you would develop a chart, you should ask students to implement it on their own. Cooperative groups are ideal for helping learn and extend expertise with the strategy. Your role should gradually become one of providing feedback, informally observing, discussing, and reinforcing independence and transfer. As with most content-area reading/writing/learning strategies, you can improve the likelihood that students will use this strategy on their own if you demonstrate how

K	W	L
Volcanoes help form mountains. The Rocky Mountains are very tall.	Do mountains grow? How do they erode? Why are the Rockies taller than the Smokies?	Mountains form when heat within the earth pushes up bedrock. Lava forces its way up and hardens into rock, causing mountains to grow bigger. Rain and wind wear them down. Mountains are part of a cycle—ocean sediment to solid rock pushed up to form mountains, then worn down into the sea again. Mountains in the eastern U.S. are very old. Mountains in the West are not as old.

FIGURE 5.3   An Eighth Grader's KWL Chart for the Formation of Mountains

using KWL to activate prior knowledge and set purposes for reading facilitates their class performance and helps meet your expectations for learning.

Anticipation Guides

Another highly regarded strategy for activating prior knowledge of text topics and helping students set purposes for reading is the **anticipation guide**. You should be somewhat familiar with this strategy already since you have been asked to complete an anticipation guide for each chapter of this book. This strategy involves giving students a list of statements about the topic to be studied and asking them to respond to them before reading. Guides are particularly useful when they provoke disagreement and challenge students' beliefs about a topic. They should reinforce relevant prior knowledge and modify misconceptions about the topic (Duffelmeyer & Baum, 1992; White & Johnson, 2001). This function seems especially important given research evidence indicating that students' existing prior knowledge and biases will be superimposed on text information when the two are at odds (Marshall, 1989). In other words, if misconceptions about a topic are not cleared up before reading, they may still exist after reading.

Anticipation guides should contain statements that are text and reader based. In addition, Duffelmeyer (1994) recommends the inclusion of certain

By completing the anticipation guides in this book, you know the strategy as a student might come to know it.

statements that force students to reconsider existing beliefs. He suggests that four kinds of statements have the potential to do this: (1) those that are related to the major ideas students will encounter; (2) those that activate students' prior knowledge; (3) those that are general rather than specific; and (4) those that challenge students' beliefs. We recommend that guide statements be written to appear correct but incompatible with the information students will encounter or to seem incorrect yet compatible with the information to follow.

The response format for anticipation guides should follow criteria similar to those of study guides. Students should not be asked to write extended answers to questions that resemble discussion or essay questions. Instead, have students respond with simple check marks or brief statements. But make sure the guide includes a feature that tests and confronts students' beliefs. Additionally, we suggest that guides have the extended feature (Duffelmeyer & Baum, 1992). This feature requires students to verify their responses after reading and encountering new content. This form of accountability guards against students making random responses without careful thinking.

Look at Part I of the anticipation guide designed for a health class shown in Figure 5.4. We would like you to respond to this guide so that you will have a better understanding of the points we have just made.

If we had assigned you to use this anticipation guide for an upcoming reading assignment or lecture on diet and nutrition, we would ask you first to meet in small groups and then, with the entire class, to discuss your viewpoints and share information and ideas. As you and other students debate and defend your responses, we would remain neutral by not giving away answers or taking over the discussion. Periodically, we would restate points of view or try to clarify ideas.

The extended feature of this guide is presented in Part II (Figure 5.5). It adds further learning potential to the activity by forcing you to self-interrogate and interact more elaborately with the text. Part II requires you to find ideas and information from the text or the lecture that either reinforce and verify your existing beliefs, force them to be altered or modified, or require you to completely reject them. During reading and exploration of a topic, as you encounter information related to the statements in Part I of the guide, you are asked to indicate whether the text or lecture material supports or does not support what you had previously asserted. In Part II you would be required to write where you found information that supported your initial anticipations. This can be written in the form of page numbers from a textbook, or class note entries. You would also write information that *corrects* unanticipated information.

As you can see, the anticipation guide takes advantage of prediction as a powerful prereading tool. It forces students to think about what they already know and believe about a topic and then confirm, modify, or disconfirm existing beliefs. Working with anticipation guides helps create the urge in students to know more. They confront the topic ideas and information purposefully and enthusiastically (Hurst, 2001; Strange & Wyant, 1999)).

Like study guides, discussed in Chapter 3, anticipation guides can be created for virtually any content or topic. The guide in Figure 5.6, for example, was given to students by a science teacher to stimulate prior knowledge about pollution

---

Directions: Read each statement. If you believe that a statement is true, place a check mark in the *Agree* column. If you believe the statement is false, place a check mark in the *Disagree* column. Be ready to explain your choices.

Agree   **Disagree**

_____   _____   1. About 45% of the total food dollar is spent on food away from home.

_____   _____   2. More cookbooks are being purchased today than ever before.

_____   _____   3. Soft drinks are essentially sugar.

_____   _____   4. The average person's diet consists of between 60% and 70% fat and sugar.

_____   _____   5. People are eating fewer fruits today than in the 1940s.

_____   _____   6. Many so-called primitive cultures have more nutritious diets than many affluent Americans.

_____   _____   7. Vitamin C has been used effectively to treat mental diseases.

FIGURE 5.4   Anticipation Guide for Diet and Nutrition: Part I

Directions: Now you will be reading and listening to information related to each of the statements in Part I of this guide. If the information you read supports your choices in Part I, place a check mark in the *Support* column. If the information does not support your choices, place a check mark in the *No Support* column. Write in your own words the relevant text and/or lecture information for your answer.

	Support	**No Support**	**Text/Lecture Information**
1.	_____	_____	_____
2.	_____	_____	_____
3.	_____	_____	_____
4.	_____	_____	_____
5.	_____	_____	_____
6.	_____	_____	_____
7.	_____	_____	_____

FIGURE 5.5   Anticipation Guide for Diet and Nutrition: Part II

---

and the environment. In this guide, students first guessed answers to the questions related to real-world problems with pollution. Guesses, in this case, serve as predictions. Then, as students read and studied the topic, they returned to the guide statements and verified the correctness or incorrectness of their initial answers. The situations and questions are designed to encourage various levels

Part I

Directions: Below are statements and situations related to the environment. If you agree with the statement, place a check mark in the *Agree* column. If you disagree with the statement, place a check mark in the *Disagree* column. Be prepared to explain your responses.

Agree   Disagree

_____   _____   1. A poor landowner wants to sell his land to a large chemical refinery. The environ-mentalists say there is an endangered species on the land. The court says he can't sell the land. Do you agree with the court ruling?

_____   _____   2. It doesn't matter if I recycle my aluminum cans or not. One person doesn't make a difference.

_____   _____   3. A small business garage owner goes to a vacant lot to empty motor oil into the ground. The police pick him up for suspicious behavior and find out what he has been doing. He is fined $50,000, which ruins his business and forces him into bankruptcy. Do you agree with the judgment? He says everybody else does it, so what difference does it make?

_____   _____   4. Your next-door neighbor has a beautiful yard. He sprays the plants almost every day. He never seems to be picking weeds; instead, he sprays his lawn with poison. Do you agree with his technique?

_____   _____   5. A man and his family saved for years to buy the home of their dreams. After they moved in, the younger child became very ill. He had headaches most of the time. The man eventually found out that he had bought a house on top of an old land-fill. He sued the real estate agent and lost the case. Do you agree with the court ruling?

_____   _____   6. The richest and most diverse terrestrial ecosystems on earth are the tropical forests. Some people want to develop this land for cattle grazing. Do you think that would be a good idea?

Part II

Directions: Now that we have studied facts and issues related to environmental pollution, look back at your responses to the statements in Part I. If you found support for your response, check the *Support* column below; if you didn't find support for your response, check the *No Support* column. Regardless of what column you check, write a sentence in your own words explaining your response.

	Support	No Support	Your Explanation
1.	_____	_____	_____
2.	_____	_____	_____
3.	_____	_____	_____
4.	_____	_____	_____
5.	_____	_____	_____
6.	_____	_____	_____

FIGURE 5.6   Anticipation Guide for the Topic of Environmental Pollution

of thinking, challenge students' beliefs, and focus on the key issues and points of the topic.

Although these formal examples of anticipation guides suggest a great deal of preparation time, they can be prepared very quickly and without burdensome planning or time-consuming clerical tasks. The guide statements require the most effort to compose but can be crafted during planning periods or even before class. Once the statements are developed, you can write them on the board or the overhead. To the left of the statements reserve a "Before Reading/Learning" column with "true/false" or "agree/disagree" categories. To the right of the statements place the same response options but in the "After Reading/Learning" column. Below each statement, students can write supporting information, such as the page and paragraph number where the information was found. Students should copy the statements into their notebooks with the date and title, so they can hand in their completed guides for a grade.

By forcing students to make and defend predictions, guides can help sustain interest in topics, promote active involvement with text and in discussion, and facilitate assimilation of new information into existing schemata (Merkley, 1996/97).

Lesson Impressions

This strategy helps students activate prior knowledge by developing an **impression** of what the forthcoming lesson will cover. It can be used before exposing students to content regardless of how information and ideas are delivered. In other words, this readiness strategy is equally effective for the variety of typical information sources in middle and secondary schools, such as reading material, a lecture, a guest speaker, a video, a CD-ROM, and a field trip. Lesson impressions can increase motivation by heightening anticipation and providing a meaningful purpose for learning.

The basic process of conducting a lesson impression begins with presenting students a list of words and phrases taken directly from the material to be covered. For example, Renard, an eighth-grade reading teacher, put the following words and phrases on the overhead: *CDs, penny, music, club, hidden commitments, contract, monthly selections, "return to sender," rip-off.*

The next step is to have students write what they think they are about to learn by creating a short description or narrative in which all of the words are used. Renard asked his students to write the words in their notebooks and directed them to craft short compositions on what they thought the lesson would be about, making sure to use all the words.

When students finish writing, they should be given the opportunity to exchange their written impressions with a peer. In this way, they can compare and contrast one another's predictions about the content to be covered in the forthcoming lesson, which acts to heighten their anticipation. Eventually, as many students as possible should be invited to share what they have written with the entire class. The goal is to gather a variety of impressions so that students are left with a sense that theirs or any one of their classmates' may be the most accurate.

In response to the lesson impression words Renard gave his students, Juwon created a kind of personal story about the topic. He read to the class:

> I saw an ad in a magazine that said I could buy 10 *CDs* for a *penny* if I joined this *music club*. They had all this cool music so I decided to join. After getting my first 10 choices, I received a *contract* that had all these *hidden commitments*, like I had to pick out so many *monthly selections* or I'd have to pay for those CDs that were only a penny. By then I knew this was a *rip-off*, so I packed everything back up in the box and wrote *"return to sender."*

At this point in the strategy process, you are ready to expose students to the information. It is a good idea to have them pay close attention to how what they're about to learn jibes with their readiness phase impressions. Some teachers require students to keep a record of the similarities and differences between their impressions and the actual content by creating a Venn diagram or a compare/contrast chart. We recommend such practices because they add an accountability feature that raises the level of assurance students are remaining engaged throughout the lesson.

After hearing from several others, Renard then passed around an article entitled, "Ten CDs for a Penny? If It's Too Good to Be True, It Probably Isn't." Students paired up and read sections of the short article aloud together, trading off reading paragraphs. Renard stopped them at regular intervals to ask questions and get responses based on their predictions in their lesson impressions.

Tammy, an eighth-grade science teacher, presented her students with the following words by writing them on the board:

breathing	oxygen	inhale	exhale
nose	carbon dioxide	vocal cords	lungs
mucus			

Next, she asked her students to write for 5 to 7 minutes using as many of these words as possible in their short compositions. Tammy said they could write what they expected to hear during the upcoming presentation on the human respiratory system. She urged students to be creative, incorporating the words in a song, poem, or story.

Many of the students wrote what they knew about the respiratory system, which helped Tammy discover the extent of their prior knowledge. Others who were more comfortable with the content chose to be creative and were eager to share their work before her presentation began. Tammy found her students paying closer attention during the lesson. Since she had not picked up their compositions, several students corrected their stories with the information they gleaned from the presentation. It was clear the lesson impression strategy had engendered focused listening and heightened motivation to learn due to students' desire to compare their impression texts with the content of the Tammy's presentation.

When Tammy asked students after her presentation what they liked or disliked about the strategy, their responses were consistent. They liked the

Along with factual content, lesson impressions can be just as effective when students use words to predict story content.

freedom to be creative and to have a default option in case the creative juices weren't flowing. The students further commented that they thought the lesson impression activity helped them focus on information about the respiratory system of which they were unsure. Two examples of the students' readiness compositions are below:

Student 1:

My *breathing* takes in air that contains *oxygen*. It goes through my *nose* and the *mucus* cleans the air before it enters my *lungs*. But first it goes through the *vocal cords*. After it enters my lungs, I *exhale* the *carbon dioxide* that I don't need.

Student 2:

My *nose* is very big although I'm very small. When I sneeze my *mucus* goes all over the wall. My lungs are *breathing oxygen* that's a proven fact. I exhale *carbon dioxide* and that's all I have to say about that. Please don't ask me to sing this hour, Because with my *vocal cords* the notes will be awfully sour.

SQPL

SQPL stands for Student Questions for Purposeful Learning. The strategy helps students ask questions that are important to them before reading and learning. By doing so, students heighten anticipation and engage in more purposeful exploration of the topic as they search for answers to their questions.

The first step entails crafting a thought-provoking statement and presenting it to students. A ninth-grade science teacher, Roberta, prepared her class to read an article on genetic engineering by writing this statement on the board:

Since scientists have already cloned animals as large as sheep, making exact replicas of dogs, cats, and even human beings through the process of cloning may be possible within the next few years.

The next step is to allow students to pair up and brainstorm questions they would like to have answered based on the statement. After asking her students to turn to their neighbor, Roberta told them to come up with three questions they would like answered about the statement on the board. While students worked together on their questions, Roberta moved throughout the room to monitor their progress and help clarify the assignment.

The next step involves eliciting the students' questions and writing them on the board or overhead. The goal here is to gather a variety of questions by making sure each student pair contributes at least one of its questions. We recommend that you highlight or star questions asked by more than one pair of students; these become class consensus questions. You can also consolidate questions by combining similar ones.

Roberta went around the room and gathered questions from each of the student pairs, writing them on the board. After every student had an opportunity to add a question to the total, Roberta drew the class's attention to those questions that were essentially the same, and added stars next to those questions.

Some questions, such as *How do you clone someone?* had five stars, since at least five separate pairs of students came up with the same or highly similar question. Another question *Who will get cloned?* was repeated four times, and *How much does it cost?* had three stars.

At this stage, students are ready for the presentation of the information. Like all of the readiness strategies discussed in this section and chapter, SQPL is adaptable to virtually any information source, such as reading material, lecture, discussion, video, and the Internet. Students should be directed to pay close attention to information that answers the questions the class generated, especially class consensus questions.

Roberta handed out to her students the article entitled, "Can Humans Be Cloned Like Sheep?" She alerted the class that as information is encountered that answers one of the readiness questions, the information should be written in their notebooks. Throughout the reading of the article, Roberta stopped students periodically to discuss the piece in general and answers to student questions in particular.

SQPL gives students a stake in the learning, which will improve their attitudes and increase their attention.

It is important to point out that student-generated readiness questions should not be the only perspectives students have of the content. SQPL should be one strategy among many and should not comprise the overall exploration of the topic. SQPL helps students make an investment in the learning process, since they become gatherers of information based on their own inquiry and not on prompts given them by the teacher or the textbook. Nonetheless, student questions may fail to cover critical information. Therefore, you will need to employ other strategies and methods to ensure all important aspects of the topic are considered by students.

WRITING TO PREPARE STUDENTS FOR READING AND LEARNING

Writing is especially well suited for preparing students to read and learn (Weech, 1994; Zamel, 2000). Writing before learning from text or a lecture allows students to explore what they already know about a topic, thereby building a bridge from their prior knowledge and experiences to the new information (Hamann, Schultz, Smith, & White, 1991). It also is an effective medium for self-reflection. Students can decide where they possess sufficient knowledge and where gaps in knowledge exist. Based on this information, they can seek people and resources to expand their knowledge base. Writing as a readiness-to-learn strategy can also increase student motivation and interest.

Readiness Writing to Learn Content Vocabulary

Sena teaches 10th-grade geometry. She had been frustrated with the ways she was teaching vocabulary—using rote memorization techniques, drill sheets, and glossaries. Last year Sena decided to try to make vocabulary learning in geometry class more fun for her students and herself by using a creative writing activity.

Early in the new school year, Sena had her students form groups of three and then gave all her students a list of terms they would encounter often in geometry along with their definitions. After going over the terms and clarifying the simple definitions, Sena asked her students to write a story with the words. Students were to use at least five of the geometry terms in their story and use them in an everyday rather than a geometry context. To help clarify the assignment, she wrote on the board, "The sheriff called out, 'Come out with your hands up; we have you circumscribed!' "

The groups worked happily on this assignment, laughing and exclaiming quietly as they completed their stories. All the while, Sena worked on a story of her own. When they had finished, volunteers from each group were asked to share their stories with the class. One group had written the following story:

> A very pretty girl stood nervously as not one but two boys expressed their *paralleled* love for her. Now, her little love *triangle* had been discovered, and she had to choose between the two. She took a stick and *circumscribed* an *area* in the dirt around them. The boys were to fight it out. One of the boys was quick and punched the other bigger boy on his *square* jaw. The big boy fell to the ground, and the girl happily accepted the winning boy's love *axiom*. As the new couple walked away, their arms formed an *angle* that would last forever.

Over different content in the same geometry class, Sena used the same vocabulary-writing strategy as readiness. One of her students wrote:

> I remember the day my life was *intercepted* by the man who I would later marry. He rode into town on horseback, a stranger whose face I had never seen before. Apparently, he was involved in a dangerous *triangle* of crime and deceit, for when he rode up to the saloon he was angrily confronted by a group of men who were up to no good. He kept his cool, even as they forced him to an open *quadrant* of town. A couple of men drew two *circles* in the dirt and demanded that there be a shoot-out to settle their dispute. Just as it was about to begin our eyes met and we both sensed a strong desire to meet. When the dust settled and I found courage to open my eyes, I was relieved to see him walking straight toward me. I have to admit the danger is what initially attracted me to him, but my gut feeling did not lie for we will be together for all *infinity*.

Examples of writing in math can be found throughout this book. See Chapters 3 and 7 for additional ideas.

The writing strategy turned out to be fun and helped lay the foundation for future learning of key geometry terminology. Sena noticed that as these terms began to appear and be used in class, her students were much more prepared for them and seemed better able to grasp their meanings in the context of geometry.

Writing Solutions to Problems Posed Before Reading

Many of the purpose-setting activities just discussed can be easily adapted to include a writing component. For instance, a seventh-grade geography class preparing to study the Kalahari bushpeople was asked to write a solution to this problem:

> The men have gone to work the big farms for harvest season. The women and children have not eaten meat in several weeks. One morning a herd of giraffe are spotted in the bush nearby. Because you are the most experienced hunter, you are asked to kill a giraffe. You are sent off alone with only a spear. How will you succeed?

In small groups, the students were given the chance to discuss ideas for solving the problem before writing. After composing their answers, several volunteers shared them with the class. Some of the more inventive solutions are as follows: Dig a big hole and cover it with grass and leaves so that the giraffe will fall into it; wait hidden in a tree that has the giraffe's most irresistible leaves, and when the giraffe comes by to eat, lasso it. Other solutions anticipated what really happens: Put poison on a spear tip, sneak up on a giraffe, and spear it. Many students embedded their solution in stories. The teacher then asked the class to read the text, which explained bushpeople hunting strategies and included a description of a giraffe hunt. As they read, students compared their solutions with the text's.

Learning Logs

Another outstanding way of using writing to help students prepare for learning by thinking about new knowledge in terms of preexisting knowledge is with **learning logs** (Newkirk, 1986; Lee, 1997). First introduced in Chapter 3, this writing strategy involves students in keeping notebooks in content classrooms to record what they already know about a topic; what they desire to know about the topic; and then, after reading, lecture, and class discussion, an amalgamation of these two aspects with what they have learned (Audet, Hichman, & Dobrynina, 1996). The amalgamation is in essence a revision of their first interpretations of the content.

Learning logs give journal writing a content focus by helping students document what they know and what they are learning.

Cassie kept a learning log in sixth-grade social studies class, in preparing to read and study a unit on the American Revolution, a topic which she felt she had a great deal of familiarity with. She wrote at length about how the war started, some of the battles, Washington's role, the effect of losing on the British and victory on the colonies, and so on. She had little to ask of herself in terms of what she further desired to learn; she thought she had the Revolutionary War down cold. She wrote in her log, "I want to refresh my memory." But then her teacher gave the class a trade book to read as a prelude to reading the text—*Thomas* (1998) by Bonnie Pryor. Cassie had never read a fictionalized account of the Revolutionary War and was doubtful about whether she could discover any new fact or detail that had been overlooked by her present or past texts. As she read the book, though, a change began taking place, as reflected in the entries in her log:

> I didn't know families were split about how they felt about the war. I didn't realize there were so many colonists who were against the war and for the British. I wonder how these people were treated during the war?

Further into the book, she found an answer to her question:

I can't believe how cruel the colonists who supported the war were to those who didn't support the war. They were treated like enemies. Thomas was not helping the Americans. He and his family were just minding their own business, and for that he gets captured and his family's cabin is burned. I wonder what's going to happen to Thomas and his mom, and his little sisters for that matter.

The trade book forced Cassie to reconsider her beliefs about the Revolutionary War in light of some new and, to her, startling information. The learning log facilitated this process of reinterpretation. When Cassie completed the book, she wrote another extended entry in her log, where she recorded the same facts she had written before reading the book but this time qualifying each fact with new information and ideas she had gleaned from the trade book.

PRETEACHING CRITICAL VOCABULARY AND CONCEPTS

Graphic Organizers and Word Webs

Schema theory informs us that it is best to preteach the overarching concepts and terms that provide the mental framework for building new knowledge structures (Dye, 2000; Robinson, 1998). One excellent way to teach terms and concepts directly is with **graphic organizers** (Egan, 1999; Robinson, Katayama, & DuBois, 1998) and **word webs** (Johnson & Rasmussen, 1998). These are diagrams of the relationships among the key concepts and terms. The main difference between the two is that the graphic organizer is a teacher-provided structured overview, whereas the word web is developed by students with teacher guidance.

The graphic organizer in Figure 5.7 was given to eighth graders in a history class before they began reading in their texts about the Industrial Revolution. An organizer such as this enables students to see the structure of the text material and anchors in memory the big ideas to which details and facts can be attached.

Seeing relationships among terms and concepts will help students learn new content and make studying easier.

Word webs are created by branching off from a major concept the related terms and concepts, much like a planet ringed with clustering satellites. The result is a graphic representation of the relationships among concepts and related terminology that approximates a cognitive network of related ideas, or a schema. These semantic networks help students explore and expand their associations with a central concept, thereby building schemata. Figure 5.8 provides a glimpse of a classroom teacher's effective use of a word web strategy to preteach the critical concept of *prejudice.*

Darrell, preparing his 10th-grade music students for a unit on orchestra, had them pair up for a strategy that combined word webbing and writing. Darrell walked around the room and gave each pair of students a photograph of a particular musical instrument found in orchestras. He told students they would be responsible for brainstorming as many words as they could related to their

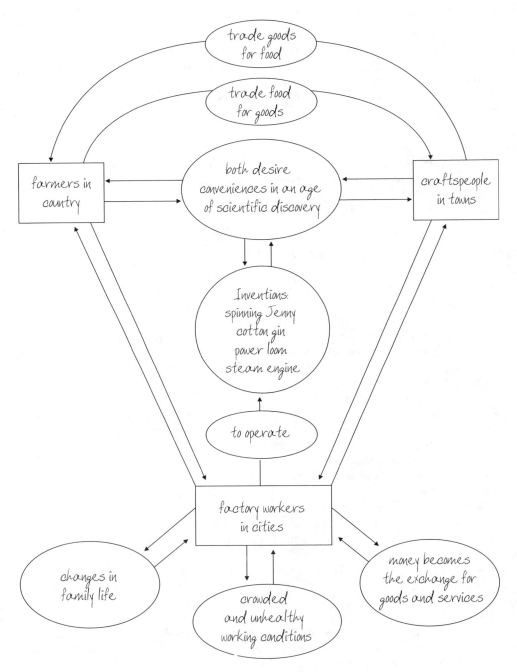

FIGURE 5.7 Graphic Organizer for the Industrial Revolution

Margaret teaches 11th-grade gifted English. In planning a unit around the concept of prejudice, she had selected a trade book to use with her students that told a story of racism and prejudice in recent U.S. history. The book was *Farewell to Manzanar* (Houston & Houston, 1974), a true account of Jeanne Wakatsuki and her family, who spent the World War II years in an internment camp off the West Coast of the United States. Before assigning any reading of the book, Margaret wanted to remind her students of examples of prejudice they were already familiar with to sensitize them to the issues of prejudice and to engage them in a lengthy discussion of the concept. Margaret first worked with the whole class to create a word web for the broad concept *racial prejudice*. She wrote the words on the board, circled them, and then helped the class come up with an array of related ideas, examples, and terminology. At the conclusion of this activity, the class was divided into groups of four or five, and each group was asked to develop its own word web for one major case of racial prejudice, such as "Nazism," "South African Apartheid," "Southern Blacks in the 1950s," and "Japanese Americans during WWII." Groups were asked to put their webs on transparencies to share them with the class. After working for several minutes, spokespersons from the various groups were asked to share their group's web and explain the rationale for its terms and groupings. The group working with "Southern Blacks in the 1950s" presented the following word web:

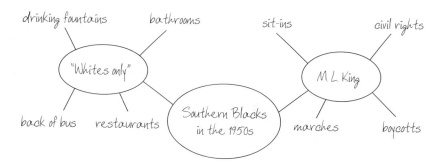

"Well, we knew there were lots of places where blacks couldn't go," said one spokesperson, "and there were signs that said 'Whites only,' or something like that, so we used it as one of our subcategories. Then we listed some of the places where blacks couldn't go . . . like they couldn't use certain bathrooms and drinking fountains . . . and they had to sit in the back of the bus . . . and they couldn't eat in certain restaurants . . . we could have listed more places. We also thought about Martin Luther King, because he was trying to change all that back then, so we listed some of the things he did to try to get rights for blacks. We couldn't remember much about the boycotts and marches, so we just said that." "Didn't they also go to restaurants that were supposed to be for whites and just take up all the seats and stay there?" a student asked. "I guess they did, so we could include . . . what would you call that? "Margaret helped out, "They were called 'sit-ins.' That's an excellent word map." After each group's spokesperson had an opportunity to present and explain its word web, answer questions, and gather feedback and additional ideas from the class, Margaret then focused the discussion on the commonalities among the major cases of racial prejudice that were depicted in the word maps. The class derived three: (a) one group feels superior to another group, often based on physical characteristics, (b) the superior group denies the rights of the other group, and (c) the superior group often uses violence to gain an advantage over the other group. Students were then asked to pay close attention to the novel they were about to read, *Farewell to Manzanar,* and to be prepared to discuss how the case of prejudice in the story shares common characteristics with the other forms of prejudice discussed in the class that day.

FIGURE 5.8   Classroom Example of Students' Creation of Word Webs to Prepare for a Unit on Prejudice

FIGURE 5.9   Student-Generated Word Web for "Piano" in 10th Grade Music

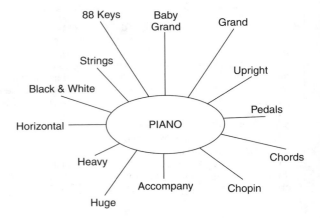

instrument. He further instructed his students to write the name of the instrument on a piece of paper and circle it. Then he demonstrated on the board how they were to radiate lines off the circled term and write all the related words that come to mind. Tim and Darcy created the word web in Figure 5.9 for "piano."

Next, Darrell asked each pair of students to use their brainstormed words to create a diary entry, poem, rap, letter, memoir, dialogue, newspaper article, or some other form. When finished, students were asked to read what they had written to allow their classmates a chance to guess the instrument. Tim and Darcy's poem based on their word web terms read:

> What kind of instrument might I be,
> I am a *huge, heavy* monstrosity.
> I can harmonize, *accompany,* play solos with delight.
> I have *88 keys* in both *black* and *white.*
> Sometimes I am *upright* or *horizontal* as I stand.
> If I am horizontal, they call me a *baby grand.*
> The *keys* strike *strings* which make a beautiful sound.
> Playing *chords* and sweet *tones* can always be found.
> So *Chopin* is the master, we certainly must say,
> Because he wrote music for all of us to play.

Both graphic organizers and word webs help students focus on the information you deem most important in the text. At the same time, they assist students in assimilating and clustering additional details. (Chapter 6 provides a detailed explanation of how to design and use graphic organizers, as well as many other effective vocabulary strategies.)

 Before writing your suggestions for Theresa in the Case Study, go to *http://www.prenhall.com/brozo,* select Chapter 5, then click on Chapter Review Questions to check your understanding of the material.

CASE STUDY REVISITED

Remember Theresa, the eighth-grade social studies teacher? She was preparing for a unit on the early Americans. Take a moment to write your ideas for Theresa to help her students prepare to study this content and become engaged in learning.

Theresa introduced students to a prereading activity on the first day that we thought was exceptional. She began by involving the class in a discussion of the role of archaeologists in understanding the relationship of artifacts to past societies. She then explained that one way to understand the past is to relate it to the present, and one way they could do that was by making a time capsule. After defining a time capsule, she asked students to think of objects they felt would be important to include in one that would be buried today and excavated 1,000 years later. Theresa jotted down ideas on the board and asked students to explain why their particular object would help people living 1,000 years later to understand what life was like today. Clearly, the purpose of exploring the idea of a time capsule was to motivate students to learn about the past by making it relevant to their own lives. The students were genuinely enjoying this activity, as reflected in interchanges such as this:

Student 1: Did you see that Coke commercial where this class sometime way in the future is walking through a 20th-century ruin and they find a Coke bottle?

Class: Yeah, I've seen that.

Theresa: What does a bottle of Coke say to these future people about ourselves and our culture?

Student 1: That we like to drink Coke.

Theresa: Would it? How could you be sure? Let's say people aren't drinking Coke a thousand years from now, and let's say these people you're talking about also found a tattered T-shirt with "Madonna" written on it, and a broken television or computer. How would they piece together the way we lived if this is all they found?

Student 2: They might think Madonna was our president or something.

Student 3: They might not even know what a television or computer was. I read a science fiction story about these people who could put this machine on their heads, like a headset, and see images in their heads and feel what you would feel if you were there.

Theresa: That's interesting. So they might not even be able to recognize that it was a television or computer or exactly what it was used for, especially if it was really badly broken up. Do you see now how hard it would be for future people to describe who we were and how we behaved from the few things they might find?

Student 4: Maybe if we put a Coke can in our time capsule, we should tape a piece of paper to it that tells what it is and all about it.

Theresa: If the paper didn't crumble and rot away, that would be very helpful for future people. Good idea. Unfortunately for archaeologists, the original inhabitants of North America didn't leave written directions and explanations with all of their artifacts.

Student 5: Didn't they draw pictures in caves of hunting buffalo and stuff like that?

Theresa: That's right, and those wall paintings help us quite a bit, but they don't tell the whole story. For instance, the wall pictures don't tell whether men and women married like they do today, or whether one man could have several wives. They don't tell us if the Indians were nomadic or whether they lived in one place for long periods of time. Did these people have music or play games, etc.?

Eventually, the class formulated a list of things to put in their time capsule. It was fascinating to listen to the students rationalize why certain items would be appropriate to include. For instance, one young man wanted to contribute his tennis shoes; one was green, the other orange, and both were untied. He argued that they would reflect what young people are like today. The class concluded that his mismatched tennis shoes would give a misleading impression because only a small minority dress that way. Instead, it was decided that pictures from magazines depicting many different fashions would be better. Another student said the time capsule should have a CD of contemporary music. This didn't seem feasible, the class agreed, because in 1,000 years, probably no means of playing the CD would exist.

The final list included a Coke can, accompanied by a picture of someone drinking from a can of Coke, a copy of *Time* magazine, several photographs of cars, fashions, stereos, TVs, computers and other high-tech electronics, houses, lyrics and sheet music to a couple of popular songs, and a class portrait. The activity culminated at week's end with a ceremonial burial on a section of the school grounds of a time capsule (actually a large plastic canister) containing the items the class had decided on.

Theresa conducted a couple of other readiness activities during the week, including a word scavenger hunt, which involves students in a game for learning key words from their readings (see Chapter 6 for details), and viewing a film that traced the journey of the first people to emigrate from Europe to the area we now call Iowa. Students were also provided with a structured overview of the migration patterns, names, and terms associated with the first Americans.

This case study makes clear how varied and yet how effective creative and meaningful activities before reading about and studying class topics can be. It demonstrates how a talented teacher takes her students far beyond the traditional boundaries of a content area lesson in preparing them for learning by generating interest in the topic and activating and building appropriate prior knowledge for the content to be learned.

————◄o►————

SUMMARY

Because we believe that the degree of success with a topic of study in the content areas depends on how well students are prepared for learning about the topic, we have devoted most of this chapter to presenting a range of classroom practices that teachers in middle and secondary schools have used to hook their students into the topic. The examples included here represent only a few of the potentially endless possibilities for getting students excited about the content to be read and studied.

We hope these guidelines and examples help you become more sensitive to the importance of providing preparation activities for all reading and learning experiences and inspire you to expand your notions about what is possible in your classroom before telling students, "Open your books and begin reading Chapter 7."

In the next chapter, you will read more about some of the vocabulary strategies briefly discussed in this chapter. You will also discover a range of additional word-learning strategies designed to expand students' understanding of course concepts.

REFERENCES

Alexander, P., & Jetton, T. (2000). Learning from text: A multidimensional and developmental perspective. In M. Kamil, P. Mosenthal, P. D. Pearson, & R. Barr (Eds.), *Handbook of reading research* (Vol. 3). Mahwah, NJ: Lawrence Erlbaum Associates.

Alvermann, D., O'Brien, D., & Dillon, D. (1990). What teachers do when they say they're having discussions of content area reading assignments: A qualitative analysis. *Reading Research Quarterly, 25,* 296–322.

Alvermann, D., Peyton Young, J., Weaver, D., Hinchman, K., Moore, D., Phelps, S., Thrash, E., & Zalewski, P. (1996). Middle and high school students' perceptions of how they experience text-based discussions: A multicase study. *Reading Research Quarterly, 31,* 244–267.

Anderson, R. (1984). Role of the reader's schema in comprehension, learning, and memory. In R. Anderson, J. Osborn, & R. Tierney (Eds.), *Learning to read in American schools: Basal readers and content texts.* Hillsdale, NJ: Erlbaum.

Anderson, R., & Nagy, W. (1992). The vocabulary conundrum. *American Educator, 16,* 14–18, 44–47.

Audet, R., Hichman, P., & Dobrynina, G. (1996). Learning logs: A classroom practice for enhancing scientific sense making. *Journal of Research in Science Teaching, 33,* 205–222.

Barnitz, J. (1994). Discourse diversity: Principles for authentic talk and literacy instruction. *Journal of Reading, 37,* 586–591.

Barton, J. (1995). Conducting effective classroom discussions. *Journal of Reading, 38,* 346–350.

Bean, T. (2000). Reading in the content areas: Social constructivist dimensions. In M. Kamil, P. Mosenthal, P. D. Pearson, & R. Barr (Eds.), *Handbook of Reading Research* (Vol 3). Mahwah, NJ: Lawrence Erlbaum Associates.

Beck, C. (1999). Francine, Kerplunk, and the Golden Nugget—conducting mock trials and debates in the classroom. *The Social Studies, 90,* 78–84.

Bintz, W. (1993). Resistant readers in secondary education: Some insights and implications. *Journal of Reading, 36,* 604–615.

Boswell, J. (1979). *The life of Samuel Johnson.* New York: Viking Press.

Brozo, W. G. (2002). *To be a boy, to be a reader.* Newark, DE: International Reading Association.

Brozo, W. G., Valerio, P., & Salazar, M. (1996). A walk through Gracie's garden: Literacy and cultural explorations in a Mexican-American junior high school. *Journal of Adolescent & Adult Literacy, 40,* 164–171.

Cameron, J., & Pierce, W. (1994). Reinforcement, reward, and intrinsic motivation: A meta-analysis. *Review of Educational Research, 64,* 363–423.

Carr, E., & Ogle, D. (1987). K-W-L Plus: A strategy for comprehension and summarization. *Journal of Reading, 30,* 626-631.

Carr, S., & Thompson, B. (1996). The effects of prior knowledge and schema activation strategies on the inferential reading comprehension of children with and without learning disabilities. *Learning Disabilities Quarterly, 19,* 48-66.

Clary, L. (1991). Getting adolescents to read. *Journal of Reading, 34,* 340-345.

Deci, E., Koestner, R., Ryan, R., & Cameron, J. (2001). Extrinsic rewards and intrinsic motivation in education: Reconsidered once again. *Review of Educational Research, 71,* 1-51.

Dermody, M., & Speaker, B. (1999). Reciprocal strategy training in prediction, clarification, question generating and summarizing to improve reading comprehension. *Reading Improvement, 36,* 16-23.

Dewey, J. (1913). *Interest and effort in education.* Boston: Houghton Mifflin.

Duffelmeyer, F. (1994). Effective Anticipation Guide statements for learning from expository prose. *Journal of Reading, 37,* 452-457.

Duffelmeyer, R., & Baum, D. (1992). The extended Anticipation Guide revisited. *Journal of Reading, 35,* 654-656.

Dye, G. (2000). Graphic organizers to the rescue! Helping students link—and remember—information. *Teaching Exceptional Children, 32,* 72-76.

Eccles, J. S., Wigfield, A., & Schiefele, U. (1998). Motivation to succeed. In W. Damon (Series Ed.) & N. Eisenberg (Ed.), *Handbook of child psychology: Social, emotional, and personality development* (5th ed., Vol. 3). New York: Wiley.

Edwards, S. (2001). Bridging the gap: Connecting school and community with service learning. *English Journal, 90,* 39-44.

Egan, M. (1999). Reflections on effective use of graphic organizers. *Journal of Adolescent & Adult Literacy, 42,* 641-645.

Frager, A. (1993). Affective dimension of content area reading. *Journal of Reading, 36,* 616-623.

Gaultney, J. F. (1995). The effect of prior knowledge and metacognition on the acquisition of a reading comprehension strategy. *Journal of Experimental Child Psychology, 59,* 142-165.

Gillet, J., & Temple, C. (1986). *Understanding reading problems: Assessment and instruction: Instructor's manual* (2nd ed.). Boston: Little, Brown.

Green, T. (2000). Responding and sharing: Techniques for energizing classroom discussions. *The Clearning House, 73,* 331-334.

Guthrie, J., & Wigfield, A. (1997). *Reading engagement: Motivating readers through integrated instruction.* Newark, DE: International Reading Association.

Guthrie, J., & Wigfield, A. (2000). Engagement and motivation in reading. In M. Kamil, P. Mosenthal, P. D. Pearson, & R. Barr (Eds.), *Handbook of reading research* (Vol. 3). Mahwah, NJ: Lawrence Erlbaum Associates.

Guzzetti, B., & Williams, W. (1996). Changing the pattern of gendered discussion: Lessons from science classrooms. *Journal of Adolescent & Adult Literacy, 40,* 38-47.

Hamann, L., Schultz, L., Smith, M., & White, B. (1991). Making connections: The power of autobiographical writing before reading. *Journal of Reading, 35,* 24-28.

Hartman, D. (1995). Eight readers reading: The intertextual links of proficient readers reading multiple passages. *Reading Research Quarterly, 30,* 520-561.

Hayden, R. (1995). Training parents as reading facilitators. *The Reading Teacher, 49,* 334-336.

Hayes, D. A., & Tierney, R. J. (1980). *Increasing background knowledge through analogy: Its effects upon comprehension and learning* (Tech. Rep. No. 186). Urbana: University of Illinois, Center for the Study of Reading.

Herz, S., & Gallo, D. (1996). *From Hinton to Hamlet: Building bridges between young adult literature and the classics.* Westport, CT: Greenwood Press.

Hidi, S., & Baird, W. (1988). Strategies for increasing text-based interest and students' recall of expository texts. *Reading Research Quarterly, 23,* 465-483.

Hidi, S., & Harackiewicz, J. (2000). Motivating the academically unmotivated: A critical issue for the 21st century. *Review of Educational Research, 70,* 151-179.

Horn, E. (1937). *Methods of instruction in social studies.* New York: Scribner's.

Hoss, M. (1991). Guest speakers are our favorite inexpensive reference tool. *Illinois Libraries, 73,* 540-542.

Hurst, B. (2001). The ABCs of content area lesson planning: Attention to basics, and comprehension. *Journal of Adolescent & Adult Literacy, 44,* 692-693.

Illich, I. (1970). *Deschooling society.* New York: Harper & Row.

Johnson, A., & Rasmussen, J. (1998). Classifying and super word web: Two strategies to improve productive vocabulary. *Journal of Adolescent & Adult Literacy, 42,* 204-207.

Kiefer, B. (2001). Understanding reading. *School Library Journal, 47,* 48-52.

Larson, B. (1999). Influence on social studies teachers' use of classroom discussion. *The Social Studies, 90,* 125-132.

Lee, E. (1997). The learning response log: An assessment tool. *English Journal, 86,* 41-44.

Marshall, N. (1989). Overcoming problems with incorrect prior knowledge: An instructional study. In S. McCormick & J. Zutell (Eds.), *Cognitive and social perspectives for literacy research and instruction.* Chicago: National Reading Conference.

Mathison, C. (1989). Activating student interest in content area reading. *Journal of Reading, 33,* 170-177.

Matulka, D. (1997). *Picture this: Picture books for young adults.* Westport, CT: Greenwood Press.

McKenna, M., Kear, D., & Ellsworth, R. (1995). Children's attitudes toward reading: A national survey. *Reading Research Quarterly, 30,* 934-956.

McKeown, M., Beck, I., Sinatra, G., & Loxterman, J. (1992). The contribution of prior knowledge and coherent text to comprehension. *Reading Research Quarterly, 27,* 78-93.

Merkley, D. (1996/97). Modified anticipation guide. *The Reading Teacher, 50,* 365-368.

Moje, E. (2000). *"All the stories that we have": Adolescents' insights about literacy and learning in secondary schools.* Newark, DE: International Reading Association.

Mosenthal, P. (1999). Understanding engagement: Historical and political contexts. In J. Guthrie & D. Alvermann (Eds.), *Engaged reading: Processes, practices and policy implications.* New York: Teachers College Press.

Nagy, W. (1997). On the role of context in first- and second-language vocabulary learning. In N. Schmitt & M. McCarthy (Eds.), *Vocabulary: Description, acquisition and pedagogy.* Cambridge: Cambridge University Press.

Nagy, W., Anderson, R., & Herman, P. (1987). Learning word meanings from context during normal reading. *American Educational Research Journal, 24,* 237-270.

Newkirk, T. (1986). *To compose: Teaching writing in the high school.* Portsmouth, NH: Heinemann.

Ogle, D. (1986). K-W-L: A teaching model that develops active reading of expository text. *The Reading Teacher, 39,* 564-570.

Parker, W. (2001). Classroom discussion: Models for leading seminars and deliberations. *Social Education, 65,* 11–15.

Pearson, P. D., & Johnson, D. D. (1978). *Teaching reading comprehension.* New York: Holt, Rinehart & Winston.

Poling, L. (2000). The real world: Community speakers in the classroom. *Social Education, 64,* 8–10.

Pressley, M. (2000). What should comprehension instruction be the instruction of? In M. Kamil, P. Mosenthal, P. D. Pearson, & R. Barr (Eds.), *Handbook of reading research,* (Vol. 3). Mahwah, NJ: Lawrence Erlbaum Associates.

Prouty, J. L., & Irby (1995, February). *Parent involvement: Integrated packets.* Paper presented at the Student/Beginning Teacher Conference, Nacogdoches, TX.

Renninger, K., Hidi, S., & Krapp, A. (1992). *The role of interest in learning and development.* Hillsdale, NJ: Erlbaum.

Robinson, D. (1998). Graphic organizers as aids to text learning. *Reading Research and Instruction, 37,* 85–105.

Robinson, D., Katayama, A., & DuBois, N. (1998). The interactive effects of graphic organizers and delayed review on concept application. *The Journal of Experimental Education, 67,* 17–31.

Ruddell, R. (1995). Those influential literacy teachers: Meaning negotiators and motivation builders. *The Reading Teacher, 48,* 454–463.

Schiefele, U. (1996). Topic interest, text representation, and quality of experience. *Contemporary Educational Psychology, 21,* 3–18.

Spilich, G. J., Vesonder, G. T., Chiesi, H. L., & Voss, J. F. (1979). Text processing of domain-related information for individuals with high and low domain knowledge. *Journal of Verbal Learning and Verbal Behavior, 18,* 275–290.

Strange, T., & Wyant, S. (1999). The great American prairie: An integrated fifth-grade unit. *Social Education, 63,* 216–219.

Symons, S., & Pressley, M. (1993). Prior knowledge affects text search success and extraction of information. *Reading Research Quarterly, 28,* 250–263.

Tobias, S. (1994). Interest, prior knowledge, and learning. *Review of Educational Research, 64,* 37–50.

Tyson-Bernstein, H. (1988). *A conspiracy of good intentions.* Washington, DC: Council for Basic Education.

Unrau, N., & Ruddell, R. (1995). Interpreting texts in classroom contexts. *Journal of Reading, 39,* 16–27.

Wade, S., Schraw, G., Buxton, W., & Hayes, M. (1993). Seduction of the strategic reader: Effects of interest on strategy and recall. *Reading Research Quarterly, 28,* 92–115.

Weech, J. (1994). Writing the story before reading it. *Journal of Reading, 37,* 364–367.

White, B., & Johnson, T. S. (2001). We really do mean it: Implementing language arts standard #3 with opinionnaires. *The Clearing House, 74,* 119–123.

Wilkinson, L., & Silliman, E. (2000). Classroom language and literacy learning, In M. Kamil, P. Mosenthal, P. D. Pearson, & R. Barr (Eds.), *Handbook of reading research* (Vol. 3), Mahwah, NJ: Lawrence Erlbaum Associates.

Wyatt, C., & Willis, C. (2000). Students make the grade. *The Science Teacher, 67,* 40–43.

Zamel, V. (2000). Engaging students in writing-to-learn: Promoting language and literacy across the curriculum. *Journal of Basic Writing, 19,* 3–21.

YOUNG ADULT BOOKS

Anaya, R. (1990). Salomon's Story. In C. Tatum (Ed.), *Mexican-American literature.* Orlando, FL: Harcourt Brace Jovanovich.

Anaya, R. (1972). *Bless me, Ultima.* New York: Warner.

Bredeson, C. (2001). *Mount Saint Helens volcano.* New York: Enslow.

Cisneros, S. (1990). Three wiseguys: Un cuento de navidad. In C. Tatum (Ed.), *Mexican-American literature.* Orlando, FL: Harcourt Brace Jovanovich.

Claybourne, A. (2000). *Read about volcanoes.* New York: Millbrook Press.

Fleischman, S. (1995). *The abracadabra kid: A writer's life.* New York: Beech Tree.

Hickman, H. (1998). *Rocket boys: A memoir.* New York: Delacorte.

Houston, J., & Houston J. (1974). *Farewell to Manzanar.* New York: Putnam.

Lee, H. (1960). *To Kill a Mockingbird.* New York: Warner Books.

Maurer, R. (1995). *Rocket! How a toy launched the space age.* New York: Crown.

Mowat, F. (1995). *Born naked.* New York: Houghton Mifflin.

Pryor, B. (1998). *Thomas.* New York: Morrow Junior Books.

Shimony, A. (1997). *Tibaldo and the hole in the calendar.* NY: Springer-Verlag.

Sutin, L., Sutin, R., & Sutin, J. (1996). *Jack and Rochelle: A Holocaust story of love and resistance.* St. Paul, MN: Graywolf Press.

VanRose, V. (2000). *Volcano and earthquake.* New York: Dorling Kindersley.

CHAPTER SIX

Developing General and Content-Area Vocabulary Knowledge

ANTICIPATION GUIDE

Directions: Read each statement carefully and decide whether you agree or disagree with it, placing a check mark in the appropriate *Before Reading* column. When you have finished reading and studying the chapter, return to the guide and decide whether your anticipations need to be changed by placing a check mark in the appropriate *After Reading* column.

	BEFORE READING		AFTER READING	
	Agree	*Disagree*	*Agree*	*Disagree*
1. Only high-risk students need to be taught vocabulary words.	_____	_____	_____	_____
2. A student with a deficient vocabulary will probably also have comprehension problems.	_____	_____	_____	_____
3. A student who can define a word for the teacher understands the word.	_____	_____	_____	_____
4. The dictionary is the best way for students to learn word meanings.	_____	_____	_____	_____
5. Teaching students 20 words a week from a list of high-utility words should improve their vocabulary.	_____	_____	_____	_____
6. The best format for evaluating students' word knowledge is a multiple-choice test.	_____	_____	_____	_____
7. English teachers are the ones who should develop students' word knowledge.	_____	_____	_____	_____

The goal for vocabulary development is to insure that students are able to apply their knowledge of words to appropriate situations and are able to increase and enrich their knowledge through independent encounter with words. . . . [T]he best way to reach this goal is to help students add to their repertoires both specific words and skills that promote independent learning of words, and also to provide opportunities from which words can be learned.

—Beck and McKeown (1991)

What does it mean to "know" a word? That question has been debated for about 50 years, starting with Cronbach (1942), who suggested that word knowledge existed in dimensions. In the vernacular, to know a word means to be able to define it. But is this an adequate measure of one's word knowledge? When asked what the word *light* meant, 4-year-old Ryan's reply was "It comes from the sun and helps us see things." However, he had no idea what "light as a feather" meant, nor did he know the meaning of light in the sentence "I saw the birds light on the tree." Does Ryan really know the word *light*?

Go to *http:// www.prenhall. com/brozo*, select Chapter 6, then click on Chapter Objectives to provide a focus for your reading.

One of the primary goals of vocabulary development at the middle and high school levels is not simply to increase the breadth of students' vocabularies (i.e., the number of words for which students have a definition), but also to increase the depth and precision of their word knowledge. In other words, the goal is to help students develop a full and complete understanding of words in order to understand the concepts they encounter across the content areas. This is especially important because most students are expected to read textbooks packed with concepts and technical vocabulary that they need to understand fully if they are to understand and learn (Blachowicz & Fisher, 2000). If too many general or technical words puzzle students as they read, they often skip the words or give up and thus become frustrated outsiders to the learning process.

We also know that understanding a content-area word or concept means more than knowing a definition to that word (Nagy & Scott, 2000, Stahl, 1999). If vocabulary knowledge is more than definitional in nature, what are the processes or dimensions involved? Although there are a variety of ideas on this issue (e.g., Laufer, 1998; Stahl, 1999), we have found that students who are learning general or technical vocabulary words should be involved in processes and activities that stress the following:

Understanding a word at the conceptual level involves students in many thought processes.

1. Recognizing and generating the critical attributes, characteristics, examples, and nonexamples of a concept.

2. Sensing and inferring relationships between concepts and their own background information or prior knowledge.

3. Discovering comparisons and contrasts between different concepts to determine meaningful similarities and differences.

4. Determining superordinate and subordinate concepts related to the targeted concept.

5. Applying the concept to a variety of situations.

6. Creating new examples and applications for the targeted concept.

In this chapter, we present a variety of teacher-directed and student-initiated vocabulary strategies that capitalize on these six processes involved in learning words beyond the definitional level. You will notice that the strategies discussed are intended to expand students' comprehension of content-area concepts, whether oral or written. We believe the best way to develop word knowledge is by capitalizing on the same effective teaching strategies discussed in previous chapters and throughout this book. Teacher demonstrations and modeling, small-group interactions, class discussions, writing activities, and reciprocal teaching are all powerful teaching tools. As you read this chapter, you will see how these teaching strategies can be effectively used to help students develop their vocabulary knowledge before they read, while they read, and after they read.

CASE STUDY

Rafalar, curriculum director of the Winter Park School District, analyzed the results of the competency-based reading test that was given to eighth graders in the spring. Much to her dismay, the vocabulary scores were again low. She called the principals to highlight her concerns and to recommend that a district committee be formed to investigate the problem and offer some specific solutions. Consequently, a committee was formed of teachers who taught eighth graders across the district's middle schools. They met regularly during the school year to discuss the problem in more depth, but they could not agree on what should be done. Several committee members thought the language arts teachers should be responsible for improving the vocabulary scores. Other members complained that the additional burden of teaching vocabulary words would rob them of precious instructional time. And three members wanted the school to purchase a computer program promising to teach students 50 words a week. Patience was wearing thin as the school year drew to a close.

To the Reader:

As you read and work through this chapter on expanding vocabulary and concepts across the content areas, consider ways in which this committee could solve their problem. Think about the characteristics of effective vocabulary instruction, the varied ways to come to know a word, and possible strategies that this school district might incorporate into the middle school curricula.

————◁o▷————

DEFINITIONAL VERSUS CONCEPTUAL UNDERSTANDING OF WORDS

One of the underlying themes of this chapter is that word-learning strategies should require students to combine new text information with their prior knowledge to yield conceptual understanding of words. The admonitions of our best vocabulary writers and researchers are entirely consistent with this theme (e.g., Nagy, 1988; Stahl, 1999). Earlier in this chapter, we mentioned 4-year-old Ryan, who had partial definitional understanding of the word *light*. But Ryan did not have a conceptual understanding of light that would have allowed him to interpret its meaning in a variety of contexts.

Stahl (1986, 1999) has made the distinction between definitional and contextual word knowledge. **Definitional knowledge** is essentially knowing a dictionary-like definition for a word. It is important word knowledge, but it limits understanding of the word to restricted contexts. **Contextual understanding**, on the other hand, means that the reader has a sophisticated schema for the word that facilitates meaningful interpretations in a variety of contexts.

To help you understand the important distinction between definitional and contextual word knowledge, we have prepared an exercise for you. For the following sentence, two key words have been defined. In the space provided, write what the statement means in your own words.

Surrogate: judge or magistrate
Testator: on making a claim on a will
The learned surrogate has held that an intent to have an apportionment will be imputed to the testator.

In your own words:

_____

_____

_____

For the next sentence, the topic area is provided. Given the topic, write in your own words the special definition of the two italicized words in the sentence.

Topic: commodities futures
Live hogs *found* November *unchanged.*

Your definition of *found:*

_____

_____

_____

Your definition of *unchanged:*

_____

_____

_____

Now that you have finished the exercise, some explanation is in order. In the first sentence, you undoubtedly discovered that even with a couple of the key terms defined, you were still unable to make sense of it. Why? Because the meaning of the sentence is larger than the sum of the definitions of each of its words. To state it another way, to understand this sentence, you must connect individual definitions to a broad context of meaning. You must possess the schema for these words, for without a schema, the sentence is an unintelligible collection of fragments of definitions. If, however, you were a lawyer of contracts and estate settlements, this sentence would be perfectly understandable.

What about the second sentence? Were you able to supply the appropriate special definitions for the commonly understood words *found* and *unchanged?* If not, it is likely due to the fact that your schema for the language of commodities futures is not especially well developed. Once again, without the necessary schema, or relevant prior knowledge, the sentence is as oblique as a line from a surrealistic poem. Of course, if you are a member of the Chicago Board of Trade familiar with hog futures in the commodities market, the expression would make perfect sense to you.

The difficulty you probably experienced in defining the words in this exercise is not unlike the problems many middle school and high school students often encounter when trying to read their content-area textbooks. When students are not given adequate preparation for dealing with the critical terms and concepts in the text, or strategies for discovering word meaning while reading, comprehension can proceed only haltingly or may break down altogether (Blachowicz & Fisher, 2000; Stahl, 1999). For the two sentences you were given, knowledge of the words and, most important, of the concepts they represent is essential if they are to be understood. How students acquire this important prior knowledge, and how they use strategies for elaborative understanding of words and concepts, are the major themes of this chapter.

Word knowledge has a significant impact on students' reading comprehension.

As you now know from your own experience, definitional word knowledge does not imply conceptual understanding of a word. It is, however, an aspect of word knowledge that allows readers to bring to mind an appropriate schema to aid them in interpreting word meanings in various contexts. Therefore, the principles and strategies of effective vocabulary instruction discussed in this chapter are not meant to make students experts at reciting definitions. If a strategy or program focuses only on correctly matching a word to a definition, then what is obtained is limited in vision and probably has a low chance of being transferred to students' actual reading, writing, listening, or speaking tasks (Nagy & Scott, 2000; Simpson & Randall, 2000). Before examining strategies that content-area teachers can use to help their students understand content-area vocabulary, we present six guidelines that should be considered when planning instruction.

GUIDELINES FOR EFFECTIVE VOCABULARY INSTRUCTION

Most individuals would agree that no single method, material, or strategy will consistently guarantee that students will improve their word knowledge. Therefore, it seems advantageous for teachers to select a variety of approaches for the general and technical vocabulary words in their content area. In addition, the following seven guidelines, gleaned from research studies, should be considered when planning vocabulary lessons:

Content-area teachers can use these guidelines to plan their vocabulary lessons.

1. Teach vocabulary in context.
2. Emphasize students' active role in the learning process.
3. Give students tools to expand word knowledge independently.
4. Reinforce word learning with repeated exposures over time.
5. Stimulate students' awareness and interest in words.
6. Build a language-rich environment to support word learning.
7. Encourage students to read widely.

Teach Vocabulary in Context

Researchers who have reviewed the literature on vocabulary instruction have concluded that vocabulary is best taught in a unifying context (Stahl, 1999). Words taught in the context of a content area such as biology will be learned more effectively than words taught in isolation because context allows students to integrate words with previously acquired knowledge. The implication, of course, is that students will not improve their long-term vocabulary knowledge and understanding by memorizing the definitions of a list of essential words that high school students should know.

Thus, content-area teachers need to select or have students select the targeted words for study from textbooks, newspapers, magazines, or novels. For example, if students are reading a short selection from a speech textbook on words and their meaning, words such as *arbitrary, connotation, denotation,* or *syntax* could be studied. Another alternative is to group general words into themes. For example, an English teacher could organize a lesson around a set of adjectives that negatively describe a person's actions (e.g., *lax, infantile, obsequious, narcissistic)*. Whatever approach is used to provide a context and an organizing schema, remember that lists of words that are introduced on Monday and tested on Friday will probably be forgotten on Saturday.

Emphasize Students' Active Role in the Learning Process

The importance of students' active participation and elaborative processing in learning new words is a consistent theme across the research literature (Blachowicz & Fisher, 2000; Nagy & Scott, 2000; Simpson & Randall, 2000). Stahl (1985, 1999) described active involvement of the learner as "generative processing." Generative or elaborative processing engages students in activities such as (1) sensing and inferring relationships between targeted vocabulary and their own background knowledge, (2) recognizing and applying vocabulary words to a variety of contexts, (3) recognizing examples and nonexamples, and (4) generating novel contexts for the targeted word. In contrast, an example of passive involvement related to vocabulary instruction would be worksheet-type activities asking students to select definitions, whether in multiple-choice or matching formats, or to fill in empty blanks with a word from a list.

Give Students Tools to Expand
Word Knowledge Independently

Vocabulary development involves both the "what" and the "how." The "what" involves students in learning new words taken from their textbooks or other reading assignments. The "how" is equally important because it involves students in learning strategies for unlocking words on their own or independently. Think about it this way: If you teach students some words, they will be able to recognize and add those particular words to their repertoire; but if you teach students some independent word-learning strategies, they will be able to expand their vocabulary continually and to read and understand many more texts once they leave your classroom.

We are not suggesting that content-area teachers discontinue their instruction of important words and concepts taken from their units of study. Instead, we make the point that classroom teachers should strike a balance between these two approaches. Students should be exposed to and actively involved in the learning of key terms and concepts related to text topics. In this case, developing broad understanding of a set of critical vocabulary is relevant and purposeful, as it will contribute to greater comprehension of the text. Indeed, we provide many strategies for this purpose in this chapter. Too often, however, word-specific methods for teaching vocabulary involve handing students a list of arbitrarily selected words without demonstrating a clear connection between remembering definitions and meaningful learning. Teachers should also help students become independent word gatherers by helping them develop effective generative strategies (Simpson & Randall, 2000).

Reinforce Word Learning With Repeated Exposures Over Time

Students' word knowledge takes time to develop and increases in small, incremental steps. Although it is impossible to identify a specific time frame for all students, we do know from the research literature that word ownership is reinforced when students receive multiple exposures to targeted words in multiple contexts (Blachowicz & Fisher, 2000; Stahl, 1999). A math teacher puts this principle into practice by building vocabulary through (1) extensive discussions of key terms and symbols exploring what students already know about them, (2) previewing how the words and symbols are used in their math textbooks, (3) asking students to record the words and symbols in a vocabulary notebook, (4) practicing the words and symbols with a variety of activities and exercises that require students to think and write rather than circle answers, and (5) reviewing and testing in a cumulative fashion. These approaches to reinforcing vocabulary ensure students' elaborative understanding and hasten their spontaneous use of the words in spoken and written contexts.

Stimulate Students' Awareness and Interest in Words

As teachers, we all know the role that interest plays in our content-area classrooms. That is, when students are interested in what they hear in class or read about in an assignment, this interest will significantly increase their attention, effort, persistence, thinking processes, and performance. Unfortunately, commercial materials and assignments that ask students to look up 20 words in the dictionary and write sentences using them do not interest or motivate most middle school and high school students. What we need to do as teachers is to increase students' awareness of words and to create situations in which learning new words is a valuable knowledge-seeking activity.

Go to Web Resources for Chapter 6 at *http://www. prenhall.com/brozo* and look for additional ideas for building students' interest in words.

The best starting point for building word enthusiasm is with you, the teacher. We can hardly expect our students to become sensitive to words and interested in expanding word knowledge if we cannot demonstrate interest in words ourselves. More than 30 years ago Manzo and Sherk stated that "the single most significant factor in improving vocabulary is the excitement about words which teachers can generate" (1971, p. 78). Such a statement still holds true today. As we emphasized in previous chapters, modeling is a powerful teaching tool. If you want students to learn certain words, then talk about words you recently heard on a television show or read in the newspaper. Show students that you use the dictionary to look up words you do not understand or for definitions you need to clarify so that they realize that vocabulary acquisition is a lifelong goal. During class discussion, in conversation with students, or when responding to journal or other student writing, use words you want them to integrate into their written and spoken vocabularies. Above all, be playful with words and exhibit enthusiasm for words. We know a 10th-grade teacher who does just that as she monitors the hallway between periods. As students enter her class she greets them with comments that use their vocabulary words in playful ways (e.g., "Josh, you certainly look disgruntled today. Did the soccer coach yell at you last night?"). The repartee usually continues, with students picking up the word play until class begins.

Another way you can be playful with words is to share with students memorable stories and histories of words. We know one sixth-grade middle school team that selects and discusses with their students one word each week that has an unusual origin or history. For example, during the first week of school they taught the word *berserk*. This word originated from Norse mythology. Berserk was a fierce man who used no armor and assumed the form of a wild beast in battle. Supposedly, no enemy would touch him. Today, if you are described as *berserk,* you are wild, dangerous, and crazed. The sixth graders had fun with that word, describing their friends, their brothers and sisters, and their first week in a middle school as berserk. More important, the sixth-grade teachers discovered that their students remembered and then used those words as they were writing and speaking.

If you are interested in finding other words such as *berserk* that have fascinating origins, the sources for these stories can be found in reference books such as Funk's (1950) *Word Origins and Their Romantic Stories*. Other such books that are excellent sources are listed in Figure 6.1. Students might also be interested in checking the Internet for websites that discuss word origins.

Go to Web Resources for Chapter 6 at *http://www. prenhall.com/brozo* and look for some websites that discuss word origins.

Build a Language-Rich Environment to Support Word Learning

We know from the research that students with strong expressive and receptive vocabularies are the ones who are immersed in home and school environments characterized by "massive amounts of rich written and oral language" (Nagy & Scott, 2000, p. 280). Teachers can best promote vocabulary growth by working

Asimov, I. (1961). *Words from the myths*. Boston: Houghton Mifflin.
Asimov, I. (1969). *Words of science and the history behind them*. New York: New American Library.
Asimov, I. (1972). *More words of science*. Boston: Houghton Mifflin.
Funk, C. (1973). *A hog on ice and other curious expressions*. New York: Harper & Row.
Funk, W. (1950). *Word origins and their romantic stories*. New York: Funk & Wagnalls.
Grambs, D. (1986). *Dimboxes, epopts, and other quidams*. New York: Workman.
Jacobson, J. (1990). *Tooposaurus: A humorous treasury of top-o-nyms (familiar words and phrases derived from place names)*. New York: Wiley.
Safire, W. (1982). *What's the good word?* New York: Times Books.
Tuleja, T. (1987). *Namesakes: An entertaining guide to the origins of more than 300 words named for people*. New York: McGraw-Hill.
Urdang, L., Hunsinger, W., & LaRoche, N. (1991). *A fine kettle of fish and other figurative expressions*. Detroit: Visible Ink Press.

FIGURE 6.1   Books About Interesting Word Origins

Oral language activities help build students' understanding of new words.

with students to create an environment where new words are learned, celebrated, and used in authentic communication tasks. Students should be given opportunities to experiment with using words in low-risk situations, to discuss new ideas daily, to talk freely and openly about how text concepts relate to their real-world concerns, to read works in a variety of text genres related to concepts, and to write purposeful and meaningful texts that employ key words and demonstrate understanding of important concepts.

> We know teachers who frontload their instruction by emphasizing the oral language use of new words long before students are asked to write about the words. In Tom's sixth-grade remedial reading class his students have the opportunity to "try out" a sentence orally using a new word with their partners in order to receive their feedback and suggestions. Then his students share their sentences orally with the entire class. Hence, after 15 minutes, these students hear countless examples of how to use a targeted word correctly and how not to use the word. These oral language activities help Tom's at-risk students understand the connotative nuances and syntactic rules that govern word knowledge and ensure that they can pronounce the words correctly.

Other teachers have told us that they reinforce and extend vocabulary learning by providing regular writing experiences to help their students become more aware of contextual meanings and their lack of specific vocabulary. In addition, the revision and editing stages of the writing process become excellent opportunities to engage students in searches for "that one perfect word" that conveys the precise meaning they have in mind.

Encourage Students to Read Widely

In Chapter 1 we pointed out that many middle school and high school students do not choose to read as a recreational activity. In fact, books and other reading matter are not part of their lives outside the walls of our classrooms. Ironically, students who do read widely and frequently have the breadth and depth of word knowledge necessary for success in school and in life (Cunningham & Stanovich, 1991; Stahl, 1999). They are also the students who perform better on standardized achievement tests such as the Scholastic Aptitude Test.

The implication for content-area teachers is obvious: If we want our students to understand what they read in our courses, we must encourage them to read beyond what they are assigned to read in our classrooms. Content-area teachers should also keep in mind that what students read is not as important as the fact that they are reading. Forcing students to read the "important" works or classics will not instill a love of reading and may, in fact, cause negative reactions. Rather than the classics, many teachers like to stimulate recreational reading by encouraging students to read newspapers, magazines, short stories, and adolescent novels.

Other teachers have discovered that they can hook their students into recreational reading by reading out loud to them a few minutes each class period. Surprising as it may seem, adolescents do enjoy hearing these oral interpretations of enticing books and short stories. Researchers have also found that students, especially those with lower vocabulary knowledge, will learn a few new words (Stahl, 1999). In Chapter 8 we discuss in detail ways to encourage students' love and interest in reading.

High school teachers should read aloud to their students on a regular basis.

SELECTING KEY TERMS AND CONCEPTS

Learning a new word or key concept for a content area is obviously a complex task dependent upon students' prior knowledge and experiences. Graves (1987) has suggested that three tasks are involved in word learning. The first task is learning a new word for a concept when the student understands the concept but has not heard of the label for that concept. For example, most students understand the processes involved in defense mechanisms such as rationalization because they have all rationalized their behaviors in some way. The label, however, will probably be new to them. Words such as these are not as difficult to teach students because they have the experiences to draw upon to understand and learn them.

The second and third tasks involved in word learning are more difficult because students are not as familiar with the underlying concept. With the second task, students are learning a new concept for a known word. In psychology and mathematics, for example, the word *set* has a different meaning from what students understand the word to mean when they talk about having to "set the table for dinner." The third task involves students in learning a new concept for which they have no label and minimal, if any, understanding or background. These tasks challenge both students and teachers. For example, in an ecology unit the concept *eutrophication* (a gradual and natural process that turns lakes into marshes because of an excess amount of algae) is probably new to most 10th graders, as is the label. Hence, the science teacher would need to spend more time on this word than on others such as *mercury, detergents,* or *biodegradable.* In addition to understanding the three tasks involved in learning a word, it is important to understand the types of vocabulary in a content area.

Types of Vocabulary

If you were to skim a chapter in this textbook, you would probably discover that the vocabulary words could be classified in two ways. The first type are **general words** that are not particularly associated with any single content area and could be found in any newspaper or weekly magazine. For example, a science teacher who asked his ninth-grade students to read a brief excerpt from Rachel Carson's book *Silent Spring* identified the following general words that he thought should be taught: *maladies, blight, moribund, specter, stark,* and *droned.* A British journalist could have easily used some of these same words to describe a winter day in London because they are common to many communication situations.

The second type are the **technical vocabulary words** that are unique to a particular content area or take on a specialized meaning when used in that content area. Technical words include general words that are used in a specialized way and technical words that have only one distinct meaning and application—the second and third tasks involved in word learning. Examples of the former are words such as *table, matter, set,* or *drive,* which take on specialized meanings depending on the content area. Examples of the latter include words such as *alveoli* in science, *sonority* in music, and *matte effect* in art.

A Process for Selecting Words to Teach

Because it is impossible to teach all the general and technical words from a content-area reading assignment, an important first step in teaching vocabulary is to decide which terms and concepts should be taught. Traditionally, teachers have used the textbook as a guide, focusing on the words highlighted in the text. Basing vocabulary instruction on these words alone, however, may not meet your overall goals for teaching the content or unit. Researchers have made it clear that students will learn what is emphasized. If instruction focuses on the important and meaningful details, concepts, and issues, those things will be what students learn and remember. Vocabulary instruction, then, should focus on words related to those important ideas. Sometimes the words the textbook author has chosen to highlight will match the concepts you choose to emphasize; sometimes they will not. It is important, therefore, that you have a system for selecting the appropriate vocabulary terms that help students better understand the key ideas of the unit.

Another issue related to selecting words to teach is that it is impossible to teach students every word they may not fully understand in their texts. Time constraints alone preclude our doing so. Any of you who have tried to identify and teach all the words in a text you think might cause your students difficulty have discovered that your entire lesson can be taken up with vocabulary instruction. It is simply not feasible to attempt to teach every word that might potentially pose trouble for your students. We submit that a far more efficient and effective approach is to select the salient terms and concepts, those that carry and represent the most important ideas, and teach them well. A thorough and elaborative understanding of those vocabulary terms will, in turn, contribute to your students' enhanced understanding of the text itself.

Content-area teachers should focus on key vocabulary words since it is difficult to teach them all.

The following process should help you determine what vocabulary words should be taught as a part of a unit of study:

1. Determine what you want your students to learn as a result of reading and studying the content. We might call this the **theme** of the unit. For instance, a music teacher may want students to develop a sense of musical interpretation after covering a unit on opera; an art teacher may wish students to develop a sense of character as a result of reading stories with well-developed characters for a unit on portrait painting; a history teacher covering the Vietnam War may stress the danger of foreign intervention in civil strife.

2. Identify **key terms** that are related to the unit's theme. For example, considering the theme of Sparta and its unique political structure, the teacher would likely select technical terms such as *euphors, assembly, council of elders,* and *helots* because they are important words related to the theme.

3. Decide on appropriate strategies to introduce and reinforce the words. For example, the words related to Sparta could be arranged into a graphic organizer, a strategy introduced in Chapter 5 and discussed in more detail later in this chapter.

4. Identify the general words that are not necessarily central to the theme of the unit but that lend themselves to various word-learning strategies that promote independence, such as modeling words in context.

You should not underestimate the importance of these first steps in teaching key terms and concepts related to a unit of study. The more discretionary you are in selecting vocabulary that potentially has the highest payoff regarding comprehension, the greater the likelihood that students will learn the designated content-area material.

TRADITIONAL APPROACHES TO VOCABULARY INSTRUCTION

In this section, we examine two traditional approaches to teaching vocabulary—context clues and the dictionary. This section could have also been titled "Caveats to Vocabulary Instruction" in that we directly discuss the limitations of using context clues and the dictionary, two very traditional and prevalent approaches. Although we offer several caveats to each approach, we also outline ways in which teachers can encourage students to use context clues and the dictionary as methods of vocabulary development.

Using Contextual Analysis

Contextual analysis refers to our attempt to understand the meaning of a word by analyzing the meaning of the words that surround it. Put another way, contextual analysis is figuring out a word by the manner in which it is used in a textbook, novel, or magazine. For example, one way in which we figure out the meaning of words is by using extended descriptions or appositives such as the following:

> There was a strange sound *emanating* from the hood of my car. When I opened the hood, I found a stray cat huddling to keep warm and meowing in fear.

> The *decadent,* or overindulgent, society in which we live spoils children by buying them whatever they see on television.

Learning words from context is not as easy as we imagine.

On the surface, the idea of learning words from context makes a lot of sense. Logical as it may seem, however, the research on students' incidental learning from context seems to indicate that some learning will occur, but the effect is not very powerful, especially with a single encounter of the targeted word (Beck & McKeown, 1991; Nagy & Scott, 2000).

One reason the utility of contextual analysis is challenged is that previous studies have used contrived, unnatural texts as their materials of study and high-frequency words as their target of study (Nist & Olejnik, 1995). The following examples illustrate the oversimplified exercises that have been used in studies and in workbooks designed to teach students how to use context clues. Can you figure out the meaning of the italicized nonsense words?

> The boys bought their tickets for the brand new outer space movie and entered the theater with mystic expectation all over their *whitors.*

> Some even looked alive, though no *fome* flowed beneath the skin.

> A little later as he sped southward along a Florida *uwurt,* he was stopped by a state police officer.

If you were able to figure out that *whitors* means "faces," *fome* means "blood," and *uwurt* means "highway," congratulations. But is your performance on these sentences indicative of your genuine ability to use contextual analysis? Imagine students who correctly complete 20 sentences similar to those you have just tried. The students may be left with the impression that they have mastered the use of context for determining word meanings. Then imagine their enthusiastic attempt to apply their new skills with a real passage from a history textbook.

To understand the possible frustrations students encounter when told to "use the cues around the word to find its meaning," read the following passage about the Andersonville Prison. As you read, think about the difficulty a ninth grader might have in trying to determine the meanings of the italicized general words using contextual analysis.

> Prisoners from the North during the Civil War who found themselves in Andersonville had to contend with unhealthful, *debilitating* conditions as well as *depredations* by their fellow inmates, who frequently stole food, clothing, and whatever other necessities for survival they could lay their hands on. The Andersonville Raiders were a large, organized group of thieves and murderers. For nearly four months these *notorious predators* controlled what went on inside the prison, committing robbery and murder on a daily basis. Finally, after six leaders were captured and a quick trial by fellow inmates, they were hanged on July 11, 1864.
>
> When the war ended, the *emaciated* survivors of Andersonville returned to their homes amidst *strident* demands in the North for swift *retribution.* It was claimed that prison commanders were responsible for deliberately planned *atrocities.* *

As you undoubtedly discovered, trying to figure out the meaning of such words as *emaciated* and *atrocities* using context alone is difficult. Schatz and Baldwin's (1986) research concurs. In this study, instead of using high-frequency words and researcher-made passages, they chose to use low-frequency words and passages from history and science textbooks. They found the use of context clues ineffective in helping students determine the meanings of those targeted low-frequency words. This is a critical aspect of contextual analysis because students' textbooks are typically lean on clues, and students need to learn how to cope with those contexts.

We can help students effectively use context clues with several different teaching techniques.

If real text is not always so generous in providing clues to the meaning of unknown words, should we teach our students to use context clues? The answer to that difficult question is a qualified "yes," if the instruction is explicit. That is, teachers should model, provide students realistic practice and feedback, and emphasize the metacognitive nature of using context clues. Let's consider two specific approaches to using context clues that satisfy these requirements: previewing in context and Possible Sentences (Moore & Moore, 1986).

Previewing in Context

Previewing in context is a teacher-directed activity that relies on modeling and demonstrating to students how word meanings can sometimes be inferred from the context. Modeling how you go about finding clues to word meanings

---

*Adapted from B. Bowles, "Prison Site in Georgia Marks Civil War Horror," *Detroit News*, December 11, 1988, p. 11-H.

with actual content reading materials allows students to see the practical application of this skill. As an example of how modeling can be used to help students understand some of the key vocabulary in the passage about the Andersonville Raiders, consider these previewing-in-context strategies employed by a ninth-grade teacher.

First, she read the text carefully and identified general and specific key vocabulary and all the words and terms likely to pose difficulty for her students. Her list included the following words:

debilitating	predators
strident	inhumane
depredations	emaciated
retributions	notorious
atrocities	expired

Next, she considered the list and pared it down to those words she felt were essential to the overall understanding of the material and consistent with her unit objectives. She included those words that could be used most instructively for teaching contextual analysis. The reason for this step was both to avoid spending too much valuable class time on teaching vocabulary and to leave several unfamiliar words for the students to analyze independently. Through this process, her list was limited to the following:

debilitating	emaciated
predator	expired
inhumane	

When she directed students to each word and its surrounding context, she "thought out loud," modeling using the context to determine word meanings. She questioned students to help them discover a word's probable meaning in the existing context. Some of her specific strategies follow.

1. She spent a considerable amount of time activating students' prior knowledge for the topic. She knew that most of her ninth graders had some information about prison conditions in general. Perhaps they had seen TV documentaries of World War II concentration camps or had read about what it is like to be in prison. Using what her students already knew about the topic, she made it easier for them to figure out many difficult words in this passage, especially the word *emaciated.*

2. She reminded students of what they already knew about syntax and word order in sentences. This clue was helpful in narrowing the contextual definition of *debilitating* because it appeared between a modifier *(unhealthy)* and a noun *(conditions).*

3. She activated students' prior knowledge acquired in studying other subjects. She thought it likely that the students had encountered the word *predator* in science class as a technical vocabulary word. They were shown how to apply their understanding of the word in science to this context.

4.   She impressed on the students the importance of taking advantage of any obvious clues provided. For instance, in the last sentence, the students were given an obvious clue to the meaning of *expired*—died, which was used earlier in the sentence.

5.   She alerted students to clues within words—for example, *in* in the word *inhumane.*

6.   She made students aware of the idea that context is more than just the few words surrounding an unknown word or the sentence in which the unknown word appears. She helped expand their notion of context to include information and ideas within, before, and after the passage.

7.   She demonstrated checking the dictionary to validate her hunches about the meaning of a word.

Previewing in context is an honest way of demonstrating how challenging it is for readers to employ contextual analysis for determining word meanings in text. Although students' attempts to use context clues may not always produce precise meanings, the use of contextual analysis in conjunction with other sources and approaches should increase their comprehension and understanding.

Possible Sentences

Possible Sentences is a teacher-directed prereading activity that prepares students for the technical and general vocabulary they will encounter in a reading assignment (Moore & Moore, 1986). During this activity, students make predictions about content, establish connections between words and concepts, write, discuss, and read their assignments carefully to verify their predictions. Stahl and Kapinus's (1991) research with fifth graders indicated that the Possible Sentences activity improved students' written recall and long-term understanding of word meanings as well as their reading comprehension.

Possible Sentences involves students in writing, discussing, and reading activities.

The Possible Sentences activity requires minimal advance material preparation but a considerable amount of teacher time in thinking and planning. First, the teacher identifies the general or technical vocabulary that is key to the theme of the unit and is adequately defined by the context. For this activity to succeed, at least five to eight words should be taken from a subsection of a chapter rather than three or four words dispersed across an entire chapter. For example, in the Andersonville Prison excerpt, the following words could be used for part of the lesson:

debilitating   predators   inhumane   expired

Teachers need to select the targeted words carefully because students must be able to verify their predictions by reading the text during the third step.

During the second step, the teacher asks students to select at least two words from the list and generate one sentence that they think might possibly be in the text. Students can either write their sentence before sharing or dictate their sentences to the teacher spontaneously. As students share their predicted sentences, the teacher writes them on the overhead transparency or chalkboard.

Moore and Moore (1986) stress that it is important for the teacher to write the sentences just as they are dictated, even if students provide inaccurate information or use the word incorrectly. With the Andersonville Prison excerpt, students might pair the following words in this manner:

In the Andersonville Prison the *predators expired.*

During the Civil War the *inhumane* generals were *debilitating.*

Note that the second example uses the word *debilitating* in a syntactically incorrect manner, but the teacher recorded it. This sharing of predicted sentences should continue until all the words on the list have been included in at least one sentence.

In step three, the teacher asks the students to read their text to verify the accuracy of the sentences the class created. Once students have finished their reading, during step four they evaluate the predicted sentences. Moore and Moore (1986) recommend that students ask these questions to evaluate the sentences: (1) Which sentences are accurate? (2) Which need further elaboration? (3) Which cannot be validated because the passage did not deal specifically with them? For example, with the first possible sentence cited previously, the teacher would want the students to realize that the predators did die, but not a natural death. The Possible Sentence merely needed more elaboration (i.e., "The predators were caught, tried, and expired as a result of hanging"). With the second Possible Sentence, students will need to discuss the meaning and use of the word *debilitating,* but the context should provide an adequate model for making their evaluations and revisions.

In the fifth and final step of Possible Sentences, students are asked to create new sentences using the targeted words. This activity can be a homework assignment for the next class period, or it can occur during class as students work in pairs or share in the large-group discussion. As students share these sentences, everyone should be involved in checking the text and the agreed-on definitions generated during class discussion.

On the plus side, the Possible Sentences activity involves students in the elaborative thinking processes that characterize active learning. However, as with any teacher-directed activity, it will not work with all units of study. This is especially true for units containing a lot of technical vocabulary for which students may not have any prior knowledge.

Previewing in context and Possible Sentences are two teacher-directed strategies for helping students become more comfortable in using contextual analysis to unlock the meaning of difficult words. If students can learn how to use context clues in conjunction with other word-meaning approaches, they will increase their chances of understanding content-area vocabulary.

Using the Dictionary

If you have ever asked someone the meaning of a word, you were probably told to "look it up in the dictionary." You probably can also recall the frustration you felt as you tried to make sense of the entry once you found the word. Often you were given a definition that would help only someone who already knew the meaning of the word. For example, look up the meaning of the word *conservative* in your dictionary. Did you find a definition similar to this one?

"of or relating to a philosophy of conservatism" (*Webster's Ninth New Collegiate Dictionary*)

Did that definition help you? More important, would that definition help your students understand the word *conservative?* Dictionaries are not a panacea for learning the meanings of unknown words.

Interpreting a dictionary entry and identifying an appropriate and useful definition requires sophisticated thinking skills (Scott & Nagy, 1997). Thus, if students are not taught how to use a dictionary, they will have several predictable problems. One such problem is that many students target only a part of the definition, ignoring the rest of the entry. In fact, many students do not read beyond the first definition, even though some dictionaries place the oldest and least used definition first. For example, the first meaning of *excoriate* in *Webster's Collegiate Dictionary* (10th ed.) is to "tear or wear off the skin of." Imagine the difficulty students might have in comprehending text if they had only that definition for *excoriate*. A recent magazine article described how Washington officials were about to *excoriate* the FBI for the way in which agents conducted an investigation. With only the first definition, students would have a rather grisly interpretation of what the FBI was about to endure. However, had students read the second definition, they would have discovered that the word also means to "denounce or censure strongly."

A second common problem students have with interpreting entries is that they find a familiar word in the definition and attempt to substitute it for the unknown word. Nist and Olejnik (1995) cite a good example of this with the word *liaison.* They point out that the dictionary definition of the word is "a close relationship, connection, or link." One of their students who read that definition substituted the familiar word *connection* for *liaison* and wrote the following sentence: "The storm caused a *liaison* between the two islands."

A third problem students have in using the dictionary is that they cannot construct an adequate and precise meaning from the vague and disjointed fragments provided in the dictionary entries. As McKeown (1990) points out, dictionaries give "multiple pieces of information but offer no guidance in how they should be integrated" (p. 6). Nist and Olejnik (1995) provide an excellent illustration of this problem with the word *vacuous.* The dictionary entry for *vacuous* is "devoid of matter, empty, stupid, lacking serious purpose." Unable to synthesize the vague parts of this definition, one of Nist's students wrote this sentence: "The glass was *vacuous* because I was thirsty and drank all the Gatorade."

Do these problems that students have with dictionaries mean that we, as teachers, should avoid the dictionary in our classroom? Of course not. What we want to stress is that the dictionary, with all its limitations, can be a tool in building word knowledge. However, it should be used in conjunction with personal experiences and textual context if students are to learn the meanings of unknown words. In short, dictionaries can validate students' hunches about words.

Students need help in using a dictionary since it is not "user friendly."

From our experiences as teachers, we believe that students must be taught how to use and interpret the dictionary if we want them to construct useful and precise definitions. How can we help students use the dictionary? Perhaps the most important thing we can do is to avoid giving students lists of words to look up in the dictionary. Without the context of a sentence or paragraph, students will not be able to construct an appropriate definition for the general or technical word and consequently will not be able to apply the word correctly.

We can also help students if we teach and reinforce the following ideas about the dictionary:

Students need to know these four basic ideas on how to use a dictionary.

1. *The format and organization of a dictionary entry.* For example, each dictionary has its own system or hierarchy for arranging definitions. Many dictionaries, such as *Merriam-Webster's Collegiate Dictionary Tenth Edition,* list definitions in order of historical usage, thus making their last definition the most current or most widely used. However, others list the most current or widely used definition first. Students need to know that this information can be found by reading the user's guide or introduction.

2. *The abbreviations and symbols in an entry.* Dictionary entries contain numerous abbreviations and symbols that initially confuse students. These must be mastered so that students can decipher the entries. For example, it is important for students to know that "n, pl" stands for the plural noun form of a word.

3. *The etymological information in a typical entry.* Etymological information usually occurs between square brackets [ ] and may appear before the definitions or after them. Inside the brackets are the origins of a word and some interesting stories connected with words such as *meander* or *snafu.* In addition, students may see how the word has changed meaning over time.

4. *How to select the most appropriate definition for the situation in which they encountered the word.* Because words have meaning only when placed in context, it is important for students to learn how to select the correct definition in a dictionary. This is difficult for students for many reasons. One reason is that dictionary entries contain definitions for words used as different parts of speech and for words used in specialized areas. For example, the word *anchors* can be a noun and a verb and can occur in nautical and sports situations.

Contextual analysis and dictionaries are two ways in which students can add to their understanding of new words from a content area. However, content-area teachers can use more powerful approaches to build students' vocabulary knowledge.

TEACHER-DIRECTED APPROACHES FOR BUILDING VOCABULARY KNOWLEDGE

Be sure to check Chapters 3, 5, and 9 for other teacher-directed activities that help students understand new words at a conceptual level.

In this section, we outline several different ways in which teachers can introduce and reinforce the general and technical vocabulary words that are important to students' understanding of content-area concepts. Using the principle that students will understand and remember more when they experience concepts in a direct and relevant fashion, we begin by explaining firsthand concept development. The next approach, semantic-feature analysis, emphasizes the importance of students' elaborative understanding of key content-area vocabulary. We should point out that Chapter 5 offers several other strategies similar to semantic-feature analysis that can be used to teach and reinforce vocabulary—strategies such as the graphic organizer.

Activities Encouraging Firsthand Concept Development

The terminology in content textbooks is often sterile, abstract, and lifeless, which makes this content especially difficult to understand and retain and leaves students unmotivated to read. Standing before the class and stating glossary-type definitions of textbook vocabulary merely reinforces students' passivity. We need to find ways of making key terms and concepts come alive for students so that they are motivated to read and learn.

Firsthand concept development refers to a variety of approaches that provide students with direct ways of experiencing words (Sartain & Stahl, 1982). Direct or firsthand involvement with words can include dramatized experiences, demonstrations, case studies, field trips, exhibits, television shows or movies, or computer simulations. The premise underlying this vocabulary approach is that information stored in long-term memory is undoubtedly a result of a great deal of mental, emotional, and physical involvement with the content.

Ideally, students should be given opportunities to have direct contact with all the words they encounter. For instance, students about to study a unit about meteorology could be allowed to hold and inspect a barometer or a rain gauge. Unfortunately, many technical vocabulary words are too abstract to be easily represented by a physical object brought into the classroom. Therefore, you must invent ways to make abstract terminology tangible for students. We will examine how three different content-area teachers' inventions or approaches helped their students experience concepts in a firsthand manner. Bernard used a demonstration, Margo involved her students in a scavenger hunt, and Guy photographed his students demonstrating adjectives.

Demonstrations

Bernard, a senior high psychology teacher, used an inventive activity to help his students experience and understand a key concept they were preparing to read about in their textbooks. The topic was human memory, and the class was asked to write 10 things they did the first day of second grade. Over the initial moans and groans, Bernard insisted that each student list 10 items within a couple of minutes to "play the game" properly. Eventually, all students were busy working on their lists. When they were finished, Bernard asked them to read the items on their lists and to talk about how they produced the items they could not recall with certainty. Students read off such things as "met the teacher," "talked with my friends from first grade," "took my seat," "received my books," and so on. Most said they could not remember all the details about what they did the first day of second grade, but they listed the things they assumed they had done. Afterward, Bernard explained that the students had been "confabulating" by creating their lists on the basis of related experience rather than definite memory.

Defined in the traditional way, with a textbook definition, *confabulation* is a sterile term. When students were allowed to experience confabulation firsthand, however, they had an experience to which they could affix the meaning of the concept in memory. In turn, the textbook chapter on memory should be easier to understand. Bernard said that his students remembered the meaning of *confabulation* and other concepts long after the unit in which they appeared had been completed if he tied an experience to the process of learning the terms. Firsthand concept development allows for greater student involvement in learning new terminology and concepts, which then encourages deeper understanding of the concepts and improves the likelihood that the textual information you are stressing will be easier to comprehend. Word scavenger hunts also have this potential.

Word Scavenger Hunts

All of us have participated in a real scavenger hunt at some time in our lives. Remember the thrill and excitement of competing with other teams in trying to be the first to gather assorted items in a limited time? Scavenger hunts for helping students build word meanings by collecting real items and pictures are valuable because they are fun, develop cooperative learning skills, and require active involvement. These elements of the strategy ensure that vocabulary learning will be more memorable (Moore, Moore, Cunningham, & Cunningham, 1986).

An eighth-grade science class developed a genuine "learning frenzy" when given the opportunity to work in cooperative groups and compete with other groups in a **word scavenger hunt.** The teacher, Margo, had selected vocabulary words from a textbook chapter on astronomy, words for which she thought students could find actual objects, models, or pictures. She included the key terms that the students needed to learn to gain a full understanding of the important content of the astronomy unit. In compiling her master list, which follows, she included technical words she knew would be easy to collect as well as difficult words:

comet	meteor	pulsar	nova	cosmic dust
red giant	sextant	black hole	radiation	big bang
telescope	asteroid	gravity	radar	crater

Margo divided her class into teams of four students and explained the scavenger hunt to be sure that all of them understood the rules and purpose. She accomplished this by asking students to share their experiences with scavenger hunting. She then specified the conditions of the competition:

- Students must bring in objects and pictures by a certain date.
- No team should reveal to any other team which items they collected and where they found the items until the hunt is over.

As she handed out the master list of content vocabulary words to each team, Margo explained that teams would earn 3 points for an actual object, 2 points for a model or facsimile, and 1 point for a picture. A few students asked if they were allowed to draw or trace, and Margo said that such art would be admissible; however, the drawing should reflect genuine effort and should not be something put together minutes before the conclusion of the hunt. She went on to explain that an object or a picture cannot count for more than one word. Teams were then given the opportunity to assign specific roles to each of their members and to discuss strategies for finding words. Teams were allowed 1 week to complete the hunt.

During the week, teams met a couple of times to update their progress in finding words and to revise their strategy, if necessary. Periodically, they were reminded to maintain secrecy about the status of the hunt, which heightened the suspense of the competition. By midweek, some students were complaining that they could not find an object or a picture for certain words. Margo told them that it might be impossible to collect objects or pictures for every word. Statements of this kind inevitably push teams to search out difficult words with renewed vigor just to prove the teacher wrong.

At week's end, the teams were allowed to go over their findings and tally the points. Margo double-checked the teams' figures and looked over the drawings to make sure they clearly represented the words and were not thrown together haphazardly. Finally, the team with the most points was declared the winner. They were allowed to gloat over their victory only briefly, however, because Margo rewarded each team for its efforts with an opportunity to display and publish its work.

Giving them the following options, Margo asked the groups to select what they wished to do with their findings and provided the necessary materials to get them started:

- Collages with the words on cards appropriately arranged
- Slide shows developed by photographing the objects and pictures and writing a brief explanation
- Picture books with photographs and illustrations accompanied by a brief explanation
- Newspapers or comic books with pictures and illustrations accompanied by stories
- An exhibit table with objects labeled and briefly described

Not only are word scavenger hunts fun, but they also go a long way toward building relevant prior knowledge for the chapter or unit. Hunts allow students to explore the topic by collecting and reading about key vocabulary words taken from the content. Students gather a great deal of information about the topic and develop an interest in it. The benefits of the hunt last throughout and beyond the unit. For instance, in the classroom just described, students were surrounded during the unit with reminders of the topic's key terms in the form of collages on the wall, a display corner in the back of the room, and books featured on the classroom library shelves.

The hands-on approach to gathering pictures and objects for words makes scavenger hunting a sound instructional strategy for enhancing students' interest in learning, their vocabulary understanding, and their reading comprehension.

Photographed Vocabulary

Teachers tell us adjectives work the best for this activity.

Another approach providing firsthand and interesting involvement with a word has been labeled **photographed vocabulary** (Stanley, 1971). This approach involves photographing students as they demonstrate the meaning of one word in a tableau. Guy, a language arts teacher for students who speak English as a second language, uses photographed vocabulary because it capitalizes on his students' "unabashed vanity and love of drama." He told us that he begins the process by selecting a list of 25 "actable" words that the class had previously encountered and discussed. The adjectives the students were to act out or dramatize described people in positive or negative ways and included words such as *studious, timid, sinister,* and *eccentric.* Guy then used the following steps to introduce the activity:

1. He told the students that each of them would have responsibility for demonstrating to the class a word from the list. Their demonstration would have to be in a tableau or frozen representation because they would be photographed. While each student was doing his or her tableau, the rest of the class would be writing down the word they felt was being acted out. The entire class would have the list of 25 words, their definitions, and sentences using the words. The students who correctly matched the words to the tableaus would receive 5 extra-credit points.

2. Guy then asked each student to draw from a hat the word he or she would demonstrate. Students were told to be ready with their tableau in 3 days.

3. The next day, the principal visited the class and modeled how she would do a tableau for the word *exasperated.* Guy modeled the word *eccentric.*

4. The day before the assignment was due, Guy checked with all students to make sure they were prepared and offered suggestions for those still groping for ideas.

5. On the day of the photographing, Guy listed the students' names on the board in the order of presentation. As the students posed, he took the pictures and the rest of the class worked to match the word to the tableau.

As a follow-up to the assignment, Guy placed all the pictures on the bulletin board. Even 3 weeks later, students still gathered around the board to check the pictures and discuss the words. Guy told us that this was probably one of the best assignments he had done that year because the students were actually incorporating the words into their writing and speaking, the real touchstone of any vocabulary approach.

Semantic-Feature Analysis

As stated throughout this chapter, to read successfully in the content areas, students must have a deep, elaborative understanding of important concepts. **Semantic-feature analysis** is a highly effective technique for reinforcing the vocabulary essential to understanding important concepts (Johnson & Pearson, 1984; Stahl, 1999).

Semantic-feature analysis is also a superb way to reinforce the concepts in a content-area unit.

Semantic-feature analysis involves building a grid in which essential vocabulary is listed on one axis of the grid and major features, characteristics, or important ideas are listed on the other axis. Students fill in the grid, indicating the extent to which the key words possess the stated features or are related to important ideas. Once the grid is completed, students are led to discover both the shared and unique characteristics of the vocabulary words.

Figure 6.2 is a word grid created for a study of polygons. Notice that the vertical axis contains the names of geometric figures, whereas the horizontal axis contains important features or characteristics of these figures. The extra spaces allow students to add more vocabulary and features as they work through the reading material.

Another example of the use of word grids (see Figure 6.3) is provided by Aaron, a 10th-grade government teacher, who is particularly effective in teaching key terms and concepts with semantic-feature analysis. He begins by asking his class for the names of fruit, writing them on the blackboard in a vertical list as students call them out. After several fruits are listed, he writes a couple of general features of fruit along the top horizontal axis of the grid, such as "tree grown" and "edible skin"; then he asks for additional features. Finally, he asks the class to consider each type of fruit and whether it possesses any of the listed features. As they go down the list of fruit, they discuss each one relative to the characteristics listed across the top, and Aaron puts a 0, 1, or 2 in the box where the fruit and feature meet on the grid. A 0 indicates that the fruit possesses none of that feature, a 1 indicates that it possesses some of that feature, and a 2 means that it possesses all of the feature. When the grid is entirely filled in, Aaron explains to the students how they can, at a glance, determine the key characteristics of a particular fruit, as well as the similarities and differences between the fruits.

By involving students in the construction of a simple word grid, Aaron introduces them to the semantic-feature analysis process. He goes on to explain how to build word grids for the key vocabulary in their textbook. To help students discover how the grid-building process can be applied to the content vocabulary in their texts, he presents a grid based on a section of a recently completed chapter on the Fifth Amendment to the Constitution. Aaron tells them that in building the grid, he first read the selection and identified the major ideas.

	opposite sides parallel	equilateral	equiangular	4-sided	3-sided
square					
rectangle					
triangle					
rhombus					
trapezoid					

FIGURE 6.2   Word Grid for Polygons

	edible skin	tree grown	bunches	citrus	fleshy
banana	0	2	2	0	2
peach	2	2	0	0	2
orange	1	2	0	2	0
apple	2	2	0	0	2
grapes	2	0	2	0	2
grapefruit	0	2	0	2	0

FIGURE 6.3   Word Grid for Fruit

The Fifth Amendment			
*Citizens' right to remain silent Capital crime Infamous crime Indictment	Double jeopardy *Private property cannot be taken Due process	Just compensation Deprived Compelled Offense	*Doesn't apply to military cases *Citizens' right to avoid self-incrimination

FIGURE 6.4   Key Vocabulary for a Word Grid for the Fifth Amendment

Next, he listed in a phrase or a single word the vocabulary that represented or was related to each idea. This was followed by an examination of the list to determine which words represent the biggest ideas (indicated by asterisks in Figure 6.4).

Then Aaron identified the words representing the important details related to the major ideas. At this point, he says, he now had enough information to organize the vocabulary and major ideas into a grid, with the major ideas across the top and the related vocabulary listed on the side (Figure 6.5).

Aaron then walks students through the process of deciding on components of the grid, discussing with them the relationship between each major idea and each vocabulary word as they fill in the grid together.

Later, as his students improve their ability to design word grids, Aaron gives them increasing responsibility to complete grids on their own. This is accomplished by providing them with partially filled-in grids containing a few key vocabulary words and major ideas or essential features. As students move through the chapter or unit of study, they expand the grid work to include additional vocabulary and features.

These students are also allowed plenty of time for class discussion and for review of the vocabulary and major ideas. They are given the opportunity to work in cooperative groups where they share their entries on the grids and review each vocabulary word, noting the pattern of numbers (0, 1, 2).

Teachers tell us they like semantic-feature analysis because it requires minimal preparation on their part yet provides students an excellent review for a unit of study. More important, they have discovered that the grid encourages students to think critically and divergently as they determine the relationships between key vocabulary and major concepts.

These approaches to vocabulary development—firsthand concept development and semantic-feature analysis—are typically used by the content-area teacher to improve conceptual understanding. In the next section, we present some ways in which content-area teachers can teach students independent strategies for building their own vocabularies.

The Fifth Amendment

	citizens' right to remain silent	private property cannot be taken	doesn't apply to military cases	citizens' right to avoid self-incrimination
capital crime				
infamous crime				
indictment				
double jeopardy				
due process				
just compensation				
deprived				
compelled				
offense				

FIGURE 6.5   Word Grid for the Fifth Amendment

PROMOTING INDEPENDENT WORD LEARNING

In order for students to increase their vocabulary knowledge, they must have a variety of generative or independent word-building strategies.

As we made clear earlier in this chapter, content-area teachers should be concerned about two vitally important aspects of vocabulary development. One is to teach key vocabulary and concepts that students need in order to understand the important content, whether in a listening or reading situation. The previous section demonstrated several effective ways in which classroom teachers can help their students develop elaborative understandings of critical terms and concepts. Another equally important aspect of vocabulary development is to teach students a variety of strategies for independently gathering and learning new

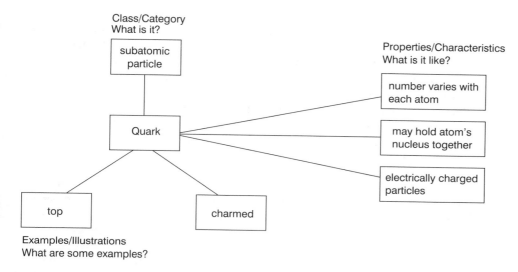

FIGURE 6.6 **Word Map for _Quark_**

words. This section describes two generative strategies—word maps and concept cards—that can be used across the content areas.

Word Maps

Students will become more independent in their vocabulary learning if we provide instruction that gradually shifts the responsibility for generating meanings for new words from us to them. One effective way of encouraging this transition is with word maps. Schwartz and Raphael (1985) developed this strategy for helping students establish a concept of definition for content-area words. The strategy stresses the importance of teaching students how to use context clues independently, how to determine if they know what a word means, and how to use prior knowledge to enhance their understanding of words.

To build a **word map**, students write the concept being studied, or the word they would like to define, in the center box of a map, such as _quark_ in Figure 6.6. Next, in the top box they write a brief answer to the question "What is it?" This question seeks a name for the class or category that includes the concept. In defining _quark,_ the category is a "subatomic particle." In responding to the question to the right, "What is it like?" students write critical attributes, characteristics, or properties of the concept or word. In the example, three critical properties of quarks are listed. The question along the bottom, "What are some examples?", can be answered by supplying examples of different kinds of quarks, such as _top_ and _charmed._

Teaching students how to create word maps gives them a strategy for generating word meanings independently. Because of the checking process they go through in asking questions about the context, this strategy also fosters self-monitoring and metacognitive thinking (Schwartz, 1988). The goal, therefore, is

Word maps help students realize that "knowing" a word involves more than just recognizing or reciting a definition.

to help students internalize this test-questioning process for all of the important words they must learn. All of us ask similar questions when we encounter unfamiliar words in context, though we rarely, if ever, draw (as in the form of a word map) the information we are seeking about the words. Think of the word map as a visual representation of students' thought processes while trying to figure out word meanings in context. Eventually, after they have demonstrated an understanding of the process by creating appropriate word maps, students should be shown that they do not have to create a map for every word they do not know. Instead, they should go through the questioning process in their heads, as mature readers do.

To help you understand how students can be taught to use word maps in the classroom, we describe the experiences of Tonya, an eighth-grade science teacher. She began her vocabulary lesson by displaying the structure of the word map and introducing it as a visual guide to remind her students of what they needed to know to understand a new, important word or concept. As the components of the map were discussed, she supplied a concept and filled in answers to the questions on the map with information from a recently studied chapter in their science textbook.

Tonya then directed students to the chapter they were about to read and, with their help, identified a key concept occurring in the first few pages: *conifer.* She asked the students to work in cooperative groups to find information in their texts and in their heads to answer the questions on the word map. As they read about conifers, they discussed the relevant information that helped define the concept and inserted it into the appropriate spaces on the map they were creating. When they completed their maps, Tonya modeled how information about class/category, properties/characteristics, and examples related to the concept could be pulled from the context. She talked about how contexts vary from *complete* (containing rich information) to *partial* (containing scanty information). She encouraged students to include their own information and ideas, especially with stingy contexts, to further their understanding of the word. Drawing on the input from groups, the whole class then worked together to create a word map for *conifer* (see Figure 6.7).

At this point, Tonya asked her students to write a definition for *conifer* based on the word-map activity. Afterward, she asked them to work in their cooperative groups and evaluate each other's definitions to determine if they were complete and, if not, to write down whatever additional information was needed. Definitions were then returned to their owners, who responded to the group's feedback. With their maps and definitions completed, students were shown that their work can serve as excellent study aids for rehearsal and long-term retention of the concept.

Tonya ended the day's lesson by assigning the students to create word maps for three other key concepts in the chapter. Before leaving, students began their assignment by identifying the possible concepts in the chapter. This procedure of modeling and assigning continued throughout the semester until Tonya was sure that students knew how to apply the word-map strategy independently to

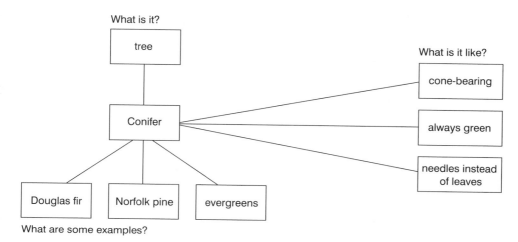

FIGURE 6.7 **Word Map for** *Conifer*

their science vocabulary. She also encouraged students to try applying it to their other courses.

Word maps can help students guide their search for new information, monitor their learning of vocabulary, and improve understanding and recall of content-area concepts.

Concept Cards

Concept cards are another strategy students can use to learn difficult general or technical vocabulary (Nist & Simpson, 2001). You may have used these in your own studying but probably called them *flash cards*. Even though **concept cards** have the same format as flash cards in that they allow students to test themselves, we prefer the term *concept cards* because they involve students in learning more than just definitions for difficult terminology. As illustrated in Figure 6.8, on the front of the concept card, students write the targeted word and the superordinate idea for the word. On the back of the card, they provide the following information, when appropriate: (1) definition(s), (2) characteristics or features, (3) examples from the text and/or personal experiences, and (4) personal sentences. The card in Figure 6.9 illustrates how one 12th grader used concept cards to study the technical terms in her business course. Notice how she adapted the card to fit her purposes.

Students can use either 4×6 or 3×5 index cards, but it is important that they use cards rather than pieces of notebook paper because the cards encourage students to test themselves rather than to look at the terminology passively. Cards are also more durable and portable, allowing students to study them while standing in line, riding the bus, or waiting for class to begin.

These concept cards are more than flash cards!

FIGURE 6.8 Content of a Concept Card

SUPERORDINATE IDEA

TARGETED WORD

[FRONT OF THE CARD]

1. Definitions

2. Characteristics: features

3. Examples (text or personal)

4. Personal sentences

[BACK OF CARD]

Carol, a teacher for gifted seventh graders, asks her students to create concept cards for the words she identifies and for the words they choose to learn. The general words she selects for their study come from their integrated history and literature units. Each week she also asks her students to select three unfamiliar words from their own reading that they would like to learn. Because she wants her students to understand the original context and to apply the word to new situations, Carol asks them to write the original sentence on the front of the card and at least one original sentence on the back. Figure 6.10 illustrates a concept card a student made for the word *turgid* that came from a short story.

There are 2 types

FORMAL ORGANIZATION

FIGURE 6.9   A Concept Card by a 12th Grader for Technical Terms in a Business Course

1. Clearly defined relationships, channels of communication, and delegation of authority.

2. Characteristics: clearly defined authority relationships, well-developed communication systems, stable/permanent, capable of expansion.

3. Tools of formal organizations include charts, policy manuals, organization manuals.

4. Example: where my father works (IBM).

To determine the students' accuracy in finding the most appropriate dictionary definition and their precision in writing a sentence that uses the words correctly, Carol usually checks the cards while students are working in groups on another activity. By doing these quick checks of the cards, she knows what words need to be emphasized the next day during discussion. Carol is a strong believer in taking time to discuss words so students can hear the various definitions and sentences that their classmates have written. She tells us that the nuances and connotations of words are not learned from the dictionary; rather, they are learned from "trying on the words and playing with them" in an environment that invites experimentation.

FIGURE 6.10 Concept Card for the Word *Turgid*

adjective

TURGID

The 13-page text includes a poem, an introduction, and a *turgid* opening chapter interpreting the First Seal.

1. Excessively ornate, flashy, wordy, and pompous in style or language

2. Synonym: *bombastic*   Antonym: *plain, simple language*

The minister's turgid sermon put everyone to sleep on the warm Sunday evening.

Carol models for the students how they should study their concept cards because she has discovered that many of them merely look at the front of their cards and then at the back without testing themselves or reciting aloud. While modeling, she makes sure that students realize the importance of saying the definitions and sentences aloud. Moreover, she stresses the importance of practicing from front to back and from back to front on the cards and the usefulness of making piles of cards representing the words that are known and the words that need further study. Carol has been requiring students to make concept cards for about 5 years. She has noticed a substantial improvement in their retention of the words and, more important, their use of the words in their written work.

Word Sorts Using Concept Cards

A **word sort** is an excellent reinforcement activity that students can use with their concept cards. During a word sort, students group their cards into different categories with common features. There are two types of word sorts: closed and open (Gillet & Kita, 1979).

With the *closed sort,* students know in advance the categories in which they must place their cards. For example, the students in Carol's class were asked to sort their concept cards into positive adjectives and negative adjectives. Thus, students sorted words such as *turgid, pretentious, neurotic,* and *condescending* into the negative adjectives category and words such as *charismatic* and *diligent* into the positive adjectives category. Carol tells students to do this activity in small groups and then asks each group to explain and justify their groupings. Being able to manipulate the concept cards makes the word-sort activity more interesting and flexible for students.

Open sorts require students to determine ways in which their general or technical vocabulary can be grouped. Therefore, students search for relationships that might exist among the words rather than depending on the teacher to provide that structure. In a ninth-grade science class, students were studying pollution and were asked to group their concept cards into one or more categories. The following words share some common categories:

Open word sorts engage students in higher levels of thinking and processing.

biodegradable	photosynthesis
leaching	surface mining
incineration	acid mine drainage
silting	reclamation projects

Can you group the words into some categories? With open sorts, there are no correct categories. Instead, what is important is that students can explain and justify how they grouped the words (Durso & Coggins, 1991). Possible sorts or categories with the preceding words include the broad category of land pollution. On a more specific level of sorting, categories might include causes of land pollution (e.g., silting, acid mine drainage, leaching) and solutions (e.g., biodegradable, reclamation projects). Because open sorts demand more elaborative thinking, they probably should be preceded by several closed-sort activities. Students, however, enjoy both types of activities. More important, teacher preparation for this activity is minimal.

In this section, we have discussed two strategies for helping students learn the meanings of technical and general vocabulary independently in their content area courses. In the next section, we examine how content-area teachers can reinforce and evaluate students' understanding of words with activities similar to word sorts.

ACTIVITIES FOR REINFORCING AND EVALUATING WORD KNOWLEDGE

Go to Web Resources for Chapter 6 at *http://www. prenhall.com/brozo* and look for some additional ideas on reinforcing and evaluating students' vocabulary knowledge.

As mentioned earlier in this chapter, one characteristic of effective vocabulary instruction is that teachers reinforce students' word learning over time. That is, once targeted vocabulary words have been introduced and discussed, students need to practice those words in a variety of new situations. Therefore, fewer words will be taught, and more instructional time will be provided for meaningful reinforcement activities and cumulative review if we want to promote students' understanding of content-area textbooks.

The first reinforcement strategies discussed, imagery and keywords, can be used across the content areas to help students learn technical and general words.

Imagery and Keywords

Have you ever created a mental picture to remember a difficult word or procedure? Many of us do this routinely because we know that images can be powerful reminders. For example, if the targeted word you need to learn is *acrophobia,* what mental picture could you use to remember that the word means fear of high places? One option would be to focus on the first part of the word, *acro,* and develop the image of an acrobat who is afraid of heights walking on a tightrope high in the sky. You could follow up with a sentence such as this: "The acrobat, who has always been afraid of high places, suffered from acrophobia." When we make pictures in our minds to help us remember what a word means or how it relates to another word or superordinate concept, we are using the strategy of **imagery**. Research suggests that imagery can be a powerful tool for reinforcing vocabulary knowledge because students are actively involved in their learning (e.g., Levin, 1993; McCarville, 1993).

Imagery and keyword strategies are excellent ways to help students learn technical vocabulary.

The **keyword strategy** differs slightly from imagery in that we think of catchy phrases or sentences related to the word we want to remember. For example, if you were having trouble remembering *amorous,* you might think about a phrase such as "more love for us," which sounds like *amorous* but has a synonym for the word in it. Although the research findings on the keyword and imagery strategies are positive and promising, they will not work for every vocabulary word or for every student. In addition, it is important to remember that students' personal images or catchy phrases will always be more powerful than the images or phrases provided by their teacher.

TEACHING Learners DIVERSE

Dale, a 10th-grade biology teacher, uses a combination of imagery and keywords to help his students with learning disabilities remember difficult definitions and relationships between concepts. During his unit on the endocrine system, he modeled the procedures he used in creating images and keywords to remember the functions of the glands and hormones in the endocrine system. One of his students, Lara, had difficulty applying the strategies, so Dale met with her during homeroom to help her. The lesson follows.

Dale: Lara, let's start with the pituitary gland and the thyrotropic hormone. To remember the definition, we need to think of something memorable from part of the word *thyrotropic.* I'll start first, and then I'll have you help me. When I hear the word *tropic,* I think of the jungles where rain stimulates extreme growth. Thyrotropic hormones stimulate growth in the thyroid, the other part of the word. Do you see what I did, Lara? I took parts of the word that I could remember because they were already familiar to me. Then I made up a sentence to help me remember the definition. Which word would you like to try next?

Lara: I missed *prolactin* on the pop quiz. Can we try this one?

Dale: Okay, Lara. Let's look at the word carefully—each letter and the parts. Can you divide the word into familiar parts?

Lara: Well, there is the word *pro,* which means a professional, in the word *prolactin.* There is also the word *tin.*

Dale: Okay, Lara. Will either of them help you remember the definition of *prolactin,* a hormone that stimulates milk production?

Lara: No, I don't see how.

Dale: Okay. Let's see if we can play with the middle part of the word, *lac.* This part of the word sounds like what word in our language, Lara?

Lara: Lack?

Dale: That's right! Has your mother ever told you that you lack milk— that you should drink more milk if you hope to be healthy?

Lara: Yes! And I hate the stuff.

Dale: Could we use the letters *l-a-c* to remind us of milk? Many people *lack* the correct amount of milk.

Lara: Yes, but what about the *pro* part of the word?

Dale: Good question. Could we use *pro* to remind us in some way that prolactin is a hormone that stimulates milk? Think about this for a moment, Lara.

Lara: (a few seconds later) Yes! Professional athletes should not suffer from a lack of milk. Will that work?

Dale: Will it work for you, Lara? That is what makes the difference.

Lara: Hmm. Yes, I can use that—it makes sense. Professional athletes should not suffer from a lack of milk. Prolactin stimulates milk production.

Dale: Let's review before we go to the next word, Lara. Give me the definitions of *thyrotropic* and *prolactin.*

Lara: Prolactin stimulates the production of milk, and the thyrotropic hormone stimulates the thyroid. This is easy.

Dale: The next hormone you missed on the quiz is *thyroxine.* Lara, what are the steps in this process of remembering a definition of a difficult word?

Notice how Dale encourages Lara to state the steps of this vocabulary strategy before she applies the strategy independently to another word. Had Lara not been able to use the strategy after this individual lesson, Dale would have shown her another strategy to help her keep straight the definitions and functions of the 47 different technical terms in this unit. He tries to present a variety of choices for his students with learning disabilities because he knows that students learn in different ways. With Lara, however, imagery and keywords worked once she realized the processes involved in them. We should point out, however, that students need not have a learning disability in order to benefit from using imagery or the keyword strategy.

Activities and Test Formats That Reinforce and Evaluate Word Learning

If students are to learn their targeted words at a full and conceptual level of understanding, the activities and test formats we select for reinforcement and evaluation should match that level of thinking. Evidence suggests, however, that commercial materials typically use multiple-choice and matching formats as the main method of reinforcement and testing (Simpson & Randall, 2000). We know that these formats do not challenge students to demonstrate their full understanding of words (Beck & McKeown, 1991; Blachowicz & Fisher, 2000). Rather, when students circle letters or draw lines to match a definition to a word, they are passively involved in guesswork. Even asking students to write a definition of a word from memory does not stimulate conceptual understanding. Therefore, alternative reinforcement and evaluation activities are needed.

Constructing creative and appropriate reinforcement and evaluative activities can be challenging. However, several activities and formats can be incorporated into any classroom routine, homework assignment, or unit exam. In fact, we know several content-area teachers who begin their class each day with one of these reinforcement activities on the overhead projector. These activities and formats involve students in a variety of elaborative thinking processes. Some of these activities and test formats follow.

Statement Plus a Request

These formats will ensure that your students will learn the words.

With the **statement plus a request** activity, students read two related statements, each containing the same targeted word. The second statement, however, asks students to demonstrate their knowledge of the word by exceeding the usual simple definition. In a sophomore history class, a teacher included this question on her unit test:

> *Directions:* Read the first statement carefully. Then read the second statement and answer it. Pay close attention to the italicized word.
>
> 1. *Statement:* Robert LaFollette was a *Progressive* with many ideas on what he wanted changed in Wisconsin.

2. *Request:* What are some of the *Progressive* ideas that Robert LaFollette had?

Exclusion

Henry (1974) states that excluding is one of the basic operations involved in concept development. When students practice **exclusion,** they discriminate between, negate, and recognize examples and nonexamples. The following example is a sample from an algebra teacher's homework assignment:

> *Directions:* Choose the one equation in each group that does not relate to the others and should be excluded. Write the letter of it in the blank after "Exclude." In the blank labeled "General Concept," write the concept that describes the remaining words.

Exclusion Activities

1. a. $x^2 - y^2 = (x + y)(x - y)$
   b. $x^2 + 5x + 6 = (x + 3)(x + 2)$
   c. $ax^2 + a^2x = ax(x - a)$
   d. $3x^2 + 4x^2 + 1 = 7x^2 + 1$

   Exclude: _____
   General Concept: _____

The following example of an exclusion item is from a French teacher's unit test:

1. la glace   la moutarde   le gâteau   la tarte

   Exclude: _____
   General Concept: _____

Paired Word Questions

The long-term vocabulary study by Beck, Perfetti, and McKeown (1982) employed a question-asking activity that paired two targeted words. To answer these *paired word questions,* students must understand the underlined concepts or words and then determine if any relationships exist between them. The following example is one of several items that an art teacher uses during class when he pairs words for a review. Notice that he tests both technical *(avant-garde)* and general *(incoherent)* vocabulary word knowledge:

> *Directions:* Answer the following questions as completely as possible, making sure you demonstrate your full knowledge of the underlined words.

1. Would an *avant-garde* painting be *incoherent?* Why or why not?

The next example is from a review activity that a ninth-grade physical education teacher included in a unit on nutrition and fitness:

1. Would an individual with *hyperlipidemia* be a candidate for *coronary heart disease?* Why or why not?

   2. Would an individual who had a *calorie deficit of 3,500 kcal* lose 1 pound of *adipose tissue?* Why or why not?

Seeing the Big Picture

With the format called **seeing the big picture,** students are asked to select the word or phrase that subsumes all the other words or phrases. By completing such an item, students demonstrate that they can discriminate the difference between a major concept and a detail or supporting idea. The following example illustrates how a mathematics teacher used the format in one of her review activities:

> *Directions:* Look at the group of words below and select the one word or phrase that subsumes the other four. Circle it.
>
> 1. Distributive properties, axiom, multiplicative inverse, cancellation law, additive identities

Analogies

Analogies are multifaceted in that they can involve students in knowing the synonyms or antonyms of targeted words or can encourage students to sense the relationships between words in a variety of ways. In fact, there are probably 50 different formats to the analogy. The following example is from a French teacher's homework assignment:

> *Directions:* Fill in the blank with the appropriate vocabulary word. You may use each word only once.
>
> 1. beau : mauvais :: froid : _____

The next analogy is from an 11th-grade art class. The teacher had just finished a unit on film and used items such as this for a review activity:

> 1. celluloid : film :: matte effect : _____

Paired Word Sentence Generation

Traditional sentence-writing activities have never been considered particularly creative or productive. However, **paired word sentence generation** forces students to demonstrate their conceptual understanding of both words and to seek out their implied relationship in order to write a sentence that uses the words correctly. The following example illustrates how a history teacher used this format to reinforce important vocabulary words in a class activity.

> *Directions:* You will find two words below that I have purposely paired because they have some relationship to each other. Your task is to write one sentence that uses both of the words correctly and clearly demonstrates your understanding of them and their relationship to each other. You will be asked to share your sentence with the class and to explain why you paired the words as you did. The first item has been done for you as an example.

1. muckrakers, *McClure's Magazine*

The muckrakers included journalists and novelists who wrote magazines such as *McClure's Magazine* and books such as *The Jungle* to expose the evils and corruption in business and politics.

2. Wisconsin idea, referendum

The next example comes from a music teacher's lesson.

Directions: Write a sentence using the following word pairs. I have purposely paired the two words because they have some relationship to each other.

1. cadence, afterphase
2. binary form, ternary form

Because these alternative activities and formats may initially confuse or surprise the students, a few important guidelines about their use should be remembered (Nist & Simpson, 2001). First, match the reinforcement or evaluation activity to the unit objectives or goals. Students can demonstrate only the level of conceptual understanding that they have been involved in during the unit. Second, vary the activities and formats across the school year and within the units of study. For example, a history teacher might include five exclusions, five analogies, and five paired word sentence-generation activities into a unit test to represent the different thinking processes underlying conceptual understanding. Finally, inform, practice, and discuss the differing activities and formats with students, especially before they see them on a test. If students are not accustomed to a new activity or test format, their response or score could mask their real understanding. In fact, it is always a good idea to provide a sample item, as did the history teacher for the paired word activity.

Make sure you always provide your students practice and debriefing sessions when you use a different type of evaluation format.

CASE STUDY REVISITED

We now return to the Winter Park School District, where a districtwide committee of teachers has been meeting throughout the school year to solve the problem of extremely low vocabulary scores in the eighth grade. After reading this chapter, you probably have some ideas on how the committee could solve this problem. Take a moment now to write your suggestions.

By the end of the school year, Rafalar, the curriculum director, and the eighth-grade teachers on the committee had reached only one decision. One eighth-grade science teacher had discussed an article he had read on the characteristics of effective vocabulary instruction, prompting the committee to decide that there were no "quick fixes" and that no single type of commercial material would fully address their school's problems. Perhaps that decision was the most important because it removed as an option the vocabulary computer program that several members were urging the school to adopt. The committee members realized that the computer program expected students to learn the targeted words in lists with no context and that only rote-level definitional knowledge was emphasized on the activities and quizzes.

Before writing your suggestions for the committee, go to *http://www.prenhall.com/ brozo*, select Chapter 6, then click on Chapter Review Questions to check your understanding of the material.

Hence, they were concerned about whether students would learn the words well enough to be able to apply them to new situations.

Although the committee did reach agreement on the use of commercial materials for the Winter Park School District, they still disagreed about the language arts teachers' role in improving students' vocabulary. Some teachers saw the teaching of vocabulary as a time-consuming intrusion into an already hectic teaching schedule. Moreover, they viewed vocabulary instruction as a natural and logical part of a language arts curriculum. Consequently, the curriculum director suggested that the issue be tabled for a while, at least until they had finished their intensive study of vocabulary acquisition.

During the summer, the committee members were provided with a stipend to read and plan further. The curriculum director had the money for the study because expensive commercial materials had not been purchased from the school budget. At their first meeting, she suggested that the committee begin with some general goals rather than adopting commercial materials or another school's approach. With the focus of establishing specific goals for vocabulary instruction at their school, the teachers read intensively about vocabulary development and kept personal learning logs. They chose articles from journals in their own content area, articles from the *Journal of Adolescent & Adult Learning,* and recent books on the topic published by professional organizations such as the International Reading Association. A major breakthrough occurred when one of the more vocal and negative teachers read a review of the literature explaining how vocabulary knowledge was closely related to students' understanding of what they read. She shared that information with the rest of the committee and made a rather compelling case for the importance of vocabulary knowledge to content-area learning. From that point on, very few committee members wanted only the language arts teachers to assume responsibility for vocabulary development.

After considerable reading and discussion, the committee developed the following goals for the school district:

1. The students should develop a long-term interest and enjoyment in developing and refining their vocabulary.

2. The students should learn some independent strategies for learning new technical and general vocabulary words.

3. The students should become skilled in the use of the dictionary and, when appropriate, contextual analysis.

Pleased with their goals, the committee members decided that their next step was to outline how each goal could be incorporated into their own curriculum and how the departments could reinforce each other. They also decided that these goals should not be limited to the eighth-grade teachers but should involve all middle school teachers and their students. Their reasoning was that an effective program of vocabulary improvement needed to be comprehensive and cumulative if real growth and change were to occur.

The language arts teachers decided that they would teach students interesting word histories and origins via Greek and Latin mythology. The social studies teachers decided to implement "The Word of the Week," which they would choose together from something they had heard on the news or read in a newspaper. This word would be placed on the bulletin board, discussed on Monday, and reinforced throughout the week. The science and math teachers incorporated that idea with a slightly different twist. Modifying Haggard's (1982) vocabulary self-collection strategy, they had their students select the word or symbol for the week that they wanted to study.

The committee members decided that they also needed to identify the technical vocabulary they would teach their students for each of their units, making sure that they did not try to teach too many words. They had read about the importance of teaching words intensively rather than extensively. The science teachers recommended that they should share these words with each other so they could gain a big-picture perspective of the words students were being asked to learn.

Of course, the committee did not agree on everything. By the end of the summer, they were still debating who should be responsible for teaching the fundamentals of how to use the dictionary. In addition, some teachers wanted everyone to agree that they would assign students to complete concept cards for all the new vocabulary. The others, while conceding the importance of teaching students a vocabulary strategy, wanted more flexibility in selecting the strategies. They all agreed, however, on the importance of selecting and teaching vocabulary strategies that would foster students' conceptual understanding of important new words.

Because the school year was about to begin, the committee decided to implement the first two goals and to evaluate the impact of their unified effort at the end of the school year. They concluded, however, that students' scores on the competency-based reading test would probably not increase suddenly as a result of these small steps toward their unified effort to improve word knowledge and reading comprehension. From their readings and discussions, they realized that their goal of improving students' vocabulary knowledge would involve a long-term commitment by every middle school teacher.

——◄○►——

SUMMARY

In this chapter we stressed the importance of students having an elaborative understanding of technical and general vocabulary in order to improve their content-area learning. Because simple definitional knowledge of a word is not sufficient for textbook comprehension, teachers will need to stress the context links from what students know to what they will learn. This contextual understanding of content-area terms and concepts can be facilitated by teacher-directed approaches such as Possible Sentences, firsthand concept development, and semantic-feature analysis.

Teachers should stress the vocabulary of their content area as they encourage students to become independent word learners. We therefore discussed vocabulary strategies such as word maps and concept cards that students can use as they read and study their assignments. Whether they are teacher directed or student initiated, these vocabulary strategies become even more powerful and useful when anchored in content-area lessons that emphasize teachers' demonstrations, modeling, small-group interactions, class discussion, and reciprocal teaching. None of these strategies is mutually exclusive; they can and should be used together. For instance, combining strategies such as firsthand concept development with previewing in context will have a stronger and more long-lasting effect than either of these strategies alone.

Like nearly all of the methods presented in this book, the vocabulary strategies discussed here will not always engender immediate enthusiasm for learning words or produce an immediate impact on reading comprehension. Teachers must take time to warm students up to these methods and must allow their students to develop expertise in using the vocabulary strategies.

Finally, remember that any method, regardless of its novelty, will eventually become ineffective if overused. Therefore, it is wise to vary the vocabulary strategies and reinforcement activities often to sustain students' excitement. In the end, however, any vocabulary development strategies that require students to process terms and concepts in elaborative, meaningful, and unique ways will help them understand words and text more fully and retain important concepts and ideas much longer.

REFERENCES

Beck, I., & McKeown, M. (1991). Conditions of vocabulary acquisition. In R. Barr, M. Kamill, P. Mosenthal, & P. D. Pearson (Eds.), *Handbook of reading research* (Vol. 2). New York: Longman.

Beck, I., Perfetti, C. A., & McKeown, M. (1982). The effects of long-term vocabulary instruction on lexical access and reading comprehension. *Journal of Educational Psychology, 74,* 506–521.

Blachowicz, C. L., & Fisher, P. (2000). Vocabulary instruction. In M. Kamil, P. Mosenthal, P. D. Pearson, & R. Barr (Eds.), *Handbook of reading research* (Vol. 3, pp. 503–523). Mahwah, NJ: Lawrence Erlbaum Associates.

Bowles, B. (1988, December 11). Prison site in Georgia marks Civil War horror. *Detroit News,* p. 11-H.

Cronbach, L. J. (1942). An analysis of techniques for systematic vocabulary testing. *Journal of Educational Research, 36,* 206–217.

Cunningham, A., & Stanovich, K. (1991). Tracking the unique effects of print exposure in children: Associations with vocabulary, general knowledge, and spelling. *Journal of Educational Psychology, 83,* 264–274.

Durso, F. T., & Coggins, K. A. (1991). Organized instruction for the improvement of word knowledge skills. *Journal of Educational Psychology, 83,* 108–112.

Gillet, J., & Kita, M. J. (1979). Words, kids, and categories. *The Reading Teacher, 32,* 538–542.

Graves, M. F. (1987). The roles of instruction in fostering vocabulary development. In M. McKeown & M. Curtis (Eds.), *The nature of vocabulary acquisition.* Hillsdale, NJ: Erlbaum.

Haggard, M. R. (1982). The vocabulary self-collection strategy: An active approach to word learning. *Journal of Reading, 26,* 203–207.

Henry, G. H. (1974). *Teach reading as concept development: Emphasis on affective thinking.* Newark, DE: International Reading Association.

Johnson, D. D., & Pearson, P. D. (1984). *Teaching reading vocabulary.* New York: Holt, Rinehart, & Winston.

Laufer, B. (1998). What's in a word that makes it hard or easy: Some intralexical factors that affect the learning of words. In N. Schmidt & M. McCarthy (Eds.), *Vocabulary: Description, acquisition, and pedagogy* (pp. 140–155). Cambridge, MA: Cambridge University Press.

Levin, J. R. (1993). Mnemonic strategies and classroom learning: A twenty-year report card. *Elementary School Journal, 94,* 234–244.

Manzo, A., & Sherk, J. (1971). Some generalizations and strategies to guide vocabulary acquisition. *Journal of Reading Behavior, 4,* 78–89.

McCarville, K. B. (1993). Keyword mnemonic and vocabulary acquisition for developmental college students. *Journal of Developmental Education, 16,* 2–4, 6.

McKeown, M. G. (1990, April). *Making dictionary definitions more effective.* Paper presented at the annual meeting of the American Educational Research Association, Boston.

Moore, D. W., & Moore, S. A. (1986). Possible sentences. In E. K. Dishner, T. W. Bean, J. E. Readence, & D. W. Moore (Eds.), *Reading in the content areas* (2nd ed.). Dubuque, IA: Kendall/Hunt.

Moore, D. W., Moore, S. A., Cunningham, P. M., & Cunningham, J. W. (1986). *Developing readers and writers in the content areas.* New York: Longman.

Nagy, W. E. (1988). *Teaching vocabulary to improve reading comprehension.* Newark, DE: International Reading Association.

Nagy, W. E., & Scott J. (2000). Vocabulary processes. In M. Kamil, P. Mosenthal, P. D. Pearson, & R. Barr (Eds.), *Handbook of reading research* (Vol. 3, pp. 269–284). Mahwah, NJ: Lawrence Erlbaum Associates.

Nist, S. L., & Olejnik, S. (1995). The role of context and dictionary definitions on varying levels of word knowledge. *Reading Research Quarterly, 30,* 172–193.

Nist, S. L., & Simpson, M. L. (2001). *Developing vocabulary concepts for college thinking.* Needham Heights, MA: Allyn and Bacon.

Sartain, H., & Stahl, N. A. (1982). *Techniques for teaching language of the disciplines.* Pittsburgh: University of Pittsburgh Press.

Schatz, E. K., & Baldwin, R. S. (1986). Context clues are unreliable predictors of word meanings. *Reading Research Quarterly, 21,* 439–453.

Schwartz, R. M. (1988). Learning to learn vocabulary in textbooks. *Journal of Reading, 32,* 108–118.

Schwartz, R. M., & Raphael, T. E. (1985). Concept of definition: A key to improving students' vocabulary. *The Reading Teacher, 39,* 198–205.

Scott, J., & Nagy, W. (1997). Understanding the definitions of unfamiliar verbs. *Reading Research Quarterly, 32,* 184–200.

Simpson, M. L., & Randall, S. (2000). Vocabulary development at the college level. In R. Flippo & D. Caverly (Eds.), *Handbook of college reading and study strategy research* (pp. 43–73). Mahwah, NJ: Erlbaum.

Stahl, S. A. (1985). To teach a word well: A framework for vocabulary instruction. *Reading World, 24,* 16–27.

Stahl, S. A. (1986). Three principles of effective vocabulary instruction. *Journal of Reading, 29,* 662–668.

Stahl, S. A. (1999). *Vocabulary development.* Cambridge, MA: Brookline Books.

Stahl, S. A., & Kapinus, B. (1991). Possible sentences: Predicting word meanings to teach content area vocabulary. *The Reading Teacher, 45,* 36–43.

Stanley, J. (1971). Photographed vocabulary. In M. G. McClosky (Ed.), *Teaching strategies and classroom realities.* Englewood Cliffs, NJ: Prentice Hall.

CHAPTER SEVEN

Writing as a Tool for Active Learning

ANTICIPATION GUIDE

Directions: Read each statement carefully and decide whether you agree or dis-agree with it, placing a check mark in the appropriate *Before Reading* column. When you have finished reading and studying the chapter, return to the guide and decide whether your anticipations need to be changed by placing a check mark in the appropriate *After Reading* column.

	BEFORE READING		AFTER READING	
	Agree	*Disagree*	*Agree*	*Disagree*
1. Writing assignments should be reserved for English courses.	___	___	___	___
2. Everything a student writes should be evaluated and graded.	___	___	___	___
3. Writing tasks are best used after students have read their textbook assignments.	___	___	___	___
4. Longer writing assignments are better than shorter ones.	___	___	___	___
5. The best way to respond to students' papers is to write extensive comments on them.	___	___	___	___

Low stakes writing helps students involve themselves more in the ideas or subject matter of a course. It helps them find their own language for the issues of the course; they stumble into their own analogies and metaphors for academic concepts. Theorists are fond of saying that learning a discipline means learning its discourse. That is, students don't know a field until they can write and talk about what is in the textbook and the lectures in their own lingo, in their informal home or personal language.

—Elbow (1997, p. 7)

As Elbow and others (e.g., Herrington, 1997; Fitzgerald & Shanahan, 2000) have pointed out, when teachers incorporate writing strategies into their content areas, they add a powerful vehicle for enhancing their students' learning. For example, a middle school math teacher used writing to help her students with units on multiplication and geometry. The students wrote explanations that described how to do something, defined new words, and explained their errors on quizzes and homework. At the end of the two units, the teacher found that her students who had used writing as a way of learning mathematics scored significantly better on their posttests than did students who had participated in more traditional activities (Jenkinson, 1988). Writing not only facilitates the learning of content-area concepts but also engages students in higher thinking and reasoning processes, especially when they synthesize ideas from a variety of sources (Hynd, 1999; Shanahan, 1997).

Go to *http://www.prenhall.com/brozo*, select Chapter 7, then click on the Chapter Objectives to provide a focus for your reading.

In this chapter we examine the ways in which content-area teachers can capitalize on the many advantages of writing without sacrificing instructional time or adding another responsibility to their incredibly busy days. Our basic theme is this—reading and writing are processes that actively involve students in constructing meaning, in monitoring what they understand, and in refining their conceptual knowledge. As such, when writing is integrated into the existing curriculum, both teachers and students profit immensely.

CASE STUDY

Dave, a first-year teacher, is a member of the biology department at an urban high school. His students are those who do not plan to attend college, and thus they differ from the students he dealt with during his practice teaching. Dave is a bit frustrated because his first unit did not go well. The students appeared to be bored with the chapters he assigned, and many did not complete any of the homework. In fact, out of his five classes, only 10 students received an A or B on the first unit exam. Dave's department chairperson has urged him to be stricter with the students. Another new teacher in the English department with whom he shares lunch duty has suggested that he incorporate more relevant reading materials and assignments into his units. Dave considers the English teacher's recommendation more intriguing than the chairperson's but does not know where to begin. He knows he wants to motivate his students to see biology as relevant to their lives, but he needs direction in planning his next unit. As you read this chapter, think about how Dave might incorporate writing and any other strategies into his next unit on the environment.

READING AND WRITING AS CONSTRUCTIVE PROCESSES

If your friend observed you reading this book and asked for a synopsis, you probably could provide one with a quick glance at the table of contents. What if, however, you were asked to write a summary? Could you complete this task as quickly and easily? Find out by writing a five-sentence summary of the key ideas of the first six chapters. You can place your summary here:

_____

_____

_____

_____

Did you think about the ideas before you began to write your summary? Did you revise your ideas several times? Are your thoughts about the key ideas presented in this book more focused than when you first started to think about the task? Did you learn anything as a result of your writing? If you answered yes to any of these questions, you have experienced the power and permanence of writing. Just as reading is more than moving your eyes across the page, writing is more than "putting ideas" on paper.

Research and theory suggest that reading and writing are not mirror images of each other but "separate, overlapping processes" that provide students alternative ways of constructing meaning (Shanahan, 1997). When students read an assignment from a textbook or write a paper, they are involved in the active process of building their own text world or internal configuration of meaning. Simply put, when students grapple with questions such as "How can I factor a polynomial?" or "How can I explain in my own words the relationship between time, velocity, and distance?" they are beginning to construct meaning and create their own text.

The writing process, not unlike the reading process, has overlapping and recursive stages (Tierney & Pearson, 1983). Although the labeling of these stages is considerably diverse, the motif common to all appears to be a concern for **prewriting**, **writing**, and **postwriting**. Just as active learners use what they already know and set purposes before they begin to read, they also spend extended periods of time before the actual writing to plan, to discover ways of approaching the task, to self-question, and to identify purposes. This stage of the composing process is often ignored because of an inordinate concern for a written product that will be evaluated by the teacher. If students could be provided with more time in class to brainstorm ideas and to discuss writing plans with their peers and their teachers, the quality of their writing would significantly increase (Sargent, 1997).

The writing process includes recursive stages.

The second phase of the writing process focuses on the initial draft. At this point the writer is engaged in the enormous struggle to get words onto paper and into sentences, paragraphs, and sections. As with the reading process, the writer works to make things cohere and fit between the whole and parts and among the parts. Most writers, however, do not follow an orderly process in this initial drafting. Often teachers do not allow enough time in class for this initial drafting or they allow no time at all. Instead, they assign the writing to be done outside of class, where other classmates and the teacher are not available for support and coaching. If students could write their initial drafts during class, teachers would then gain the timely opportunity to meet with their students to discuss their problems in getting ideas down on paper. Moreover, these mini de-briefing sessions can often save teachers considerable evaluation time on the subsequent final product.

The third phase of the writing process involves revising, editing, proofreading, and polishing for readability and interest so that the text is ready for sharing with an audience. Just as active readers pause to reflect on their ideas and then reread to verify, elaborate, or evaluate, mature writers take time to read, reflect on, and evaluate their writing as another would. By taking the role of the reader during this third phase of the writing process, students begin to see their "writing" as a piece of "reading" that must make sense to another individual.

The intensity and willingness that students devote to any of these phases depend on the two conditions that we, as teachers, can control. First, most students have a naive idea of what it takes to be a good writer, just as they do of what it takes to be a good reader. To them, good writing has correct spelling and grammar, whereas good reading is the accurate pronunciation of words. When teachers share with them the processes of their own writing tasks, students are surprised to discover that professionals or mature writers must evaluate and revise extensively before they concern themselves with the surface features of spelling and grammar. Second, students who have never written for anyone but the teacher often feel that their ideas are not worthy of extended writing and revision or that the teacher already understands the ideas, so there is no need to be explicit and clear. They also have difficulty believing in a real audience because the writing task to them is no more than an occasion for a grade. Teachers can change this misconception by providing their students with real and intriguing audiences for their writing so that the urgency of communicating ideas becomes a passion and a drive (Light, 2001).

In short, teachers can help their students understand these recursive and overlapping stages by reserving time in class for brainstorming, planning, drafting, revising, editing, proofreading, and sharing.

HOW CAN THE WRITING PROCESS HELP THE CONTENT-AREA TEACHER?

Content-area teachers rely heavily on their textbooks, lectures, demonstrations, and question-answer sessions as means of transmitting information to students (Wade & Moje, 2000). Unfortunately, many students begin to expect teachers to tell them the important information so that they do not have to think about

Go to Web Resources for Chapter 7 at *http://www. prenhall.com/brozo* and look for more information on the writing process.

ideas. Often textbook assignments are not read; at best, the ideas are quickly memorized for examinations and then forgotten. In short, students become passive learners, sponges soaking up details to pass exams.

The following example from a high school government class demonstrates how the sponge theory operates:

Ernesto assigns his 11th graders to read the first part of Chapter 2, which describes the characteristics of public opinion, and to come to class prepared for discussion. In their reading, the students come across one of the characteristics of public opinion, latency, and its corresponding definition—an opinion not yet crystallized or formed.

Marty, an especially diligent student, repeats that definition several times before coming to class, confident that he is prepared for discussion or an unannounced quiz (for which Ernesto is infamous). Ernesto lives up to his reputation. He asks the students to list and define the five characteristics of public opinion and to give an example of each. Marty, confident of the definition of latency, writes the words "not yet crystallized" but gives no example. In fact, none of the students give examples, and they complain loudly about this aspect of the exam. "There were no examples in the textbook! You are not being fair! We really did read the assignment."

Was Ernesto unfair? Did Marty really understand the concept *latency* or the words "not yet crystallized"? Should Ernesto's students be expected to create examples of concepts? Although we believe that Ernesto was justified in not accepting rote memorization by his students, we also believe that he could have prevented this minor student revolt by integrating the processes of reading and writing into his lesson plans. The combined use of reading and writing in this government class would have provided the students with more opportunities to construct their own definitions of the key concepts (e.g., *latency*) and to discover whether or not they understood. Writing is a potent means of learning that can help passive memorizers become active learners and thinkers.

Writing is a powerful means for learning because the more students manipulate content, the more they are likely to remember and understand that content (Elbow, 1997). When students are asked to write about content-area concepts, they must select and then organize words to represent their understanding of what they have read. To accomplish this, they must relate, connect, and organize ideas from the text. They must establish systematic connections and relationships between words and sentences, the sentences in paragraphs, the paragraphs in texts, and the paragraphs across texts. They must also build interrelationships between the ideas stated in the texts and their own prior knowledge, background, and purposes for reading. These are active processes. In contrast are the passive processes that the students probably employed when they read about the characteristics of public opinion: calling out the words, locating definitions or details, and memorizing word for word those definitions or details. Had they been required to write in some manner about the reading assignment, they would have been better prepared for Ernesto's exam.

Ernesto could have incorporated writing into his classroom routine in three basic ways. Perhaps the most common use of writing is to help students consolidate and review key ideas and experiences once they have finished reading. Ernesto's students could have been assigned to write a brief summary of the chapter's key ideas. In giving the assignment, he could have emphasized the importance of translating ideas into their own words and of creating examples. The students could have compared their summaries at the beginning of the class before the "infamous" and expected quiz.

Writing activities can also be used before students read in order to motivate, to focus their attention, and to help them draw on relevant knowledge and experience (Fitzgerald & Shanahan, 2000). This is the stage at which Ernesto could have capitalized on the power of writing. He could have introduced the chapter and unit by asking the students to take 5 minutes to describe in their journals the typical American's opinion about capital punishment for mass murderers. Then he could have asked them to describe their own opinions. After several students had shared their journal entries with the class, Ernesto could have asked the students to brainstorm reasons why there were so many differences in opinion across the classroom. His students would then have been better prepared to read about the five characteristics that influence political opinion, having brainstormed several of them already.

Finally, writing can be used in the content-area classroom to help students think critically and creatively about concepts (Herrington, 1997). This type of writing asks students to explore relationships among concepts, develop classification systems, trace causes and effects, and speculate about future developments—all higher level and elaborative thinking processes. For the chapter on public opinion, Ernesto could have asked his students to poll a representative sample of 25 individuals about an important issue and then to summarize and explain these findings in light of what they have learned thus far about public opinion.

Throughout this book you will find techniques and activities that capitalize on the power of writing.

In short, writing is valuable to you because students cannot remain passive if they are asked to put their ideas on paper. Writing activities demand participation by every student, not just those who volunteer. More important, writing activities can quickly demonstrate which students understand and where the understanding breaks down so that reteaching can be planned. In the next section we discuss several important guidelines for the use of writing in the content-area classroom.

GUIDELINES FOR THE USE OF WRITING ACROSS THE CONTENT AREAS

You can maximize the potential of writing in your classroom if you remember that writing is a process that may or may not end in a written product that will be handed in for a grade. Admittedly, there are occasions when you will want your students to write answers to essay questions in a biology class or to summarize their findings in a lab report for a chemistry class. These are "high-stakes" assignments that are evaluated formally and thoroughly. However, a considerable amount of writing should be informal or "low-stakes" writing (Elbow,

1997). According to Elbow, low-stakes writing assignments are "frequent, informal assignments that make students spend time reflecting in written language on what they are learning from discussions, readings, lectures, and their own thinking" (p. 7). As such, students may complete the writing assignments during class or as homework. These pieces that students write for themselves are considered low stakes because they do not have a major impact on their course grade. In other words, students need not write a formal paper and have you evaluate that paper for them to profit from their writing. The following six guidelines describe more specifically the implications of the process approach to writing assignments.

First Identify Your Unit's Objectives and Then Consider the Options

Before designing a writing activity, ask yourself what you want your students to learn from a unit of study. Armed with that information, you can then decide if writing is your best alternative or if it would be more appropriate for the students to create a map or chart or complete a study guide. If you determine that a writing activity would be appropriate, then you will need to decide whether that activity will be either low stakes or high stakes. In contrast to the informal orientation of low-stakes writing assignments, high-stakes assignments, such as major research papers at the end of a unit of study, adhere to the writing process and involve students in planning, drafting, revising, and editing. Students' final versions of those papers have been crafted to demonstrate their knowledge of a certain concept or body of knowledge, and we, as teachers, are judging their knowledge and writing and making suggestions for how to improve both. Obviously, there are many options to consider.

Ask Students to Write Frequently

This second guideline may seem to be in contradiction to the first guideline. However, we want to stress the importance of asking students to write on a regular basis rather than reserving it solely for high-stakes situations such as "the term paper." Consider this analogy to running. If you had a choice of running just one marathon or several different races of shorter duration, what event do you think would provide you the most experience and information to guide you as an athlete? As runners who have run both marathons and shorter races, we know that the 26 miles involved in a marathon truly wear down the body and mind. On the other hand, we have profited from the shorter road races because they have provided us considerable feedback on our running prowess. So it is with writing. Students learn when provided with numerous opportunities and with frequent feedback situations. Frequent writing in content-area classrooms will ensure that students are "warmed up and more fluent" about a concept and that their high-stakes writing tasks, if assigned, will be "clear" and free from "tangled thinking" (Elbow, 1997, p. 7).

You do not have to assign term papers or research projects to capitalize on the usefulness of writing.

We know a history instructor, Bryant, who has discarded the term paper routine and replaced it with four "one-page" memos that his students write throughout the semester. Bryant is extremely pleased with this change because he and his students have observed growth and improvements in their writing and critical thinking.

Vary Assignment Formats and Perspectives

If students only summarize what they have read or heard during class, they are not experiencing the full magnitude of writing as a means of learning content-area concepts. Writing is particularly powerful when students are invited to respond or react personally to an idea, event, or issue. When students are asked to think how an issue such as isolationism relates to them or how a story such as "The Lottery" is important to them, they are involved in "constructed knowing" (Belenky, Clinchy, Goldberger, & Tarule, 1986). Writing tasks that encourage students to construct knowledge and to become involved in their learning need to be more creative than "summarize the key ideas in this essay or chapter." In fact, an overreliance on "spitback" assignments can discourage many students (Herrington, 1997).

The options in Figure 7.1 emphasize the many exciting formats or discourse modes for content-area writing assignments. These assignments, such as writing complaints or time capsule lists, help students feel more comfortable with writing by taking on inviting, engaging, and motivating tasks that facilitate active learning.

In addition to varying the formats you offer your students, it is also productive to vary the perspectives or voices that students could take when they write. For example, we know a 10th-grade biology teacher, Gretel, who asks her students to describe in writing the functions of the endocrine system by taking the

Abstracts	Correspondence	Jokes and riddles	Rebuttals
Advertisements	Demonstrations	Journals, diaries	Recipes
Advice columns	Dramatic scripts, plays	Letters (personal,	Requests for information
Announcements	Editorials	public)	Resumés
Applications	Eulogies	Limericks	Reviews
Biographical sketches	Feature stories	Mottoes, slogans	Scripts, skits, puppet
Brochures	Forms	News stories	shows
Cartoons	Games and puzzles	Oral histories	Songs, ballads
Case studies	Guess who/what	Pamphlets	Stories
Character sketches	descriptions	Parodies	Tall tales
Children's books	Historical "you are	Petitions	Technical reports
Coloring books with text	there" scenes	Posters, flyers	Telegrams
Commercials	Inquiries	Proposals	Time capsule lists
Complaints	Instructional manuals	Protests	Word problems

FIGURE 7.1   Possible Writing Formats

perspective of one of the secreted hormones. One student in her class took the perspective of glucose and wrote a letter to his cousin who was recently identified as being a diabetic. In sum, using a variety of writing formats and perspectives provides students an extra challenge and an opportunity to display their creativity and understanding of important content-area concepts.

Design Writing Assignments That Have a Real and Immediate Audience

Whether it be other students in the class, other students in the school, community members, or individuals who support a particular cause in Washington, DC, students need an audience for their writing. By having a real and immediate audience, students will be able to decide how to state their position, what information to include, and what format best serves their needs. Students also take more care in choosing their words, explaining their ideas, and proofing their papers when they view their writing as an opportunity to communicate with another individual (Herrington, 1997; Light, 2001). In other words, when students write only for their teachers, they will see their audience as someone who "knows it all" already and whose primary reason for reading their work is to give them a grade.

MEETING THE NEEDS OF DIVERSE LEARNERS IN THE CONTENT-AREA CLASSROOM

We know a teacher who provides a message board inside her classroom for her students with learning disabilities to use as a means of communicating with each other. The message board also provides these struggling students relevant reasons and authentic audiences for their written messages. Rather than pass notes during class, a forbidden activity in most classrooms, the students in Maureen's classroom are allowed to write notes to one another and to post them on the board before or after class. Maureen's basic rules for the written messages are that they cannot contain profanity, gossip, ridicule, or inappropriate topics. Students have honored her rules and have used the message board to talk with their friends about content-area concepts, current events, or ideas they have encountered in the media. For example, two of her students carried on this conversation in writing:

Dear Kurt,
Yesterday I was talking with Sean and he told me that extinct animals have been found frozen in ice. I don't believe him, do you?
Neal

Dear Neal,
It's true. I saw a television show about it. They found one of them long-haired elephants. There's a book in the resource center that has pictures of them. Want to see?
Kurt

Dear Kurt,
Okay. What are you doing sixth period? I think I can meet you in the resource center at that time.
Neal

And so go the typical kinds of exchanges that Maureen's students pin to the message board. The same idea, of course, could be implemented in your classroom if you placed all your students' e-mail addresses on a listserv.

Provide Sufficient Time for Prewriting Activities

We believe that front-loading an assignment is the best way to ensure quality thinking and learning from students. When you front-load a writing assignment, you take class time for prewriting activities. Prewriting activities are especially important if you want students to profit from their writing experiences.

Fortunately, there are a variety of prewriting activities to help students decide on a topic, brainstorm possible ideas, see connections among ideas, and try out the ways in which those ideas could be stated. Some of these activities involve students in brainstorming and predicting questions, such as the DR-TA activity discussed in Chapter 3 or the KWL strategy discussed in Chapter 5. Other activities involve students with computer programs such as Inspiration (2000). These programs assist students in seeing the interrelationships between ideas and help them develop concept maps, a strategy discussed in Chapter 9.

Finally, many prewriting activities capitalize on the power of oral language or talk. Oral language activities are especially advantageous to struggling readers who may lack experience in the more formal modes of academic thinking and expression (Sweet, 1997). For example, in one study researchers found that middle school students wrote more persuasive papers after they had the opportunity to role-play their intended audience before they began writing (Wagner, 1987). In addition to Discussion Webs and word fluency activities (see Chapters 3 and 4), content-area teachers can assign students to work in pairs and ask each other questions to help them plan their writing. Rubin and Dodd (1987) recommended the following questions for partners to ask each other during the prewriting phase:

Just as oral language activities are advantageous to vocabulary and comprehension growth, so they are for helping students write "untangled" prose.

1. What are you going to write about?
2. What are the two most important parts of your topic?
3. What evidence or support will you use?
4. How will you begin? What information could you include in your introduction?
5. Do you have a thesis statement in mind?
6. Who will be the intended audience for your thesis?
7. What might be a good title for your paper?

Publish and Celebrate Your Students' Writing

The final phase of the writing process, postwriting, includes publishing. By publishing we mean that when students finish a piece of writing, it is shared and made public. When students realize that their work will be "published," they know they have an audience and thus a reason for working diligently in revising, editing, and proofreading. Content-area teachers can display their students' work in booklets, in school newspapers, or on a link or bulletin board site for their website. Students can also share their work by reading it aloud to their classmates; you too should share your writing with your students.

Adhering to these six guidelines should enhance the quality of writing that students produce when they interact with content-area concepts in your classroom. In addition, one critical aspect—assignment making—must be addressed in detail. If you wish, consider it the seventh guideline.

Go to the Web Resources at http://www.prenhall.com/brozo and look for additional ideas on how to help students publish and discuss their writing.

STARTING RIGHT WITH AN EFFECTIVE WRITING ASSIGNMENT

What causes fuzzy thinking and bad writing on the part of your students? Many individuals believe the culprit to be ineffective or unclear assignments. Even though bad writing assignments are never intentional, their effect is the same. Bad writing assignments can become good assignments when certain information is communicated to the students orally and in writing. When you communicate your writing assignment to your students, they will first need to know the purpose of the assignment, the topic, the audience, and the options or possible formats. A specific statement of **purpose** (e.g., "to understand the impact of words on interpersonal communication") will help students understand why this writing is being done. The **topic** for the writing assignment usually originates from content and course objectives, but you will need to specify how you want the students to narrow that focus without dictating their thesis. The **audience** will determine the background knowledge, vocabulary, and opinions of the individual who will read the writing, whether that is you, the teacher, another student, or a small child in the community. Ideally, writing assignments should provide students with several suggestions about possible **modes** or **formats** rather than just a single option such as the essay. Even the most reluctant student will become intrigued by writing a letter to the editor of a local newspaper or an imaginary diary.

An effective writing assignment should also include information on the recommended process, steps, or strategies that a student might use to complete the assignment. In addition, your writing assignment should include information on your expectations for (1) length; (2) level of polish; (3) format; (4) grammar, mechanics, and spelling; and (5) method of evaluation. The following writing

Poorly constructed assignments will create "fuzzy" thinking and "tangled ideas" on the part of your students.

assignment was used by Jan, an 11th-grade American history teacher, for the unit on the Progressives. Note that she specifies the mode that she wants the students to use, but she gives them choices within that mode.

> We have been studying the Progressive Era for the past week. This assignment will help you summarize the key issues and assess the impact of this intriguing period in our history. I want you to imagine that you are either Dan Rather or Diane Sawyer and you will be interviewing Robert LaFollette or Alice Paul, who have briefly returned from the dead. What would Rather and Sawyer want to ask these individuals? What would the television viewers want to know about these people and this time in history? You are to write out Rather's or Sawyer's questions and LaFollette's or Paul's replies. Then close the interview with a written commentary by Rather or Sawyer that evaluates the impact of LaFollette or Paul and the Progressive Era. Your audience will be television viewers unfamiliar with this historical period.
>
> Your first step in doing this assignment will be to review the relevant readings that we have done this week. You should also watch several news shows so that you can get an idea of the range of questions that could be asked. In class on Wednesday you will have time to brainstorm and role-play with a partner. By Thursday I want you to be prepared for the first draft, which we will write in class.
>
> In grading this assignment I will use these criteria:
>
> 1. Your understanding of the Progressive Era and its impact on history.
> 2. Your creativity and imagination, as demonstrated by your ability to write meaningful and interesting questions, responses, and a commentary.
> 3. Your quality of writing. It should be clear and free of gross mechanical and spelling errors.
>
> The final draft, which is worth 50 points, will be due at the beginning of class on Tuesday. Please use ink and write on every other line. As for length, the bare minimum is three pages of normal handwriting. These papers will be shared in class.

After assigning this writing activity, Jan also shared some examples of interviews and commentaries from a unit on the Vietnam era so that her students could visualize the finished product. She told us that the time she spends front-loading a writing assignment really pays off in the quality of work she receives from the students.

Because content-area teachers can use a variety of writing strategies in their classroom, these strategies will be discussed throughout the remainder of the chapter. It should be pointed out, however, that writing as a way of learning content-area concepts permeates this textbook; thus, you will find many other ideas throughout the textbook.

WRITING ACTIVITIES THAT PREPARE STUDENTS FOR LEARNING

As discussed in Chapter 5, one way to stimulate students to process and think more elaboratively about content-area concepts is to help them make connections between what they already know or want to know and what they are about to read and study. Remember the ease of reading a difficult Russian novel like *War and Peace* after you had viewed the movie? The ease of remembering a fact-filled history chapter on the Civil War after you had visited the Shiloh and Gettysburg battlefields during your summer vacation? Your students can gain the same advantage if you provide relevant and concrete classroom activities such as discussing, brainstorming, organizing, and writing responses before they read their text assignments. The Guided-Writing Activity and learning logs provide these opportunities.

The Guided-Writing Activity

The **Guided-Writing Activity** (Smith & Bean, 1980) is a research-validated instructional strategy that involves students in discussing, listening, reading, and writing about content-area concepts. The steps of this strategy are as follows:

1. On the first day, activate the students' prior knowledge on the topic of study by brainstorming and listing ideas on an overhead or chalkboard.

2. Ask the class to organize and label the ideas collectively.

3. Then ask the students to write individually on the topic using this information.

4. In preparation for the second day, have the class read the text and revise their explanatory writing.

5. In class on the second day, give a follow-up multiple-choice and essay exam on the text's key ideas.

To visualize how the Guided-Writing Activity could be incorporated into a content-area classroom, let's examine Lila's eighth-grade health class. Lila began the lesson by asking her students to write any ideas, definitions, or emotions that came to mind when they heard the words *stress* or *stressful*. She then circulated around the room and asked the class to share what they had written while a student wrote these ideas on the chalkboard. The students' reactions were varied. Some mentioned how their parents complained of too much stress in their executive-level jobs, and others commented on the stress their mothers felt in trying to raise a family alone and perform a full-time job at the same time. Some students pointed out that newspapers and television shows constantly focus on how to control stress to prevent serious illnesses. A few students discussed the stress they felt in trying to be accepted by the best college.

When Lila was sure that everyone had contributed, she asked the students to help her categorize the list of ideas and emotions on the board. The categories that emerged from this discussion were (1) the causes of stress, (2) the feelings associated with stress, (3) the dangers of stress, and (4) the cures for stress. Next, she asked the students to preview (see Chapter 9) their chapter to discover which of these ideas would be included in their next assignment. The students quickly pointed out that all four ideas were included in the chapter's boldface headings. Lila then asked them to determine the headings in the textbook that were not included in their list. One student suggested that the dangers of stress were subdivided into the physical and mental effects of unrelieved stress, a distinction they had not made in their own list. Another student pointed out that there was a separate section on adolescent stress in the chapter—a comment that generated considerable discussion and excitement.

Lila closed the class period by telling the students to read the chapter, to focus on gathering information on those four areas, and to be prepared for discussing and writing during the next class period. On the second day, Lila began her lesson by asking the students to take out the entry they had written about stress the day before and to reread it for possible revisions. Her directions were: "Imagine that you are explaining the concept of stress to a younger brother or sister. What would you add to your original entry? Jot these ideas down." After a few minutes, she asked the students to share and discuss their ideas. As she recorded their ideas on the board, she was surprised by the number of students who volunteered and eagerly participated in the discussion. In fact, the discussion took longer than she had expected. On the third day of class, Lila returned to the writing task and asked the students to revise their original entry on stress, keeping in mind their audience, a younger brother or sister. Although this activity was not the end of her unit on stress and health, it does illustrate how one teacher used writing as a means of helping students make connections between what is to be learned and what is already known.

Learning Logs

As noted in Chapter 5, learning logs are notebooks that students keep in order to record ideas, questions, and reactions to what they have read, observed, or listened to in class. Learning logs can also be used to help students prepare for learning by thinking about new knowledge in terms of their preexisting knowledge (Santa & Havens, 1991). For example, Clarese, an eighth-grade math teacher, asks her students to write a learning entry for each unit of study. Her students respond to a variety of open-ended probes designed to stimulate their reflection and to provide her valuable assessment information on their knowledge and possible misconceptions about a mathematical concept. For a unit on averages, Clarese began the lesson by asking the students to answer the following questions:

1. Where have you heard about averages?
2. Who uses averages and for what?
3. How are averages used?
4. What do you know about forming an average?

Learning logs work
especially well in math and
science classes.

As a follow-up to these open-ended probes, Clarese asks her students to share their log entries with their study partner before sharing them with the entire class. Clarese believes that writing activities such as these help her teach more effectively because she learns so much about her students in a short amount of time.

Rosa, a tenth-grade biology teacher, also likes to have her students write in their learning logs before she begins a new unit or lesson. Sometimes she initiates her students' thinking and writing by asking them to preview the next assigned chapter. When students preview chapters in their biology textbook, they examine the title, headings, subheadings, charts, summaries, and questions. Based on this preview, the students then write in the learning logs what they already know or think they know about the topic. After reading the text chapter or a section of it, Rosa then has her students write another entry focusing on what they learned and noting any misconceptions in their original log entries.

The following example illustrates one student's learning log entries before and after reading a chapter on the human brain.

Learning Log Entry Written Before Reading

In this chapter I'm going to learn about the human brain. I know the brain is split into a right and left half. I think the halves control different things, but I'm not sure what. I also know that when someone has a stroke, blood vessels break in the brain.

Learning Log Entry Written After Reading

I learned that the two halves of the brain are called the right and left cerebral hemispheres. But, really, there are four main parts of the brain: the medulla oblongata, the pons, the cerebellum, and the cerebrum. I also learned that a stroke is caused by a blockage in the arteries in the brain. This keeps the brain from getting enough oxygen, and it becomes damaged.

As these entries demonstrate, the student was able to use writing as an aid in the process of constructing meaning from the text. The first entry served as a reflection of prior knowledge, whereas the second entry allowed the student to reconsider his initial understandings (e.g., the nature of strokes) and derive new understandings based on his reading of the text. Other examples of learning logs can be found in Chapter 5. In the next section we examine writing strategies that will help students summarize, organize, and monitor their understanding of content-area concepts.

WRITING ACTIVITIES THAT ENCOURAGE STUDENTS TO CONSTRUCT MEANING AND TO MONITOR THEIR UNDERSTANDING

As explained in Chapter 2, active learners can summarize and organize key ideas and monitor their understanding so that they know when they know and know when they are lost. Most middle school and high school students are not active learners but rather memorizers who can regurgitate textbook or teacher statements with minimal understanding and involvement (Alexander & Jetton, 2000). Even though it is admittedly difficult to move a student from memorization, this transition can be facilitated through the use of strategically planned writing assignments. The writing activities, however, must require students to do more than merely answer teacher- or text-posed questions with one-word answers. In this section, we will describe four activities to help students construct meaning and monitor their understanding. All of these low-stakes writing activities can be easily integrated into the classroom routine and require minimal teacher preparation and response. More important, they are inviting and approachable for students who have minimal writing skills.

In this section you will discover four writing activities to help your students become more active in their learning.

Quick Writes

Have you ever begun a class by asking the infamous question "Are there any questions about the assigned reading?" If your students are like most adolescents, the result is an uncomfortable silence. Rather than asking a question that rarely will be answered, ask your students to take out their learning logs or a piece of paper and spend 3 minutes in a **Quick Write.** Quick Writes have also been called *one-minute papers* or *admit/exit slips.* Regardless of the name or the duration, these informal writing activities are low-stakes assignments that can stimulate discussion or encourage passive students to reflect and think about a content-area concept. Quick Writes can be used before students read or listen to a class discussion, after they have read, or during a discussion as a way of focusing and summarizing. In this section we examine the use of Quick Writes as a way to help students summarize, organize, and monitor their understanding.

You can use a variety of prompts or probes with a Quick Write. We like these two questions because they can be modified for any content-area classroom: (a) What is the big point, the main idea, that you learned (from your reading assignment, from class today)? (b) What is the muddiest point? What don't you understand from (your reading, the discussion, the lab)? Some teachers, especially in chemistry or physics courses, ask students to list the pages that were confusing to them. We have collected these Quick Write probes from other content-area teachers:

■ Write on the board an interesting quotation from the reading assignment or a statement of opinion (e.g., "The pituitary gland is the most important gland in the endocrine system") and ask the students to explain their stand on the statement.

Content-area teachers love to begin their classes with these Quick Write ideas.

■ To emphasize a new and important technique that has just been introduced in science, industrial arts, or home economics class, stop and ask students to write for 5 minutes to describe the technique to another student who was absent from class. This has also been called "Yesterday's News" and can be modified for any content area where you want students to write a summary of the concepts discussed in the previous class (Fisher, 2001).

■ To focus a class discussion that becomes rambling or dominated by just a few students, stop and ask the class to write for 5 minutes. They could respond to the question "What are we trying to explain?" or to the assignment "Restate the key points that have been made thus far."

■ To help students reflect on the key ideas of a specific unit, ask them to review their notes and assigned readings and then to write. This activity works best when announced in advance so that students can think and plan for a while. Such a synthesis is also especially advantageous for the students as a means of preparing for an examination.

■ To help students predict what might happen next in a lesson or during a lab or demonstration, use the "Crystal Ball" prompt. Students write their predictions and explain why they believe they are right.

Once your students have completed their Quick Write in the time you specify, ask volunteers to read their entries or place them in partners to share. If you do the Quick Writes at the end of the hour (i.e., exit slips), collect the students' responses so that you can read them over quickly before class meets again. In the next section we describe another low-stakes writing activity similar to the Quick Write—the microtheme.

Microthemes

Microthemes are assignments so short that they can be written on a single 4×6 index card and read within minutes (Bean, Drenk, & Lee, 1982). They are productive in the content areas because they ask the students to do a small amount of writing preceded by a great deal of thinking. Microthemes can also be designed to emphasize different content-area objectives. The most common microtheme asks students to summarize key ideas from a reading assignment, demonstration, experiment, or lecture in their own words. The advantage of students' summaries recorded on an index card is that the cards are much easier to handle and carry home for your perusal. Students also feel less intimidated when they have only an index card to fill.

The following probes illustrate how Ann, a ninth-grade math teacher, uses the microtheme to encourage students to state in their own words their conceptual understanding of exponents.

Integral Exponents

Rule 7 is in addition to previous ones you have worked with in other chapters. In your own words, explain what this rule means and how you might use it to simplify 2^{-4} and $1/4^{-3}$.

Rational Exponents

1. Define *radical, radicand, index,* and *principal root.* Identify each in an example you supply.

2. The *cube root* of a number means _____.

The secret to the microtheme is in the format of the card. Students must carefully plan what they will say and how they will say it because they receive only one index card to record their ideas. They also learn that more is not always better. Just as a poet carefully chooses words for each poem, so will the students as they write a microtheme. What they write depends on your course objectives and content because these variations are only a beginning.

Microthemes are small in size but large in the thinking processes students use.

Once the students have completed their Quick Write or microtheme, the next step is for you to decide what you will do with their written work. You have several options. First, you could simply go on with the lesson and hope that the writing has served its purpose in helping students summarize, organize, and monitor their understanding of key concepts. Second, you could give the students an immediate chance to ask questions and clear up any confusion they may have discovered while they were writing. They could pose questions for you to answer or issues to clarify, or they could turn to a neighbor to share their answers and resolve their difficulties together. As the students work, you could circulate around the room to eavesdrop and troubleshoot. Finally, as previously mentioned, you could collect the cards and read them for your own information. The students' writing becomes excellent feedback on whether they learned what you had tried to teach that day.

Some content-area teachers grade this type of writing by awarding several points for each microtheme. Others prefer to award pass/fail credit in their gradebooks. Regardless of the evaluating procedure or question posed for the students' writing, Quick Writes and microthemes can facilitate student learning and provide immediate feedback on your teaching effectiveness.

Double-Entry Journals

When students write in a journal they can summarize and react to ideas, but they also can reflect on their processes of making sense of what they are reading or learning in a content area. Such journal entries are called **double-entry formats** (Calkins, 1986). With this format, students use the left-hand column of an evenly divided note page to copy directly from a text quotations, statements, theories, definitions, and other things that are difficult to understand, interesting, of key importance, or require clarification. On the right-hand side, students record whatever thoughts, questions, or comments come to mind as they attempt to make sense of what was copied. Figure 7.2 is an example of a double-entry format that one ninth-grade student, Chris, created for his reading assignment in a government course. The text he copied on the left-hand side of the paper came from a chapter discussing political opinions and attitudes that Chris found confusing. Notice Chris's comments on the right-hand side. By examining his journal entry, his government teacher was able to determine what concepts were troubling him and what strategies he was using to make sense of his reading. More important, Chris gained some information about himself through his writing. The last comment made by Chris was a very honest and perceptive observation about textbooks that typifies the feelings of some students who are very

Text	Responses to Text and Strategy Concerns
Political attitudes may exist merely as potential. They may not have crystallized. But they still can be very important, for they can be evoked by leaders and converted into action. Latent opinions set rough boundaries for leaders.... *Source:* J. Burns, J. Peltason, & T. Cronin (1984). *Government by the People* (p. 175), Englewood Cliffs, NJ: Prentice Hall.	I know that this section is supposed to define the key word *latent* because the boldface heading tells me this. However, I am having problems finding a definition. Help! *Okay*—I think the second sentence helps me, but I will need to look up the word *crystallized*. I think, right now, that latent opinions are opinions not formed, but existing as potential for leaders and other people who wish to influence us. *Whew!* I will read on since our teacher has told us that authors often take several pages to define a word. This is hard work and I think the textbook authors made it even harder for us.

FIGURE 7.2   Entry in a Double-Entry Journal

metacognitively aware. Those comments, however, do not occur as a result of one double-entry journal assignment. Teachers must provide modeling and guidance to develop their students' metacognition.

Framed Paragraphs

Some students are so intimidated by writing that they cannot seem to begin the process, even if they view the assignment as intriguing and captivating. In addition to the microtheme, framed paragraphs are another way to provide students with guidance and structure so that they can overcome their paralysis when asked to think and write about content-area concepts. As illustrated in Figures 7.3 and 7.4, **framed paragraphs** are skeletal paragraphs with strategically placed transitions or cue words that signal to students a particular way to think and write about a concept (Vacca, Vacca, & Gove, 1995). After students have read an assignment or viewed a demonstration, they complete the framed paragraphs by writing in the missing words and by creating their own sentences in order to produce a total paragraph or mini-essay about a particular topic. Students can then share their framed paragraphs in small groups or with their study partners.

Manuel was a _____ student. He decided to do a pantomime of Ritchie Valens's "La Bamba" at the school's talent show because _____ . As he watched the various acts done by his classmates, he was _____ . When he went up on stage he felt _____ . Once he began dancing and pantomiming, he _____ . Then suddenly in the middle of his act, _____ . He felt very _____ but decided to keep _____ . Once the talent show was over, the audience _____ . Manuel was surprised because _____ . Ricardo and Manuel's father thought Manuel had _____ . That night when Manuel was alone in his room, he decided _____ . The irony of this story is _____ .

FIGURE 7.3   Framed Paragraph About "La Bamba"

The animal kingdom can be divided into vertebrates and _____ . Vertebrates are animals with a _____ , whereas invertebrates are animals _____ . There are four identifying features of invertebrates. The first distinguishing feature biologists use to group invertebrates is _____ . The name of that subgroup is _____ and an example of such an animal in that subgroup is _____ . The second distinguishing feature is _____ . The name of that subgroup is _____ and an example is _____ . The third _____ _____ . The fourth _____ _____ .

Of all the invertebrates, I have had the most encounters with _____ . As I read about invertebrates, it seems to me that most of them live _____ . In addition, it seems interesting to me that _____ .

FIGURE 7.4   Framed Paragraph for a Unit on Invertebrates

Framed paragraphs can be constructed for narrative text and emphasize the elements of narrative structure such as plot, setting, characters, and theme. The narrative framed paragraph in Figure 7.3 was written by a sixth-grade teacher to accompany a story that he liked to teach his struggling readers. Framed paragraphs can also be created for expository text and emphasize patterns of organization such as problem-solution or comparison-contrast. The framed paragraph in Figure 7.4 was written by a eighth-grade general science teacher in order to help his students become more aware of the categories, examples, and characteristics of invertebrates and vertebrates.

Many teachers like to use framed paragraphs at the beginning of the school year in order to ease students into the process of writing about content-area concepts. After students build their confidence and fluency in writing, the cues in framed paragraphs are reduced so that students then write using alternative formats. Because the framed paragraph and microtheme are not intimidating in their structure and format, your less skilled students will experience success in their writing.

Framed paragraphs provide structure to struggling readers and learners.

WRITING ACTIVITIES THAT ENCOURAGE STUDENTS TO ELABORATE AND THINK CRITICALLY

Although there is not a mass of research studies that prove in a definitive manner that writing activities will improve students' critical thinking in a content area, we do know that reading and writing can be effectively combined to support and augment students' thinking about concepts. That evidence originates not only from empirical studies, but also from a variety of classroom teachers (e.g., Elbow, 1997; Fitzgerald & Shanahan, 2000; Light, 2001; Randall, 1996; Tierney, Soter, O'Flahavan, & McGinley, 1989). Hence, we feel comfortable in describing techniques that content-area teachers have found to be useful.

In this section we examine two activities that challenge students to extend and reformulate ideas and to think critically: the reader response heuristic and analytical writing assignments. In addition, we share two techniques to help you frame and design creative writing assignments.

Reader Response Applied to Expository Text

As we said earlier, meaning does not reside in any written text. Rather, meaning or comprehension emerges from an interaction among the reader, the text, and the context. This concept puts into perspective your reaction to the reading assignments in your educational methods courses. When you first read those seemingly dry and boring textbook chapters, you almost certainly had no students of your own and no specific problems to solve (e.g., How do I motivate adolescents?). Hence, you probably remember little or nothing from them, even though you were a fluent and highly competent reader. This phenomenon also affects your students as they read unless they are provided with opportunities to explore the connections between what they already know, feel, and want to know and the information contained in their textbooks.

One way to help students make those connections is through the reader-response heuristic. A *heuristic* is a method of inquiry, and the **reader-response heuristic** is a method of self-inquiry in which readers write about their own responses to certain aspects of the text. The reader-response heuristic asks readers first to write what they perceive in the text, then to explain how they feel about what they see, and finally to discuss the thoughts and feelings emanating from their perceptions (Petrosky, 1982). This is a personal type of writing, which is very different from summary-type writing. Summaries are often audience-oriented tasks in that they are written exclusively for other individuals to read. By contrast, reader-response tasks exist for the learner and the reader. Summaries and brief essays require writers to support stances and assertions with public-based information. Conversely, reader-response tasks value the examples, beliefs, and assumptions of the students.

These three generic questions help students make personal connections with text.

We suggest these three generic questions to guide students in making connections to expository text:

1. What aspect of the text excited or interested you most?
2. What are your feelings and attitudes about this aspect of text?
3. What experiences have you had that help others understand why you feel the way you do?

To visualize how the reader-response journal entry would work in a content-area classroom, consider Rodney's 11th-grade history and current events class. He introduced the activity by presenting model answers he had created, talking his students through while paying special attention to the way they attempted to answer these three main questions in the self-inquiry process. Rodney's essay was a response to an article in *Newsweek* about the former system of apartheid in South Africa. He emphasized how this statement of feeling—that the United States should be doing more to abolish racial segregation in South Africa—was explained and supported by his personal experience of witnessing racial prejudice when he was in the Navy in South Carolina during the early 1960s. He then assigned students to go through the same process of discovering personal connections with several different articles from *Newsweek*. One student, Eric, read an article about Arab-Israeli relations. His ideas blossomed as he moved from brief responses to the three questions to a multiple-page essay. Eric's first response follows:

> Whenever I read that there might be peace among Arabs and Israelis I get real excited. I believe that when they can figure out how to solve the problem for the Palestinians, the entire Middle East will become peaceful. I know Arabs and Jews can live in peace and happiness. I'm part Lebanese and I have friends who are Jewish. If we can get along why can't they? Instead, they fight and every day more people die. My mom told me Lebanon used to be a beautiful country. Now its people and its economy are ruined. (Brozo, 1988, p. 3)

Eric's writing partner thought he had a good start and suggested he find an experience to give his feelings and ideas some authority. Together they brainstormed possible personal connections, which helped Eric explore the roots of his feelings. Rodney worked with them too, encouraging and pushing Eric to be more specific about why he felt that way. In the third draft, which follows, Eric created an essay that demonstrated a genuine sensitivity to his readers by linking the text to his strong feelings and attitudes and by explaining his feelings with a vivid experience.

> Whenever I read that there might be peace among Arabs and Israelis I get real excited. I believe that when they can figure out how to solve the problem of the Palestinians, the entire Middle East will become peaceful. It seems like all the problems exist because of the Palestinian issue. I can just think of a time when Israelis and Arabs will work, play, and grow together. I know Arabs and Jews can live in peace and happiness. I hope it happens in my lifetime. [Eric's answer to question one]

I feel so deeply about this issue for two reasons. First, I hate war and how it ruins a country's economy and most importantly, its people. And second, I'm part Lebanese, yet I have real good friends who are Jewish. [Eric's feelings]

Last year I rode twice a week to basketball practice with a Jewish guy named David. I felt close to David right away. We shared ideas and feelings about basketball and our girlfriends and geometry. We talked very personally. We became close even though we didn't get together that often outside of basketball practice.

One day David asked about my ethnic background. He was Jewish and proud of it. But who was I? An American who happens to be part Lebanese (I'm also part Italian and Irish) only by chance. I mean I could have just as easily been born an African bushman or an Alaskan Indian. My nationality is not a big deal to me. So I didn't know what to say at first to David. I was afraid to tell the whole truth. Then I thought, I like and trust this guy as a friend—he has told me many things about his Jewishness expecting me to accept and respect him, so why should I feel different?

"I'm half Lebanese," I said.

David smiled, "We're cousins. I knew there was something special about us. Salam ah likum," he said.

"Shalom," I replied. [Eric's personal experience]

(Brozo, 1988, pp. 14–15)

With the reader-response heuristic and the assistance of both his writing partner and Rodney, Eric was helped to see how his interpretations of the text on Arab-Israeli relations were mediated by his feelings and experiences. His moving responses also created a good, solid essay that supports assertions with an excellent example derived from personal experience.

The next step in the process is the sharing of essays. Rodney found it to be a particularly exciting phase of the lesson because multiple viewpoints were exchanged, questioned, and debated. This sharing also gave his students a wider audience and extended feedback for the revision process.

The reader-response heuristic can be easily modified for any content area. Because these three questions were intended only to be generic stimuli, you can create content-specific questions relevant to your course objectives and your students. Remember, not every student-response entry must be turned into an essay like Eric's. Your students will profit immensely just from the processes of interpreting, questioning, and reacting.

Analytical Writing Assignments

A variety of writing activities encourage students to think analytically about content-area concepts.

One way we can enhance our students' ability to think critically is to provide them analytical writing assignments that challenge them to speculate, reformulate an understanding, or apply a concept to an important issue or problem. An added advantage to such analytical writing assignments is that students find such tasks to be inviting and challenging (Fisher, 2001; Herrington, 1997). Because analytical writing assignments require students to manipulate a smaller number of concepts in more complex ways, they are particularly attractive to content-area teachers who rightfully worry about reading countless pages written by their students. Although no strict rule or mnemonic applies to creating analytical writing assignments, we will share three different, but not mutually exclusive, ideas: thesis-support writing, data-provided writing, and concept application writing.

The **thesis-support writing** assignment can help students discover issues and develop arguments and stances that are supported with empirical evidence. When writing a thesis-support paper, students must often go beyond the textbook to build a logical, cohesive argument. When students think about and research a particular issue, they actively master the unit's objectives. Most important, they begin to realize that their textbook presents only one point of view and that all content areas are in a constant state of controversy and flux.

An example of a thesis-support writing assignment developed by a seventh-grade general science teacher follows:

> Directions: The purpose of this assignment is to provide you with an opportunity to examine an issue in depth by taking a stand and developing a logical argument for that stand. You have two choices, so read the choices below carefully and select one of them. Then determine which side you wish to defend for that issue. For the side you have selected, write a microtheme that defends that position. Use evidence and reasoning from your textbook, from our discussion in class, or from the film we watched in class. Write your final draft on the index card you have been given. Class time will be provided for brainstorming, planning, and prewriting. HAVE FUN WITH THIS!
>
> 1. The diversity theory has/has not been proven.
>
> 2. People do a lot to the environment that encourages/prevents animal extinction.

The teacher discussed and distributed several examples of thesis-support microthemes after announcing the assignment. Following a discussion of the assignment, he invited the class to help him do an analysis of this seemingly simple assignment so that they could plan appropriately. In addition, he provided one class period for the students who had selected the same issues to meet, debate, and brainstorm. Several days later, he set aside a class period for the students to write their initial draft so that he could be available while they wrote. The teacher reported that the students did have fun with this assignment and, more important, did better than usual on their unit exam.

A second type of analytical writing is the **data-provided** paper. With such an assignment students are provided with data in a list of sentences or in a graph, table, or chart. They must arrange the data in a logical order, interpret what they see as trends and patterns, and then offer, in writing, their conclusions or generalizations. This type of writing assignment is especially useful for students who ignore or who cannot accurately interpret important visual aids, especially in math or science classes.

We know a geography instructor, Deb, who assigns her students several analytical writing assignments throughout her course rather than the ubiquitous research paper (Martin, personal communication, 2001). She particularly likes the data-provided assignment because it helps her students fully understand important concepts like the population pyramid and the patterns of immigration in the United States. In order to complete the data-provided assignment on these two concepts, Deb provides her students a table that describes the total population of the United States in 1996 and another table that describes the immigrant population in 1996. She then outlines a series of steps that require her students to use the data as they calculate percentages and plot the percentages on two different empty pyramid graphs that she has provided them. Once her students have manipulated the data and drawn their interpretations, Deb then asks them to write about the data with probes and questions such as these: (a) Compare the two pyramids you have created. How is the pyramid for immigrants different from the one for total population? How do you explain these differences? (b) How are the immigrants affecting the U.S. population structure? (c) What implications will the Baby Boom generation have for American society in 20 years?

Because students write a limited amount of expository text in response to the data, the evaluation process of these papers moves very quickly for the content-area teacher. However, that "limited amount" of writing is preceded by an immense amount of thinking, planning, and revising on the part of the students so they can explain and defend their interpretations and conclusions.

The third type of analytical writing assignment is the **concept application** paper. With such a writing assignment the content-area teacher asks students to apply important concepts to a different, novel situation or problem not discussed in class or in the textbook. As explained in Chapter 5 and elsewhere (e.g., Elbow, 1997; Lenski, Wham, & Johns, 1999) students learn concepts at a deeper level of understanding when they are asked to solve problems using what they know and what they have learned. Although you can organize a concept application writing assignment in a variety of ways, most of them focus on a situation or scenario that you have created. These situations can be brief, such as this one given by a 12th-grade physics teacher: Write an essay explaining to a 10th-grader why an airplane flies. Assume no knowledge on the part of the student. Hence, you will probably have to discuss the Bernoulli equation that we studied last week in this course (Herrington, 1997).

Writing activities that require students to apply concepts to new situations or problems work especially well in the sciences.

These situations can also be far more comprehensive. Deb, the geography instructor, has discovered that her students really enjoy her assignment called "The Geography of Breakfast" (Martin, 2001). This writing assignment requires her students to understand and apply the concept of the food chain to their daily breakfast routines. She sets up the assignment in this manner:

> Choose three breakfast items. If the breakfast items are processed food, such as cold pizza, choose the ingredients, such as cheese or tomatoes. For each of these three ingredients or items, answer the following questions:

a. What is the breakfast item or ingredient?

b. In what ways is your breakfast regionally or culturally specific? Who else, living where, is likely to eat the same kind of breakfast as you do? Who is unlikely to eat the same kind of breakfast, and why? (HINT: *Look for the "made in" or the company's address.*)

c. What does the food's packaging tell you and not tell you about the origin of the ingredients?

d. For each of the three items or ingredients, use knowledge you already have, the course textbooks and atlas, and as many additional sources of information as you need, to describe something about the three of the nine elements in the food chain. (EXAMPLE: *Wheat used to make the bagel is grown in the Midwest, processed in Texas, and consumed in Georgia. That is approximately a "B" answer—for a higher grade, elaborate on these elements using the descriptions/discussions in the text.*)

Notice that Deb provides hints to the students and suggestions as to sources they might use to write their paper. As mentioned earlier, you will receive quality written products when you front-load a challenging assignment. That is, you will need to inform students of what you expect, provide them positive and negative examples, suggest possible resources or steps they might take in their thinking and writing, and explain the grading criteria you will use with their papers. In the next section we will address the issue of formulating assignments that encourage students to be creative and imaginative.

Writing Assignments That Encourage Creativity

We know it is challenging to design unusual and intriguing assignments that will stimulate students into thinking creatively about concepts. Sometimes our "creativity" well seems almost dry or empty. Fortunately, two acronyms can guide us in the process of designing creative assignments: RAFT (Santa, Havens, & Maycumber, 1996) and SPAWN (Martin, Martin, & O'Brien, 1984). These two acronyms are particularly helpful because they encourage students to take perspectives different from their own and to write using alternative discourse modes. In addition, both acronyms provide students choices and a sense of control, important motivational factors (Turner, 1995).

Teachers tell us that these two acronyms help them develop creative writing assignments for their students.

RAFT stands for *role of the writer* (is the author a thing, a concept, a person, an animal?), *audience* (to whom is the author writing?), *form* (what format or discourse mode is the author going to use?), and *topic* (what topic is the author writing about?). Deborah, a seventh-grade health teacher, introduced RAFT during her unit on nutrition because she wanted her students to bring closure to the unit with a creative writing task. After providing her students several examples of how RAFT could be operationalized, one of her students, Chris, decided to use RAFT for his paper. Using RAFT, his writing assignment took on this focus:

R: I am vitamin D (the concept).

A: Jack's body (the audience).

> **F:** I will write a letter (the format).
>
> **T:** I will inform Jack what I will do for him (topic).

Chris's letter is illustrated in Figure 7.5.

The second way you can design creative writing assignments is by using SPAWN. **SPAWN** stands for *special powers, problem solving, alternative viewpoints, what if,* and *next.* Each is a category of writing assignments that can encourage students to move beyond the memorization of facts. To construct such an assignment, you can select one of the categories from SPAWN and combine it with the most appropriate writing form. (Refer to Figure 7.1 for some examples of writing forms that are creative and nontraditional.)

Beth is a 10th-grade English teacher who decided to use the SPAWN mnemonic to help her construct possible writing topics for the book *Farewell to Manzanar* (Houston & Houston, 1974). The book fit perfectly into the sophomores' unit on prejudice and injustice because it describes the internment of a Japanese girl in an American camp on the West Coast during World War II. Although Beth likes to give her students wide choices for their writing, she also knows that they appreciate some suggestions. Thus, she distributed the following ideas:

Option 1: Special Powers

You have the power to change any event in *Farewell to Manzanar.* You must write and tell what event you changed, how you changed it, why you changed it, and what could happen as a result of the change. For instance, what if Rodine's mother had welcomed Jeanne into the Girl Scouts? Would that affect just that part of the story, or might Jeanne's life have been totally different if she had been accepted right from the first?

After you have completed the written section of this assignment, I will meet in a group with everyone who elected to do this assignment. We will discuss the changes that have been made and the possible consequences.

Dear Jack,

I would like to introduce myself. I am vitamin D. I am found in many dairy products such as milk and cheese. I promise if you eat me, you will have strong bones and teeth. I can even help you to grow old and be a healthier person. Have you seen the television commercial for milk? That commercial is all about me. I am the reason milk is so good. So, I recommend that you eat foods that contain me. I also recommend that you drink milk. If you do these things, I will do my best to help you.

Sincerely,
Vitamin D

FIGURE 7.5   Example of RAFT

Option 2: Alternative Viewpoints

We heard Jeanne's viewpoint on her friendship with Rodine. We were told of their experiences as their friendship began to grow through their years at Cabrillo Homes and during junior high school. After entering high school, they began to drift apart. What is Rodine's viewpoint? What happened according to her perspective? How did she feel?

Pretend that you are Rodine. Write several journal entries in which you discuss the beginning of the friendship, a few of the high points, and the time when you finally realized that you were no longer special friends. You will have the chance to share this with others who do this same assignment.

Option 3: What If?

What if this story took place in Japan after World War II? Rodine's father was in the army as an officer in the occupational forces. He wanted her to become familiar with the Japanese culture, so she attended a Japanese school, where she was the only white person. Jeanne was in her class. Starting with Rodine's first day in class, write a story of the experiences Jeanne and Rodine had. How would life be different now that Rodine is the minority and Jeanne is the majority? You may tell your story from either Jeanne's or Rodine's point of view. You will have the opportunity to meet with others in the class to share your story and to discuss the approach that they followed for the same assignment.

Beth reported that the students enjoyed these writing options and that several of them used the SPAWN mnemonic to create their own assignments. More important, this writing assignment measured more completely her students' achievement of unit objectives than any multiple-choice exam she could have created.

Diverse writing tasks are available for content-area courses—assignments that effectively smuggle oral and written language into the curriculum, assignments that motivate and intrigue, and assignments that can maximize students' learning and thinking. Several issues must be resolved, however, before teachers and students feel comfortable in using writing as a way of learning. In the next section we discuss four of these issues.

CRITICAL ISSUES CONCERNING THE USE OF WRITING AS A MEANS OF LEARNING

The decision to use writing as a means of encouraging students' active learning changes the way many teachers view their content area, the writing process, and their responsibilities in negotiating the two. As a result, numerous questions and issues are posed that need to be addressed. We deal with five of the more urgent and far-reaching of these:

1. grading and responding to students' writing
2. student involvement in evaluation

3. the use of writing in a testing situation to evaluate students' mastery of concepts

4. the research paper

5. the use of computer technology

Sane Methods for Grading and Responding

In a classic study several years ago, a researcher discovered in his interviews with teachers that many were hesitant to incorporate writing into their units of study because of the overwhelming amount of work that would be generated by the 100 or more students they see each day (Pearce, 1983). Over the years, we have collected specific techniques from other teachers and from our own experiences that have made it feasible for students to write and teachers to survive. These techniques acknowledge that teachers have personal lives and thus prefer not to spend the weekend glued to the kitchen table writing comments to students about their written work. All of the techniques are based on the premise that responding is more important than grading in the writing process and in students' mastery of content-area concepts. The following are some general guidelines to expedite the process of responding and grading:

These 10 ideas should help you in providing your students with feedback on their writing.

1.   Remember the purpose of each writing assignment and keep content the center of your focus. If students write a learning log entry or an exit slip, the purpose is to help them construct meaning or to monitor their understanding of a content-area concept. Hence, the evaluation process should reflect their participation and nothing more. If, however, the students have worked their way through the processes of writing and class time has been provided for feedback at each stage, evaluate the writing as a final draft. Students should be told in advance the importance of their spelling, grammar, and mechanical errors in the total evaluation process. As discussed earlier, the assignment-making process should be thorough to inform students of your expectations and purposes.

2.   Avoid zealous error detection as you respond to your students' writing because this type of response can consume huge amounts of your time and energy. Remember that students are more likely to make mechanical errors when they first begin to write on a topic that is unfamiliar or new to them.

3.   Write at least one supportive comment or reaction. Sometimes a large "yes!" does the trick or a statement such as "You have provided lively and credible examples." Some content-area teachers like to place wavy lines under ideas that are particularly insightful and straight lines under ideas that are unclear or fuzzy.

4.   Use green, purple, or orange pen, or better yet, use a pencil—any color but red, which connotes a highly punitive message.

5.   Use abbreviations for comments you frequently make. For example, instead of writing "Elaborate More" countless times, write EM. Provide students with a list of your abbreviations.

6.   Troubleshoot many of the errors that students commonly make by providing them with class time, in advance of the due date, to read and edit their assigned

partner's rough draft. This will save you time and provide them with more sensitivity and appreciation for the writing and thinking processes.

7. Consider the possibility of not collecting and grading every low-stakes assignment, especially microthemes, Quick Writes, or reader-response entries. Many teachers put a check mark in the upper corner after quickly skimming to make sure the assignment is complete. On other occasions, especially with multiple journal entries or summaries, some teachers determine in advance the one that they will grade thoroughly or ask the students to select their best papers to be graded.

8. Severely limit the length of some assignments, as with the microthemes, which are written entirely on an index card. The important criterion should not be length, but rather the students' effectiveness in judiciously selecting the words they will explain or defend. Space limitation not only will save you time, it will also educate your students so that they will not always equate length with quality.

9. Stagger your writing assignments across your classes so that you do not require all your students to hand in their work at the same time. For example, your first- and second-period classes could hand in their writing on Mondays, your third- and fourth-period classes on Tuesdays, and your fifth- and sixth-period classes on Wednesdays.

10. Perhaps the most important thing to remember about grading is to think and plan carefully before assigning. Writing tasks do not facilitate all types of course objectives and help all types of students.

In addition to these general grading suggestions, you can develop some forms (checklists, primary trait evaluation guides, and rubrics) to help decrease the time devoted to providing students with quality comments and responses to their written work. These forms, which can be adapted to any content area and any assignment, are discussed next.

Students and parents appreciate those forms because they provide a specific and organized way to view your comments.

Checklists

Checklists contain the general criteria you wish to focus on when you read students' writing, whether their thesis statements or their use of support to defend a position. Rather than writing the same comment over and over again (e.g., "Be more specific," "Support your statements"), you merely circle the item on the checklist. In addition, the checklist allows you to indicate the level of competence the student displayed on the checklist's criteria. Figure 7.6 illustrates a type of checklist that Luna, a health teacher, used when she evaluated her students' papers on heart disease. Notice that it concentrates on content development and organization. You could easily modify such a checklist by adding different criteria.

Primary Trait Evaluations

Much like the checklist, with **primary trait evaluations** teachers focus on the desired traits they want in their students' writing. For example, if Luna had done a primary trait evaluation on her students' essays, it probably would resemble Figure 7.7. You have likely constructed something similar and called it your

	Below Average	Average	Above Average
1. The essay has an introduction.	_____	_____	_____
2. The essay answers the question and provides key ideas from the text or lecture.	_____	_____	_____
3. The essay provides support for each of the key ideas.	_____	_____	_____
4. The essay personalizes the information by relating it to situations beyond the text and lecture.	_____	_____	_____
5. The writing is clear and organized.	_____	_____	_____
6. The essay summarizes the findings.	_____	_____	_____

FIGURE 7.6   Checklist for Grading a Health Essay

1. The essay lists five of the nine factors impacting heart disease. (age, sex, race, genetic factors; cholesterol and triglycerides; hypertension; diabetes; obesity; smoking; type A behavior; stress; inactivity)	<u>5 points</u>
2. The essay explains these five factors with statistics, examples, support.	<u>15 points</u>
3. The essay relates these factors to personal situations (i.e., the author assesses his/her own risk of developing heart disease).	<u>15 points</u>
4. The essay is clear and well organized.	<u>5 points</u>
	TOTAL <u>40 points</u>

FIGURE 7.7   Primary Trait Evaluation of Health Essay

"grading template." We suggest that you write brief comments on students' papers and focus on one or two primary traits, especially with students' first efforts in writing about a concept. In addition, it has been recommended that content-area teachers write questions rather than comments such as "Be specific" (Lunsford, 1997). Questions force students to solve problems and interact with the material. For example, instead of writing the comment "Be specific," Luna could write a question such as this: "Can you convince me that fitness relates to general health?"

Rubrics

A **rubric** gives content-area teachers more structure for their responses because it summarizes the traits or criteria, as well as the characteristics of high-quality and low-quality papers. Using the rubric as a guide, the teacher can quickly read

An "A" Essay Would Contain

1. An introduction or thesis statement
2. A list of the factors (five minimum) impacting heart disease
3. Explanations, examples, statistics for each of the five factors
4. A personal application or assessment (i.e., the author would assess himself/herself about the risk of developing heart disease)
5. An implication statement discussing solutions
6. Very good organization, few mechanical errors

A "B" Essay Would Contain

1. An introduction or thesis statement
2. A list of the factors (five minimum) impacting heart disease
3. Explanations, examples, statistics for four of the factors
4. An attempt of a personal application
5. A summary statement
6. Good organization, few mechanical errors

A "C" Essay Would Contain

1. A list of the factors (five minimum) impacting heart disease
2. Explanations, examples, statistics for three of the factors
3. A conclusion or summary
4. Fair organization, some mechanical errors

A "D" Essay Would Contain

1. A list of the factors (three or four) impacting heart disease
2. Explanations, examples, statistics for two of the factors
3. Below-average organization and many mechanical errors

An "F" Essay Would Contain

1. A list of the factors (fewer than three) impacting heart disease
2. Explanations, examples, statistics for one factor
3. A list of points, poor organization, many mechanical errors

FIGURE 7.8   Scoring Rubric for a Health Essay

the students' work and respond specifically and appropriately. For Luna's assignment, the rubric might resemble Figure 7.8.

Regardless of the form you select, it is a good idea to introduce it with the assignment and ask the students to attach it to their writing assignment. In that way, the form becomes a concrete reminder for students of what the criteria will be for your responses and eventual evaluation. In the next section, we will discuss how students can participate and assist in the evaluation of their writing.

Effective Activities for Involving Students in Evaluation

Students should be involved in evaluating their writing and other students' writing if we want them to gain independence as learners and consumers of print.

Because many students have been conditioned to respond only on a mechanical level (i.e., "Did I misspell any words?") to their writing, this self-evaluation or peer evaluation takes time to develop. The advantages far outweigh the disadvantages, however, especially in terms of lightening your responsibilities as the sole responder and evaluator. In addition, if students can identify or troubleshoot some common writing problems during class, they can use that information once they begin to revise their final product.

Over the years, we have discovered several activities that help students learn how to evaluate and respond to writing. We have found it best to begin with a whole-class activity that involves students in judging optimal and nonoptimal written models. Another name for this activity is "The Good, the Bad, and the Ugly" because good writing samples as well as bad ones are shared with the students. It is best not to use actual student work but rather to create samples of student writing that typify what "past students" have written. Usually these samples are combinations of students' work and teachers' concerns about common writing problems. The three essays in Figure 7.9 illustrate what one English teacher developed to help students evaluate short essays objectively. The essays were on the abstraction process and fit nicely into her unit on language. See if you can determine the "good," the "bad," and the "ugly" in these essays.

Students are told to read the samples and then assign a grade to each. After grading each sample, they are to rank the writing samples from best to worst. Once they have completed these tasks, the teacher leads a discussion on the grades, ranks, and students' rationales. From our experiences with this activity, students become highly motivated to participate and defend their judgments.

When students feel comfortable with the concept of evaluating and responding to their classmates' writing, it is a good idea to pair them for peer evaluation of a writing assignment they have recently drafted. Begin by emphasizing the basic rules for peer evaluation: Be positive and be specific. Then explain the process: One student will read his or her paper while the other student listens, using a set of questions to guide the feedback given to the writer. The questions should vary according to the content area and assignment; the following typify some that can be used:

1. What did you like best about your partner's paper?
2. What could be added to make the paper more interesting?
3. What facts, ideas, and evidence could be added to strengthen your partner's paper?
4. What parts are not clear?
5. What two parts should be changed or revised?

To help students remember what their partner has recommended, it is a good idea to provide students with a form, such as the one in Figure 7.10. After the student reads her paper, the partner shares his ideas and responses to the questions as they talk. It is important that they talk to each other about the writing rather than just exchange forms. After the talking and responding, they switch roles. If the activity is difficult for the students or if they feel uncomfortable

When students are involved in peer review, they learn a lot about the writing process.

EXAMPLE 1

We employ categories for the purpose of classifying the stimuli. We note the similarities and the differences. Like the English bulldog and Labrador.

The abstraction process could be termed a stereotyping process. Rather than do that, we employ abstractions and stereotypes. Like doctors.

Abstractions can cause some real problems in interpersonal communication. General semanticists have suggested that the abstraction process causes us to overlook the differences in people and things simply because they are all in the same category.

Always try to check with them to make sure that our responses to words are compatible with theirs.

EXAMPLE 2

The abstraction process is of interest to interpersonal communication. When we use the abstraction process, we employ categories for the purpose of classifying the stimuli we perceive. To conceive of the category *dog,* it is necessary for us to abstract from each of these furry creatures those characteristics they all have in common. To do this, we note the similarities but also overlook the differences.

When we categorize we obviously overlook some significant differences. An English bulldog is short, bowlegged, and waddles. On the other hand, a Lab is incredibly graceful, can jump, and has long silky hair. Yet these two dogs have much in common. Both are interested in chasing birds, barking at strangers, and playing with balls and sticks.

Abstractions can be good in that they help us deal with the incoming stimuli in our day-to-day world and provide us with some predictive ability. However, the abstraction process can also cause some real problems. We often assume that the characteristics of a category will hold true for every member. General semanticists have suggested that the abstraction process causes us to overlook the differences in people and things simply because they are all in the same category.

One way to avoid these kinds of errors with the abstraction process is to use indexing, dating, and quotation marks. What it involves is marking a word by the use of numbers or quotes or dates to indicate that dog 1 is different from dog 2. This should remind us that all dogs are not necessarily friendly and that we must test this assumption with each dog.

EXAMPLE 3

When we use the abstraction process, we employ categories for the purpose of classifying the stimuli we perceive. To conceive of the category *dog,* it is necessary for us to abstract from each of these furry creatures those characteristics they all have in common. An English bulldog is short, bowlegged, and waddles. On the other hand, a Lab is incredibly graceful, can jump, and has long silky hair. Yet these two dogs have much in common. Both are interested in chasing birds, barking at strangers, and playing with balls and sticks.

Abstractions provide us with some predictive ability. The abstraction process could also be termed a stereotyping process. Although the abstraction process is useful, there are some real problems it can create in interpersonal communication. General semanticists have suggested that the abstraction process causes us to overlook the differences in people and things simply because they are all in the same category.

One way to avoid these kinds of errors is to use indexing and dating. Like dog1, dog2, and dog3.

FIGURE 7.9 "The Good, the Bad, and the Ugly" Exercise

initially, you can model the procedure for the class by becoming the partner who responds.

A third activity can be done in small groups. A volunteer in each group reads his paper. Then the other members of the group state ideas from their papers that either were or were not present in the paper just read. Each member of the

---

Author's Name: **Peer Reviewer's Name:**

Authors: Read your paper aloud to your reviewer.

Reviewer: Answer the questions below so that the author has a written copy of the comments you will provide orally.

1. This paper is mainly about
2. The best part of the author's paper was
3. These parts of the author's paper were not clear to me:
   a.
   b.
   c.
4. I think the author's paper could be strengthened by:
   a.
   b.
   c.
5. I think the paper could be even more interesting if the author would

Reviewer and Author: Talk to each other about your ideas.

FIGURE 7.10 Student Evaluation Form for Working in Pairs

group must respond. Because all students are required to participate, they profit from hearing how others have interacted with the targeted concepts. This information should assist students in revising their papers once they leave class. Moreover, this activity can serve as an excellent review for an examination.

Using Writing to Test Learning

If you have ever used an essay examination in your class as a means of measuring student learning, you probably have shared the reactions of most teachers: "No more essays!" "These students can't write, so why should I waste my time grading these pitiful excuses for essay answers!" or "Did these students even study?" Although the most judicious use of writing is not for testing or evaluating, essay examinations should not be avoided just because students initially are inept with them. As stated in Chapter 4, writing is one of the best means, next to a conference with each student, to assess how well students can think analytically about content. If we expect our students to synthesize, evaluate, and apply course objectives to new contexts, we should design evaluation measures that are sensitive to those objectives. In short, true-false and multiple-choice questions should not be the only examinations students take.

How then do we prepare students to be adept at taking essay examinations? One way to help students through their first essay test is by teaching them the processes involved in **PORPE** *(predict, organize, rehearse, practice, evaluate),* an essay preparation strategy built on research and theory in writing and metacognition (Simpson, 1986). In the initial validation study, the high-risk college freshmen trained in PORPE as a means of preparing for a psychology

PORPE provides students a way to study for essay and short-answer exams.

exam performed significantly better than an equivalent group answering short-answer questions (Simpson, Hayes, Stahl, Conner, & Weaver, 1988). Not only were these students' essays superior in content, organization, and clarity, but their scores on the multiple-choice exam were also significantly superior to those of the control students. This study demonstrated that any student, with assistance from the teacher, can learn how to apply the steps of PORPE to improve in essay and multiple-choice test performance.

PORPE's first step, **predict,** asks students to generate some potential questions that would make good essays. To help students at this point, teachers should introduce the language used for writing essay examinations by providing them with a glossary of commonly used essay-question words such as *explain, discuss, criticize, compare,* and *contrast.* Once students understand the meaning of these essay-word starters, teachers can involve them in brainstorming possible essay questions from a specific chapter. Often the main difficulty students have with essay prediction is that they focus on minute details rather than key ideas. Thus, teachers should try telling them to check the boldface headings and summaries for possible essay topics. Essay prediction is not easy, but all students can learn this important step if given considerable guidance. The following questions illustrate some of the questions students predicted for their essay test on the Modernist movement in an art appreciation course:

1. Discuss the individuals and types of art that influenced the Modernist movement in painting.

2. Compare and contrast Kandinsky with Picasso.

3. Trace the development of the Modernist movement in the United States, noting influential artists as well as critics.

The second step in PORPE, **organize,** involves students in gathering and arranging the information that will answer the self-predicted essay question. This step is very much like brainstorming and prewriting in that students map or outline answers in their own words. Content-area teachers can help students with this step by sharing their own maps or outlines that answer a predicted essay question. Students can also work in pairs to brainstorm their own organizational structure for another predicted essay question. Representatives from each pair could then present and discuss their structure and rationale on the chalkboard. As a final step, students could develop their own map or outline for a different essay question and receive brief written or oral feedback from the teacher. This step encourages students to develop connections among ideas so that the course content becomes reorganized into a coherent structure instead of memorized as a list of unrelated bits of information.

The third step of PORPE, **rehearse,** engages students in the active self-recitation and self-testing of the key ideas from their maps or outlines. At this point, teachers should stress the difference between the processes of *recall* and *recognition* so that students will accept and internalize the need for a rehearsal step in their study. Most of the students we have worked with think that studying is the same as looking at the information, and they see no difference in demands between essays and multiple-choice exams. One of the major reasons students have difficulty writing essay answers is that they have not spent the concentrated time rehearsing information to transfer it to long-term memory.

To help students rehearse, we have found it useful to incorporate the talk-through strategy (see Chapter 9) at this stage. During class, students meet with their partners and practice talk-throughs for a specified amount of time. After discussing and evaluating each other's talk-through, students write, from memory, an answer to one of their self-predicted essay questions.

The fourth step, **practice,** is the validation step of learning because students must write from recall the answers to their self-predicted essay questions in preparation for the real examination. Before students begin their practice, content-area teachers should provide them with many examples of essay answers, good and bad, and discuss their relative merits. Teachers can also reduce students' anxiety by outlining the procedures for writing an effective answer in an actual testing situation. For example, students should be taught to read each question carefully before they begin to write, underlining key words. Next, they should be encouraged to sketch their outline or map in the margin of their test paper before they begin writing. Once they begin answering the question, they should make sure that their opening sentence rephrases the essay question and/or takes a position. Finally, students should reread the essay question to ensure that they have answered it directly.

The final step of PORPE, **evaluate,** requires students to evaluate the quality of their practice answers. To facilitate this process, students are given a checklist that requires them to read and evaluate their text as would a teacher. The checklist in Figure 7.11 helps students to evaluate, completely and objectively both their essay answer and their readiness for the real examination. Content-area teachers can introduce this final step of PORPE by arranging brief sessions when students read, discuss, and evaluate the merits of various essay answers. Once students become more accustomed to evaluating writing with a checklist, they can work in pairs to evaluate each other's essays and evaluate their own answers independently.

Even though the steps of PORPE will take some additional class time, it is important to remember that not only will students learn how to prepare for and take an essay exam, but they also will learn important course concepts. In addition, the PORPE strategy can help students prepare for multiple-choice exams, especially when the questions ask them to draw conclusions and apply information to new contexts. Thus, the essay test should not be feared by students or teachers but used when appropriate and when students have been taught the *how.*

The Research Paper

Research and the processes inherent in research are not reserved just for the classroom. Our students need to know how to become critical consumers of information if they are to thrive in a society saturated with conflicting information. Their employers also expect them to be capable researchers and problem solvers who are comfortable in identifying potential sources of information,

Directions: Evaluate the quality of your answer by using this checklist. If you score *above average* on the six questions, you are probably ready for the exam. If, however, you find some of your answers to the predicted essay questions to be *below average* or *average,* go back to your notes, annotation, and strategies. Examine your organization (STEP TWO) again—did you leave out some key ideas or details? Repair and then go through the steps again—PREDICT, ORGANIZE, REHEARSE, PRACTICE, AND EVALUATE.

EVALUATING PRACTICE ESSAY ANSWERS

	Below Average	Average	Above Average
1. I directly answered the question that was asked.	1	2	3
2. I had an introductory sentence which restated the essay question and/or took a position on the question.	1	2	3
3. I organized the essay answer with key ideas or points which were made obvious.	1	2	3
4. I included in the answer *relevant* details or examples to prove and clarify each idea.	1	2	3
5. I used transitions in the answer to cue the reader. (e.g., First, Finally)	1	2	3
6. My answer made sense and demonstrated a knowledge of the content.	1	2	3

Source: From "PORPE: A Writing Strategy for Studying and Learning in the Content Areas," by M. L. Simpson, 1986, *Journal of Reading, 29,* p. 411. Reprinted by permission of the author.

FIGURE 7.11   Student Checklist for Self-Evaluation

analyzing that information in a critical fashion, and making informed decisions (Mendrinos, 1997). Some content-area teachers choose to use the research paper as a vehicle to teach these important yet demanding thinking skills.

Because of these sophisticated demands inherent in a research paper, students and teachers often become frustrated and disillusioned. Students are frustrated because they do not understand the intricate and time-consuming processes involved in writing from multiple sources. Teachers are frustrated because the products students hand in are not what they have anticipated. Moreover, in some situations students have inadvertently plagiarized ideas because they have copied text rather than paraphrasing and summarizing. What is the solution? Should content-area teachers avoid research papers or written reports? We think a better solution is to define clearly the goals of such assignments and to provide specific interventions that will help students during the processes of researching, reading, planning, and writing. Moreover, we would recommend that students write several brief research papers or memos rather than one lengthy one.

The goals of a research paper can vary along a continuum, with one goal emphasizing knowledge telling and the other knowledge transformation (Nelson & Hayes, 1988). Knowledge telling requires students to locate and summarize what other individuals have stated about a certain topic. For example, a student in a history course might decide to do a research paper on blacklisting or the Red Scare. Knowledge transformation involves students in reading and evaluating information in terms of a specific question or goal they have established for themselves. A student doing a research paper of this type would selectively read, evaluate, and synthesize information from the sources with the goal of answering a question, such as whether or not the activities and behaviors of people during the Red Scare are in any way characteristic of the present era. Knowledge telling differs significantly from knowledge transformation in that students must plan, evaluate, and synthesize more with the latter. If teachers want students to do the type of critical thinking and writing involved in knowledge transformation, then they should inform students of that expectation when giving the assignment. Otherwise, students typically will reinterpret the research report as an assignment in which they gather information and then record it in a paper.

Research papers have the potential of being positive experiences that involve students in many sophisticated reading and thinking processes.

In addition to informing students of the goals of a paper, content-area teachers can assist students by guiding them through the recursive processes or stages involved in writing a research paper:

1. selecting a topic or issue that is of high interest
2. getting started and narrowing the focus of the topic or issue by doing some initial reading and thinking
3. searching for more relevant sources and taking notes using your own organizational system rather than the author's
4. thinking and planning the structure of the paper
5. returning to the library or Internet for additional sources to fill out your structure
6. writing the first draft
7. evaluating, revising, and editing with the audience in mind
8. writing the final version of the paper

Students also need to understand the time frame necessary to move from stage 1 to stage 8. Our experience suggests that students often miscalculate the time necessary to find the appropriate sources in the library. More important, they underestimate the time that must be devoted to the stages that follow the research, thinking that the paper can be written the night before the deadline.

Use these six ideas to help your students avoid last-minute efforts with their research papers.

You can help your students progress through the stages of writing a research paper if you follow these six recommendations. First, you should provide a reading list or key words that students can use in their library or computer searches. In some situations it might be helpful to teach students how to use search tools and conduct Boolean searches if your school does not have a learning specialist with these skills. Second, you should probably review the characteristics of scholarly sources and credible Internet sites in your content area. As explained in Chapter 3, students should be taught how to judge the authority and intent of authors and the accuracy and objectivity of their ideas.

Third, you can ask students for progress reports in the form of learning log entries or Quick Writes where students discuss what they have done and list their concerns or questions. These entries can be shared with the teacher and with other students in group problem-solving sessions during class. Some teachers ask students to hand in writing products as a way of ensuring that students are progressing. For example, students can hand in their initial reference list, outline, or notes to demonstrate that they are on task. Such work, handed in early, also allows you to give your students specific feedback. If you collect the students' first draft of their research paper, as many writing experts would recommend, it is often useful to ask the students to include a brief cover note to their draft (Herrington, 1997). In this brief note the students would indicate what they are most satisfied with at this point (e.g., their thesis statement), what they are still working on or what is still troubling them (e.g., organizing, finding sources), and what they would like feedback on (e.g., am I specific enough in my analysis?). This cover letter could be addressed to you, the teacher, or to a peer who might also read the draft.

Fourth, teachers can help students by demonstrating and providing examples of organizational formats for summarizing and synthesizing ideas from multiple sources. As explained in Chapter 9, students have significant difficulties in synthesizing from multiple sources (Simpson & Nist, 2001). The study sheet and the chart or map are certainly appropriate ways to organize and synthesize ideas for the research paper. In addition to these formats, some teachers have found I-Charts (Hoffman, 1992) to be particularly beneficial for students (see Figure 7.12).

Randall (1996) used a modification of the I-Chart with her eighth graders during an interdisciplinary unit on the wilderness and the environment. She found the organizational strategy to be highly effective, especially with her struggling readers. Her students also raved about the usefulness of the I-Chart, many of them offering testimonials such as "It saved my life" and "I rate it a 10." As illustrated in Figure 7.12, the I-Chart provides students a format to summarize important facts from multiple sources under a topic heading. Such a format assists students in paraphrasing ideas and in sensing patterns across sources. As one student in Randall's class said, "They keep your stuff straight and in order" (Randall, 1996, p. 541).

Fifth, you can require students to present to the class an oral report of their paper one week before the written report is due. In this way, students are forced to think about and organize their ideas for an audience other than the teacher. When students realize that they will be presenting their work to a real audience, they tend to adapt and transform the information they have gathered to meet the needs of their uninformed listeners (Nelson & Hayes, 1988).

Finally, you can help students by giving them in advance the criteria that will be used to grade or evaluate their work. As mentioned earlier in this chapter,

---

TOPIC: _____

Name:
Subtopic:
What do I already know about this topic?

_____

Source #1   **MY NOTES**

_____

Source #2   **MY NOTES**

_____

Source #3   **MY NOTES**

_____

Facts I find interesting:

Key words:

New questions I should research:

FIGURE 7.12   I-Chart Format for Synthesizing Sources

explicitly describing writing assignments can prevent bad writing. Students should understand the role of mechanics, organization, content, and writing style in the grading process. Some teachers use a checklist and ask students to attach it to the first page of their paper. The checklist incorporates the grading criteria and helps students evaluate their work before handing it in. We think this is a good idea that can make the grading process somewhat easier. Following these six suggestions should prevent the nightmares that occur for students and teachers when research papers have not been fully thought through and mentored.

The Role of Computer Technology During the Writing Process

The use of computers is addressed more fully in Chapter 10, but it is appropriate to outline briefly how the computer can be used during the writing and learning process. As you undoubtedly have already discovered, computer technology can be initially intoxicating for students. They hope that the computer can think for them and miraculously generate quality text with little or no effort in a short period of time. We must remind students that this technology is not inherently advantageous to the writing process. When used correctly and insightfully, however, a word processing program can develop students' understanding of and sensitivity to how they write and can thus increase their control over their writing process.

Research tends to support these intuitions about computer technology and writing (Bangert-Drowns, 1993; Kamil, Intrator, & Kim, 2000). That is, it seems that word processing programs can help your students produce longer documents and better-quality writing, especially when the recursive stages of prewriting, writing, and postwriting are stressed. As Kamil et al. stated, "Process writing predates the advent of word processors, but the two concepts seem to be so matched that they seem to have sprung from the same intellectual root" (p. 773). In the next section we examine the role of the computer during each of these three stages.

Research suggests that word processing programs can help students produce better quality writing.

Prewriting Stages

A word processing program can be advantageous at the prewriting stage by reducing the anxiety some students feel about writing, especially those who will tell you that they know nothing about the topic or are unsure of where to begin. With a word processing program, students can freely and quickly brainstorm ideas, especially if they know the keyboard. They can then delete, add, and rearrange those ideas into groups, and those ideas can then be labeled and ordered. If students suffer from the "fuzzy-thinking" syndrome during their planning, they can stop and practice what Flower (1985) describes as *nutshelling*. Nutshelling is helpful to students who have brainstormed many ideas but who lack a focus or precise direction. To **nutshell** on the computer, students must compress into a sentence the key idea they would like to write about and then teach that idea to someone else before they move any further in the composing process. The following example of nutshelling came from a student who was writing an essay about the novel *The Contender.*

> Through boxing and his interactions with several different people, Alfred learned that he could be a contender in life.

By taking the time to nutshell, this student began to understand what he wanted to say about the book he had just read.

In addition to brainstorming and nutshelling, **invention programs** encourage students to generate ideas and sense relationships across ideas. These programs provide students with questions or prompts (e.g., "What are the good consequences of your topic?" "Whom do you consider an authority on your topic?") that help students consider what they already know about a topic and what they still need to research or explore. Other computer programs, such as Inspiration (2000), help students visualize interrelationships between ideas using concept maps.

Writing Stages

Word processing programs have many advantages at this stage of the writing process. If students know the keyboard, they can be more effective and efficient because their thoughts are almost always ahead of their fingers when they write by hand. With the computer, students are more likely to experiment by trying out ideas, erasing ones they do not like, skipping ahead, and then returning to reword difficult introductions or transition sentences. They even can write two different versions of a sentence or paragraph, marking one with parentheses or capitals, either of which can easily be deleted later. In short, word processing programs encourage flexibility and efficiency during the drafting stages of writing.

Postwriting Stages

The postwriting stages of the writing process include revising, editing, and proofreading. After the draft has been saved, downloaded, and copied, students will be able to read and revise and/or share copies with their peers or teachers for feedback. Alternatively, students could share their documents with their classmates by sending them via an e-mail attachment. These typed, double-spaced drafts are far more readable, and gross mistakes, such as misspellings and punctuation omissions, are obvious. Moreover, students are more likely to accept the suggestions for major revisions given by teachers and peers because the computer makes draft writing so easy. Instead of saying "Do I have to do this whole thing over?" students are more likely to say "How else can I make this draft better?" The word processing program allows them to insert new text, combine paragraphs, move entire paragraphs or pages to different places, or delete unnecessary text. In addition, when students use the "comment" function and the "track changes" functions of Microsoft Word, they are collaborating with their peers.

Several word processing commands and software packages can help students with their editing. Some word processing programs have search commands that can identify a character or string of characters, such as a word or a mark or punctuation. The computer will then scan the entire text, stopping each time to highlight the designated character(s) so that the student can change or correct it. The search-and-replace command locates a character and automatically replaces it with another (e.g., *effect* for *affect*). Many word processing programs have a spelling checker, and some have a thesaurus to help students with word choices.

As you can see, word processing programs and software packages have the potential to help your students during the writing process. Because we realize that every teacher does not have access to 30 computers, we offer the following suggestions for capitalizing on the computers to which your students do have access:

1. Make sure that middle school students are taught basic typing and keyboard skills so that they can improve their fluency and speed on the computer.

2. Have students write their first draft in pencil. When they are done, they can sign up for a 20- to 30-minute session on the computer.

3. Ask students to work in pairs on the computer. One student who knows the keyboard can type her paper while the other student reads it to her. Then the students can switch roles.

4. Reserve a certain amount of computer time for printing the students' writing so that they have a written product that can be taken home for reading, revising, and editing.

5. Allow students to decide whether they want to use the computer for brainstorming, drafting, or revising.

Although it is advantageous to use the computer and computer software programs, we should point out the obvious: this technology will not automatically increase students' ability to communicate in writing about content-area concepts. What does make a difference in students' learning is how computers are integrated into the process approach to writing and into the classroom environment (Kamil et al., 2000).

CASE STUDY REVISITED

At the beginning of this chapter, we described the problems that Dave was experiencing in his first year of teaching biology to non-college-bound students. After reading this chapter, you probably have some suggestions on how he could motivate his students to become more active participants and learners. Write your suggestions now.

Before writing your suggestions for Dave, go to *http://www.prenhall.com/brozo*, select Chapter 7, then click on Chapter Review Questions to check your understanding of the material.

After talking to the English teacher and doing some of his own research and planning, Dave decided to spark his students' interest in the environment unit in several ways. Because the unit was to last approximately 9 weeks, he felt he had the time to assign some literature and expository pieces other than just the textbook. In addition, he decided to involve his students actively by asking them to write about their concerns and questions rather than having them merely answer the questions at the end of the textbook chapter.

Dave began the unit with an activity designed to assess his students' present attitudes toward the environment. The students were prepared for a lecture and a textbook assignment when they entered class on the second day of the unit. Instead, they were greeted with Dave's slides of beautiful outdoor scenes and Jethro Tull's "Songs from the Woods" playing in the background. As the song faded, Dave shifted the slides to scenes of human filth and flotsam. Slides of dumps, incinerators, and cities were now shown, and the background music was John Prine's "Paradise." When the slides and song were finished, Dave handed out the following questionnaire:

Directions: Answer as completely as possible. There are no right or wrong answers, so feel free to express yourself.

1. Briefly, tell me how the slide presentation made you feel.

2. What was the message of the second song, "Paradise"?

3. Is there a place outdoors that you especially like to go? Where? Why?

4. Have you ever thought or read or heard about the ideas presented today? If so, tell me about them in more detail. What was the source of those ideas?

Dave read his students' responses before he assigned the next activity, which was designed to provoke them into comparing their personal feelings about the environment with society's attitudes. When his students entered the classroom on the third day, he handed them "a letter from archy," excerpted from *from the lifetimes of archy and mehitabel* by Don Marquis (1950), and asked them to read it. The English teacher had suggested this particular piece to Dave, and he found it especially relevant.

Dave then divided the students into groups of five and gave them a study guide to provide a focus for their discussions. He circulated around the room as they discussed the questions, joining groups and provoking them to think beyond the obvious. One of the statements on the study guide required them to estimate the date of the letter. As Dave interacted with each group, he found that they were shocked to learn that the letter had been written in 1935.

Dave then brought the class together to brainstorm all the actions and decisions people have made that have ignored archy's warnings. Because of recent media coverage, the students were quickly able to list problems like the greenhouse effect, acid rain, deforestation, and the loss of wildlife. At the end of the hour, he told his students that they were going to focus on one issue: the loss of wildlife.

On the next day of class, Dave handed out copies of Farley Mowatt's *Never Cry Wolf* (1963) and said they would be reading the book for the next few days. To establish an overall purpose for their reading, he asked the students to focus on three questions: (1) Why was the wolf endangered? (2) What was the likely future of the wolf? (3) What must we do to prevent its extinction? He then read aloud the first few pages to elicit their interest and assigned the first 30 pages. Each day the students gathered in their groups to discuss and then write a group response to the "Question for the Day" that Dave had written on the board (e.g., "What were the reasons for Farley's boss giving him this assignment?" "What do you think Farley is going to find out about the wolf?"). When the students finished the book, Dave gave each of them an index card and asked them to respond to the three focus questions he had asked the first day. After reading the students' microthemes, Dave led a class discussion of the book and the three questions. He was pleased with this activity because most of his students had actually read the book and some reported that it was their first.

Because Dave's next unit objective was to have his students localize and personalize the issue of endangered species, he obtained a list of locally endangered animal and plant species from the Department of Natural Resources and asked each student to select a species from the list. The librarian and the English teacher suggested that he give his students a lot of structure for the assignment, so Dave distributed a handout outlining his expectations:

You are to select one of the species from the list and gather information about its problem of survival. Specifically, I want you to include the following information in your paper: (1) past and present range and population,

(2) length of time it has been endangered, (3) reasons for its being endangered, (4) why it is important that this species survive, and (5) actions currently being taken to improve its chances for survival.

You will have 2 weeks to complete this assignment. Your first step in doing the assignment will be to use the classroom library and any resources I have listed for you on the accompanying page. Read extensively and take notes for about 4 days. On the fifth day, begin organizing your ideas into an outline or map, making sure you have answered all five questions. On the sixth day, you will deliver a 3-minute presentation to the class on what you have learned thus far about your endangered species. Rough drafts of your written paper will be due on October 15. I will read them and provide you with feedback. The final paper will be due October 30.

In grading this assignment, I will use these criteria:

1. How well you answered the five questions concerning your species. Were you complete? Accurate? Did you explain yourself clearly so that your best friend could understand? This part is worth 35 points.

2. Your spelling, mechanics, and grammar. This part is worth 15 points. As to length—there are five questions, so I expect three pages as a minimum.

Most of Dave's students attempted to do the assignment, so he was pleased. He realized, however, that he probably should have started on a smaller scale with a less intimidating discourse mode. After chatting with the English teacher during lunch, he decided to try letter writing because it was a less formal type of writing and was closer to talking, something with which his students had lots of experience.

The next week, Dave began his final activity for the unit. The class brainstormed what could be done to stop or slow down the process of environmental degradation. When Dave asked his students what they could do, he received many blank stares. He then suggested to them that education was one answer and that they could be a part of that educational process by becoming informed and involved. Dave explained that involvement can occur in many forms, and that letter writing was one powerful and permanent means of disseminating ideas. With that introduction, he told each student to write a letter to his or her senator or representative asking for support of legislation they considered important for the protection of wildlife. After discussing the proper form for a letter to a government official, the students were given time to begin their rough drafts. Dave provided feedback on all rough drafts, and by the end of the week he had 24 letters to mail to Washington, DC. Many students doubted whether they would receive a response, but within a month, all of Dave's students had received replies from the senators and representatives. Copies of the 24 letters were placed on Dave's bulletin board and shared with group members. Even after 4 months and several other units of study, the students still gathered at the bulletin board to read those letters and to discuss the status of their environment.

Dave is still struggling with ways to involve his students with the biology curriculum. He has some good days and some bad ones, but he feels that his students are certainly more involved than they were before, when he taught only from the textbook.

—————◄O►—————

SUMMARY

In this chapter we have demonstrated that the writing process can be a powerful tool in helping students learn content-area concepts. Writing, like reading, is a constructive process that can stimulate passive learners to become active learners as they grapple with the task of putting their own words on paper. Although low-stakes writing assignments can be extremely useful in teaching content, teachers must also remember that writing is not a product, but a process with overlapping and recursive stages. With high-stakes writing assignments, sufficient instructional attention and time must be allotted to these stages so that students plan, draft, revise, edit, proofread, and polish their writing before the possibility of grading is even considered. For those teachers wondering how to evaluate students' writing, we offered some practical grading guidelines and suggestions to make the task easier and more reasonable.

This chapter was organized on the assumptions that writing can be used to help students (1) prepare for their reading assignments, lectures, demonstrations, and class discussions; (2) summarize and organize concepts and monitor their understanding of those concepts; and (3) think critically and creatively. Using those three assumptions, we presented a variety of activities—the Guided-Writing Activity, learning logs, Quick Writes, microthemes, the double-entry journal, framed paragraphs, the reader-response heuristic, and analytical writing assignments—to stimulate students to attain higher levels of thinking. For those teachers who are interested in computers or who have access to computers in their classroom, we also recommended some materials and activities for word processing programs. Any of these writing activities could easily be incorporated into content-area lesson plans to challenge and motivate even the most reluctant learner.

REFERENCES

Alexander, P. A., & Jetton, T. L. (2000). Learning from text: A multidimensional and developmental perspective. In M. Kamil, P. Mosenthal, P. Pearson, & R. Barr (Eds.), *Handbook of reading research* (Vol. 3, pp. 285–310). Mahwah, NJ: Lawrence Erlbaum Associates.

Bangert-Drowns, R. L. (1993). The word processor as an instructional tool: A meta-analysis of word processing in writing instruction. *Review of Educational Research, 63,* 69–93.

Bean, J. C., Drenk, D., & Lee, F. D. (1982). Microtheme strategies for developing cognitive skills. In C. W. Griffin (Ed.), *New directions for teaching and learning.* San Francisco: Jossey-Bass.

Belenky, M., Clinchy, B., Goldberger, N., & Tarule, J. (1986). *Women's ways of knowing.* New York: Basic Books.

Brozo, W. (1988). Applying the reader-response heuristic to expository texts. *Journal of Reading, 32,* 140–145.

Burns, J., Peltason, J., & Cronin, T. (1984). *Government by the people.* Englewood Cliffs, NJ: Prentice Hall.

Calkins, L. M. (1986). *The art of teaching writing.* Portsmouth, NH: Heinemann.

Elbow, P. (1997). High stakes and low stakes in assigning and responding to writing. In M. Sorcinelli & P. Elbow (Eds.), *Writing to learn: Strategies for assigning and responding to writing across the disciplines* (pp. 5–13). San Francisco: Jossey-Bass.

Fisher, D. (2001). "We're moving on up": Creating a schoolwide literacy effort in an urban high school. *Journal of Adolescent & Adult Literacy, 45,* 92–101.

Fitzgerald, J., & Shanahan, T. (2000). Reading and writing relations and their development. *Educational Psychologist, 35,* 39–51.

Flower, L. (1985). *Problem solving strategies for writing.* New York: Harcourt Brace Jovanovich.

Herrington, A. J. (1997). Developing and responding to major writing projects. In M. Sorcinelli & P. Elbow (Eds.), *Writing to learn: Strategies for assigning and responding to writing across the disciplines* (pp. 53–66). San Francisco: Jossey-Bass.

Hoffman, J. V. (1992). Critical reading/thinking across the curriculum: Using I-Charts to support learning. *Language Arts, 69,* 121–127.

Houston, J. W., & Houston, J. (1974). *Farewell to Manzanar.* New York: Bantam.

Hynd, C. R. (1999). Teaching students to think critically using multiple texts in history. *Journal of Adolescent & Adult Literacy, 42,* 428–436.

Inspiration [Computer software]. (2000). Retrieved from http://www.inspiration.com.

Jenkinson, E. B. (1988). Learning to write/Writing to learn. *Phi Delta Kappan, 69,* 712–717.

Kamil, M. L., Intrator, S., & Kim, H. (2000). The effects of other technologies on literacy and literacy learning. In M. Kamil, P. D. Mosenthal, P. D. Pearson, & R. Barr (Eds.), *Handbook of reading research* (Vol. 3, pp. 771–788). Mahwah, NJ: Lawrence Erlbaum Associates.

Lenski, S. D., Wham, M. A., & John, J. (1999). *Reading and learning strategies for middle and high school students.* Dubuque, IA: Kendall/Hunt Publishing.

Light, R. J. (2001). *Making the most of college: Students speak their minds.* Cambridge, MA: Harvard University Press.

Lunsford, R. F. (1997). When less is more: Principles for responding in the disciplines. In M. Sorcinelli & P. Elbow (Eds.), *Writing to learn: Strategies for assigning and responding to writing across the disciplines* (pp. 91–104). San Francisco: Jossey-Bass.

Marquis, D. (1950). *from the lifetimes of archy and mehitabel.* Garden City, NY: Doubleday.

Martin, C. E., Martin, M. A., & O'Brien, D. G. (1984). Spawning ideas for writing in the content areas. *Reading World, 11,* 11–15.

Mendrinos, R. B. (1997). *Using educational technology with at-risk students.* Westport, CT: Greenwood.

Mowatt, F. (1963). *Never cry wolf.* Boston: Little, Brown.

Nelson, J., & Hayes, J. R. (1988). *How the writing context shapes college students' strategies for writing from sources* (Tech. Rep. No. 16). Berkeley: Center for the Study of Writing, University of California at Berkeley.

Pearce, D. (1983). Guidelines for the use and evaluation of writing in content class-rooms. *Journal of Reading, 27,* 212–216.

Petrosky, A. R. (1982). From story to essay: Reading and writing. *College Composition and Communication, 33,* 19–36.

Randall, S. N. (1996). Information charts: A strategy for organizing students research. *Journal of Adolescent & Adult Literacy, 39,* 536–542.

Rubin, D. L., & Dodd, W. M. (1987). *Talking into writing: Exercises for basic writers.* ERIC Clearinghouse on Reading and Communication Skills. Urbana, IL: National Council of Teachers of English.

Santa, C., & Havens, L. (1991). Learning through writing. In C. Santa & D. Alvermann (Eds.), *Science learning: Processes and applications.* Newark, NJ: International Reading Association.

Santa, C., Havens, L. & Maycumber, E. (1996). *Project CRISS: Creating independence through student-owned strategies.* Dubuque, IA: Kendall/Hunt.

Sargent, M. E. (1997). Peer response to low stakes writing in a WAC literature classroom. In M. Sorcinelli & P. Elbow (Eds.), *Writing to learn: Strategies for assigning and responding to writing across the disciplines* (pp. 41–52). San Francisco: Jossey-Bass.

Shanahan, T. (1997). Reading-writing relationships, thematic units, inquiry learning . . . In pursuit of effective integrated literacy instruction. *Reading Teacher, 51,* 12–20.

Simpson, M. L. (1986). PORPE: A writing strategy for studying and learning in the content areas. *Journal of Reading, 29,* 407–414.

Simpson, M. L., Hayes, C., Stahl, N., Conner, R., & Weaver, D. (1988). An initial validation of a study strategy system. *Journal of Reading Behavior, 20,* 149–180.

Simpson, M. L., & Nist, S. L. (2001). Encouraging active reading at the college level. In C. Block & M. Pressley (Eds.), *Comprehension instruction: Research-based practices* (pp. 365–379). New York: Guilford Press.

Smith, C. C., & Bean, T. W. (1980). The guided writing procedure: Integrating content reading and writing improvement. *Reading World, 19,* 290–294.

Sweet, A. (1997). A national perspective on research intersections between literacy and visual/communicative arts. In J. Flood, S. Heath, & D. Lapp (Eds.), *Handbook of research on teaching literacy through the communicative and visual arts* (pp. 264–285). New York: Simon and Schuster.

Tierney, R. J., & Pearson, P. D. (1983). Toward a composing model of reading. *Language Arts, 60,* 568–580.

Tierney, R. J., Soter, A., O'Flahavan, J., & McGinley, W. (1989). The effects of reading and writing on thinking critically. *Reading Research Quarterly, 24,* 134–173.

Turner, J. (1995). The influence of classroom contexts on young children's motivation for literacy. *Reading Research Quarterly, 30,* 410–441.

Vacca, J. L., Vacca, R. T., & Gove, M. K. (1995). *Reading and learning to read.* New York: HarperCollins.

Wade, S., & Moje, E. (2000). The role of text in classroom learning. In M. Kamil, P. Mosenthal, P. D. Pearson, & R. Barr (Eds.), *Handbook of reading research* (Vol. 3, pp. 609–628). Mahwah, NJ: Lawrence Erlbaum Associates.

Wagner, B. J. (1987). The effects of role playing on written persuasion: An age and channel comparison of fourth and eighth graders. *Dissertation Abstracts International, 47,* 4008A.

CHAPTER EIGHT

Literature Across the Curriculum and Throughout Life

ANTICIPATION GUIDE

Directions: Read each statement carefully and decide whether you agree or disagree with it, placing a check mark in the appropriate *Before Reading* column. When you have finished reading and studying the chapter, return to the guide and decide whether your anticipations need to be changed by placing a check mark in the appropriate *After Reading* column.

	BEFORE READING		AFTER READING	
	Agree	*Disagree*	*Agree*	*Disagree*
1. Using novels and picture books in the content areas is a recent innovation.	____	____	____	____
2. Trade books can educate the heart and the mind.	____	____	____	____
3. Certain trade books supply many useful facts about a variety of topics.	____	____	____	____
4. Literature has limited utility in science and math classrooms.	____	____	____	____
5. Middle and secondary students enjoy being read to just as much as younger learners do.	____	____	____	____

Real books are wonderful. These are the books you find in public places like libraries, bookmobiles, bookstores, and sometimes even in supermarkets. Real books rest beside your bed, clutter the coffee table, and stand on shelves at the ready—waiting to be lifted, opened and brought to life by your reading. Real books—each one with its own individual binding, each one sized just right for the story it houses—are written by authors who know how to unlock the world with words and to open our eyes and our hearts. Each real book has its own voice—a singular, clear voice—and each speaks words that move us toward increased consciousness.

—Peterson and Eeds (1990)

Many junior and senior high school students receive their first serious look at different cultures, historical eras and events, politics, and scientific advances of the human race through content-area textbooks. As we stated earlier, because of the demands of limited space, adoption committees, and readability constraints, textbook publishers often present a distilled version of content-area information. Emphasis is placed on important facts, broad views, pivotal characters, and general effects on whole populations, resulting inevitably in a detached tone and dry material. But we must not forget that within each of these cultures, social movements, historical eras, and scientific advances lie richly detailed stories about the people who made them or who watched them being made and were affected by them. The narrative element—the stories that lie within all human interactions—is often left out of many content-area lessons. Yet, it is narrative that can bring the content to life.

One of the most instructive precedents for bringing content material to life is Selma Lagerlof's book *The Wonderful Adventures of Nils* (1912), an earlier edition of which had been written for and adopted by the public schools of Sweden in 1907. This is a rare example of textbook and trade book successfully written as one. In this adventure-filled story, Nils, a boy-turned-to-elf, sails back and forth across Sweden astride a barnyard goose as the author subtly acquaints the reader with an encyclopedia of knowledge about that country. Lagerlof recognized the value of story and exploited it fully by stringing dry, educational subjects on the thread of exciting adventures and the engaging character of Nils Holgersson.

Children learn to read with stories. In fact, their early reading experiences involve stories exclusively. So it is not surprising that for many children the transition to content textbooks employing expository structures leads to their first difficulties with reading (Quiocho, 1997; Richgels, Tomlinson, & Tunnell, 1993). We believe that one effective response to the difficulties students may experience with reading textbooks, not only in the transitional middle grades but in secondary school as well, is for the content-area teacher to continue to exploit students' past successes with literature by using children's and young adult books in conjunction with textbooks.

In Chapter 2, we described some important instructional requisites for developing the higher levels of literacy many middle and secondary students seem to lack. Trade books, when used appropriately with textbooks, can become a powerful teaching tool for expanding literacy. This approach builds relevant prior knowledge, capitalizes on the student's skill in reading narrative, engenders interest and motivation, and consequently promotes a deeper understanding and appreciation of the content in both trade books and textbooks (Austin, 1998; Tomlinson, Tunnell, & Richgels, 1993).

This chapter has two main thrusts. It is devoted primarily to ways in which young adult literature can be skillfully integrated into the content curriculum to make it more palatable, comprehensible, and memorable. Additionally, we discuss ways in which teachers can encourage students to make reading an integral part of their lives outside the classroom.

Go to *http:// www.prenhall.com/ brozo*, select Chapter 8, then click on Chapter Objectives to provide a focus for your reading.

Fiction and nonfiction trade books written for adolescents can be used to help teach nearly any content-area subject.

CASE STUDY

Linda is a high school teacher who has two junior-level American history classes. In planning the unit "Immigration to the United States," she established three primary goals. First, she wanted her students to recognize and appreciate that the United States is made up of immigrants from virtually every country of the world who have played a role in the creation of our country and our culture. Second, she wanted her students to recognize, explain, and describe the concept of *cultural diversity* and determine the advantages and challenges that cultural diversity has brought to this country. Finally, she wanted her students to recognize and appreciate both the specific contributions and the specific problems associated with Jews and African Americans in the United States.

During the year, the class discussed immigration several times as it related to various eras of our country's history. For example, students studied Spanish, French, English, German, and Swedish immigration during colonial times, Irish immigration in the 1820s and 1840s, and the forced immigration of blacks into slavery.

To the Reader:

As you read and work through this chapter on the use of literature to improve content learning and develop the reading habit, consider ways in which Linda could incorporate young adult books and other literature sources into her unit in order to meet her goals. Think about how the strategies described and those from your own experience and imagination could be applied to the teaching of a unit on immigration.

————◄○►————

WHAT IS YOUNG ADULT LITERATURE?

According to Donelson and Nilsen (1997), any literature read by young adults is considered young adult literature. Although we know that adolescents read a large variety of texts, a certain type of literature is especially relevant to their interests and needs. For our purposes, young adult literature, adolescent literature, and trade books for young adults all refer to books written or marketed primarily for teens and preteens.

There are several major genres or types of young adult books. Indeed, the world of young adult literature is wonderfully rich, with countless high-quality books of fiction and nonfiction that cover a wide range of topics.

- *Historical fiction:* Historical fiction allows adolescents to appreciate important historical events in human terms through the eyes of adolescents who lived through them (Spencer, 1994). Because these books deal with events of the near and distant past, they often have a timeless quality that permits their use for many years (Elkassabany, Johnson, & Lucas, 2000).

- *Coming-of-age books:* Most young adults enjoy reading books about characters who are grappling with the transition from childhood to adulthood. These books are capable of moving young adults toward maturity (Estes, 1994).

- *Science fiction:* Young adults who are interested in science are often great fans of science fiction (Westcott & Spell, 1999). By the same token, quality science fiction books can play an important role in developing students' interest in science (Hartwell & Cramer, 1994).

- *Fantasy:* It is thought that fantasy may be the most appropriate genre to meet the needs of adolescents who are trying to discover where they fit into the world (Gooderham, 1995). The dominant theme of fantasy books is the quest for good and truth.

- *Mystery and suspense:* This genre has been a timeless favorite among young adults, going back to the Nancy Drew and Hardy Boys books. Today, many excellent tales of mystery and suspense are available to adolescents (Kerby, 1996).

- *Nonfiction:* An important genre of adolescent literature, nonfiction books written for young adults draw them into the reading and learning process the way no textbook ever could (Jones, 2001). Nonfiction books, often referred to as *informational* books, are typically written by authorities who cover topics from dinosaurs to dating using engaging and informative writing styles and writing from the perspectives of young adults. According to some (Sebesta & Donelson, 1994; Sullivan, 2001), nonfiction is the most frequently read literature among adolescents.

In this chapter and in this book we make essentially one broad recommendation: regardless of the genre, use as many types of trade books and alternative text sources as your resources will allow to complement and enrich the teaching and learning of content-area subjects.

GUIDELINES FOR INTEGRATING LITERATURE INTO CONTENT CLASSROOMS

The contributions that young adult literature can make to the teaching of subject matter are limited only by your own sensibilities because the union of trade book and textbook seems to rest on firm theoretical underpinnings (Richgels et al., 1993). Researchers (Alexander, Kulikowich, & Hetton, 1994; McPhail, Pierson, & Freeman, 2000; Dillon, 1989) have shown that attitudinal and motivational factors have a direct influence on students' literacy development and content learning. Pennac (1994) has observed that teenagers will quickly turn off to reading if they find texts difficult or boring. On the other hand, Guthrie and Wigfield (2000), in reviewing research on the influence of affect in the reading process, observed that when students find reading pleasurable and interesting,

Students' motivation to learn will likely increase when they are allowed to read interesting trade books.

their positive attitudes toward reading rapidly become generalized to most other subjects, which leads to a deeper love of reading as a primary source of information and enjoyment. Furthermore, students' reading comprehension has been shown to be greater with high-interest materials because interesting material maintains their attention more effectively and provides motivation (Baker, Afflerbach, & Reinking, 1995; Frager, 1993; McDaniel, Waddill, & Finstad, 2000).

Although literature can be a powerful motivator for reading and writing, combining its use with content-area textbooks is also compelling from a schema-building perspective. In earlier chapters you learned that schema theorists posit that the more developed the knowledge structures readers possess about a particular topic, the greater the likelihood they will be successful in dealing with new information related to that topic. The most important instructional implication of schema theory is that teachers should build bridges between new information to be learned and students' prior knowledge (Hartman, 1995). Stories written in familiar narrative style can provide the background information and call to mind related ideas, building the foundation for easier assimilation of new textual information (McMackin, 1998).

Vye, Rowe, Kinzer, and Risko (1990) point to another major advantage of combining textbooks with trade books. When literacy instruction is kept separate from mathematics, science, and social studies, students believe that math knowledge is relevant only in math class, science knowledge only in science class, and social studies only in social studies class. Labeling this compartmentalized approach to teaching and learning "inert" knowledge, Brandsford and Vye (1989) demonstrated that using literature in social studies helps to circumvent this problem. By integrating literature into the social studies classroom, the teacher in their research project was able to help students use the cross-curricular content to better understand the social studies information and the functionality of their learning.

The union of trade book and textbook can be supported theoretically, as we have shown, and has been widely recommended in the literature for virtually every content area (Austin, 1998; Jacobi-Karna, 1995; Lightsey, 1996; Lombard, 1996; Miller-Hewes, 1994; Pappas & Barry, 2001; Royce & Wiley, 1996).

The duration and scope of any lesson or series of lessons that integrates trade book and textbook will depend on the topic and on your judgments and preferences. Throughout this book we have noted the benefits of planning and teaching in units, whereby students experience a series of lessons often lasting up to several weeks that revolve around a unifying theme with related subtopics. The primary benefit of this approach to both you and your students is time—sufficient time to investigate a topic thoroughly through reading, discussion, writing, and research and, therefore, time to get interested in and excited about learning while producing considered responses. The following guidelines and methods are most applicable to unit-based teaching.

Identify Salient Themes and Concepts

The process of identifying important themes and concepts for a unit of study is essential for integrating appropriate trade literature. Trade books and textbooks should be bridged by overarching themes and concepts related to the most important information and ideas of the unit. The process involves, first, deciding what you want your students to know as a result of the unit and then using this theme as a guide, identifying the related concepts and subtopics.

Textbooks are usually organized by units, which makes them helpful in identifying broad themes for unit plans. As we have recommended before, however, you should develop unit themes that are meaningful to you and your students, regardless of the extent to which the topics are dealt with in the textbook. In this way, you can take advantage of your own and your students' special skills or interests. We have stressed the importance of this step many times throughout this book. It involves deciding what students should take away from their study of the content so that instruction can focus on the ideas and information that are most important to you and your students.

Unfortunately, although textbooks are excellent dispensers of facts, they often lack explicit development of important themes. Therefore, you must infer essential ideas and information from them. Try asking yourself the following questions as you look over a textbook unit:

- What are the driving human forces behind the events?
- What phenomena described in the textbook have affected ordinary people (including me and my students) or may do so in the future?
- What universal patterns of behavior related to this reading should be explained?

Answers to these questions will go a long way toward helping you decide what students should know as a result of the unit and thereby will provide direction for selecting appropriate trade books to tie in with the theme. For example, when Debbie, a seventh-grade social studies teacher, applied these questions to the textbook's unit on Australia, she inferred that *the geography of a place affects the lives of its inhabitants*. This theme seemed particularly apparent in the case of Australia, with its curiously evolved wildlife and bush country lifestyles, so Debbie believed that this would be an advantageous context in which to teach it.

To further illustrate the process of establishing important themes related to textbook topics, consider the following excerpt about the Nazis, the Jews, and the Holocaust taken from an eighth-grade history/social studies book. Indeed, the quoted paragraphs are the extent of text related to the Holocaust in this history book. As you read the excerpt, ask yourself the three questions just posed. Then write down a theme you believe would be important to teach in relation to this content.

As Allied forces were advancing, they found prison camps called *concentration camps* in various parts of Germany. The Nazis had herded millions of people into these camps. The largest group of prisoners was made up of Jews, both from Germany itself and from the conquered countries. Other prisoners included thousands of non-Jews who had opposed the Nazis.

Deciding what's most important to teach will make the selection of appropriate trade books easier.

Many people had died of disease and starvation in the camps. Thousands of others had been put to death, most commonly in gas chambers. This was part of Hitler's plan to kill off all the people he considered "unacceptable." No one was spared—not even the young and the very old. Six million Jews and perhaps as many non-Jews were murdered in what is now known as the Holocaust (that is, the terrible destruction). (Graff, 1980, p. 660)

You probably found that this preceding text is like most textbook prose. It covers the facts but offers few ways of identifying the underlying critical themes and concepts. By asking our three recommended questions, however, we believe you can identify one of the most important themes of this content—*the dangers of prejudice*—only hinted at in the sweeping, factual account of Nazism and the Holocaust.

After establishing a theme for a unit of study, we recommend you explore the content further to identify important concepts and subtopics related to the unit's theme. To accomplish this, we suggest you create a visual display or a web (Pappas, Kiefer, & Levstik, 1999). Beginning with the unit topic or theme written in the center of a large piece of paper, you, with help from your students, generate related subtopics and write them around the main topic. These ideas may come directly from the text or from prior knowledge. Figure 8.1 is an example of a web constructed by Debbie and her seventh-grade social studies class for their unit on the American Civil War.

The connections between subtopics (indicated by the broken lines in Figure 8.1) are indicative of another important benefit of unit teaching: The scope of a unit is broad enough to reveal relationships between different aspects of a topic, thereby helping students knit information together, expand schemata, and improve their overall understanding of the topic. With the completed web, Debbie then decided which subtopics were most relevant to the theme of the unit. Rarely is there time to cover every aspect of a topic generated in the webbing process, and some subtopics must be deemphasized or omitted entirely—even though the information may be covered in the textbook. Finally, under the subtopic headings to be included in the unit, Debbie listed related literature and activities (Figure 8.2). We will talk more about how Debbie organized instruction with multiple trade books later in this chapter.

Drawing out the relationships among unit topics and subtopics can lead to good decisions about what content should be stressed.

Identify Appropriate Literature to Help Teach Concepts

Once an important theme for the unit is established and related subtopics and concepts have been identified, the next step is to find trade books that are thematically and conceptually related.

Becoming more knowledgeable about young adult books is made easier by the many bibliographies, reference guides, lists, and reviews of current young adult literature available to all of us in school and local libraries as well as on the Internet. Librarians can work with you to locate helpful print and electronic sources. In most cases, the literature selections in these guides are based on

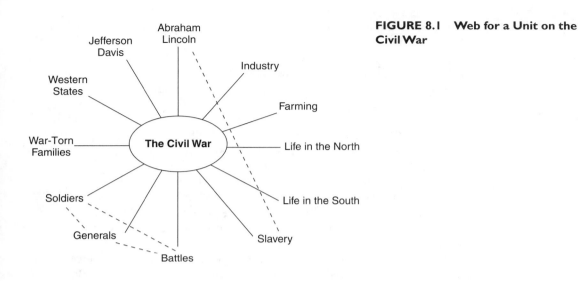

FIGURE 8.1   Web for a Unit on the Civil War

FIGURE 8.2   Web for a Unit on the Civil War, Including Appropriate Young Adult Books

quality, and reading levels are often included. Some of the most helpful references are found in Figure 8.3.

Regarding our topic of Jews in Europe during World War II, we find a wealth of related young adult novels listed in these references, including one of our timeless favorites, *Friedrich* (Richter, 1970), and many other fine selections emerging each year, such as *The Key Is Lost* (Vos, 2000), *Escape to the Forest* (Radin, 2000), *No Pretty Pictures* (Lobel, 1998), *Katrina: A Novel* (Winter, 1999), *Behind the Bedroom Wall* (Williams, 1999), *Jacob's Rescue* (Drucker, 1994), *The Night Crossing* (Ackerman, 1995), and *The Hunted* (Carter, 1994).

Once a book or collection of titles is located, the most enjoyable aspect of this process begins—you get to read the books before using them in class. We have found that as teachers begin a reading program of their own, they rediscover their love of good literature, they develop fresh perspectives on the topic, and their enthusiasm for teaching grows.

Boundless rewards await the history teacher who intends to incorporate trade books, such as those mentioned previously, into a unit on the Holocaust. In *Friedrich* the reader meets a German boy and his Jewish playmate and learns how both are gradually victimized by Nazi propaganda and pogrom during the years 1925 to 1942. In *The Key Is Lost,* 12-year-old Eva Zilverstijn recounts the horrors of survival in Nazi-occupied Holland. This gripping story is made all the more urgent by the use of the present tense. Eva and her sister are separated from their parents and must depend on the kindness and risk-taking of others to survive. *Escape to the Forest* is a highly accessible novel that would be an ideal choice to introduce middle grade students to the realities of the Holocaust. Sarah, a young Jewish girl, and her family are forced into a small ghetto in Poland. Eventually the Germans arrive and order them and their Jewish neighbors onto a train bound for Treblinka. Sarah manages to escape into the forest in search of other families hiding from the Nazis.

No Pretty Pictures is yet another memoir of a young Jewish girl hiding from Nazis and surviving completely dehumanizing conditions. This haunting first-person account will keep adolescent readers riveted from the first to the last page. Katrina, the main character of the book by the same name, becomes like so many Jewish children in eastern Europe during the early 1940s—a wanderer. Separated from family, hiding in farmhouses, and finally sheltered in a Christian orphanage, Katrina tells her story of a life of displacement and constant fear while Slovakia is overrun by Germans and their colluders. In an interesting twist, *Behind the Bedroom Wall* introduces us to Korinna who discovers her German parents are harboring a Jewish family in a secret space in their house. Being a loyal member of the Hitler Youth, Korinna is appalled by this discovery, and the novel's tension centers on whether her beliefs in the Nazi party are strong enough that she would turn in her own parents.

Jacob's Rescue also is set amidst the madness of anti-Semitism in eastern Europe. In this gripping, action-filled tale, the Roslans, a Warsaw couple, do everything imaginable to save and protect Jacob, a Jewish boy, from the ever

Adamson, L. G. (1998). *Notable women in American history: A guide to recommended biographies and autobiographies.* Greenwood Press.

Adamson, L. G. (1998). *American historical fiction: An annotated guide to novels for adults and young adults.* Greenwood Press.

Adamson, L. G. (1998). *World historical fiction: An annotated guide to novels for adults and young adults.* Greenwood Press.

Adamson, L. G. (1999). *Notable women in American history: A guide to recommended biographies and autobiographies.* Greenwood Press.

Adamson, L. G. (2002). *Thematic guide to the American novel. Recreating the past: A guide to American and world historical fiction for children and young adults.* Greenwood Press.

American Library Association. (2000). *Best books for young adults* (2nd ed.). American Library Association.

Beers, K., & Samuels, B. (1998). *Into focus: Understanding and creating middle school readers.* Christopher-Gordon Publishers.

Bogart, G. L., & Carlson, K. R. (2000). *Senior high school library catalog.* H. W. Wilson.

Calvert, S. (1997). *Best books for young adult readers.* Bowker.

Carroll, P. S. (1999). *Using literature to help troubled teenagers cope with societal Issues.* Greenwood Press.

Carter, B. (2000). *Best books for young adults.* American Library Association.

Children's Science Book Review Committee. (1994). *Appraisal: Science books for young people.* National Science Teachers Association.

Donelson, K., & Nilsen, A. P. (1997). *Literature for today's young adults* (5th ed.). Scott, Foresman.

Dresang, E. (1999). *Radical change: Books for youth in a digital age.* H.W. Wilson.

Drew, B. (1997). *The 100 most popular young adult authors: Biographical sketches and bibliographies.* Libraries Unlimited.

Dreyer, S. S. (1993). *The book finder: A guide to children's literature about the needs and problems of youth aged 2–15.* American Guidance Service.

Dwyer, J. (1996). *Earth works: Recommended fiction and nonfiction about nature and the environment for adults and young adults.* Neal-Schuman.

Gillespie, J. T. (1998). *Guides to collection development for children and young adults.* Libraries Unlimited.

Helbig, A., & Perkinis, A. (1997). *Myths and heroes: A cross-cultural guide to literature for children and young adults.* Greenwood Press.

Herald, D. (1997). *Teen genreflecting.* Libraries Unlimited.

Herz, S., & Gallo, D. (1996). *From Hinton to Hamlet: Building bridges between young adult literature and the classics.* Greenwood Press.

FIGURE 8.3   A List of Useful Guides to Young Adult Books

Holsinger, M. P. (1995). *The ways of war: The era of World War II in children's and young adult fiction*. Scarecrow Press.

Howard, E. (1997). *America as story: Historical fiction for secondary schools* (2nd ed.). American Library Association.

International Reading Association. Books for adolescents. *Journal of Adolescent & Adult Literacy*. 800 Barksdale Road, P.O. Box 8139, Newark, DE 19711. Reviews of current young adult literature appear in all nine issues of the volume year.

International Reading Association. Children's choices. *The Reading Teacher*. The list appears in the October issue of each volume year.

Jones, P. (1999). *Connecting young adults and libraries*. Neal-Schuman.

Kan, K. (1998). *Sizzling summer reading programs for young adults*. American Library Association.

Kaplan, J. S. (1999). *Using literature to help troubled teenagers cope with identity issues*. Greenwood Press.

Kaywell, J. (1999). *Using literature to help troubled teenagers cope with family issues*. Greenwood Press.

Mediavilla, C. (1999). *Arthurian fiction: An annotated bibliography*. Scarecrow Press.

New York Times Book Review, 299 W. 43rd St., New York, NY 10036. The weekly edition of book reviews includes reviews of new books for teens and preteens.

Schecter, I. R., & Bogart, G. L. (1995). *Junior high school library catalog*. New York: H. W. Wilson.

Sullivan, E. (1999). *The Holocaust in books for youth*. Scarecrow.

The School Library Journal. P.O. Box 1978, Marion, OH. In the nine issues published annually are reviews of current young adult literature.

VanMeter, V. (1997). *America In historical fiction: A bibliographic guide*. Libraries Unlimited.

Webb, C. A. (1993). *Your reading: A booklist for junior high and middle school students*. National Council of Teachers of English.

Wurth, S. (1992). *Books for you: A booklist for senior high students*. National Council of Teachers of English.

Young Adult Services Division of the American Library Association. *Best books for young adults,* published annually.

Zvirin, S. (1996). *Best years of their lives: A resource guide for teenagers in crisis* (2nd ed.). American Library Association.

FIGURE 8.3   A List of Useful Guides to Young Adult Books—Continued

widening net of Nazi surveillance. An easier read for less able students, *The Night Crossing* follows Clara and her Jewish family on their frightful escape from Nazi-controlled Austria to their eventual freedom in Switzerland. *The Hunted* has a thrilling plot based on the heroism of Italian soldiers in southern France who, after Italy surrendered to the Allies, took extraordinary action to save

Jewish children and carry them to safety across the border into their now liberated home country.

On reading these stories, you will note that they and others like them are, first of all, human. You will understand that the effects of distant, large-scale events such as war will become real to students only when translated into terms of what they mean to characters such as Friedrich, Katrina, and their parents, friends, and neighbors. After hearing her teacher read *Behind the Bedroom Wall*, for example, an eighth-grade student commented, "This book describes the life of these people so well you'd think that Sophie, Rachel, Korinna, and the other people were a part of your own family." Were it not for works of literature like these, most historical events of national and international scope and most notable human achievements and tragedies would remain for many young adults distant or even mythical notions with no emotional connection to their own lives and experiences.

A second notable characteristic of quality young adult literature is that the authors take time to describe the effects of large-scale events on ordinary people. Within the narration of realistic human interaction, concepts can be made understandable and real to young readers. Earlier, we referred to prejudice as an important concept to be explored in the study of Nazism and World War II. Excellent passages exploring the nature of this concept can be found in all of the previously mentioned books. Consider, for example, the following passage from Richter's *Friedrich*. In it, the 13-year-old Jewish boy is trying to retrieve his clothes from a swimming pool attendant in Germany in 1938.

> "Just take a look at this!" the attendant said. "You won't get to see many more of them." Everyone could hear his explanation: "This is one of the Jewish identification cards. The scoundrel lied to me. He claims his name's Friedrich Schneider—it's Friedrich *Israel* Schneider, that's what it is—a Jew that's what he is! A Jew in our swimming pool!" He looked disgusted.
>
> All those still waiting for their clothes stared at Friedrich.
>
> As if he could no longer bear to touch it, the attendant threw Friedrich's identification card and its case across the counter. "Think of it! Jewish things among the clothes of respectable human beings!" he screamed, flinging the coat hanger holding Friedrich's clothes on the ground so they scattered in all directions. (Richter, 1970, pp. 76–77)

When reading passages such as this, students cannot help but be affected by the injustice and humiliation suffered by this character they come to know as decent, likable, and intelligent. Furthermore, the theme of the dangers of prejudice—its meaning, its effect on people, and its often terrible results—is made startlingly clear. After reading *Friedrich*, a seventh-grade student wrote:

> The book made you feel how you would have felt if you were Jewish or German at the time. I learned how brave the Jewish family was in the book.

Trade books bring to life abstract ideas and collections of facts.

I also learned how cruel and unthinking people can be and not caring and thinking that these people are the same as we are—human. Another thing I learned is that war is horrible. I hope, even though I doubt it, that there will be no more wars and discrimination in this world. The book really touched me.

Organize the Content and the Classroom for Literature

Clearly, good literature affects young adults deeply; even so, teachers who have never used trade books often ask us questions such as "How can I find the time to work literature into my daily plans when I barely have enough time to cover the chapters?" or "I have 20 to 25 students per class. How can I manage my classroom if I use literature, the textbook, and other sources?"

Good historical fiction doubles as a motivator and useful resource of accurate information.

The first concern is easy enough to understand when you consider the fragmented, fact-laden curricula within which so many content-area teachers try to operate. Not only is each content area taught as a separate entity, but each subject is broken down into bits of information that students are required to memorize (Bean, 2000; Brown, Collins, & Duguid, 1989; O'Brien, Stewart, & Moje, 1995). Almost invariably, so much time is spent learning the small details that no time is left to experience holistic treatments of the topic and to understand the big picture. As a result, many students rarely enjoy or see the point in studying history or science facts, forget them, and often have to relearn them the next year. In contrast, time spent reading good literature can be both efficient and effective because it gets students interested in learning the content and, when the books are chosen appropriately, can serve as a source for content instruction (Bean, Kile, & Readence, 1996; George & Stix, 2000; Lott & Wasta, 1999). For example, one of the trade books used in Debbie's unit on the Civil War was Hill's (2000) *A Voice from the Border*. From this book, students learned accurate information about one of the most war-torn states of the nation, Missouri. They discovered historically sound facts and information about Unionists and Secessionists battling each other and setting up rival governments in the same state. At the same time Debbie's students benefited from the experience of reading a whole, well-written historical novel with an exciting main character, 15-year-old Reeves, and an important message about slavery and civil strife.

We believe the best way to approach the problem of finding time for trade literature is to choose the most important themes and overarching concepts to be taught and then place instructional emphasis on this information. Naturally, some of the textbook content is not as pertinent to the important themes as other content and, consequently, should be given less attention; deciding on a focus thus frees up time that can be spent on relevant, important information. For example, in his unit on the American Revolution, Frank decided to emphasize three important themes: (1) freedom, both for countries and for people, has a price (the heavy toll of war, even on the victor; the responsibilities that accompany self-government and personal independence); (2) war affects all citizens of a country; and (3) alternatives to war exist. Frank then selected several possible trade books that would help to reinforce these themes, finally deciding to use one primary book, *Johnny Tremain* (Forbes, 1945), and to suggest others for students' independent reading. *Johnny Tremain* is a classic of accurate and compelling historical fiction. By its copyright, this may seem to be a dated work for today's adolescents, but because its subject matter centers on events in our nation's past more than 200 years ago, it has a timeless quality that makes it as relevant now as ever. Next, Frank went through the 12 chapters in the text unit and, keeping his salient themes in mind, made decisions about how to teach each chapter (Figure 8.4) and listed potential writing activities for many of the chapters (Figure 8.5).

We can address the second concern—how to manage the content classroom with literature—by describing the experiences of three different teachers whose approaches represent three management systems.

Chapter	Suggested Activity
1	Life in New England—Students read; compare with trade book; write (see writing suggestions).
2	Work, Church, & School same as Chapter 1.
3	Life in Southern Colonies Teacher lecture—brief.
4	Life in Middle Colonies Teacher lecture—brief.
5	Life in the Wilderness Teacher lecture; book talk: *Distant Thunder* (Moore).
6	Government in the English Colonies Teacher lecture; debates (see writing suggestions).
7	Furs and Farming in New France Teacher lecture—brief.
8	French & English Fight Students read; map study; develop time line, write (see suggestions); book talk and sharing: *The Matchlock Gun* (Edmonds).
9	England Tightens Its Grip Students read.
10	Colonists Become Angry Students read; prioritize value of ways to cause change; compare text & trade book; write (see suggestions); book talk and sharing: *My Brother Sam Is Dead* (Collier & Collier).
11	Liberty or Death Students read; list causes of war, rank order, & defend rankings.
12	New Nation Is Born Students read; discuss Johnny Tremain's change of mind.

FIGURE 8.4   American Revolution: Teaching Ideas

Chapters 1 & 2

Let Johnny Tremain have a dialog with a person of today about the living conditions in the 1700s. Make comparisons.

Write a position paper for living in the 18th century or today.

Compare & contrast women's roles in the 18th century and today, based on reading in *Johnny Tremain*.

Chapter 6

Debate: Develop arguments explaining the points of view of British and colonists. Placards and posters can support either side.

Chapter 8

Thumbnail sketches of important Revolutionary War personalities.

Newspaper articles for *Colonial Times*.

Editorial about British taxation.

Dialog between a colonist and King George III.

List personal freedoms you have and value today. Which of these can be traced to the events of the 1770s? Which were actually fought for in the Revolutionary War?

Chapter 10

Prioritize relative value of various means of gaining one's ends and producing change.

1. Voting
2. Physical force
3. Vigilante (scare) tactics
4. Terrorism
5. Diplomacy

Chapter 12

You have just read *Johnny Tremain*. What part of this story did you react to most strongly? Do you see any connection between this part of the story and your own life?

FIGURE 8.5   American Revolution: Suggested Composition Assignments

Don uses the simplest of systems. He reads to his ninth graders literature that is thematically linked to the science topics under consideration. When studying the topic of genetics and genetic engineering, for instance, Don read Kress's (1996) *Beggar's Ride*. Two hundred years in the future, regular human beings hate and fear the Sleepless and the SuperSleepless, genetically modified humans who are immune to disease and hunger and need no sleep. Don made other books available to students that were related to the topic of genetic alteration, including *Dead Water Zone* (Oppel, 1993), about a teenager trying to find his genetically stunted younger brother in the polluted ruins of an American city; *Virus Clans* (Kanaly, 1998), about viruses that evolved billions of years ago on a distant planet and then spread to Earth where they have been directing evolution; and *The Hot Zone* (Preston, 1995) that tells the dramatic and chilling story of an ebola virus outbreak in a suburban Washington, DC lab.

Combining classic novels with current information books, Don has been able to include young adult literature in nearly all of his units. For example, Farley Mowat's *Never Cry Wolf* (1979), about a scientist's struggle to survive and study wolves in the Arctic Circle, was read during the study of scientific explorations of the Arctic. Along with Mowat's narrative, Don used *Buried in Ice: The Mystery of a Lost Arctic Expedition* (Beattie & Geiger, 1992), with its vivid, gripping photographs of mummified explorers found in the Arctic permafrost, to grab his students' interest in the topic. Isaac Asimov's (1966) *Fantastic Voyage* was used in conjunction with a unit on the systems of the body. His students also used Schultz's (1992) light and informative *Looking Inside the Brain* during this unit.

As Don reads, he asks his students to be active listeners, paying attention not only to plot developments but also to how the ideas in the story relate to those in the text. With this approach, only a single trade book is needed. Don reads 15 to 20 minutes daily and is able to complete a book of average length in 2 ½ weeks. Over 9 months, he often reads as many as 15 books to his classes. Over the same period, he exposes his students to countless other novels, picture books, and informational books.

As an alternative to the teacher's reading aloud, the whole class can read a single book. Patty's eighth-grade social studies classes read Margaret Peterson Haddix's (1998) *Among the Hidden* during a unit on political systems. This trade book dovetailed nicely with her textbook instruction, which focused on the theme of ways in which governments can control citizens. Haddix's novel follows the life of Luke, a 12-year-old boy living in a future where the Population Police enforce the law limiting a family to only two children. As a third child, Luke has spent his entire life in fear and isolation on his family's farm, until he meets another "third." Students read the trade book and the textbook as homework and then engaged in classroom activities designed to help tie the two texts together. For example, they developed a chart that depicted the similarities and differences between Luke's society and that of present-day communist China.

A more complex but exciting and powerful management system involves student-directed, cooperative learning groups for reading and sharing multiple novels (Burns, 1998). Earlier, we described how Debbie, a seventh-grade social studies teacher, builds webs for her units to identify salient concepts and subtopics and appropriate literature. For her Civil War unit she decided to focus on the subtopics of slavery, the major battles, and war-torn families. She secured sets of four of the following trade books: *A Voice from the Border* (Hill, 2000), *Soldier's Heart* (Paulsen, 1998), *The Unwritten Chronicles of Robert E. Lee* (Herrin, 1989), and *Stealing Freedom* (Carbone, 2001).

Debbie then introduced the books through book talks and allowed students to form their own cooperative groups based on self-selection of these four books. Independent reading schedules were set for each book, and each group member was given a daily assignment that related to the reading.

Figures 8.6 to 8.9 provide a more detailed description of cooperative literature group members' assignments. The student assigned to be the "literary

---

Reading Assignment _____ Date _____ Name _____

LITERARY LUMINARY—guides oral reading for a purpose

Page	Reason (1–5)	Plan for Sharing Reading

Choices Could Include

1. Good dialog between characters

2. Vivid description

3. Setting a mood

4. Examples of:
   a. Simile/metaphor
   b. Flashback or foreshadowing
   c. Other literary device

5. Other instance of the author's craft

Source: From *Using Novels in the Classroom: A Management System*, by B. Abraham. Unpublished manuscript.

FIGURE 8.6   Literary Luminary for a Cooperative Learning Assignment

Good literature can be incorporated into the content classroom in several ways, depending on your resources and willingness to experiment.

luminary" identified three to five passages in that day's assignment for discussion or oral reading (Figure 8.6). The "vocabulary enricher" prepared a list of four to six unfamiliar words or word usages for discussion (Figure 8.7). The "discussion director" prepared five to eight questions about the assignment (Figure 8.8). The "checker" questioned each group member about completion of the assignment, evaluated participation, and urged everyone to enter into the discussion (Figure 8.9). Discussions focused on daily independent reading assignments that were usually completed the day before at home.

In the beginning, Debbie carefully modeled each cooperative group assignment and helped students tie together trade and text learning through questions and discussions. Debbie devised these cooperative learning group roles because they contribute to students' learning in the manner she desires. It is important to note that you can create your own cooperative learning group roles, depending on what kinds of learning you want to take place within the groups.

Such a system is admirably suited to teaching units because a variety of trade books, each emphasizing a different aspect of the unit theme, will contribute

Reading Assignment _____ Date _____ Name _____

VOCABULARY ENRICHER—clarifies word meanings and pronunciations

Page	Word	Definition	Plan

Presentation Plan Possibilities

1. Have the group find the word and figure out the meaning from context clues.
2. Use the dictionary. Choose the correct definition.
3. Use a thesaurus. Find a synonym to substitute in the sentence.

_____

Source: From *Using Novels in the Classroom: A Management System*, by B. Abraham. Unpublished manuscript.

FIGURE 8.7   Vocabulary Enricher for a Cooperative Learning Assignment

much to the scope and depth of students' understanding (Elbaum, Schumm, & Vaughn, 1997). In Debbie's unit on the Civil War, one group of students reading *The Unwritten Chronicles of Robert E. Lee* learned of the great deeds and masterful battle strategies of Lee, Stonewall Jackson, and other prominent Confederate generals. Another group looked at the life in the state of Missouri during the war, where families and friends were torn apart by their strong feelings over slavery and secession in *A Voice from the Border*. Another group of students read a compelling narrative of the horrors of combat from the perspective of a 15-year-old Union recruit in *Soldier's Heart*, while in *Stealing Freedom*, students learned of the brutality and hardship of slavery from the story of 12-year-old Anna Weems who, separated from her family, makes a dramatic escape on the Underground Railroad.

Reading Assignment _____ Date _____ Name _____

DISCUSSION DIRECTOR—asks questions to increase comprehension

Why do you think the author put _____ in this place in the story?

How is _____ like/different from _____ ?

If you had been _____ how would you have _____ ?

How did you feel about _____ ?

What happened after _____ ?

What do you think caused _____ ?

Compare _____ .

If the author had left out _____ how would the story have been changed?

Summarize _____ .

Predict _____ .

What happened that you think will be important later on?

Who? Where? When? _____

_____

Source: From *Using Novels in the Classroom: A Management System,* by B. Abraham. Unpublished manuscript.

FIGURE 8.8   Discussion Director for a Cooperative Learning Assignment

Reading Assignment _____ Day # _____ Name _____

CHECKER—checks for completion of assignments, evaluates participation, helps monitor discussion for equal participation

Names	Job	Done?	Participation or Cooperation	Read Assignment

Participation Key:

✔ for each answer

+ for other contributions and cooperative behaviors

− for interrupting, distracting, "goofing-off" incidents

Reading Key:

+ appears to have read

− little, if any, proof

Process Evaluation:

Our group _____

_____

_____

Source: From *Using Novels in the Classroom: A Management System,* by B. Abraham. Unpublished manuscript.

FIGURE 8.9   Checker for a Cooperative Learning Assignment

TEACHING WITH TRADE BOOKS AND TEXTBOOKS: A SYMBIOSIS

Precisely how you develop plans for relating literature to themes and concepts in the text will depend on your individual style. Generally, you should be prepared to use texts and trade books interchangeably throughout any teaching sequence. Toward that end, we recommend the following instructional combinations that are likely to deepen students' understanding of content material.

Use the Trade Book as a Schema and Interest Builder

Science

A sixth-grade science teacher had her students read Robert Lipsyte's *The Chemo Kid* (1993) as a prelude to a unit on ecology. The story is about two boys who try to stop the pollution of their town's reservoir. The adventures the boys have and the lessons they learn set the stage for the theme of the ecology unit and class discussion by establishing an overall picture of how a human can live and thrive in harmony with nature. In addition, the story gave students a store of unusual, dramatic examples of the interdependence of species, food chains, and habitats, which they then read about in expository form in their science textbooks. Other excellent selections for this topic include Monica Hughes's (1993) *Invitation to the Game*, Mack McDevitt's (1995) *Engines of God*, and Karen Hesse's (1995) *Phoenix Rising*.

Mathematics

Tenth-grade students were introduced to the study of geometry by reading and exploring Doris Schattschneider's (1990) *Visions of Symmetry: Notebooks, Periodic Drawings, and Related Works of M. C. Escher*. The repetitive patterns in Escher's drawings provided students with excellent models for creating their own repetitive designs. Students read about Escher's descriptions of his drawings—"regular division of the plane." Then they were given the opportunity to find examples of a variety of regular geometric shapes in Escher's works. Students enjoyed finding parallelograms, rhombi, hexagons, rectangles, triangles, and squares in the artist's other-worldly illustrations. These patterns were found on floors, walls, pillars, and even some of Escher's creatures, which seem to grow out of geometric patterns. With these experiences, the 10th graders were much more enthusiastic about continuing their study of geometry.

Students in a senior math class were introduced to probabilities and inferential statistics with the book *Death Qualified: A Mystery of Chaos* (Wilhelm, 1991). Barbara Holloway quits her own law practice to help her father in a murder case. In so doing, she enters a new world of fractuals, chaos theory, and computers—necessary for developing the case for the modern attorney.

Other good books to use with middle and upper grade students in conjunction with math content include Joan Bauer's (1997) *Sticks* and Alan Ritchie's (1991) *Erin McEwan, Your Days Are Numbered*.

Physical Education

Before starting the softball season, a physical education teacher read aloud to his students the interesting sports novel *Striking Out* (Weaver, 1993). Billy Baggs, the central character in the story, possesses almost unbelievable pitching and hitting ability, yet his struggle to find himself and realize his potential while dealing with the hardships of family and farm life nearly cause him to lose everything. The teacher used this particular book because he wanted his students to develop realistic expectations for themselves as ball players and as teenagers. The novel allowed students to become aware of their own strengths inside and outside of sports.

Over the past decade or so, numerous quality fiction and nonfiction trade books for young adults with sports themes and sports characters have become available. For the middle grades and less able high school reader there is *At the Plate with Mark McGwire* (Christopher, 1999), *Brett Favre* (Dougherty, 1999), *Kobe Bryant: Basketball Big Shot* (Savage, 2000), and *Muhammad Ali: Athlete, Activist, Ambassador* (Duplacey, 1999). Sports books with female protagonists and about women athletes are on the increase as well. Some of the best fictional narratives are *Goalie* (Shreve, 1999) and *Forward Pass* (Dygard, 1999). Information picture books in this same genre include *In These Girls, Hope Is a Muscle* (Blais, 1996), *Winning Ways: A Photohistory of American Women in Sports* (Macy, 1996), and *Venus to the Hoop* (Corbett, 1998).

A group of senior high students who had volunteered to be counselors for summer camp were asked to read *Downriver* (Hobbs, 1991) in their training class. In the book, four 15-year-old Outward Bound trainees, better known among themselves as "hoods in the woods," steal their guide's equipment and raft and attempt to take on the mighty Colorado River on their own. They learn about responsibility the hard way, with disastrous consequences. The seniors read and discussed the book each evening. Although they enjoyed the gripping adventure and the adolescent mischief, the book forced them to look seriously at their role as counselors and served as a focal point for discussions about behavioral problems and health emergencies.

English

Trade books can serve as excellent sources for preparing students to learn almost any topic.

In preparation for reading, studying, and doing dramatic interpretations of William Shakespeare's *Hamlet*, an English teacher had her 12th-grade students read Grant and Mandrake's (1990) picture book version of the play. Lavishly illustrated, this work remains faithful to the story and retains much of the original dialog and narration. Although the teacher knew there is no substitute for the actual work, she nonetheless recognized the value of this illustrated book for introducing her students to the exciting world and remarkable ideas of *Hamlet*. In this way the book served as a bridge to the original, offering students a story with rich artwork and skillful expressions of Hamlet's anguish and torment.

Because you know which concepts and information will be encountered later in the textbook, when choosing to read literature orally, you can easily highlight key passages by reading them with particular emphasis or by reading them again after cueing the students. When trade books are read independently or in small groups, you can alert students to these passages before reading. You can also use discussion and demonstrate context strategies for learning terminology that appears in the trade book and later in the textbook.

One benefit of using good literature in content classes is that the interest factor is built in. Good narrative, by its very nature, drives readers and listeners on to discover what happens next. But you should not depend on reading alone to build schemata. Because students learn best through active participation, you should encourage discussion and written responses after daily reading sessions. Worthwhile topics could include favorite passages, alternative courses of action for characters, characters' personalities, and possible future developments in the story.

Use the Trade Book to Extend Textbook Ideas

During reading, students can work in small groups to discuss particular issues focused on in the text and elaborated on in related trade books. Students can share what they have found to be particularly informative sections of the trade book or passages that support and extend the text. For instance, the teacher and class could read a section of text and then search trade books for additional and supporting information, as occurred in the following classroom examples.

Social Studies

Eighth-grade students studying the Age of Exploration in the New World in their social studies texts also read in small groups Scott O'Dell's timeless trilogy *The Captive* (1979), *The Feathered Serpent* (1981), and *The Amethyst Ring* (1983), which chronicle the 16th-century world of the Maya, Aztec, and Inca empires, respectively. Students were asked to find passages in the trade books describing events from the indigenous people's point of view, a perspective often omitted in textbook treatments. Likewise, students found passages that helped to explain how and why a mere handful of Spaniards were able to overtake three enormous empires. As we have noted before, too often the driving human forces behind important historical events are not made clear in textbook accounts. In O'Dell's trilogy, however, the reader is brought face-to-face with the greed and religious zeal that drove many explorers and their followers to fanatical behavior.

MEETING THE NEEDS OF DIVERSE LEARNERS IN THE CONTENT-AREA CLASSROOM

Gary, an experienced teacher of 14 years, teaches general biology in a high school set in an economically depressed area of an inner city. African Americans and Latinos/Latinas comprise nearly 90% of the student body. Because of the special concerns his students bring to his classroom, Gary has become a resourceful teacher who is constantly searching for new ways to make his instruction more responsive to the needs of his students.

His classroom is an inviting setting for a young researcher and scientist. Next to his door in the hall is a large glassed-in display case that he and his students redo with each new six-week grading period. During a unit on "food chains," for example, the display included the book *Never Cry Wolf* by Farley Mowat (1979), a collage in the shape of a wolf's head composed of pictures of animals that wolves prey upon, a pair of binoculars, and a field book with pencil. The walls of his room are laden with posters, charts, student work, and photographs of field trips Gary and his students have taken over the past few years to such interesting places as the Elk Repopulation Center in Great Smoky Mountains National Park, the Florida Everglades, and the North Carolina Outer Banks. Three large lab tables hold animal specimens in jars, petry dishes, various artifacts from the natural world (e.g., rocks, grasses, mosses, snake skins, owl pellets, etc.), a large aquarium, and microscopes. Against one wall is a row of eight computers; against another are two large bookshelves—one filled with science-related paperbacks and magazines, the other holds reference and informational books.

Gary's C-Block class had 24 students. The topic for the day's lesson was "Population Crashes," which Gary had projected on a large screen in the front of the room from his computer. After employing a 10-minute PowerPoint presentation that defined and characterized causes and effects of population crashes in the natural world, Gary asked students to work in pairs to seek out as much evidence and as many examples as they could find of such population crashes using the print and nonprint resources available to them. Students were given a recording sheet to document their research. Tremayne and Elton used a total of four different information sources. They began by thumbing back through the novel *Never Cry Wolf* which the class had been reading, and wrote down information related to Mowat's description of what happens to the vole population when too many wolves are killed or relocated. They moved from the novel to Internet and found a site devoted to problems related to overpopulation of humans. Elton remembered something he had seen in a magazine related to human overpopulation and went to the bookshelf returning with a copy of Smithsonian. He and Tremayne looked through the article together and took notes. Finally, the two boys used one of the scientific reference books to look up information on Thomas Malthus—a person Gary mentioned in his presentation—for more leads about population crashes. There was a general biology textbook, but only a couple of students were consulting it for information.

Gary then passed out copies of *Never Cry Wolf* and organized a review of the last chapter read. The review was in a "popcorn" format whereby Gary gave the class the first critical event of the chapter, then waited for other students to stand up and supply a statement about what happened next. Using this approach, the class was able to cover most of the chapter plot within 5 minutes.

Gary then invited volunteers to come to the front of the class and take parts reading the next chapter aloud. In this chapter, a bush pilot and a party of hunters make camp near to where Farley is conducting his research of the wolf pack. He and the hunters have a threatening encounter. Gary took the role of narrator while the others read parts for Farley and members of the hunting party. Students seemed eager to participate and after a couple of pages a new set of students came to the front of the class to continue the read aloud. Gary was patient with all students and waited until one asked for help with a word before he or a classmate provided it.

At several points in the action, Gary invited class members who were not reading aloud to ask questions of the students who were. This seemed to keep everyone focused on the plot. Student questions were mostly verbatim level. Gary welcomed all of them, however, while modeling higher level thinking questions.

Gary has a strong desire to help his students develop independent learning skills, so he always includes opportunities for them to explore topics on their own. Gary allows his students to use other resources than the textbook, because as he says, "That's what researchers do." When information is needed in his classroom, students are used to going to whatever sources are available. Gary knows the textbook is written at a level that's too difficult for many of his students, so he doesn't rely on it. By allowing his class to read about class topics from sources that may be easier for them, they tend to stay on task.

Gary uses novels because he wants his students to be interested in science. He recognizes that if the only way they received science is through a textbook, they would never want to explore science further or become scientists themselves. He is also sensitive to the fact that his kids are generally poor readers and the only way they'll get any better is if they get time to read in school. In addition to Farley Mowat's book, Gary has his class read *The Boys from Brazil* (Levin, 1977) when teaching about genetics and *The Chemo Kid* (Lipsyte, 1992) when covering a unit on toxic chemicals in the environment.

Music

A 12th-grade music teacher asked her orchestral class to read *Lohengrin* as they prepared for a performance of the overtures that accompany Wagner's enchanting opera. Much more than a libretto, *Lohengrin,* written by the composer, resembles a novella. Because of its length, the story of Lohengrin is well developed and character descriptions are rich. These features make the book ideally suited to instruction in musical interpretation. As the young musicians read the book, they also worked on the music. Cooperative groups were formed on the basis of orchestral sections (strings, woodwinds, percussion instruments, etc.). During each class session, groups were responsible for reflecting on the story, discussing plot and character, and then, based on story interpretations, presenting possible musical interpretations. After whole-class discussions and teacher input, the student musicians attempted to operationalize their interpretations in rehearsals.

Terrence used reading and writing in his music composition class. Every week his inner-city students gathered newspapers and used the headlines for inspiration in their composing. In another example, his class read a book about musical instrument makers of medieval times. The book was filled with illustrations of instruments, some rather exotic, that have long since vanished. The author explained how some contemporary craftspersons were attempting to recreate these extinct instruments. This book inspired the class to create their own instruments. Using junk from garages, closets, attics, and alleys piled in the classroom, students fashioned horns, drums, and stringed instruments. With this motley assemblage, they wrote and performed an original composition. The female students were complaining that they were reading about and hearing compositions only by male composers. Terrence acquired information on and addresses of several contemporary female classical music composers, and his students wrote letters to them. A couple of them wrote back, sending samples of their work on tape and CDs, along with sample scores. The class performed a composition given them by one of the women and allowed her to listen and watch via a telecommunications hookup.

There are several excellent books for adolescents with opera and oratorio themes. Among them are such picture books as *Aida* (Price, 1990), *Turandot* (Mayer, 1995), and *Messiah: The Wordbook for the Oratorio* (Handel, Illus. Moser, 1992). Other picture books with classical music themes include *Mozart Tonight* (Downing, 1991), *Wolfer: The First Six Years In the Life of Wolfgang Amadeus Mozart* (Weil, 1991), *Ludwig van Beethoven* (Thompson, 1990), *Sleeping Beauty: The Story of the Ballet* (Horosko, 1994), and *Tchaikovsky Discovers America* (Kalman, 1995).

To bring middle and high school students to a better appreciation of jazz music, teachers can read and make available *Hip Cat* (London, 1996), *Jazz: My Music, My People* (Monceaux, 1994), and *Satchmo's Blues* (Schroeder, 1996).

Teachers searching for contemporary books with music themes will find a nice variety. Among the best novels written for today's music-loving youth are *Tribute to Another Dead Rock Star* (Powell, 1999), *Drive* (Wieler, 2001), *Do Angels Sing the Blues?* (LeMieux, 1999), *The Maestro* (Wynne-Jones, 1996), and *The Rose That Grew from Concrete* (Shakur, 1999).

History

For the study of the American Revolution, a 10th-grade history teacher selected the following themes: Broaden the students' awareness of all the colonists' attitudes toward the war, and sensitize them to the tragic consequences war brings its participants. She selected the trade book *My Brother Sam Is Dead* (Collier & Collier, 1974) to use in conjunction with text study. In this story, students learned about the hardships and realities of the war as told by Tim Meeker, a young boy who watches his loyalist father be killed by bandits and his brother Sam, unjustly accused of stealing by his comrades in the colonial army, hanged.

Directions: Listed across the page are 9 events or statements from *My Brother Sam Is Dead*. Listed down the left side are the names of characters involved in the story plot. In each box indicate whether that character would agree or disagree with the words stated above. Use the symbols in the key below. You must make some inferences to answer the questions. Be prepared to support your answers with examples from the book.

Key: **A** = Agree **D** = Disagree **X** = Doesn't apply **?** = Not enough info	Children should respect and obey their parents.	Battles of Lexington and Concord.	Men should be free to govern themselves.	Render unto Caesar the things that are Caesar's.	I'm an Englishman but have more say in government as a colonist.	The end justifies the means.	I'm interested in making a living but not in fighting a war.	I'm just against wars.	Declaration of Independence.
Sam Meeker, rebel soldier									
Mr. Meeker, Sam's father									
Mrs. Meeker, Sam's mother									
Tim Meeker, Sam's brother									
Mr. Beacher, minister									
Betsy Read, Sam's girlfriend									
Col. Read, Betsy's father									
Mr. Heron, Meekers' neighbor									
General Putnam									
Captain Betts									

FIGURE 8.10   Study Guide for *My Brother Sam Is Dead*

As students read chapters in their textbook and trade book, they responded to study guides (discussed in Chapter 3) that were designed to help students see connections between material in both sources, apply their new learning beyond the parameters of the unit, and involve them in dynamic class discussions. In the first guide (Figure 8.10), students were asked to make inferences about the attitudes of story characters. In this way, students were helped to understand the various points of view on the war. With another study guide (Figure 8.11), students were asked to consider the human elements of war—so poignantly brought out in the trade book—by reminding them that the problems and

"Principle, Sam? You may know principle, Sam, but I know war. Have you ever seen a dear friend lying in the grass with the top of his skull off and his brains sliding out like wet oats? Have you ever looked into the eyes of a man with his throat cut and the blood pouring out between his fingers, knowing that there was nothing you could do, in five minutes he would be dead, yet still trying to beg for grace and not being able because his windpipe was cut in two? Have you ever heard a man shriek when he felt a bayonet go through the middle of his back? I have, Sam, I have. I was at Louisbourg the year before you were born. Oh, it was a great victory. They celebrated it with bonfires all over the colonies. And I carried my best friend's body back to his mother—sewed up in a sack."

Both men had their own principles. Think about what your principles might be about war and the exercise of our freedoms. Immense human sacrifice was made by both sides during the American Revolution. Thomas Paine, a patriot, wrote, "The cause of America is in a great measure the cause of all mankind." What do you think he means by this? Was there another way besides war to achieve the same end? "Could the United States have made its way without all that agony and killing?" ask James and Christopher Collier.

Part I. Pretend you are a United States senator. Indicate whether you would vote yes or no on the suggested imaginary bills on the floor of the United States Senate. Give your reason.

U.S. Senate bill, proposed   *Reason*

_____   The U.S. government should lift the oil
embargo on Iraq.

_____   The U.S. government should cut spending on
nuclear arms.

_____   The U.S. government should create a fund to
give aid to other countries' rebels or patriots.

Write a bill of your own to be voted on.

FIGURE 8.11   Study Guide for *My Brother Sam Is Dead*

---

conflicts the revolutionists faced are still real today where other wars are being waged.

In a study of immigrants to the United States in the early 20th century, Tom read aloud to his juniors from the award-winning book *Letters from Rifka* (Hesse, 1992). Rifka and her Jewish family flee Russia in 1919 to avoid Russian soldiers and a pogrom. Her dream of finding a new, safe world is finally realized when the family arrives in America. Rifka records her journey in her treasured volume of Pushkin poetry, bringing the reader intimately close to her ordeal: humiliating examinations by doctors and soldiers; deadly typhus; separation from family, friends, and homeland; deadly ocean storms; detainment on Ellis Island; and the loss of her beautiful golden hair.

In nearly every case, students prefer reading stories about content-area topics rather than textbook treatments.

While studying the details and facts of immigration in their textbooks, students in Tom's class were discovering the human drama of immigration through the words in Rifka's diary. Tom had his students trace Rifka's journey on a map of Europe and the United States. Students compared immigration procedures on Ellis Island, as discussed in the textbook, with Rifka's experiences. He also had them adopt the persona of an immigrant and create a record of that person's experiences in the form of a diary or personal travelogue modeled after Rifka's. Students were given regular opportunities to read entries from their diaries to the class.

Mathematics

Lori had been struggling to help her geometry students expand their perceptions of geometry and to look for real-life parallels to geometric terms, postulates, and theorems. Her efforts accomplished little until she boldly decided to have her class read and discuss novels. She began her search for appropriate literature with some incredulity, but with the help of a local reference librarian she soon discovered several books that appeared ideally suited to teaching geometry, including Abbot's (1927) *Flatland*, Hinton's (1907) *An Episode in Flatland*, and Dewdney's (1984) *The Planiverse*. She finally chose *Flatland,* a 19th-century British novel of science fiction, as an important tool in trying to humanize students' understanding of geometry.

In *Flatland,* all of the characters are two-dimensional geometric figures that represent different social classes. The first part is essentially a social satire. In the second part, the main character travels to other dimensions to describe the relative merits of different points of view. *Flatland* can be read for its straight geometric descriptions as well as for its social commentary and satire.

Lori found that *Flatland* could be incorporated into her geometry course without ignoring any of the basic material. She tied the book to a unit in the textbook dealing with geometric models of the universe. Class discussion centered on the basic plot: its purpose and social context; details of Flatland, other lands, and their inhabitants; and the symbolism. In small groups, students were asked to brainstorm solutions to problems in Flatland (not explained by the author) such as rain and snow patterns, locomotion, food, and writing. Then the whole class compared their solutions. As a writing activity, students were asked to select a known person and tell which Flatland class (geometric figure) he or she would be in and why.

Lori's geometry unit was very well received. Many students asked that more novels be used in the class. Lori found her efforts worthwhile because she was able to get to know her students better, how they thought and felt, as a result of the many opportunities to interact during the unit. She also accomplished her goal of humanizing the learning of geometry.

In Latife's physics class, she read aloud during the first grading period *The Uncertainty Principle* (Sommers, 1990). The central character in the story, Kathy, quits the cheerleading squad and takes physics instead. To the dismay of all the boys in class, she excels. For the first time in her life she feels a genuine challenge and begins to dream and plan for a future as a physicist. There are obstacles, of course, among them Kathy's father, who can't accept the idea of sending his daughter to Cal Tech. Latife used this book as a prod, especially for the girls in class, to keep up the work and effort and to accept problems in physics as challenges to be met and overcome.

French

To help a group of first-year students develop an appreciation for the similarities and differences in French and American cultures, Faith had her students read *Mystery of the Metro* (Howard, 1987). In this story, a 16-year-old American girl finds herself alone in France and is forced to deal with all of the challenges of getting by in a foreign country. The story also has a tinge of mystery that makes it even more engaging. As students read the book, Faith had them compare the French styles of eating, transportation, and other customs with the American way of life. Students were also required to research a particular aspect of French culture that presented the main character in the book with problems and report back to the class.

Current Events

Glen's senior class was focusing on the former system of apartheid in South Africa. Resources for the unit included government and United Nations reports, essays by Nelson Mandela, music lyrics by black South African folk songwriters, and three young adult books. One was the beautifully photographed *Mandela: An Illustrated Autobiography* (Mandela, 1996) accompanied by a text that contains an extraordinary amount of detail about his personal life and the history and politics of anti-apartheid. The others were two masterful novels written by Norman Silver. *No Tigers in Africa* (Silver, 1990) tells the story of Selwyn Lewis and his white racist upbringing in Cape Town, South Africa. When his family moves to England, however, Selwyn's new experiences force him to confront his racism and look within himself to find moral solutions to prejudice. In *An Eye for Color* (Silver, 1991), Basil Kushenovitz narrates interconnecting stories about growing up white and Jewish in Cape Town. About his ambivalent position in a racist culture, Basil says that like a lizard, "My one eye sees one thing, and my other eye sees something quite different." Basil must try to reconcile his split vision—between his comforts and others' deprivation, between what is expected of a white man and what he himself is willing to become. Glen's goal in having his students read both of Silver's honest and painful novels was to rivet them to the compelling human stories of apartheid, making it possible for them to understand that racist systems leave victims on both sides of the color/culture fence.

Science

Gordy found the ideal novel to use in conjunction with his 10th-grade general biology students' study of molecular processes of life. *The Children Star* (Slonozewski, 1999) features mind-bending genetic engineering of circular and tire-shaped creatures that have evolved triple DNA and exotic amino acids. The sinister side to the plot is that these bizarre life forms plan to overrun a race of humans. Gordy read the novel aloud to his class and exploited it both for its interesting and scientifically sound information about genetics and for its more challenging theme of the dangers of uncontrolled and unregulated manipulation of the genetic code. His students were required to keep a notebook of information gleaned from the novel that related to the biology textbook's treatment of the same topic. Gordy also had his class confront ethical issues of genetic engineering through debates and role-plays.

An eighth-grade teacher captured her students' attention and enthusiasm for learning by using the illustrated informational book *Looking Inside Sports Aerodynamics* (Schultz, 1992). Filled with young teens' favorite sports figures, from Michael Jordan in basketball to Monica Seles in tennis, this colorful, enjoyable book deals with unseen forces that affect objects in motion. By combining sports and science, the teacher found that students learned the facts of aerodynamics and understood the principles more thoroughly than when the textbook was the sole resource.

In another classroom, Gail taught a unit on the consequences of science and technology through the use of science fiction. Her goal was to promote problem-solving skills and help students clarify values regarding scientific technology. Knowing that science fiction can motivate students to take a greater interest in science (Schmidt, 1996), Gail used *Star Trek: The Next Generation* (Bornholt, 1989) to instigate discussion on controversial issues associated with cloning. In the story, members of the *Enterprise* spaceship, while on a planet populated by original clone settlers, are asked to allow their own tissues to be used to spawn a new generation of clones to replace a line that is malfunctioning. The crew members refuse, but find that their tissues have been stolen while they were rendered unconscious. They return to the planet and destroy their clone look-alikes. The colony claimed that without the new clones they would die out in a few generations.

Given these story events, Gail posed the following question to her students and asked them to take a stand on a values continuum: Did the *Enterprise* crew members have the right to destroy the clones?

Pro-choice	Right-to-life
Do not provide tissue for cloning	Provide tissue for cloning

First, students were asked to write their positions on their own. Then they went to the board and plotted their positions on the values continuum by writing their names along it. This was followed by small-group interaction to crystallize their positions and respond to those of others. The activity concluded with class discussion. Gail has found science fiction to be a rich resource for teaching science because it motivates students to become more active learners and thinkers.

Art

Many students who are not blessed with artist's hands can learn something of how the artist sees the world through related trade books (Hurst, 1995; Stover, 1988; Tallman, 1990; Whitin, 1996). Cal, a high school art teacher, began to recognize the connection between good books and art appreciation after reading sleuth books by Gash and Malcolm relating to crimes in the art world. This led him to investigate books for adolescents that would help students who struggle with drawing and painting assignments gain some insights into the way artists see the world and approach compositions. In his search he found several good books and began using them in his art classes. Among students' favorites are *The Broken Bridge* (Pullman, 1992), *Unfinished Portrait of Jessica* (Peck, 1991), and *Shizuko's Daughter* (Mori, 1993) where young people learn about art while grappling with typical adolescent concerns; *Visions: Stories about Women Artists* (Sills, 1993), the lives and visions of women who share a commitment to art and creative imagination; and *I, Juan de Pareja* (de Trevino, 1965), which deals with the slave and friend of the Spanish painter Velasquez who becomes a painter himself under the tutelage of his master. Cal has read these books aloud to his students, drawing their attention to their central theme: the artist's struggle to capture a vision on canvas. In addition, he has found that his students come to care deeply for the engaging characters, both fictional and real, who populate these books, thus learning things from them about artistic expression that Cal himself cannot teach.

Because art is visual, it makes sense to enrich the art class with young adult picture books that have painting and drawing themes. Wonderfully illustrated books for the art class include *Redoute: The Man Who Painted Flowers* (Croll, 1996), *A Blue Butterfly: A Story about Claude Monet* (LeTord, 1995), *Leonardo da Vinci* (Stanley, 1996), *Rosa Bonheur* (Turner, 1991), *Pish Posh, Said Hieronymous Bosch* (Willard, 1991), and *The Painter's Cat* (Wooding, 1994).

Use Follow-Up Activities That Allow Students to Personalize New Trade/Text Knowledge

Because follow-up activities often help students to assimilate concepts and information and allow you to evaluate students' learning and to check for misconceptions, they are essential to a complete teaching and learning experience with trade books and textbooks.

With writing, drama, and art, all viable discourse forms, and with the array of electronic and graphic media available in today's schools, follow-up activities that help students synthesize textbook and trade book learning can be as diverse as the people who create them. The following strategies, which are drawn from the same classroom experiences referred to throughout this chapter, are representative of the unlimited possibilities for rewarding follow-up activities. Moreover, they facilitate deep, meaningful comprehension of the critical unit themes and concepts.

Writing

Writing activities can be as simple as on-the-scene descriptions of places or events mentioned briefly in the text and detailed in a trade book or letters to historical figures from students who assume the persona of fictional characters. Both activities allow students to use factual knowledge in a personal way. A more involved writing activity is composing a dialog between historical figures and fictional characters. One teacher had students write dialog between Sarah, from *Escape to the Forest* (Radin, 2000), and Hitler. A science teacher asked students to present a conversation between a fictional and a real-life character based on a study of the environment and the novel *Deadeye* (Llewellyn, 1991). The main character, Harry, a teenager on a sailing vacation off the coast of Scotland, becomes embroiled in a dangerous plot to foil criminals dumping toxic waste into the North Sea. Students wrote and presented imaginative scenes involving Harry and an industrial polluter. These composing activities elicited responses in which concepts, issues, and information were reviewed and reconsidered. As an overall review of the Civil War unit, groups of students wrote and illustrated an informational picture book containing facts from both the textbook and their trade books. Fact sheets were written about the Aztec chieftain Montezuma as one culminating activity for students studying exploration of the New World. Students finishing their unit of the American Revolution assumed the persona of a character from *My Brother Sam Is Dead* (Collier & Collier, 1974) and composed a short diary from April 1775 through April 1776. They also wrote personal letters from Tim Meeker to George Washington explaining his feelings about the war and its effects on the Meeker family.

Writing provides students the medium for thinking creatively and critically about newly learned content.

Drama

Drama, unrehearsed and without an audience, serves students well in providing nonthreatening, active contexts for trying out new roles and language forms and experiencing different perspectives. Students can extemporaneously reenact scenes or events mentioned in their reading, or use text material and stories to provide models for original scenes pertaining to the same concepts. Informal, on-the-spot interviews of characters or figures encountered in texts or trade books allow students to play with newly acquired content-area ideas, concepts, and facts as they formulate questions and answers. Interviewers armed with facts reported in their texts and the knowledge of the characters from trade book reading interviewed peers posing as Friedrich (Richter, 1970) and his German friend as they lived through different stages of the Nazification of Germany, Tina (Leonard, 1988) in her search for her mother, Jesse and her friends (Hobbs, 1991) as they embark on their perilous journey down the Colorado River, Julian Escobar (the main character, a young seminarian, in *The Captive,* by O'Dell, 1979) in the Mexican jungle, and the Redding townspeople gathered to watch the execution of Sam Meeker (Collier & Collier, 1974). For the World War II unit, some students interviewed local people who actually lived in Europe during the war as a means of personalizing and extending their knowledge of that era.

Adolescents enjoy opportunities to "act out" scenes from trade books.

Radio plays are a natural adjunct to reading and writing. In this dramatic form, students select a scene or invent a probable scene from a historical event, write a script with dialog and action, and tape-record it with sound effects for later "broadcast." Free of the demands of staging and acting, students can concentrate on accurate representation of facts, characters' motives, and appropriate language production. Imagine the language and composing skills, thinking, and relevant concepts and information called into play by students who recon-structed the scene surrounding Pizarro's decision to burn his ships off the Mexican coast to prevent his fearful, disgruntled soldiers from deserting. Drama—an enjoyable, valuable form of composition—is too seldom used in our middle and secondary school classrooms.

We recommend activities that require students to plan, think, and, in many cases, write and revise. Although these can be time-consuming processes, we believe much is gained from higher order follow-up activities, including abun-dant oral and written language production; opportunities for independent thinking and decision making; and application of newly acquired concepts, ideas, and information. As you begin and continue to integrate trade books into your curriculum, we think you will agree that its benefits more than justify the time it requires.

PROMOTING LIFELONG READING HABITS

We now shift our attention away from specific instructional strategies that com-bine textbook and trade book learning to ways in which classroom teachers can help students develop the reading habit by encouraging them to read outside of school as well as inside the classroom for information, self-growth, and the sheer pleasure of reading.

In Chapter 1, we described the growing phenomenon of aliteracy—capable readers choosing not to read. We argued that the seeds of aliteracy are planted when reading lessons become drudgery; when the books students must read are uninspiring or have little connection to their real-world needs, concerns, and in-terests; and when reading is perceived as a separate subject instead of a func-tional tool for intellectual and personal growth. Unfortunately, many students who enter junior and senior high school rarely read, not because they can't but because they won't. Some have given up reading altogether and will likely be-come nonreading adults (Davidson & Koppenhaver, 1993; Weeks, 2001).

Because many adolescents are reluctant readers (Bintz, 1993), all teachers have a responsibility to do more than teach the content in their subject areas. Teachers must try to reach students by developing curricula that encourage them to read interesting and personally meaningful books and that help them realize reading for its own sake can be a pleasurable and rewarding experience.

Helping reluctant readers become regular readers is critical because they are likely to have the most difficulty learning content-area material.

What Classroom Teachers Can Do to Keep Students Reading

When Bill, the first author of this textbook, began his first job out of college teaching English in an all-black high school in rural South Carolina, he came face to face with adolescents who in the words of Sven Birkerts (1994) "had never bathed in the energies of a book" (p.18), young people who could not read at a level necessary to understand and enjoy the stories and plays in the required literature anthology. William, a 6-foot-7 17-year-old in one of Bill's 11th-grade classes, leaned close to his ear as he handed out textbooks on the first day of class and whispered, "I don't know how to read." Bill came quickly to the realization that in order to engage William and his classmates as readers at all, he would need to use alternative text sources.

His first experiment with literature that he hoped his students would find more accessible and personally meaningful was Alice Childress's (1974) *A Hero Ain't Nothing But a Sandwich*, a coming-of-age story for an adolescent boy in Harlem. Bill's class was transformed by this book. Attendance and behavior problems dropped noticeably. Students were anxious to read on and clamored for more of the same when the book was concluded. Even William made modest progress that year.

Of course, as authors of this book, our own literate histories have been very different from those African American teens growing up in hot, dusty tobacco country, whose ancestors were share croppers and, only a few generations before that, human chattel on the farms and plantations of the deep South. For us, like Sven Birkerts:

> Reading was once, in childhood, a momentous discovery. The first arrival was so stunning, so pleasant, that (we) wanted nothing more than a guarantee of return—Here was the finding of a lens that would give (us) a different orientation to what was already, though only nascently, the project of (our lives). (p. 35)

Separately, we recall vividly the exhilaration of finding a new favorite book as a young child. For Bill it was a new Stephen Meader novel at age 10 in the Montieth Branch Library on a rainy summer morning in Detroit. He'll never forget sitting atop his upper bunk in the attic of his family's small, clapboard house—in one of hundreds of blocks of blue-collar neighborhoods in a working class city—reading *Lumberjack, Whaler 'Round the Horn*, or *Boy with a Pack*. For Michele, the co-author of *Readers, Teachers, Learners*, it was the *Nancy Drew* and *Madeline* books.

These book encounters were identity-affirming and even life-altering experiences for us, as similar encounters with print have been and will always be for countless men and women who found their own points of entry into literacy as children or youth. And this leads us to the crucible of our message in this section of the chapter. Where we begin our literate journeys may have little resemblance to where we find ourselves at any future place on that journey or certainly where the journey concludes. What is important is that a point of entry is found for every young person because, as we believe, there may be multiple roads to engaged reading, but only by taking the path of literacy can there be any hope at all that for a rewarding and meaningful life (Young & Brozo, 2001a).

All teachers can help students find entry points into active literacy and be their guides on the journey to lifelong reading.

Although each of our literate journeys is private and unique, what all of us share is that from the first stirrings of excitement brought about by print encounters as children and teens, we have come this far, to this point in time where the life-altering and consciousness-expanding power of literacy continues to be realized. Because we simply do not know where young person's first exciting print experiences will take him or her, we as teachers must do all we can to help teens and preteens find their entry points into literacy with texts that interest them and that capture their imaginations (Young & Brozo, 2001b).

Classroom teachers who employ strategies similar to those described in this chapter will go a long way toward helping middle school and secondary students take their first steps down a path of active literacy. These strategies are meant to encourage students already in the reading habit to read even more and to rekindle a desire to read among students whose interest has faded. Along with these strategies, there are many additional ways to promote engaged reading by content-area teachers and in the content-area classroom.

Discover and Use Students' Interests

In Chapter 4 we offered some suggestions for assessing students' interests to introduce them to informative and exciting books that match their interests. We reiterate the importance of discovering the particular interests of the students in your classroom, not only to turn them on to your subject but to turn them on to reading (Ivey & Broaddus, 2001).

A simple sentence-completion inventory, such as those suggested in Chapter 4, can reveal a great deal about what students find pleasurable. Remember that students who may be nonreaders or reluctant readers will have little to say in response to questions or incomplete statements about reading. Therefore, interest inventories should reveal more than reading interests; they should uncover students' real-world interests, concerns, needs, dreams, and hobbies.

Teachers who use journals often get to know their students in ways that would be impossible with simple inventories and questionnaires. In journals, students often disclose important aspects of their lives related to their community, family, and peer relationships. They write about what makes them laugh and cry. With this information, a teacher is better able to respond with appropriate suggestions for reading material that speaks to their real-world concerns. For instance, a high school English teacher who learned that one of her students was a single mother responded in the young woman's journal with suggested books about teenage moms trying to stay the course in school and plan for a better future for themselves and their children. She recommended two realistic novels that deal with these challenges honestly, *Spellbound* (McDonald, 2001) and *Like Sisters on the Homefront* (Williams-Garcia, 1995)

The first step in matching good books with readers is discovering students' outside-of-school interests and needs.

Other teachers have used letters from reluctant readers to gain insights into their reading and outside interests (Isakson, 1991). Receiving letters from students and writing letters back to them makes it possible for the teacher to offer book suggestions in a nonthreatening and confidential way. One 10th-grade student confided in a letter to his teacher that he loved "stuff" about the Civil War but was having a difficult time finding books on the topic that were easy for him to read. The teacher loaned him a copy of *Civil War! America Becomes One Nation* (Robertson, 1992), a photographic picture book written in a lively and accessible style—just right for the student. He eventually wrote back that it was one of the best books about the Civil War he had ever read and wondered if the teacher had more suggestions.

Demonstrate That Reading Is Valued

Teachers who are bored with their own texts can hardly be expected to entice students into the "literacy club" (Sanacore, 1996). Likewise, if students believe that only the teacher and the text possess the important and correct ideas and information, they will likely remain uninvolved and uninterested readers.

Creating an atmosphere in the classroom in which you and your students are free to share enthusiasm for books is the best way we know to demonstrate that reading is valued (Gambrell, 1996). To do this, time must be allocated for building and browsing through the classroom library and visiting the school library to select books, magazines, and newspapers for recreational reading, sharing books, and gathering students' responses and reactions to books.

Sanacore (1992) recommends cluttering the classroom with as much print material as possible. In an environment where students are surrounded by reading material of all varieties, they are more likely to browse and read some of these materials. Instead of becoming anxious over what students choose to read, we should be reminded of Nell's (1988) discovery that as readers become more experienced in reading for pleasure, they tend to select appropriate materials. Making the environment conducive to reading by arranging a few comfortable reading spots with good seating and lighting and adding colorful posters, book jackets, and mobiles for decoration will make it clear to students that you value pleasurable personal reading (Clary, 1991).

Given current and foreseeable demographic and achievement trends, content-area teachers should make every effort to keep print material in their classrooms that will appeal to a variety of tastes, cultural backgrounds, and abilities. In Figure 8.12 is a list of resources teachers can access to find appropriate contemporary multicultural literature for their students. To make literature available to students who have become disengaged readers because most classroom texts are too difficult, Figure 8.13 presents resources for identifying picture books for young adults. Teachers of middle grades and secondary-level students who are having particular difficulty getting reluctant boys to read will find in Figure 8.14 a list of helpful books devoted to boys and reading. Each of these figures directs you to our companion website where many additional resources can be found online.

Within a print-rich classroom, there must also be time for pleasure reading. We strongly recommend a **sustained silent reading (SSR)** program as a useful strategy to encourage the leisure reading habit. SSR provides you and your students with time to do nothing but read in an atmosphere free of assignments, grades, and reports. Students are allowed to read anything that interests them. For many, SSR may be the only free reading time all day. Ideally, the entire school should be involved in SSR, even though you and your classroom alone can have a successful program. SSR programs have been shown to promote more positive attitudes toward reading (Davis, 2001) and greater independence (Sanacore,

One of the best ways to demonstrate to students that reading is valued is to provide daily opportunities in the classroom for self-selected reading.

Books

Brown, J., Stephens, E., & Salvner, G. (1998). *United in diversity: Using multicultural young adult literature in the classroom.* Urbana, IL: National Council of Teachers of English.

Kuipers, B. (1995). *American Indian reference and resource books for children and young adults* (2nd ed.). Greenwood Village, CO: Libraries Unlimited.

McCaffrey, L. (1998). *Building an ESL collection for young adults.* Westport, CT: Greenwood Press.

Reed, A. (1999). *Multicultural literature anthology.* Reading, MA: Addison-Wesley.

Rochman, H. (1993). *Against borders: Promoting books for a multicultural world.* Chicago, IL: American Library Association.

Roscow, L. (1996). *Light 'n lively reads for ESL, adult, and teen readers: A thematic bibliography.* Greenwood Village, CO: Libraries Unlimited.

Totten, H., Garner, C., & Brown, R. (1996). *Culturally diverse collections for youth.* Neal-Schuman.

Valdez, A. (1999). *Using literature to incorporate multicultural education in the intermediate grade school level.* Upper Saddle River, NJ: Prentice Hall.

Willis, A. I. (1998). *Teaching multicultural literature in grades 9–12: Moving beyond the canon.* Norwood, MA: Christopher Gordon.

Articles

Ford, D., Tyson, C., Howard, T., & Harris, J. (2000). Multicultural literature and gifted black students: Promoting self-understanding. *Roeper Review, 22,* 235–241.

Godina, H., & McCoy, R. (2000). Emic and etic perspectives on Chicana and Chicano multicultural literature. *Journal of Adolescent & Adult Literacy, 44,* 172–179.

 Go to Web Resources for Chapter 8 at *http:www.prenhall.com/brozo* and look for multicultural literature.

FIGURE 8.12   Multicultural Literature Resources for Teachers of Young Adults

1994). The following sections present a few guidelines for your classroom SSR program.

Give students assistance in finding something to read.   In time, most students will come prepared for SSR with material selected in advance. Others, particularly reluctant readers, may need help in finding something to read. Talk with these students about their interests, and allow them to visit the classroom or school library to select a book, magazine, newspaper, or other reading material that matches their interest.

Accept any reading material that students bring for SSR.   Avoid the tendency to push your tastes on students, even if they have selected material you

Books

Benedict, S., & Carlisle, L. (1992). *Beyond words: Picture books for older readers.* Portsmouth, NH: Heinemann.

Hall, S. (2001). *Using picture storybooks to teach literary devices: Recommended books for children and young adults.* Westport, CT: Greenwood.

Kiefer, B. (1995). *The potential of picture books.* Englewood Cliffs, NJ: Prentice Hall.

Matulka, D. (1997). *Picture this: Picture books for young adults.* Westport, CT: Greenwood Press.

Tiedt, I. M. (2000). *Teaching with picture books in the middle school.* Newark, DE: International Reading Association.

Articles

Carr, K., Buchanan, D., Wentz, J., Weiss, M., & Brant, K. (2001). Not just for primary grades: A bibliography of picture books for secondary content teachers. *Journal of Adolescent & Adult Literacy, 45,* 146–153.

Hadaway, N., & Mundy, J. (1999). Children's informational picture books visit a secondary ESL classroom. *Journal of Adolescent & Adult Literacy, 42,* 464–475.

Matthews, R., Mingrone, M. C., Zuidema, L., & Macia, E. (1999). What picture books do you recommend for use in the English language arts classroom? *English Journal, 88,* 27–33.

 Go to Web Resources for Chapter 8 at *http:www.prenhall.com/brozo* and look for picture books for young adults.

FIGURE 8.13 Picture Book Resources for Teachers of Young Adults

consider to be of poor literary quality. The key is that you are providing a supportive environment for students to read material that is meaningful to them. One qualifier: Many teachers experienced with SSR programs find that they must eventually make it clear that certain material is absolutely inadmissible, such as pornography. You may want to head off any problems before they occur by restricting certain materials that are clearly inappropriate for the SSR program.

Never link reports or grading to SSR.   SSR is free reading. The best way to undermine this intent is by turning SSR into schoolwork. Occasionally, school-related activities will flow naturally from SSR reading. For instance, a student may use a book being read in SSR for a research project or story writing, but these activities should never become requirements. SSR should allow students to explore the pleasures of reading. Your support of the program will clearly demonstrate that you value daily reading of personally meaningful and interesting materials.

Use as much time as you can allow for SSR.   For adolescents, SSR periods of 15 minutes or more should be the goal. Keep in mind that those 15 minutes

Books

Brozo, W. G. (2002). *To be a boy, to be a reader: Engaging teen and preteen boys in active literacy.* Newark, DE: International Reading Association.

Gurian, M. (2000). *What stories does my son need?* New York: Tarcher/Putnam.

Millard, E. (1997). *Differently literate: Boys, girls and the schooling of literacy.* London: Taylor & Francis.

Odean, K. (1998). *Great books for boys.* New York: Ballantine.

Rand, D., & Parker, T. (2000). *Black books galore! Guide to great African American children's books about boys.* Somerset, NJ: John Wiley & Sons.

Articles

Brozo, W. G., & Schmelzer, R. V. (1997). Wildmen, warriors, and lovers: Reaching boys through archetypal literature. *Journal of Adolescent & Adult Literacy, 41,* 4–11.

Brozo, W. G., Walters, P., & Placker, T. (2002). "I know the difference between a real man and a TV man": A critical exploration of violence and masculinity through literature in a junior high school in the 'hood'. *Journal of Adolescent & Adult Literacy, 45,* 530–538.

 Go to Web Resources for Chapter 8 at *http:www.prenhall.com/brozo* and look for books for reluctant male readers.

FIGURE 8.14   Teacher Resources for Helping Reluctant Male Readers

may be the only time all day that many students read self-selected materials simply for pleasure or personal use.

Foothills High School, described in Chapter 4 for its informed use of low-stakes reading achievement testing, exemplifies how teachers can work together to ensure students have regular opportunities for engaged reading. After several meetings at which teachers tried to determine how faculty in all subject areas could make a contribution to the school's reading improvement goals, they decided to establish a sustained silent reading program. In order to launch the program successfully, several preparation steps were taken:

■ A survey was administered to students early in the new school year to reveal the kinds of topics they would most like to read about and their various areas of interest outside of school.

■ With this information, the department head of English and the librarian purchased hundreds of young adult paperback novels using funds from a Goals 2000 grant. It's worth noting that up to this point, the Foothills High library had very few young adult novels on its shelves. This is all too common in many high schools where the emphasis in acquisitions is on reference materials, computer software, magazine subscriptions, and adult best-sellers.

■ A book drive was organized to acquire even more print material for the planned SSR program. Teachers in every classroom asked students to donate to the school a paperback and/or magazine from home that they had read. Several large "book drops" were set up around the campus, and within just a few weeks most were piled high with student donations.

■ Input from teachers had revealed that their biggest concern about the program was that students would not have access to or find something worth reading during SSR. To meet this challenge, class sets of paperbacks, newspapers, and magazines were compiled. Several metal racks collecting dust in a storage room of the old junior high school were discovered and wiped clean. These were stuffed with the various print material and placed in each teacher's room.

■ A contest was held among the student body to come up with the best name for Foothills High School's new reading initiative. After voting on several entries, students selected "Reading Cyclone" after the name of their mascot.

■ Finally, to inaugurate the program, a ceremony was held. Sweatshirts had been made with a Reading Cyclone logo designed by students and worn by faculty, administrators, and guests. After a reading rally held in the gym, where a star football player from the local university spoke, everyone present on the campus, including clerical, custodial, and food service staff, read silently for 20 minutes.

■ Reading Cyclone now takes place three days per week for twenty minutes during homeroom, from about 9:40 to 10:00 A.M. It is prompted from the office by a student right after he or she makes daily announcements, though teachers find the prompting isn't really necessary. Because plenty of print sources are available to students in every classroom, teachers have been pleased to find students looking forward to the quiet "down time." Teachers have also discovered the value of Reading Cyclone for eliminating student disruptions during homeroom. Another important benefit is the opportunity teachers have to model the enjoyment of reading and to reinvigorate their own independent reading habits.

Read Aloud to Students

Earlier in this chapter, we mentioned that reading aloud is one way to integrate trade books into content-area classrooms. Reading aloud to students on a regular basis is also an excellent way to motivate them to read and is a highly pleasurable experience for listeners of any age (Daisey, 1993; Erickson, 1996). Jim Trelease, the noted storyteller, says teachers should read aloud "to reassure, to entertain, to inform or explain, to arouse curiosity, and to inspire—and to do it all personally" (1989, p. 2). We recommend that you try to recreate the same intimate atmosphere of a parent reading a favorite story to a child (Mathews, 1987). In a warm, trusting environment, you and your students can "get lost" in books. Read-aloud resources can range from short, appealing magazine articles to full-length novels. Sharing with students a variety of materials through

Students of all ages derive great pleasure from listening to teachers read books aloud.

read-alouds models expressive reading, transmits the pleasure of reading, and invites listeners to be readers while expanding their tastes (Richardson, 1994, 2000).

The following read-aloud guidelines offered by Erickson (1996) have proven to be highly useful for identifying and working with quality selections:

- The books hold the interest of both teacher and students.
- The books stimulate discussion.
- The books lead to additional readings.
- The books involve dilemmas whose solutions are open-ended.
- The books include main characters who are both male and female.
- The books have authors from many cultures.
- The books match listeners' social and emotional levels.

Other aspects of read-alouds that we have found critical to their success include (1) practicing reading aloud a selection beforehand, (2) stopping the selection if it clearly doesn't work for your students, (3) keeping each read-aloud to about 15 or 20 minutes, and (4) encouraging but not insisting on discussion of the selection.

We have witnessed teachers take risks with hundreds of selections, abandoning many but keeping many that students enjoy. Over the course of a few years, you will develop a growing collection of "winners" that will appeal to most all middle and high school students.

Make Reading Fun

Many teachers and parents are quick to point out that reading cannot possibly compete with television viewing as a leisure-time activity. It is well documented that most adolescents spend several hours per day watching TV (Minow & Lamay, 1996; Neuman, 1988). It is also apparent that reading performance is negatively correlated to TV viewing, especially for those who watch 4 or more hours daily (Donahue, Voelkl, Campbell, & Mazzeo, 1999). A surprising finding by Neuman, however, is that students choose to watch TV during their leisure time because it is more interesting than other activities, such as reading. In other words, take TV out of the lives of students who are not interested in reading, and those students will fill the void with other nonreading activities. Get those students more excited about books, however, and they will consciously make time for reading, even if it means eliminating some TV viewing. One way to help students choose reading as a leisure-time activity is to make it fun.

We must remember that junior and senior high school students enjoy playing with language and should be encouraged to read books that are fun. Reed (1988) recommends that teachers, and parents suggest humorous young adult books such as joke books and even comic books, especially for reluctant readers, to keep them active members of the literacy club. These books can act as a bridge to more sophisticated reading materials.

A seventh-grade teacher we know demonstrates how enjoyable reading can be through read-alouds. Regionalized versions of well-known fables and fairy tales from such books as Chase's (1948; 1943) *Grandfather Tales* and *Jack Tales* have become perennial favorites. The Christmas season is made all the more festive with humorous holiday favorites such as Garner's (1995) *Politically Correct Holiday Stories: For an Enlightened Yuletide Season* and Jacobs's (1973) *Cajun Night Before Christmas*. The teacher involves students in role-plays to her compelling narration. The texts and her interpretations often leave the class full of laughter. She has noted the influence of the read-alouds on her students' own enthusiasm for reading these and other humorous books.

Humorous books have helped many reluctant readers find entry points into active literacy.

Make Reading a Real-Life Experience

As we have emphasized throughout this chapter, your goal as a teacher is to do more than teach the content of your subject area. You must also be involved in reaching students through reading to help them take responsibility for their own literacy development beyond the schoolroom. This can be accomplished by taking every opportunity to bring real-world reading materials into the classroom so that, through interesting and meaningful classroom activities, adolescents come to understand how reading needs to be a part of their adult lives. Newspapers, magazines, and various other print sources found in the adult world should be used in daily classroom instruction and made available in the classroom library or reading corner.

A prime example of integrating everyday reading materials into classroom instruction comes from a literature teacher who was helping his students understand *metaphor*. He knew that metaphors are often found in newspapers. Because they are inexpensive, easy to obtain, and contain articles that are generally short and concise, newspapers are a good source for figurative language instruction.

The teacher began by distributing to small groups of students headlines that used metaphorical language, such as "Still Limping, Oil Patch Exits Intensive Care" and "Experts Zero in on Magic Bullet to Kill Cancer Cells." Using a reciprocal teaching strategy (explained in Chapters 2 and 3), the teacher modeled a question-asking and -answering process out loud to demonstrate for students how he interpreted the metaphors in the headlines. For instance, with the first headline, he began by asking "What is an oil patch?" Then he dug into the article until he found information that helped him answer the question. The oil patch is a group of four states whose net worth and economic stability depend heavily on the production and sale of oil—namely, Louisiana, Oklahoma, Colorado, and Texas.

The next question he asked was, "In what way could four oil-producing states exit intensive care?" He pointed out that the statement clearly made no sense if interpreted literally, which, by default, made it a metaphor. This question led immediately to his next question, "Who would normally exit, 'limping,' from the intensive care ward?" Students were quick to respond by identifying a sick or injured person who is getting better but is basically still ill or injured. In this way students began to see the similarities between the oil patch and a patient just released from intensive care.

At this point, the teacher asked students working in their groups to come up with an explanation of the metaphor. Most were able to explain that the oil-producing states were in trouble but were in far better financial shape than they were a few years ago, just as the hospitalized person who limps out of intensive care is still in trouble but in better physical condition than not long before.

The teacher went on to engage students in a discussion of why the author chose to use a metaphorical headline in the first place. To make the article more attractive and "catchy" was one explanation. Another was that the author was "teasing" readers to entice them to read the article. The teacher pointed out that by linking the troubled economies of distant states with something familiar— hospitals, illness—the author was trying to make his subject accessible to more readers.

There are many more examples of teachers who routinely integrate real-life reading materials into their content instruction to help students see connections between literacy development inside and outside the classroom boundaries.

Using print material from popular media and the everyday world makes learning more engaging for adolescents.

- A health teacher has students bring in menus from restaurants and cookbooks from home when working on food preparation and nutrition.
- A business education teacher, for his unit on career explorations, brings in several examples of employment applications. He also urges students who may be applying for part-time jobs to bring in their applications.
- A chemistry teacher asks students to bring in labels from household cleaning products and foods indicating that certain chemicals are being used.
- A government teacher uses popular news magazines to relate text topics to current events.
- An accounting teacher asks students to bring in actual bills and account statements to teach accounting terms and budgeting.
- A math teacher asks students to write/create math problems using tables, maps, and graphs from the local newspaper.

The list could go on and on because the possibilities for integrating everyday reading materials into the content classroom are virtually limitless.

According to Davidson and Koppenhaver (1993), adolescents today live in a world of instant food, appliances, entertainment, and information. Unfortunately, the technology that makes life easier for young adults is also decreasing their motivation to develop literacy skills beyond the classroom. To help students see the importance and utility of real-world literacy, we recommend that teachers bring into the classroom familiar, everyday texts that students encounter outside school. These strategies, along with others that emphasize the personal-growth benefits and pleasure of leisure reading, are the best ways we know to encourage young adults to make reading an integral part of their lives.

CASE STUDY REVISITED

Remember Linda, the history teacher? She was preparing a unit on "Immigration to the United States," and we asked you to think of trade book strategies that might be helpful to her as she developed activities for her students. Write your suggestions now.

Before writing your suggestions for Linda, go to *http:// www.prenhall.com/brozo,* select Chapter 8, then click on Chapter Review Questions to check your understanding of the material.

Linda taught the unit using the history textbook and a variety of trade books. She chose books for their quality representation of the immigrant experience of four primary ethnic groups: (1) European Americans (*Immigrants,* Sandler, 1995), (2) African Americans (*The Slave Dancer,* Fox, 1973), (3) Asian Americans (*I Am an American,* Stanley, 1994), and (4) Hispanic Americans (*Spanish Pioneers of the Southwest,* Anderson, 1989; *Voices from the Fields,* Atkin, 1993). Additional sources included Mitsumasa Anno's *Anno's U.S.A.* (1983) and a featured article in *The Atlantic Monthly* called "The Price of Immigration" (Kennedy & Borjas, 1996).

The class began the study of immigration by reading, analyzing, and discussing *Anno's U.S.A.* in small groups and then as a class. Each student was asked to look for historical and literary events, figures, and ideas found in the book. This wordless picture book was a favorite among many of Linda's students. Some of them borrowed the book over and over again, impressed that the Japanese author knew so much about the United States but that they knew so little about the country and history of Japan. *Anno's U.S.A.* provided Linda's American history classes with an excellent introduction to the topic of immigration through detailed and accurate illustrations.

Linda then introduced the other trade books with brief booktalks. She divided the class into small groups and assigned each group one of the books. As she circulated among the groups, they talked about what they read and what they saw in the illustrations. As each group finished, she asked them to write down their reactions to what they read: what they liked and did not like, what the illustrations brought to the text, what the illustrations told them that the text did not, and what overall impressions they had after reading.

Each group was responsible for making a daily oral report summarizing what had been read and learned from the trade books. In this way, all students could gain essential content about the immigration experience for different major ethnic groups.

Students who read *Immigrants* thoroughly enjoyed sharing with their classmates information about transatlantic travel by young European children without parental supervision and guidance, procedures on Ellis Island, and life on Hester Street in New York City at the turn of the century. The group representing Asian American immigrants discovered fascinating information about early Japanese and Chinese settlers and workers in the Western United States. This group was especially taken by the treatment of Japanese American citizens during World War II. Separate groups read and shared their trade books about Hispanic immigrants. In *Spanish Pioneers of the Southwest,* students learned how Spanish, Mexican, and Native American cultures combined to form a unique blend of original American customs among the early immigrants to the territory once called New Spain. In *Voices from the Fields,* students were brought face-to-face with Mexican American children and youth living a hazardous yet proud itinerant life as farmworkers. All of these engaging informational picture books provided a refreshing contrast to their regular textbook reading and class discussion.

During this time, Linda also read *The Slave Dancer* to both classes so that her students would have a clearer understanding of black immigration. In it, students learn about Jesse, a New Orleans boy who is kidnapped and taken aboard a slave ship where he's forced to play his fife so that the slaves will dance and maintain their good physical condition. Students also learned a wealth of information about how slaves were obtained in Africa and the routes taken to bring them to the United States. They enjoyed the novel immensely. In discussion groups, they explained the role of African tribal chiefs who sold blacks to white captains like Cawthorne (the captain of the ship in the story); they described the living conditions aboard the slave ship; and they debated the reasons for slavery in America.

The next activity also involved small-group and then class discussion as Linda asked students to brainstorm possible ways of sharing the material they found in their trade books. After they compiled a list of activities and projects, she asked each student to pick an activity or project to do individually and share it with the class. (Figure 8.15 shows the list of activities the students brainstormed.) As a class, they focused on the contributions of each of the major ethnic groups to the culture of the United States.

After students completed the trade books and Linda finished reading *The Slave Dancer* to the class, they turned their attention to the issue of cultural diversity, its advantages and challenges, and the specific contributions and problems that have resulted from America's brand of cultural diversity. Using the article on immigration in *The Atlantic Monthly,* the class explored a variety of social, economic, and political issues surrounding current immigration practices and policies in the United States. These ideas were handled in a number of lively discussions. Topics included anti-semitism and racism in the last decade, the recent arrests of white supremacy group members, U.S. Supreme Court decisions, the Ku Klux Klan and the American Nazi Party, superiority, inferiority, economic disparity, and even the firing and censorship of athletic officials after their racist remarks about black athletes.

The classes charted the problems each major group of immigrants has faced in American society and the ways in which society has sought to address and solve those problems. Linda's students did not affix blame to any one racial or ethnic group; rather, they recognized that we are all responsible for the problems and for finding the solutions.

———◄○►———

SUMMARY

This chapter has been devoted to two themes: (1) strategies for combining trade book and textbook instruction in the content-area classroom and (2) strategies for helping students develop lifelong reading habits.

Anno's U.S.A.

1. Draw a map of the United States to show Anno's route.
2. Draw a time line to accompany the pages of the book.
3. Write a text for several pages of the book. Choose an age group and an audience to write it for.
4. Analyze a page with historical and literary explanations.
5. Write a list of questions to ask the author and then incorporate them in a letter.
6. Choose an activity or write a paper explaining an incident or a character found on a page of the book.
7. Add a double-page spread to update the book to 1998.
8. Add a double-page spread to include the history of Pearl City.
9. Construct a model of a page or part of a page.
10. Share the book with a younger student and provide the student with explanations.
11. Design a cover or book jacket for *Anno's U.S.A.*

Immigrants

1. Write a list of questions and possible answers for a European immigrant from the book.
2. Dramatize the above interview and tape-record it.
3. Contact a recent immigrant, develop a list of questions, interview the immigrant, and then write a report of the interview.
4. Write a description of an immigrant from the book's first week in the United States.
5. Write a diary as the narrator of life aboard ship.
6. Read and discuss the book with younger students.
7. Research some aspect of immigration (transportation, routes, conditions aboard ship, Ellis Island, etc.) and prepare a written report.
8. Design a cover or a book jacket for *Immigration*.
9. Research and write a short paper on why people from a particular European country immigrated to the United States.
10. Research conditions in one European country that led to the immigration of some of its citizens to the United States.
11. Research the contributions made by a European immigrant to the United States.

Spanish Pioneers of the Southwest

1. Keep a journal for 1 week as if you were one of the pioneer children.
2. Make a model of the *placita* where the Baca family lived.
3. Create articles for a pioneer newspaper (front page, cartoon, living, entertainment, etc.).
4. Create a colorful map that charts the path taken by the Baca family.

Voices from the Fields

1. Write a letter to a congressperson explaining the living conditions of migrant farmworkers and asking for policies to help improve them.
2. Create a map that charts the travel of a farmworker family for 1 year.
3. Write dialog and reenact a scene between farmworkers and farm owners.
4. Interview a current or former migrant farmworker and present the results of your interview.
5. Write and perform a rap or Tejano song about your life as a farmworker.

The Slave Dancer

1. Design a cover or a book jacket.
2. Design a picture book based on one aspect of the book.
3. Write a letter to the main character expressing your thoughts and opinions about slave trading.
4. Write a book review.

FIGURE 8.15 **Project Choices for Immigration Unit**

First, we presented a theoretical rationale, specific recommendations, and practical considerations for integrating young adult books and textbooks into content-area teaching. We have shown that the practical use of trade books can be supported by theories of learning. Trade books can help students build on past literacy successes, create interest and motivation, and develop schemata.

In this chapter we provided an in-depth explanation of how trade books and textbooks can be used together. Specific instructional recommendations were made for (1) developing a unit overview and identifying key themes and concepts within the unit topic, (2) choosing trade books to help teach concepts, (3) teaching with textbooks and trade books, and (4) following up a unit of study with exciting learning activities.

The union of textbook and trade book is feasible and has produced elaborate processing of textual information, greater enthusiasm for learning, and long-term recall in field tests that have been conducted in junior and senior high schools (Brozo & Tomlinson, 1986, 1987). The probability of success with this approach is enhanced when teachers responsible for content-area subjects look for opportunities to integrate trade books with their texts and when the literacy support staff work with these teachers to help bring about such an integration. Moreover, using trade books in content classrooms should not be perceived as a device or gimmick to create interest in a topic on Monday that is forgotten by Friday. To use trade books and textbooks effectively, you need to make long-range plans, carefully considering how each unit's themes and salient concepts will be developed, and how trade books and text will interplay from the introduction to the conclusion of the unit.

Good literature, once discovered, sells itself. Students return again and again to favorite books, and teachers who know good, young adult literature find ways to use it in their classes. The key is knowing the literature. Unfortunately, many teacher training and certification programs still offer literature courses as electives only. We endorse the trend toward making these courses mandatory and further suggest that all content-area methods courses include a literature component to increase the likelihood that students will graduate with skills and knowledge related to using trade books across the curriculum. Most important, we recommend that you establish and maintain an independent reading program of literature geared to the students and subject you teach.

The content areas deal with interesting, vital information, but if you rely on textbooks as your sole teaching resource, you may render this information dry and lifeless. Use trade books in conjunction with texts to help ensure that students are more actively involved in learning and that the vitality and spirit inherent in the content-area material are kept alive.

Finally, this chapter discussed ways in which the classroom teacher can demonstrate the importance and pleasure of developing independent reading habits. Students who are led to see the connection between their real-world needs, concerns, and interests and books, newspapers, magazines, and the myriad print sources in the adult world will likely remain active, lifelong members of the literacy club.

REFERENCES

Alexander, P., Kulikowich, J., & Hetton, T. (1994). The role of subject matter knowledge and interest in the processing of linear and nonlinear texts. *Review of Educational Research, 64,* 210–253.

Austin, P. (1998). Math books as literature: Which ones measure up? Use of trade books rather than textbooks in schools. *New Advocate, 11,* 119–133.

Baker, L., Afflerbach, P., & Reinking, D. (1995). *Developing engaged readers in school and home communities.* Mahwah, NJ: Lawrence Erlbaum Associates.

Bean, T. (2000). Reading in the content areas: Social constructivist dimensions. In M. Kamil, P. Mosenthal, R. Barr, & P. D. Pearson (Eds.), *Handbook of Reading Research,* (Vol. 3). Mahwah, NJ: Lawrence Erlbaum Associates.

Bean, T., Kile, R., & Readence, J. (1996). Using trade books to encourage critical thinking about citizenship in high school social studies. *Social Education, 60,* 227–230.

Bintz, W. (1993). Resistant readers in secondary education: Some insights and implications. *Journal of Reading, 36,* 604–615.

Birkerts, S. (1994). *The Gutenberg elegies: The fate of reading in an electronic age.* New York: Fawcett Columbine.

Brandsford, J., & Vye, N. (1989). A perspective on cognitive research and its implications for instruction. In L. Resnick & L. Klopfer (Eds.), *Toward the thinking curriculum: Current cognitive research.* Alexandria, VA: Association of Supervision and Curriculum Development.

Brown, J., Collins, A., & Duguid, P. (1989). Situated cognition and the culture of learning. *Educational Researcher, 18,* 32–42.

Brozo, W. G., & Tomlinson, C. (1986). Literature: The key to lively content courses. *The Reading Teacher, 40,* 288–293.

Brozo, W. G., & Tomlinson, C. (1987, October). *A trade book/textbook approach versus a textbook-only approach on student learning and attitudes during a social studies/history unit.* Paper presented at the meeting of the College Reading Association, Baltimore, Maryland.

Burns, B. (1998). Changing the classroom climate with literature circles. *Journal of Adolescent & Adult Literacy, 42,* 124–129.

Clary, L. (1991). Getting adolescents to read. *Journal of Reading, 34,* 340–345.

Daisey, P. (1993). Three ways to promote the values and uses of literacy at any age. *Journal of Reading, 36,* 436–440.

Davidson, J., & Koppenhaver, D. (1993). *Adolescent literacy: What works and why* (2nd ed.). New York: Garland.

Davis, J. (2001). Heritage Hills tops in school reading. *Indiana Courier Press*, February 11, 142.

Dillon, D. (1989). Showing them that I want them to learn and that I care about who they are: A microethnography of the social organization of a secondary low track English Reading classroom. *American Educational Research Journal, 26,* 227–259.

Donahue, P., Voelkl, K., Campbell, J., & Mazzeo, J. (1999). *NAEP reading report card for the nation and the states.* Washington, DC: U.S. Department of Education.

Donelson, K., & Nilsen, A. (1997). *Literature for today's young adults* (5th ed.). New York: Longman.

Elbaum, B., Schumm, J., & Vaughn, S. (1997). Urban middle-elementary students' perceptions of grouping formats for reading instruction. *The Elementary School Journal, 97,* 475–499.

Elkassabany, A., Johnson, C., & Lucas, T. (2000). How do you incorporate history into the English curriculum. *English Journal, 89,* 26–30.

Erickson, B. (1996). Read-alouds reluctant readers relish. *Journal of Adolescent & Adult Literacy, 40,* 212–214.

Estes, S. (1994). *Growing up is hard to do: A collection of booklist columns.* Chicago: American Library Association.

Frager, A. (1993). Affective dimensions of content area reading. *Journal of Reading, 36,* 616–622.

Gambrell, L. (1996). Creating classroom cultures that foster reading motivation. *The Reading Teacher, 50,* 14–25.

George, M., & Stix, A. (2000). Using multilevel young adult literature in middle school American studies. *The Social Studies, 91,* 25–31.

Gooderham, D. (1995). Chidren's fantasy literature: Toward an anatomy. *Children's Literature in Education, 26,* 171–183.

Graff, H. F. (1980). *The free and the brave.* Chicago: Rand McNally.

Guthrie, J., & Wigfield, A. (2000). Engagement and motivation in reading. In M. Kamil, P. Mosenthal, R. Barr, & P. D. Pearson (Eds.), *Handbook of Reading Research* (Vol. 3). Mahwah, NJ: Lawrence Erlbaum Associates.

Hartman, D. (1995). Eight readers reading: Intertextual links of proficient readers reading multiple texts. *Reading Research Quarterly, 30,* 520–561.

Hartwell, D., & Cramer, K. (1994). *The ascent of wonder: The evolution of hard science fiction.* New York: TOR Books.

Hurst, C. (1995). Bringing art into the library. *Teaching Prek-8, 26,* 84–86.

Isakson, M. (1991). Learning about reluctant readers through their letters. *Journal of Reading, 34,* 632–637.

Ivey, G., & Broaddus, K. (2001). "Just plain reading": A survey of what makes students want to read in middle school classrooms. *Reading Research Quarterly, 36,* 350–377.

Jacobi-Karna, K. (1995). Music and children's books. *The Reading Teacher, 49,* 264–270.

Jones, P. (2001). Nonfiction: The real stuff. *School Library Journal, 47,* 44–45.

Kennedy, D., & Borjas, G. (1996, November). The price of immigration. *The Atlantic Monthly, 278,* 51–77.

Kerby, M. (1996). Mystery books. *School Library Media Activities Monthly, 12,* 18–21.

Lightsey, G. (1996). Using literature to build fifth grade math concepts. *Reading Horizons, 36,* 412–419.

Lombard, R. (1996). Using trade books to teach middle level social studies. *Social Education, 60,* 223–230.

Lott, C., & Wasta, S. (1999). Adding voice and perspective: Children's and young adult literature of the Civil War. *English Journal, 88,* 56–61.

Mathews, C. (1987). Lap reading for teenagers. *Journal of Reading, 30,* 410–413.

McDaniel, M., Waddill, P., & Finstad, K. (2000). The effects of text-based interest on attention and recall. *Journal of Educational Psychology, 92,* 492–502.

McMackin, M. (1998). Using narrative picture books to build expository text structure. *Reading Horizons, 39,* 7–20.

McPhail, J., Pierson, J., & Freeman, J. (2000). The role of interest in fostering sixth grade students' identities as competent learners. *Curriculum Inquiry, 30,* 43–70.

Miller-Hewes, K. (1994). Making the connection: Children's books and the visual arts. *School Arts, 94,* 32–38.

Minow, N. & Lamay, C. (1996). *Abandoned in the wasteland: Children, television, and the First Amendment.* New York: Hill & Wong.

Nell, V. (1988). *Lost in a book: The psychology of reading for pleasure.* New Haven, CT: Yale University Press.

Neuman, S. B. (1988). The displacement effect: Assessing the relation between television viewing and reading performance. *Reading Research Quarterly, 23,* 414–440.

O'Brien, D., Stewart, R., & Moje, E. (1995). Why content literacy is difficult to infuse into the secondary school: Complexities of curriculum, pedagogy, and school culture. *Reading Research Quarterly, 30,* 442–463.

Pappas, C., & Barry, A. (2001). Examining language to capture scientific understandings. *Science and Children, 38,* 26–29.

Pappas, C., Kiefer, B., & Levstik, L. (1999). *An integrated language perspective in the elementary school* (2nd ed). White Plains, NY: Longman.

Pennac, D. (1994). *Better than life.* Toronto: Coach House.

Peterson, R., & Eeds, M. (1990). *Grand conversations.* Richmond Hill, Ontario: Scholastic-TAB.

Quiocho, A. (1997). The quest to comprehend expository text: Applied classroom research. *Journal of Adolescent & Adult Literacy, 40,* 450–455.

Reed, A. J. S. (1988). *Comics to classics: A parent's guide to books for teens and preteens.* Newark, NJ: International Reading Association.

Richardson, J. (1994). Great read-alouds for prospective teachers and secondary students. *Journal of Reading, 38,* 98–103.

Richardson, J. (2000). *Read it aloud! Using literature in the secondary content classroom.* Newark, DE: International Reading Association.

Richgels, D., Tomlinson, C., & Tunnell, M. (1993). Comparison of elementary students' history textbooks and trade books. *Journal of Educational Research, 86,* 161–171.

Royce, C., & Wiley, D. (1996). Children's literature and the teaching of science: Possibilities and cautions. *The Clearinghouse, 70,* 18–23.

Sanacore, J. (1992). Encouraging the lifetime reading habit. *Journal of Reading, 35,* 474–477.

Sanacore, J. (1994). Lifetime literacy through independent reading: The principal is a key player. *Journal of Reading, 37,* 602–606.

Sanacore, J. (1996). An important literacy event through the grades. *Journal of Adolescent & Adult Literacy, 39,* 588–591.

Schmidt, G. (1996). Of pulp, substance, and science fiction. *Children's Literature Association Quarterly, 21,* 45–60.

Sebesta, S., & Donelson, K. (1994). *Inspiring literacy: Literature for children and young adults.* New Brunswick, NJ: Transaction.

Spencer, P. (1994). *What do young adults read next? A reader's guide to fiction for young adults.* Detroit: Gale Research.

Stover, L. (1988, September). What do you mean, we have to read a book for art class? *Art Education,* 8–13.

Sullivan, E. (2001). Some teens prefer the real thing: The case for young adult nonfiction. *English Journal, 90,* 43–47.

Tallman, S. (1990). Cultural literacy. *Arts, 64,* 17–18.

Tomlinson, C., Tunnell, M., & Richgels, D. (1993). The content and writing of history in textbooks and trade books. In M. Tunnell & R. Ammon (Eds.), *The story of ourselves: Teaching history through children's literature.* Portsmouth, NH: Heinemann.

Trelease, J. (1989). *The new read-aloud handbook*. New York: Penguin.

Vye, N., Rowe, D., Kinzer, C., & Risko, V. (1990, April). *The effects of anchored instruction for teaching social studies: Enhancing comprehension of setting information*. Paper presented at the meeting of the American Educational Research Association, Boston.

Weeks, L. (2001, May 14). Aliteracy: Read all about it, or maybe not—Millions of Americans who can read choose not to. Can we do without the written word? *Washington Post*, C1.

Westcott, W., & Spell, J. (1999). Tearing down the wall: Literature and science. *English Journal, 89,* 70–76.

Whitin, P. (1996). Exploring visual responses to literature. *Research in the Teaching of English, 30,* 114–140.

Young, J. P., & Brozo, W. G. (2001a, April). *Boys will be boys, or will they? A critical dialogue about boys and literacy*. Paper presented at the annual convention of the International Reading Association, New Orleans, LA.

Young, J. P., & Brozo, W. G. (2001b). Conversations: Boys will be boys, or will they? Literacy and masculinities. *Reading Research Quarterly, 36,* 316–325.

YOUNG ADULT BOOKS

Abbot, E. (1927). *Flatland*. Boston: Little, Brown.

Ackerman, K. (1995). *The night crossing*. New York: Random House.

Ackerman, K. (1990). *The tin heart*. New York: Atheneum.

Anderson, J. (1989). *Spanish pioneers of the Southwest*. New York: E. P. Dutton.

Anno, M. (1983). *Anno's U.S.A.* New York: Philomel.

Archer, J. (1999). *A house divided: The lives of Ulysses S. Grant and Robert E. Lee*. Minneapolis, MN: Econo-Clad Books.

Asimov, I. (1966). *Fantastic voyage*. Boston: Houghton Mifflin.

Atkin, S. B. (1993). *Voices from the fields: Children of migrant farmworkers tell their stories*. Boston: Little, Brown.

Ayers, K. (2000). *North by night*. New York: Yearling.

Bauer, J. (1997). *Sticks*. New York: Bantam Books.

Beattie, O., & Geiger, J. (1992). *Buried in ice: The mystery of a lost Arctic expedition*. Toronto: Madison Press Books.

Beatty, P. (1990). *Eben Tyne, powdermonkey*. New York: Morrow.

Beatty, P. (1992). *Who comes with cannons?* New York: Morrow.

Blais, M. (1996). *In these girls, hope is a muscle*. New York: Warner Books.

Bornholt, J. (1989). *Star Trek: The next generation*. New York: Dell.

Burchard, P. (1995). *Charlotte Forten: A black teacher in the Civil War*. New York: Crown.

Carbone, E. L. (2001). *Stealing freedom*. New York: Young Yearling.

Carter, P. (1994). *The hunted*. New York: Farrar Strauss & Giroux.

Chase, R. (1943). *Jack tales*. Boston: Houghton Mifflin.

Chase, R. (1948). *Grandfather tales*. Boston: Houghton Mifflin.

Childress, A. (1973). *A hero ain't nothin' but a sandwich*. New York: Coward, McCann, and Geoghegan.

Christopher, M. (1999). *At the plate with Mark McGwire*. Boston: Little Brown.

Collier, J. L., & Collier, C. (1974). *My brother Sam is dead*. New York: Scholastic.

Collier, C., & Collier, J. L. (1997). *With every drop of blood*. New York: Laureleaf.

Connelly, B. (1997). *Follow the drinking gourd*. Rabbit Ears Press.

Corbett, S. (1998). *Venus to the hoop: A gold medal year in women's basketball.* New York: Anchor Books.

Croll, C. (1996). *Redoute: The man who painted flowers.* New York: Putnam.

de Trevino, E. (1965). *I, Juan de Pareja.* New York: Farrar, Straus & Giroux.

Dewdney, A. K. (1984). *The planiverse.* New York: Poseidon Press.

Dougherty, T. (1999). *Brett Favre.* Brookshire, TX: ABDO Publishing Co.

Downing, J. (1991). *Mozart tonight.* New York: Simon & Schuster.

Drucker, M. (1994). *Jacob's rescue: A Holocaust story.* New York: Yearling Books.

Duplacey, J. (1999). *Muhammad Ali: Athlete, activist, ambassador.* Warwick, CA: Woodside Publishing.

Dygard, T. (1999). *Forward pass.* Minneapolis, MN: Econo-Clad Books.

Edmonds, W. (1991). *The matchlock gun.* New York: Troll.

Fleischman, P. (1993). *Bull Run.* New York: HarperCollins.

Forbes, E. (1945). *Johnny Tremain.* Boston: Houghton Mifflin.

Forman, J. (1992). *Becca's story.* New York: Scribners.

Fox, P. (1973). *The slave dancer* (E. Keith, Illus.). New York: Bradbury.

Freedman, R. (1989). *Lincoln: A photobiography.* New York: Clarion.

Garner, J. (1995). *Politically correct holiday stories: For an enlightened Yuletide season.* Thorndike, ME: G. K. Hall.

Grant, S., & Mandrake, T. (1990). *William Shakespeare's Hamlet.* New York: Berkley.

Haddix, M. P. (1998). *Among the hidden.* New York: Aladdin Paperbacks.

Handel, G. F. (1992). *Messiah: The wordbook for the oratorio.* New York: HarperCollins.

Hansen, J. (1992). *Which way freedom?* New York: Avon.

Herrin, L. (1989). *The unwritten chronicles of Robert E. Lee.* New York: St. Martin's Press.

Hesse, K. (1992). *Letters from Rifka.* New York: Henry Holt.

Hesse, K. (1995). *Phoenix rising.* New York: Puffin.

Hesse, K. (1999). *Light in the storm.* New York: Scholastic.

Hill, P. S. (2000). *A voice from the border.* New York: Avon Books.

Hinton, C. H. (1907). *An episode in flatland.* London: Swan Sonnenschein.

Hobbs, W. (1991). *Downriver.* New York: Macmillan.

Hopkinson, D., & Ransome, J. (1993). *Sweet Clara and the freedom quilt.* New York: Random House.

Horosko, M. (1994). *Sleeping beauty: The story of the ballet.* New York: Atheneum.

Houston, G. (1996). *Mountain valor.* Madison, WI: Turtleback Books.

Howard, E. (1987). *Mystery of the metro.* New York: Random House.

Hughes, M. (1996). *Invitation to the game.* New York: Pocket Books.

Hunt, I. (1965). *Across five Aprils.* New York: Grosset & Dunlap.

Jacobs, H. (1973). *Cajun night before Christmas.* New York: Pelican.

Kalman, E. (1995). *Tchaikovsky discovers America.* New York: Scholastic.

Kanaly, M. (1998). *Virus clans.* New York: Ace Books.

Kress, N. (1996). *Beggar's ride.* New York: Tor Books.

Lagerlof, S. (1912). *The wonderful adventures of Nils* (V. S. Howard, Trans.). New York: Doubleday, Page.

LeMieux, A. C. (1999). *Do angels sing the blues?* Minneapolis, MN: Econo-Clad Books.

Leonard, A. (1988). *Tina's chance.* New York: Viking.

LeTord, B. (1995). *A blue butterfly: A story about Claude Monet.* New York: Doubleday.

Levin, I. (1977). *The boys from Brazil.* New York: Dell.

Lipsyte, R. (1993). *The chemo kid.* New York: HarperCollins.

Llewellyn, J. (1991). *Deadeye.* New York: Summit Books.

Lobel, A. (1998). *No pretty pictures: A child of war.* New York: Greenwillow.

London, J. (1996). *Hip cat.* New York: Chronicle Books.

Love, D. A. (1998). *Three against the tide.* New York: Holiday House.

Lowry, L. (1994). *The giver.* New York: Dell.

Lyon, G. (1991). *Cecil's story.* New York: Orchard/Watts.

Macy, S. (1996). *Winning ways: A photohistory of American women in sports.* New York: Henry Holt.

Mandela, N. (1996). *Mandela: An illustrated autobiography.* Boston: Little Brown.

Mayer, M. (1995). *Turandot.* New York: Morrow Avon.

McCurdy, M. (1994). *Escape from slavery: The boyhood of Frederick Douglass in his own words.* New York: Alfred A. Knopf.

McDevitt, J. (1995). *Engines of God.* New York: Ace Books.

McDonald, J. (2001). *Spellbound.* New York: Farrar, Strauss & Giroux.

McKissack, P. (1997). *A picture of freedom.* New York: Scholastic.

Monceaux, M. (1994). *Jazz: My music, my people.* New York: Alfred Knopf.

Moore, R. (1991). *Distant thunder: A sequel to the Christmas surprise.* Scottdale, PA: Herald.

Mori, K. (1993). *Shizuko's daughter.* New York: Henry Holt.

Morris, G. (1990). *The last confederate.* Minneapolis, MN: Bethany House.

Mowat, F. (1979). *Never cry wolf.* New York: Bantam Books.

Murphy, J. (1992). *The long road to Gettysburg.* New York: Clarion.

Murphy, J. (2000). *The long road to Gettysburg.* New York: Clarion.

O'Dell, S. (1979). *The captive.* Boston: Houghton Mifflin.

O'Dell, S. (1981). *The feathered serpent.* Boston: Houghton Mifflin.

O'Dell, S. (1983). *The amethyst ring.* Boston: Houghton Mifflin.

Oppel, K. (1993). *Dead water zone.* Boston: Little Brown.

Paulsen, G. (1998). *Soldier's heart.* New York: Delacorte.

Peck, R. (1991). *Unfinished portrait of Jessica.* New York: Delacorte Press.

Perez, N. (1990). *The slopes of war.* Boston: Houghton Mifflin.

Pinkney, A. D. (1999). *Silent thunder.* New York: Hyperion Books.

Powell, R. (1999). *Tribute to another dead rock star.* New York: Farrar, Straus & Giroux.

Preston, R. (1995). *The hot zone.* New York: Doubleday.

Price, L. (1990). *Aida.* New York: Harcourt Children's Books.

Pullman, P. (1992). *The broken bridge.* New York: Alfred A. Knopf.

Radin, R.Y. (2000). *Escape to the forest.* New York: HarperCollins.

Reeder, C. (1998). *Across the lines.* Madison, WI: Turtleback Books.

Richter, H. P. (1970). *Friedrich* (E. Kroll, Trans.). New York: Holt, Rinehart & Winston.

Rinaldi, A. (1988). *The last silk dress.* New York: Holiday.

Rinaldi, A. (1994). *In my father's house.* New York: Scholastic.

Ritchie, A. (1991). *Erin McEwan, your days are numbered.* New York: Random House.

Robertson, J. (1992). *Civil War! America becomes one nation.* New York: Alfred A. Knopf.

Sandler, M. (1995). *Immigrants.* New York: HarperCollins.

Sargent, P. (1988). *Alien child.* New York: Harper & Row.

Savage, J. (2000). *Kobe Bryant: Basketball big shot.* Minneapolis, MN: Lerner Publishing Group.

Schattschneider, D. (1990). *Visions of symmetry: Notebooks, periodic drawings, and related works of M. C. Escher.* New York: W. H. Freeman.

Schroeder, A. (1996). *Satchmo's blues.* New York: Doubleday.

Schultz, R. (1992a). *Looking inside sports aerodynamics.* Santa Fe, NM: John Muir.

Schultz, R. (1992b). *Looking inside the brain.* Santa Fe, NM: John Muir.

Shakur, T. (1999). *The rose that grew from concrete.* New York: Simon & Schuster.

Shreve, S. (1999). *Goalie.* Minneapolis, MN: Econo-Clad Books.

Shura, M. F. (1991). *Gentle Annie: The true story of a Civil War nurse.* New York: Scholastic Books.

Sills, L. (1993). *Visions: Stories about women artists.* Morton Grove, IL: Albert Whitman.

Silver, N. (1990). *No tigers in Africa.* New York: E. P. Dutton.

Silver, N. (1991). *An eye for color.* New York: E. P. Dutton.

Slonozewski, J. (1999). *The children star.* New York: Tor Books.

Sommers, B. (1990). *The uncertainty principle.* New York: Fawcett.

Stanley, D. (1996). *Leonardo da Vinci.* New York: Morrow.

Stanley, J. (1994). *I am an American.* New York: Crown.

Thomas, V. M. (1997). *Lest we forget: The passage from Africa to slavery and emancipation.* New York: Crown.

Thompson, W. (1990). *Ludwig van Beethoven.* New York: Penguin.

Turner, R. M. (1991). *Rosa Bonheur.* Boston: Little Brown.

Vos, I. (2000). *The key is lost.* New York: HarperCollins

Weaver, W. (1993). *Striking out.* New York: HarperCollins.

Weil, L. (1991). *Wolfer: The first six years in the life of Wolfgang Amadeus Mozart.* New York: Holiday House.

Wieler, D. (2001). *Drive.* Toronto: Groundwood Books.

Wilhelm, K. (1991). *Death qualified: A mystery of chaos.* New York: St. Martin's Press.

Willard, N. (1991). *Pish posh, said Hieronymous Bosch.* New York: Harcourt Brace.

Williams, L. (1999). *Behind the bedroom wall.* Minneapolis, MN: Econo-Clad Books.

Williams-Garcia, R. (1995) *Like sisters on the homefront.* New York: Puffin Books.

Winter, K. (1999). *Katrina: A novel.* New York: Scholastic.

Wisler, G. C. (1991). *Red cap.* New York: Lodestar/Dutton.

Wisler, G. C. (1994). *Mr. Lincoln's drummer.* Birmingham, AL: Lodestar Books.

Wooding, S. (1994). *The painter's cat.* New York: Putnam.

Wynne-Jones, T. (1996). *The maestro.* London, UK: Orchard Books.

CHAPTER NINE

Study Strategies

ANTICIPATION GUIDE

Directions: Read each statement carefully and decide whether you agree or disagree with it, placing a check mark in the appropriate *Before Reading* column. When you have finished reading and studying the chapter, return to the guide and decide whether your anticipations need to be changed by placing a check mark in the appropriate *After Reading* column.

	BEFORE READING		AFTER READING	
	Agree	*Disagree*	*Agree*	*Disagree*
1. Research has shown that there is a best strategy for studying.	_____	_____	_____	_____
2. Most adolescents reread and memorize as their method of studying and preparing for exams.	_____	_____	_____	_____
3. The gifted, AP, and college-bound students know how to study.	_____	_____	_____	_____
4. Task knowledge is a must if students are to profit from the use of a strategy.	_____	_____	_____	_____

Shifting the responsibility for learning from the teacher to the student and improving the capabilities of students for engaging in self-directed learning might be expected to have benefits for both students and teachers. First, with respect to teachers and schools, these changes might provide an economical way to increase total learning without the need to allocate additional teaching or instructional time.... Giving students more responsibility for their learning might also be expected to reduce somewhat the burden that teachers bear for effecting student achievement. Having students share in this responsibility might be expected to reduce teachers' anxiety that they alone are the cause of students' successes and failures.

—Thomas, Strage, and Curley (1988)

As the preceding quotation suggests, students who are strategic learners will profit, as will their teachers. Students will profit because the use of study strategies is positively related to their academic performance. In general, students who use strategies that demand their critical thinking and elaboration are more likely to do better on their assignments, exams, and papers (Simpson & Nist, 1997; Weinstein, Husman, & Dierking, 2000).

Study strategies are deliberate, planned, and conscious activities that students select to achieve a particular goal. Students typically employ study strategies when they need to retain material for the purpose of taking a test, writing a paper, participating in class discussion, or any other demonstration of their learning. When does the need for strategy training begin? As soon as students are required to retain material for a later purpose, typically when they encounter their first expository textbook—around fourth grade.

As we mentioned in Chapter 2 in our fifth principle of active learning, middle school and high school students must have a variety of strategies to be effective in their studying and learning. Researchers have suggested that the strategies we teach students should include important cognitive and metacognitive processes such as being able to:

 Go to *http:// www.prenhall. com/brozo*, select Chapter 9, then click on Chapter Objectives to provide a focus for your reading.

The focus on creating strategic learners is a win-win situation for everyone—students, teachers, and parents.

1. select important ideas and restate them in your own words.

2. reorganize and elaborate on these ideas.

3. ask questions concerning the significance of targeted information and ideas.

4. monitor when you know and when you do not understand.

5. establish goals and define your tasks.

6. evaluate plans and reflect on the strategies you selected.

Because of their importance, these cognitive and metacognitive processes are reflected by the strategies we present in this chapter.

We should also note that this chapter is an extension of Chapter 3; both describe and discuss how to build active learners. Whereas Chapter 3 emphasizes teacher-generated strategies that encourage elaborative processing of text and reflection (e.g., discussion webs and study guides), this chapter emphasizes student-initiated strategies that promote strategic reading and independent learning. In particular, this chapter is devoted to ways of incorporating strategy training into your classroom instruction.

CASE STUDY

Jan is an English teacher who teaches several different classes of gifted students who all plan on attending college. Although most of them are receiving good grades in advanced courses such as chemistry and world history, Jan knows that these students have mediocre study habits. She has discovered in conversations with her students that they do not read their textbooks, choosing instead to listen carefully in class as the teachers discuss the material. The district coordinator for gifted education has provided Jan with a workbook that contains study tips and memory enhancement exercises, but her students have complained bitterly about the exercises. Jan also feels a certain amount of pressure from the parents who have told her on various occasions that they expect the high school to prepare their children for the rigors of college.

To the Reader:

As you read and work through this chapter on study strategies, decide what Jan might do to improve her approach with these gifted students. Consider the guidelines and strategies we examine and how Jan might use this information to help her students become more active learners.

◄◦►

GUIDELINES FOR TEACHING STUDY STRATEGIES

In order to develop active learners who have a variety of strategies for learning in your content area, there are some basic guidelines drawn from current research and theory. The eight guidelines presented in this section describe the conditions that are necessary for students to become active learners. A discussion of these guidelines follows.

Emphasize the Importance of Task Knowledge

Imagine that you are training to run a machine in a factory, and you prepare for your job by reading a manual about how to operate it. You read the manual a couple of times, skimming over it before you begin working. Then you are put on the machine and told to get started. Every few minutes you need to consult the manual; eventually, the machine breaks down, and your boss is at your throat. The reason for your failure? A clear mismatch between the way you trained and the task's demands.

Now imagine that a student is studying for a biology test by using flash cards with the names of the hormones secreted by the endocrine system on one side and their definitions on the other. On the test, students are asked to interpret several diagrams, explaining the relationship between the hormones and their impact on other glands and human behavior. What grade would you predict for this student? Would she pass the test? Was there a match between the way she studied and what she needed to know for the test?

Like the factory worker, this student experienced a mismatch between the strategy and the demands of the task. That is, the biology test required the students to integrate the information about the hormones in the endocrine system. The student, however, focused on rote memorization of definitions rather than the relationships between concepts.

These two examples point out the importance of the principle of **transfer appropriateness**. This principle states that the more appropriate the match between a study process and an academic task, the more easily information can be transferred to long-term memory. When students select strategies that match the tasks they have been assigned, their academic performance will be enhanced (Nist & Simpson, 2000). Conversely, many failures or mediocre performances by students can be explained by a mismatch between their perceptions of the task and their teacher's perceptions (Simpson & Nist, 1997).

The implication of this principle is that students must be taught how to analyze the tasks they will encounter in their content-area courses. Tasks, according to Doyle (1983), can be characterized in terms of their products and thinking processes. The products are the papers, projects, lab reports, or tests that students must complete for a course. More important than the product are the thinking processes that students must employ in order to complete the product. For example, if students are assigned a paper for a government class, that paper is the product. If the teacher asks the students to read an editorial by George Will and critique it, the thinking processes for that paper are far more involved than those required for a paper summarizing Will's key ideas. Students must be able to determine and understand the levels of thinking demanded in their academic tasks. More important, they need to be shown that it is acceptable for them to seek information about the nature of their tasks and about other ways they will be held accountable for their learning. With that information, they can make informed decisions about which study strategy to employ.

Not only should we teach students how to analyze an academic task such as the one required by the government teacher, but we, as teachers, should provide clear and explicit information about what we want students to do and how we want them to do it. By sharing product and process information with our students, we ensure that they will have the task knowledge to make informed strategy decisions.

When teachers are explicit about the tasks they assign, students find it easier to learn.

Remember the When, Why, and How of Strategy Use

In Chapter 2, we described active learners as those who have knowledge (i.e., declarative, procedural, and conditional) and control of strategies. Here we reiterate that active learners need to develop a repertoire of adaptive, flexible strategies and an ability to use the most appropriate ones to match the task demands of the content areas they are reading and studying. To do this, we need to teach students the *when,* or best specific applications of the strategy; the *whys,* or advantages; the limitations; and the *hows,* or steps of the strategy. If students lack procedural and conditional knowledge about a strategy, they will not be likely to abandon their typical approaches of memorizing, which they find more comfortable and accessible, in favor of more elaborative and appropriate strategies (Nist & Simpson, 2000; Hofer, Yu, & Pintrich, 1999).

Take the Time to Develop Students' Strategic Expertise

Pressley (2000) and others have pointed out that students do not quickly transfer or use a new strategy they just have been taught. Most study strategies involve complex processes that cannot be mastered in brief teaching lessons or artificial exercises packaged in workbooks. Admittedly, students may learn the steps of a strategy from such instructional approaches, but they will not gain the conditional and procedural knowledge necessary for them to transfer the strategy to their own tasks.

We believe it is critical for any teacher interested in training students to use study strategies to accept this principle; otherwise, the teacher and the class may give up on a strategy, in spite of its potential, too early, before students have had a chance to develop control and expertise.

We can help students employ effective strategics if we provide them explicit instruction and useful feedback.

Validated training approaches and models (e.g., Pressley, 2000; Simpson, Hynd, Nist, & Burrell, 1997) are numerous, but they all agree that instruction should be direct, informed, and explanatory. In other words, students can be taught to employ a strategy if they receive intensive instruction over a reasonable period of time that is characterized by (1) a description of the strategy and its characteristics, (2) an explanation of why the strategy is important, (3) think-alouds about how the strategy is used, including the processes involved, (4) explanations as to when and where it is appropriate to apply the strategy, and (5) guidelines for evaluating whether the strategy is working and what to do if it is not. In addition, teachers should provide students with strategy examples from their content-area textbooks or materials, guided practice during class, and qualitative feedback on their strategy attempts.

We have found it takes at least a few weeks before students begin to feel comfortable with a particular strategy. One way we have found to facilitate this process is by allowing students to practice the strategy with material that is easy to understand. In this way, students avoid overcrowding the cognitive workbench and can focus most of their attention on learning the strategy. Gradually, we increase the difficulty of the material until students demonstrate that they can apply the strategy to their own textbooks. This may take several weeks, but the time is well spent because our primary goals of study strategy training are to develop students' strategic expertise and ultimate independence in learning.

Know the Study Strategies You Teach

We could restate the principle "Know the study strategies you teach" by saying "Practice what you preach." In our experience, students respond most favorably to strategy instruction when the teacher is credible and enthusiastic. This means you must be familiar with the strategies you offer. If you plan to teach your students a text-study system, for instance, you need to know the system inside and out, including its strengths, limitations, and applications. One way to gain this knowledge is to learn and practice the system with your school reading. If you are taking university course work, use the strategy you are teaching your students in your own studying. Then, when students have questions about the strategy, you will be able to answer them from firsthand experience. Examples of your own strategies can also be illuminating for students because they often hold the misconception that "sophisticated readers" can read and remember everything on the first try. One of our graduate students shared with her students the chart she had created to learn the different theories of reading as one way of explaining the strategy of comparison and contrast charts. Students are sensitive to your attitudes about what you teach; if you can demonstrate your belief in the value and utility of study strategies, they will respond to your enthusiasm.

Create Situations in Which Students Can Transfer Strategies to Realistic Content-Area Tasks

Students need real, meaningful purposes for reading and studying. To teach them how to take notes in a particular way that has little to do with how they are actually supposed to organize and process the material in your class and other classes may mean that they will know how to take notes your way, but they will find no reason to do so. What good is it that students can list the steps of a strategy or complete a workbook activity using that strategy? As we have said many times, strategies should never be taught in isolation from authentic reading and study tasks.

One way to increase the likelihood that students will actually use the strategies they are taught is by linking strategy training to learning across the content areas. A nearby high school provides an example of this approach. The high school requires all incoming first-year students to take a reading and study skills course during their first quarter. The course is designed to teach them how to read and study their textbooks, manage their time, and prepare for and take tests. In addition, they are taught to take notes from their class discussions or lectures in a specific form, called the *split-page method* (Palmatier, 1973). Split-page notes are taken on note paper that is divided into two columns, the left side for key idea statements or questions and the right side for the information presented during class (this method is explained in greater detail later in this chapter). Here is what is so special about the way students in this high school learn this strategy: Although they are taught and practice the strategy in reading class, they are given the opportunity to apply it in their biology class. Biology teachers reinforce this method of note taking by talking to their students about how split-page notes can be taken for text content and for their lectures. To facilitate this process, they show students examples of their lecture material organized in the split-page format, and they constantly remind and encourage students to use the method. In sum, all teachers must carefully orchestrate strategy transfer.

An all-school approach helps to build active, strategic learners.

Acknowledge the Importance of Students' Belief Systems

As mentioned in Chapter 2, students' "will" is as important as their strategy "skill" (Paris, Lipson, & Wixson, 1983). Equally important are the beliefs students have about learning. Rather than attributing academic success to chance or the whims of a teacher, active learners with high **self-efficacy** ratings attribute what they learn to their own effort and strategy use. In contrast, students with low self-efficacy are more likely to attribute their failures to external factors (e.g., the test was not fair) or to a fixed ability that they cannot change (Zimmerman, 2000). For example, it is not atypical to hear adolescents say something like this: "I am not good at math and never will be." As a result, these students decide to give up before they even enter the classroom or at the first setback or challenge. Interestingly, you will find that students' self-efficacy varies across the content areas. For example, a student may have a strong sense of self-efficacy in a history course but feel totally overwhelmed or frustrated in an English course that requires her to write critical or creative responses to what she reads (Hofer & Pintrich, 1997).

Because some students believe learning involves only the memorization of facts, they perceive most academic tasks as situations involving minimal effort or mental energy. As a result, it will be difficult for you to convince them that they need to use strategies that encourage them to think critically and elaboratively about content-area concepts. The best way to counteract students' naive conceptions about learning is to persuade them that learning is often hard and rarely quick or absolute.

Encourage Students to Modify Strategies to Meet Personal Needs and Styles

The consummate active learner understands the tasks, understands how he learns best, and then selects and modifies strategies to meet his needs.

It never fails. After a semester of teaching study strategies, say a note-taking system, none of the students' notes look exactly like ours or like anyone else's in the class. But this should be expected because there are no prototypes, no answer keys. We all make choices and decisions based on what we think is the most important information to include in our notes, and we modify the format to fit those perceptions. Students need to be able to make these choices and changes. After all, each of our study needs is personal, and what better time to learn how to stress personal adaptations than when students are being trained to use study strategies? Help students develop ownership of the strategies by allowing them to decide how study strategies should be modified to meet their needs.

The fundamental point is this: Do not be too prescriptive, mechanical, or formulaic when teaching students study strategies. Otherwise, you shift emphasis away from your intention of having students modify study processes to making judgments about their products.

Use Homework and Other Assignments to Reinforce Study Strategies

The topic of homework is often overlooked in teacher education programs. Yet, anyone who is or has been a middle school or high school teacher knows that students who read and study do so at home. We also know from research studies that students spend very little time reading and doing assigned work outside of the classroom because they know they can rely on their notes and teacher-provided review sheets to pass their exams (Campbell, Voekl, & Donahue, 1997; Moje, 1996).

We briefly take up this topic here because we believe that homework, when appropriately designed and assigned, can play an important role in reinforcing students' study strategies and in encouraging students to read their textbooks. Our data for this discussion do not come from empirical research but rather from anecdotal evidence, interviews with content-area teachers, and our teaching experiences with high school and college students.

Classroom teachers interested in helping students see the connection between how they read and study their textbooks and the course expectations and requirements should assign homework that asks students to integrate particular strategies with the learning of the course content. For example, a biology teacher who wants her students to learn the different glands and hormones in the endocrine system could assign homework requiring them to create a chart to summarize those concepts. In class, the students could brainstorm what information might be contained in the charts (e.g., locations, functions) and examine possible formats. The following day, students could meet in groups to compare and discuss their charts and identify any ambiguous information. The teacher could also give the students a quiz about the endocrine system, allowing them to use their newly created charts. In this way, the teacher receives feedback on how students are progressing in their mastery of the study strategy simultaneously with how well they are learning the course content.

In addition to these ideas for using homework to apply newly learned study strategies, we offer the following guidelines for assigning strategy homework:

- Study strategy homework assignments should be made as a result of careful initial planning of a unit's themes and concepts.

- Homework should be related to the amount of instruction given and the time spent teaching a study strategy.

- If study strategy homework is given, it should be given to all students, and adjustments should be made for various ability levels.

- Homework should be used as feedback on students' progress toward strategy mastery.

- Study strategy homework should be meaningful and functional.

- Specific feedback should be provided on students' homework assignments in a timely fashion.

Students frequently perceive homework as an infringement on their time for extracurricular activities, part-time jobs, or recreation. When homework is given judiciously and when it is meaningfully related to the course expectations, there is a greater chance that it will be completed. In turn, students who practice applying strategies to their course content will become competent readers and successful independent learners.

Based on these eight guidelines of effective study strategy instruction, we next describe some basic processes that are important to almost any content area.

BASIC PROCESSES IMPORTANT TO ACTIVE LEARNING

Students who are active learners understand how their textbooks are organized, how to interpret and record an assignment, how to begin reading their assignments, and how to interact with the material. As content-area teachers, we cannot assume that students have mastered these basic processes in the elementary grades.

Knowing the Format and Organization of a Textbook

Never assume that students understand the format of your textbook or that they know how to use all of its special features.

One basic strategy that students often overlook is the effective use of the textbook. We have known college students who have carried their psychology textbook around for 6 weeks without knowing that there was a glossary at the back or that a list of key terms was included at the end of each chapter. If students can learn how their textbook is organized and capitalize on those features as they read and study, they can increase their concentration, understanding, and remembering.

Carolina, an eighth-grade social studies teacher, had attended a district workshop where the speaker stressed the importance of introducing the format and organization of textbooks to students. Before the workshop she had assumed, as had many other teachers, that most students take the time to explore their textbooks once they receive them. Like most, she had merely handed out her textbook and assigned the first chapter of reading. Taking part of a class period to explain the "obvious characteristics" of a textbook seemed a bit unnecessary, but she decided to give it a try. She began her discussion by explaining that textbooks contain only the theories, perspectives, and conclusions of certain scholars under contract from a publisher. She then asked the students to read the title page and preface of their textbook to gain information about their authors. The students discovered that three individuals had written their text. After a discussion about the authors, Carolina stressed that the content of all their readings would be filtered through the biases and personal opinions of the authors.

After that brief orientation, which many students found intriguing, Carolina distributed a textbook introduction activity designed to orient her students further to their textbook (Figure 9.1). In the workshop, she had learned that many students know neither where important textbook parts are located nor how they function. She therefore paired her students and gave them 15 minutes to familiarize themselves with the parts of the textbook through the questions on the activity sheet. Each chapter, as the students soon discovered, had a general introduction; a summary that listed key ideas; and boldfaced headings, subheadings, and italicized words. Carolina closed the period with a discussion of how these aids could help them as they read and studied their first assignment.

Carolina received positive feedback from her students on this lesson and decided to incorporate it into her beginning-of-the-year routine. We know some

Title of textbook _____
Author(s) _____
Copyright date _____ Has the book been revised? _____

1. Read the **preface** carefully and completely. Summarize briefly what it says.
2. Find the **table of contents.** Answer these questions after studying it:
   a. Are the chapters broken down into many or few subheadings?
   b. Can you list five or six major topics included in the table of contents?
3. Find the **index.** On what page does it begin? Name two or three types of information you find there.
4. Find the **glossary.** How can it help you?
5. Find the **appendix.** What type of information can you find in it?
6. Find one **bibliography.** List two authors or titles that interest you.
7. Examine Chapter 1. Check the organizational features available in this textbook:
   a. Introduction _____
   b. Marginal notes _____
   c. Italicized or underlined words _____
   d. Boldfaced headings _____
   e. Pictures _____ Graphs _____ Maps _____ Charts _____
   f. Internal summaries _____ Summary _____
   g. Questions at the end _____

FIGURE 9.1   Getting Acquainted With Your Textbook

school districts insist that all teachers take the time during the first week of school to introduce their textbook with an activity like the one in Figure 9.1. The form can obviously be modified to fit any content-area textbook. What Carolina and many other teachers hope is that students will become critical and savvy consumers of text who will conduct their own "get-acquainted" activities before they begin reading.

Interpreting and Recording Assignments Correctly and Completely

If students are to select the appropriate strategies, they must understand all the nuances of their academic tasks. They must also record these tasks or assignments correctly and completely so that they can refer to them while they read and study at home. We, as content-area teachers, can help students in two fundamental ways. First, we must constantly strive to provide students tasks that are explicit and descriptive. For example, a sophomore English teacher we observed provided her students with the following task information:

> On Friday you will have an essay exam on the five short stories we have studied thus far. The essay questions will ask you to analyze how the themes of these short stories are alike and different. Your essay will be evaluated on

how well you answer the questions and provide specific examples of your points. I will not be grading on spelling and mechanics, but I do expect organization in the form of thesis statements. The exam is worth 80 points, 40 points per essay. Any questions?

Notice that she shared with her students the following task information: (a) what they will be doing—taking an essay exam; (b) what thinking processes they would be involved in—analyzing the short stories in order to compare and contrast them; (c) what overall point value would be assessed and when it would occur; and (d) what criteria she would use to evaluate their essay answers—their written answers must be organized, answer the question, and provide specific examples.

The second way we can assist students to become independent learners is to provide them questions they should ask themselves about an assignment or task they must complete. For example, the following are predictable questions that students could use for almost any course:

Some teachers have posted these six questions on their school's web page in order to help parents as they interact with their children.

1. What is the assignment? What am I to produce? What is the purpose of the assignment?

2. What resources should I use? Textbook? Class discussion notes? Computer databases? Outside reading? Videos? Class demonstrations or laboratory experiments?

3. What are the requirements for format, length, or size? Must the assignment be typed? In ink? Stapled?

4. When is the assignment due? Are there any penalties for late work?

5. How will this assignment be evaluated? How much does it count in the total evaluation process?

6. Do I understand all the words that the teacher used to explain the assignment?

The last question is particularly critical because we often use words such as *critique* or *respond creatively* when we give students assignments, assuming that they know what we mean. More often than we would like, students do not understand these words and the processes they embody (Simpson & Nist, 1997, 2001).

We know a team of seventh-grade teachers that have these six questions listed on a poster in their classroom in order to encourage students to "get all the information" when they write their assignments in their notebooks. In addition, they encourage and reinforce students to ask questions about assignments. A serendipitous result of training students to record their assignments in this fashion has been vocal endorsement from the students' parents, who are frequently bewildered by what homework their children should be doing each night. These six questions have reduced students' and parents' bewilderment and frustration.

Previewing

Dominique and Turkessa were preparing to go to a performance of the local symphony. As they were dressing, Turkessa suggested that they read about the composer, Bach, to learn about his life and musical philosophy. Dominique rummaged through their stacks of books in the basement and eventually found the trusty music appreciation text he had used years ago in undergraduate school. He read aloud about Bach as they finished dressing and continued reading to Turkessa as she drove downtown. They arrived at Symphony Hall early and read further from the program about the compositions to be performed that evening. By the time the first note sounded, they had established a context for the music that greatly aided their interpretation and appreciation of what they heard.

This kind of context setting is at the heart of the **previewing strategy**. Students often seem to begin a reading assignment much like those people who entered Symphony Hall and scurried to find their seats just before the conductor's entrance on the stage. The music rushed over them, but because they did not plan for listening, they may not have known what the composer intended to communicate with his music. Likewise, when students are expected to gain a complete understanding of their text but approach their reading by opening their books to the beginning of the assignment and simply plowing forward, they fail to prepare for the flood of words they encounter and may find themselves in the middle of the chapter unsure about what the author is trying to convey.

To prepare for the reading assignments, students should be taught how to preview. The previewing strategy is a logical follow-up to learning the format and organization of a textbook because it requires students to know and use those features. As students preview, they read the introductory paragraphs, summaries, topic markers or boldfaced headings, visual aids, summaries, and questions or problems provided by the author. Once students have previewed these text features, they need to take a moment to reflect on this information, allowing the ideas to sink in. By previewing, students should be able to answer questions such as these: (a) What is the chapter about? (b) What are some key terms I will learn? (c) How should I read this chapter and divide up this task? We know several 10th-grade history teachers who demonstrate the steps of the preview strategy during the first month of school. Gradually, they shift the responsibility to their students to preview their assignments by assigning them to complete a worksheet similar to the one in Figure 9.2. This particular example guides students through the process of identifying key ideas and seeing the relationships between these ideas.

Why should students preview? Because students may initially resist such a strategy, it is important to discuss the advantages of previewing with them. In these discussions, stress the fact that previewing provides a meaningful organization of the material to be learned. As students read introductory paragraphs and look over headings and subheadings, they will form a mental outline of the major topics and subtopics. This information will provide students with the data

Previewing has so many advantages, but students often overlook this basic strategy.

Directions: We previewed most of the chapter in class. In order to understand how the chapter is organized, complete the following skeletal outline. You can do this by identifying the author's major headings and subheadings. As you do this activity, be thinking of possible test questions.

The Age of Jackson: Chapter 10

  I. The New Two-Party System Develops (**1st MAIN TOPIC**)

    A. Adams's election enrages Jacksonians

    B. Adams's policies are unpopular

      1.

      2.

    C.

    D.

    E.

 II. Jackson Shows a New Presidential Style (**2nd MAIN TOPIC**)

    A. Common people become leaders

      1.

      2.

      3.

      4.

    B. Jackson removes the Indians

      1.

      2.

      3.

      4.

    C.

III. (NOW, YOU FINISH THE OUTLINE. THERE ARE A TOTAL OF FOUR MAIN TOPICS IN THIS CHAPTER.)

FIGURE 9.2   **Previewing Activity**

they need to make judgments about their readiness to learn the material, the difficulty of the material, and the actions they may need to take to learn the material. In addition, when students take the time to preview their textbooks before they read, they should observe an improvement in their reading fluency, concentration, and comprehension.

As a strategy, previewing is neither relevant nor appropriate for all texts and tasks. Some texts are not considerately organized, and many literature anthologies do not contain textbook markers or summaries. Hence, students will need to modify the preview strategy (i.e., read the first sentence of each paragraph when there are no textbook markers) or select a more appropriate strategy. Occasionally, some teachers may not want their students to read and study an entire chapter but instead may tell them to memorize specific processes, steps, or formulas. For example, if a chemistry teacher told her class that all they would be required to know from Chapter 3 in their textbook was the symbols and atomic weights for five specific elements, extensive previewing would not be appropriate. This example points again to the importance of students' knowing what they will be responsible for as a result of reading and studying so that they can employ the most relevant study strategy (Zimmerman, 2000).

Previewing, although not a panacea, certainly will engage students in more active reading and learning. Moreover, previewing is one of the strategies that can be initially introduced by teachers, modeled and reinforced, and then gradually shifted to students for their own responsibility and control.

Once students have previewed their text and started their reading, they must be able to identify and transform key ideas using their own words. We address that essential process next.

Summarizing Revisited

All of us summarize many times during the course of a day. When you ask your colleague in the hall, "How are you?" and she says, "Fine," she is summarizing—categorizing her collective experiences and feelings and labeling them with a single word. When you ask a fellow student about the weather and he says, "Gloomy," this also is a summary, the selection of a single word that embraces a variety of weather characteristics. Across the content areas, the ability to summarize text is perhaps one of the most essential reading skills. In fact, if you return to Chapters 2 and 3 and review the five principles that characterize active learners, you will note that summary generation involves students in all of them. Because summarizing involves students in so many cognitive and metacognitive processes, it takes time to develop expertise in summarizing. If, however, students can learn how to construct a summary using their own words, their understanding and metacognition will be enhanced. In addition, students can use their self-generated summaries to study and prepare for examinations. For example, Simpson and Nist (1990) found that students who had been trained to summarize and annotate key ideas performed significantly better on three different content-area exams than students who used traditional study methods (e.g., rereading, memorizing). Even more interesting was the finding that the students who had summarized and annotated spent half as much time studying as their counterparts who were using passive techniques.

In Chapter 3 we discussed and illustrated the power of modeling the steps involved in creating a summary. Throughout this textbook we have also suggested ways in which students can summarize what they read even though they are not allowed to annotate directly in their textbooks. In Chapter 3 we introduced the technique called the "pop quiz with an index card" that provides students a format, the index card, as a way to summarize and monitor

---

To the Student: I have checked the areas you need to work on in order to improve your summaries. Please read the checklist carefully and incorporate these suggestions when you revise your summary.

_____1. Your summary represents the author's key ideas. Good work!

_____2. You need to use your own words when summarizing the text.

_____3. Your summary focuses too much on unimportant details.

_____4. Your summary needs to focus more on key ideas and less on details.

_____5. You need to be briefer in your summary.

_____6. You need to be more specific and not so vague with your summary.

_____7. Your summary needs to show the relationships between ideas.

FIGURE 9.3   Summary Checklist

their understanding. In Chapter 7 we also shared the microtheme and exit/admit slips as two other summarizing formats. Another alternative to these formats is to suggest to your students that they summarize important ideas on yellow stickies or Post-it notes. We know a lot of students who strongly endorse this summarizing format.

When you use a checklist, you can provide students with quick, specific feedback on their attempts to master a process or strategy.

Whatever the format, it is also important to provide students feedback on their attempts to summarize or to employ any new technique or strategy (Simpson & Nist, 2001). Of course, concrete, specific feedback takes considerable time, especially when you see more than 100 students in one day. In order to provide their students quality feedback in an expedient manner, some teachers we know like to use a checklist. The checklist in Figure 9.3 is similar to one used by a global studies teacher at a local ninth grade. He tells us that he can review a class set of summaries in about 15 minutes when he uses a checklist.

In sum, if you want your students to be able to summarize what they read or hear or see in your class, they need specific steps, a format, and feedback on the quality of their summaries.

STRATEGIES FOR TAKING CLASS NOTES

If you have ever wondered why it is so difficult for your students to take notes during class discussions or during one of your demonstrations of a concept, consider all the prerequisite skills involved in note taking. Students must be able to:

1. paraphrase and summarize
2. select key ideas and discard irrelevant details
3. establish purposes for listening or observing
4. identify organizational patterns such as problem–solution or cause–effect
5. record information quickly using abbreviations and symbols

In addition to these skill prerequisites, students need some prior experiences or background information to make sense of the concepts being discussed or presented during class. In sum, taking class notes is a difficult skill for most middle school and high school students. In fact, note taking is a difficult skill for most college students (Simpson & Nist, 1997). Fortunately, this skill can be taught and reinforced across the content areas.

We have collected a variety of suggestions from content-area instructors about how they teach note taking. The following are some of the activities they use:

1.   Begin the year with a discussion of your classroom note-taking expectations. Include the *why* of taking notes, whether you will check notes, how notes will be used, and in what you would like the notes to be kept (i.e., in a spiral or three-ring notebook).

2.   Discuss the qualities of good notes in your course. Include general physical formats, organization, and content. Show examples of your own class notes or previous students' notes via handouts, the overhead projector, a web page on the computer, or the bulletin board.

3.   Model note-taking behaviors by using a *framed outline* during class. At the beginning of class, distribute a handout with the major points to be covered that day but with ample room for the development of your ideas. Specific cue words could be added for students with learning disabilities (e.g., "The second step of the tennis serve"). Then deliver your presentation and fill in the major points and details on the framed outline using the overhead projector. Require students to add your notes to their framed outline. Repeat this procedure at least once a week and gradually reduce the cues until you no longer present the notes on the overhead or on the framed outline.

4.   Teach the patterns of organizations that are common to your content area (e.g., comparison–contrast, sequence). For example, after discussing the problem–solution organizational format, the science teacher could deliver a brief lecture and assign students to note the nature of a problem, the courses of action proposed, and the advantages and disadvantages of the solutions.

5.   Teach and model physical and verbal cues that teachers commonly use during class presentations. Include physical cues such as tone, facial expressions, pace, and gestures. Include verbal cues such as "Now we will consider the second point" or "In summary." Reserve time in class to discuss the students' notes to check if they recorded the important points that were cued.

6.   Teach the common symbols and abbreviations and those unique to your specific content area. For example, students should be taught to use abbreviations such as *ex* to represent *examples* and = to represent the words *equals* or *equivalent*. Government teachers should teach students to use abbreviations such as *jud* and *leg* to represent the words *judiciary* and *legislation*.

In addition to these activities, it is important for content-area teachers to continually reinforce the usefulness and advantages of taking class notes.

Students will not continue to use a strategy unless they see it as effective and worthy of their effort (Weinstein et al., 2000). You can reinforce and reward your students in a variety of ways for taking class notes. We particularly like these four ideas and have found them to be successful with middle school and high school students:

1. Give unannounced quizzes in which students can use their class notes. Make sure that the questions asked pertain to the information and concepts you presented during the class. Students will quickly learn that it is important to listen and take detailed, organized notes.

2. After some instruction on how to take class notes, collect students' notes without warning, either at the end of the class period or the next day. Evaluate the notes and then discuss them the next day with the students.

3. Have a weekly review of class notes. Ask questions that could be answered by using the notes. Points could be awarded for correct answers. This procedure could also be used at the beginning of each class period.

4. Provide students with class time to review their notes with a partner, especially after an important lesson or before a test or quiz.

You will need to model good note-taking procedures and reinforce students on taking notes during class.

The Split-Page Note-Taking Format

Some content-area teachers like their students to take class notes in a predictable format such as the **split-page format** (Palmatier, 1973). With this format, during class students record their notes on the right-hand side of a piece of paper. Later, perhaps as a class assignment, they write on the left-hand side of the paper key idea statements in order to reduce the information and to see the big picture. The notes in Figure 9.4 illustrate how one student used the split-page format in his math class. In addition to writing key idea statements in the left-hand margin, students could be assigned to incorporate key ideas from their textbooks or other sources. In that way, they can collect and synthesize all the information about a particular concept.

Bob, a 10th-grade biology teacher, teaches his students the split-page format. He begins by asking them to take notes during class in their usual fashion. This assignment provides him and his students with some self-assessment data. Samples of actual notes produced by students are put on the overhead projector and analyzed. Bob asks the students to consider the note samples relative to the goals of studying, which stimulates discussion of the relevance and transfer appropriateness of note-taking strategies. When he introduces split-page notes, he first describes the format; then, unrehearsed, he creates a set of notes. This gives students a view of Bob's thoughts and decisions during the note-taking process. In addition, Bob demonstrates how he would study the notes by covering the right column and using the left-column entries as recall prompts, and vice versa.

"To Be Good Is Not Enough When You Dream of Being Great" 1/16/97 ①

	* Problem
	Find the slope of a line tangent to the
What is the slope	parabola $y = x^2$ at (x, x^2)
of a line tangent to	
$y = x^2$ at	
(x, x^2)?	
How do you find	* The slope of the line thru P & Q is given by
the slope of a	$M_{PQ} = \dfrac{(x+h)^2 - x^2}{(x+h) - x}$
tangent line?	
	* To find the slope of a tangent line, let
	$h = 0$. Equivalently, let Q tend to p.
Simplify the	* Simplify $\dfrac{x^2 + 2xh + h^2 - x^2}{h} = \dfrac{2xh + h^2}{h}$
equation	
$x^2 + 2xh + h^2 - x^2$	$= \dfrac{h(2x + h)}{h} = 2x + h$ So: $M_{PQ} = 2x + h$

FIGURE 9.4 Sample of Split-Page Notes from a Math Course

When students take class notes, they are involved in several elaborative reading and critical thinking processes. These processes cannot be mastered in a week or two. We emphasize that if you believe a study strategy is worth teaching, students should be given the opportunity to learn it well. More important, students need to develop facility with the strategy so that they can personalize it to the task and the course in a controlled, comfortable manner. In the next section we discuss some strategies that will assist students in synthesizing information from multiple sources.

STRATEGIES FOR SYNTHESIZING MULTIPLE SOURCES

If you teach students how to synthesize ideas from multiple sources, you have taught them a valuable skill.

Students have great difficulty organizing and synthesizing ideas from multiple sources (Moje, 1996; Simpson & Nist, 2001). Thus, when you assign students to write a paper or present a speech using several outside sources, or when you ask them to combine their class notes with the information presented in their textbooks, what they produce will often be mediocre, at best. Moreover, students may inadvertently resort to copying what they have read and listing these "borrowed ideas" without thinking about overall patterns or generalizations. What students need are organizational strategies that stimulate them to synthesize and think about content-area generalizations. We will discuss three such strategies in this section: mapping, synthesis journals, and study sheets. Please note, however, that students could certainly use several of the strategies discussed elsewhere in this text (e.g., charting in Chapter 3 or Information Charts in Chapter 7) as a strategy for synthesizing and organizing.

Mapping

Carol, resource-room teacher for students with learning disabilities, was working recently with her students on study strategies. Instead of talking to them about strategies, she spent the day meeting with students individually to discover what their study needs were and how they were presently trying to meet those needs. While sitting with Mark, a congenial, conscientious 12th grader, she listened as he tried to explain the characteristics and relationships among the three major aspects of Freud's theory of personality. He was studying for a test in his psychology course. As Mark moved back and forth from *id* to *ego* to *superego,* Carol soon became lost and said, "I need to see what you're talking about. Can you draw me a picture?" As Mark drew and Carol questioned, they created a diagram to represent Freud's theory (Figure 9.5). When finished, they both looked at the diagram they had created and realized they had taken their understanding of the material to a new level. The diagram was an attempt to infer and make clear the organization and relationships in the content. Mark and Carol then talked about how students can create diagrams of complex material to use as study aids. Mark agreed that drawing out how ideas are related forces students to get their thoughts together.

Mark's discovery that creating a diagram of the material helped organize his thinking and provided a useful study aid is perhaps the best way to learn the value of the *mapping strategy.* Like other elaborative study processes, however, mapping should not be taught as a series of steps that, when followed, will automatically lead to greater comprehension and retention. Instead, students should discover through experimentation an approach to mapping that is personally meaningful and appropriate to the study task. The reason is that there is actually no set way to map content.

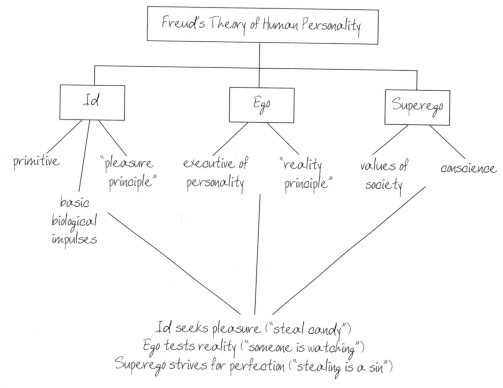

Id seeks pleasure ("steal candy")
Ego tests reality ("someone is watching")
Superego strives for perfection ("stealing is a sin")

FIGURE 9.5   Map for Freud's Theory of Human Personality

The material itself, the individual style and preference of the reader, and the study demands will all influence any map design. Notice how the specific designs of the examples of maps in Figures 9.6 and 9.7 differ yet retain these common features:

- The major theme, topic, or concept is emphasized.
- Other important ideas, concepts, and terms are boxed, circled, or otherwise set off in some way.
- Lines are used to connect related ideas.
- Information becomes more specific as map lines radiate from the major theme or topic.

We encourage students who prefer to create maps and other diagrammatic representations of text to develop a sensitivity to the clues the author provides to the organization of the content so that they can create the most accurate and useful map. For example, some content may best be represented by a cycle or flow chart, whereas other content may best be summarized in a tree diagram.

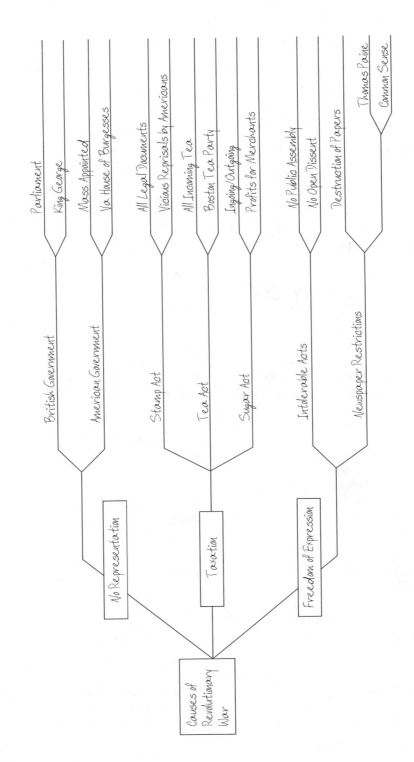

FIGURE 9.6 Map for the Causes of the Revolutionary War

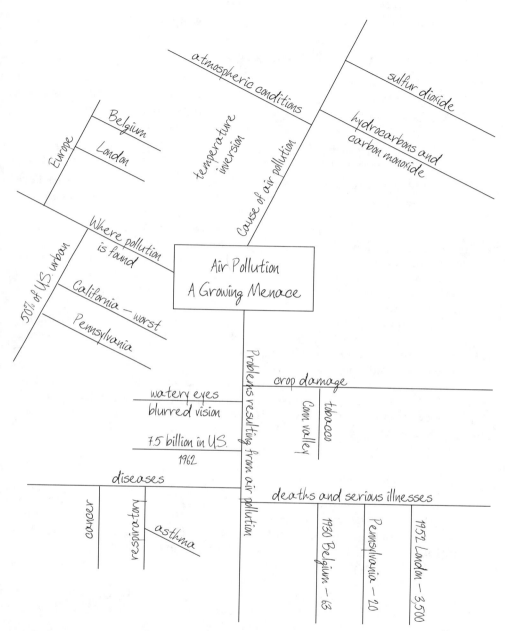

FIGURE 9.7 Map of a Chapter on Air Pollution

The following suggestions have also helped students as they map sections from their textbooks:

1. Read and think about the information before beginning to map.

2. Make sure you do not crowd your map with information because you want a memorable and precise image from which to study. Consider using legal-sized or computer paper and colored pencils and pens to differentiate ideas and make them stand out visually.

3. The act of constructing a map is a way of studying, but you will learn even more if you review your map by talking through the ideas.

Our experiences with teaching the mapping strategy have led us to believe that students either initially love the strategy or find it confusing and cumbersome. Hence, we have found it useful to encourage students to try out the strategy before rejecting it as a possible way to study. The best way to encourage students to try out any strategy is to begin with some structured practice on easy, interesting material. With the mapping strategy, you can provide initial structure by asking students to complete a skeletal or unfinished map in small groups or pairs. Students can then discuss the experience and brainstorm ways to study from their finished product.

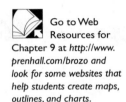

Go to Web Resources for Chapter 9 at *http://www. prenhall.com/brozo and look for some websites that help students create maps, outlines, and charts.*

You may remember that a graphic organizer, useful as a readiness strategy (see Chapter 5), is a visual representation of the key vocabulary and concepts in a text that the teacher creates and gives to students. Although maps often strongly resemble graphic organizers, the major difference between the two is that maps are student-generated. This is a critical difference. Providing students with organizational aids will promote learning; however, teaching students how to generate their own strategies will ensure that they become successful independent learners. As teachers, we need to determine how to walk that fine line between providing and promoting content-area learning.

Synthesis Journals

Synthesis journals (Burrell & McAlexander, 1998) are not really journals per se but a format that encourages students to identify, organize, and then synthesize various perspectives on an issue. As illustrated in Figure 9.8, when completing a synthesis journal, students determine and then write in the appropriate place the viewpoints and statements of authors they have read, of their teacher, of their classmates, and finally, their personal viewpoints. The center is reserved for the students to synthesize the viewpoints and then write a generalization. The synthesis journal entry in Figure 9.8 was created by a seventh grader during a unit in his health course about drug use and adolescents.

Synthesis journals obviously have many advantages. Not only do they encourage students to think critically about an issue and synthesize multiple sources, but they also stimulate students to identify and explain various perspectives, a problem many middle school and high school students have with their writing (Burrell & McAlexander, 1998). Moreover, synthesis journals give students a strategy

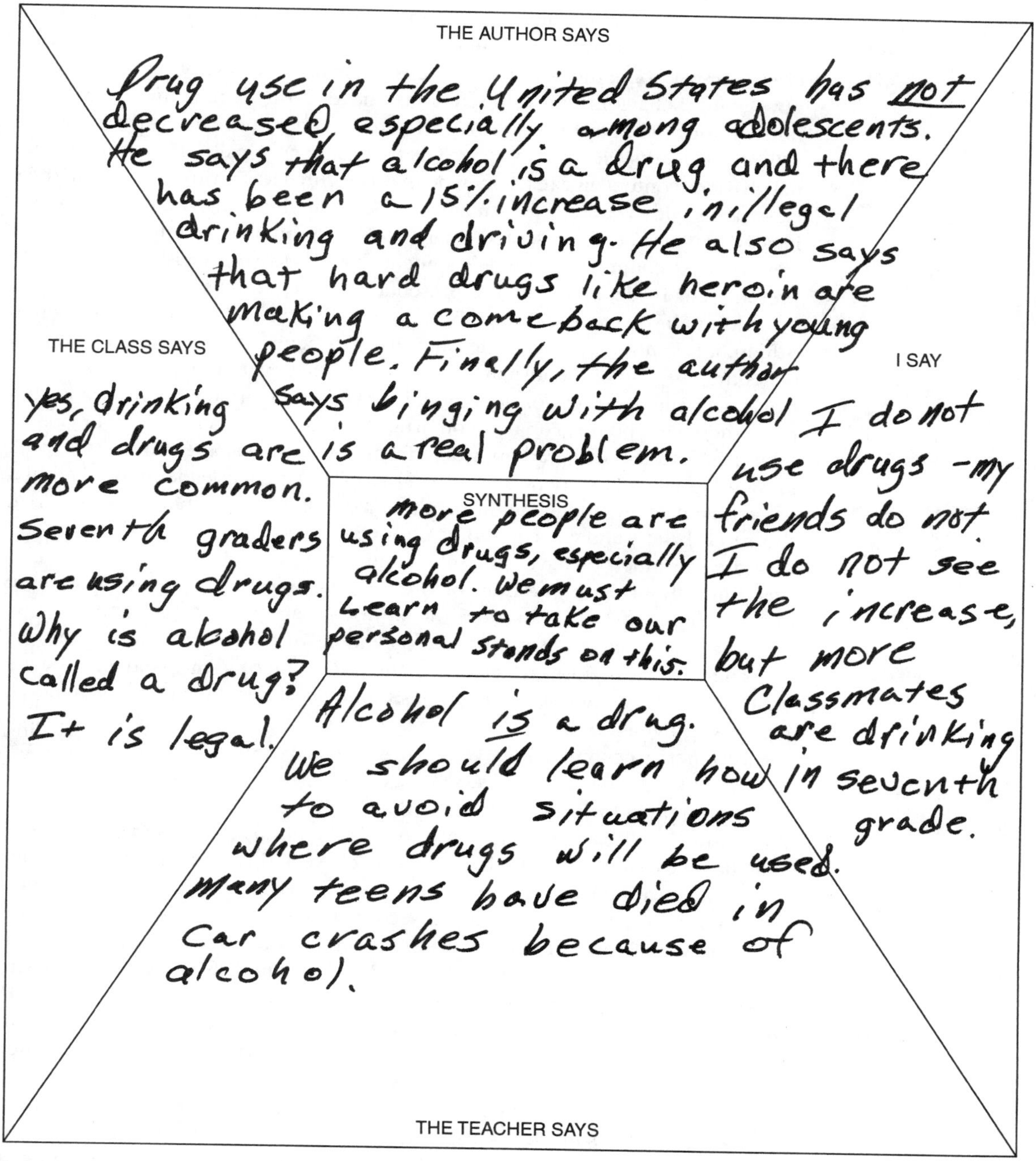

THE AUTHOR SAYS

Drug use in the United States has <u>not</u> decreased, especially among adolescents. He says that alcohol is a drug and there has been a 15% increase in illegal drinking and driving. He also says that hard drugs like heroin are making a comeback with young people. Finally, the author says binging with alcohol is a real problem.

THE CLASS SAYS

Yes, drinking and drugs are more common. Seventh graders are using drugs. Why is alcohol called a drug? It is legal.

SYNTHESIS

More people are using drugs, especially alcohol. We must Learn to take our personal stands on this.

I SAY

I do not use drugs - my friends do not. I do not see the increase, but more classmates are drinking in seventh grade.

THE TEACHER SAYS

Alcohol <u>is</u> a drug. We should learn how to avoid situations where drugs will be used. Many teens have died in car crashes because of alcohol.

FIGURE 9.8   A Synthesis Journal

that assists them in taking notes during discussions. Far too often, what the teacher says in class during a discussion becomes more important than what other classmates say about the issue being discussed. In fact, we have observed students' note-taking behaviors during discussions and discovered that they rarely took notes. If they did, they included only what the teacher said. The synthesis journal validates students' viewpoints as well as the teacher's. Finally, the synthesis journal provides content-area teachers who may use only a few written sources in their classrooms with a strategy for students to use in summarizing and thinking about ideas that have been presented orally during a unit. For example, under the "Author Says" column in Figure 9.8, students could write the ideas and viewpoints presented in a video, film, or class presentation by a guest speaker.

Although you can use the synthesis journal in many ways with your students, Adrian, a seventh-grade health teacher, likes to begin by explaining to the students the purpose of the format. She tells them that every perspective on a controversial issue deserves consideration; the synthesis journal recognizes and supports these viewpoints. For a unit on drug abuse and teenagers, Adrian begins by asking the students to read an article from a local newspaper about two well-known high school students, a football player and a cheerleader, who died in a car accident while under the influence of alcohol. She tells them to summarize the article briefly and write it in the "Author Says" section. For students who tend to write too much or have difficulty summarizing key ideas, she suggests that they think about these questions before they start writing: (1) What is the topic of this assignment? (2) What does the author say about the topic? and (3) How does the author explain, support, and defend his or her position on this topic?

The next day in class, Adrian begins the discussion by asking students to share what they have written in their synthesis journals about the author's viewpoint. Before she invites students to share their own perspectives in a class discussion, she asks them to complete the "I Say" corner. Because Adrian reserves the synthesis journal for the more controversial issues in her health course, it does not take much prompting for students to voice their opinions after writing them. Perhaps the most difficult part of the lesson is to stop the discussion so that students will take the time to record what other students believe in the "Class Members Say" section. Adrian leads the discussion but also offers her viewpoints, giving her seventh graders opportunities to fill in the last section— "The Teacher Says."

During the last 15 minutes of class, Adrian asks the students to fill in the middle section, "Synthesis." Because this synthesis was initially difficult for her students, Adrian had explained what was meant by a synthesis and then modeled the process for them on an easier topic. In addition, she described how other students had completed their "Synthesis" section on issues they had discussed in her health course. The next day in class, Adrian asks students to share what they have written. For this unit on drugs, she has students meet with their study partners to read each other's entries. Adrian's unit does not end with the synthesis journal, but it certainly starts it in the right direction. She believes that the synthesis journal, like the Discussion Web, encourages her students to think critically about highly charged issues like the ones she addresses in her health course.

Study Sheets

Study sheets are similar to maps and charts in that they help students summarize and organize ideas from a variety of sources. Kent, a 10th-grade American history instructor, teaches his students how to create study sheets because he found the strategy extremely helpful when he was a student. He introduces the study sheet strategy during his Civil Rights unit in which students read several different newspaper articles published during the 1950s and '60s and an excerpt from a recent book by John Lewis. In addition, all his students watch a television documentary about the Civil Rights movement. Kent selected these sources carefully so that they illustrated perspectives similar to and different from the ones contained in his students' history textbook.

Darrell, one of Kent's students, created the study sheet illustrated in Figure 9.9. Notice how Darrell organized the information into smaller categories (e.g., events, groups and their beliefs) and combined ideas from a variety of sources (e.g., documentary, textbook, newspaper articles). Darrell and the other students learned a considerable amount of information merely from the decisions they had to make about the categories and subcategories and their arrangement. Fortunately, Kent had frontloaded the assignment at the beginning of the year when he told his students that history was not so much about dates and wars as it was a story about people, groups, and significant events. Kent also made sure his students understood that their history textbook was just one version of the "story" written by several different authors. Hence, his students were accustomed to reading history with that lens or perspective rather than the traditional perspective that history is "just facts" (Hynd, 1999).

The beauty of the study sheet strategy is that it can be modified to fit almost any content area.

Kent tells us that his students use their study sheets in a variety of ways during the Civil Rights unit—as a resource for class discussions and small-group projects and as a test preparation strategy for the essay exam that formally closes the unit. Although Kent personally prefers the study sheet strategy, he also knows that it is important to teach his students a variety of organizing strategies and then to orchestrate situations where they can choose the ones they prefer.

The three study strategies discussed in this section will definitely help students organize and synthesize information from multiple sources and facilitate their active learning. Because metacognitive awareness is also an essential characteristic of active learners, in the next section we examine strategies for developing this characteristic.

STRATEGIES FOR CREATING METACOGNITIVE AWARENESS

As we stated in Chapter 2, active learners are metacognitively aware; that is, they know when they understand a concept and when they are lost and need to "fix up" their difficulties. Metacognitively aware students also evaluate the strategies and techniques they are using in terms of their goals. The three strategies

Topic: Civil Rights movement during the early 1960s	
Leaders	**Groups**
James Farmer: member of CORE, planned Freedom Rides James Meredith: integrated University of Mississippi, March Against Fear Martin Luther King: campaign in Alabama, March on Washington, wins Nobel Peace Prize S. Carmichael: registers voters in Mississippi; suggests the need for Black Power Malcolm X: spokesperson for Black Muslims	CORE SCLC SNCC (changes direction under Carmichael) Black Panthers
Significant Events	**Legislation**
Sit-ins (Greensboro, SC, in 1960) Freedom Riders to Alabama, Mississippi Attempts to integrate universities (Alabama, Mississippi, and James Meredith, Georgia) MLK's campaign in Birmingham, AL (1963) MLK's March on Washington (1963) Explosion in Alabama church that kills four girls (1963) Violence in Selma, Alabama (MLK, Carmichael, and Malcolm X work to register voters in 1965) SNCC launches voter registration in Mississippi (1966) March Against Fear (1966)	*Boynton v. Virginia* Public Order Laws Civil Rights Act of 1964 24th Amendment Voting Rights Act of 1965

FIGURE 9.9   Study Sheet on the Civil Rights Movement

we discuss in this section—self-generated questions, talk-throughs, and strategy evaluation—should help middle school and high school students to become more metacognitively aware.

Self-Questioning Strategies for Expository Text

We could ask students to answer the questions provided by the authors of our textbooks. Such a task, however, probably does not mesh with the goals and activities of our units of study. Moreover, these text-provided questions do not teach students how to ask their own questions or interrogate the texts they read. Yet, the ability to generate and then answer appropriate questions is essential to becoming metacognitively aware (Pressley, 2000).

One strategy for increasing students' active processing of text is to teach them how to pose and then answer task-relevant questions about what they study. Because nearly every form of testing comprises questions, asking and answering questions while studying makes good sense. The key, of course, is knowing the kinds of questions to ask.

Students can learn how to ask thought-provoking questions by using high-utility stems as question starters (King, 1992). The following question stems are useful in most content areas:

1. In my own words, what does this term mean?
2. What are the author's key ideas?
3. What is an example of . . . ?
4. How would you use . . . to . . . ?
5. What is a new or different example of . . . ?
6. In my own words, explain why . . . .
7. How does . . . affect . . . ?
8. What are the results or consequences of . . . ?
9. What are the likenesses between . . . and . . . ?
10. How is . . . different from . . . ?
11. What are the advantages of . . . ?
12. What are the disadvantages/limitations of . . . ?
13. What are the functions of . . . ?
14. What are the characteristics of . . . ?
15. Do I agree or disagree with this statement: . . . ?
16. What were the contributions/influences of . . . ?
17. How would you evaluate . . . ?

These research-validated question stems help students ask meaningful questions.

King found that students working in pairs who generated elaborative answers to question stems like those in the preceding list perform better on a content-area objective test than those who did not.

Students have options in organizing and answering their questions about expository text. They could, as did the subjects in King's studies, meet in pairs and quiz each other. They could also write their questions and answers in a format that encourages self-testing. One such format is the questions–answers strategy.

Questions–Answers Strategy

Figure 9.10 illustrates how one student used the **questions–answers strategy** to prepare for a test in an ecology course. When the questions and answers are written and organized this way, students can test themselves by folding the paper in half and reading the questions aloud. They can also test each other because a permanent written artifact is available for them to share. Because the questions–answers strategy is written, it also can be handed in to teachers for

Questions	Answers
1. What is the major source of solid waste?	Agriculture
2. What is the effect of silting on our environment?	Silting reduces oxygen production and the food supply for fish; also fouls spawning beds of fish.
3. What causes acid mine drainage?	
4. What is the danger of acid mine waste?	
5. Why was DDT banned?	
6. What chemical compound affects the central nervous system of humans and animals?	
7. What is the specific problem associated with thermal pollution?	
8. Give an example of a material that is *not* biodegradable.	

FIGURE 9.10   Questions–Answers Strategy in Preparing for a Test

their feedback. For example, by looking at the students' self-generated questions, teachers can determine what misconceptions or difficulties students are encountering with a particular concept.

Questions like the ones in Figure 9.10 do not spout from students' mouths at the first try. In fact, we have found that modeling, coaching, and specific feedback are necessary in teaching students how to ask and answer meaningful questions. One math teacher we know distributes index cards to his students and requires them to write a question every day of the year. He collects the cards, groups the questions, and then responds to them at the beginning of class. Although it may take time to teach this strategy, the results are worth the effort because students learn how to control and monitor their own learning. In the next section, we discuss how this strategy can be modified to narrative text.

Narrative Text and Self-Generated Questions

In Chapters 2 and 3, we presented the idea that texts have predictable structures and that we can teach students to take advantage of inherent properties of text to improve their reading and studying. One way to capitalize on the predictable rhetorical structure of narratives is to ask and answer questions related to story elements. The following are typical of the kinds of questions that could be asked:

1. Who is the main character?

2. What did you learn about the main character from his actions? From what he said? From what others said about him?

3. How is the setting important to this story? Could this story have taken place somewhere else?

4. What are the goals of the main character? Of the supporting characters?

5. How does the main character attempt to achieve these goals?

6. Is the main character successful in reaching his goals?

7. What is the author saying about human nature?

In a classic study conducted many years ago, Singer and Donlan (1982) devised such a set of story-structure questions and taught them to 11th-grade students. They found that compared with a group of students who simply read and reread, the students who asked questions of the story elements had a more complete understanding of the stories.

A ninth-grade literature teacher, Guy, taught his students to use the story-structure questions as a basis for creating their own questions. Guy told us this questioning process was useful because it aided his students' understanding of short stories, which in turn enlivened the class discussions. To reinforce the relevance of this study strategy, the connection between these tasks and studying stories through questioning was made explicit by giving the students typical discussion and exam questions and relating them to specific questions based on the story-structure questions. Modeling the process of question construction, Guy described how he created specific questions to prompt his understanding of essential elements in simple, familiar stories. He then asked students to work in small groups to generate questions for other simple, familiar stories. Gradually, students began working with the stories from their literature anthology. Figure 9.11 illustrates one group's set of questions developed for Hemingway's "The Short Happy Life of Francis Macomber," a short story in their literature anthology.

What is most impressive about story-structure questions is that they reflect the student's attempt to personalize and control the questioning process. Students learned that questioning can be modified to match the structure of a story and to focus their attention on its most important aspects.

The Talk-Through

If you have ever verbally rehearsed what you wanted to tell the life insurance agent who kept pestering you with phone calls, you have conducted a talk-through. A **talk-through** is a study strategy that involves verbal rehearsal of content-area concepts (Simpson, 1994). Many of the study strategies previously discussed (e.g., mapping) rely on written products. The talk-through, by contrast, involves students in expressing and explaining themselves orally. In fact, the talk-through is very much like teaching, except that the audience is imaginary. We tell students that when they conduct talk-throughs, they should imagine themselves giving a lecture on a topic to an uninformed audience. We urge students with learning difficulties to pace the room, gesture, and talk. We know one student who stood on the top of her desk and delivered her talk-throughs as a way of preparing for her essay exams in history.

Since most of us have used informal talk-throughs to practice delivering important information, it is not surprising to learn that talk-throughs as a study strategy can improve understanding and remembering of content-area concepts.

The Leading Character

Who is Francis Macomber?
What do we learn about him from what Wilson and Margot say about and to him?
What do we learn from what the author says about him?

The Goal

Why does Macomber want to kill the lion?
What does this reveal about Macomber's personality?

The Obstacles

What prevents Macomber from killing the lion?
Why does Macomber go after the buffalo with such a vengeance?

The Outcome

Why did Macomber run from the grass when the lion charged?
What does this reveal about his character?
Was Margot trying to shoot Macomber or the buffalo?

The Theme

Macomber's struggle is with himself and his self-confidence. He also struggles with the forces of nature in the lion and buffalo. And he struggles with his wife because of what she thinks about him.

FIGURE 9.11   Story-Specific Questions Based on Story-Structure Questions for Hemingway's "The Short Happy Life of Francis Macomber"

Simpson's (1994) research demonstrated that students who had been trained to generate talk-throughs performed significantly better on an objective exam (i.e., multiple-choice and true-false) and an essay exam than their counterparts who were not so trained. Even more interesting was the finding that these students predicted more accurately their overall performance on the test and on each item. In other words, the subjects who did talk-throughs were more metacognitively aware of their performance on the exam than their counterparts.

Talk-throughs can be used in any content area, but they must be tailored to the demands of the course. Depending on the course, a talk-through could contain any of the following information:

1. key ideas, using the student's own words
2. examples, characteristics, processes, steps, causes, effects
3. personal or creative reactions
4. summary statement or generalizations
5. personal applications or examples

Consequently, an effective talk-through in an American history class would probably differ from an effective talk-through in a geometry or physical education course.

Talk-throughs are especially useful for math and science courses.

Ann, an algebra teacher, has found that students profit from using the talk-through strategy in her classes, especially when it comes to internalizing the steps for solving word problems. She begins the school year by teaching the following steps to her students:

1. Read the problem carefully, underlining key words or phrases.
2. Reword the problem using the necessary facts.
3. Ask yourself, What problem do I have to solve? What is unknown?
4. Translate the reworded problem into an equation.
5. Solve the equation.
6. Check the answer by substituting the answer in the equation. Ask yourself, Does this answer make sense?
7. State the answer to the problem clearly.

Ann posts these seven steps on her bulletin board and distributes them to every student on a bookmark. Throughout the first 9 weeks, she provides her own talk-throughs on how to implement the seven steps with sample problems taken from the textbook. However, Ann has added an extra dimension to the talk-through: She uses the chalkboard as a support to her talk-through, sketching situations and setting up equations from the word problems. She has found that the verbal and visual involvement of the talk-through has greatly increased the attention and subsequent learning of her students with learning disabilities.

The following is an example of a talk-through that one of Ann's students, Damien, did at the chalkboard for his classmates:

This is the problem. "As a chef's assistant in a fancy restaurant, Kendra earns in 1 year a salary of $19,000. This is two fifths of the head chef's salary. What is the head chef's salary?" First, I will reword the problem. Two fifths of the head chef's salary is Kendra's salary. I was able to reword the problem because I knew that the word *this* in the second sentence referred to Kendra's salary. I also took out the extra words and reduced the problem to just the necessary facts and words. Second, I will translate these 10 words into symbols and numbers to create an equation. My goal for this problem is to find the chef's salary, which I do not know. Thus, I will represent this *unknown* with an X (he uses the chalkboard to do this and to reinforce the rest of his talk-through). I do know Kendra's salary: It is $19,000. I also know that two fifths of the chef's salary, or 2/5 of X or 2/5 *times* X, is $19,000. Or, stated in another way, 2/5 times X = $19,000 *or* 2/5 (X) = $19,000. I used the parentheses to stand for "multiplied by." Now I am ready to solve the problem, which is step five of the process.

Although many of the math problems in Ann's class could probably be answered without using the seven steps or the talk-through, Ann believes that verbal rehearsal on the simple problems will help students later on in the school year with the more demanding problems.

We have found from our experiences with the talk-through strategy that it helps to explain to students the steps in developing an effective talk-through. A talk-through like Damien's involves considerable cognitive and metacognitive effort and planning. The following steps, although generic, can be modified according to the content area:

1. Think about the key ideas, trends, issues, and problems. Make sure you are using your own words when you explain them.

2. Organize the key ideas in some way. This can be done on an index card, but be brief because these notes are meant only to prompt your memory.

3. Find a quiet place, close your textbook or class notes, and use your card to deliver your talk-through out loud.

4. After practicing your first talk-through, check your card to make sure you were precise and complete. Ask yourself if you made sense.

5. Find someone to listen to your talk-through. Ask your audience if you made sense.

Because Ann knows that her students will not use the talk-through strategy unless they find it has more benefits than costs, she asks them to generate a list of advantages to the strategy after they have used it several times. The following comments typify what Ann's students and other students have seen as the advantages of the talk-through strategy: (1) Talk-throughs help me determine what information I know and what information is still unclear. (2) Talk-throughs improve my understanding of key terms because I am using my own words. (3) Talk-throughs help store information in my long-term memory. (4) Talk-throughs make me more actively involved in my learning. Making these advantages explicit is a necessary part of strategy instruction because students need to know the "why" as well as the "what" and the "how" if they are to adopt new study routines or strategies.

Encouraging Students to Evaluate and Reflect

Active learners reflect upon the strategies they have employed and evaluate whether these strategies were appropriate for the task and content area (Simpson & Nist, 2001). In addition, active learners determine whether their self-selected strategies were appropriate for themselves as learners and make adjustments, when necessary, to remedy the situation and improve their academic performance. Reflecting and evaluating in this manner are highly sophisticated processes that make students even more metacognitively aware and successful in their independent learning across the content areas (Zimmerman, 2000). Moreover, when students are engaged in activities that require them to reflect and evaluate, they are less likely to attribute their performance to luck, inherent skill, or "tricky" test questions that the teacher created.

Because most students do not take the time to evaluate the effectiveness of their study techniques, teachers need to know a variety of ways to encourage students to do so.

Content-area teachers can employ a variety of ways to encourage their students to reflect and evaluate about their performance. One effective technique is to ask students to write a learning log entry once they have finished taking an exam. In this paragraph, students could describe in detail how they read and studied, discuss whether their strategy choices were appropriate, and predict their performance. If you tell students it is important to be honest in writing their entry, you will gain some useful assessment information about them. More important, by thinking about their strategies and whether they were appropriate, your students will realize that they are the ones in control of their academic performance, not you.

Kim, a 10th-grade biology teacher, asked her students to write a learning log entry immediately after they had finished their exam. Then two days later, after discussing the exam during class and going over the answers, Kim asked them to reread their entry. She then assigned her students to write a second entry describing what they had learned about themselves and what they would do differently had they had the opportunity to retake the exam. One student, Jason, wrote the following evaluation paragraphs, labeled *before* and *after*. As you read them, think about his strengths and weaknesses as an active learner and what he learned about himself.

Jason's Evaluation Paragraphs

BEFORE: Well, I predict that I will get an A on this test. I have always been smart in science. The test was about what I expected—not too hard, not too easy. I didn't think we would have to diagram the female reproductive cycle—that was a surprise. I studied by skimming the chapters and looking at my notes during homeroom. I probably studied about 10 minutes—science is my thing, so I really did not need to study much. By the way, did we talk in class about the regulation of glucose?

AFTER: Well, I guess I did not do as well as I predicted—I got a D on the test. I missed all the questions on the diagrams. My other science teachers never asked me to label and explain diagrams. I probably should have read the chapters rather than skimming them. I also should have looked at my class notes longer. If I could take the test again, I would certainly study longer, and I would memorize those diagrams you discussed with us in class. Otherwise, if I could take this test over, I probably would not change my strategies that much. I learned from this first test that biology may be different from general science.

What did you learn about Jason? What did you decide his strengths were? His weaknesses? After receiving Jason's evaluation paragraph, Kim hypothesized that Jason was not using active strategies for studying. He was merely skimming or looking at material—very passive strategies. Because Kim requires her students to integrate concepts, Jason's strategies were definitely not appropriate for the thinking processes she emphasizes in her course. Moreover, Jason probably was not listening intently in class because Kim had stressed the importance of studying the diagrams and being able to explain how hormones interact with each other. Kim decided to watch Jason carefully and to work on his definitions of what it means to read and study in a biology course. Kim, however, was not the only individual who gained important information from the learning log entries. Jason and Kim's other students were gathering important information about themselves as learners in biology.

Directions: In order to help improve your exam performance, I must know more about the techniques you are using to read and study. Please note that I am interested in how you really studied, not in how you wished you had studied. Be honest as there is no penalty for telling me that you did not read your assignments or did not do any chemistry problems. FILL IN THE BLANKS AND CHECK THE STATEMENTS THAT PERTAIN TO YOU.

YOUR NAME: _____

Estimate the amount of time you spent studying for this exam: _____ (hours/minutes)

When did you begin your serious studying? _____ (the night before, etc.)

I did these things to study for the Chemistry Exam:

_____ 1. I read my assignments on a daily basis.

_____ 2. After I read a chemistry assignment, I summarized the key ideas on a piece of paper, sticky note, or index card.

_____ 3. I identified the material that I did not understand so I could ask questions in class.

_____ 4. I reviewed my class notes on a daily basis.

_____ 5. I read the lab manual and took the self-check quiz before I did the experiments in lab.

_____ 6. I solved the assigned chemistry problems without looking at the solutions at the back of the book.

_____ 7. I did extra chemistry problems at the end of each chapter.

_____ 8. I did talk-throughs of the key concepts in the chapters.

_____ 9. I quizzed myself or asked someone to quiz me over the key concepts.

_____ 10. Describe any other methods you used to study _____

_____

FIGURE 9.12   Strategy Evaluation Checklist for Chemistry

In addition to the learning log, content-area teachers can encourage students to evaluate their own strategies and techniques by asking them to complete a checklist similar to the one in Figure 9.12. This particular checklist was developed by Nicole, a chemistry teacher, who was concerned about her students and their reactions to the first chemistry exam. Many of her students were dismayed by their mediocre performance and were making comments in class similar to these: "I am just not good in chemistry." "I studied for eight hours last night and still received a C in the exam." "I am not going to try anymore, because when I study I still fail." Nicole knew these students were not reading and studying appropriately but wanted them to draw that conclusion. Hence, she listed on the checklist all the strategies and techniques that she knew were task appropriate and productive for learning chemistry.

The following day Nicole distributed the checklist and asked her students to complete it. She stressed that the checklist, if done honestly, would help them

The students who received an A or B on the exam

Studied an average of 2 hours for the exam

Began their studying at least two days before the exam

Reported an average of 4.8 different strategies

Used these techniques:

(a) They all did extra chemistry problems

(b) They all summarized what they read

(c) They all reviewed their class notes on a daily basis

(d) They all asked questions during class

The students who received a D or F on the exam

Studied an average of 2.8 hours for the exam

Began their studying the night before the exam

Reported an average of 1.7 different strategies

Used these techniques:

(a) They all read their assignments

(b) They did most of the assigned problems

FIGURE 9.13   Overhead Summarizing Checklist Data for Nicole's Class

determine what they needed to do to improve their exam performance. That evening Nicole divided the checklists into categories: students that received an A or B on the exam and students who received a D or F. She then read each checklist and coded the strategies that the students checked so that she could identify the strategies used by the high-performing students and the low-performing students. Although she knew what trends would emerge from this data analysis (e.g., the students who solved all the problems in the workbook were the ones who did well on the exam), she also knew her students would perceive the data from the checklists as extremely credible and useful.

Armed with the data and the trends, Nicole went to class the next day and presented the information to her students on an overhead. In Figure 9.13 you will note the trends that Nicole discussed with her students. As you can see, the students who received an A or B on the first exam were the ones who were reading and studying on a daily basis, solving all the assigned problems, and asking questions during class to clarify concepts. Nicole also found no differences between the high-performing and low-performing students in terms of the amount of time spent studying. As expected, this information about time really surprised her students.

After a discussion of the trends, Nicole asked her students to return to the checklist and circle the strategies and techniques they would be willing to try out for the next exam. This particular step was important because it placed the responsibility on the students to reflect on the techniques they had been using and to consider the possibility of changing to some more productive ones. Nicole tells us that the time spent on the checklist and the debriefing of the trends from the checklist has been time well spent. During the semester she has observed numerous students making significant changes in their reading and studying behaviors. Because of the success of this lesson, Nicole decided to place the checklist on her WebCT as a link for parents so they, too, have a sense of how their children should be reading, studying, and thinking about chemistry.

In sum, content-area teachers can use a variety of strategies to encourage students to monitor their understanding and to evaluate the ways in which they approach their reading and studying. As always, we would remind you that throughout this textbook we describe techniques and strategies to help your students become metacognitively aware and active in their learning (e.g., Chapter 3 and Chapter 7). We began this chapter with a quote by Thomas et al. (1988) who suggested that the emphasis on active learning is beneficial for both the student and the teacher. We end this chapter with that same thought stated in another way: When we build active learners, we are building learners for the future.

CASE STUDY REVISITED

Before writing your suggestions for Jan, go to *http://www.prenhall.com/brozo*, select Chapter 9, then click on Chapter Review Questions to check your understanding of the material.

Return to the beginning of the chapter, where we described Jan, the English teacher concerned about her gifted students' study strategies. After reading this chapter, you probably have some ideas about how she could be more creative and effective in her teaching. Take time now to write your suggestions.

As Jan was searching for instructional answers for her gifted students, a situation serendipitously occurred in their AP history class that stimulated considerable discussion and complaining. Most of Jan's students felt that their most recent essay exam in history had been unfair and far too demanding. Jan therefore decided to talk to her colleague and running partner who taught the history class. Theo was more than happy to share the questions and some insights with Jan. It seems that the essay questions required students to read and synthesize several written sources about isolationism. Some of the questions asked students to form generalizations and another question asked them to compare and contrast some of the theories.

Armed with this information, Jan went to class the next day and asked her students to evaluate their exam performance by writing an paragraph that addressed several questions (e.g., How long did you study?, Describe how you read and studied, What techniques did you use?). That night as she read the students' paragraphs Jan discovered that several of them did not read all the assigned material and that a significant number of them waited until the night before the exam to finish their reading. She also learned that most of the students reported no special techniques or strategies to organize the multiple sources. Jan found her first "hook" for teaching her students more powerful study strategies—their success in AP history.

She began her new unit with a discussion of how historians read and think about texts. She decided to do this because she had read several articles in professional journals that suggested that students' beliefs about knowledge and learning influence how they choose to read and study. As the discussion progressed, Jan learned from her students that they believed history consisted of facts. Their beliefs certainly explained their frustration when asked to form their own generalizations about a concept such as isolationism.

Although the lesson was illuminating for Jan, it was not particularly productive for her students. They remained unconvinced and irritated about their low exam grades. Jan needed to return to her classes armed with some specific processes and strategies. The next day she decided to teach her students how to corroborate, an essential higher level thinking process, by using the charting strategy. Corroboration involves students in comparing and contrasting texts with another, a process that her students had skipped in their study procedures. Rather than use the history curriculum, Jan decided to introduce the usefulness of charts with the short stories they had been reading in her class. The students selected several characters from the stories and then worked in pairs to compare and contrast them on several different features. Once all the students had completed their charts, Jan then debriefed the experience, stressing the advantages of the chart as a visual organizer and a preparation step for writing.

Two days later Jan followed up the initial charting lesson by explaining to her students that they would be creating another chart in order to compare and contrast historical figures such as Churchill and Wilson. After brainstorming all the possible characteristics that could be used on the vertical axis of their charts (e.g., individual's background, beliefs), Jan placed the students in pairs to work. In order to emphasize the benefits of the charting strategy, the next day Jan gave the students a quick pop quiz over the content in their charts. The students were thrilled to discover that they "aced" the quiz because they had remembered all the information in their charts. This situation provided Jan a perfect opportunity to discuss other ways in which to organize and synthesize ideas.

In addition to organizing, Jan taught her students an essay preparation strategy called PORPE (Simpson, 1986). The students first practiced the five steps of PORPE (Predict, Organize, Rehearse, Practice, and Evaluate) during their unit on contemporary American poets. Then they applied the steps of PORPE to their history class in order to prepare for their midterm exam in Theo's class. For both situations Jan led them through the process of predicting good essay questions by using the question stems developed by King (1992).

During the school year, Jan also read a few articles about the teaching of study strategies in professional publications such as the *Journal of Adolescent & Adult Learning*. From her reading, she realized that she needed to demonstrate for her students how they should modify their reading methods for the different courses they were taking. Her students were particularly impressed by her verbal demonstrations or think-alouds because they had always thought they should read their chemistry assignments in the same way they should read their literature or history assignments.

As Jan looks to the next semester, she is excited. Her students participate more in class and do not complain as much about their assignments, even though they are probably doing more work than they did when they completed workbook pages. Many of her students are reading and listening more actively, but some are not monitoring their understanding. With those students she hopes to introduce self-questioning and the talk-through strategy. The first semester has taught Jan many things. Most important, she has realized that students will not be able to transfer study strategies to their own tasks if they do nothing but complete workbook activities.

———————◄○►————————

SUMMARY

Study strategies should be taught as processes instead of as a series of steps that, when followed, will automatically produce greater learning and retention. We have emphasized the learner as an important part of strategy instruction. Without giving students opportunities to help shape the study strategies they are being taught, we run the risk of offering them a series of meaningless formulas that have little relevance to their genuine study needs. This has important implications for content-area teachers who want their students to be active rather than passive learners. Your role should be to inform students of each study process and its best possible applications, and then to guide them in developing personally meaningful adaptations that transfer to actual study tasks.

We purposely limited our presentation to a few effective study-reading processes because we wish to reiterate the idea that it takes a great deal of time to develop expertise in using them. We also made it clear that no single text-study strategy will be appropriate for every study need. Consequently, students should be encouraged to learn a few flexible, meaningful study processes so that they can select the most appropriate one for their purposes and tasks. Finally, we stressed that the development of strategic, active learning should be the goal of every content-area teacher.

REFERENCES

Burrell, K. I., & McAlexander, P. J. (1998). Ideas in practice: The synthesis journal. *Journal of Developmental Education, 22,* 20–22, 24, 26, 28, 30.

Campbell, J. R., Voelkl, K., & Donahue, P. L. (1997). *Report in brief: NAEP 1996 trends in academic progress.* Washington, DC: National Center for Education Statistics.

Doyle, W. (1983). Academic work. *Review of Educational Research, 53,* 159–199.

Hofer, B. K., & Pintrich, P. R. (1997). The development of epistemological theories: Beliefs about knowledge and their relation to learning. *Review of Educational Research, 67,* 88–140.

Hofer, B. K., Yu, S. L., & Pintrich, P. R. (1999). Teach college students to be self-regulated learners. In B. Zimmerman & D. H. Schunk (Eds.), *Self-regulated learn-*

ing and academic achievement: Theory, research, and practice (pp. 57-85). New York: Springer-Verlag.

Hynd, C. (1999). Teaching students to think critically using multiple texts in history. *Journal of Adolescent & Adult Literacy, 42,* 428-436.

King, A. (1992). Enhancing peer interaction and learning in the classroom through reciprocal questioning. *American Educational Research Journal, 27,* 664-687.

Moje, E. B. (1996). "I teach students, not subjects": Teacher-student relationships as contexts for secondary literacy. *Reading Research Quarterly, 31,* 172-195.

Nist, S. L., & Simpson, M. L. (2000). College studying. In M. Kamil, P. Mosenthal, P. D. Pearson, & R. Barr (Eds.), *Handbook of reading research* (Vol. 3, pp. 645-666). Mahwah, NJ: Lawrence Erlbaum Associates.

Palmatier, R. A. (1973). A notetaking system for learning. *Journal of Reading, 17,* 36-39.

Paris, S. G., Lipson, M. Y., & Wixson, K. K. (1983). Becoming a strategic reader. *Contemporary Educational Psychology, 8,* 293-316.

Pressley, M. (2000). What should comprehension instruction be the instruction of? In M. Kamil, P. Mosenthal, P. D. Pearson, & R. Barr (Eds.), *Handbook of reading research* (Vol. 3, pp. 545-561). Mahwah, NJ: Lawrence Erlbaum Associates.

Simpson, M. L. (1994). Talk throughs: A strategy for encouraging active learning across the content areas. *Journal of Reading, 38,* 296-304.

Simpson, M. L., Hynd, C. R., Nist, S. L., & Burrell, K. I. (1997). College academic assistance programs and practices. *Educational Psychology Review, 9,* 39-87.

Simpson, M. L., & Nist, S. L. (1990). Textbook annotation: An effective and efficient study strategy for college students. *Journal of Reading, 34,* 122-131.

Simpson, M. L., & Nist, S. L. (1997). Perspectives on learning history: A case study. *Journal of Literacy Research, 39,* 363-395.

Simpson, M. L., & Nist, S. L. (2001). Encouraging active reading at the college level. In M. Pressley & C. Block (Eds.), *Reading comprehension instruction.* New York: Guilford Publications.

Singer, H., & Donlan, D. (1982). Active comprehension: Problem-solving schema with question generation for comprehension of complex short stories. *Reading Research Quarterly, 17,* 166-186.

Thomas, J. W., Strage, A., & Curley, R. (1988). Improving students' self-directed learning: Issues and guidelines. *Elementary School Journal, 88,* 313-326.

Weinstein, C. E., Husman, J., & Dierking, D. R. (2000). Self-regulation interventions with a focus on learning strategies. In M. Boekaerts, P. Pintrich, & M. Zeidner (Eds.), *Handbook of self-regulation* (pp. 727-747). San Diego, CA: Academic Press.

Zimmerman, B. J. (2000). Attaining self-regulation: A social cognitive perspective. In M. Boekaerts, P. Pintrich, & M. Zeidner (Eds.), *Handbook of self-regulation* (pp. 13-39). San Diego, CA: Academic Press.

CHAPTER TEN

Expanding Literacy and Content Learning Through Computer Technology

ANTICIPATION GUIDE

Directions: Read each statement carefully and decide whether you agree or disagree with it, placing a check mark in the appropriate *Before Reading* column. When you have finished reading and studying the chapter, return to the guide and decide whether your anticipations need to be changed by placing a check mark in the appropriate *After Reading* column.

	BEFORE READING		AFTER READING	
	Agree	*Disagree*	*Agree*	*Disagree*
1. Computer technology is incompatible with a language-based approach to content-area teaching.	_____	_____	_____	_____
2. Computers are limited learning tools in the content classroom.	_____	_____	_____	_____
3. Reading and writing are necessary skills for operating computers effectively.	_____	_____	_____	_____
4. The Internet can be used to promote higher level thinking in virtually every content area.	_____	_____	_____	_____
5. Word processing is the only computer application supportive of students' literacy growth.	_____	_____	_____	_____
6. Electronic field trips will be possible in this decade.	_____	_____	_____	_____
7. Databases and spreadsheets are difficult to use in content areas other than math and science.	_____	_____	_____	_____

… [W]hen students work with computer technology, instead of being controlled by it, they enhance the capabilities of the computer, and the computer enhances their thinking and learning.

—Jonassen (1996)

The overriding principle that guides our selection of strategies for this book is that they engage students in ways that lead to meaningful and active learning. It is clear that computer technology holds great promise for engaging students and helping them think in meaningful ways (Burbules & Callister, 2000). Computer technology also poses challenges. Principle among them is the possibility that students who are steeped in information technologies will never get initiated into the conversations that mediate critical cultural knowledge and wisdom. As illustration, consider the experience Burniske and Monke (2001) had with a senior high student who didn't know how to use the information technology medium, with which he was so proficient, to fulfill a project assignment on TV news bias because he had no understanding of the terms "liberal" and "conservative." This was an A student who had taken the most advanced computer courses the district had to offer, who could design amazing visual displays using publishing programs, spreadsheets, and databases. But he was also a student, as the authors noted, who had become so distracted by his extensive computer education that he had failed to become prepared for critical citizenry. The point we make in this chapter is that we as teachers of adolescents should not mindlessly embrace the promises of the computer revolution. Instead, we should use information technologies only when they further our goals of fostering informed *and* critical thinking, media *and* traditional print literacy, high interest *and* meaningful learning.

Go to *http://www.prenhall.com/brozo*, select Chapter 10, then click on Chapter Objectives to provide a focus for your reading.

Over the past 10 years remarkable developments in hardware, software, and access to information have made computers more integral to public and private life than ever before (Negroponte, 1995; Warschauer, 1999). For example, consider the explosion of interest in the Internet. Ten years ago, few teachers even knew of its existence. Just a few years ago, many more teachers knew of its existence but only a small number used it. Today, however, teachers all over the globe, from remote villages to major cities, have knowledge of and experience with the Internet (Loveless & Ellis, 2001; Ryder & Graves, 1997). Other computer technologies, such as telecommunications, multimedia, and word processing, have seen similar growth.

In this chapter we will explore these and other types of computer technology and their use in middle and secondary school classrooms. We will also provide useful information for helping teachers become more informed about these technologies while developing strategies to use them with their students.

CASE STUDY

José and his colleagues in the science and math department of a large urban high school received a state-funded technology grant. The grant was designed to be used by teachers of math and science to train their students in the ways in which computer technology could improve learning in those subjects. José received funds to purchase computers, computer software, networked Internet connections, and teacher training in the new uses of computer technology.

In staff development workshops, José discovered a number of exciting applications of computer technology to his biology subject matter. In one workshop session, he and other faculty were asked to think of ways of using the computer to facilitate their students' learning of especially challenging content. José's students seemed most challenged by the sheer volume of detail they were required to learn. For example, for the study of cell types in advanced biology, students had to learn and remember hundreds of facts related to 10 to 20 different cell types. They were having a great deal of difficulty organizing and remembering this information. José had tried to devise study schemes for his students, but they were either too complex or did not provide motivation.

To the Reader:
As you read and study this chapter, think about José and his goal to help his students organize their biology content more effectively. What computer-based strategies could José use to achieve this goal?

PRINCIPLES GUIDING THE USE OF COMPUTER TECHNOLOGY IN CONTENT-AREA CLASSROOMS

As we have noted, the overriding criterion teachers of adolescents should apply when considering the use of information and communications technologies in their lessons is the extent to which these technologies will promote expansive learning and critical thinking. We believe, as others (Leu, 2000) do, that teachers who create learning contexts where the importance of critical reading and writing abilities is valued will find appropriate ways to integrate computer technology in support of traditional literacy and content learning. The principles below should be used to help guide your decisions about how best to link information and communications technologies to your content-area lessons.

Principle 1: Provide Opportunities for Creative Uses of Computer Technology

Casting aspersions on computer technology as a tool for learning in schools is akin to heresy in today's high-tech world. We have come to accept the sanguine pronouncements of computer industry spokespersons, bandwagoning policy makers, and well-intentioned educational administrators without challenge. Yet, as some people in the popular media (Mathews, 2000) and others who develop and study these new technologies (Burbules & Callister, 2000; Leu, 2000; March, 2000) admit, the research basis for grand claims about computers and student learning may yet be quite difficult to defend. What does seem to be known about the value of computer technology for teaching and learning is that achievement is more likely to rise if schools use computers in interesting and creative ways instead of mostly for drill in basic skills (Wenglinsky, 1998). In fact, using computers for drill, practice, and entertainment was found to depress achievement. The idea is that it's not how much time students spend on computers but the quality of use that relates to higher achievement. Unfortunately, most research with computers has explored new ways of presenting and acquiring basic information, shedding scant light on how new knowledge is acquired and used in productive ways (Healy, 2000).

Quality, more so than quantity, of computer time is related to higher student achievement.

This principle also emphasizes that computer technology should be exploited for its unique instructional capabilities and not simply as a medium for re-presenting predictable worksheet tasks in a visual format. Interesting and creative uses of computer technology are more likely to enhance learning and develop higher level thinking skills. Computers and other electronic media can help students visualize content to be learned in novel ways. For example, virtual reality programs and programs that allow students to work with geometric figures in hyperspace are made possible only through computer-based instructional technology (Marcus, 1995).

The computer activities described a bit later in this chapter all emphasize the ways in which the technology can be used creatively for engendering higher level thinking and knowledge acquisition.

Principle 2: Use Computer Technology in Ways That Promote Critical Reading

With the advent of widespread access to computer technologies in homes and schools, our ideas about literacy have undergone major transformations. As we described in the first chapter, literacy is no longer viewed solely as the ability to decode and encode printed words. Proponents of new and multiple literacies (Alvermann, 2002; Brindley, 2000; Lankshear, Gee, Knobel, & Searle, 1997; Luke & Elkins, 1998) assert that a much broader conception of what it means to be literate encompasses all forms of symbolic communication enacted by adolescents and influencing their lives and learning. This conception must include, of course, information and communications technologies. Preparing students for a post-typographic world—that is, a world where traditional print literacy is no longer essential—is presented by some (Reinking, McKenna, Labbo, & Kieffer, 1998) as incumbent upon the responsible educator. Post-typographic literacies are seen as vital tools students must have in order to navigate within and "read" our increasingly complex global society (Anderson & Lee, 1995; Gee, 1996; Leu, 2000). We agree with the late Brazilian scholar and activist, Paulo Freire (1987), who insisted that in order to read the word, we must also be capable of reading the world. Critically reading the world and the word should, therefore, be a vibrant feature of instruction with computers in the content-area classroom.

Once again, however, a word of caution is warranted. Hundreds of books on the market today list thousands of opportunities for using information and communications technologies in the classroom. Yet, at the same time, Monke (2001) points out, there is a "disappointing shortage of thoughtful literature devoted to discussing the sobering flip side of opportunity—responsibility" (p. 203). We must never forget that although we may have become excited by and proficient with computer technologies and the different formats they provide for representing meaning (Kress, 1998), we, as teachers, bring a sophisticated grounding in traditional print literacy to these new communications media. Therefore, we believe it is our collective responsibility to ensure language curricula for middle and secondary school students helps them find their entry points to engaged print literacy even while we take advantage of new and promising benefits of electronic technologies.

Computer literacy should be used to enrich and complement traditional print literacy, not replace it.

The astronomer, Clifford Stoll (1999), warns that scientists may use computers in their research, but they did not learn science through computers. Computers can yield answers to specific questions but they do not necessarily inspire scientific curiosity or give understanding. In a similar vein, it is the responsibility of those of us who began so modestly down our own literate paths—who now after years of traditional print explorations have come to pride ourselves on our sophisticated and flexible discourses—not to assume that young people can somehow use computer technologies to short-circuit the journey we have taken to arrive at a point of critical literacy abilities. Put another way, teachers of adolescents should find uses of computer technology that enrich and reinforce students' abilities to critically read print and the electronic media that display and transmit it.

Each year, the Internet grows exponentially. This mind-boggling expansion of Web connections has created a greater need than ever before for critical consciousness and critical reading. Burbules and Callister (2000) describe the opportunity and problems of unrestricted self-expression on the Internet in this way:

> Participants in this environment often need to read and evaluate so much material, from so many sources, that it becomes impossible to maintain a critical discerning attitude toward it all. The very volume and number of voices has a kind of leveling effect—everything seems to come from the same place and nothing seems much more reliable than anything else. This makes the need to evaluate the value and credibility of what one encounters on the Internet a crucial skill if one is to be an active beneficiary of the available information and interaction. (p. 71)

Because of ease of accessibility and hypertext, or the linking nature of the Internet, we urge content-area teachers in the middle and upper grades to foster in students a form of critical reading of the Internet medium itself (Burbules, 1998; Peters & Lankshear, 1996).

Principle 3: Use Computer Technology in Ways That Promote Authentic Communication

Our best thinking about the most effective way to teach comprehension makes it clear that students need ample time for reading and writing for authentic purposes (Fielding & Pearson, 1994). One of the most promising features of computer technology for promoting authentic communication is the Internet. Unlike previous technologies such as television and radio, once thought to have the potential to transform education, the Internet offers teachers and students a blend of communication and retrieval functions within a worldwide framework. More significantly, although the Internet is an electronic network, it nonetheless runs on literacy (Mike, 1997). Even for skeptics of computers as learning tools, it is indisputable that reading and writing are essential for electronic navigation and information retrieval (Ryder & Graves, 1997).

The reading and writing involved in typical computer tasks in schools can provide some of that much needed time for authentic literacy activities. Consider the literacy requirements of a ninth grader's computer research of the rocky planets in our solar system. First, he must read a variety of directions for accessing specific "hits" to review. Next, he must follow additional directions to find texts and other information about the planets of interest. All the while, the student is reading, making critical judgments, and typing key words and phrases to hone his search. There may come a time when students will be able to complete similar tasks with mere voice activation, but for the foreseeable future, reading and writing skills will continue to be a necessity for school-related computer tasks.

Sophisticated reading and writing skills are necessary for complex computer-related tasks in school.

Internet communication should be exploited as a medium for providing an authentic sense of audience for literacy activity. Composition research using that medium has demonstrated its potential for helping students develop audience sensitivity and writing skills (Hawisher & Selfe, 1998). Students who communicate on the Internet are writing for an actual audience of one or perhaps hundreds or thousands. Likewise, students who read Internet communications become part of an audience. Teachers can take advantage of this experience by helping students develop audience sensitivity with writing assignments on the Internet for various purposes. For example, students can engage in activities as simple as writing missives to chat groups and letters to electronic pen pals, to more complex communication tasks as formal inquiries to experts, companies, and organizations and creating home pages and publishing e-zines (Internet magazines and newspapers).

Principle 4: Use Computer Technology in Ways That Increase Student Motivation for and Interest in Purposeful and Meaningful Learning

The strongest advocates for the use of computer technology in teaching and learning claim its most appealing feature is that students are automatically interested in and motivated by computers (Healy, 2000). This high level of enthusiasm has resulted in a generation of young people Rushkoff (1996) calls "screenagers" who represent for him a desirable model of a new form of consciousness that thrives in the state of chaos found in digital and cyber worlds. But just because young adults enjoy looking at computer screens doesn't mean that should influence our decision about computer use for student learning.

Those of us with teenagers of our own know there are many things that hold their attentions but are not necessarily and unequivocally good for them. TV viewing and eating junk food quickly leap to mind.

In spite of the cautions against using computers for learning solely on the basis of student interest, there is a growing body of research to support the motivating effects of computers when used with students in school-based learning (Leu, 2000). Bridging student motivation with constructive learning is, as we have been saying throughout this book, the artful task of the content-area teacher. One of our expressed goals in this text is to help teachers develop students who are motivated and independent learners. Learning independently means that students are able to construct their own knowledge rather than simply recall information supplied by teachers (Bean, 2000; Simons, 1993). Salomon (1993) argues that unlike most other tools for learning, computers can serve as intellectual partners that take on unproductive memorizing tasks while allowing learners to think more deeply and meaningfully.

One way to think about this is to consider how scientists and mathematicians who have come into their own in the past 20 years have done so in the age of computers. And yet, no one claims that these thinkers and scholars are less capable than their predecessors because of computer technology. On the contrary, computers have become a necessary tool allowing scientists and mathematicians to find practical expression for their most imaginative ideas. For instance, it is safe to say that without computers to handle the staggering number of calculations necessary for manned exploration of the moon and the planets, our space program would be far less advanced than it is today. The point is that when computers are used as partners in learning, students and teachers alike can free their imaginations to explore content on a more meaningful and critical level than they might without this technology.

In the next section of this chapter you will read descriptions of several teachers exploiting the full potential of computer technology for content-area learning. We especially like the approaches and strategies used by these teachers because in one form or another, the four principles presented previously undergird their practice, which is marked by creativity, opportunities for critical thinking, authentic communication, and meaningful learning.

When computers are used as partners in learning, students and teachers can free their imaginations to explore content on a more meaningful and critical level.

TEACHING AND LEARNING STRATEGIES THAT INTEGRATE COMPUTER TECHNOLOGY ACROSS THE CURRICULUM

Fifteen years ago, when we were finishing the final draft of the first edition of this book, we made some predictions about trends in schools' use of computer technology most likely to expand in the future. We're proud to say that our predictions have been highly accurate. For example, we said that telecommunications, multimedia, and databases would become increasingly prominent in educational computing. A safe prediction, you might say. However, at that time, it was impossible for us to know with certainty how rapidly instructional computing would change the way we think about teaching and learning. Some (Newby, Stepich, Lehman, & Russell, 1996) have speculated that if the automobile industry had progressed as quickly as the computer industry, we would be able to own a vehicle capable of traveling at jet engine speeds while getting a million miles to the gallon, for only a few dollars! Over the past 10 years, personal computers have become remarkably more powerful, more compact, and less expensive, making it possible for a single machine to handle a number of complex tasks. Four areas of computer technology are changing the face of education in junior and senior high schools in virtually all subject areas: (1) *telecommunications,* including *networking;* (2) *word processing,* including *desktop publishing* and creating *home pages;* (3) *database management systems;* and (4) *multimedia.*

Telecommunications

Telecommunications technology involves electronic communication of information using computers. Although telecommunications has been in use for some time in business and industry, a growing number of telecommunications applications are being explored in schools. Massive webs of phone lines, bulletin board systems, and international networks are now available to bring a world of people and information within reach for teachers and students (Burniske & Monke, 2001; Harris, 1994; Kelly & Wiebe, 1994; Loveless & Ellis, 2001).

Communicating with computers has provided teachers in all subject areas with powerful support for literacy and content learning (Beach & Lundell, 1998). Today, with advances in telecommunications technology along with steadily declining costs for the use of this technology, electronic links between students and teachers have become an affordable and effective option for delivery of instruction. Teachers who value students' active exploration of information and collaborative exchange of ideas will find numerous applications of telecommunications technology (Armstrong, 1995).

The Internet, including e-mail, is one of the most common ways in which teachers can use telecommunications technology.

Using the Internet as a Languaging and Learning Tool

Content-area teachers in middle school and senior high school around the country are exploring new ways of helping their students learn via telecommunications. In the following section we will describe several examples of teachers using e-mail, threaded discussions, and the Internet to engage students in meaningful learning projects. Common to all of these activities is the use of computers for authentic and purposeful communication. In this way, we hope you will see how students' language and literacy skills, necessary for electronic communication, can be used and reinforced (Blase, 2000; Grabe & Grabe, 1998) while learning content from virtually any content area.

Foreign language. Janette, a Spanish teacher, and her class had been studying the cultures of Spain for several weeks (as described in Newby et al., 1996).

Her students enjoyed reading about the people from different regions of Spain, and she wanted them to have the opportunity to interact directly with Spaniards. As a student herself, Janette had carried on a pen pal relationship with a young girl from Barcelona. She remembered how enjoyable it was to write and receive letters with interesting information and items, such as stamps, coins, and photographs. Eventually the exchange of letters dwindled and then stopped as the girls grew older, but Janette always regretted never being able to meet and speak with her pen pal in person. Janette's knowledge of telecommunications technology helped her decide to arrange for an audio teleconference between her Spanish language students and students from Spain, which led to establishing an electronic pen pal relationship between the two classes.

After making arrangements with a high school English language teacher in Seville, Janette and her students prepared questions for their Spanish counterparts. Using a speakerphone from the school's technology center, Janette called the classroom in Seville and the two classes held a 20-minute conversation. The students in Spain got to practice their English, while Janette's students got to practice their conversational Spanish. In the end, everyone seemed to understand each other, and both classes of students were enthusiastic about continuing to interact.

Learning to communicate in a new language is made easier when students from differing countries can have daily exchanges via e-mail.

After the teleconference, Janette had her students initiate e-mail conversations with their new pen pal class in Spain. Students were able to practice their writing skills while gaining valuable cultural and language information from their electronic pen pals. Janette felt that the experience had been a success, since several of her students continued to correspond with Spanish students months after they were introduced to the long-distance education technologies.

Social studies. As middle school students in a small community in Alaska began to prepare for their class trip to Disney World in Orlando, Florida, they tried something a little different (as described by Roblyer, Edwards, & Havriluk, 1997). In April they established a computer link with eighth-grade students in Orlando. Using e-mail, students exchanged information, eventually met each other in Orlando, and continued to contact one another after the trip via e-mail. The Alaskan students were mostly native Alaskans, so they were able to share a great deal about their culture and daily lives with the Orlando junior high students while gaining greater knowledge of telecommunications technology.

Biology. Students in Wisconsin established e-mail links with classrooms all along the migratory route of the whooping crane. Students initiated reports on the movement of the cranes during their migration and created an informational guide to their migration habits.

A group of 10th-grade biology students in Massachusetts used the National Geographic Society's Kids' Net to tap into a national science project. Kids' Net was designed for science classrooms around the country to share in-class science experiments. The students tried various experiments with seeds that had been sent into space aboard the space shuttle to see how space travel had affected them. After collecting data on their experiments, the students sent their results across the country through Kids' Net on the Internet.

Science.   Although land-locked, middle graders in Iowa kept track of a U.S. Coast Guard "tall ship" during a training journey using telecommunications technology. Students gathered updates on its movements and activities through the SAILING forum, which can be accessed through the Internet. The topic was of great interest to the students and included a variety of related learning experiences. Students researched more about the ship. They adopted a sailor or cadet aboard the ship and exchanged e-mail letters and pictures. They read books such as *Mutiny on the Bounty* because the Coast Guard ship was following a route similar to Captain Bligh's. Log sheets were kept, and weekly updates via computer were received. Students learned about time zones, the international date line, and the weather's effects on the seas. They also developed their map-reading skills. Telecommunications technology stimulated and supported the students' exploration of a 20th-century sailing voyage.

Mathematics.   High school students in several cities throughout the country polled the local population on their views of national issues, such as gun control, smoking bans in public places, female presidential candidates, and abortion. Using e-mail, the classes exchanged the data they collected, and all the participating schools shared in an overall analysis of the findings.

Across the curriculum.   For more than a decade classrooms from countries in virtually every part of the globe have been partnering in the Learning Circles Project. The project facilitates cooperation through telecommunications among a small group of classrooms for exploring and seeking solutions to social, environmental, and geopolitical problems (Riel, 1993; Riel & Fulton, 2001). Students discover the varied perspectives their peers in other locations and cultures have on these problems. These multiple perspectives form the basis for testing theories and possible solutions. Internet and multimedia tools give students involved in the collaboratives access to information no single school could possibly acquire. Learning Circles provides students an electronic forum for gaining new knowledge, appreciating diverse points of view, and writing collaboratively with a community of their peers who share an equal commitment to tackling important global issues. The outcome of the project is the publication of jointly authored booklets and papers based on the students' collaborative problem solving. Several Learning Circles projects have taken place over the past few years, including the following:

Go to Web Resources for Chapter 10 at *http://www. prenhall.com/brozo* and look for Learning Circles.

Internet tools make unique learning collaborations possible.

■ Students in Saudi Arabia, along with their partner students in other countries, explored solutions to problems in the Persian Gulf. The students discussed issues such as world dependence on Arabian oil, political freedom, and religious and cultural conflicts.

■ West Virginia students have held conferences with prison inmates to discuss a range of social issues. Inmates provide information from their personal life experiences so that students can better understand the origins of crime.

■ Students from several urban areas around the country collaborated on studies of homelessness, illiteracy, and substance abuse. Data were compiled and written in a booklet, *Investigating Society's Problems.*

■ Students from Belgium worked with collaborating schools in the United States and other industrialized nations on a research project concerned with excessive packaging of goods. They gathered local products and evaluated them from the standpoint of their pricing and their effects on the environment.

Riel & Fulton (2001) found that because students' electronic communication and project publications were part of a discourse for a large networked audience of their peers, they were more fluent, better organized, and more clearly written than compositions produced merely for a grade. Electronically supported collaborative authoring involving partner students around the world resulted in better use of grammar and syntax as well.

Threaded Discussions

Threaded discussions bring teachers and students together electronically to dialog about content-area topics.

Social studies.   A threaded discussion is a form of electronic communication that promotes collaboration and interaction among students by providing a cyber-environment for recording responses and engaging in critical dialog over relevant issues from the content classroom (Nichols, Wood, & Rickelman, 2001).

Using Microsoft Office FrontPage (Barron & Lyskawa, 1998), Holli and her sixth-grade students carried out a threaded discussion based on Opinionnaire statements (White & Johnston, 2001) related to an article on teen alcohol abuse. Figure 10.1 presents the Opinionnaire statements that were used as prompts for an online, threaded discussion as well as excerpts from the discussion that took place online among the students and between Holli and her students.

The first thing we hope you will recognize in the threaded discussion are the rich and considered responses made by students. This was possible because instead of controlling the lesson, computer technology provided a new and creative dimension of communication that made an instructional strategy Holli had been using even more successful.

Virtual Field Trips

Experiential learning is one of the most highly valued forms of learning promoted in this book. We believe strongly that when students are given the opportunity to explore content firsthand, they are much more likely to learn information and ideas and to commit new learning to memory than they are without direct experience. A common source of frustration among teachers, however, is the lack of resources to make experiential learning through field trips possible. Adding to the problem are increasing liability risks of moving students bodily from the school grounds to the field and back. Undoubtedly, there are countless "Ms. Frizzles" out there who would like nothing more than to hop on a magic bus and journey to some new exotic locale for virtually every topic

This is an on-line Opinionnaire to be used for an article we will be reading on teen alcohol abuse. All sixth grade students should post their responses and explanation for each statement from the Opinionnaire. If someone posts a response different from yours, please respond to the sender. Be sure to post any comments, personal opinions, and guesses related to the upcoming article. Once you have read the article post new responses.

The content frame shows the title of all articles posted to the discussion. When you select a title it will load the corresponding article into this frame.

You should also feel free to:

* Post a new article and start a new thread
* Search the articles for a particular word or phrase

Remember also that each article has links to let you continue the thread and navigate the article list.

Please post your reactions to the following opinion statements and tell why.

From: Holli   **Date:** 10/14/01   **Time:** 10:15:11 AM

Alcohol must not be really bad for teens otherwise kids in Europe wouldn't be allowed to drink beer and wine just like the adults.

From: Dez   **Date:** 10/14/01   **Time:** 10:47:03 AM

I've heard of that. Don't real young kids get to drink with their parents, like in Italy and France? So maybe if we grew up drinking with our families we wouldn't want to get drunk as teenagers.

From: Truann   **Date:** 10/14/01   **Time:** 1:04:32 PM

I disagree with the statement and with Dez. I think kids who drink probably grow up to be even worse drinkers. Alcohol is a drug that's in your body all the time if you drink everyday.

From: Truann   **Date:** 10/15/01   **Time:** 3:01:55 PM

The article agrees with my opinion and not the statement. Teenagers in Europe abuse alcohol just as much as teens do in America. It says that in some countries like Finland and Russia teenagers are the worse drinkers of all.

From: Holli   **Date:** 10/15/01   **Time:** 3:22:41 PM

I remember on a trip I took to Scandinavia a few years ago how surprised I was to see so many young people overdrinking in public. During the summer it stays light well into the evening, as late as 10:00 or 11pm, so teenagers stay out very late. Do you think teens around the world abuse alcohol because they're trying to act like adults and because of peer pressure?

From: Fareed   **Date:** 10/15/01   **Time:** 3:27:13 PM

Adults abuse alcohol so kids do too. That's what we see so why do adults expect us to be any different?

From: Corinne   **Date:** 10/16/01   **Time:** 8:42:38 AM

I agree with Fareed. How can parents and teachers say don't drink when they drink? I'll bet everyone in this class has beer or wine at home. It's like smoking, too. Parents always tell their kids, "Don't smoke" but then smoke. I think kids won't drink if they have parents who don't drink.

FIGURE 10.1   Excerpts From a Threaded Discussion Based on Opinionnaire Statements

in the curriculum. Fortunately, this goal is rapidly becoming more achievable through the use of telecommunications technology.

Taking a field trip electronically turns students into "virtual travelers" capable of going to places they could only imagine. Unlike prerecorded video programs of distant places, virtual field trips make it possible for students to interact with other learners, teachers, researchers, scientists, and technicians at remote locations (Mather, 2000). Using two-way voice and video, students communicate with peers and local experts as they explore interesting locations around the world, such as the Guatemalan rain forest or an Antarctic research station. With the development of telerobotics tools it is now possible for students in their classrooms to reserve time on the Hubbell telescope and direct its view of space or control an underwater vehicle as it explores the unique seabed of Monterey Bay.

Go to Web Resources for Chapter 10 at *http://www. prenhall.com/brozo* and look for Jason Project.

Science. One of the most exciting electronic field trip projects available to teachers today is the Jason Project. Through a complex network of advanced satellite technology, underwater robotics, two-way audio, and television screens, viewers at participating schools in many locations in the United States and other countries can observe actual exploration sites and participate in the exploration itself. Jason, a remotely operated vehicle for underwater navigation and research from which the project gets its name, has made it possible for students to go on interactive scientific explorations of sites such as the Mediterranean Sea, the Galapagos Islands, and the bottom of Lake Ontario. The project allows students live participation via satellite-delivered images and two-way audio interaction. Teachers and students can pose questions, receive answers, and conduct remote experiments. Special curriculum guides are developed and can be obtained to help teachers and students study and prepare for each expedition. During Jason's expedition, students and teachers record its progress, communicate through e-mail and real-time video, and participate by completing assignments and experiments.

A recent Jason Project entitled "Hawaii: A Living Laboratory" took students electronically to the most isolated chain of islands in the world. Formed by volcanic activity, the Hawaiian Islands are a unique site for the study of tectonics, ecology, lava flows, steam vents, and much more. Three high school students from Hawaii, Jeff, Maren, and Joe, were chosen to join the Jason expedition team. Better known as student argonauts, these teenagers stayed "wired" for voice and video while in the field with the researchers, so they could communicate with students all over the United States participating in Jason. The student argonauts also kept an electronic field journal accessible to classrooms nationwide. When an eighth grader in North Dakota asked Maren to describe a steam vent, the North Dakotan students watched and listened as Maren trudged cautiously near where vapor plumes rose with force from the volcanic rock. Maren's description of the phenomenon was in the kind of terms adolescents use with one another—plain-speak.

Across the curriculum. An increasing number of middle and secondary schools are creating high-tech links with resource-rich museums as a virtual solution for problems associated with conventional field trips. In Wisconsin, for example, a network comprised of interactive television and high-speed data transmission has been put in place that provides collaborative opportunities between students and expert staff at some of the most celebrated and revered shrines of American and world culture. Through two-way voice and video students access a museum's collections and work directly and in real-time with curators, archivists, and researchers.

In one Wisconsin high school, Waterford Union High, students from nearly all subject areas take advantage of this technology for distance learning. Some of the virtual museum trips Union High students have taken will give you a sense of the promise and possibilities of this new form of cyber travel. A history class visited the Baseball Hall of Fame in Cooperstown, New York, so they could see actual exhibits from the Negro League baseball era and discuss this period in our past with museum staff. An African American studies club journeyed to the Museum of Television and Radio in Los Angeles to learn more about the Civil Rights movement through its collection of media documentaries. The school jazz ensemble went to New York on several occasions to watch, listen to, and talk jazz with professional musicians at J@zzchool. Art students visited the Indianapolis Museum of Art to learn about the modern art movement and its statement on society and popular culture. Using this information, the students drew and painted their own works, which were critiqued by the museum curators. Finally, life science students took a trip to the Columbus zoo where they researched condors.

Virtual museum trips are a feasible alternative to being there.

Virtual field trips are becoming increasingly popular because of their ease and relatively modest expense. With insurance, travel, safety, and time issues forcing many middle and secondary schools to limit or even eliminate conventional field trips, we're likely to see tremendous growth in electronic explorations over the next several years.

Opportunities for electronic communication in the classroom are endless, limited only by the imagination of teachers and students. As Roblyer and colleagues (1997) point out, the biggest challenge is for teachers to take the first step. We believe that as teachers become more familiar with the benefits of communicating via computers across distances, an increasing number from all content areas will take advantage of this technology for motivating students to read, write, and exchange meaningful information.

Word Processing for Meaningful Communication

Word processing is, at its simplest, typing on a computer. Word processing programs facilitate nearly any assignment or activity that was previously done by longhand or a typewriter. Word processing is more versatile and powerful than older writing methods. Since a word-processed document is typed and formatted on a screen before being printed, editing, revising, and correcting can all take place before a finished written product is produced.

Those of us who have been around long enough to remember know what writing and publishing were like before access to computers became easy and commonplace. Today, it's difficult to imagine writing for work or recreation without computers. Although the advantages of word processing are obvious to most of us, there has been some dispute over whether this new technology actually helps produce better writing (Halio, 1990; Gamble & Easingwood, 2000). Nevertheless, we believe that writing as a conceptual and creative process is facilitated by productivity tools such as word processors. That is why we have included examples of teachers and students using computers for word processing in other sections of this book, such as in Chapter 7.

Applications of word processing programs are becoming increasingly varied. Students and teachers alike are using word processing for creating imaginative documents, brochures, books, newsletters, and more with desktop publishing programs. Other programs have been developed to facilitate student note taking. Word processors are now being used to create home pages and other printed information on the World Wide Web.

Desktop Publishing

Desktop publishing software gives teachers and students more powerful formatting capabilities for printed material than regular word processing programs. Recently, older distinctions between word processing and desktop publishing software have disappeared since word processors are now including more and more desktop publishing features (Roblyer et al., 1997). With desktop publishing, users have a great deal of control and flexibility in the composition and layout of the printed page, including text and graphics. Today many schools are using high-quality desktop publishing software to produce colorful and visually appealing school newspapers and yearbooks, and illustrated material for the classroom.

Mathematics. Sixth-grade students at a middle school in the Southwest planned all of the second semester for a math fair in early May. Not only did individuals and groups work tirelessly on projects to be displayed at the fair, but students also worked diligently to make the fair one of the best the school had ever had. Early in the planning stages for the fair, the classes decided to emphasize publicity of the event as a way of increasing participation by the school and the community. Hector, one of the math teachers, aided students in their publicity efforts by introducing them to desktop publishing. Using Microsoft's Publish It! software, Hector taught students how to create a variety of eye-catching and professional communications combining page setup, text format, and graphics elements.

Desktop publishing offers students a way of combining fun and purposeful communication with content-area topics.

Students first learned how to design their own stationery, blending the school's mascot, an owl, with their own creative arrangement of print and figures. The desktop publishing program made it possible to generate colorful flyers and brochures describing the upcoming math fair. These were mailed in the desktop-generated envelopes to local businesses, churches, and school and community organizations. Additionally, large posters were created and displayed throughout the school and community. With the desktop publishing software, students even discovered the ease of creating a math school newsletter containing updates on the math fair events. The newsletter featured students who had records of high achievement in math, real-world math problems, and a math "puzzler."

The students' advertising campaign paid off. The math fair brought more people to the school to observe, judge, and participate in related activities than any previous math fair. Desktop publishing provided students with an important tool for promoting their event and helped them learn valuable information about using the computer.

Computer-Assisted Outlining and Concept Mapping

Another way to use word processing as a learning tool involves computer-based outlining and concept mapping programs. Outlining and mapping are a couple of the most commonly recommended strategies for organizing textbook and classroom information. That's why we offer suggestions for teaching text organization strategies to students in Chapter 9. As we discuss in that chapter, organizational strategies have been found to be an excellent way to promote active learning (Anderson & Armbruster, 1984; Brown & Campione, 1996) and provide students with a record of study for future use, such as in tests, projects, and class discussion (Nist, Simpson, Olejnik, & Mealey, 1991).

Even though students are often urged to incorporate lecture and class information into a unified note-taking format, many will tell you that creating paper-and-pencil outlines or hand-drawn maps can be very inefficient. This is because it is difficult and messy to reorganize, make room for new information, show new relationships, and elaborate on prior information using paper and pencil. Scratch-outs and erasures, changes and additions written in between lines and in margins, drawings, and arrows inevitably force students to recopy everything they've written or to try to learn and study from disorganized notes.

Anderson-Inman (1995–1996), at the Center for Electronic Studying at the University of Oregon, has been investigating ways in which teachers can help students improve their independent study skills by using the computer to record and organize information. Her work has led to the development of computer-based outlining and concept mapping (Anderson-Inman & Horney, 1997) programs designed to make note taking easier and more efficient for students.

Outlining programs operate similarly to word processing programs, but the typed text consists only of formats into an outline. Electronic outlining is an effective form of recording and organizing information from the text and the class (Horney & Anderson-Inman, 1992) for the following reasons: (1) expandability—students can modify electronic outlines in an infinite number of ways; (2) focusability—program functions such as "hide" and "show" allow students to display particular sections of their outline for concentrated attention; and (3) juxtaposability—electronic outlines allow students to bring together two or more sections from different places in the outline for instant and easy comparisons and for information elaboration. Afterward, the sections can be returned to their original places in the outline.

Electronic note taking makes organizing, outlining, and linking information especially easy for students who have difficulty writing.

A variety of concept mapping programs are available to allow users to craft visual representations of ideas and information from text and lecture depicting content links and concept interrelatedness. With the appropriate software, students can use laptops or Palm Pilots with keyboards to design a web that best reflects the organization of the information. The programs allow students to create their own shapes and shading, type in notes, and add connectors with explanations.

Go to Web Resources for Chapter 10 at *http://www. prenhall.com/brozo* and look for Inspiration Software.

Music. Music students in a ninth-grade class created electronic outlines for the topic of historical periods of music (Figure 10.2). The students were taught a five-step process for creating the outline using Inspiration software. First, they went through the primary music textbook and crafted a skeletal outline of the chapter's major headings and subheadings. Second, they summarized textual information using important words and phraseology under each heading in the skeletal outline. Third, they read information on the topic in alternative text sources supplied by the teacher and inserted relevant information in the outline. Fourth, class notes from teacher- and peer-led discussions and demonstrations were integrated into the outline. Finally, students restructured the headings and subheadings by adding and consolidating and rearranged information in the outline to fit the new structure. When their outlines were completed, the music teacher showed students how they could use the outlines to prompt themselves during study and test themselves in anticipation of a test on the content.

Meeting the Needs of Diverse Learners in the Content-Area Classroom

Patrick was awarded a BellSouth grant that made it possible for him to buy 20 Dell laptops for use by the inclusion students in his classes. He asked for the computers so he could combine technology with the study of U.S. government with the expectation that it would ease the note-taking process for his students with learning disabilities and improve their listening and concentration skills. One of the ways this was accomplished was by teaching students how to make electronic notes from class lectures, discussions, and readings. With Inspiration's integrating diagramming software, Patrick taught his students how to organize course information by mapping content and using it as a basis for studying and preparing for debates and tests. Prior to this technology-assisted approach, all of his students but particularly his inclusion students required steady coercion to take longhand notes. Most failed to keep organized or complete notes, for all of Patrick's chidings, until the laptops were assigned. Once the special education students caught on to the versatility and ease of the Inspiration format, they never looked back. Patrick reported that their level of attention in class has increased noticeably, as evidenced by how frequently they now ask clarifying questions, indicating they're becoming more critical listeners, and the quality of the maps they are producing (see Figure 10.3 for an example of a

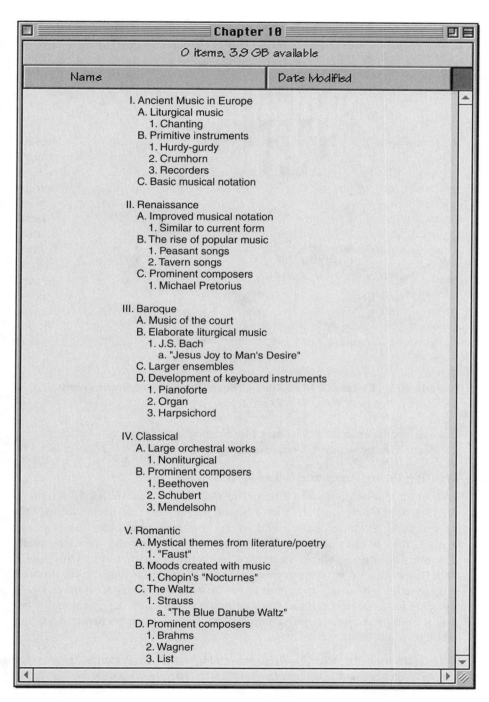

I. Ancient Music in Europe
   A. Liturgical music
      1. Chanting
   B. Primitive instruments
      1. Hurdy-gurdy
      2. Crumhorn
      3. Recorders
   C. Basic musical notation

II. Renaissance
   A. Improved musical notation
      1. Similar to current form
   B. The rise of popular music
      1. Peasant songs
      2. Tavern songs
   C. Prominent composers
      1. Michael Pretorius

III. Baroque
   A. Music of the court
   B. Elaborate liturgical music
      1. J.S. Bach
         a. "Jesus Joy to Man's Desire"
   C. Larger ensembles
   D. Development of keyboard instruments
      1. Pianoforte
      2. Organ
      3. Harpsichord

IV. Classical
   A. Large orchestral works
      1. Nonliturgical
   B. Prominent composers
      1. Beethoven
      2. Schubert
      3. Mendelsohn

V. Romantic
   A. Mystical themes from literature/poetry
      1. "Faust"
   B. Moods created with music
      1. Chopin's "Nocturnes"
   C. The Waltz
      1. Strauss
         a. "The Blue Danube Waltz"
   D. Prominent composers
      1. Brahms
      2. Wagner
      3. List

FIGURE 10.2   Electronic Outline for Periods of Music

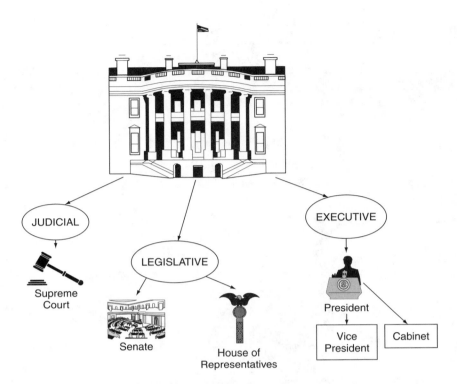

FIGURE 10.3 Electronic Note Taking: Map of Branches of Government

> map produced in Patrick's class). More significantly, Patrick's inclusion students have shown overall improvement in their attitudes and achievement.

Creating Home Pages and Other Web Writing

An ever increasing number of teachers and students are creating information on the Internet by designing their own **home pages**, screens on the World Wide Web that identify a particular site. It seems to be a natural progression for students as they become skillful at accessing information on the Web; eventually, they are not satisfied with this activity and want to create their own information. Home page construction seems to support active learning, group problem solving and planning, and interactive teaching (Ryder & Hughes,1997). Students have created various types of home pages, including personal home pages, multimedia newspapers, online portfolios, class supplements, and community resources.

Art. A group of students in a high school art class were prompted to develop a home page for other art students after they found it difficult to locate resources on contemporary artists and art movements. The advantage of the Internet over the limited resources available in their school's library became immediately apparent to the students when they initiated their search on the World Wide Web for information about current active artists. Hundreds of relevant sites were identified that included artists' names, biographies, illustrations of their works, and more. The art students decided to design their home page with a collage of photographs of original works they had done. They entitled their home page "The Demon of Curiosity: A 12th Graders' Guide to Modern Art" after a painting by Penck done in the 1980s. The site was designed as a resource for any student wishing to gather information about the current art scene. Students included a brief history of their effort to create the site as well as art autobiographies, links to relevant Internet sites, additional readings about artists and their work, and suggestions of assignments and activities to develop modern painting and sculpting techniques.

Students from any content classroom can be responsible for creating and maintaining websites, thereby linking literacy and content learning.

Word processing technology generally has been viewed as the most versatile tool for teaching and learning in most subject areas. In communication, it offers significant advantages over traditional writing tools such as typewriters and paper and pencil. Word processors eliminate many of the difficulties associated with editing and producing texts. With sophisticated desktop publishing capabilities, students can integrate word processing with graphics to create professional-looking materials. Finally, when word processing is combined with the World Wide Web to create home pages and websites, students can make their texts available to a global audience.

English. Kehus (2000), a high school English teacher, has created a forum on the Internet for adolescents to publish their work. The website allows teen writers to submit their completed work for review and possible publication, submit drafts of work for feedback, post messages about their work and the work of others on the site, and exchange points of view about writing with others from around the country. The goals of the website are to provide young adults an authentic purpose and audience for their writing and to create an electronic space for teens to become part of a broad, literary community (Rheingold, 1993). Those teachers who have opened opportunities for young adults to publish on and compose for the Internet (Hunt, 1996) understand the power of writing for the potentially vast, unseen audience out there looking in on their CRTs and LCDs. Student writers for the Internet are often inspired to write more and to create higher quality texts. Electronic networks mediating student writing can also help break down, at least on a cyber-level, the barriers that keep many of us separated in life, culture, ethnicity, and economics.

 Go to Web Resources for Chapter 10 at *http://www. prenhall.com/brozo* and look for Kehus.

Meeting the Needs of Diverse Learners in the Content-Area Classroom

Close on the heels of e-mail has come a new medium for student writing on the Internet—electronic magazines or *e-zines*. Already there are hundreds of these cyber-creations available on the Web covering every imaginable area of interest, with a growing number designed and composed by young adults.

E-zines are ready-made vehicles for using Web-based software to link purposeful writing with subject matter.

Irene's third-block general science class was comprised of 22 freshmen, 12 of whom were receiving special education services and all of whom resided in the inner-city neighborhood around the school. To maximize motivation and engagement, she worked tirelessly to make the learning personally meaningful and relevant to the students' lives and futures. In fact, the inspiration for a science class e-zine grew out of a project tied to one of the class topics, viral diseases. Working collaboratively with her students, Irene helped them explore the extent of diseases such as AIDS and hepatitis in their own community. The class began their investigation by doing e-based searches of local newspapers and conducting phone interviews. With Irene's support, students organized a panel of community volunteers, patients, social workers, and experts to dialog with class and guests on the relationships between viral diseases and conditions of poverty, malnutrition, poor health care, race, gang violence, teen pregnancy, and other factors. Her students videotaped the panel discussion and later when they were replaying it, realized they had something quite special and worthy of sharing with a much wider audience. Since theirs was a technology high school, endowed with state-of-the-art computer labs, high-speed Internet connections, and plenty of innovative software, Irene knew the technology infrastructure would support sophisticated Internet publishing. Her students loved the idea, so they all went to work.

Irene began by assigning the class into teams to tackle different parts of the project. One team focused on the technology; another, the content; and a third, promotional and advertising concerns. The content group operated in much the same way students do when they publish a school newspaper. They wrote informational stories, editorials, events summaries, and public information announcements all based on their work during the study of viral diseases, including, of course, the wealth of information gathered from the panelists. The technology group helped Irene create and design the e-zine. Using Adobe PageMaker, they first formatted the e-zine for regular content, including columns for articles. Next, they experimented with on-screen palettes to find the right logos to drag onto the documents and colors to make the product visually appealing. The advertising group spent time brainstorming a title for the e-zine and ways of ensuring an audience of potential readers would be aware that it was available. Among all of the interesting titles this group pitched to the rest of the class, "Science in the City" was the one that clicked. The class decided to publish three more editions during the balance of the school year focusing on major units: environmental pollution, human reproduction, and fueling and maintaining the human machine.

With the launching of "Science in the City," Irene's class had a new and entirely deserved sense of pride about their learning. More important, they developed a heightened sense of responsibility and accountability that comes with producing an e-zine, improved research skills, writing and spelling skills, and critical thinking skills.

Expanding Learning in Content Classrooms With Databases and Spreadsheets

Databases are extremely versatile computer programs that allow students to collect, organize, and retrieve information. Databases are popular computer applications second only to word processing programs (Jonassen, Peck, & Wilson, 1999). Similar to phone books, recipe files, and catalogs, databases enable students to find, cross-reference, classify, and sort data and search for specific topics and information quickly and easily. Most libraries store reference materials, including encyclopedias, in databases. The exceptionally large storage requirements for works such as encyclopedias, the complete works of Shakespeare, and world almanacs require the optical storage technologies of **CD-ROMs**. Similar to audio CDs, CD-ROMs can store hundreds of millions of bits of information. One small CD can hold up to 250,000 pages of information, making it possible to store entire reference works on a single CD, along with an extensive index that allows searchers to access the information within seconds. Using CD-ROMs, students have been able to expand their research skills, improve their ability to organize information, and learn a great deal about a particular topic by authoring their own databases (Turner & Dipinto, 1992). Teachers have found databases excellent ways of developing higher level thinking skills through questioning (Hancock, Kaput, & Goldsmith, 1992; Merkley, Schmidt, & Allen, 2001).

Spreadsheets are computerized, numerical record-keeping systems. A spreadsheet is composed of a grid, table, or matrix with columns and rows. Each cell may contain values, formulas, or functions, using either numbers or words. Spreadsheets are used to store, calculate, and present information. Most spreadsheet programs allow the learner to display information in a variety of ways, including graphs and charts. Spreadsheets help users manage numbers in much the same way that word processors help them manage words. In fact, Bozeman (1992) described spreadsheets as a way to "word process numbers" (p. 908). Teachers from a variety of content areas have used spreadsheets to engage and support problem solving and other forms of higher level thinking.

Following are brief descriptions of how databases and spreadsheets have already been used by middle and secondary school teachers to improve student motivation and learning in content classroom.

Social studies. An eighth-grade social studies teacher had her class compile a database on current events using information from local newspapers about happenings in countries around the world. Each student was assigned 10 newspaper articles per quarter, which were summarized in a database field that included the country, subject, date, title, publication, and student's name. At the end of the year, the class organized their articles into their own encyclopedia containing more than 2,000 newspaper articles. The students developed a convenient retrieval system for accessing articles with key words.

Current events. Tenth graders engaged in a letter-writing campaign to political prisoners, which grew out of a unit on Amnesty International, and built

Artist	Birth	Movement	Death
Leonardo DaVinci	1452	High renaissance	1519
Édouard Manet	1832	Impressionism	1883
Vincent Van Gogh	1853	Impressionism	1890
Salvador Dali	1904	Surrealism	1983
Frida Kahlo	1910	Surrealism	1954
Henri Matisse	1869	Fauvism	1954
George Bellows	1882	Realism	1925
Käthe Kollwitz	1867	Expressionism	1945
Jackson Pollock	1912	Abstractionism	1956
Andy Warhol	1928	Pop art	1987
Mildred Howard	1945	Postmodernism	

FIGURE 10.4 Database of Artists

Spreadsheets and databases are versatile programs that allow vast amounts and types of information to be organized and easily retrieved.

databases to keep track of their prisoners. They entered such information as the reason for the arrest, the length of the prison term, the current length of imprisonment, the reason for incarceration, health status, and addresses of persons or groups to contact. With the database, they could monitor changes concerning the prisoners, update the record on any prisoner as new information became available, and analyze the information for patterns such as similarities among charges brought against prisoners.

Databases and the Internet

Combining use of the Internet with database systems is an excellent way for teachers to exploit both technologies. Students researching information on the World Wide Web can use a database for organizing and storing information, making study and recall of the information convenient and easy.

Art.   An art teacher had his students research information about artists ranging from Leonardo DaVinci to Frida Kahlo. Using a database program, students first created a framework for recording critical information about each artist, including dates of birth and death and the movement he or she represented or defined (Figure 10.4). Students searched websites with information about the artists, downloaded and printed what they wanted to retain, and then placed the relevant information in the database. When the databases were completed, students printed them and used them to recall information for class discussion and study for a test.

Kinesiology.   Each student in a middle school physical education class was required to maintain a database for the entire school year for recording personal information related to each exercise and athletic activity (Figure 10.5). The purpose of the assignment was to help students learn important information about fitness and muscle development while tying this information to class sports and

Activity	Equipment	Type of Motion	Muscle Group	Benefits
sit-ups	none	sitting, bending	abdominis	toning stomach
walking	shoes		longus, lateralis	toning, cardiovascular
cycling	bicycle	pedaling	femoris, soleus	toning, cardiovascular
running				
curls				
chin-ups				
push-ups				

FIGURE 10.5   Database for Personal Exercise and Health

activities. Students recorded the type of activity (basketball, sit-ups, flag football, etc.), necessary equipment, the type of motion required to perform the activity, the primary muscle groups involved, and the cardiovascular and other fitness benefits. Students also made notes on their databases of particularly useful websites for acquiring additional information relevant to the activity. Using their direct experience and information from the Internet, the students filled in their databases. Throughout the year, they used their databases to retrieve specific information as needed for class participation and examinations. The teacher often asked students to show the rest of the class an especially helpful website and explain how it was used.

Spreadsheets in the Content Classroom

Science.   As Earth Day approached, a junior high science teacher had his students develop a spreadsheet assignment for analyzing lunchroom trash (Ramondetta, 1992). Students spent a week organizing trash items into recyclable and nonrecyclable categories, weighing trash samples, and projecting annual waste and costs. Using color pie charts, bar graphs, and grids, students organized and exhibited their findings at the school's Earth Day fair and assembly. Thought-provoking questions were included with the exhibit to help students understand the seriousness of the problem.

In another science class, sixth graders created a spreadsheet to display information concerning relative gravity on Earth and the other planets. The students designed a grid with statistics on all the planets and individual bar graphs comparing Earth with each planet. Feeding the spreadsheet program with the appropriate formulas for calculating relative gravity, students filled in columns with each planet's relative gravity and their body weight on Earth. The program then automatically calculated the students' weights on the other planets. The information was blown up and put on a large chart board to be displayed in class during the study of gravity.

Mathematics.   High school math students were given the assignment of calculating the dimensions of the Milky Way. Using a scale model, they plugged their formulas into a spreadsheet that provided a calculation function. This function proved to be critical as students modified their formulas up to the last minute and used the spreadsheet to recalculate all of the new values based on the formula changes. As a result of this project, students developed a much better appreciation for the enormity of space.

Algebra. To better organize and understand nonlinear equations, an algebra teacher had her students develop a spreadsheet (Figure 10.6). The spreadsheet was created as students moved through the text and class material on hyperbolas. As students learned new examples, these were added to the spreadsheet along with additional characteristics and definitional information. When the spreadsheet was completed, the teacher showed her students how to use it to study and prepare for tests she designed based on how the information in the spreadsheet was organized. For example, she asked students to compare and contrast different types of hyperbolas and to describe a particular hyperbola based on its critical features.

Database management systems offer teachers and students organized formats for storing and retrieving information. Higher level thinking skills can be fostered through the use of this computer technology as students comprehend and analyze information to be included in the databases. Furthermore, students

	Intersects itself	Function?	Has a defined range	Has a defined domain	Has an x^2 term	x^2 term + or −	Has a y^2 term	y^2 term + or −	Coefficient of x^2 and y^2 terms are equal
Parabola									
Parabola									
Parabola									
Parabola									
Circle									
Ellipse									
Hyperbola									
Hyperbola									

FIGURE 10.6 Spreadsheet for Nonlinear Equations in Algebra

can gain an encoding and recall benefit when they are given responsibility for putting information into the database and creating a record of their study for a later purpose, such as a quiz, test, or class discussion.

Hypertext, Hypermedia, and Multimedia

Hypermedia is a hybrid term that combines **hypertext**, the nonsequential linking of e-based textual information, and **multimedia**, such as photos, video, art, graphics, animation, and audio, to create an interactive computer-mediated experience for participants (Landow, 1992; Tolhurst, 1995). Given students' familiarity with electronic images, multimedia and hypermedia presentations in schools are growing in popularity because they are excellent for gaining and holding attention and because they are multisensory (Jonassen, 1996; Reinking et al., 1998). Student-developed multimedia, hypermedia, and hypertext projects have also been shown to promote critical literacy (Myers & Beach, 2001), strengthen written and oral communication skills (Browning, 2000), increase motivation, and further creative processes (Troxclair, Stephens, Bennett, & Karnes, 1996).

With the development of software such as Storyspace (Bolter, Smith, & Joyce, 1990) HyperCard, CD-ROM Bookshelf, HyperStudio (Wagner, 1997–1998), and SuperLink, it is possible to create and use databases containing an enormous amount of multidimensional information (Bolter & Grusin, 2000; Kozma, 1991, 1994).

Physics. A high school physics teacher had her students create a hypertext database on Nobel Prize winners in physics over the past 10 years. First, using the Internet to establish an initial roster of prize winners, students developed links to news stories, books, scholarly articles, their university and research centers' home pages, three-dimensional models of their award-winning work, photos of the physicists, biographical information, and more. When the projects were completed, they were "tested" by other students working through the stacks and links of information in each database on the physicists to determine ease of access and creativity in making connections. In the course of this project, students demonstrated imagination and a great deal of valuable research experience.

History. Dillner (1994) describes the work of an American history teacher who created a hypermedia database for the Bill of Rights. She designed the computer-based lesson to be friendly to even her most inexperienced computer users. When students turned on the classroom computer, a title page with the words *The Bill of Rights* and a graphic of an American flag appeared on screen, while the music of "Yankee Doodle" flowed from the computer speakers. When the song ended, directions appeared on the screen. Using the mouse, students highlighted an arrow at the bottom of the screen and a new page appeared. The new page was a menu with a list of all 10 amendments. Students were asked to highlight an amendment to acquire more information about it. For example,

Go to Web Resources for Chapter 10 at *http://www. prenhall.com/brozo* and look for Hypermedia and Hypertext Software.

Many adolescents are highly motivated to use computers to manipulate images, text, and sound in the content classroom.

highlighting "Right to Bear Arms" brought on a screen with the amendment title surrounded by five choices *(Interpretation, Definition, On Your Own, Examples, Assignments)*. When students highlighted *Examples,* a videotaped clip ran of a student broadcaster and student actors replaying the scene of the day former president Ronald Reagan and his press secretary, James Brady, were shot by John Hinckley. The video was accompanied by audio information about how, since the assassination attempt, James and Sarah Brady have been lobbying against Americans' easy access to handguns. The other choices on each of the amendment screens provided additional media support for learning about the amendments and directing learning of the textbook chapter on the Bill of Rights.

History/culture.   Patterson (2000) had her middle school students use Storyspace (Bolter, Smith, & Joyce, 1990) to build hypertexts around research they were conducting in American history and culture. For example, during the study of Native Americans, students created biographical webs for Sitting Bull and Sacagawea with links to important related events in history. Students made Native American poetry webs with links to critical information about Native American culture and history.

For the study of slavery, Patterson developed a joint project with students in Ghana, Africa, to help write a more complete history of the slave trade. The African students began the story with information about how slaves were captured in Africa, while Patterson's middle graders finished the story by describing the slave experience in the southern United States. Based on their research, students then composed hypertext narratives with links to information about slavery.

Science.   Some highly motivated junior high students worked together to create a touch-sensitive multimedia kiosk that was installed at a local zoo (Beichner, 1994). Using HyperCard and other hypermedia technology, they designed an information program, working with an on-screen audio recorder, a video tool to operate the videodisc player, color painting and text tools, and a data-linking tool for connecting pieces of information. Hot spots were created on the screen that, when touched by zoo visitors, made it possible to see and hear animals, gather additional information, and even obtain printouts, such as a map and student-generated questions and comments about zoo animals. Students demonstrated great enthusiasm for this project because they saw a real-world connection between their developing technology and science skills and the product of their efforts—the information kiosk for zoo visitors.

Social studies.   Middle school students, using the tools available in HyperStudio, created a hypermedia presentation on the Civil Rights movement of the 1960s for a class project during African-American History Month. Their research resulted in several hypermedia topics of interest, including music, images (photographs and video), major players, historical background, and more. The program was on display in the school library during February for all students to access. By clicking on a topic of interest, students could read about Rosa Parks, see a video clip of George Wallace, or listen to President John Kennedy make a brief speech.

Hypermedia technology seems to be an ideal way to motivate today's youth to explore information in realistic and multimodal ways. Integrating sights, sounds, texts, graphics, and computers into an overall presentation can be an enriching and memorable learning experience for students in virtually all subject areas. Hypermedia and hypertext projects are becoming excellent alternatives to traditional papers and tests as measures of students' overall understanding of a unit or topic. The projects students create can also become part of the classroom collection of resources to be accessed by future students to enrich their learning.

ACCESSING AND ASSESSING COMPUTER TECHNOLOGY

Because of the rapid developments in computer technology, keeping up with innovations in hardware, software, and related technologies is a daunting task, especially for busy teachers. Perhaps the most challenging task for the classroom teacher is the selection of appropriate software. Although computers have the potential to improve teacher effectiveness, this can occur only when quality computer programs are put in the hands of quality teachers. Concerns about quality software are especially critical for those of us promoting the integration of literacy processes into content-area classrooms.

Although a daunting task, keeping abreast of computer technology is simpler for content-area teachers by accessing information on the Internet itself.

Considering the four principles described at the opening of this chapter, we recommend that instructional software be selected on the basis of whether it contains meaningful content and can be used for purposeful learning. In addition, software programs should require active participation by the learner and emphasize elaborative and creative thinking instead of repetitive drill. Vigorous efforts have been made over the past 10 years to change the nature of software for students from computerized workbooks to interactive, generative learning tools (Leu, 2000). Therefore, it is important to evaluate closely any computer products that may be potentially useful in your classroom.

One fairly easy way to find out about new developments in computing hardware and appropriate software is by exploring the Internet itself. Some of the best sites are designed just for teachers. Reviews of software can also be found in educational computing and general microcomputer magazines as well as in professional journals. A list relevant publications can be found in Figure 10.7.

Before writing your suggestions for José in the case study, go to *http://www.prenhall. com/brozo,* select Chapter 10, then click on Chapter Review Questions to check your understanding of the material.

CASE STUDY REVISITED

After exploring this chapter, you should now have many new ideas about how to use computer technology in the content classroom for increasing student motivation and active involvement and for promoting higher level thinking. José, the biology teacher who is the focus of this case study, was fortunate enough to discover

Byte
One Phoenix Mill Lane
Peterborough, NH 03458

Computer Assisted English Language Learning Journal
International Society for
    Technology in Education (ISTE)
1787 Agate St.
Eugene, OR 97403-1923

Computer Science Education
Ablex Publishing Corp.
355 Chestnut St.
Norwood, NJ 07648

Computers and Education
Michigan Technological University
Department of Humanities
Houghton, MI 49931

Computers and Education
Pergamon Press
600 White Plains Rd.
Tarrytown, NY 10591-5153

Computers, Reading and Language Arts
Modern Learning Publishers, Inc.
1308 E. 38th St.
Oakland, CA 94602

Curriculum Product News
Educational Media, Inc.
992 High Ridge Rd.
Stamford, CT 06905

ED-TECH Review
Association for the Advancement of
    Computing in Education (AACE)
Box 2966
Charlottesville, VA 22902

Educational Technology
720 Palisade Ave.
Englewood Cliffs, NJ 07632

Instruction Delivery Systems
Communicative Technology Corp.
50 Culpepper St.
Warrenton, VA 22186

Interactive Learning Environments
Ablex Publishing Corp.
355 Chestnut St.
Norwood, NJ 07648

Internet World
20 Ketchum St.
Westport, CT 06880

Journal of Adolescent & Adult Literacy
International Reading Association
800 Barksdale Rd.
Box 8139
Newark, DE 19714-8139

*Journal of Computers in Mathematics
    and Science Teaching*
AACE
Box 2966
Charlottesville, VA 22902

Journal of Computing in Teacher Education
ISTE
1787 Agate St.
Eugene, OR 97403-1923

Journal of Educational Computing Research
Baywood Publishing Co., Inc.
26 Austin Ave.
Box 337
Amityville, NY 11701

Journal of Educational Multimedia and Hypermedia
AACE
Box 2966
Charlottesville, VA 22902

Journal of Research on Computing in Education
ISTE
1787 Agate St.
Eugene, OR 97403-1923

Learning and Leading with Technology
    (formerly *The Computing Teacher*)
ISTE
1787 Agate St.
Eugene, OR 97403-1923

**FIGURE 10.7   Journals, Magazines, and Technology Websites for Middle
and Secondary School Teachers**

MacWorld
MacWorld Communications, Inc.
501 2nd St.
San Francisco, CA 94107

Multimedia Schools
Information Today Inc.
143 Old Marlton Pike
Medford, NJ 08055-8750

PC Magazine
Ziff-Davis Publishing Co.
One Park Ave.
New York, NY 10016

Personal Publishing
Hitchcock Publishing Co.
191 S. Gary Ave.
Carol Stream, IL 60188

Research in Science & Technological Education
Carfax Publication Co.
Taylor & Francis
325 Chestnut St., Suite 800
Philadelphia, PA 19106

The Reading Teacher
International Reading Association
800 Barksdale Rd.
Box 8139
Newark, DE 19714-8139

School Library Journal
Box 1878
Marion, OH 43305

School Library Media Activities Monthly
LMS Associates
17 East Henrietta St.
Baltimore, MD 21230-3910

Science Teacher
1742 Connecticut Ave. NW
Washington, DC 20009

Teaching and Computers
Scholastic, Inc.
Box 2040
Mahopac, NY 10541-9963

Tech Trends
Association for Educational Technology
   and Communications
1025 Vermont Ave. NW, Suite 820
Washington, DC 20005

Techniques
Association for Career & Technical Education
1410 King St.
Alexandria, VA 22314

Technology & Learning
600 Harrison St.
San Francisco, CA 94107

Telecommunications in Education
   (T.I.E.) News
ISTE
1787 Agate St.
Eugene, OR 97403-1923

T.H.E. Journal–Technological Horizons in Education
150 El Camino Real
Tustin, CA 92680

Via Satellite
Phillips Business Information, Inc.
7811 Montrose Rd.
Potomac, MD 20854

Windows Magazine
CMP Publications
600 Community Dr.
Manhasset, NY 11030

Windows Users
Wandsworth Publishing, Inc.
831 Federal Rd.
Brookfield, CT 06804

The Writing Notebook, Creative Word
   Processing in the Classroom
Box 1268
Eugene, OR 97440-1268

 Go to Web Resources for Chapter 10
at *http:/www.prenhall.com/brozo* and
look for Technology Websites.

**FIGURE 10.7   Journals, Magazines, and Technology Websites for Middle
and Secondary School Teachers** (*continued*)

some of the outstanding instructional applications of computer programs for help-ing his students better organize, analyze, and study biology information.

José brainstormed with another biology teacher and decided that a database management system held the most promise for helping their students organize a large number of related bits of information. José used the Microsoft Works inte-grated software package provided with the DOS-based computers purchased through his school's grant.

José introduced his students to the database management system approach to organizing and studying by presenting a database he had completed as an example. José knew that with the students' first exposure, it was critical that the database not be too complex, leading to possible frustration and failure. Wisely, he began with a familiar database of lunch menu items from the previous month, his likes and dislikes, meat and vegetable content, and choice of beverage. First, he projected his database on a large screen using a liquid crystal display (LCD) acquired with grant monies. LCD panels are compact, flat units that fit on top of overhead projectors and allow large groups equal viewing access to computer screen information. After explaining how he constructed his database, he posed several questions to the class, and then had them work in pairs using the database to answer the questions.

José's next step was to have students complete a partially completed database by using their biology textbooks to fill in the gaps. This approach is highly consistent with the ways teachers can help students enjoy the encoding benefits of learning we describe in this book. Again, working in pairs, his students keyed in information re-lated to several different animals, their diets, and their habitats. Several sessions were spent monitoring and coaching the students and demonstrating the desired thinking and computer skills needed to complete the database. Students were encouraged to ask frequent questions of José and their peers as they gained greater facility and con-fidence in using the process of database construction.

At this stage, José was ready to begin applying the database technology to the study of cell types. As before, he placed a database (this time, blank) on the overhead projector using an LCD panel. Students sat in pairs around a common terminal, with their own blank database on-screen and their textbooks open to the chapter on human cells. José read through the chapter with his students and engaged them in discussion about key terms and descriptions of cell types. As they progressed through the first few pages of the chapter and talked about in-formation they were learning about cells, José demonstrated on the overhead how and where to place critical information into their databases. Finally, es-sential categories were agreed upon and written into their database grids; these included cell type, shape, function, and location (Figure 10.8). With each subse-quent class session, as students read, studied, and engaged in meaningful learning activities related to cells, they were given the opportunity to input relevant in-formation into their databases. At the end of each class session, José engaged stu-dents in an exchange of questions about their expanding databases. Students asked questions of each other and of José, as he asked questions of them in a model/elicit format. In this way, José was stimulating critical decision making and higher level thinking as he prepared his class for a test on the material at the end of their study of the chapter. Through this process, students were able to see

Type of Cell	Shape	Function	Location
astocyte	radiating	supply nutrients	central nervous system (CNS)
basal	cube-like	make new cells	stratum basale
cardiac muscle	branched	pump blood	around heart
erythrocytes	disc	move O_2, remove CO_2	blood plasma
fibroblast	flat	fiber production	connective tissue
keratinocytes	round	strengthen cells	stratum basal
osteoclast	ruffled	bone restoration	bone
sensory neurons	long, thin	impulses to CNS	cell body
simple columnar	columnar	secretion, absorption	digestive tract, glands
simple squamous	flat	diffusion of materials	lungs, blood vessels, kidneys
skeletal muscle	long	movement, posture	bone, skin
smooth muscle	disc	movement	organ walls

FIGURE 10.8   José's Class Database

how test-like questions were related to their databases and could be answered using information in their grids.

José was proud to report that after his class created, queried, and studied their databases on cells, they scored higher on his chapter test than any previous group. His colleague, who used the same approach, had similar results. Students demonstrated much more enthusiasm for learning the content of the chapter using the computer and reported that they could concentrate and understand the material more easily using a database.

◄○►

SUMMARY

There has been incredibly rapid growth in instructional applications of computer technology over the past couple of editions of *Readers, Teachers, Learners*. We believe the ultimate outcome of this growth is the inevitable use of computers as teaching and learning tools in an increasing number of middle and secondary schools. We also believe that with this growth comes responsible use of computer technology for meeting the learning needs of adolescents. Consequently, we advocate in this chapter that teachers use computers in meaningful ways to encourage active learning, to provide students with opportunities for unique learning experiences, and to help them organize and synthesize information across the content areas. Teachers of today and the future will need to increase their knowledge of classroom applications of computer technology to be wise and purposeful consumers. It is our hope that with this knowledge, teachers will discover ways to make computers a tool compatible with the other interactive, pro-social, language-based strategies recommended throughout this book.

REFERENCES

Alvermann, D. (2002). *Adolescents and literacies in a digital world.* New York: Peter Lang.

Anderson, J., & Lee, A. (1995). Literacy teachers learning a new literacy: A study of the use of electronic mail in a reading education class. *Reading Research and Instruction, 34,* 222–238.

Anderson, T. H., & Armbruster, B. B. (1984). Content area textbooks. In R. Anderson, J. Osborn, & R. Tierney (Eds.), *Learning to read in American schools: Basal readers and content texts.* Hillsdale, NJ: Erlbaum.

Anderson-Inman, L. (1995–1996). Computer-assisted outlining: Information organization made easy. *Journal of Adolescent & Adult Literacy, 39,* 316–320.

Anderson-Inman, L., & Horney, M. (1997). Computer-based concept mapping: Enhancing literacy with tools for visual thinking. *Journal of Adolescent & Adult Literacy, 40,* 302–306.

Armstrong, S. (1995). *Telecommunications in the classroom.* Palo Alto, CA: Computer Learning Foundation.

Barron, A., & Lyskawa, C. (1998). *Microsoft FrontPage.* Cambridge, MA: International Thompson Publishing.

Beach, R., & Lundell, D. (1998). Early adolescents' use of computer-mediated communication in writing and reading. In D. Reinking, M. McKenna, L. Labbo, & R. Kieffer (Eds.), *Handbook of literacy and technology: Transformations in a post-typographic world.* Mahwah, NJ: Erlbaum.

Bean, T. (2000). Reading in the content areas: Social constructivist dimensions. In M. Kamil, P. Mosenthal, P. D. Pearson, & R. Barr (Eds.), *Handbook of reading research,* (Vol 3). Mahwah, NJ: Lawrence Erlbaum Associates.

Beichner, R. J. (1994). Multimedia editing to promote science learning. *Journal of Educational Multimedia and Hypermedia, 3,* 55–70.

Blase, D. W. (2000). A new sort of writing: E-mail in the English classroom. *English Journal, 90,* 47–51.

Bolter, J. D., & Grusin, R. (2000). *Re-mediation: Understanding new media.* Boston: MIT Press.

Bolter, J. D., Smith, J., & Joyce, M. (1990). *Storyspace.* Cambridge, MA: Eastgate.

Bozeman, W. (1992). Spreadsheets. In G. Bitter (Ed.), *Macmillan encyclopedia of computers.* New York: Macmillan.

Brindley, S. (2000). ICT and literacy. In N. Gamble & N. Easingwood (Eds.), *ICT and literacy: Information and communications technology, media, reading and writing.* London: Continuum.

Brown, A., & Campione, J. (1996). Psychological theory and the design of innovative learning environments: On procedures, principles, and systems. In L. Schauble & R. Glaser (Eds.), *Innovations in learning: New environments for education.* Mahwah, NJ: Erlbaum.

Browning, T. (2000). Hypermedia design in the English classroom. In D. Hickey & D. Reiss (Eds.), *Learning literature in an era of change: Innovations in teaching.* Sterling, VA: Stylus.

Burbules, N. (1998). Rhetorics of the Web: Hyperreading and critical literacy. In I. Snyder (Ed.), *Page to screen: Taking literacy into the electronic era*. London: Routledge.

Burbules, N., & Callister, T. (2000). *Watch it: The risks and promises of information technologies for education*. Boulder, CO: Westview Press.

Burniske, R., & Monke, L. (2001). *Breaking down the digital walls: Learning to teach in a post-modem world*. Albany State University of New York Press.

Dillner, M. (1994). Using hypermedia to enhance content area instruction. *Journal of Reading, 37*, 260-270.

Fielding, L. P., & Pearson, P. D. (1994). Reading comprehension: What works. *Educational Leadership, 51*, 62-68.

Freire, P. (1987). *Literacy: Reading the word and the world*. South Hadley, MA: Bergin & Garvey.

Gamble, N., & Easingwood, N. (2000). *ICT and literacy: Information and communications technology, media, reading and writing*. London: Continuum.

Gee, J. (1996). *Social linguistics and literacies: Ideology in discourses* (2nd ed.). London: Falmer Press.

Grabe, C., & Grabe, M. (1998). *Learning with Internet tools: A primer*. Boston: Houghton Mifflin.

Halio, M. P. (1990). Student writing: Can the machine maim the message? *Academic Computing, 6*, 18-19.

Hancock, C., Kaput, J. J., & Goldsmith, L. T. (1992). Authentic inquiry with data: Critical barriers to classroom implementation. *Educational Psychologist, 27*, 337-364.

Harris, J. (1994). Teaching teachers to use telecomputing tools. *The Computing Teacher, 22*, 60-63.

Hawisher, G., & Selfe, C. (1998). Reflections on computers and composition studies at the century's end. In I. Snyder (Ed.), *Page to screen: Taking literacy into the electronic era*. London: Routledge.

Healy, J. (2000). *Failure to connect: How computers affect our children's minds—for better or worse*. New York: Simon and Schuster.

Horney, M. A., & Anderson-Inman, L. (1992, April). *Computer-based outlining programs as tools for gathering, organizing and studying information across the curriculum*. Paper presented at the annual conference of the American Educational Research Association, San Francisco.

Hunt, V. (1996). The Raptor Project. In C. Edgar & S. Wood (Eds.), *The nearness of you: Students and teachers writing on-line*. New York: Teachers and Writers Collaborative.

Inspiration Software, Inc. (1995). *Inspiration 4.1*. Portland, OR: Author.

Jonassen, D. H. (1996). *Computers in the classroom: Mindtools for critical thinking*. Englewood Cliffs, NJ: Prentice Hall.

Jonassen, D., Peck, K., & Wilson, B. (1999). *Learning with technology*. Columbus, OH: Merrill.

Kehus, M. (2000). Opportunities for teenagers to share their writing online. *Journal of Adolescent & Adult Literacy, 44*, 130-134.

Kelly, M. G., & Wiebe, J. H. (1994). Telecommunications, data gathering, and problem solving. *The Computing Teacher, 21*, 23-26.

Kozma, R. (1991). Learning with media. *Review of Educational Research, 61*, 179-211.

Kozma, R. (1994). Will media influence learning? Reframing the debate. *Educational Technology Research and Development, 42,* 5-17.

Kress, G. (1998). Visual and verbal modes of representation in electronically mediated communication: The potentials of new forms of text. In I. Snyder (Ed.), *Page to screen: Taking literacy into the electronic era.* London: Routledge.

Landow, G. P. (1992). *Hypertext: The convergence of contemporary critical theory and technology.* Baltimore, MD: Johns Hopkins University Press.

Lankshear, C., Gee, J., Knobel, M., & Searle, C. (1997). *Changing literacies.* Cambridge, England: Open University Press.

Leu, D. (2000). Literacy and technology: Deictic consequences for literacy education in an information age. In M. Kamil, P. Mosenthal, P. D. Pearson, & R. Barr (Eds.), *Handbook of reading research* (Vol. 3). Mahwah, NJ: Lawrence Erlbaum Associates.

Loveless, A., & Ellis, V. (2001). *ICT, pedagogy and the curriculum: Subject to change.* London: RoutledgeFalmer.

Luke, A., & Elkins, J. (1998). Reinventing literacy in "new times." *Journal of Adolescent & Adult Literacy, 42,* 4-7.

March, T. (2000). "Are we there yet?" A parable on the educational effectiveness of technology. *Multimedia Schools, 7,* 54-55.

Marcus, S. (1995). E-meliorating student writing. *Electronic Learning, 14,* 18-19.

Mather, M. A. (2000). Exhibits alive! Museums, schools, and technology work together. *Technology & Learning, 21,* 57-62.

Mathews, J. (2000). High-tech heretics. *Washington Post,* May 2, A11.

Merkley, D., Schmidt, D., & Allen, G. (2001). Addressing the English language arts technology standard in a secondary reading methodology course. *Journal of Adolescent & Adult Literacy, 45,* 220-231.

Mike, D. (1997). Internet in the schools: A literacy perspective. *Journal of Adolescent & Adult Literacy, 40,* 4-13.

Monke, L. (2001). In dreams begins responsibilities. In R. Burniske & L. Monke (Eds.), *Breaking down the digital walls: Learning to teach in a post-modem world.* Albany State University of New York Press.

Myers, J., & Beach, R. (2001). Hypermedia authoring as critical literacy. *Journal of Adolescent & Adult Literacy, 44,* 538-546.

Negroponte, N. (1995). *Being digital.* New York: Alfred A. Knopf.

Newby, T., Stepich, D., Lehman, J., & Russell, J. (1996). *Instructional technology for teaching and learning.* Englewood Cliffs, NJ: Prentice Hall.

Nichols, W. D., Wood, K., & Rickelman, R. (2001). Using technology to engage students in reading and writing. *Middle School Journal, 32,* 45-50.

Nist, S. L., Simpson, M. L., Olejnik, S., & Mealey, D. L. (1991). The relation between self-selected study processes and test performance. *American Educational Research Journal, 28,* 849-874.

Patterson, N. (2000). Weaving a narrative: From teens to string to hypertext. *Voices From the Middle, 7,* 41-47.

Peters, M., & Lankshear, C. (1996). Cricial literacy and digital texts. *Educational Theory, 46,* 51-70.

Ramondetta, J. (1992). Learning from lunchroom trash. *Learning Using Computers, 20,* 59.

Reinking, D., McKenna, M., Labbo, L., & Kieffer, R. (1998). *Handbook of literacy and technology: Transformations in a post-typographic world.* Mahwah, NJ: Erlbaum.

Rheingold, H. (1993). *The virtual community: Homesteading on the electronic frontier*. Reading, MA: Addison Wesley.

Riel, M. (1993, April). *The writing connection: Global learning circles*. Paper presented at the annual meeting of the American Educational Research Association, Atlanta.

Riel, M., & Fulton, K. (2001). The role of technology in supporting learning communities. *Phi Delta Kappan, 82*, 518-523.

Roblyer, M. D., Edwards, J., & Havriluk, M. A. (1997). *Integrating educational technology into teaching*. Upper Saddle River, NJ: Prentice Hall.

Rushkoff, D. (1996). *Playing the future: How kids' culture can teach us to thrive in an age of chaos*. New York: HarperCollins.

Ryder, R. J., & Graves, M. F. (1997). Using the Internet to enhance students' reading, writing, and information-gathering skills. *Journal of Adolescent & Adult Literacy, 40*, 244-254.

Ryder, R. J., & Hughes, T. (1997). *Internet for educators*. Upper Saddle River, NJ: Prentice Hall.

Salomon, G. (1993). On the nature of pedagogic computer tools: The case of the writing partner. In S. P. LaJoie & J. Derry (Eds.), *Computers as cognitive tools*. Hillsdale, NJ: Erlbaum.

Simons, P. R. (1993). Constructive learning: The role of the learner. In T. Duffy, J. Lowyck, & D. Jonassen (Eds.), *Designing environments for constructive learning*. Heidelberg, Germany: Springer-Verlag.

Stoll, C. (1999). *Why computers don't belong in the classroom and other reflections by a computer contrarian*. New York: Doubleday.

Tolhurst, D. (1995). Hypertext, hypermedia, multimedia defined? *Educational Technology, 35*, 21-26.

Troxclair, D., Stephens, K., Bennett, T., & Karnes, F. (1996). Teaching technology: Multimedia presentations in the classroom. *Gifted Child, 19*, 34-47.

Turner, S. V., & Dipinto, V. M. (1992). Students as hypermedia authors: Themes emerging from a qualitative study. *Journal of Research on Computing in Education, 25*, 187-199.

Wagner, R. (1997-1998). *HyperStudio Workbook*. El Cajon, CA: Roger Wagner Publishing.

Warschauer, M. (1999). *Electronic literacies: Language, culture, and power in online education*. Mahwah, NJ: Erlbaum.

Wenglinsky, H. (1998). *Does it compute? The relationship between educational technology and student achievement in mathematics*. Princeton, NJ: Educational Testing Service.

White, B., & Johnson, T. S. (2001). We really do mean it: Implementing language arts standard #3 with opinionnaires. *The Clearing House, 74*, 119-123.

CHAPTER ELEVEN

Becoming an Effective Content Literacy Professional

ANTICIPATION GUIDE

Directions: Read each statement carefully and decide whether you agree or disagree with it, placing a check mark in the appropriate *Before Reading* column. When you have finished reading and studying the chapter, return to the guide and decide whether your anticipations need to be changed by placing a check mark in the appropriate *After Reading* column.

	BEFORE READING		AFTER READING	
	Agree	*Disagree*	*Agree*	*Disagree*
1. To answer questions about the best instruction to provide students, teachers should rely solely on expert opinion and research.	_____	_____	_____	_____
2. Introducing new ideas is usually a smooth and enjoyable process for all involved.	_____	_____	_____	_____
3. Change, no matter how minor it may seem to others, can be difficult for most teachers.	_____	_____	_____	_____
4. Meaningful change in teaching methods can happen only if teachers work alone.	_____	_____	_____	_____
5. Reflective teachers are constantly striving to understand how to provide more effective instruction.	_____	_____	_____	_____

I have to learn beyond my classroom. I have to put myself in situations that challenge my thinking, my comfort. I take courses that push my knowledge. I find myself hiding behind other students, hoping the professor won't call on me because I'm having trouble understanding the vocabulary and the concepts. But I push myself to figure it out. I listen hard. I reread. I rewrite what I think. And I try to relate it all to my experiences. I have to be a learner in and out of my classroom so I won't lose sight of what it's like for my students—so I will continue to hear their voices.

—Rief (1992)

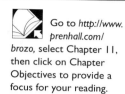
Go to *http://www.prenhall.com/brozo*, select Chapter 11, then click on Chapter Objectives to provide a focus for your reading.

J ust as effective reading does not result from prescriptive teaching, effective teaching cannot be achieved by following a set of prescriptions. What makes content literacy professionals effective is often what makes them unique. They create classroom learning environments and engage students in experiences that break from tradition, that make learning exciting and memorable. The strategies in this book, then, should be viewed as examples of possibilities that, when modified to fit your needs, your students' needs, and the instructional context, will lead to greater learning and enthusiasm for learning.

This chapter deals with several important issues related to literacy professionalism as it concerns middle and secondary classroom teachers and student literacy. First, we explore personal, contextual, and political factors that influence teachers' use of innovative reading and learning strategies. Within this discussion, we propose a model of teacher change. We then discuss how teacher reflections and classroom action research can provide teachers with insights into themselves, their evolving philosophies of teaching, and their students. We also present collaborative strategies for solidifying support among teachers and students, parents, other teachers, and administrators. We argue that through these collaborative relationships, teachers become more effective in arousing students' enthusiasm for learning, increasing content-area learning, and expanding literacy. As part of this discussion, we present guidelines for developing professional learning communities and examples of teachers involved in teacher study groups. We conclude this chapter with descriptions of schoolwide literacy efforts in four different settings. Based on these descriptions we ask you to envision yourself in a middle or secondary reading program playing the most effective role possible in expanding literacy for adolescents.

CASE STUDY

Melinda hadn't used centers for 10 years, since the last time she taught first grade. But last summer just before the new school year, she decided to see if her sixth graders would get just as excited about centers as her little ones did. Melinda, a language arts teacher, knew a change was needed in her classroom, though she had been uncertain about exactly what and how to change. Student performance was not necessarily slipping; it was Melinda's own sense of professionalism that impelled her to explore other instructional possibilities for her sixth graders. Remembering vividly how centers helped her children solve problems, work cooperatively, use their imaginations more creatively, and enrich their skills, Melinda reasoned that centers could bring about the same results with older readers and learners, provided that they were designed appropriately. Part of her goal in implementing centers was to determine their effectiveness throughout the year so that modifications could be made whenever needed.

To the Reader:
As you explore Chapter 11, consider all of the possible steps Melinda can take to study the effectiveness of her centers. Keep in mind that the context for this research is an actual sixth-grade language arts classroom, with all of its dynamics and complexities. Also keep in mind Melinda's goals for the centers.

————◀◎▶————

LITERACY INNOVATIONS IN THE CONTENT CLASSROOM: CHALLENGES TO CHANGE

Those of us who teach content-area reading courses for undergraduate and graduate preservice and in-service teachers from a variety of subject area disciplines are engaged in a constant struggle to convince our students that the methods we advocate have validity. A ubiquitous concern is that we are being hypocritical as teachers of teachers if we tell our students to teach content in a way that makes it personally meaningful and functional to their students while we discuss and demonstrate strategies that are not functional or personally meaningful to our own students (Short & Burke, 1989).

Over the past several years, numerous explanations have been offered for why classroom teachers do not practice the strategies learned in content reading courses (Bintz, 1997; Holt-Reynolds, 1992; O'Brien, Stewart, & Moje, 1995; Palmer & Stewart, 1997; Ratekin, Simpson, Alvermann, & Dishner, 1985; Ruddell & Sperling, 1988; Sturtevant, 1993; Sunderman, Amoa, & Meyers, 2001; Wilson, Konopak, & Readence, 1992). Collectively, these reasons include the following:

Literacy innovations must be relevant to teachers' and students' needs in order to be effective.

- Teachers construct simplified approaches to content instruction based on the perceived constraints of their particular school setting.
- Teachers view content reading and writing strategies as instructionally worthless because they were learned from lecture and textbooks, essentially in isolation from real classroom settings with groups of students. They have not been able to try out the strategies, observe them in practice, or make judgments and decisions about them.
- The organization and power structure of schools inhibit teachers' attempts to try new ideas such as content reading and writing strategies. Preservice teachers are also acutely sensitive to the potential ramifications of nonconformity and innovation.
- Teachers perceive that content reading and writing strategies encroach on valuable time spent covering content.
- Teachers perceive that content reading and writing instruction does not produce measurable gains on standardized tests, where such tests are seen as the most important gauge of successful teaching.

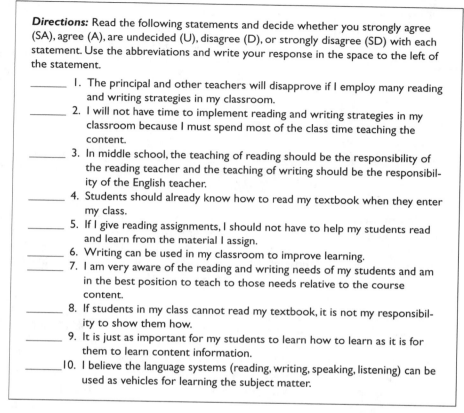

Directions: Read the following statements and decide whether you strongly agree (SA), agree (A), are undecided (U), disagree (D), or strongly disagree (SD) with each statement. Use the abbreviations and write your response in the space to the left of the statement.

_____ 1. The principal and other teachers will disapprove if I employ many reading and writing strategies in my classroom.

_____ 2. I will not have time to implement reading and writing strategies in my classroom because I must spend most of the class time teaching the content.

_____ 3. In middle school, the teaching of reading should be the responsibility of the reading teacher and the teaching of writing should be the responsibility of the English teacher.

_____ 4. Students should already know how to read my textbook when they enter my class.

_____ 5. If I give reading assignments, I should not have to help my students read and learn from the material I assign.

_____ 6. Writing can be used in my classroom to improve learning.

_____ 7. I am very aware of the reading and writing needs of my students and am in the best position to teach to those needs relative to the course content.

_____ 8. If students in my class cannot read my textbook, it is not my responsibility to show them how.

_____ 9. It is just as important for my students to learn how to learn as it is for them to learn content information.

_____ 10. I believe the language systems (reading, writing, speaking, listening) can be used as vehicles for learning the subject matter.

FIGURE 11.1 Inventory of Attitudes and Beliefs About Implementing Reading and Writing Strategies in Your Content Classroom

To determine your own attitudes and beliefs about teaching reading and writing strategies in your classroom, follow the directions in Figure 11.1 to complete the inventory of attitudes and beliefs about implementing reading and writing strategies in your content classroom.

STRATEGY, TEACHER, AND ORGANIZATIONAL CHARACTERISTICS INFLUENCING THE KNOWLEDGE AND USE OF READING AND WRITING STRATEGIES

When considering influences on the extent to which reading and writing strategies are implemented in the classroom, it becomes readily apparent that teacher, strategy, and structural characteristics are most critical (Albright, 2001;

Richardson, 2001; Sunderman, Amoa, & Meyers, 2001). These are discussed in the following paragraphs.

Strategy

For any new strategy to be effectively incorporated into practice, teachers must perceive it in one or more of the following ways:

1. The new strategy must have an advantage over alternatives. We believe it has been made abundantly clear in this book that integrating strategies for reading, writing, and literacy development within the content classroom affords a number of advantages over traditional instructional delivery systems. Students can learn more quickly and easily by improving the process of acquiring the content. They can become more motivated to learn, remember, and apply the content when innovative language-learning strategies are used as vehicles for expanding knowledge. The teacher can become more enthusiastic and involved in the teaching–learning process when there are abundant opportunities for demonstrations, multidirectional interactions, reflections, and personal and group explorations.

Teachers must recognize the advantages of new strategies over ones they are currently using if they are to be incorporated into their repertories.

2. The new strategy must be compatible with what the teacher already knows or believes. What do you know and believe about teaching reading in middle and secondary school? In this book we have attempted to expand your understanding of the reading process and your knowledge about how best to teach reading and writing in the middle and secondary school classroom. The research-grounded foundations of language-based teaching in Chapter 1 and principles of active learning in Chapter 2 derive from our current knowledge about literacy. If these principles already guide your practice or will serve you in that way in the future, then the ideas and strategies in this text for promoting expansive literacy in middle and secondary schools will be more readily incorporated into your teaching repertoire.

3. The new strategy must not be too complex. Although it is true that the reading process comprises many complex interactions, we have tried to point out that it is also true that teachers can be effective if they recognize self-evident truths about learning. For instance, it does not take volumes of research to tell us that students will be more motivated to read and learn if we give them something interesting to read. By the same token, students will become better language users if we give them plenty of opportunities to use language in meaningful and functional ways. We have purposely tried to eliminate unnecessary complexity from our discussions and have not laden our explanations of reading and writing processes and strategies with dense, abstract theoretical terminology because we believe that theory and practice are transactional (Burnaford, 1996; Valli & Price, 2000; Korthagen & Kessels, 1999). In other words, reading theory ought to be grounded in experience (Bloome & Harste, 2001; Wells, 1992). In this connection, we have tried to demonstrate what competent language teachers and users do to facilitate text comprehension.

4. The new strategy must be tried out and/or observed in practice. For some of you who have yet to enter a classroom, nearly every teaching strategy discussed by a professor or presented in a textbook must seem a bit hollow and leave you a bit incredulous. We are especially sensitive to these reactions among students. Although the laws of physics prevent us from projecting you into an actual classroom/instructional setting, we have tried our best to offer realistic applications for the strategies discussed. The constant references to actual classroom practices and anecdotal evidence for the successful implementation of strategies are intended to help you see how the strategies worked in one setting and reflect on the possibilities for you and your classroom.

Effective teachers shape strategies to fit their particular classroom contexts.

Teacher

It goes without saying that the teacher plays the most important role in student learning. Excellent strategies in the hands of disinterested teachers are likely to have little impact on student achievement. Conversely, highly creative, skilled, and enthusiastic teachers can elevate student achievement regardless of the instructional scheme (c.f., Bond & Dykstra, 1967). Although this has been commonly understood for many years, it hasn't inhibited educational administrators and policy makers from repeatedly insisting that teachers employ the newest "best practice." It is naive to expect significant changes in student learning will occur as a result of such curricular impositions (Sunderman, Amoa, & Meyers, 2001).

Those who have investigated the complexities of teacher change (Hargreaves, 1995; Richardson, 2001) claim that teachers are highly likely to accept and put into practice innovative literacy and learning strategies if they (1) view themselves as supportive and productive; (2) have open lines of communication in the classroom and with colleagues and others in the profession; (3) are self-initiating, cooperative, and highly motivated; and (4) are intellectually curious. Furthermore, in order to have realistic expectations that teachers will modify their instructional approaches, those desiring change must provide contextualized models, opportunities for experimentation and reflection, and appropriate resources (DuFour & Eaker, 1998; Marshall, Pritchard, & Gunderson, 2001).

Organization

Several factors related to the organizational system of the school, including communication networks through which teachers obtain new information about reading and writing, can strongly influence how much a teacher knows about innovative reading and writing strategies and whether knowledge is translated into practice.

The Ease or Difficulty of Access to Professional Development Opportunities

The ease or difficulty of access to professional development opportunities is directly related to how much support is provided to a teacher for professional development, as reflected by a school's formal policies that structure a teacher's time and activities. For instance, ease of access to professional workshops and conferences and access to professional journals can dramatically influence a teacher's knowledge and use of reading and writing strategies (Weller & Weller, 1999). Some school systems have formal policies that provide many opportunities for professional development, whereas the opportunities in other systems are less formalized and less abundant (Hargreaves, 1995).

The Extent to Which Change Agencies Are Highly Formalized

In the complex organizational system of many schools, responsibility for change is often centralized and highly formalized. In some school systems, boards, superintendents, and principals are the exclusive change agencies responsible for implementing formal policies related to such issues as standardized testing and textbook adoptions, which in turn influence curriculum choices and changes. It has been found that in organizations where the change agencies are not so formalized, innovative teaching strategies are more easily and quickly implemented in classrooms. For example, professional learning communities and study groups—discussed in detail later in this chapter—invest considerable decision making about the direction and process of change in teachers themselves (Murphy & Lick, 1998). Faculty control over curricular change has been shown to be much more effective than administrative threats and mandates (Arter, 2001).

Faculty control over curricular change has been shown to be much more effective than administrative threats and mandates.

Before teachers will take full advantage of content literacy strategies, they should be informed of the realities of school organizations in which they must function on a day-to-day basis (O'Brien, Stewart, & Moje, 1995; Sunderman, Amoa, & Meyers, 2001). They should be given the opportunity to explore reasons behind an organization's resistance to change and the social and political constraints that define school policy and acceptable and unacceptable literacy teaching practices (Albright, 2001).

SUPPORTING MEANINGFUL CHANGE IN TEACHER PRACTICE

As you might infer, promoting change in the ways middle and secondary school teachers integrate and apply content area literacy strategies is not always a simple or clear-cut process. Educational innovations do not happen in schools merely because politicians or administrators say they should. Over the past decade, the literature on teacher change suggests that ignoring teachers' beliefs and personal attributes (Brozo, Brobst, & Moje 1994–1995; Griffiths & Tann, 1992; Richardson, Anders, Tidwell, & Lloyd, 1991), classroom cultures (Moje, Brozo, & Haas, 1994), the structure and organization of schools (Hargreaves, 1995), the importance of reflective inquiry (Rallis & MacMullen, 2000), and teachers' knowledge of the realities of their own teaching situations—referred to as *practical knowledge* (Liston & Zeichner, 1996)—in the change process could lead to disappointing results.

Researchers involved in exploring how educational innovations are adopted and used by teachers have begun to paint a more detailed picture of the variables involved in the change process. For instance, teachers are no longer viewed as intractable, ill-informed, and blindly resistant to innovation. Instead, teacher change involves a complex blend of variables ranging from personal attributes of teachers to the structure of the organizations in which they work. To understand the interrelationships among these variables more fully, Richardson (1990) proposed that the following questions should be explored:

- *Who is in control of change?*

  Teachers should feel a genuine sense of investment in the change process.

  Teachers should see a relationship between their efforts and change outcomes.

  Teachers should be provided with opportunities to reflect on their practical knowledge, theoretical frameworks, and activities associated with the educational innovation.

- *What is significant and worthwhile practice?*

  Teachers must be actively involved in making judgments about which changes are worthwhile and significant.

- *What is the context of change?*

  Individual teacher change should be viewed within the context of the culture and norms of teachers, administrators, other school personnel, and students in a particular school.

Based on these questions, Figure 11.2 depicts the critical variables in promoting meaningful change in teacher practice. The model suggests that changes in teaching practices are most likely to come about when teachers' own beliefs, attitudes, theories about learning and teaching, and everyday knowledge about the realities of teaching are taken into account when they are introduced to an educational innovation. *Structural support* refers to all of the ways school administrators and staff can support each other in the change process, including providing necessary and desired resources, sustained commitment to staff development, incentives for change that teachers perceive as meaningful, and time to solve problems and commiserate collectively. A critical component of this model is the need for teachers to reflect on the change process (Moallem, 1997) to assess regularly the efficacy of the educational innovation and the ways in which it is being implemented.

CHARACTERISTICS OF EFFECTIVE TEACHERS

Although effective teaching cannot be distilled, bottled, and taken as an elixir, we know that effective middle and secondary classroom teachers exhibit certain general characteristics that can serve as guidelines for helping you become a better teacher.

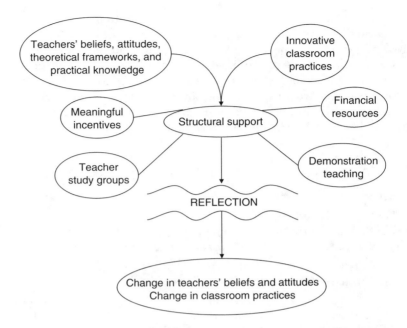

FIGURE 11.2 Key Components for Promoting Meaningful Change in Teaching Practice

Effective Teachers Are Reflective Teachers

Reflective teaching is a powerful way to consider your teaching carefully and to become a more thoughtful and alert student of teaching (Bullough & Gitlin, 1995; Tremmel, 1993). First, we know what doesn't constitute reflective teaching (Zeichner & Liston 1996):

> If a teacher never questions the goals and the values that guide his or her work, the context in which he or she teaches, or never examines his or her assumptions, then it is our belief that this individual is not engaged in reflective teaching. (p. 1)

Moallem (1997), on the other hand, provides a useful definition of *reflective teaching,* which demands contextualized problem solving that goes beyond sole reliance on theories and techniques:

> Although research-based knowledge may help teachers identify the best method for reaching a specified goal, it does not help them prioritize goals. Teachers have to resolve the context-bound problems of practice by mentally experimenting and manipulating contextual factors, generating alternative hypotheses about the problem, and mentally testing these hypotheses in order to come up with a discovery that leads to action. (p. 143)

Reflective teachers do not rely on routine, tradition, and authority to simplify their professional lives, nor do they uncritically accept the everyday reality of schools. Instead, they constantly and carefully reconsider beliefs and practices (Anders, Hoffman, & Duffy, 2000; Valli, 1993).

Reflection allows the teacher to examine critically the assumptions that schools make about what are and are not acceptable goals and practices. According to McLaughlin (1992), although teachers must work within some constraints, they often accept as predetermined by authority or tradition far more than is necessary. In other words, although it may be true that school structures place constraints on teachers' practices and decision making, a fair degree of latitude exists nonetheless. For instance, teachers within the same school vary widely on such matters as evaluation and classroom management practices, goals, political beliefs, treatment of special needs students, and adherence to textbooks. We believe there is ample room for teachers to exercise their professional prerogative and individuality in teaching.

Reflective teachers critically examine classroom practices and school policies to make their work more responsive to student needs.

Urging you to be a reflective teacher, then, means urging you to depend on yourself as a decision maker and to trust your judgments based on what you know and believe.

Reflection and Developing a Personal Philosophy of Teaching

Reflective thinking can be a tool for helping you develop and refine your personal philosophy of teaching, your professional identity. Reflection forces you to engage in inquiry about teaching that ultimately requires self-analysis and appraisal. If you reflect on your professional experience throughout your career, your personal philosophy of teaching will evolve over the years. This evolution is a sign of professional growth.

One way to become a reflective teacher, to determine where you stand and what you believe relative to your specific school environment, is to record events and your analysis of them in a *reflective thinking journal (RTJ)*. Keeping a daily or weekly journal allows you to keep track of events and reflect privately on what they mean to you and what they mean within a broader context. What happened? Why did it happen? What was my role? What beliefs did my actions reflect? Did my actions reflect beliefs and assumptions of which I was not aware? Did the consequences of my actions raise doubts or reinforce beliefs? How should I act in the future based on what happened?

An RTJ not only can lead you to discoveries about how you teach, but it also can help you teach. It can offer you a way to think about strategies, to plan their implementation, to question the social and dynamic conditions that will influence their success, to appraise their effectiveness, and to reconsider and modify them (Santa, Short, & Smith, 1993).

Maintaining a reflective teaching journal that documents and analyzes classroom practice will increase professionalism and improve instruction.

We suggest the format depicted in the sample RTJ in Figure 11.3. Any format is adequate, however, if it helps you focus on particularly significant events and facilitates the recording of necessary information about events and analysis of events. A discussion of the components of the RTJ follows.

Event	Analysis Reflections
I began Chapter 7 a little differently today. Instead of jumping into the text like I normally do, I asked the class to write before they read the chapter. The chapter was concerned with important environmental issues related to nuclear power, and I asked students to get together in small groups and talk about possible solutions to the nuclear energy problems and then write a short paper discussing their solutions. Collective groans went up when I explained the assignment. It took a few students several minutes to find a group. As I moved around the room, I discovered that many students were not participating in the group discussions; some were staring out the window or had their heads on the desk; some were talking about anything but the topic. I asked them to hand in their papers at the end of the period—I got 7 out of 27 back!	I'm not sure what happened, but this strategy of writing before reading sure fell on its face. I felt embarrassed and confused. I wanted to demand that students get involved and take advantage of this "fun," different approach to the chapter, but it didn't make any sense to try that. They seemed just as confused and unenthusiastic as I must have appeared. As I think some more on it, I'm beginning to realize that I came out of nowhere with this exercise. The class has done very little group work and not much writing other than term papers and reports. Maybe if we try this again—but move into it more gradually and I prepare the class for writing—I might get a better response. I think I also have to get clearer in my head why I'm asking students to do this in the first place. I read that it was a good idea; perhaps I need more information.

FIGURE 11.3   An RTJ: Sample Format and Entry for an 11th-Grade Earth Science Classroom

Events.   Select one or two events that you felt were significant. They may be significant because what you tried to teach or what you observed bothered you (such as the earth science teacher's concern about trying a prereading writing assignment); excited you; caused you to rethink your initial ideas, plans, or goals; or convinced you that your initial ideas were valid. Whether your events reflect successful or unsuccessful experiences or something in between, they are significant if they provide fodder for reflection and learning.

Describe the significant event(s) in detail. Think about what you felt during the event(s), how you perceived your students' responses to your actions and words, and who or what significantly influenced and shaped the outcome of the event(s). Rich description here will provide you with the material you need for further analysis and reflection in the other section of the journal.

Analysis/reflection.   In this section of the journal, you should include a discussion of *why* the event was significant to you and how you interpret it. Posner (1985) points out the critical importance of this section:

Try to figure out what you accomplished, identify problems that emerged and how you plan to follow up, and distill from the episodes what you learned. This last point is the most important. You may have learned what works in this situation and what does not. If so, describe what you conclude. But you may also have learned something about your philosophy of teaching (your perspective). Does the episode confirm your ideas or force you to reconsider them? Maybe initial ideas you held rather dogmatically depend, to a large extent, on the situation that affected the applicability of the ideas. (p. 25)

After analysis and reflection, you may be left with more questions than answers. We view questions as an essential part of the inquiry process of reflective thinking. The RTJ can be used to search for answers to your questions, explore your evolving feelings and philosophy about teaching, and help you modify approaches over time.

To help you "experience" reflective thinking, take a moment to do a reflective thinking exercise. Set up a piece of notebook paper in the format shown in Figure 11.3, using the headings "Event" and "Analysis/Reflection." Fill in this "page" of an RTJ based on one of the following: (1) a strategy you implemented in your classroom, (2) a strategy you observed a teacher implement, or (3) a recent classroom experience in which you were a student. Try to provide a full description of the event and a complete analysis of and reflection on the event.

In summary, reflective teaching is a process that causes teachers to think deeply about their experiences and calls on them to self-assess and produce insights and new perspectives that will guide their practice.

Effective Teachers Use the Research Process as a Learning Process

Effective teachers expand their knowledge about their practice and themselves in many ways. They learn by reading the professional literature, by observing students in their own classrooms, by observing teachers and students in other classrooms, by reflecting on their observations alone and with others, and by sharing their knowledge and experience. They also learn through critical reflective inquiry and systematic investigations of their teaching effectiveness (Goff, 1996; Lytle, 2000). According to Harste (1988), "As a learning process, nothing beats research" (p. 9).

Teacher researchers, interested in improving practices within their own settings, engage in inquiry to better understand their students, themselves, and their particular educational environment. In simple terms, teacher researchers use research to do a better job of teaching (Branscombe, Goswami, & Schwartz, 1992; Zeichner, 2001).

Classroom action research is research undertaken by teachers to improve practice. It can also be used to provide verification and produce evidence that certain strategies are making a difference (Cochran-Smith & Lytle, 1993;

Go to Web Resources for Chapter 11 at *http://www. prenhall.com/brozo* and look for teacher research.

Evans, Lomax, & Morgan, 2000). You and most teachers work hard and are constantly searching for new methods and strategies to improve instruction, but rarely do you gather the kind of proof about the effectiveness of your strategies that makes superintendents, principals, and other teachers take notice. As a result of action research, your teaching practices improve, and support for your efforts increases. This type of research also encourages ownership of strategies and improvement in student achievement. Effective teachers view teaching as research (Baumann & Duffy-Hester, 2000).

Classroom action research helps teachers ask and answer their own questions about best practices.

We recommend a seven-phase plan for helping you conduct research in your classroom (Green, 1987): (1) identify an issue, interest, or concern; (2) seek knowledge; (3) plan an action; (4) implement the action; (5) observe the action; (6) reflect on the observations; and (7) revise the plan. To help you better understand classroom action research and how it works, we discuss the seven phases in some detail.

Phase 1: Identify an Issue, Interest, or Concern

Teachers conduct classroom research, for several reasons: (1) they want to learn more about an aspect of their students' reading and writing development; (2) they want to observe the reading and writing development of certain students (e.g., special needs students); (3) they want to observe over time students' responses to and development of particular strategies; (4) they want to observe the effect of the learning environment on student development; (5) they want to determine differences in students' responses to and development of various strategies.

For example, Michael, an 11th-grade history teacher, was dissatisfied with the departmental unit tests that had been developed before he joined the faculty. He felt they placed too much emphasis on memorization of detailed information and not enough emphasis on understanding concepts. After presenting his concerns to the history faculty and gaining their general support, he decided to test some alternative teaching strategies to determine how well students learned important history concepts.

Phase 2: Seek Knowledge

A variety of sources are available for acquiring information about teaching strategies, including (1) college undergraduate and graduate courses and notes; (2) professional books, journals, and magazines; (3) university faculty; (4) district curriculum specialists; (5) professional conferences, workshops, and in-service training; and (6) colleagues.

For example, Michael began to seek information related to teaching concepts in history. He got the idea of teaching history using a thematic unit approach centering on critical concepts from an undergraduate history methods class. He found reinforcement for the idea from presentations at a state social studies conference and from a class project in a graduate content-area reading class. Returning to the handouts and texts from the presentations and courses, he began putting together a unit plan on the Civil War. In addition, he consulted with his former university professors and the district curriculum specialist, and he brainstormed with a colleague in the history department to round out the particulars of the unit and ways in which students' knowledge of concepts could be assessed. Michael decided to focus his instruction on helping students apply their understanding of the concept of civil war to examples of civil strife that have occurred before and since and are occurring today around the globe (e.g., in the former Soviet Union and in Afghanistan).

Phase 3: Plan an Action

In this phase the teacher researcher should refine the research goals. One way to do this is to pose questions that the classroom research might help answer. Brainstorm as many questions as possible related to the issue, interest, or concern of the research. During this phase, plan how the action will be observed or assessed.

Michael formulated three main questions for his research:

1. Will students acquire the basic factual information about the Civil War (e.g., battles, generals, dates, places)?
2. Will students demonstrate an understanding of the concept of *civil war?*
3. Will students exhibit greater enthusiasm for this unit over previous ones?

To answer the first question, the existing questions on the departmental unit test would be used. In this way, his students' performance could be directly compared with the performance of students in other classes.

To answer the second question, Michael wrote some additional questions for the unit test that required knowledge and application of the critical concept. In addition, he designed an assessment requiring students to generate a personal essay that would provide insights into their ability to apply their knowledge of the concept.

To answer the third question, Michael designed an attitude and interest inventory that would be given to students at the conclusion of the unit. The inventory asked students to reflect on their learning experiences during the unit and decide how they felt about them and how they compared with other learning experiences in other history units.

Phase 4: Implement the Action

The plan that has been devised to investigate an issue, interest, or concern should be put into action. A plan of action in classroom action research generally involves a teacher's trying out a strategy or series of strategies related to the five reasons for classroom research outlined in Phase 1. The strategies may be new or they may be ones already being employed. In both cases, the teacher desires information about students' responses to the strategies and their effectiveness.

During his history unit, Michael engaged students in a variety of learning experiences intended to help them explore the concept of civil war. As students read and learned about our Civil War, they also learned about civil strife in other countries and at other times in history using fiction and nonfiction trade books, current events magazines, films and videos, discussions and debates, and the Internet, tied to a variety of strategies.

Phase 5: Observe the Action

Teacher researchers employ a variety of data-gathering methods as part of their investigations. The most common methods include observations, field notes, teacher and student journals and learning logs, interviews, and questionnaires. Normally, teachers gather feedback and interpret students' responses throughout an investigation period as a part of everyday classroom assessment.

Michael kept a daily log of classroom events in which he recorded observations, perceptions, and reflections. The log provided a means of formative evaluation concerning how well he was teaching the critical concept and the extent to which students were learning it. The log was also used to monitor students' enthusiasm and interest in the unit. With this information, he was able to make ongoing adjustments to the unit plan.

Phase 6: Reflect on the Observations

In this phase, data collected through various methods to provide information for the teacher researcher concerning the issue, interest, or concern should be collated. Teacher researchers typically analyze data informally; however, formal analyses are made in more tightly structured investigations.

Michael analyzed data from four primary sources: (1) his daily log, (2) the end-of-unit department test, (3) his end-of-unit essay test, and (4) the attitude inventory. At the conclusion of the unit, all students from all the history classes took the departmental test, the essay test, and the attitude inventory. Results clearly demonstrated that Michael's students came away from the Civil War unit with not only a collection of newly learned details but also the ability to recognize other examples of civil strife and explain their significance. Students in the other history classes seemed only to be able to demonstrate memory of detailed information.

Phase 7: Revise the Plan

A scrutiny of the results of the investigation should lead to some important decision making. The teacher researcher should ask: Were the investigation's questions answered? Is more information needed? Was useful unanticipated information obtained? Answers to these questions will help the teacher determine whether or not students benefited, further investigations should be planned, new strategies should be implemented, or changes in the way data are collected and analyzed should be made.

Michael's demonstration of the effectiveness of a concept approach to teaching history led to several important changes. It helped solidify the history faculty's resolve to place a more balanced emphasis on critical concepts and important details; departmental goals were revised; cooperation increased among the history faculty; and changes were made to the unit tests. In addition, the principal made more money available to the history department for trade books and other alternative resources.

Why do we encourage classroom action research? To reiterate, we believe there are many benefits to individual teachers and teacher teams conducting classroom-specific research. This type of research

- provides verification that instructional practices work
- promotes more open-mindedness among the faculty and the administration to try new ideas
- expands instructional possibilities and enhances a teacher's own teaching
- develops ownership of specific strategies based on theory and research
- helps teachers learn more about themselves and their students
- builds a teacher's self-confidence and feeling of empowerment

Teacher research is grounded in the everyday lives of real classrooms and offers immediately useful information.

In short, we concur with Baumann and Duffy-Hester (2000) when they point out that "teachers are in the best position to explore their own practice and to make sense of classroom worlds" (p. 94).

Effective Teachers Collaborate With Students, Teachers, Parents, and Administrators

Many people share an interest in your students' reading, writing, and learning development, including the students themselves, other teachers, parents, and school administrators. The prospects of students becoming active learners and developing lifelong reading habits greatly increase when all persons concerned work collaboratively to help students use literacy for information and pleasure. With these collaborative efforts, your teaching effectiveness increases as well.

Following are suggestions for developing collaborative relationships with teachers, parents, administrators, and students.

Let All Interested Groups Know Your Expectations for Reading, Writing, and Learning

To work collaboratively, it isn't necessary to convert others to your approach to teaching, but it is important that they be made aware of the nature of your curriculum and the rationale behind it. Otherwise, suspicion, distrust, and confusion may develop. Before others make judgments about you based on piecemeal or incorrect information, share with them as honestly and as accurately as possible your teaching philosophy and classroom strategies.

Make Sure Students Understand Your Expectations for Them as Readers, Writers, and Learners

Students must "revalue" reading and writing as meaningful, functional processes that can be used as vehicles for learning and expanding on subject matter. All the strategies discussed in this book are intended to help you incorporate into your content curriculum learning experiences that demonstrate this revaluing of literacy.

Develop Collaborative Relationships With Students

Rhodes and Dudley-Marling (1988) put it well when they said, "We can teach but we can't force learning; learning is a student's prerogative" (p. 273). Students in the middle and upper grades should be used as curricular informants and should be allowed a hand in determining course topics, materials, learning experiences, projects, and evaluation. Involving students in course decisions will encourage cooperation and commitment; they will be vested in the learning process. Without students' active involvement, the chances of expanding their content knowledge, as well as their literacy skills, are greatly diminished.

Develop Collaborative Relationships With Parents

Parents play a vital role in the literacy development and motivation of students (Bean & Valerio, 1997; Brozo, Valerio, & Salazar, 1996). Teachers and parents can work together to facilitate students' literacy at home (Tice, 2000). Most of the suggestions that teachers make to parents should be reminders of how parents have been supporting literacy at home for generations. When support for literacy at school is provided at home, students discover the importance of reading and writing (Saravia-Shore & Arvizu, 1992). Parents, in turn, can be useful informants about their students' attitudes, interests, hobbies, and other behavioral and personality insights that the teacher can use when selecting trade books and planning research projects.

One of the best ways parents can be involved in their adolescent son's or daughter's literacy development is by encouraging and modeling personally meaningful reading. Adolescents who daily catch their parents in the act of reading—whether it's an executive in Los Angeles with *The Wall Street Journal,* a hog farmer in Illinois with the farm report, or a teacher in Florida curled up on the couch with a mystery novel—are likely to develop positive attitudes about reading (DeBruin-Parecki, Paris, & Siedenburg, 1997). Encourage parents to make sure they let their adolescents observe them reading. Instead of ordering and demanding them to read, parents should set an example for their adolescents of the importance and joy of literacy.

Another way to involve parents in the literacy development of their sons or daughters is to encourage them to make a variety of reading materials available at home. A student in one of my graduate reading courses told me recently how she had been struggling to get her 12-year-old son to read. She had subscriptions to youth and teen magazines, but he wouldn't read them. She handed him one book after another, only to have each rejected. One day she left Gary Paulsen's *The Haymeadow* (1992) on his bedstand. Later that night she noticed light spilling out from under his bedroom door. To her delight, she found her son engrossed in the book. She almost had to wrestle it from him to get him to go to sleep. The next day a blizzard kept students at home, and he picked up the book

1. Use the book lists and websites in Chapter 8 and 11 as guides.
2. Check local bookstores and public and university libraries for the best source of books.
3. Consult librarians, bookstore clerks, university faculty, and teachers who are knowledgeable about young adult books.
4. Become a keen observer of your adolescent's interests, including favorite television shows, hobbies, leisure-time activities, and the kinds of books he or she had read and enjoyed in the past.
5. Consider how well your daughter or son reads when deciding the appropriateness of young adult books.
6. Take a close look at the books to determine whether they match your adolescent's interests.
7. Enroll your son or daughter in a young adult book club, or form one.
8. Be sure the main character in the book approximates the age of your adolescent. Characters who are too young are likely to be poorly received; characters who are a bit older are often preferred.
9. Try to make a variety of books available to your adolescent; then allow her or him to select a favorite one.
10. Don't impose your tastes on your adolescent; use your child's selection to guide you in selecting or purchasing future books.
11. Don't jam the books down your adolescent's throat or lay on a thick, hard sales pitch.
12. Try to increase gradually the literary quality of books.
13. Avoid the tendency to make reading a requirement at home; be patient.
14. Try to gradually induce your adolescent to select young adult books. Help by (a) encouraging regular visits to the public library and bookstore, (b) introducing librarians and clerks who are knowledgeable about young adult books and sensitive to the needs of adolescents, (c) purchasing and sharing annotated bibliographies of young adult books (see the reference guides in Chapter 8), (d) discussing the book your young adult is reading, and (e) suggesting books your young adult might enjoy.

Adapted from *Comics to Classics: A Parent's Guide to Books for Teens and Preteens*, by A. J. S. Reed, 1988, Newark, DE: International Reading Association.

FIGURE 11.4   A Parents' Guide to Selecting Books for Adolescents

on waking and stayed in bed until he was finished. "Man, that was a great book," he said. "Are there any more like that?"

Indeed, there are many more outstanding young adult books that can make the difference between whether or not adolescents become lifelong readers. Figure 11.4 presents guidelines adapted from Reed (1988) for helping parents select books for adolescents.

Establishing partnerships with parents is critical because they are in the best position to model the joys and benefits of literacy.

The best way to assist adolescents in developing the reading habit is to be a model. As adolescents observe influential adults reading functional and meaningful materials and observe adults' selection processes, they are likely to imitate this behavior. Teachers and parents can work together to discover what adolescents will enjoy reading and use thoughtful and sensitive guidance to help them become mature readers.

Develop Collaborative Relationships With Other Teachers

In Chapter 9 we described how Bob, a reading and study skills teacher, teamed up with a biology teacher to help reinforce instruction in the split-page method of note taking. The beneficiaries of their collaboration were new first-year students grappling with the demands of high school textbook reading. This example of cooperative planning between teachers demonstrates the power of collaboration as an effective way to influence teachers' beliefs about reading, writing, and learning.

Another way teachers can support each other is by collaborating on thematic units. For example, an eighth-grade history teacher teamed up with the language arts teacher on a World War I unit. In the language arts classroom, students read *No Hero for the Kaiser* (Frank, 1986), wrote responses and themes related to the book and what they were learning in the history class, researched their own family histories to determine who fought in the war, and built charts relating battles described in their history books to the effects of the battles on the characters in the trade book. They engaged in many other literacy experiences designed to integrate trade and text reading. This support of the history teacher's unit led to greater student learning of details and concepts related to World War I and increased enthusiasm for the unit on the part of the students and teachers alike. In this way, the history teacher had time to cover the content he felt was important, while the language arts teacher engaged students in functional and meaningful literacy experiences. In the process, everyone benefited.

A few middle and secondary schools have a reading specialist to serve students and teachers. If your school has such an individual, introduce yourself immediately to discover what specific services the specialist can offer you to help your students. The reading specialist can work with students from your class who are having difficulty learning your content-area concepts. The specialist will often team teach with you to develop effective study strategies for learning material from course texts and class notes. The specialist might conduct demonstration lessons for your students on certain strategies, such as mapping or the survey procedure using your content materials. The reading specialist can also provide you with teaching ideas for students who have been mainstreamed into your classroom.

Finally, you should develop an effective relationship with your school librarian. Librarians can be invaluable friends and colleagues when you plan units and projects with your students. Librarians are excited about identifying relevant resources for your upcoming topics. They can provide your class with helpful presentations and demonstrations in using reference material, accessing computer databases, and conducting research. Don't forget, as mentioned in Chapter 8, librarians are your best link to quality young adult books.

As the previous examples demonstrate, changing the practice of a couple of teachers can make a significant difference in the academic lives of the students they teach. However, to achieve broad-based change in literacy teaching and learning, middle and secondary school teachers need to work in purposeful groups to solve complex problems and bring about a more responsive curriculum. A promising development in this connection is the rise of what has become variously referred to as teacher study groups (Murphy & Lick, 1998), teacher learning teams (Arter, 2001), professional learning communities (DuFour & Eaker, 1998), and peer coaching (Beavers, 2001). We prefer the term *professional learning community* and will describe its characteristics and examples next.

As we stated earlier in this chapter, ultimately, teachers make or break educational innovation. Policy makers can enact the laws, administrators can supply the pressure, staff developers can present the innovative strategies, but teachers make the decision to change or not to change the ways they teach. The growing realization among those seeking restructuring of the curriculum, modifications of school policies, or enhancing faculty professionalism is that without teacher support and ownership of the processes involved in making these changes, success will always remain illusive. Professional learning communities comprised primarily of teachers (but extended when appropriate to include as co-partners administrators and parents) who are vested with the responsibility of setting curricular direction are more likely to bring about school improvements (Tichenor & Heins, 2000). Putnam and Borko (2000) assert, "For teachers to be successful in constructing new roles they need opportunities to participate in a professional community that discusses new teacher materials and strategies and that supports the risk taking and struggle entailed in transforming practice" (p. 8).

Professional learning communities have three main purposes (DuFour & Eaker, 1998):

- to help educators implement curricular and instructional innovations
- to engender collaborative planning for school improvement
- to provide educators a forum for studying current research regarding teaching and learning

In professional learning communities teachers themselves ask critical questions about their practice and build a collaborative framework for finding answers. In this way, teachers take control of their learning by actively participating in problem-centered discussions and activities (Crowther, 1998).

Learning communities are comprised of small groups of professionals who agree to research an area of concern, experiment with possible solutions, and meet regularly for a specified period of time to share and reflect upon lessons learned in the classroom. Although there are numerous suggestions for improving the likelihood that professional learning communities will be successful

Teacher study groups are seen now as one of the best ways to develop professional learning communities in schools.

 Go to Web Resources for Chapter 11 at *http://www. prenhall.com/brozo* and look for teacher study groups.

(Murphy, 1999), we found in our own work with teachers in a study group at Foothills High School that the following guidelines were critical:

Important criteria should be established to ensure the success of professional learning communities.

■ *Participants should choose areas of concern that are meaningful to them.* Throughout this book we have been emphasizing the importance of giving students as many opportunities as possible for learning in ways that are personally meaningful to them. We urge this approach because it fits nicely with how learning occurs best in our own adult lives. We found that teacher study group attendance and involvement remained high when group members were allowed to identify aspects of a school issue that were relevant to them.

Any number of issues can form the focus of professional learning communities provided each member of the community or study group has a common reason for joining. For example, teachers in a California middle school formed a study group that included parents to deal with concerns about large numbers of failing ESL students. In a Cincinnati high school teachers came together around the common need to deal more effectively with the educational and social welfare of a growing number of students who were from homeless backgrounds. At Foothills High a teacher study group was established by the principal to respond to problems posed by 30% of the student body reading significantly below grade placement.

■ *All individuals should participate voluntarily.* Teachers are more likely to get and remained involved in professional learning communities if the first guideline above is sincerely honored. Once again, lessons from students are instructive here. Adolescents are required to attend school but we cannot force them to read, learn, and stay engaged in classroom activities. Instead, students have to voluntarily decide to involve themselves in the flow of instruction. The chances of their involvement increase significantly if they are offered interesting and personally meaningful learning opportunities. Similarly, teachers who volunteer to become a part of professional learning communities tend to remain actively involved and share their enthusiasm with others in the school (Ross, Rolheiser, & Hogaboam-Gray, 1999).

The principal of Foothills High School conducted a survey of his faculty to gather information about their perceptions of struggling readers in their classrooms. Based on the results, he invited particular teachers who noted the most serious problems to join in a collective effort to find possible solutions. Not everyone accepted his invitation, but a study group was ultimately formed comprising the librarian, two teachers from English, and one each from special education, biology, business education, and history. Although participation in the professional learning community at Foothills High was voluntary, the principal did create incentives for joining and staying involved. He gave special recognition to group members at faculty and board meetings. He also allowed the teachers to earn staff development points by attending discussions, participating in activities, and documenting new schoolwide reading initiatives and strategies used in their classrooms.

■ *Participants should select their own resources for becoming informed and launching new initiatives.* When given the time and support to do so, teacher study groups can demonstrate skill and resourcefulness in identifying appropriate directions and tools for change (Murphy & Lick, 1998). For example, one member of the Foothills High group had recently completed graduate course work in literacy, the textbooks for which included current chapters and articles pertinent to the focus of their professional learning community. These she disseminated among the members, who read and discussed them. Another member of the group had attended a grant writing workshop conducted by state department personnel to learn about applying for Reading Excellence Act monies. She proposed they write a grant that required collaboration with a local university. That's how we became involved in the reading efforts at Foothills High.

■ *Participants should negotiate adequate time for implementation and reflection.*   Administrators who are fully committed to the success of professional learning communities know that time is a vital resource. Group members should be able to meet regularly and participants should be allowed time in lieu of other duties, such as faculty meetings, to maximize attendance. At Foothills the principal made arrangements for study group members to have a full-day retreat to plan and write the REA grant. He also permitted group members to exit whole-staff faculty meetings early to conduct their own sessions.

Professional learning communities are springing up throughout the country as teachers, administrators, and parents grapple with new and evolving learning concerns for adolescents. Some, like the National Council of Teachers of English Reading Initiatives (Smith & Hudelson, 2001), enjoy official sponsorship by a prominent literacy organization. The Reading Initiative supports teachers and administrators who engage in focused study, conversation, reflection, and problem solving of concerns particular to their school sites by providing participants a one-year NCTE membership, subscription to an NCTE journal of their choice, and registration to the NCTE annual convention. Others are formed with the help and prodding of university faculty (Tichenor & Heins, 2000). Most, however, are led and monitored by teachers. Regardless of the particular ways in which professional learning communities are formed, they all share a common purpose—to create collegial, supportive school cultures with expressed visions and directions for professional development and school improvement (Marshall, Pritchard, & Gunderson, 2001).

Any teacher, new or experienced, can be the instigator for a professional learning community in his or her school.

We urge you to get involved in study groups at your school or to form a study group yourself if one doesn't already exist. Raise the idea with your principal and colleagues as an alternative to traditional staff development, which is usually composed of a few days of in-service workshops every year presented by "experts" who may have little appreciation for the particular needs and issues of teachers and students at your site. The funds used to cover workshop speakers' expenses could be spent on books, journals, computer access, and pay for substitute teachers to spell study group participants while they observe programs and strategies in other schools or do off-site materials and information gathering. Start simple to make the prospects more inviting, such as the approach we observed in one of the middle schools we visited, which the teachers called "The

Friday Five." Every Friday afternoon five teachers with a common planning period met as a study group for 45 minutes to explore topics related to reading and writing and to support one another's efforts to implement new literacy strategies in their classrooms. The key is that you take control of your own expanding sense of professionalism through inquiry, problem solving, and, most important, peer collaboration.

■ *Participants should agree in advance on the kinds of activities the group and each team member should be involved in and hold each other accountable for fulfilling those tasks.* The Foothills High professional learning community members agreed in one of their first team meetings that each session would be taken up with (1) discussing instructional implications of articles and chapters read, (2) proposing reading strategies and efforts designed to leaven the achievement levels of struggling readers and enrich the literate culture of the school as a whole, (3) sharing progress and seeking feedback on classroom strategies, and (4) preparing for the next topic, charge, and/or reading. Between sessions, participants agreed to work on the grant proposal, locate additional relevant books and articles, do the required reading, and try out certain strategies in their classrooms.

■ *Participants should report to the entire staff on a regular basis.* Keeping administrators and other faculty fully apprised of developments that grow out of the work of professional learning communities is critical to overall school change. Since team members at Foothills High were responsible for proposing and helping launch literacy initiatives that would eventually require the support of every teacher, open communication was critical. Before submitting their REA grant, members of the study group needed to be certain the project features were feasible, and sensitive to the needs of students in their particular school. Reporting to the entire staff was also meant to ensure faculty across all content areas as well as administrators could "buy in" to the initiatives proposed and to gather additional suggestions for improving the ultimate literacy program that would be put into place at Foothills.

Develop Collaborative Relationships With Administrators

In most buildings, school principals, supervisors, and other administrators possess a great deal of decision-making power. Therefore, they can be important allies. The extent to which they share their power may depend on how actively you cultivate cooperative relationships with them.

Since school administrators are powerful decision makers, cultivating collaborative relations with them is vital.

We recommended earlier that to begin, you should make clear your expectations for the learning environment in your classroom. Most administrators are happy to hear of your innovative efforts and are more likely to provide support if they are kept abreast of the reading, writing, and learning strategies you are attempting to incorporate into your classroom. Principals can play an instrumental role in developing and implementing a sustained silent reading or writing program. They can find funds for alternative resources, such as trade books, and can provide the necessary support for book drives, sales, and other plans you devise for finding books and raising money for books. Administrators can help create a supportive environment for teacher collaboration and classroom research. With your cooperation, they can help arrange important and enlightening in-service training and facilitate parent–teacher programs. They can also make critical links to community resources for donations of reading, writing, and other curricular materials.

The more you communicate with administrators about your students' growth, the greater the chance that they will appreciate your efforts, understand your needs, and support your curricular changes.

One last word about collaboration. We do not want to give the impression that students, parents, teachers, and administrators are the only individuals who can contribute to the overall learning and literacy development of your students. We recommend that you also develop links with other members of the community who can assist you, including local poets, writers, musicians, senior citizens, retired teachers, university student volunteers, and others. Sometimes persistent inquiry can lead to the discovery of some wonderful local resources. Recently, for example, one of our students, an English teacher, while preparing a unit on the Arthurian Legend, found out about a local group of actors known as the Guild of Creative Anachronisms. Several members came into his classroom dressed in Arthurian garb and gave an exciting and informative demonstration on the life, culture, and music during that period and place in history. This strategy enlivened the unit and provided his students with a truly unforgettable experience.

Effective Teachers Employ Innovative Strategies That Link Content and Literacy Learning

All of the ideas in this book for expanding reading, writing, and other language processes are suggestions, ways of demonstrating possibilities. These suggestions come from our own work, from research, and most prominently from the exceptional teachers who have developed them and used them successfully. They are to be considered guidelines because, obviously, not all will work in your particular setting and not all of the suggested strategies will work in precisely the ways we describe. Effective teachers are constantly on the lookout for new ideas, suggestions, and strategies that they can modify and adapt to their particular needs. This process of modification and adaptation is innovation. In fact, we expect that the strategies we suggest will take on new shapes and forms in the hands of generative teachers.

For example, a 10th-grade music teacher who wished to incorporate trade books into her music classes was having difficulty finding appropriate young adult fiction books that dealt with music themes. She solved this problem by locating and bringing in the original stories for the suites her students were performing. Together, they read the stories, analyzed them, and based much of their musical interpretation on what they learned about the characters and the action. In another example, a sixth-grade science teacher created a language-rich environment in his classroom by establishing a class library, including a variety of science text-books and information books dealing with many different topics, science magazines, young adult fiction books with science themes, picture books, biographies of scientists, and other young adult books unrelated to science but available to students who simply wished to read. Next to the shelved books was an old overstuffed couch, a couple of beanbag chairs, and a table with chairs for relaxation reading and personal research. Students were given opportunities during nearly every class period to use the class library to work on personal and class projects and to simply read as their interests dictated.

To restate our key point, you do not become an effective teacher by simply following the suggestions of others. Teaching effectiveness will result if you create new strategies based on reframing and expanding existing strategies that are more ideally suited to the needs and interests of you and your students.

Effective Teachers Understand Literacy Processes

A common concern among the teachers we meet is expressed in the question "How can I stay abreast of all the new trends and developments in the fields of reading and writing?" In response, we strongly advocate that teachers take graduate courses in reading or as part of a graduate or certification program and attend workshops and conferences on reading and writing. Another inevitable answer we must give to this question is that to become aware of current teaching developments in reading and writing, you must read the professional literature. As we have shown, teacher study groups and professional learning communities can encourage reading and inquiry. We admit, however, that trying to decide what professional literature to read can be a daunting task. Some guidelines follow.

Become a member of the International Reading Association (IRA) and the National Council of Teachers of English (NCTE). As a member of either of these organizations, you will receive a journal that deals with reading and writing issues, concerns, and practical teaching suggestions for adolescent students. IRA members find the *Journal of Adolescent & Adult Literacy* most helpful for presenting many fresh ideas each month on such topics as teaching vocabulary, writing in the content areas, and using young adult literature. NCTE's *English Journal* and *Voices From the Middle* are also valuable resources for teachers looking for ideas and strategies to facilitate middle grades and high school students' literacy abilities. Select two or three articles from these journals every month and read them closely. Integrate the ideas and suggestions into your instructional plans, and modify them to meet your particular needs. In this way, you will gain regular exposure to the current perspectives on reading/writing processes and on developing skill at translating ideas and others' suggestions into your own personally meaningful and useful strategies.

These organizations are offering an increasing array of electronic services. More and more journals are available online, eliminating the need for shelving and storage space and allowing archival searches and retrievals. Chat room and

Go to Web Resources for Chapter 11 at *http://www.prenhall.com/brozo* and look for professional organizations.

Threaded discussions and chat rooms offer teachers a window on the practices and ideas of their peers from around the country and the world.

threaded discussion opportunities for teachers are other new features of membership. In these cyber-environments teachers pose questions and describe problems, seeking input from kindred spirits. These sites are also sources for detailed explanations of successful educational innovations tried out by teachers working with young adults.

Another benefit of membership in IRA and NCTE is the availability of discounted books on a wide range of reading/writing topics, most of which can be purchased only through these professional organizations. New books are added annually. As you peruse the IRA or NCTE catalog, you will undoubtedly find three or four publications on topics of interest. Regularly reading these publications will help to expand your knowledge about reading and writing processes. It will also provide you with many more strategies for developing these language processes and helping students use them in learning your classroom content.

International Reading Association
800 Barksdale Road
P.O. Box 8139
Newark, DE 19714-8139

National Council of Teachers of English
1111 Kenyon Road
Urbana, IL 61801

Given the staggering number of journals that publish reading and writing articles and the professional texts that appear annually, we suggest that you ease into the current literature in a modest way. Set aside a couple of hours per week to devote to reading journals and books. After reading a journal article or book, jot down notes about the topics on an index card and file the card or establish an electronic database so that you can consult it when you need some ideas for teaching course content using reading and writing strategies. As suggested earlier, seek out like-minded colleagues interested in meeting regularly to discuss articles from journals. Like book clubs these teacher study groups can heighten your motivation to read, analyze, and apply new content literacy innovations.

A second common concern, related to the one just discussed, is expressed in the question "How do I determine whether reading strategies are appropriate for my students and are based on sound theory and research?" This question, dealing with how to choose appropriate, sound, research-based strategies for teaching reading and writing, is not easily answered. Perhaps the biggest challenge for the concerned professional is to determine the most important criteria related to a research study or methods paper: Is the research based on actual practice in actual school settings with students like mine, or is it based on populations of students and conducted in contexts dissimilar to my own?

It is safe to say that because of the mind-boggling number of research studies and reports that continually appear in the professional literature, many literacy professionals, including those in higher education, do not always know what is research based. To confound matters, articles appearing in the same journal often contain conflicting findings. So it is not surprising to find many concerned teachers confused about how best to teach reading and writing.

One way of breaking through the confusing maze of reading research is to follow our advice given in previous sections of this chapter in our discussion of reflective teaching, classroom research, and professional learning communities. Begin defining your personal philosophy about teaching language processes. Your philosophy will be influenced by what you have learned and are learning about reading and writing from course work, journals, textbooks, other teachers, your students, and, most important, your own classroom research experiences and reflections. Then look for and generate strategies that are consistent with your evolving knowledge about yourself and your students and about the best conditions for teaching and learning. Also, seek support from colleagues by forming study groups that make reading and analyzing the professional literature enjoyable and relevant.

We certainly hope that as your developing philosophy evolves, it encompasses beliefs consistent with language-based teaching:

1. Students grow in language when it is whole, meaningful, and functional.
2. All classrooms should immerse students in a language-rich environment.
3. The learning environment should be arranged to promote and encourage regular and frequent student–student interactions.
4. Teachers should demonstrate the reading, writing, and learning processes they expect their students to acquire.

If your beliefs about language development are similar, then it should be easy for you to modify and adapt the strategies contained in this book to help improve your ability to develop your students' content knowledge and literacy. Also, as you read about other strategies that may derive from a different philosophical base, you will be better able to decide what, if any, aspects of the strategies can be adapted for your use and what can be left out of your instructional practices.

Effective Teachers Establish Personal Reading Programs

Middle and secondary school teachers often protest when we suggest that they should read several young adult books every year so that they can use good books to enlist their students in the *literacy club,* as Frank Smith (1985) terms it. "We haven't the time," they respond. "We're too busy with our required work to read all those books."

We are not naive; we understand the time constraints placed on secondary school teachers. Teaching often entwines itself around teachers' entire lives, so that outside the classroom they are thinking about their students, their existing methods of instruction, and new ways to improve their instruction, as well as grading papers and preparing lessons. Yet many teachers also have a family, children, house chores, and cooking and may even be taking additional university courses. Teachers lead incredibly busy lives! However, reading young adult books may be as integral to your role as a teacher as any other teaching-related activity.

We can reach adolescents in many ways. Experienced and insightful teachers often discover how to capitalize on subtle teaching moments that are not part of a preconceived lesson or curriculum. We know, for instance, that young adults can be dramatically influenced by teachers who simply show genuine concern for them as individuals with real-world needs and problems. Often, books recommended to teenagers by a concerned teacher can make a significant difference in the young adults' lives, their way of viewing a problem or relationship, their strategies for coping with a personal difficulty, or their interest in knowing more about a topic. It is not uncommon for us to learn from our undergraduate and secondary reading students that certain books that really moved them as teenagers were recommended by teachers. One student recalled how in seventh grade he was talking with his English teacher, whom he regarded as a friend, about the difficulty he was having in geometry. The teacher suggested that he read the book *The Planiverse* (Dewdney, 1984), which describes life in a two-dimensional world. The student became very excited about the ideas in the book and began approaching his geometry lesson with renewed enthusiasm, which helped him pass the course. Another student recounted how her music teacher, who knew she was pregnant, passed her the book *Spellbound* (McDonald, 2001), which tells the story of single-mother Raven who has aspirations for college but must struggle to finish high school, work, and raise a baby at the same time. It wasn't the book itself that made a difference in her ability to cope, she said, but the fact that her teacher cared enough for her to suggest the book.

Being a regular reader of books for young adults makes you a credible model of active literacy and a helpful resource.

Young adult books can obviously play a more direct role in lesson planning and content-area instruction, as demonstrated in Chapter 8. Because of the tremendous influence these books can have on students' lives, we recommend that all teachers become knowledgeable about how to use adolescent literature to stimulate students' interest in the topic of study, to help them learn the content information in a more palatable way, and to reach them by introducing them to books related to their needs outside of the classroom. To get started on a personal reading program, we suggest that you take as little as 15 minutes a day to read a young adult book. Try reading the book before bed. We think you will discover that this kind of teaching preparation is much easier and much more exciting than traditional school-preparation tasks. You will have the pleasure of enjoying quality literature while learning about the power of books for reaching the students in your classroom.

The following list indicates where you can find young adult books for your own reading and for stocking your classroom library:

- locally owned bookstores and bookstore chains
- supermarkets, drugstores, and discount department stores
- used-book stores
- libraries (will often sell duplicate or unused books at a fraction of the original cost)
- book fairs

- book clubs (paper and illustrations are often inferior, but the prices are low)
- garage sales
- discount book sites on the Internet

CREATING A SCHOOLWIDE LITERACY EFFORT

Middle and high school teachers have always recognized that adolescents who encounter difficulties learning can usually attribute their frustrations to major shortcomings in their reading ability, but the needs of these students have gone unmentioned in public debates about education and in popular media (Buehl, 1998). Vacca (1998) describes a condition of benign neglect toward adolescent literacy as evidenced by minuscule funding for research in secondary reading, a dearth of reading teachers and specialists at the secondary level, and the stark absence of dialog about adolescent literacy development at state departments of education and in Washington, DC. Instead, the overwhelming share of federal education dollars is being allocated to fund early intervention programs, particularly for children in preschool through third grade. No one would argue with the wisdom of this priority. Clearly, front-loading children's academic needs makes good sense. However, the reality is that in spite of all the funding for programs and presidential pronouncements such as "All children will be reading on grade level by grade three," many students, perhaps as high as 30%, at the middle and secondary school levels continue to struggle as readers and learners (Hargis, 1999). All adolescents will be in need of the kinds of advanced literacy and learning skills advocated in this textbook.

More than 60 years ago Blair (1941) conducted a survey of high school principals to determine what kinds of reading services were being provided students. Since then there has been only one update of common secondary reading practices across the United States in the manner of Blair (Barry, 1997). This in itself suggests an overall lack of interest in the topic. Nonetheless, positive signs for secondary reading did emerge from Barry's study. Encouraging was the finding that 67% of the respondents from high schools in 48 states and the District of Columbia said they maintain a program for adolescent struggling readers. Equally promising is the finding that 66% of high school reading programs are staffed by either reading teachers and specialists or those with special reading endorsements. The majority of respondents indicated their schools were moving away from special remedial reading classes and pull-out programs to more of a curriculum-integrated approach. Reading teachers and specialists were reported to be spending more of their time collaborating with content-area teachers and providing staff development for their colleagues in reading strategies across the curriculum.

Another encouraging trend is an increase over the past 20 years in the number of middle and secondary school teachers who have received systematic training in content literacy strategies (Romine, McKenna, & Robinson, 1996). Although training alone will not automatically translate into changes in teacher practice, content-area reading course requirements are a step in the right direction. Teachers with this training can play critical roles as instigators of professional learning communities or in paired collaboration with subject area specialists to infuse language-based teaching into all classrooms.

Most promising of all, perhaps, has been the formation and work of the Commission on Adolescent Literacy. The International Reading Association Board of Directors formed the commission in 1997 and charged it with reflecting "on the current state of affairs of adolescent literacy" revitalizing "professional interest in and commitment to the literacy needs of adolescents" and advising and making "recommendations to the Board concerning future directions for the field of adolescent literacy" (Moore, Bean, Birdyshaw, & Rycik, 1999, p. 100). Two years after its formation, the commission put forward a landmark position statement that describes seven program principles for supporting adolescent literacy growth:

- Adolescents deserve access to a wide variety of reading material that they can and want to read.

- Adolescents deserve instruction that builds both the skill and desire to read increasingly complex materials.

- Adolescents deserve assessment that shows them their strengths as well as their needs and that guides their teachers to design instruction that will best help them grow as readers.

- Adolescents deserve expert teachers who model and provide explicit instruction in reading comprehension and study strategies across the curriculum.

- Adolescents deserve reading specialists who assist individual students having difficulty learning how to read.

- Adolescents deserve teachers who understand the complexities of individual adolescent readers, respect their differences, and respond to their characteristics.

- Adolescents deserve homes, communities, and a nation that will support their efforts to achieve advanced levels of literacy and provide the support necessary for them to succeed.

The Commission on Adolescent Literacy's position statement specifies what quality literacy should be for teens and preteens.

Principles and admonishments do not in themselves transform literacy teaching for adolescents; that can only happen when middle and high school teachers and administrators decide to commit themselves to responsive literacy instruction for all students. Just such a commitment has been made by faculty and principals in schools from Georgia to Indiana to California where effective and exemplary reading programs based on guiding principles similar to those of the Commission on Adolescent Literacy are in operation. What follows is a description of four schoolwide reading efforts, including the initiatives that we were a part of at Foothills High School. The main purpose of these program descriptions is to help you (a) appreciate what has been done in real schools to further the literacy growth of adolescents, (b) envision possibilities for whole school literacy reform in your own middle or secondary school, and (c) imagine the best role you might play as a content-area teacher, special education teacher, reading teacher, librarian, principal, or reading specialist within such programs.

Winder-Barrow High School, Barrow County, Georgia

In this rural consolidated high school of approximately 1,650 students, a reading program was implemented in 1994 and has since been identified in the state of Georgia as exemplary (Weller & Weller, 1999). Along with this recognition came an $18,000 grant. The state provides funding through its Innovative Program grant in order to support the documentation of the program's effectiveness and the dissemination of information about its positive features to assist other schools in the state that are attempting to implement their own secondary reading programs.

Winder-Barrow High calls its program POWER (Providing Opportunities With Everyday Reading). It targets both reading in the content areas and independent reading. Like many secondary reading initiatives, POWER grew out of a concern over declining test scores on state-mandated standardized achievement measures and teachers' frequent comments that students could not read their course textbooks. The principal lobbied for and received a full-time reading teacher who, along with a couple of subject area teachers, accompanied him to facilitators training in content-area reading. He also paid all teachers in the high school a stipend from staff development funds to attend a summer workshop taught by the teacher facilitators. This approach has been so successful other teachers who have become expert in the use of reading strategies in their own classrooms now help teach the summer content reading course for all new hires. An advanced course on reading across the curriculum was made available to Winder-Barrow High teachers a couple of years ago, and nearly the entire faculty has taken it.

In addition to content-area reading, the other critical component of POWER is sustained silent reading (see Chapter 8 for a complete description SSR). Twice weekly during students' 25-minute study hall just after lunch they participate in SSR. The grant helped supply every teacher with reading materials, including young adult novels, paperbacks, magazines, and newspapers to make it easier for students to find something to suit their tastes and ability levels.

Although reading test scores have increased significantly for Winder-Barrow over the past few years leaving other districts desirous to copy the POWER program, all of the teachers involved in POWER point to its flexibility as the critical component of success. Teachers aren't required to use particular content reading strategies for any number of times per week. Instead, they are urged to make a commitment to teach using the reading strategies of their choosing as derived from their course work at least twice per week. Virtually the entire staff reports doing so. Importable features of Winder-Barrow High's approach to developing a schoolwide reading program include:

- holding many formal and informal faculty meetings to discuss the importance of reading

- making research results in the area of secondary content-area reading available to teachers

- recruiting teacher leaders who believe in the importance of reading at the secondary level

- allotting funds for groups of teachers to visit other school systems with successful reading programs

- providing peer coaching and forming teacher collegial groups in support of teachers' efforts to implement reading strategies in their classrooms

- establishing a reading committee dedicated to expanding the effectiveness of reading initiatives in the school

Heritage Hills Junior-Senior High School, Lincoln City, Indiana

One of the 2001 winners of the Indiana State Reading Association's and International Reading Association's Exemplary Reading Program Awards, Heritage Hills Junior-Senior High School embraces the idea that the one sure way to improve students' reading abilities is by giving them as much time as possible to engage in sustained print encounters (Davis, 2001). What we find most admirable about this school is the way in which its principal, faculty, and parents threw their entire support behind the elegant notion (presented as Foundation 3 of language-based teaching in Chapter 1) that more reading makes better readers (Smith, 1985). This is so self-evidently true and is, without exception, endorsed by the entire professional literacy community, yet too few schools provide adolescents a regular forum for "just plain reading." Heritage Hills, however, is one of the few bright examples of the literacy possibilities when real reading is the centerpiece of the curriculum.

But it wasn't always that way. For years, teachers at this rural southern Indiana school held the view about young adults and reading that most at the secondary level hold—it is something you do in elementary school. Once again, declining test scores on the Indiana Statewide Testing for Educational Progress forced faculty and administrators to take a hard look at what was being done in the name of reading for their students. A reading comprehension study group was formed that included teachers, parents, and staff to investigate directions for improvement. Along the way, the group encountered and read *The Power of Reading* (Krashen, 1993) and was so impressed with its message that it decided to put into action three simple yet powerful recommendations:

- Develop a print-rich school environment of authentic reading material.

- Give students numerous formal and informal opportunities to read authentic material.

- Create opportunities for teachers and students to serve as literate role models.

Reading in the content areas, sustained silent reading, and long-term professional development are common features of most schoolwide literacy initiatives.

The most prominent feature of the program is 20 to 30 minutes of sustained silent reading (SSR) at the beginning of each day. Referred to as "read-ins" this time is inviolate. Everyone reads, including teachers, administrators, janitors, food handlers, aides, parents, and anyone else who might be in the school building. In this way, students are provided structured time to read independently texts of their choosing while faculty and staff model authentic literate behavior.

As with virtually all other SSR programs, Heritage Hills had to get prepared by stocking classroom libraries. It has taken a few years to build each one, but there is now an average of 300 books per classroom, along with numerous magazines and newspapers. Teachers are given time to travel to bookstores, book fairs, and book sales in the area to enrich their stocks. Once a year seventh graders take a field trip to a local bookstore chain to buy a book of their choosing. Each student is given money from the football concessions fund with which to purchase books.

Another important aspect of the Heritage Hills program involves students from the Junior-Senior High going once a week to the elementary school to read to children there. This activity heightens the adolescents' sense of responsibility as reading role models and sends a powerful message to kids that athletes and other teens enjoy and value reading.

Heritage Hills has also begun a volunteer summer staff development program called "Journey" that provides reading strategy training. The training has resulted in more teachers employing literacy activities in their subject area classrooms. Several teachers participate in professional development activities for teachers and administrators from other schools around the state who come to observe the Heritage Hills reading program in action.

The read-ins, role modeling, and literacy across the curriculum efforts have resulted in dramatic increases in student reading achievement as measured on the state test. But more important, student attitudes toward reading have improved and the entire literate culture of the school and community has changed. Students who had never picked up a book before to read for pleasure are going through 10 to 20 books per year; parents are reporting their teen and preteen sons and daughters spending more time at home reading; and teachers are witnessing an increase in book exchanges among students and more book talk.

"Tubman" High School, San Diego, California

Unlike Winder-Barrow and Heritage Hills schools, "Tubman" is an urban high school with a student population that reflects the demographics of most large cities: all qualify for either free or reduced lunch, 96% are ethnic minorities, and 46% are English language learners (Fisher, 2001). A few years ago Tubman's achievement test scores placed it among the lowest in the state of California, but with the implementation of a schoolwide literacy effort, state accountability targets have been met and reading achievement gains continue to be realized. Three initiatives identified by teacher focus groups at Tubman account for the changes in student reading scores: (1) staff development that was focused and required accountability, (2) daily independent reading and regular teacher-student conferences, and (3) block scheduling.

An obvious thread that runs through each of the secondary reading program descriptions thus far is the importance of effective staff development. At Tubman the staff development committee identified particular reading across the curriculum strategies all teachers were expected to incorporate into their lessons. These included writing to learn, K-W-L charts, concept mapping, reciprocal teaching, vocabulary instruction, note-taking techniques, and read-alouds. In-service workshop facilitators presented these strategies at the beginning of the year using examples from a variety of content areas. But instead of assuming exposure was enough, the committee and school administrators provided additional monthly meetings to allow teachers to discuss their challenges and successes implementing the selected strategies. These meetings were held during the school day to ensure maximum attendance and participation.

To ensure all teachers were making an honest effort to employ the content reading strategies, 10 were randomly chosen and agreed to be observed on three separate unannounced occasions by school administrators. The administrative team prepared well for these observations by attending and participating in all staff development activities and by developing a sophisticated understanding of each of the strategies. Afterward, teachers and administrators met to debrief. Feedback was given and, when appropriate, arrangements were made for individual teachers to receive additional support from their colleagues who had demonstrated expertise in strategy applications. The strength of this approach is that it goes well beyond the traditional approach to staff development, the limitations of which we described earlier in this chapter, by providing scaffolding to teachers in the form of ongoing feedback, modeling, and support.

Another common theme among the secondary reading programs we have described thus far is the provision of sustained silent reading. Tubman High implemented this component of their reading program by doing the following. First, teachers in discussion groups agreed that a "sacred" time for reading should be set aside each day, but were not satisfied with an initial proposal to require SSR time during each English class. In order to make certain the entire faculty was playing a supporting role in the overall reading program, teachers agreed that 20 minutes would be added to the block after lunch, so students and teachers in all classrooms could participate in SSR. This had a potent effect on students who were able to see their math, chemistry, and even physical education teachers reading. During the first year of SSR a $50,000 library grant was used to purchase books that could be rotated into every teacher's classroom. In addition, teachers were budgeted $500 to acquire extra books for their classroom collections. In the following year, teachers received $800 for such purchases.

An added feature to independent reading time is the teacher-student conference. During SSR, students are called individually to the teacher's desk to chat for three to five minutes about the particular material they're reading. Students usually give retellings and answer a few general questions. At this time teachers can offer any needed assistance in helping students locate interesting and readable texts. Student responses are summarized either on index cards or in a log. Although the accountability of conferencing raise the stakes a bit for SSR, if conducted in a supportive atmosphere, these sessions need not inhibit students' self-selections nor limit the pleasure that comes with recreational reading.

The third key component Tubman High teachers recognized as contributing to the reading achievement gains made by their students was block scheduling. Four blocks of 90 minutes each comprise a school day. Although not necessarily the norm in American high schools, blocks have been shown to provide teachers with the necessary time to explore topics in more depth than is possible when the day is carved into several brief 45-minute periods (Benton-Kupper, 1999). With 90 minutes, content-area teachers at Tubman were able to work into their daily instruction the required seven critical reading strategies. For example, a science teacher could begin class with a read-aloud, introduce the material with the K-W-L strategy, demonstrate note taking and concept mapping with textbook content, and still have time for a lab activity.

The block schedule also helped facilitate professional development. In the past, when workshops were held only after school, teachers who also coached or supervised a club would often have to miss these important sessions. The staff development committee took this into account when it planned content-area reading workshops, deciding instead to schedule them during teachers' planning periods. Once a month for nine months during teachers' prep time they attended a 90-minute workshop on content-area strategies. As a result, at the end of the year everyone had been exposed to the same strategic instruction.

As Fisher (2001) notes, Tubman's success has been due to sustained professional development and a school structure that accommodates educational innovation. Recognizing what we have been saying throughout this chapter that student success, especially in challenging urban settings, is contingent upon high-quality teachers, Tubman's principal noted, "Our students don't just need good teachers, they need great teachers who are provided with the right resources to be successful. To improve, we have to support the teachers" (Fisher, 2001, p. 100).

Foothills High School—*Reading Cyclone*

Two major components of Foothills High School's reading program, *Reading Cyclone,* have already been described in this book. In Chapter 4 we discussed how low-stakes standardized reading achievement testing was used as a pre/post-measure to determine whether or not growth in reading skill had occurred for students. In Chapter 8 we recounted the steps taken by faculty and staff to launch a sustained silent reading initiative as part of *Reading Cyclone.* Achievement testing and SSR are features shared by the three previously described secondary reading programs. Some additional unique elements comprised the overall program, including (a) in-class demonstration teaching, (b) textbook readability study, (c) remedial reading tutoring, and (d) the development of curricular readers.

It has been made clear based on virtually all reading programs that have demonstrated effectiveness that comprehensive staff development is essential.

Professional learning communities and study groups, peer collaboration, regular feedback sessions, and in-service workshops have been the most common forms of professional development for middle and secondary school faculty implementing new reading initiatives. Not as common are in-class teaching demonstrations conducted by a workshop leader or consultant. As we explained earlier in this chapter, in-service workshops typically fail to bring about lasting change because there are few provisions for supporting teachers' sustained efforts to implement literacy and learning innovations presented by an "expert" on one day or one afternoon. To improve on this approach, the schools described previously have built some form of continuous feedback, support, or even accountability into the process. Foothills accomplished this by requesting us to provide not only two full-day workshops at the beginning of the school year, but then to go into teacher's classrooms throughout the year and conduct lessons using the strategies demonstrated in the workshops.

Demonstration teaching strategies included many of those described in *Readers, Teachers, Learners.* For example, we conducted a lesson impression in a 10th-grade history class preparing to read a piece on the Civil War by Stephen Crane. Afterward, during the history teacher's planning period, we met to reflect on the effectiveness of the strategy and discuss ways he might begin to use it himself. During the following week, we worked with the teacher to develop a lesson impression for another Civil War topic and textbook chapter. After observing the lesson, we met again with the teacher to offer feedback and respond to his questions concerning different possibilities for implementing the strategy with other content and making it even more engaging for his 10th graders. Within three or four attempts to employ the strategy, the teacher had reached a level of comfort and confidence with lesson impressions, incorporating it into his instructional repertoire. With in-class modeling and subsequent support of teachers' efforts to apply content reading innovations, we observed many changes in instructional approach.

MEETING THE NEEDS OF DIVERSE LEARNERS IN THE CONTENT-AREA CLASSROOM

Several activities were undertaken at Foothills High to deal in a comprehensive way with struggling readers. Achievement testing had revealed nearly 25% of the student population was reading two or more years below grade placement. This meant the variability in reading in most classes was substantial. In one remarkable situation it was discovered a certain junior-level classroom had a range of reading ability stretching from second grade (special education inclusion students) to a grade level of 18.5!

Accommodating the disparate literacy needs of students has always been a challenge for teachers, especially those in middle and senior high school who see themselves first and foremost as subject matter experts. Even for skilled reading teachers providing effective instruction for all students with ability ranges as dramatic as the previous example is extremely challenging. Nonetheless, provisions can be made to make classroom life more engaging and meaningful for even the most seriously deficient reader.

One of the first things we did was conduct readability studies of all high school textbooks. Using computer programs for ease of calculation, we compiled textbook readability scores of particular classes along with the reading achievement levels of the students in those classes. This information was made available to the teachers of the classes, so they were able to see graphically which students would likely have difficulty profiting from independent textbook reading as well as those who would not be able to engage in textbook reading at all. Our frequent observations in content classrooms reinforced for us the fact that most of the struggling readers were out of the flow of instruction, were frequently off task, and were not doing assigned readings.

Armed with this information, we brainstormed with teachers as many feasible approaches we might take in making their instruction more responsive to students who were struggling. Three mutually supportive strategies were put into action. First, we located public domain and copyright-free materials from the Internet and government publications that were topically related to the material being covered in the various subject classrooms. For example, in 10th-grade biology, we located texts that matched nearly all of the topics from the course syllabus, such as cell division, genetic engineering, cloning, and viral diseases. We then used readability guidelines to modify the texts to make them easier to read, eventually compiling a set of curricular readers for each classroom. These readers were printed with colorful clip art to make them more visually appealing. Subject area teachers worked closely with us throughout the identification, modification, and design process so they felt comfortable creating curriculum readers themselves.

Creating reading/learning centers in the content-area classroom was another strategy implemented in tandem with curricular readers. When teachers think of centers, they think first of very young children moving from area to area to engage in individual or small group activities at elaborately designed work stations. Although it is true centers are far more common in the early grades, they are not unheard of in middle and secondary school classrooms, but they are likely to be referred to euphemistically to make them more acceptable to older students, such as "research stations" or "cooperative learning corners." The centers at Foothills High were carrels with trays of readings and teacher-made worksheets. During the 90-minute class period when individual textbook reading and seatwork were assigned, students who had been identified on testing and through teacher observation as two or more years below grade placement went to a carrel to read and respond to questions over a modified, easier-to-read text. When in carrels we observed students who formerly might fail to bring their book to class, remain off task during seatwork, or even sleep attending to text, remaining engaged with print for extended periods of time, and completing worksheet activities. This meant that in spite of their reading deficiencies, students could get desperately needed experience with printed material that, unlike the class textbook, was readable. Furthermore, instead of failing to gain any content knowledge at all because of subject matter difficulty, these students were slowly building up a store of relevant content information, improving the possibility for new learning.

A third approach used to help struggling readers build confidence, increase their motivation to read, and expand reading skill was cross-age tutoring in the form of buddy readers (Jacobson, Thrope, Fisher, Lapp, Frey, & Flood, 2001). Twice per week a group of 17 students was escorted by a teacher's aide across a short path to the elementary school where they spent 45 minutes reading aloud to first- and second-grade children and making books together. The high schoolers and youngsters reported favorably on this experience. For the elementary students, reading one-on-one with teenagers, some of whom were football and basketball standouts, was a real thrill. For the Foothills High students planning for these book shares meant reading and rereading, and generating discussion questions. The bookmaking aspect of their work meant they had to improve their compositional and spelling skills, too.

CASE STUDY REVISITED

We hope that as a result of reading and studying this chapter you now have a much better idea about how a teacher like Melinda can go about systematically and contextually discovering the best ways to implement centers for junior high students in her language arts classroom. In this chapter we described processes of reflection and steps in teacher research that allow teachers to ask and answer their own "local" questions about student learning. Take some time now to write your suggestions for Melinda.

Before writing your suggestions for Melinda, go to the Companion Website at *http://www.prenhall.com/ brozo* and select Chapter 11 to complete the Chapter Review Questions.

Melinda began the process of introducing centers to her sixth graders by talking with colleagues about the feasibility of using centers with older students. The feedback she received was frank and useful, with overall support for her ideas. In fact, one other sixth-grade language arts teacher wanted to keep in close touch during the implementation process to discover whether centers might also work for him. One extremely helpful recommendation from other teachers was for Melinda to give her centers a name more appropriate for sixth graders. The idea was to eliminate any possible childish associations students might have with centers. With the brainstorming help of her colleagues, Melinda decided to call her centers *language think tanks*. Melinda also had a discussion with the curriculum director in her school district, who loaned her an IRA publication entitled *Teachers as Researchers: Reflection and Action* (Santa, Short, & Smith, 1993). With this book as a guide, Melinda organized a plan of action for implementing centers.

Although time consuming and not always a high priority, Melinda followed one of the book's suggestions and kept a log or, as she called it, a *research journal* throughout her teaching with centers. In the journal she recorded just about anything that came to mind regarding this aspect of her teaching. Some of her entries consisted of questions, others of inner talk about her doubts or concerns; still others described actual scenes and observations of students using centers. Melinda tried to make entries while observing students, though more often than not, she found herself later in the evening with a cup of coffee in one hand and her pen in the other trying to reflect on the experiences of the day, groping through her memory for anything that might inform her about the effectiveness of the centers.

After using the centers for a couple of weeks, Melinda began to modify her observations and analysis. It soon became apparent that trying to account for the responses of all her students to the centers would be an overwhelming task, so she decided to track three particular students. She identified the students she believed would provide highly useful information about the effectiveness of the centers. One student, Tony, was a high performer; another student, Amy, was average; and Kaley was below average. These students became informants both through direct observation of their work in the centers and via formal and informal interviews Melinda had with them throughout the year.

Melinda focused her exploration of the centers' effectiveness by asking three broad questions: (1) Will students find centers enjoyable and motivating, resulting in more task-focused activity? (2) Will students' reading, writing, and language abilities improve through the use of centers? (3) Will students work more cooperatively to solve problems and share language? Melinda employed a variety of methods for gaining information to answer each of these questions, including observation notes, informal and formal interviews, assignments and other materials completed at the centers, and quiz/test results.

One of the first discoveries resulting from her scrutiny of the three students was that the term *language think tank* appeared to be acceptable. Students were using the term themselves; Tony even began calling them *LTTs*—an acronym that caught on. This certainly was an indication that students were finding centers interesting, if not entirely engaging.

Kaley seemed to be taking the fullest advantage of the centers. In her observation notes, Melinda noted that Kaley was spending most of her time on the center's activities and completing her assignments on time. For example, in one note Melinda observed Kaley sitting at an LTT devoted to the study of cover material for young adult books. The goal was to look over at least three books, read all the cover text, inside and out, and then rate the cover information using a sheet with scaled questions and open-ended questions. Kaley was seen completing this activity with enthusiasm and focus. She was proud to describe for the class her finding: that of the four books she reviewed, the most enticing cover material concerned *Maniac Magee* (Spinelli, 1990), followed by *Monkey Island* (Fox, 1991), *The Crossing* (Paulsen, 1987), and *Off and Running* (Soto, 1996). Her detailed explanation of the features of each book made it abundantly clear to Melinda that this center activity was valuable as a language builder and motivator for Kaley.

To see how effective centers were in promoting group problem solving and cooperation, Melinda formed groups of three, including one group consisting of her three students of concern: Amy, Tony, and Kaley. Their center activity involved creating poems from a bag filled with words and expressions cut out of magazines. Then the students were asked to identify all of the possible figures of speech evident in the poems and to share their results with the class. Melinda observed how Amy, who was normally uncomfortable working in groups, took on a leadership role, directing Tony and Kaley through this activity with confidence and enthusiasm.

Every couple of weeks, Melinda found time to gather feedback from her three students on the centers. From these conversations, she learned which centers were most motivating and which activities needed to be modified. For example, one of the LTTs for grammar was designed to drill students on parts of speech using traditional approaches. Melinda felt that this practice was necessary and that coaching in a center might create more of an incentive to complete the work. All three of her students told her, however, that this was one of their least favorite LTTs. Amy suggested that music lyrics be used to study parts of speech. Picking up on that suggestion, Melinda set up a listening center with rap, folk, country, and rock music. With printed lyrics available, students listened to the music and did a variety of grammatical analyses, such as (1) identifying parts of speech, (2) looking for and correcting subject–verb agreement errors, and (3) identifying figures of speech. This LTT quickly became one of the most popular with the three students and the rest of the class.

At midyear, Melinda took stock of her centers, noting some significant results that helped answer her guiding questions. First, overall, centers appeared to be motivating for most students. As the year progressed, there was less and less grousing and grumbling about center work. Students seemed to enjoy being able to get out of their seats and move around the classroom from center to center. Their behavior appeared to be focused and task related when they worked at centers. Second, Melinda noted improvement in writing and grammar, which she attributed at least in part to the centers. Her three student informants, especially Kaley and Amy, showed good progress from August to December, as evidenced on quiz grades and themes. Finally, Melinda found ample evidence that the centers instigated freer language exchanges among students. Center group work was often the most enjoyable for the class, and students often generated high-quality answers and solutions to language-related problems.

Answering classroom questions through a systematic approach is one of the best ways for you to discover the effectiveness of your teaching. Melinda's discoveries about the centers impelled her to continue their use and modification throughout the year. She now collaborates with her language arts team, all of whom have adopted centers, improving and refining them through regular and frequent discussion and feedback from her colleagues. These developments would not have been possible without Melinda's initiative and willingness to introduce an instructional innovation into her classroom and her commitment to scrutinize and reflect on her teaching in order to maximize student success.

———◇———

SUMMARY

This chapter was devoted to issues related to teacher professionalism. We organized the chapter around factors that influence the degree of literacy instruction that classroom teachers provide and around characteristics of effective teachers.

We know that middle and junior and senior high school teachers must deal with real and perceived constraints on what they can do in the classroom. We suggested that innovative literacy strategies are likely to find their way into the classrooms of teachers who (1) are able to explore their own beliefs, theories, and practical knowledge when preparing to implement an innovative literacy practice; (2) are provided with the necessary support from administrators and staff to follow through with implementation; and (3) are given plenty of opportunities to reflect on the change process.

We describe characteristics of effective teachers that contribute significantly to students' achievement and attitudes. In particular, we have much to learn about teaching effectiveness from teachers who are reflective; who test their strategies in classroom action research; who understand the importance of providing literacy instruction within the content classroom; and who develop collaborative relationships with students, parents, teachers, and administrators.

We conclude this chapter with descriptions of four secondary schoolwide literacy efforts as scenarios of possible initiatives in your own school and the possible role you can play in support of such literacy initiatives.

REFERENCES

Albright, J. (2001). The logic of our failures in literacy practices and teaching. *Journal of Adolescent & Adult Literacy, 44,* 644–658.

Anders, P., Hoffman, J., & Duffy, G. (2000). Teaching teachers to teach reading: Paradigm shifts, persistent problems, and challenges. In M. Kamil, P. Mosenthal, P. D. Pearson, & R. Barr (Eds.), *Handbook of reading research* (Vol. 3). Mahwah, NJ: Lawrence Erlbaum Associates.

Arter, J. (2001). Learning teams for classroom assessment literacy. *NASSP Bulletin, 85,* 53–65.

Barry, A. (1997). High school reading programs revisited. *Journal of Adolescent & Adult Literacy, 40,* 524–531.

Baumann, J., & Duffy-Hester, A. (2000). Making sense of classroom worlds: Methodology in teacher research. In M. Kamil, P. Mosenthal, P. D. Pearson, & R. Barr (Eds.), *Handbook of reading research* (Vol. 3). Mahwah, NJ: Lawrence Erlbaum Associates.

Bean, T., & Valerio, P. C. (1997). Constructing school success in literacy: The pathway to college entrance for minority students. *Reading Research Quarterly, 32,* 320–327.

Beavers, D. (2001). Professional development: Outside the workshop box. *Principal Leadership, 1,* 43–46.

Benton-Kupper, J. (1999). Can less be more? The quantity versus quality issue of curriculum in a block schedule. *Journal of Research and Development in Education, 32,* 168–177.

Bintz, W. (1997). Exploring reading nightmares of middle and secondary school teachers. *Journal of Adolescent & Adult Literacy, 41,* 12–25.

Blair, G. M. (1941). Remedial-reading programs in senior high schools. *The School Review, 49,* 32–41.

Bloome, D., & Harste, J. (2001). Teaching, learning, and growing as a member of a professional education community. *Language Arts, 79,* 38–39.

Bond, G., & Dykstra, R. (1967). The cooperative research program in first-grade reading instruction. *Reading Research Quarterly, 2,* 5–142.

Branscombe, N., Goswami, D., & Schwartz, J. (1992). *Students teaching, teachers learning.* Portsmouth, NH: Heinemann.

Brozo, W. G., Brobst, A., & Moje, E. B. (1994–1995). A personal story of teacher change. *Childhood Education, 71,* 70–73.

Brozo, W. G., Valerio, P. C., & Salazar, M. (1996). A walk through Gracie's garden: Literacy and cultural explorations in a Mexican American junior high school. *Journal of Adolescent & Adult Literacy, 40,* 164–170.

Buehl, D. (1998). Integrating the "R" word into the high school curriculum: Developing reading programs for adolescent learners. *NASSP Bulletin, 82,* 57–66.

Bullough, R., & Gitlin, A. (1995). *Becoming a student of teaching: Methodologies for exploring self and school context.* New York: Garland.

Burnaford, G. (1996). A life of its own: Teacher research and transforming the curriculum. In G. Burnaford, J. Fischer, & D. Hobson (Eds.), *Teachers doing research: Practical possibilities.* Mahwah, NJ: Erlbaum.

Cochran-Smith, M., & Lytle, S. (1993). *Inside outside: Teacher research and knowledge.* New York: Teachers College Press.

Crowther, S. (1998). Secrets of staff development support. *Educational Leadership, 55,* 75.

Davis, J. (2001). Heritage Hills tops in school reading. *Indiana Courier Press,* February 11, 1B.

DeBruin-Parecki, A., Paris, S. G., & Siedenburg, J. (1997). Family literacy: Examining practice and issues of effectiveness. *Journal of Adolescent & Adult Literacy, 40,* 596–605.

DuFour, R., & Eaker, R. (1998). *Professional learning communities at work: Best practices for enhancing student achievement.* Bloomington, IN: National Educational Service.

Evans, M., Lomax, P., & Morgan, H. (2000). Closing the circle: Action research partnerships towards better learning and teaching in schools. *Cambridge Journal of Education, 30,* 405–419.

Fisher, D. (2001). "We're moving on up": Creating a schoolwide literacy effort in an urban high school. *Journal of Adolescent & Adult Literacy, 45,* 92–101.

Goff, S. (1996). Experienced teachers and action research: A model for professional development. In G. Burnaford, J. Fischer, & D. Hobson (Eds.), *Teachers doing research: Practical possibilities.* Mahwah, NJ: Erlbaum.

Green, J. L. (1987). *Colloquial materials.* Unpublished manuscript. Columbus: The Ohio State University.

Griffiths, M., & Tann, S. (1992). Using reflective practice to link personal and public theories. *Journal of Education for Teaching, 18,* 69–84.

Hargis, C. (1999). *Teaching and testing in reading: A practical guide for teachers and parents.* Springfield, IL: Charles C. Thomas.

Hargreaves, A. (1995). *Changing teacher, changing times: Teachers' work and culture in the postmodern age.* New York: Teachers College Press.

Harste, J. C. (1988). Tomorrow's readers today: Becoming a profession of collaborative learners. In J. Readence & R. S. Baldwin (Eds.), *Dialogues in literacy research. Thirty-seventh yearbook of the National Reading Conference.* Chicago: National Reading Conference.

Holt-Reynolds, D. (1992). Personal history-based beliefs as relevant prior knowledge in course work. *American Educational Research Journal, 29,* 325–349.

Jacobson, J., Thrope, L., Fisher, D., Lapp, D., Frey, N., & Flood, J. (2001). Cross-age tutoring: A literacy improvement approach for struggling adolescent readers. *Journal of Adolescent & Adult Literacy, 44,* 528–536.

Korthagen, F., & Kessels, J. P. (1999). Linking theory and practice: Changing the pedagogy of teacher education. *Educational Researcher, 28,* 4–17.

Krashen, S. (1993). *The power of reading.* Englewood, CO: Libraries Unlimited.

Liston, D., & Zeichner, K. (1996). *Culture and teaching.* Mahwah, NJ: Erlbaum.

Lytle, S. (2000). Teacher research in the contact zone. In M. Kamil, P. Mosenthal, P. D. Pearson, & R. Barr (Eds.), *Handbook of reading research* (Vol. 3.) Mahwah, NJ: Lawrence Erlbaum Associates.

Marshall, J., Pritchard, R., & Gunderson, B. (2001). Professional development: What works and what doesn't. *Principal Leadership, 1,* 64–68.

McLaughlin, M. (1992). What matters most in teachers' workplace context? In M. McLaughlin & J. Little (Eds.), *Cultures and contexts of teaching.* New York: Teachers College Press.

Moallem, M. (1997). The content and nature of reflective teaching: A case of an expert middle school science teacher. *The Clearing House, 70,* 143–150.

Moje, E. B., Brozo, W. G., & Haas, J. (1994). Challenges to change: Portfolios in a high school classroom. *Reading Research and Instruction, 33,* 275–292.

Moore, D., Bean, T., Birdyshaw, D., & Rycik, J. (1999). Adolescent literacy: A position statement. *Journal of Adolescent & Adult Literacy, 43,* 97–112.

Murphy, C. (1999). Use time for faculty study. *Journal of Staff Development, 20,* 20–25.

Murphy, C., & Lick, D. (1998). *Whole-faculty study groups: A powerful way to change schools and enhance learning.* Thousand Oaks, CA: Corwin Press.

O'Brien, D., Stewart, R., & Moje, E. B. (1995). Why content literacy is difficult to infuse into the secondary school: Complexities of curriculum, pedagogy, and school culture. *Reading Research Quarterly, 30,* 442–463.

Palmer, R., & Stewart, R. (1997). Nonfiction trade books in content area instruction: Realities and potential. *Journal of Adolescent & Adult Literacy, 40,* 630–641.

Posner, G. J. (1985). *Field experience: A guide to reflective teaching.* New York: Longman.

Putnam, R., & Borko, H. (2000). What do new views of knowledge and thinking have to say about research on teacher learning? *Educational Researcher, 29,* 4–15.

Rallis, S., & MacMullen, M. (2000). Inquiry-minded schools: Opening doors for accountability. *Phi Delta Kappan, 81,* 766–773.

Ratekin, N., Simpson, M., Alvermann, D., & Dishner, E. (1985). Why teachers resist content reading instruction. *Journal of Reading, 28,* 432–437.

Reed, A. J. S. (1988). *Comics to classics: A parent's guide to books for teens and pre-teens.* Newark, DE: International Reading Association.

Rhodes, L., & Dudley-Marling, C. (1988). *Readers and writers with a difference: A holistic approach to teaching learning disabled and remedial students.* Portsmouth, NH: Heinemann.

Richardson, V. (1990). Significant and worthwhile change in teaching practice. *Educational Researcher, 19,* 10–18.

Richardson, V. (2001). *Handbook of research on teaching* (4th ed.). New York: Macmillan.

Richardson, V., Anders, P., Tidwell, D., & Lloyd, C. (1991). The relationship between teachers' beliefs and practices in reading comprehension instruction. *American Educational Research Journal, 28,* 559–586.

Rief, L. (1992). *Seeking diversity: Language arts with adolescents.* Portsmouth, NH: Heinemann.

Romine, B., McKenna, M., & Robinson, R. (1996). Reading coursework requirements for middle and high school content area teachers: A U.S. survey. *Journal of Adolescent & Adult Literacy, 40,* 194–200.

Ross, J., Rolheiser, C., & Hogaboam-Gray, A. (1999). Effects of collaborative action research on the knowledge of five Canadian teacher-researchers. *Elementary School Journal, 99,* 255–275.

Ruddell, R. B., & Sperling, M. (1988). Factors influencing the use of literacy research by the classroom teacher: Research review and new directions. In J. Readence & R. S. Baldwin (Eds.), *Dialogues in literacy research. Thirty-seventh yearbook of the National Reading Conference.* Chicago: National Reading Conference.

Santa, C., Short, K., & Smith, K. (1993). *Teachers as researchers: Reflection and action.* Newark, DE: International Reading Association.

Saravia-Shore, M., & Arvizu, S. (1992). *Cross-cultural literacy: Ethnographies of communication in multiethnic classrooms.* New York: Garland.

Short, K., & Burke, C. (1989). New potentials for teacher education: Teaching and learning as inquiry. *The Elementary School Journal, 90,* 193–206.

Smith, F. (1985). *Reading without nonsense.* New York: Holt, Rinehart & Winston.

Smith, K., & Hudelson, S. (2001). The NCTE reading initiative: Politics, pedagogy, and possibilities. *Language Arts, 79,* 29–37.

Sturtevant, E. G. (1993). Content literacy in high school social studies: A focus on one teacher's beliefs and decisions. In T. Rasinski & N. Padak (Eds.), *Inquiries in literacy learning and instruction. Fifteenth yearbook of the College Reading Association.* Pittsburgh, KS: College Reading Association.

Sunderman, G., Amoa, M., & Meyers, T. (2001). California's reading initiative: Contraints on implementation in middle and high schools. *Educational Policy, 15,* 674–698.

Tice, C. (2000). Enhancing family literacy through collaboration: Program considerations. *Journal of Adolescent & Adult Literacy, 44,* 138–145.

Tichenor, M., & Heins, E. (2000). Study groups: An inquiry-based approach to improving schools. *The Clearing House, 73,* 316–319.

Tremmel, R. (1993). Zen and the art of reflective practice. *Harvard Educational Review, 63,* 434–458.

Vacca, R. (1998). Let's not marginalize adolescent literacy. *Journal of Adolescent & Adult Literacy, 41,* 604–609.

Valli, L. (1993). Reflective teacher education programs: An analysis of case studies. In J. Calderhead (Ed.), *Conceptualizing reflection in teacher development.* Albany, NY: SUNY Press.

Valli, L., & Price, J. (2000). Deepening our understanding of praxis: Teacher educators' reflections on action research. *Teaching Education, 11,* 267–278.

Weller, D., & Weller, S. (1999). Secondary school reading: Using the quality principle of continuous improvement to build an exemplary program. *NASSP Bulletin, 83,* 59–68.

Wells, G. (1992). *Constructing knowledge together.* Portsmouth, NH: Heinemann.

Wilson, E., Konopak, B., & Readence, J. (1992). Examining content area reading beliefs, decisions, and instruction: A case study of an English teacher. In C. Kinzer & D. Leu (Eds.), *Literacy research, theory, and practice: Views from many perspectives. Forty-first yearbook of the National Reading Conference.* Chicago: National Reading Conference.

Zeichner, K., & Liston, D. (1996). *Reflective teaching: An introduction.* Mahwah, NJ: Erlbaum.

Zeichner, K. (2001). Practitioner research. In V. Richardson (Ed.), *Handbook of research on teaching* (4th ed.). New York: Macmillan.

YOUNG ADULT BOOKS

Dewdney, A. K. (1984). *The planiverse.* New York: Poseidon Press.
Fox, P. (1991). *Monkey island.* New York: Bantam Doubleday.
Frank, R. (1986). *No hero for the Kaiser.* New York: Lothrop, Lee & Shepard.
McDonald, J. (2001). *Spellbound.* New York: Farrar, Strauss & Giroux.
Paulsen, G. (1987). *The crossing.* New York: Bantam Doubleday.
Paulsen, G. (1992). *The haymeadow.* New York: Dell.
Soto, G. (1996). *Off and running.* New York: Delacorte Press.
Spinelli, J. (1990). *Maniac Magee.* New York: Harper Trophy.

SUBJECT INDEX